Juvenile Sexual Offending

Juvenile Sexual Offending

Causes, Consequences, and Correction

Third Edition

Gail Ryan

Thomas Leversee

Sandy Lane

WILEY

John Wiley & Sons, Inc.

This book is printed on acid-free paper. ∞

Copyright © 2010 by John Wiley & Sons, Inc. All rights reserved.

Published by John Wiley & Sons, Inc., Hoboken, New Jersey.
Published simultaneously in Canada.

This publication is designed to provide accurate and authoritative information in regard to the subject matter covered. It is sold with the understanding that the publisher is not engaged in rendering professional services. If legal, accounting, medical, psychological or any other expert assistance is required, the services of a competent professional person should be sought.

Designations used by companies to distinguish their products are often claimed as trademarks. In all instances where John Wiley & Sons, Inc. is aware of a claim, the product names appear in initial capital or all capital letters. Readers, however, should contact the appropriate companies for more complete information regarding trademarks and registration.

For general information on our other products and services please contact our Customer Care Department within the U.S. at (800) 762-2974, outside the United States at (317) 572-3993 or fax (317) 572-4002.

Wiley also publishes its books in a variety of electronic formats. Some content that appears in print may not be available in electronic books. For more information about Wiley products, visit our website at www.wiley.com.

Library of Congress Cataloging-in-Publication Data:

Juvenile sexual offending : causes, consequences, and correction / [edited by] Gail Ryan, Thomas Leversee, and Sandy Lane.—3rd ed.
    p. cm.
  Includes index.
  ISBN 978-470-53191-4 (pbk); 978-0-470-64669-4 (ebk); 978-0-470-64693-9 (ebk); 978-0-470-64694-6 (ebk)
  1. Teenage sex offenders. I. Ryan, Gail. II. Leversee, Thomas III. Lane, Sandy L.
  HV9067.S48J88 2010
  364.36—dc22
                                                   2010005949

Printed in the United States of America

10 9 8 7 6 5 4 3 2 1

*This book is dedicated by the editors
to the memories of Fay Honey Knopp for
her shepherding of workers in this field,
Brandt F. Steele for his fostering and mentoring
of clinicians working in child protection,
and to the young clients who have struggled
with us to achieve understanding and change in
order to stop the multigenerational cycle of abuse.*

Contents

Acknowledgments

The editors wish to thank our family members for their support of our work, as well as our many colleagues throughout the field whose sharing and collaboration have contributed to 30 years of work in this field. The patience, nurturance, and good nature of those working with these troubled and troubling youth has enriched our professional experience and enabled the advances in knowledge and practice that are apparent in this text.

Members of the National Adolescent Perpetration Network, Directors of the Kempe Center, the University of Colorado Denver School of Medicine, Department of Pediatrics, the Kempe Foundation, and the Colorado Division of Youth Corrections have provided the opportunity and necessary support for this work.

Thanks to the following colleagues who reviewed this book and provided feedback:

Magdalena Linhardt
University of Maine, Augusta
Sandra M. Todaro
Bossier Parish Community College, Lousiana

The editors especially want to thank the chapter contributers for their work, Gerry Blasingame for his input updating the special population information regarding those youth with developmental disabilities, and David Prescott for help with references.

About the Editors

Gail Ryan, MA, is a Program Director at the Kempe Center for Prevention and Treatment of Child Abuse and Neglect in Denver, and retired from the University of Colorado School of Medicine in September 2005. She continues part-time as an Assistant Clinical Professor in the Department of Pediatrics and is focusing on dissemination by teaching, writing, and training of trainers. She continues to teach a certificate course on treatment of juveniles who have sexually offended using this text. Ms. Ryan has worked at the Kempe Center since 1975, has worked with abusive parents and abused children, and provided offense-specific treatment for 11- to 17-year-old males who had molested children for 20 years, working with Jeffrey Metzner, MD. Her primary interests have been in the correlation between early life experience and dysfunctional behavior with an emphasis on prevention of the development of sexually abusive behavior in "at-risk" groups. She was awarded the National Adolescent Perpetration Network Leadership Award, 2000, The Faye Honey Knopp Award, 2003, and the Distinguished Practitioner ATSA Award, 2006. She is Director of the Kempe Perpetration Prevention Program; Facilitator, National Adolescent Perpetration Network; Facilitated the National Task Force on Juvenile Sexual Offending (1987–1993), and is a Clinical Specialist for the Kempe Center's National Resource Center. Other publications include *Childhood Sexuality: A Guide for Parents*, and *Web of Meaning: A Developmental-Contextual Approach in Sexual Abuse Treatment*. She is currently instructing trainers to use the Kempe curriculum, *Primary, Secondary, and Tertiary Perpetration Prevention in Childhood and Adolescence*, to train others in their own communities.

Tom Leversee, LCSW, is an adjunct professor at the University of Denver Graduate School of Social Work. He is a member of the Colorado Sex Offender Management Board and also provides consultation, training, and clinical services for at-risk youth. After 34 years of direct care, clinical, and administrative experience in the Colorado Division of Youth Corrections, Tom retired from his position as coordinator of sex offense-specific services in 2008. Tom was an Advisory member of the National Task Force on Juvenile Sexual Offending (1987–1993), contributing to *The Preliminary Report from the National Task Force on Juvenile Sexual Offending 1988* and the revised report in 1993. He is the author of the therapy curriculum and student manual *Moving Beyond Sexually Abusive Behavior* (NEARI Press), as well as several chapters and journal articles. Tom has extensive experience in providing clinical supervision, training, and workshops. He was awarded the National Adolescent Perpetration Network's "Pioneer Award" in 2005 for "21 years of unique contributions to prevent perpetration of sexual abuse."

Sandy Lane, BSN, was one of the pioneers in developing offense-specific treatment programming for the Colorado Division of Youth Services at the Closed Adolescent

Treatment Center from the late 1970s to the late 1980s, and subsequently was clinical coordinator at RSA, Inc. (developing one of the largest outpatient offense-specific treatment agencies in Colorado) treating children, adolescents, and adults who sexually offended. She provided extensive consultation services for programs and therapists, and was appointed to the National Task Force on Juvenile Sexual Offending from 1987–1993, and the Colorado Department of Corrections Therapeutic Community Advisory Board in 1996. She was awarded a National Adolescent Perpetration Network's "Pioneer Award" in 2005 for "21 years of unique contributions to prevent perpetration of sexual abuse." She is currently retired, and has viewed this revision of the text as one last "fling."

About the Contributors

Steven M. Bengis, Ed.D., is a recognized consultant and trainer in the United States, Israel, Canada, and New Zealand. He is President of MASOC, the professional association in Massachusetts dealing with children with sexual behavior problems and adolescents who abuse, and served on the National Task Force on Juvenile Sexual Offending (1986–1993). He facilitated creation of the *Standards of Care For Youth In Sex Offense-Specific Residential Programs*, authored several articles, chapters, and one of the first online courses on youth who sexually abuse at NEARI Online. Together with his wife, Penny Cuninggim, Ed.D., he founded and serves as Executive Director of the New England Adolescent Research Institute, Inc. (NEARI) in Holyoke, Massachusetts. Dr. Bengis has worked as a therapist both privately and in outpatient, residential, and school settings.

Christopher Lobanov-Rostovsky, works for the Colorado Division of Criminal Justice within the Department of Public Safety as the Program Director for the Colorado Sex Offender Management Board. He provides expertise regarding juveniles who have committed sexual offenses to policymakers both locally and nationally, including the Colorado State Legislature. He has delivered training and consultation around the country on the treatment and management of these juveniles based upon a 20-year work history that includes work in residential, diversion, and community-based settings.

Kevin M. Powell, Ph.D., is the clinical director and licensed psychologist at Platte Valley Youth Services Center, a 132-bed youth correctional facility, in Colorado. He is also an adjunct assistant professor at Colorado State University in the Department of Psychology. He has been working with at-risk children, adolescents, and their families for over two decades in a variety of settings, including schools, outpatient youth service agencies, inpatient hospitals, and correctional facilities. He also provides trainings on the topic of working effectively with at-risk youth, including those with sexual behavior problems.

Jerry Thomas, M.Ed., has more than 40 years of experience working with children and families, served on the National Task Force on Juvenile Sexual Offending (1986–1993), and contributed to the *Standards of Care For Youth In Sex Offense-Specific Residential Programs*. She and her son, Wilson Viar III, M.A., have worked together to author numerous textbook chapters on the importance of involving families in treatment. She was influential in pioneering child advocacy in Tennessee, and is particularly recognized for her expertise in creating and evaluating safety in child welfare settings. She has been a consultant and trainer in developing many offense-specific programs in the United States and abroad, and continues to provide expert testimony in institutional abuse cases since retiring. She is a recipient of the Beyond the Call Award, 2003, and the Faye Honey Knopp Award, NAPN 2005.

Introduction

Sexual offenses encompass a wide spectrum of behaviors in a variety of situations, victimizing many types of persons. Sexual aggression in the form of violent or sadistic rape has long been feared and punished, and other deviant sexual behaviors and paraphilias have been shunned and prohibited. Sexual deviance has generated many myths and misconceptions. In the past, sexual offenses often eluded report and recrimination because of the lack of accurate information and the reluctance of many cultures to discuss sexual issues. Juveniles who committed sexual offenses were often exempted from responsibility for their abusive sexual behaviors and many of their exploitive behaviors were considered "adolescent adjustment reactions" or "exploratory" stages of development.

As society has come to recognize the incidence and prevalence of child sexual abuse, clinical work and research have illuminated the negative impacts of early sexual exploitation on the developing child. Legal, educational, and social service approaches have been mobilized to intervene on behalf of sexually abused children. Since the 1980s, the sexual abuse of children has been defined as criminal and perpetrators are now held accountable and punishable; mandatory reporting has been legislated to aid in earlier detection; prevention messages have sought to teach children to resist and report sexual victimization, and treatment programs have evolved to treat those who are abused and those who abuse them, and also their families. The primary prevention of sexual abuse, however, is dependent on eliminating the danger or potential of sexual exploitation by stopping sexual offending. Effective intervention to prevent further offending by identified offenders and to prevent the development of offending by the next generation is ultimately the only proactive alternative in sexual abuse prevention. It is by asking the question, "Who are these sex offenders, and where do they come from?" that attention turns to children and adolescents who sexually abuse others.

Recognition that sexually abusive behaviors that begin in childhood or adolescence might continue into adulthood has led to the development of early intervention programs to address these behaviors immediately, in hopes of preventing both the victimization of others and the habituation of these behaviors. Programs for identified youth developed rapidly in the 1980s, adapting treatment strategies that were in use in adult programs, based on the belief that the adolescents who sexually offended were destined to become the adult offenders of the future, unless something interrupted that development.

As research has evolved through three decades, there is now much more known about juveniles who sexually offend, and much of the new knowledge is good news. Long-term follow-up studies continue to demonstrate much lower rates of sexual recidivism by juveniles than expected, and even less after participation in specialized treatment programs. The growing body of research and clinical knowledge has contributed to new models for understanding and responding to juvenile sexual offending, and thus necessitates the revision of this text. This third edition reveals dramatic discoveries and new approaches that were only foreshadowed in the 1997 edition.

It is now clear that many youth who commit sexual offenses in childhood or adolescence are more like other delinquents than like adult sexual offenders. Although some youth do have a "sexual deviance" problem that may continue to pose a risk across the life span, for most, the sexually abusive behavior is much more about their capacity to be abusive and their failure to perceive and/or be responsible for the harmful effects of their behavior. The fact that most do not appear to be acting on pedophilic interest is good news, as is the fact that they can become both culpable and responsible for their sexual behavior when required to do so. Nonetheless, sexual abusers of all ages continue to be characterized by denial and minimization of their past and resistance to intervention.

Treatment is often most successful when court ordered rather than voluntary, and offense-specific treatment continues to employ some nontraditional approaches.

The largest portion of juvenile sexual offenses involve victimization or exploitation of significantly younger children, and lesser portions involve harassment or violent assaults on peers, adults, or strangers. Therefore, the primary focus throughout this text is on the sexual abuse of children, and issues of peer harassment, violent offenses, and various subgroups are addressed separately only when theory or practice differs significantly. Similarly, acknowledging that the common denominator is the abusive nature of the behavior, all types of abusive behaviors are addressed, and the sexual nature of the behavior is only one aspect of the problem to be addressed in offense-specific treatment.

Clinical work with these youth builds on traditional clinical training, and specialized training prepares clinicians to treat these youth in abuse-specific/sexual offense-specific programs. This text continues to address the need for comprehensive coursework to be provided in graduate schools, as well as postgraduate certificate programs, to support educational competency for those who work with sexually abusive youth and their families. The text describes descriptive, qualitative, and empirical studies of the causes, consequences, and correction of juvenile sexual offending; suggests theoretical perspectives and clinical approaches; and creates an agenda for primary, secondary, and tertiary perpetration prevention strategies. The text is not designed to describe specific programs but to provide a base of knowledge to support decision making, program development, and case management by the multidisciplinary professionals involved in child protection, child welfare, mental/behavioral health, and juvenile corrections. Supplemental reading in sexual abuse, child development, sexuality, delinquency, aggression, and clinical practice is recommended for clinicians specializing in the treatment of sexually abusive youth.

The book presents a developmental-contextual perspective by looking at sexuality, child development, deviance, dysfunction, risk, and resilience, as these things relate to sexually abusive behaviors. The consequences for the youth, for those they abuse, and the families of each are examined; also, the role and responsibility of parents and alternative care providers in supervision and health promotion are described. Legal issues are discussed, as well as the range of services needed to meet the needs of youth who have sexually offended.

New information included in this edition reflects the curiosity and the science that has informed the development of juvenile models, which are now substantially different from traditional adult models. Appreciation of the juvenile's capacity to change supports the risk reduction–health promotion models that are characteristic of these newer approaches. Using all available knowledge, current hypotheses hold the promise of significantly reducing the incidence and prevalence of sexual abuse in future generations.

Typology research now illuminates the diversity that exists in this population in regard to subtypes, duration of offending behaviors, clinical characteristics, etiology, social and interpersonal skills, relationships, and mental health issues. Differential treatment and supervision interventions are discussed that address the individualized needs of this diverse population.

Over the past 25 years, increasingly punitive legislative and policy responses to juveniles who have committed sexual offenses fail to reflect the research. Many of the popular beliefs, trends in adult sex offender management, and community reactions continue to be applied equally to juveniles who have committed sexual offenses. The dilemma this creates is described. The dissonance between what is known about this population and legislative and policy responses is discussed, with recommendations as to how communities might proceed.

The current state of the art in evaluation and ongoing assessment methodologies and protocols are presented. The increase in empirically supported risk assessment instruments is bringing the field closer to an actuarial instrument. Evaluation and ongoing assessment is discussed from the standpoint of both the science and the art.

This third edition reflects the tremendous strides in research on brain growth and development, and the impact of positive and negative life experiences on the brain. New knowledge has important implications in understanding normal adolescent development, juvenile culpability, and the impacts of neglect or trauma on the brain. The relevance of evidence-based treatment for trauma symptoms and other mental/behavioral disorders is also discussed. In the "special populations" chapter, some new developments in meeting the special needs of children, females, developmentally disabled, and violent youth who engage in sexually abusive behavior have been added. Drawing from the research to date, a number of well grounded hypotheses are suggested regarding primary and secondary perpetration prevention.

The good news is that the work with abusive and at-risk juveniles is a dynamic and evolving field. That can also be bad news when writing a book such as this. This text captures a "moment" in time in the field, yet even as the book goes to print, new developments continue to shape the "state of the art." The continuing evolution of knowledge informs the work, but underscores the need to be thoughtful and cautious about any intervention that might potentially cause harm. It is incumbent on the professionals working with these populations to continue to learn from the emerging research and literature.

Gail Ryan, Tom Leversee, and Sandy Lane
Denver, Colorado, USA

Juvenile Sexual Offending

PART ONE

THE PROBLEM

CHAPTER 1

Sexually Abusive Youth
Defining the Problem and the Population

GAIL RYAN

S EXUALLY ABUSIVE BEHAVIOR has been defined as any sexual interaction with person(s) of any age that is perpetrated (a) against the victim's will, (b) without consent, or (c) in an aggressive, exploitive, manipulative, or threatening manner. It may involve one or more of a wide array of behaviors, and multiple paraphilias (more than one type of sexual deviancy) may be exhibited by a single individual. Molestation may involve touching, rubbing, disrobing, sucking, exposure to sexual materials, or penetrating behaviors. Rape may include any sexual act perpetrated with violence or force, although legal definitions often include penetration: oral, anal, or vaginal and digital, penile, or objectile. Hands-off offenses include exhibitionism (exposing one's genitalia); peeping or voyeurism (observing others without their knowledge or consent); frottage (rubbing against others); fetishism (such as stealing underwear, urinating on a victim, or masturbating in another's garments); and obscene communication (such as obscene telephone calls and verbal or written sexual harassment or denigration).

Definition of the acts that constitute sexual abuse cannot be approached in terms of behavior alone. Relationships, dynamics, and impact must be considered because most of the behaviors could also be nonabusive. Definitions of rape relate primarily to force and lack of consent and often include penetration. In contrast, sexual harassment is not defined by behavior, but by the perception of unwelcome advances, words, or behaviors that cause someone to feel uncomfortable or unsafe. So the act of intercourse might be abusive or not, and what might be welcome flirting with one peer might be sexual harassment of another.

In evaluating the sexual abuse of children, when adults sexually abuse a child, age differential and behavior are adequate to define the problem. In contrast, when sexual interactions involve two juveniles, age and behavior identifiers may be inadequate definitions, and further evaluation is required.

It is clear that an older adolescent sodomizing a small child is sexual abuse, but as age differences narrow and the behaviors become less intrusive and/or less aggressive, the interaction and relationship between the two juveniles needs evaluation. In any sexual interaction, the factors that define the nature of the interaction and relationship, and define the presence or absence of abuse or exploitation are consent, equality, and coercion.

Consent as a legally defined construct is based on the perceived competence or culpability of juveniles. Even older adolescents are seldom considered competent or responsible for legal consent in important decisions. In sexual issues, state laws use arbitrary ages to define an "age of consent" for engaging in sexual relationships. The age differs from state to state, but is usually between 14 and 16. These laws are not based on any scientific evidence or understanding of human sexuality, but reflect the values of the community and were historically aimed at preventing the exploitation of youth by adults. In most cases, activities with willing similar-aged peers were only charged as "statutory" crimes if a complaint was made. More recently, some states have amended "age of consent" laws to 18, essentially attempting to legislate abstinence for all youth. Such laws can result in charges for sexual offenses for nonabusive activities in dating relationships. Therefore, the need to differentiate the legal constructs from clinical concerns has become even more critical. Assessing consent in the interactions of juveniles demands more than a legal definition or an age identifier. The elements of consent are defined as follows:

Consent: Agreement including *all* of the following: (a) understanding what is proposed; (b) knowledge of societal standards for what is being proposed; (c) awareness of potential consequences and alternatives; (d) assumption that agreement or disagreement will be respected equally; (e) voluntary decision/choice; and (f) mental competence (National Task Force on Juvenile Sexual Offending, 1988, 1993). These elements are relevant in all forms of consent, not just consent for sexual behaviors, and the term "informed consent" is used to indicate culpability/responsibility for choices. Defining "informed" consent among juveniles must consider the *similarity of knowledge* regarding each of these constructs, based on age, maturity, developmental level, functioning, and experience. Unequal knowledge compromises equality and can be exploited, but equal ignorance or naiveté does not obviate consent.

Confusion in defining consent among juveniles can stem from a failure to distinguish cooperation or compliance from consent. The apparent outcome may appear identical in terms of behavior, but the intent, motivation, and perception are quite different, so the experience and impact are not the same. Whereas consent implies that both persons have similar knowledge, understanding, and choice, *cooperation* implies active participation regardless of personal beliefs or desire and may occur without consent; and *compliance* may indicate passive engagement without resistance in spite of opposing beliefs or desires (Ryan, 1988).

Equality considers differentials of physical, cognitive, and emotional development, passivity and assertiveness, power and control, and authority. Physical differences such as size and strength may be assessed with some ease; cognitive and emotional differentials may be more reflective of life experience. Thus, in similar situations, one case of two children of the same age engaging in reciprocal genital touching may be exploitive due to either a delay in the development of one child or precociousness in the development of the other, whereas a case of two juveniles with an age difference of even three or four years engaging in the same behavior may not be exploitative if the two are developmentally equal. Similarly, power and control issues and passivity and assertiveness may define the roles of two juveniles in an interaction and thus clarify the equality or inequality of the two in a particular situation. In some cases where all other factors appear equal, some subtle authority of one child over the other may exist. This authority may be explicit, as in the case of an older child who is put in charge of a younger one in a babysitting relationship or on an outing. Other examples of explicit authority are when one child is the "president of the club," the "parent," the "teacher," or the "hero" in a play situation. More subtle levels of authority may exist if one child has previously been held responsible for the other's misbehavior or due to the implications of family positions (for example, if one is the older brother, favorite child, uncle, or so on) or due to differences in self-image related to popularity, competence, talents, and success. The juvenile who feels inferior in a peer relationship may be victimized by a similar age peer, as surely as a smaller child may be victimized by an older adolescent.

Coercion, the third factor in defining abuse in juvenile sexual interactions, refers to pressures that deny the victim free choice. The factors already discussed as inequality are often the tools of coercion: perceptions of power or authority may be exploited to coerce cooperation, while size differentials may coerce compliance.

Another level of coercion involves secondary gains or losses that may result from the interaction. Secondary gains are employed in bribery to coerce cooperation or compliance in return for emotional or material gains. When money, treats, favors, or friendship are offered in return for sexual involvements, the bribe is the tool of coercion. Even more subtle secondary gains lie in nurturance and care that may be offered or withheld in abusive relationships. Secondary losses for lack of compliance may be material, but may also be perceptual in the victim's fear of rejection or abandonment—the loss of love, friendship, or caring. Threats of secondary losses may be implicit, as when the victim thinks, "Maybe he won't like me if I don't do it," or explicit, as when an offender states, "I won't like you if you don't."

Finally, coercion may be expressed through the threat of force, threats of harm, or overt violence. Threats of force or violence are more common elements of coercion than are actual acts of violence. Both threats and acts of violence are less common in the sexual abuse of children than in sexual assaults against peers or adults, since it is usually possible to coerce a child without resorting to violence or force. In cases of juvenile sexual behavior, coercion may be most employed to assure secrecy and nondisclosure, following an interaction that is perceived likely to result in negative consequences.

THE MODAL SEXUALLY ABUSIVE YOUTH

There is no single profile descriptive of every sexually abusive youth—it is possible to paint a picture of the modal (or most often identified) youth and offense as a composite, and then describe the range of characteristics that may vary from the mode.

In the early literature, many samples of sexually abusive youth were identified and described. The modal factors were quite similar in the early samples (Chabot, 1987; Farrel & O'Brien, 1988; Kerr, 1986; Ryan, 1988; Ryan, Miyoshi, Metzner, Krugman, & Fryer, 1996; Wasserman & Kappel, 1985; Wheeler, 1986). The majority of those identified youth were male (91 to 93%), and the modal age of referral was 14. These youth were most often white and living with two parental figures in the home at the time of the offense. They rarely had any previous charges for sexual offense, but very often had other sexual offenses and other victims prior to being referred. There was also one chance in three that they had been adjudicated for nonsexual delinquent behavior.

More recent research often describes particular subgroups of the whole population of youth who are known for sexual offending (see Chapter 6), or particular characteristics of interest, so recent descriptive studies of the whole population are scarce. However, developments over the past 20 years suggest that the current mode of referrals may be somewhat younger (due to earlier identification), have fewer previous victims (due to earlier interventions), and may be involved in somewhat more nonsexual delinquency.

The juvenile offense scenario most often involves a significantly younger child victim, five to eight years old, and most often a female who is not related by blood or marriage. The behavior is unwanted or confusing, involves genital touching and often includes penetration (over 60%), and involves sufficient coercion or force to overcome any resistance.

THE RANGE OF CHARACTERISTICS

Sexual abuse may be perpetrated by children as young as 3 to 5 (Cavanaugh-Johnson, 1988; Isaac, 1986), and juvenile offense referrals may include youth through ages 18 and 19. A majority of work and research with sexually abusive youth to date has focused on 12- to 18-year-olds who are adjudicated for sexual offenses; however, identification of sexually exploitive and aggressive behaviors in preschool and elementary schools by prepubescent children has increased dramatically as early childhood educators and caregivers have learned to define abuse among children and become aware of the need for early intervention (Bonner, Walker, & Berliner, 1996; Gil & Cavanaugh-Johnson, 1993). Earlier referrals of younger children contribute to a broader range of characteristics in today's samples. Also, sexual "harassment" was not defined or referred to as a "sexual offense" until recently. The influx in referrals for sexual harassment (particularly from schools) adds another subgroup of offenses that may also affect the numbers in terms of similar age victims, as well as the scenarios, locations, and characteristics of juvenile offenses.

Sexual offenses are perpetrated by juveniles of all racial, ethnic, religious, geographic, and socioeconomic groups in approximate proportion to these characteristics in the general population. Although most of these youth are living in two-parent homes at the time of discovery (70%), over half report some parental loss (such as abandonment, illness, or death of a parent); disruptions/separations due to placement of a child, or divorce, hospitalization, or incarceration of a parent. Inconsistent care, parental loss, exposure to domestic violence, and/or dysfunctional child-rearing experiences are factors overrepresented in this population.

The majority of these juveniles are attending school and achieving at least average grades, although a significant number have been identified with special problems in school, such as learning disabilities, special education needs, truancy, or behavior problems. The range of social characteristics includes every type of youngster. Samples of sexually abusive youth may contain the tough delinquent, the under-socialized youth, the social outcast, the popular star, the athlete, or the honor roll student. Few have been previously diagnosed and treated for mental illness, psychosis, or developmental disabilities, although there does appear to be an over-representation of emotional and behavior disorders, affective and attentional/hyperactivity disorders, obsessive-compulsive disorders, and posttraumatic stress disorder (Becker, Kaplan, Tenke & Tartaglini, 1991; Dailey, 1996; Ryan, 1993) and many have developmental deficits. Some are well-known for chronic nonsexual delinquency but many do not have observable personality or behavior characteristics that set them apart from their peer groups.

THE RANGE OF OFFENSE SCENARIOS AND BEHAVIORS

The juvenile's stage for sexual offenses is often their own home or the home of the other child; but it may also be outdoors somewhere in the neighborhood. Sexual assaults against peers sometimes occur in the context of a date, or a victim may be sought out, stalked, and seized in a more typical rape scenario. Assaults on older persons often occur during the commission of a robbery or burglary, typically in the home of the victim. A majority of juvenile offenses (more than 65%) involve significantly younger children—45% are siblings or other children living in the same household. Children provide easy targets as they may seek out attention or be left in the care or company of an older youth by unsuspecting adults. Over 95% of child victims of sexual abuse know the perpetrator as an acquaintance, friend, neighbor, or relative.

The sexual behaviors involved in juvenile offenses include the whole range of human sexual behavior. Some hands-off offenses such as peeping, flashing, or obscene communications may precede hands-on offenses, and sometimes continue between offenses. It is important to note too, that more normative, nonabusive sexual experiences may have preceded the juvenile's illegal behavior (Becker, Cunningham-Rathner, & Kaplan, 1986). It is clear that the sexually abusive behaviors of youth are not merely the "exploration" of curious youth, but are also not always indicative of sexual pathology. Access and opportunity may contribute to the risk.

Sometimes sexually abusive youth have abused the same victim on more than one occasion, over a period of months or even years prior to disclosure or discovery. Even with increased public awareness, they may still have multiple victims over time prior to their first arrest. The average number of victims of juvenile perpetrators in data from the 1990s was seven, and some juveniles had disclosed thirty or more. In most cases, however, an earlier age of identification is correlated with a smaller number of victims and fewer offenses. It is possible and perhaps likely that the average number of victims and/or offenses may have declined in recent years. In fact, there has been a decline in rates of child sexual abuse as a whole (Finklehor & Jones, 2004; Finkelhor, Hammer & Sedlak, 2008). However, it is not clear whether that decline includes the rate of sexual abuse of children by other children. Reliable data regarding the incidence and prevalence of juvenile sexual offenses continues to be elusive.

Although juvenile offenses may involve similar behaviors and have many things in common, each of the youths is a unique individual. Describing the modal youth or the most common abuse scenario does not constitute a profile of the sexually abusive youth or of their abusive acts. Each case requires individual assessment to describe differential diagnoses and treatment plans.

REFERENCES

Becker, J. V., Cunningham-Rathner, J., & Kaplan, M. F. (1986). Adolescent sexual offenders: Demographics, criminal sexual histories, and recommendations for reducing future offenses. *Journal of Interpersonal Violence, 4,* 431–445.

Becker, J. V., Kaplan, M. S., Tenke, C. E., & Tartaglini, A. (1991). The incidence of depressive symptomatology in juvenile sex offenders with a history of abuse. *Child Abuse and Neglect, 15,* 531–536.

Bonner, B., Walker, E., & Berliner, L. (1996). Children with sexual behavior problems: Research based treatment. Paper presented at the Eleventh International Congress on Child Abuse and Neglect, Dublin, Ireland.

Cavanaugh-Johnson, T. (1988). Child perpetrators: Children who molest children. *Child Abuse and Neglect: The International Journal, 12*, 219–229.

Chabot, H. (1987). *Interdisciplinary cooperation in juvenile justice's approach to child sexual abuse: Final report.* Tacoma, WA: Juvenile Sexual Assault Unit, Pierce County.

Dailey, L. (1996). Adjunctive biological treatments. Paper presented at the Twelfth Annual Conference of the National Adolescent Perpetrator Network, Minneapolis, MN.

Farrel, K. J., & O'Brien, B. (Eds.). (1988). *Sexual offenses by youths in Michigan: Data, implications, and policy recommendations.* Detroit: Safer Society Resources of Detroit, Michigan, Michigan Adolescent Sexual Abuser Project.

Finkelhor, D., & Jones, L. M. (2004). *Explanations for the Decline in Child Sexual Abuse Cases. Crimes against Children Bulletin.* Washington, DC: U.S. Department of Justice, Office of Justice Programs, Office of Juvenile Justice and Delinquency Prevention.

Finkelhor, D., Hammer, H., & Sedlak, A. J. (2008). *Sexually Assaulted Children: National Estimates and Characteristics.* NISMART Bulletin. Washington, DC: U.S. Department of Justice Programs, Office of Juvenile Justice and Delinquency Prevention.

Gil, E., & Cavanaugh-Johnson, T. (1993). *Sexualized children.* Washington, DC: Launch Press.

Isaac, C. (1986). Identification and interruption of sexually offending behaviors in prepubescent children. Paper presented at the Sixteenth Annual Child Abuse and Neglect Symposium, Keystone, CO.

Kerr, M. (Ed.). (1986). *An executive summary: The Oregon report on juvenile sexual offenders.* Salem, OR: Avalon Associates, Children's Services Division.

National Task Force on Juvenile Sexual Offending. (1988). Preliminary report. *Juvenile and Family Court Journal, 39*(2): 1–67.

National Task Force on Juvenile Sexual Offending. (1993). Revised report. *Juvenile and Family Court Journal, 44*(4): 1–120.

Ryan, G. (1988). The juvenile sexual offender: A question of diagnosis. Unpublished data collected by the Uniform Data Collection System of the National Adolescent Perpetrator Network. Presented at the National Symposium on Child Victimization. Anaheim, CA, April.

Ryan, G. (1993). Concurrent psychiatric disorders. Paper presented at the Annual Conference of National Adolescent Perpetrator Network, Lake Tahoe, NV.

Ryan, G., Miyoshi, T., Metzner, J., Krugman, R., & Fryer, G. (1996). Trends in a national sample of sexually abusive youths. *Journal of the American Academy of Child and Adolescent Psychiatry, 35*, 17–25.

Wasserman, J., & Kappel, S. (1985). *Adolescent sex offenders in Vermont.* Burlington, VT: Vermont Department of Health.

Wheeler, J. R. (1986). *Final evaluation of the Snohomish County prosecutor's Juvenile Sex Offender Project.* Olympia, WA: Department of Social Services, Juvenile Justice Section.

CHAPTER 2

Incidence and Prevalence of Sexual Offenses Committed by Juveniles

GAIL RYAN

ESTIMATING THE INCIDENCE and prevalence of sexual offenses has always been difficult because of many unknown variables. Social and personal processes affect victim disclosure. Victims of sexual crimes often feel responsible or guilty about their own victimization; rape victims fear publicity and the trauma of testimony. For centuries, the incest "taboo" has prevented disclosure more effectively than it prevents the occurrence, and males who are sexually victimized during childhood or adolescence tend to deny or minimize the nature of such experiences in order to preserve the image of male invulnerability. However, during the 1970s, large numbers of both men and women began disclosing that they had been sexually abused as children (Finkelhor, 1996; Timnick, 1985).

This resulted in child abuse reporting laws that had been passed in the 1960s being amended to address the needs of child sexual abuse victims for identification, intervention, and protection. As the public's awareness of the devastating impacts of childhood sexual abuse increased, reports of this abuse rose at an alarming rate. In 1976, confirmed cases of child sexual abuse represented only 3.2% of all child abuse reports; by 1982 these reports had increased to 6.9% of confirmed cases of child abuse (Russell & Trainor, 1984). The National Center on Child Abuse and Neglect (NCCAN, 1987) indicated that in 1986 there had been an estimated 2.25 million cases of child abuse reported and over 1.5 million cases confirmed that year alone, and that of those reported cases, the incidence of child sexual abuse was 2.5 children per 1,000 annually, or a tripling of reported incidence from 1976 to 1986. By 1993, child protection investigations had increased to nearly 3 million per year nationwide, but the reported rates of sexual abuse had remained stable and the demographics had not changed significantly (Snyder, Sickmund, & Poe-Yamagata, 1996). In all samples, juveniles have been the alleged perpetrators in at least 30% of reports of child sexual abuse (Finkelhor, 1996). The incidence rate of child sexual abuse confirmed by child protective services dropped to 2 per 1,000 children per year in 1994 (American Humane Association, 1996). Underreporting has continued to be a problem and a Gallup survey indicated that the true number might be as many as 19 per 1,000 per year (American Humane

Association, 1996). However, most recently, evidence of a decline in reported child sexual abuse has been systematically reviewed, controlling for every conceived reason why such data might be unreliable, and it is apparent that there has been a decline over the past decade (Finkelhor & Jones, 2004).

Although numerous studies have revealed the magnitude of the problem, none have fully defined the incidence or prevalence of child sexual abuse because data is often limited to cases handled by child protective services agencies or counts only legally defined cases. Such data may not reflect the incidence of sexual abuse of children by older juveniles for several reasons. Many reports of juvenile offenses are rejected by social service intake criteria, which exclude nonfamilial cases. Extra-familial or third-party cases are often referred to law enforcement or criminal justice, and we know that not all juvenile child sexual abuse involves sibling incest. The Uniform Data Collection System of the National Adolescent Perpetration Network reported 38.7% of cases involved siblings and 15% were crimes against peers or older individuals. The balance, 46.2%, were offenses against unrelated children; such cases, involving neighbors, friends, and acquaintances, are seldom investigated by social service systems. Although the Uniform Data Collection System's sample ($N = 1,600$) contains an enormous amount of data on cases, it cannot contribute to our knowledge of incidence or prevalence because the data came from multiple treatment providers in many states, but not every provider in any one state. One area of information in that sample does, however, support the notion that all official data underreport the true incidence: the majority of the juveniles were being referred for charges of a "first offense" and yet the average number of victims identified was seven, suggesting many unreported offenses had already occurred (Ryan, 1988; Ryan, Miyoshi, Metzner, Krugman, & Fryer, 1996).

Another source of data that could be used to further define the incidence or prevalence of juvenile sexual offending might be federal statistics on juvenile crime and delinquency. The FBI Crime Index does identify rape and other sexual offenses for both adult and juvenile perpetrators, but it reports on only cases charged, prosecuted, and found guilty. This index is not dependable data on juvenile perpetration of child sexual abuse because many of these cases go undetected, others are never brought to the attention of the juvenile or criminal justice system, others are referred to diversion or social service programs for treatment with no charges filed, and still others are dismissed or rejected for prosecution for a variety of reasons.

However, FBI crime statistics from 2003 reflect that 2.2 million (16%) of all arrests involved juveniles, of which 92,300 were arrested for "violent crimes" (including 4,240 rapes), and 18,300 for other sex offenses. Total sexual offense arrests were 22,540 (Snyder & Sickmund, 2008). The 2006 data does reflect a decline from the Office of Justice reports in 1994, which recorded 6,000 forcible rape and 17,700 other sexual offenses by juveniles: total sexual offense arrests were 23,700. These totals are not significantly different but are interesting in that they indicate fewer arrests, despite increased awareness and intolerance in the community, and the trend toward more punitive legal interventions.

The most reliable source for true incidence figures on child sexual abuse may be self-reports of past and present victims and offenders. In a *Los Angeles Times* poll in 1985 (an anonymous telephone survey of a random sample of over 2,600 American adults), 22% of the population (16% of all male respondents and 29% of all female respondents) reported having been sexually abused prior to age eighteen (Timnick, 1985). It was not possible to extract from that poll what portion of cases involved a juvenile perpetrator, but several other studies described the proportion of all child sex abuse victims who were abused by juveniles, indicating that more than half (56 to 57%) of all reports of sexual abuse of male children were perpetrated by teenagers (Rogers & Tremaine, 1984; Showers, Farber, Joseph, Oshins, & Johnson, 1983).

Knowing that 24% of reported child sexual abuse victims in 1986 were male, one can estimate that approximately 70,000 boys were reported sexually abused by juveniles during 1986. One can also hypothesize that at least half of the adult male victims disclosed by the *Los Angeles Times* poll may also have been abused by juvenile perpetrators, which would result in an estimate that 8% of all males in the general population were sexually abused by a juvenile prior to age 18.

Similarly, knowing that 15 to 25% of female child sexual abuse victims alleged molestation by a juvenile (Farber et al., 1984), one can estimate that in 1986, 60,000 to 110,000 girls were sexually abused by juveniles and approximately 5 to 7% of all females under age 18 may be sexually abused by a juvenile prior to age 18.

Even these approximations must remain suspect because it is likely that the incidence of child sexual abuse has continued to be underreported. Several more specific studies of smaller samples in defined areas have confirmed the alarming magnitude of juvenile sexual offending and suggest that many estimates are conservative. Many states have studied, counted, and described the known population of juveniles who have been either abused by other juveniles, or been abusive to other juveniles (Chabot, 1987; Kerr, 1986; State of California, 1986; Wasserman & Kappel, 1985; Wheeler, 1986). If estimates of the percentage of child sexual abuse cases perpetrated by juveniles is applied to one 1985 sample in Colorado, over 50% of the boy victims (more than 190 cases) and at least 20% of the girl victims (345 cases) would likely be attributable to juvenile perpetration (Rosenthal, Beveridge, & Associates, 1986). The substantially higher proportion of males who are molested by an unrelated third party (51%, as compared to 32% of the females) correlates with findings in many studies that females are more at risk for sexual abuse in the family and males more at risk outside the family.

Another source of information on the incidence of sexual offending by juveniles is found in the retrospective self-reports of convicted adult sex offenders. Several studies of adult offenders' self reports have agreed that over half of adult offenders began committing sexual offenses prior to age 18 (Abel, Mittelman, & Becker, 1985; Freeman-Longo, 1983). Most notably, Abel, Mittelman, and Becker (1985) report on a group of 240 adult offenders who, when guaranteed confidentiality, reported an onset of deviant sexual behavior prior to age 18 and averaged 581 attempted or completed acts against an average of 380 victims per offender throughout their lifetimes. The range of number of offenses included adults with both much lower and much higher numbers of offenses and victims. (Subsequent studies have not replicated as high averages as Abel's 1985 study, but nevertheless continue to demonstrate multiple victims and high rates of offending by those who continue as adults. Differences may be related to sample differences or accuracy of self-reports.)

All of these estimates must be approached with extreme caution because of the many unknown factors. We do not know how many sex offenders are never reported or if those who are caught are representative of all. In addition, just as the self-reports of victimization may be unreliable, the self-reports of sex offenders are highly suspect. Although it seems important to explore the question of incidence and prevalence, the scope of this book is not concerned so much with the size of the problem but rather with its causes and how it may be prevented.

REFERENCES

Abel, G. G., Mittelman, M. S., & Becker, J. V. (1985). *Sex offenders: Results of assessment and recommendations for treatment.* In H. Ben-Aaron, S. Hucker, & C. Webster (Eds.), *Clinical criminology: Current concepts* (pp. 191–205). Toronto: M&M Graphics.

American Humane Association. (1996). *Fact sheet on child sexual abuse.* Denver: Author.

Chabot, H. (1987). *Interdisciplinary cooperation in juvenile justice's approach to child sexual abuse: Final report.* Tacoma, WA: Juvenile Sexual Assault Unit, Pierce County.

Farber, E. D., Showers, J., Johnson, C. F., Joseph, J. A., & Oshins, L. (1984). The sexual abuse of children: A comparison of male and female victims. *Journal of Clinical Child Psychology, 13,* 294–297.

Finkelhor, D. (1996). *Keynote address.* Presented at the International Congress on CAN, Dublin, Ireland.

Finkelhor, D., & Jones, L. M. (2004). *Explanations for the decline in child sexual abuse cases.* Crimes against Children Bulletin. Washington, DC: U.S. Department of Justice, Office of Justice Programs, Office of Juvenile Justice and Delinquency Prevention.

Freeman-Longo, R. E. (1983). Juvenile sexual offenses in the history of adult rapists and child molesters. *International Journal of Offender Therapy and Comparative Criminology, 27,* 150–155.

Kerr, M. (Ed.). (1986). *An executive summary: The Oregon report on juvenile sexual offenders.* Salem, OR: Avalon Associates, Children's Services Division.

National Center on Child Abuse and Neglect. (1987). *Study of national incidence of child abuse and neglect.* Washington, DC: Author, December.

Rogers, C., & Tremaine, T. (1984). Clinical intervention with boy victims of sexual abuse. In S. Greer & I. R. Stuart (Eds.), *Victims of sexual aggression: Men, women, and children* (pp. 91–103). New York: Van Nostrand Reinhold.

Rosenthal, J., Beveridge, J., & Associates. (1986). *Reporting of child abuse to Colorado Central Registry.* Denver: Colorado Department of Social Services.

Russell, A. B., & Trainor, C. M. (1984). *Trends in child abuse and neglect: A national perspective.* Denver: American Humane Association.

Ryan, G. (1988). *The juvenile sexual offender: A question of diagnosis.* Unpublished data collected by the Uniform Data Collection System of the National Adolescent Perpetrator Network. Presented at the National Symposium on Child Victimization, Anaheim, CA, April.

Ryan, G., Miyoshi, T. J., Metzner, J., Krugman, R. D., & Fryer, G. E. (1996). Trends in a national sample of sexually abusive youths. *Journal of the American Academy of Child and Adolescent Psychiatry, 35*(1): 17–25.

Showers, J., Farber, E. D., Joseph, J. A., Oshins, L., & Johnson, C. F. (1983). The sexual victimization of boys: A three-year survey. *Health Values: Achieving High-Level Wellness, 7,* 15–18.

Snyder, H. M., & Sickmund, M. (2008). *Juvenile offenders and victims: 2006 National Report.* Washington, DC: U.S. Department of Justice, Office of Justice Programs, Office of Juvenile Justice and Delinquency Prevention.

Snyder, H., Sickmund, M., & Poe-Yamagata, E. (1996). *Update on violence.* Washington, DC: Office of Justice.

State of California, Department of Youth Authority. (1986). *Sex offender task force report.* Sacramento, CA: Author.

Timnick, L. (1985, August 25). The Times poll. *Los Angeles Times.*

Wasserman, J., & Kappel, S. (1985). *Adolescent sex offenders in Vermont.* Burlington, VT: Vermont Department of Health.

Wheeler, J. R. (1986). *Final evaluation of the Snohomish County prosecutor's Juvenile Sex Offender Project.* Olympia, WA: Department of Social Services, Juvenile Justice Section.

PART TWO

CAUSES: THEORY AND RESEARCH

CHAPTER 3

Theories of Etiology

GAIL RYAN

S EXUAL AGGRESSION IS a multidimensional problem without a clearly defined cause. Historically, there have been many theories advanced concerning both normative and deviant sexuality. Sexual exploitation and aggression have been considered truly deviant only in this century. Many ancient cultures viewed sexual behavior only in terms of reproduction or physical satisfaction, and thus it stood outside the context of relationships. Male dominance was the norm. More recently, sexual interactions are expected to be physically, emotionally, and psychologically meaningful in the context of a relationship. Exploitation, violence, and force are now considered both deviant and criminal. In the light of societal norms and the taboos and penalties associated with the sexual victimization of others, many hypotheses have been explored in regard to the etiology of sexually abusive behaviors.

The various theories that have received substantial attention in this century serve as a basis for understanding both the history of thinking about sexual offending and the historical basis of current approaches to treatment. Many aspects of these various theories are interwoven, and similar issues surface in the application of different theories to sexual offending. The descriptions of the theories that follow are brief; clinicians entering this field as a specialty may wish to explore more fully the works cited in each section. The evolution of theoretical explanations for sexual offending parallels the evolving consensus in the field that supports current theories and practice. Research continually depicts a very diverse population and many different developmental trajectories. To date, there is no causal variable or combination of factors that is unique to those who sexually offend. With no simple explanation of why one person does and another does not sexually offend, different theories are likely to be more or less relevant to different individuals.

PSYCHOSIS THEORY

It is ironic that the most readily acceptable theory seems to account for the smallest portion of the problem. In terms of logic and humane sensibilities, the only acceptable explanation for rape and child sexual assault is that of psychosis. The notion that these perpetrators "must be crazy" or "sick in the head" is the oldest and most widely accepted theory in the community, and yet in the vast majority of cases, there is little basis for a diagnosis of mental illness (as a causal explanation) in the sense that other personality disorders are defined. In actuality, truly psychotic sex offenders account for less than 8% of the total population of adult perpetrators (Knopp, 1984) and even less in juvenile populations. In those relatively rare cases where sexually abusive behaviors are associated with borderline, schizophrenic, or psychotic conditions, psychiatric hospitalization and treatment to control the underlying disturbance would be a prerequisite to any assessment or reduction of continued risk of sexual offense. It is not apparent in the scientific literature that psychotic features specifically support or promote sexually exploitive behavior; therefore, sexual offenses in this small proportion of cases may be symptomatic of the underlying illness rather than descriptive of the illness itself.

The psychotic offender's behavior has no less of an impact, however, than that of other offenders, and thus the concern for decisive intervention is not diminished. These offenders are the least likely to be served in the majority of specialized treatment programs and are therefore not the focus of this book.

PHYSIOLOGICAL/BIOLOGICAL THEORIES

Physiological explanations have been sought and explored to explain all types of deviance and harmful behaviors. Neurological and hormonal factors seem to be promising areas for physiological research, as either would involve measurable and potentially alterable conditions. Genetic factors are similarly relevant. However, the attraction of biological theories is not entirely scientific because any physiological cause would support a view that sex offenders are born rather than raised. This distinction is important because any inborn deviant, harmful, or repulsive condition can be approached with compassion and science without casting guilt on the postnatal environment or the individual. The notion that sexual offenders choose to behave as they do is so dissonant with our social sensibilities that an explanation that portrays the problem as beyond the control (and therefore the accountability) of offenders is in some ways more palatable. If offenders are helpless to control their behavior because of an inborn condition, then society is also helpless, and neither can be held responsible. The burden of guilt shifts to the fates.

To date, there are no identified physiological factors that differentiate those who sexually offend from those who do not. Physiological investigation is not without merit, however. Neurological research continually offers new clues to human conditions and behavior; hormonal factors are known to exert powerful influences on many aspects of psychological, emotional, and physiological functioning in ways that often affect feelings and behavior, and research showing genetic differences that create predispositions for particular disorders holds promise as well.

In the 1980s, researchers studying post-traumatic stress disorder demonstrated that for some individuals, the experience of overwhelming trauma actually changes neural pathways and/or permanently changes chemical responses in the brain to subsequent events. This area of study has been relevant to understanding many dysfunctional responses that have previously defied explanation (Van der Kolk, 1986). Research in the basic sciences that has described and illuminated brain functions, especially the neurotransmitters relating to emotional states, has supported clinical applications of pharmacological interventions in the treatment of numerous psychiatric disorders, among them post-traumatic stress disorders, attention deficits, mood disorders, obsessive-compulsive disorders, and dissociative disorders. Even though no specific neurological explanation for sexually aggressive behavior has been found, neurological factors have already been linked to emotional regulation and aggression, and discoveries about the growth, structure, and function of the brain relate to learning and memory processes.

Neurological and genetic research intersect in discoveries of differences in the structure of the brain that are genetically predetermined and have been linked to a variety of risks. One identifiable difference in the structure of the brain specifically predicts aggression. Nonetheless, like most variables, this difference only correlates with aggressive behavior when combined with exposure to aggression.

Hormonal factors have been investigated extensively in research on sexuality, but this book will not address those findings except as they concern the treatment of sexual offending. Hormonal activity is specifically relevant to sexual interests, drive, and arousal, and hormonal changes associated with puberty are particularly relevant to understanding juvenile sexuality and behavior. In some cases, elevated rates of sexual arousal are thought to be associated with compulsive sexual behaviors. For the offender who is bothered by too frequent or continual arousal, reduction of that physical condition might reduce the perceived need to engage in sexual behaviors and, consequently, might reduce the risk of offending (Berlin & Meinecke, 1981).

Physiological, neurological, or biological explanations of sexual deviance and aggression fall short in prediction because for every predisposition, external and experiential variables may moderate or exacerbate the risk of dysfunctional outcomes.

INTRAPSYCHIC THEORY

Related to, but not synonymous with, the theory of psychosis are the early theories of sexual offending as a symptom of intrapsychic conflict. Stimulated by Freud's theories of personality development, psychoanalytic approaches were used exclusively for many years and will also relate to the developmental theories covered later in this chapter. Freud's theory of personality was based on the belief that people have two basic instincts: sexual and aggressive. These instinctual drives for gratification and the external demands for socially acceptable behavior are often in conflict. Freudian theory suggests that three elements of personality (the id, the ego, and the superego) are in subconscious, internal conflict: the id, operating on the pleasure principle, seeks immediate gratification of sexual and aggressive impulses; the ego, working on the reality principle, attempts to direct impulses into socially acceptable channels; and the superego makes the moral and ethical judgments that produce shame and guilt. Freud's work advanced the theory that development from birth to maturity proceeds through various stages and that internal conflicts that interrupt this development might later manifest in dysfunctional behavior symptomatic of personality disorder.

Freud's views of the psyche are so rooted in sexuality and aggression that his theory appeared to be applicable to the manifestation of sexual aggression; and was, therefore, a preferred starting point in attempting to understand and treat sexual offenders. Although psychoanalytic and psychodynamic therapy has taught us a great deal about the origins of deviancy, it has never been shown to be consistently effective in changing sexually abusive behavior when used as an exclusive method of treatment.

As the problem of childhood sexual abuse has been explored in recent times, research has increased regarding child development and led to new scrutiny of Freudian theories. It is now thought that prior to the widespread publication of his theory, Freud was aware of the devastation and destruction of childhood sexual abuse as it was seen in the Paris morgue. As a medical student observing autopsies in the morgue, he was quite likely aware of the evidence of genital trauma in children, so prevalent in some of these young victims, that a hypothesis that children were being sexually abused by their caregivers was suggested. Historians report that Freud had in his personal library the books of Brouardel (1909), Bernard (1886), and Tardieu (1878), which described sexual violence against children (Mason, 1985). The seduction theory (Freud, 1954/1897) was built on the evidence that "real sexual traumas in childhood lay at the heart of neurotic illness" (Mason, 1985), and yet Freud later relegated clients' reports of sexual trauma in childhood to the realm of fantasy. It is probable that Freud's colleagues were so outraged at the hypothesis that client symptoms might be outcomes of childhood sexual abuse that he retreated to a position dealing with sexual issues in childhood as fantasies symbolic of developmental stages and intrapsychic conflicts (Freud, 1954/1897; Kiell, 1988). Thus, societal ignorance and the pervasive denial of the reality of childhood sexual abuse have a long history. It is also apparent that sexual conflicts of childhood have long been acknowledged to be intertwined with life's miseries, in both fantasy and fact.

As late as 1977, research into the etiology and treatment of sexual offending (see Groth, 1979) was investigating intrapsychic conflict as the causative factor in sexually exploitive behaviors. Groth conceptualized child molesters as either fixated or regressed pedophiles. Although this dichotomy has no scientific basis, it applies a Freudian style of thought to the development of the child molester. Groth and his colleagues recognized that some molesters had an exclusive interest in having sex with children, while others were also interested in sexual activities with age-mates. The resulting hypothesis was that the fixated pedophile had suffered a developmental arrest, which caused his sexual interest to remain in childhood, whereas the regressed pedophile had proceeded into adult development, but then some trauma or stress caused a regression to an earlier stage of sexual interest and behavior.

The notion that childhood trauma or adult conflicts are causal or explanatory of an adult's use of children as sexual partners is not entirely without substance, for it increases our understanding of the individual and also alerts us to the lessons of history, which can guide us toward earlier intervention and prevention. Nevertheless, the psychoanalytic approach to intrapsychic conflicts is inadequate by itself to correct the problem behavior because several other factors have also played a part in the development of sexual deviancy.

LEARNING THEORY

Learning theory relates in a basic sense to the concept of the infant mind as a blank slate that is imprinted by experience. Pavlov's dogs (Parlov, 1927) are the famous example of learned response patterns, where the simultaneous experience of a stimulus and a reward leads to a pairing of the two in a classical condition of learning. Instrumental learning theory (Skinner, 1974) illuminated the learning experience by correlating a sequence of events (a stimulus followed by a consequence). Bandura's theory of observational learning (1977) added modeling and imitation to the learning repertoire of social animals. These theories of learning have been applied to the exploration of sexual behavior and have important implications in consideration of the causes, consequences, and correction of sexually abusive behavior.

It is important to consider how learning theory may apply to the development of sexuality and sexual deviancy. Although the capacity for sexuality is inborn, and many biological factors create the preconditions necessary for sexual functions, the ways in which people manifest their sexuality are learned. The concepts of normal and deviant sexuality are based in societal norms and values, and thus evaluation of sexual behavior is based on learning what is acceptable within a given culture. The conditions that support or enable a sexual offender to circumvent social norms must be explored. If almost everyone is aware of sexually deviant behavior in the course of a lifetime, what conditions support or inhibit the manifestation of deviant behavior in the individual? Each of the learning theories offers a hypothesis.

Pavlov's theory of classical conditioning demonstrates a physiological response to the paired stimuli. In any sexual behavior, physiological arousal may be a variable. If sexual arousal is paired with deviant behavior, a condition exists whereby sexual deviance may occur. Repetition of deviant behavior would then reinforce the original pairing and support continuation of the behavior. In view of juvenile sexual offending, classical conditioning might relate to a child's early experiences of sexual arousal that occurred in the context of a deviant situation or an exploitative relationship. These conditions might include sexual victimization but could also be relevant to arousal that occurs in the context of exposure to sexually deviant or aggressive stimuli in the culture.

Similarly, Skinner's theory also pairs two factors: behavior and reward or punishment. In the scenario of instrumental conditioning, a sexual behavior might be reinforced by subsequent sexual arousal or inhibited by a negative consequence. An equally important consideration is that the reinforcement or inhibition of sexual behaviors may initially lie in nonsexual rewards or punishment. In applying this theory to the question of juvenile sexual offending, the child's early experience of sexual behavior may or may not have included sexual arousal but may have been paired with some reward or punishment.

Bandura's theory of learning through observation and imitation supports a hypothesis that learning may begin prior to experience. That one may learn through observing a model that is then practiced imitatively implies that sexual behaviors may be learned from the models available in the environment; thus, exposure to deviant models might result in the practice of deviant behaviors. It would then follow that the experience of imitating deviant models might incorporate a pairing of stimuli with either rewards or punishment that are present in the imitative experience. For the sexually abusive youth, this theory implies that the reinforcement of early imitative or reactive behaviors has led to a patterned response.

The social aspects of learning are particularly significant in regard to sexual behaviors because of the interpersonal conditions and societal judgments that define what is exploitative, and therefore criminal. Societies that do not protect their developing children from deviant modeling and experiences are at high risk of being plagued by deviant behaviors.

Learning theories are not entirely fatalistic. Research in learning addresses not only the origins of behavior but also its extinction or correction. Reduction of undesirable behaviors has been a focus of learning research; to unlearn what has been learned and to relearn more acceptable patterns has been central to behavior modification research. In sexually abusive behavior, reduction or extinction of deviant arousal patterns has been recognized as one of the necessary components in treatment, and behaviorists have applied learning theory to developing corrective techniques. Positive and negative reinforcers are employed to reshape physiological responses and decrease the likelihood of continued negative behaviors; punishment for criminal behavior attempts to override the positive reinforcers with a more powerful negative consequence, and case management often attempts to restrict or remove the offender from situations likely to reinforce continued deviant behavior.

Although psychotic, physiological, and intrapsychic theories offer partial under-standing, learning theory has provided a number of areas for consideration in both prevention and correction or control. Many clinicians treating adult sex offenders have reached similar conclusions regarding the etiology of the problem. Groth (1979); Freeman-Longo (1982); Abel, Becker, Murphy, and Flanagan (1981); and Blanchard (1974) have all suggested that deviant arousal patterns develop as the result of learned behavior and social interactions, such as sexual victimization or sexually traumatic or deviant events, exposure, or experience. Most recently, research by Burton (2003); Miner (2008); Abel and Emmerick (2005); and Hunter, Figuerado, Malamuth, and Becker (2003) have further refined characteristics of one's sexual victimization that seem to correlate with subsequent perpetration. Observations that the sexually abusive youths may have learned a distorted or confused view of sexuality invoke classical, instrumental, and observational learning hypotheses. The question of origin in the learning framework is therefore, where does the sex offender learn offending, and what are the most salient reinforcers?

Application of learning theory to the exploration of any harmful or repulsive deviancy invites resistance because of the implication of responsibility. If the sex offender "learned" his deviancy from individuals or environmental conditions, then society is forced to examine its role and responsibility in the origins of the problem. The implication of some societal omission or commission (failure of function, neglect, or abuse) has contributed to both personal and societal denial of the existence of sex crimes, especially the sexual abuse of children. The question of the origin of deviancy arises in every theory and hypothesis, and the role of sexual conflicts, learning, abuse, or trauma will be more fully explored as the various theories are integrated later in this book. It is clear that the implications of childhood learning and behavioral change are areas of importance for the exploration and understanding of the causes, consequences, and correction of juvenile sexual offending.

DEVELOPMENTAL THEORIES

Developmental theories are a primary focus of concern if the causal factors of sexual offending are to be understood and ultimately prevented. Many theories of child development have been advanced in this century and provide a basis for exploration of both normal and deviant development. Three of the more global and influential of these theories are Piaget's theory of cognitive development, Erikson's theory of psychosocial development, and Freud's theory of personality development. Each views development from birth to maturity in the context of stages, and in each case, the stages are dependent on the previous ones. Table 3.1 depicts these three primary theories as they relate to age and developmental stages. The similarities of ages and stages are immediately apparent.

Piaget (1928) begins with the sensorimotor stage, from birth to age two, in which the infant learns from interacting with the environment. Piaget asserts that the

Table 3.1
The Developmental Stages in the Theories of Piaget, Erikson, and Freud

Age	Piaget	Erikson	Freud
1	Sensorimotor	Trust vs. Mistrust	Oral
2		Autonomy vs. Shame and Doubt	
3	Preoperational		Anal
4			Phallic
5		Initiative vs. Guilt	
6			
7		Industry vs. Inferiority	
8	Concrete Operations		Latency
9			
10			
11			
12	Formal Operations	Identity vs. Role Confusion	Genital
13			
14			
15			
16			
17			
18		Intimacy vs. Isolation	
19			
20			

fundamental cognitive abilities develop in this earliest stage of life and that one cannot progress to subsequent stages until each stage of development is successfully completed. The concept of fixation in an unsuccessful stage of development is important in relation to Groth's concept of fixated pedophiles, and the concept that life views formed in the first years of life relate to both attachment theory and theories of antisocial personality.

Several other areas of Piaget's work have important implications in the occurrence of sexual exploitation. Egocentrism in infancy directs all concern and behavior toward personal interests and needs; decentration, which should occur around age two, enlarges one's view to encompass recognition of other people's feelings, ideas, and needs. These stages are especially relevant to the capacity for empathic recognition of other's cues, an identifiable deficit of many abusers. Also, accommodation and assimilation, or the processing of new experiences on the basis of past experiences, relate to the learning theories previously discussed, adding the dimension that past experiences lay the foundation for incorporating or interpreting future experiences. Concerning the recurring question of exposure to deviancy in the history of sexually abusive youth, this aspect of Piaget's work would support the hypothesis of a deviant foundation for the accommodation and assimilation of future experiences.

Erikson's theory of psychosocial development (1963) describes a variety of crises through which individuals must pass in order to achieve a mature identity. The first of these crises occurs during the first months of life, as the infant's experience inspires either trust or distrust depending on characteristics of the nurturer. During Erikson's second stage, control issues such as feeding and toilet training must be successfully resolved to attain autonomy, or the child may internalize shame and doubt regarding the failure. This concept leads to speculation that the control issues so prevalent among sexually abusive youth may relate to resolution failures in these early stages. Erikson's theories differ from Piaget's in that they suggest negative consequences of developmental failures rather than fixation; in other words, development does not stop, but the course of development is altered. Sexual identity is defined in Erikson's third stage with implications of sex role modeling by the parents. It may be assumed that parental dysfunction or loss may increase the risk of dysfunctional modeling.

Freud's theory of personality development (1965) is permeated with themes of sexual conflict: oral, anal, phallic, and genital stages are defined. The oral stage is related to adequate nurturing and gratification in feeding, the anal stage to control issues arising around bodily functions, the phallic stage to sexual identity and self-image, and the genital stage to heterosexual fulfillment. Freud's concept of a latency stage was that children were relatively free of sexual issues or interests from ages seven to eleven, although later research has disproven this (Ford & Beach, 1951). The implications of either unresolved earlier stages or traumatic sexual experiences during the oral, anal, phallic, or latent stages would be the expectation of conflict and subsequent dysfunction. The Freudian theory also advances the theory of fixation, attributing it to unresolved conflicts of the id, ego, and superego.

The application of development theory to the etiology of sexual offending was obvious in Groth's work. Also, Steele (1986) and Freeman-Longo (1982) advanced the theory that early childhood experience is of vital concern, that the family and the environment are essential influences in the development of sexuality, and that the lack of empathic care, family trauma, physical and sexual abuse, neglect, scapegoating, undefined family roles and boundaries, and exposure to sexually traumatic experiences or explicit materials in the environment may contribute to the development of sexually deviant or abusive behavior. More recent research such as Miner (2008) and Peters, McMahon, and Quinsey (1992) continue to point to early life relationships and the quality of care as influential in attachment and interpersonal relationship variables.

ATTACHMENT THEORIES

Although it is the nature of the interpersonal relationship and interaction that defines abuse, attachment theories were not initially widely applied in adult sexual offender treatment models. Yet it is apparent that many of the early childhood variables are related to early relationships (Ryan and Associates, 1998; Steele, 1987). It has been especially apparent in work with younger children that many of those with sexual behavior problems are also "attachment disordered," and Marshall, Hudson, and Hodkinson (1993) have applied attachment theories to adults and adolescents as well. Ward, Hudson, Marshall, and Siegert (1995) explored the relationship between intimacy deficits and adult sexual offending and, most recently, Miner (2008) has focused specifically on attachment in juvenile sexual offending.

Attachment models suggest that early relationships create internal representations of relationships that affect self-image and one's expectations in relationships throughout the life span. Such theories provide an explanatory bridge between developmental theories and cognitive processes.

Drawing extensively on the concept of internal working models (Ainsworth, 1989; Bowlby, 1969, 1973; Main, Kaplan, & Cassidy, 1985) that represent one's view of self and others as positive or negative, Bartholomew (1990), Bartholomew and Horowitz (1991), and others have studied the four categories of attachment in adults: (1) secure; (2) anxious/ambivalent; (3) avoidant I; and (4) avoidant II, and find that attachment style affects one's ability to achieve intimacy in personal relationships. By applying these categories in the assessment of sexual abusers, Ward, Hudson, Marshall, and Siegert (1995) were able to differentiate adult sex offender subgroups from each other in terms of motive, victim selection, grooming, coercion, and offense variables. Miner's research on attachment styles (Miner, 2008) and Kaufman's research on the "M.O." or "modus operandi" of juveniles' offenses (Kaufman, Hilliker, & Daleiden, 1996) further illuminate the variables of interpersonal relationships that relate to the patterns and differences that are evident in the offenses of juveniles. As Burton, Miller, and Shill (2002) and Abel and Emmerick (2005) have examined the nature of the relationships within which the juvenile's own sexual victimization occurred, the juvenile research, though sparse, continues to provide validation of many of the developmental antecedents overrepresented in the youth who commit sexual offenses.

COGNITIVE THEORY

Whereas Piaget's theory addresses cognitive development, cognitive/behavioral theory was widely applied to the assessment and treatment of adult sex offenders and continues to be very influential in most programming. One element of sexual offending is the thinking that allows the person to imagine his or her behavior is acceptable, justifiable, or harmless. These cognitions, which have been referred to as "distortions," thinking errors, or irrational thinking, are essential to the abusive individual's ability to overcome societal taboos against abusive behavior. Many criminal offenders think differently from nonoffenders, and it is suggested that this difference relates to those earliest developmental stages where the infant first formed his view of relationships and the world and became the basis for subsequent accommodation of his experiences.

Yochelson and Samenow published a singularly comprehensive theory of cognitive distortions or "thinking errors" in *The Criminal Personality* (1976). Their theory of "antisocial" or "criminal" has a long history in the work with sexual offenders, and cognitive restructuring is a basic tenant in cognitive-behavioral treatments. Although only 30 to 35% of adult sex offenders are diagnosed as having antisocial personalities (corresponding to similar numbers of sexually abusive youth diagnosed as conduct disordered), virtually all sex offenders, regardless of age, demonstrate some patterns of thinking that support and excuse their behavior. Thinking patterns are a product of interpretations and reactions to other life experiences and whether such thoughts are in fact "distorted" or "irrational" will be an area of inquiry in treatment. Cognitive-behavioral treatment models have proven effective in mental health treatment of many referring problems. In treating sexual offending, changing beliefs and attitudes specifically supportive of sexual deviance and abusive behavior are obviously relevant; however, changing one's view of the world confronts more embedded belief systems.

ADDICTIVE THEORY

Because physiological rewards are associated with sexual behaviors (intimacy, arousal, orgasm, and/or tension reduction), theorists have explored the "addictive" qualities of sexual offending. The role of physiological rewards refers back to Pavlov and Skinner's conditional learning theories to explain the compulsive qualities of some sexual offending. Carnes (1983) proposed a continuum of compulsive sexual behaviors, including legal, nuisance, and criminal behaviors, which become problematic because of their unmanageability and interference in other areas of functioning. Applying an addictive model to sexual behaviors, Carne's theory of sexual addiction considers faulty beliefs and impaired thinking (previously discussed in relation to cognitive theory), acknowledging that sexual behavior may become unmanageable or out of control because of the individual's preoccupation, ritualization, compulsivity, and subsequent despair. The offender sees his behavior as beyond his control.

In addictions models, distorted thinking and shamelessness are confronted, and individuals are made accountable for their behavior and its impact. Twelve-step models similar to the various "Anonymous" groups (e.g., Alcoholics Anonymous) have evolved from addictions theory in treatment of compulsive sexual behaviors. Such models explore the family of origin and current relationships for co-addictive characteristics, including poor boundaries and role reversals, control battles, unrealistic expectations, and deviant modeling of sexual attitudes and behaviors. By the early 1990s, Carnes had recognized that childhood victimization was overrepresented in the etiology of sexual addictions, and began advocating collaboration between the addictions and child abuse fields (Carnes, 1990).

FAMILY SYSTEMS THEORIES

For many years, intrafamilial sexual abuse such as spousal rape and parent-child or sibling incest was seen as a family problem separate and distinct from other types of sexual offenses. Weiner surveyed the literature on incest in 1964 and found that incest was viewed predominantly as a family dysfunction, reporting: (a) the incest perpetrator's behavior occurs "independent of general criminal tendencies"; (b) the mothers "frustrate their husbands sexually while encouraging father-daughter intimacy"; and (c) the victims "seldom resist or complain . . . and rarely experience guilt" (Weiner, 1964). All three statements are now known to be false, but they describe theories of incest prevalent through the 1960s. We now know that incest perpetrators often exhibit multiple paraphilias and other types of antisocial or abusive behaviors, that wives often are powerless in these families but are not equivocally responsible or even supportive of their husband's behavior, and that children often resist within the limits of their power to do so and often suffer long-term negative effects.

In the 1970s, the first shift in family systems thinking removed responsibility from the child victim, although mothers were still thought to play a colluding role. Giarretto (1978) continued to view incest as a family dysfunction but moved with the legal system to hold both parents accountable. Although the child was no longer considered a causal part of the problem, the family system and interrelations of the various dyads remained a focus, and marital problems were often blamed. Each family member's contribution to the pathological system that allowed and maintained the sexual abuse was explored. Zaphiris (1978) described the dynamics of the incestuous family as "conditioning" the family to allow and support the incest.

Not until the mid-1980s (see Conte, 1985; Finkelhor & Araji, 1983) was the attribution of responsibility for incest placed unequivocally with the perpetrator. This is not to say that family dynamics need not be understood and perhaps modified, but family therapy is now adjunctive to the first and primary responses of prosecution and offense-specific treatment for perpetrators and protection and therapy for child victims. Family dynamics and treatment issues will be explored in greater depth in later chapters.

INTEGRATIVE THEORIES

None of the theories outlined so far is as simple as these brief synopses suggest and all are interrelated through certain recurring themes. Integrating these theories has been an ongoing challenge, and many offense-specific treatment specialists use eclectic approaches that incorporate aspects of many theories. Each theory offers something to our understanding of the causes, consequences, and control of sexually exploitive behaviors. Few programs operate with a single, unadulterated theory; there are many integrative approaches. The integrations summarized here demonstrate how theorists have visualized various patterns or typologies as frames of reference but are by no means exclusive of the possibilities.

One of the earliest conceptualizations was Groth's (1979) application of developmental and intrapsychic conflict theories to distinguish "fixated" and "regressed" pedophiles. Although his theory has been discounted as not "evidence based," it serves as a reminder that those who molest children have different motives, patterns, and treatment needs. The search for profiles has been continual and illuminating.

In the adult field, Lanning (1987) contributed a concept of profiles based entirely on behavior patterns and related solely to law enforcement investigation. He distinguished a "situational molester" and a "preferential molester" and characterized them according to personal characteristics, motivation, victim criteria, method of operation, and use of pornography. His model continues to inform law enforcement investigation, but does not speak to etiology or correction.

Finkelhor and Araji (1983) conceptualized a four-factor model of pedophilia that identifies four areas of explanation: (1) *emotional congruence,* which explores the reasons that an adult might find it satisfying to relate sexually to a child (some possibilities include arrested development, mastery of victimization through identification with the aggressor, and, more recently, disordered attachment and the internal working model of relationships); (2) *sexual arousal to children* explores the origin of sexual preference (for example, in childhood arousal, childhood sexual trauma, operant conditioning, modeling, or misattribution); (3) *blockage* suggests factors that might prevent success in sexual relationships with equal and consenting age-mates (such as intrapsychic conflicts, fear, adult sexual trauma, poor social skills); and (4) *disinhibitors,* which interfere with normal inhibitions against such behaviors (psychosis, substance use, senility, impulse disorders, cognitions, and stress). This model expands the incorporation of multiple theories into a single framework that demonstrates the diversity and complexity of the problem. The four-factor model has significant implications in treatment, assessment, and explanation, as well as correction.

Weissberg (1982) conceptualized a simplistic view of multiple maladaptive responses to stress, which included sexual abuse and incest (as well as spousal violence, substance abuse, child abuse, and suicide). His concept identified a stressful precipitant that caused normal functioning to fail, a stage of denial, disorganization and symptom formation, and a maladaptive behavioral response. The adaptive function of the maladaptive response represents a mode of coping. While considering both predispositions and precipitating factors, Weissberg considered both etiology and treatment aimed at "promoting (more) adaptive responses": both cognitive and behavioral change.

Although Abel et al. (1984) initially took a behavioral approach in treatment, they used a "lifeline" from birth to the present, pinpointing significant events, patterns, and the escalation of dysfunction, especially experiences of victimization or loss, sexual fantasies and behaviors, and offenses, exploring etiology and maintenance of the behavior.

Prentky, Knight, Rosenberg, and Lee (1989) used a decision tree for subtyping child molesters according to: (a) the "meaning of aggression in the offense" as instrumental or expressive; (b) the "manner of relating to the victim" as objective, related, or exploitive; and (c) the "prior level of achieved relations" as either fixated or regressed (p. 240). This approach guided treatment planning and research toward differential diagnosis and treatment. Current taxonomic classification systems have implications for prediction and prevention.

DEVELOPMENTAL-CONTEXTUAL THEORY

Ryan et al. (1993) and Ryan and Associates (1998) have proposed a model that integrates theories relevant to growth and development (Strayhorn, 1988), attachment (Steele, 1987), and phenomenology (Yochelson & Samenow, 1976) in a developmental-contextual approach that supports an individualized and holistic approach to understanding all sexual abuse clients. Theories of developmental competence suggest that functional deficits and deviance are products of inadequate or dysfunctional growth. Contextual (or ecological) theories consider the interaction between individual experience and the environment as the basis of individual beliefs about self, others, and the world. Developmental-contextual models have been described by other theorists (Donovan & McIntyre, 1990; Gilgun, 1996) and are relevant to many of the juvenile models that have evolved, such as will be discussed in Chapter 7.

Sexual abusers are not born abusive. The human infant is born with the capacity to be sexual, to grow and develop, and to become both attached and autonomous. Humans naturally strive to achieve a sense of personal competence and belonging based on safety, nurturance, and intimacy in relationships.

Human growth and development are influenced by internal and external factors that interact from birth in different ways to contribute to the unique individuality of each person. Individual development becomes problematic when it undermines successful independence or relationships.

From infancy to independence, human development is distinguished by the capacity to be intellectual, sensual, and emotional (Firestone, 1990). Personal competence is dependent on mastery of skills that facilitate, operationalize, and mediate human capacity in ways that contribute to independence and interrelatedness. Deviant developments are normally subjected to corrective experiences, which are the natural consequence of useless or destructive growth.

Human development continues throughout the life span and is subject to internal and external influences that shape and change the course of development. Values, beliefs, skills, interests, and concerns change over time, most rapidly early in life. Piaget's (1963) theory posits that each stage of development builds on what has gone before. In cognitive development, the child's understanding of current events is based on his or her beliefs and understanding of earlier events, and current perceptions become the basis for understanding future events.

Developmental-contextual theory focuses on the interaction of the individual's developmental status in the context of life experiences that continually shape human functioning. What develops internally is both a product of, and an influence in, what surrounds the individual externally.

The individual and the environment are each complex puzzles with infinite pieces. In order to conceptualize what factors might be relevant to a particular problem (such as sexually abusive youth), it is useful to consider sexuality, abusiveness, and youth as three separate domains, each represented in the problem, each affording various opportunities for understanding and change. Interventions for children and adolescents who have been sexually abusive have been motivated by a belief that there might be a better prognosis for change if treatment occurred while these individuals were still growing and developing, as compared to treating them as adults. It is the youth factor that is most significant in distinguishing work with sexually abusive youth from the treatment of adult sex offenders. Therefore, a developmental perspective is particularly compelling (National Task Force on Juvenile Sexual Offending, 1993).

Contextual theories refer to the *view of the world*, which is the individual's unique way of understanding and anticipating life experiences based on diverse life experiences and the beliefs and perceptions of the individual (see Figures 3.1 and 3.2). In each domain the factors that affect outcomes can be positive or negative: for development, they may be competence, deviance, deficits, or something else. For context, they may be a positive or negative view of self, others, or the world.

As each of the domains represented in Figure 3.1 (view of self and others) and Figure 3.2 (development and context) is overlaid, the complexity of the developmental contextual view is multiplied exponentially. Developmentally, the accommodation and assimilation of each experience from birth has an impact on the phenomenological perception of the individual. The path of development is growth, and the path of context is experiential perception.

Positive Self Positive Other	Positive Self Negative Other
Negative Self Positive Other	Negative Self Negative Other

Figure 3.1   Internal Working Models

Abusive Development Deviant Sexual Context	Abusive Development Normative Sexual Context
Nonabusive Development Deviant Sexual Context	Nonabusive Development Normative Sexual Context

Figure 3.2   Interaction of Development and Context

Yochelson and Samenow (1976) had described differences in the "criminal" view of the world and characterized particular patterns of thinking as "thinking errors" and "distortions." The developmental-contextual view facilitates the exploration of this phenomenon but reframes the understanding of patterns of thinking as reflective of the individual's perceptual experience: rather than assuming distortion, such thoughts may reflect a different reality. The complexity of etiology, as well as the necessity of differential diagnosis and treatment, is apparent in a developmental-contextual approach.

CONCLUSION

Theorists, clinicians, and researchers have continued to explore the etiology, initiation, and maintenance of sexually abusive behaviors, as well as the antecedents and sequence of patterns associated with the habituation of the problem. The keys to primary and secondary prevention lie in the etiology. Just as each theory contributes to understanding differences in what might be relevant in treatment, each also contributes to understanding what must ultimately be prevented to reduce the incidence and prevalence of sexual abuse. The integration of various theories in research and practice continues to promise the most complete understanding of offending, and the new models that have evolved in the juvenile field draw on research both in and outside the field. Basic science has contributed new knowledge about human beings that was not available in the 1980s, and much of what has been learned since the first edition of this text (1991) supports optimism for success in reducing sexual victimization.

Translating knowledge into action in the community is the challenge.

REFERENCES

Abel, G., & Emmerick, R. (2005). *The Sexual Misconduct of Five Thousand Adolescent Males.* Presentation at the 20th Annual Conference of the National Adolescent Perpetration Network: Denver, CO.

Abel, G., Becker, J., Cunningham-Rathner, J., Rouleau, J., Kaplan, M., & Reich, J. (1984). *The treatment of child molesters.* Program description. [Brochure]. New York: Authors.

Abel, G., Becker, J. V., Murphy, W. D., & Flanagan, B. (1981). Identifying dangerous child molesters. In R. Stuart (Ed.), *Violent behavior: Social learning approaches.* New York; Brunner Mazel.

Ainsworth, M. D. S. (1989). Attachments beyond infancy. *American Psychologist, 44,* 709–716.

Bandura, A (1977). *Social learning theory.* Englewood Cliffs, NJ: Prentice Hall.

Bartholomew, K. (1990). Avoidance of intimacy: An attachment perspective. *Journal of Social and Personal Relationships, 7,* 147–178.

Bartholomew, K., & Horowitz, L. M. (1991). Attachment styles among adults: A test of a four category model. *Journal of Personality and Social Psychology, 61,* 226–244.

Berlin, F. S., & Meinecke, C. F. (1981). Treatment of sex offenders with antiandrogenic medication: Conceptualization, review of treatment modalities, and preliminary findings. *American Journal of Psychiatry, 138,* 601–607.

Bernard, P. (1886). *Des Attentats à la pudeur sur les petites filles.* Paris: Octave Doin.

Blanchard, E. (1974). The role of fantasy in the treatment of sexual deviation. *Archives of General Psychiatry, 30,* 467–475.

Bowlby, J. (1969). *Attachment and loss* (Vol. 1). New York: Basic Books.

Bowlby, J. (1973). *Attachment and loss* (Vol. 2). New York: Basic Books.

Brouardel, P. (1909). *Les Attentats aux moeurs.* Paris: Pref de Thionot.

Burton, D. L. (2003). Male adolescents: Sexual victimization and subsequent sexual abuse. *Child and Adolescent Social Work Journal, 29*(4): 277–296.

Burton, D., Miller, D., & Shill, C. (2002). A social learning theory comparison of the sexual victimization of adolescent sexual offenders and nonsexual offending male delinquents. *Child Abuse and Neglect, 26,* 893–907.

Carnes, P. (1983). *Out of the shadows: Understanding sexual addiction.* Minneapolis: CompCare Publications.

Carnes, P. (1990). Sexual addiction: Progress, criticism, challenges. *American Journal of Preventive Psychiatry and Neurology, 20,* 30.

Conte, J. (1985). The effects of sexual victimization on children: A critique and suggestions for future research. *Victimology, 10,* 110–130.

Donovan, D., & McIntyre, D. (1990). *Healing the hurt child.* New York: Norton.

Erikson, E. H. (1963). *Childhood and society* (2nd ed.). New York: Norton.

Finkelhor, D., & Araji, S. (1983). *Explanations of pedophilia: A four factor model.* Durham, NH: University of New Hampshire Family Violence Research Program.

Firestone, R. (1990). *The universality of emotional child abuse.* Los Angeles: Glendon Association.

Ford, C. S., & Beach, E. A. (1951). *Patterns of sexual behavior.* New York: HarperCollins.

Freeman-Longo, R. E. (1982). Sexual learning and experience among adolescent sexual offenders. *International Journal of Offender Therapy and Comparative Criminology, 26,* 235–241.

Freud, S. (1954). Letters to Wilhelm Fliess, drafts and notes: 1887–1902. In M. Ponparte, A. Freud, & E. Kris (Eds.), *The origins of psychoanalysis* (E. Mosbacher & J. Strachey, Trans.). New York: Basic Books. (Original work published 1897.)

Freud, S. (1965). *Normality and pathology in childhood: Assessment of development.* New York: International University Press.

Giarretto, H. (1978). Coordinated community treatment of incest. In A Burgess, A. N. Groth, L. L. Holmstrom, & S. M. Sgroi (Eds.), *Sexual assault of children and adolescents* (pp. 231–240). San Francisco: Lexington Books.

Gilgun, J. (1996). Human development and adversity in ecological perspective: Part I and II. *Families in Society, 77,* 395–402, 459–476.

Groth, A. N. (1979). *Men who rape.* New York: Plenum Press.

Hunter, J., Figuerado, A. J., Malamuth, N. M., & Becker, J. V. (2003). Juvenile sex offenders: Toward the development of a typology. *Sexual Abuse: A Journal of Research and Treatment, 15,* 27–48.

Kaufman, K. L., Hilliker, D. R., & Daleiden, E. L. (1996). Subgroup differences in the modus operandi of adolescent sexual offenders. *Child Maltreatment, 1,* 17–24.

Kiell, N. (1988). *Freud without hindsight.* Madison, CT: International Universities Press.

Knopp, F. H. (1984). *Retraining adult sex offenders: Methods and models.* Syracuse, NY: Safer Society Press.

Lanning, K. V. (1987). *Child molesters: A behavioral analysis.* Quantico, VA: National Center for Missing and Exploited Children.

Main, M., Kaplan, N., & Cassidy, J. (1985). Security in infancy, childhood, and adulthood: A move to the level of representation. In I. Bretherton & E. Waters (Eds.), Growing points in attachment theory and research. *Monographs of the Society for Research in Child Development*, 50, 66–166.

Marshall, W. L., Hudson, S. M., & Hodkinson, S. (1993). The importance of attachment bonds in the development of juvenile sex offending. In H. E. Barbaree, W. L. Marshall, & S. M. Hudson (Eds.), *Juvenile sex offending* (pp. 164–181). New York: Guilford.

Mason, J. M. (1985). *The assault on truth: Freud's suppression of the seduction theory*. New York: Penguin Books.

Miner, M. (2008). *What attachment theory tells us about unique risks for adolescent boys to sexually offend*. Portland: National Adolescent Perpetration Network Conference.

National Task Force on Juvenile Sexual Offending. (1988). Preliminary report. *Juvenile and Family Court Journal*, 39(2): 1–67.

National Task Force on Juvenile Sexual Offending. (1993). Revised report. *Juvenile and Family Court Journal*, 44(4): 1–120.

Pavlov, L. (1927). *Conditioned reflexes*. Oxford: Clarendon Press.

Peters, R. D., McMahon, R. J., & Quinsey, V. (1992). *Aggression and violence throughout the life span*. Newbury Park, CA: Sage.

Piaget, J. (1928). *Judgement and reasoning in the child*. London: Routledge & Kegan Paul.

Piaget, J. (1963). The attainment of invariants and reversible operations in the development of thinking. *Social Research*, 30, 283–299.

Prentky, R., Knight, R. A., Rosenberg, R., & Lee, A. (1989). A path-analytic approach to the validation of a taxonomic system for classifying child molesters. *Journal of Quantitative Criminology*, 5, 231–257.

Ryan, G., and Associates (1998). *The web of meaning: A developmental-contextual approach in treatment of sexual abuse*. Brandon, VT: Safer Society Press.

Ryan, G., Lindstrom, B., Knight, L., Arnold, L., Yager, J., Bilbrey, C., et al. (1993). *Treatment of sexual abuse in the context of whole life experience*. Paper presented at the Twenty-first Annual Child Abuse and Neglect Symposium, Keystone, CO.

Skinner, B. F. (1974). *About behaviorism*. New York: Knopf.

Steele, B. F. (1986). Lasting effects of childhood sexual abuse. *Child Abuse and Neglect: The International Journal*, 10, 283–291.

Steele, B. F. (1987). Abuse and neglect in the earliest years: Groundwork for vulnerability. *Zero to Three*, 7, 14–15.

Strayhorn, J. (1988). *The competent child*. New York: Guilford Press.

Tardieu, A. (1878). *Etude médico-légale sur les attentats aux moeurs*. Paris: Octave Doin.

Van der Kolk, B. (1986). *Psychological trauma*. Washington, DC: American Psychiatric Press.

Ward, T., Hudson, S. M., Marshall, W. L., & Siegert, R. (1995). Attachment style and intimacy deficits in sexual offenders. *Sexual Abuse: A Journal of Research and Treatment*, 7, 317–335.

Weiner, I. B. (1964). On incest: A survey. *Exerpta Criminologica*, 4, 137–155.

Weissberg, M. (1982). *Dangerous secrets: Maladaptive responses to stress*. New York: Norton.

Yochelson, S., & Samenow, S. (1976). *The criminal personality* (Vol. 1). Northvale, NJ: Aronson.

Zaphiris, A. (1978). *Incest: The family with two known victims*. Denver: American Humane Association.

CHAPTER 4

Sexuality in the Context of Development From Birth to Adulthood*

FLOYD M. MARTINSON WITH CONTEMPORARY ADDITIONS BY GAIL RYAN

S EXUALITY IS SELDOM treated as a strong or healthy force in the positive development of a child's personality in the United States. Adults are not inclined to
believe that children are sexual or that they should be sexual in any of their
behaviors. Although it is difficult to generalize in a pluralistic society, there is
typically no permission for normal child sexual experiences. Children are not taught
to understand their sexual experiences or to anticipate sexual experiences as enjoyable. Rather, they are taught to be wary of most sexual experiences, both inter-
personally and intrapsychically. Confusing societal expectations contribute to
dysfunctional sexual attitudes and behaviors.

There are conflicting and contradictory expectations in American society concerning sexuality. Despite the inhibition of sexual knowledge and experience, it is
expected that adolescents develop a secure sexual identity in preparation for
healthy adult relationships. Adults demand that adolescents develop a healthy
sexual maturity without engaging in learning experiences that make that maturity
possible (Gadpaille 1975). In one Dutch study of "unwanted" sexual behavior
among youth (N1700), researchers found that when youth explore and test the
boundaries of self and others "they run the risk of transgressing boundaries,
thereby becoming both victims and perpetrators of 'unwanted' sexual behavior"
(Bruijn, Burrie, & van Wel, 2006, p. 81). Learning about personal boundaries is only
one of the many developmental skills that support respectful and nonabusive
relationships.

Sexuality is what distinguishes sexual abuse from all other types of abuse.
To attempt to intervene in human sexual behavior without understanding
human sexuality is ill advised. Especially in work with youth, who are in the

---

*Martinson (1991, 1997, 2010); Ryan (2010).

31

midst of identity development regarding behaviors that most often occur during the prepubescent and pubescent stages of development, it is imperative to understand, and help them become able to understand, sexual development, learning, and experience in the context of their life. The goal is not to prevent and prohibit sexuality, but rather to define and develop the capacity, skills, knowledge, and motivation for healthy, nonabusive sexuality as the youth becomes an adult.

In North America, parents have operated in a "protective paradigm" (Lee, 1980) within which it is generally accepted that the proper perspective for rearing children is to protect the child from even knowing there is such a thing as sexuality. This protection, as traditionally carried out, has meant that the child was shielded from all adult, adolescent, and most childhood sexual experience. There is no modeling on the part of adolescents or adults, sex talk in the presence of children is avoided, nonlabeling or mislabeling of sexual parts and activities occurs, sexual experimentation with peers or siblings is not allowed, and sex education for younger children is minimal at best. North American children know the least about sexuality, receive their sexual knowledge at older ages, and are least prepared for adult sexual experience when compared with other English-speaking children and with Swedish children (R. I. Goldman & L. D. G. Goldman, 1982).

Nevertheless, children have capacities for sexual experiences and interactions and they do express sexual behavior in a variety of ways. An increased understanding of the child's sexual development increases awareness of the role that sexuality plays in both sexually abusive behaviors and the development of healthy or deviant sexuality. It also contributes to an understanding of the impact of sexual victimization at various ages, the ability to identify problems related to dysfunctional sexual development, and early identification of sexually abusive attitudes, interests, and behaviors.

The sexual development of the child is complex, involving a number of factors. During its intrauterine period, the fetus exhibits sensory development that continues through the neonatal stage. At birth, by interacting with the caregiver, the neonate is developing the capacity for intimacy, tactile responsiveness, and sensual interaction. In the first year, the child exhibits increased interest in bodily exploration, as well as autoeroticism and the development of orgasmic abilities. In early childhood, there is increasing social interaction, especially with peers, that may involve experimentation with sexual behaviors and intimacy. Gender roles and interactional sexual experimentation continue to develop through the preadolescent years, and during adolescence youth learn sexual and intimate behaviors that prepare them to function as adults in sexual encounters.

Each child's development and learning is markedly influenced by cultural norms and expectations, familial interactions and values, and the social/interpersonal experiences encountered. Organic capacities, cognitive development and integration, and intrapsychic influences further determine the rate and extent of sexual development. There are no predictable biological-psychological stages that occur during the stages of growing up. There is no universal ontogeny or inborn, predetermined stage in the sexual development of the child. There are, however, identifiable capacities and behaviors that appear to contribute to the child's sexual development, and research in less repressive cultures illuminates a more natural developmental path than is possible in North America.

The human organism's sensory capacity for erotic experience develops in utero. Eroticism, the condition of being physically or psychically aroused, excited, or motivated, is an integral part of human sexual functioning. The sources of the capacity and motivation for eroticism are both organic and social in nature, whether one is aroused toward oneself (autoeroticism) or by and toward another person (alloeroticism). The capacities for eroticism, begun during the embryonic stage, continue to develop through fetal, neonatal, and infantile stages given favorable conditions. There is a developmental continuum of eroticism.

SENSORY DEVELOPMENT IN UTERO

Although children do not normally have a sufficiently strong, compelling, inborn sex drive that will overcome all social obstacles to its expression, they do have significant sensory capacity and tactile responsiveness. All senses can be involved in erotic excitation and satisfaction. For humans, touch is more intimately related to erotic arousal and activity leading to orgasm than are the other senses, such as smell or taste. The sensory capacity for touch begins its development early. The fetus is responsive to pressure and touch; at times the fetus appears to move intentionally for the sensual reason of making itself more comfortable in the uterus. Just as children have the capacity to develop a very robust appetite for sexual experience, including orgasm, the fetus may also experience autostimulation before birth.

One of the earliest sensory systems to become functional in the embryonic stage is the skin (Montague, 1978), and it enables the human organism to experience its environment. The fetus is massaged with each movement of the mother as she carries on her daily activities. Stroking, massaging, and rocking of premature infants (who have missed this stimulation in the womb) have dramatic results: significant increases in body weight and improved neurological and bodily functioning. Without stimulation and activity, normal growth and maturation are hampered. The fetus is active in the womb because movement is absolutely essential to full human development. Activity reduces tensions and increases pleasurable feelings.

The areas of cutaneous reflex are generalized over the body (Langworthy, 1933), and sensate learning begins before birth and continues in the development of tensional outlets. Genital erectile capacity is in functional readiness during the fetal period (Calderone, 1983), and fetal movement similar to subsequent genital play is possible.

The fetus also becomes acquainted with its extrauterine environment through hearing. It can hear the mother's heartbeat, hears the rhythm and tone of conversations between the mother and others, and detects the difference between male and female voices (Pines, 1982). Since the mother's voice will be the one the fetus hears most regularly, and if the rhythm, intensity, and timbre of that voice provide a pleasant experience, it may well be that the fetus is prosocially primed to a positive relationship with that mother.

DEVELOPMENT OF ATTACHMENT AND SENSORY RESPONSIVENESS IN THE NEWBORN

The infant continues to develop responsiveness to sensory stimulation, beginning with the initial moments of contact with the mother, and those first social experiences become the basis for future patterns of communication and intimacy. The neonate is capable of promoting a bond with the mother immediately on birth in spite of, or perhaps because of, its total inability to fend for itself. Klaus and Kennell (1976), who coined the term *maternal sensitivity period*, see this sensitive period in the first minutes and hours after birth as vital for parent-infant attachment and the "wellspring for all the infant's subsequent attachments" to other individuals. It is also the basis for the bond with the caregiver that protects the baby from being abandoned, forgotten, or hurt in times of frustration or stress by the caregiver. The infant is totally dependent on the caregiver for food, protection, and interaction.

Infants are capable of interactional behaviors at birth and (with favorable attention and stimulation), respond to attachment behaviors (fondling, caressing, kissing, gazing at, looking *en face*, talking to, and being held close) by forming an attachment relationship. Eye-to-eye contact is an especially significant aspect of initial mother-infant interaction in the absence of definitive vocal symbols (language). A high degree of eye-to-eye contact between mother and infant contributes to the infant's cessation of crying and strengthens the bond with the caregiver (Clark-Stewart, 1973). Vocal interaction begins in the first few days of life, and the infant's motor behavior becomes synchronized with the speech behavior, matching experiential states with body language. Synchrony is an important element in mother-infant interaction. Establishing mutual attention is the first step in beginning the patterns of communication and learning (Honig, 1982).

The true locus of intimacy is in the caregiving dyad, which is necessary because of the infant's dependency and immobility. The earlier, the more, and the better the time spent together, the more intimate that relationship becomes. Attachment and intimacy result from the consistency of this relationship.

The newborn's interactive resources are meager and not symbolic. Initial motivations are not socially acquired; rather, they are physiological and psychological givens. Babies are not born with symbolic meanings associated with their needs, but they do have energy, capacities, and some inherent predispositions. Interpersonal competency begins to develop through interaction with caregivers and is enhanced by the variety and complexity of those interactions.

Although totally incapable of fending for themselves, it is not accurate to assume that babies are only passive and receptive. From the moment of birth they have an advanced sensory system (Harris, Cassel, & Bamborough, 1974) that generates internal cues and triggers the communication of needs (crying). They appear to have a "capacity for curiosity," and their first impulse is to establish contact with the outside world (Kanner, 1939). They also appear to have an "instinct to master" (Hendrick, 1942), to want to do what they are able to do, to experience and to control as large a segment of the outside world as is compatible with their limitations. Using the sensory, motor, and intellectual functions that are available to them, they take an active part in initiating the development of attachment to others. Healthy infants possess an immediate desire to use and perfect each area of functioning as soon as possible. Impulses can be regarded as yet undifferentiated desires for physical, emotional, and intellectual satisfaction (Martinson, 1973).

Ainsworth (1964) hypothesized that it is largely through an infant's own activity that attachment and bonding develop rather than through stimulation or satisfaction of needs by the caregiver. The early attachment may be defined as a unique relationship between two people that is specific and endures through time. Parent-infant bonding behaviors such as fondling, kissing, cuddling, and prolonged gazing are seen as the indicators of attachment (Klaus & Kennell, 1976). Such behaviors serve both to maintain contact and exhibit affection toward an individual.

Early interaction patterns are established at a fundamental bodily level of giving and receiving, and are biologically primed to develop reciprocal contacts and interactions (Honig, 1982). Caregiving involves extensive physical intimacy: ears, eyes, nose, hands, mouth, lips, tongue, breasts, and some genital contact. Only extensive and prolonged genital contact is excluded from normal parent-child interchanges (Levinger, 1977; Rossi, 1978). Physical handling that is gentle, firm, close, and relatively frequent has a beneficial effect on the infant's attachment and responsiveness to the mother, as well as on cognitive and motor development (Clark-Stewart, 1973). Infants who have been held tenderly and carefully tend later to respond positively to close bodily contact as well (Honig, 1982). The caregiver's own state influences the quality of interaction. It is the nonanxious parent who is most likely to hold the baby tenderly and carefully.

Intimate-sensate dyadic relationships can become so intense, consuming, and concentrated as to appear almost hypnotic or ecstatic (Burr, Leigh, Day, & Constantine, 1979). In an ecstatic state, a person is so "carried away" by the interaction that there is a suspension of voluntary action. Such ecstatic experience may occur for infants and mothers, and may even seem orgasmic. Lewis (1965) reports ecstatic behavior in infants eight to ten months old, when "in a moment of apparent delight, the child clasps the mother and begins rapid, rotating pelvic thrusts" at a frequency of about two per second and lasting ten to fifteen seconds. Thrusting behavior is later characteristic of adult coital behavior.

The most physiologically charged interactions between infant and mother occur during breast-feeding. Sucking at the breast is initially a food-getting response but involves more than mouth-breast stimulation. Suckling infants often put their fingers into the mother's mouth; she responds by smiling. Babies also pat the mother's breast while sucking or during breaks in feeding, pat her face, turn a cheek to be kissed, clasp her around the neck, lay a cheek on hers, hug, and bite (Hurlock, 1950). Bottle-fed babies who are held tenderly will exhibit similar intimate interactions during feeding.

The sensuous enjoyment of infant feeding increases the baby's desire to suckle frequently and fully, thus also stimulating the mother's secretion of milk. After feeding there is a relaxation, creating a pattern quite similar to other reinforcing behaviors that involve arousal, action, and tension reduction, such as sexual or aggressive behavior. The physiological responses of the mother to coitus and lactation are also closely allied. Uterine contractions, increased body temperature, and nipple erection occur during suckling and are also associated with sexual arousal (Newton & Newton, 1967).

The sensory and sexual responses of infant and mother to their intimate dyadic experiences appear to be almost wholly reflexive in nature—that is, neither planned nor intended—and society approves of and expects intimate infant-mother interaction. Infants are supposed to be stimulated, cuddled, fondled, and aroused by the mother from the moment of birth and emotional maturation depends on such stimulation. If one were to design an infant socialization model that was designed to lead to the development of full erotic potential and the capacity for intimacy, one could hardly improve on the model recommended for the care of infants during the first year of life. Clinical studies credit insufficient physical contact between infant and parent as related to a subsequent inability to form attachments. On the other hand, case studies attest to the disastrous consequences of parental overstimulation and continued arousal.

Behaviors associated with nurturance and hygienic care of infants is intimate and sexual, in that it involves contact with sensitive organs: lip, mouth, anus, and genitals. Breast feeding, toilet training, diapering, and bathing are not purposely sensual or sexual, and parents generally do not attribute erotic motives to their infants (even erections), most often describing infants touching their genitals as "natural self-exploration" (Roberts, Kline, & Gagnon,1978).

BODILY EXPLORATION AND AUTOEROTICISM IN THE FIRST YEAR OF LIFE

Research more than 50 years ago explored the erotic and sexual capacity of infants. The perceived intrusiveness of the methodology in some of those studies would no longer be allowed in the scientific community, but did illuminate the understanding that human sexuality is present from birth. Many of the older studies have not been replicated in more recent research because adult manipulation of children's genitals is now defined as abuse.

Adults' denial of childhood sexuality has been pervasive in North American culture, and sexual behaviors of infants and children are often referred to in the pediatric literature as "genital play." Adults often deny that children are actually sexual prior to puberty, partly because they believe that innocence and sexuality are incongruent in a child (Ryan & Blum, 1993). However, the innocence of childhood sexuality is not in its absence but in the way children think about their sexuality (Ames, 1966; Dillon, 1934; R. I. Goldman & L. D. G. Goldman, 1982). It is likely that the infant who discovers that touching their genitals feels good is not imagining elaborate sexual interactions but simply perceives that touching the genitals feels different from other touches and enjoys the feeling. It is when adults project their own understanding of sexuality onto the infant that sexuality and innocence seem incongruent (Ryan & Blum, 1993).

During the first year of life, there is progression in infants' discovery of their body and manual exploration of all parts of the body, including the genitals. Many infants find their ears and appear to derive satisfaction from pulling them or sticking their fingers in them, although this behavior gradually diminishes by six months of age (Levine, 1957). Many boys begin genital play at six or seven months, and many girls by ten or eleven months (Galenson & Riophe, 1974). This type of genital play involves fingering, simple pleasurable handling, and random exploration. Children's genital play is often inhibited by diapers and discouraged by caregivers changing soiled diapers. Some children's genital play appears to subside with repressive or punitive messages from the caregiver while others continue casual play, adding visual and tactile exploration of the genitals. Large-muscle control is sufficiently coordinated as early as six months for infants to develop rocking behavior and infants may engage in many types of rocking, swaying rhythmically, or bouncing up and down. Elevating to hands and knees and rocking forward and backward appears to be the most frequent type of rocking and is not uncommon as early as six to twelve months (Levine, 1957).

Many infants form a pattern of rocking that is likely to be much more intensely rhythmic and repeated than is manual genital play. Infants may discover the pleasure of rhythmic genital sensation through rocking activity before they have adequate hand and arm control to masturbate. Rocking appears more satisfying, for infants engaged in manual genital play may be fairly easily distracted, in contrast to infants who rock with great vigor and tension and are not easily distracted, often engaging in the activity before going to sleep and/or immediately on rising. Rocking behaviors often subside by ages 2 or 3 (Levine, 1957).

There is an important distinction between genital play and masturbation in infancy. Infants in the first year of life generally are not capable of the direct volitional behavior required for the behavior pattern that is called the masturbatory act. Some pleasure may result simply from pressing the thighs together, especially for girls. The greatest autoerotic satisfaction, and certainly the occurrence of orgasm, is dependent to a large extent on manipulations that are rhythmic and repeated. But small-muscle control is not sufficiently well-developed for rhythmic manipulation with the hand until children are approximately 2-and-a-half to 3 years old (Levine, 1957), although Kinsey (Kinsey, Pomeroy, & Martin, 1948) reported some infants under 1 year who were observed to stimulate themselves in that way. Nevertheless, the average infant is not innately motivated and lacks the muscular capacity for the degree of self-stimulation to produce orgasm.

Infants do have the physiological capacity for genital response and satisfaction. Erection in the male baby and vaginal lubrication in the female baby are present from birth. During sleep, spontaneous erection or vaginal lubrication occurs every 80 to 90 minutes throughout the life span, but only erections in male infants have been observed and recorded in any systematic way (Sears, Maccoby, & Levine, 1957). In a study of nine male babies, ages 3 to 20 weeks, Halverson (1938) noted that tumescence was observed at least once daily by seven of the nine. Tumescence was often accompanied by restlessness, fretting, or crying, and stretching and flexing the limbs stiffly. Following the detumescence, the babies appeared to be more playful and relaxed. As early as 1883, Pouillet reported that if the edge of an infant's foreskin was tickled with a feather, the penis would swell and become erect, and the infant would grab at it with his hand. Kinsey (Kinsey, 1953; Kinsey, Pomeroy, & Martin, 1948) reported that orgasm is not at all rare among preadolescent boys or girls and has been observed in infants of every age from 5 months to adolescence.

Kinsey (1948) described orgasmic activity of male infants under 1 year of age as a series of gradual physiologic changes: the development of rhythmic body movements with distinct penis throbs and pelvic thrusts; an obvious change in sensory capacities; a final tension of muscles, especially of the abdomen, hips, and back; a sudden release with convulsions, including rhythmic anal contractions; followed by the disappearance of all symptoms. A fretful baby quiets with the initial stimulation, is distracted from other activities, begins rhythmic pelvic thrusts, and becomes tense until the convulsive action, after which the child loses erection quickly and subsides into the calm and peace that typically follows orgasm for older persons. Thirty-two percent of boys 2 to 12 months old were able to reach climax. One boy of 11 months had been stimulated to 10 climaxes in an hour, and another of the same age had 14 climaxes in 38 minutes, although for most there is some time required before erection could be induced again following climax. Halverson (1938) reviewed the findings and concluded that penile erection in infants can be a purely reflexive response resulting from mechanical stimulation.

Infants have the capacity for sexual response and males are most easily observed. The stimulus for penile erection can be internal or external. A full bladder or a full bowel can initiate the reflexes, and after evacuation, the erection slowly subsides. Strong sucking or frustration in attempting to get nourishment can initiate the same penile reflexive response. When the sucking stops or the milk is easily attained, the erection subsides. Such erections, unlike the ones induced by external stimulation, are less likely to be accompanied by signs of intense pleasure followed by relaxation (Sears, Maccoby, & Levine, 1957). According to Spitz and Wolf (1946), autoerotic activity—that is, genital play—in the first 18 months of life is a reliable indicator of the adequacy or inadequacy of parenting. They found that when the relationship between mother and infant was optimal, genital play on the part of the infant was present in all cases.

During the first year of life, there are significant events that contribute to the child's erotic, sexual capacity: an attachment that becomes the basis for later capacity for intimacy; experiences of physical and emotional intimacy (hugging, kissing, clutching, petting, gazing, vocalization, stroking, sucking, and biting); sensory-erotic intimacy and response (previously described); awareness of one's body, including genitals; experience of rhythmic, pleasure-inducing behaviors; genital stimulation and response; and the capacity for orgasmic response, although the threshold of genital orgasm is high.

YOUNG CHILDREN

As infancy turns to toddler-hood, the child continues to develop erotic capacity, in part through more purposeful autoerotic behaviors. Riophe and Galenson (1981) hypothesize an endogenously rooted early genital phase that emerges early in the second year of life. In the child's interaction with self and others, the exploration of genitalia becomes increasingly influential in organizing the infant's development and forming the basic core of sexual identity. It is different from the less organized genital awareness of infancy because it appears to occur in a regular developmental sequence, is characterized by psychological awareness of the genitals, and affects all areas of functioning.

Galenson and Riophe (1974) observed that genital manipulation at 13 to 16 months is accompanied by distinct signs of pleasure, including giggling and smiling, visual and tactile attention to the genital area, and affectionate gestures and behavioral signs of feeling directed toward other people. In boys, more purposeful self-stimulation began at 15 to 16 months, whereas in girls a pattern of intermittent genital touching was noted. It is likely that adult responses to boys' and girls' genital behaviors might differ and affect these observations (Ryan et al., 1988). Much of the sexual activity at these young ages remains genital play rather than true masturbation. Levine (1957) reports that most children, even through 24 to 36 months, indulge in genital play with a certain degree of satisfaction, but in most cases without apparent orgasmic levels of excitement or stimulation.

Masturbation appears to be a common experience in the development of normal infants and children and has long been recognized as nearly universal. At 3 years old, most boys masturbate manually by rubbing the penis or by wrapping the fingers around the erect penis and moving the hand. Some boys lie on their stomachs on a flat surface and writhe while engaged in other activities such as watching television. Some raise themselves slightly and propel themselves forward and backward, rubbing the genitals against the leg of a chair or other object, and derive satisfaction in that way. In girls at 3 years old, there are manifold varieties of masturbation: placing a soft toy or blanket between the legs against the genitals and wriggling the body, manually titillating the clitoris, rubbing against objects, and, less frequently, inserting objects in the vagina (Levine, 1957). Following masturbation that leads to orgasm, children relax and sometimes go to sleep, although some may be more active for a period of time.

Masturbation, often observed among preschool-aged children (Dillon, 1934), is recognized as a tension reliever. It unquestionably increases during periods of emotional tension, but three-year-old children have also been observed to masturbate as an expression of delight when they are not tired, stressed, or unhappy (Levine, 1957). On the other hand, masturbatory behaviors also provide stimulation and are frequently observed occurring when children are bored. Adults' observations of children's sexual behaviors in early childhood settings and at home frequently report masturbatory behaviors at nap time and bedtime. Self-stimulation becomes particularly habituated among children who lack other forms of stimulation in a deprived environment, as in the case of neglect (Ryan, 2000).

How children think about sexuality raises the question of sexual "fantasy." Within every person there is a constellation of thoughts, images, wishes, and fears that differ greatly in the degree to which they are "fantastic" to the individual (Pitcher & Prelinger, 1963). It is assumed that sometime in the first year, before beginning to speak, the infant probably fantasizes, for understanding precedes speech (Gardner, 1969).

However, it is worthwhile to define what is meant by "fantasy." In adolescence and adulthood, the sexual life is informed and organized by a store of experiences, actual and vicarious. The kind and content of prior sexual experiences and exposure influence, produce, and structure subsequent sexual thoughts and experiences. Early in the literature, children's sexual thoughts were referred to as fantasy, but it is important to distinguish thoughts that simply reflect information stored in memory from a fantasy, that is a goal directed toward some future experience. The term "fantasy" was used extensively in the early psychoanalytic literature, especially in reference to sexuality, having been influenced by Freud's suggestion that allegations of adult sexual contact with children were products of "fantasy" (see Chapter 3). Fantasy was equated with being unreal, whereas today, the term "sexual fantasy" most often refers to sexual thoughts that reflect interest and desire.

At whatever age "fantasizing" or thinking about sexuality first occurs, it is the case that the thoughts/fantasy of an inexperienced person (a child) will not be as rich in content or as sexually explicit as will that of an experienced adult. In North America today, however, children are exposed to sexual learning and messages throughout the culture and community from very early ages. If sexual fantasy is defined as thoughts about sexual behavior one has not yet engaged in or experienced, the risk of children's "fantasy" being more sexually explicit is likely to have increased now as compared to children's thoughts about sexuality in the 1950s, when the culture children were most exposed to was almost devoid of sexual innuendo and stimuli.

In reference to sexual fantasies, Riophe and Galenson (1981) observed that during the infant's genital self-stimulation an "inward gaze and a self-absorbed look" seem to indicate that a fantasy feeling state had now become a regular component of the genital self-stimulation and that this new type of genital activity is true masturbation.

Because little evidence about thoughts can be collected until the child is old enough to talk, several studies relate to the fantasy content of children aged 2 years and older. Ames (1966) studied the themes or topics in stories told by 2- and 3-year-old children and found that 60% of the boys and 68% of the girls had themes of violence, along with themes of food and eating, sleep, good and bad, sibling rivalry, the possibility of castration, and reproduction. Pitcher and Prelinger (1963) analyzed stories of children 2 to 5 years old and identified eight main themes: aggression, death, hurt or misfortune, morality, nutrition, dress, sociability, and crying. Boys' themes of aggression tended to be more violent than girls, and among 2-year-olds, there were concerns about violation of body intactness (some part of the body being broken or severed), whereas this theme is almost absent in the stories of the 3-year-olds. Themes about sensory and sexual experiences were rare, another aspect that may now be changed by high exposure to these themes in North American culture.

Ames (1966) found that although kind and friendly stories were uncommon at any age (intimacy, kindness, or eroticism), they occurred most commonly at 2 and 3 years. Pitcher and Prelinger (1963) found that girls referred to love, courtship, and marriage, and were more likely than the boys to express emotion and affect. These authors found that the younger children appeared at times to make quite a transparent reference to the issue of pregnancy in their stories, but the connections of the various details tended to be illogical. They also observed that it was rare that the phenomenon of excitement or aggression between a man and woman took place in the stories. A major flaw in these studies may be that American children learn early that they must not talk about sex or family violence, and that may be why the subjects did not appear in their stories. This may also be changed by greater exposure to these issues today.

One of the most striking findings of Conn and Kanner's (1940) play interview study of 200 children aged 4 to 14 was the inability or unwillingness of the children to use words referring to sex. In the play interviews, they found that sexual fantasies accompanying masturbation—imagining sight or touch of genitals, buttocks, or breasts and thoughts of coitus—were reported by a very small number of boys below age 9 and by no girls of any age. For instance, in play interviews, the children even as young as 4 years old spoke up unhesitatingly and without embarrassment of the boy's "thing" and the girl's "thing," but other distinctions had something secret or hidden about them. It was not so much that they did not know names for the genitals—in fact, these children used 61 different names—but that they regarded the names as bad, nasty, or dirty, and hence not to be uttered. Children with such inhibitions would be unlikely to report stories they have made up about sex or sexual activity. This same phenomena has been a concern in children's ability to report sexual abuse, due to the secrecy surrounding all sexuality. The lack of permission to use explicit language is one of the most common and reasonable things child sexual abuse prevention programs have tried to address.

That children do think about sex is evident in their questions. In Hattendorf's (1932) collection of sex questions, preschoolers asked the most questions (49.1%), those from age 6 to 10 asked 40.1% of the questions, and those 10 to 14 asked only 16.8%. The questions asked most frequently concerned the origin of babies, the coming of another baby, physical differences, organs and functions of the body, the process of birth, the relation of the father to reproduction, intrauterine growth, and marriage. It is apparent that children do want to know about these matters.

Two- and 3-year-olds exhibit intimate involvement with others. Freud (1938) observed that children from 3 to 5 years old were capable of "evincing a very strong object selection which is accompanied by strong affect." Kinsey's (1953) interviews with a small sample of 2-year-olds and their mothers reveal a good deal of cuddling and kissing of parents and others by both boys and girls. Infants who are securely attached to a parent were compliant and cooperative by 21 months. Schvaneveldt, Frye, and Ostler (1970) report that children as young as 3 years old, when asked what "good" and "bad" parents do, report that good mothers kiss you and bad mothers do not, and a good father is one who kisses and hugs you and a bad father is one who is not nice to you.

By age 3 to 4, children are beginning to be socialized away from body contact with self and others (Lewis, 1965). Children begin early to sense consciously that touching patterns (as part of their tactile communication system with their parents) have gradually become nonreciprocating. Blackman (1980) has shown that at least by the age of 4, children no longer have permission to touch their parents to communicate their needs. Beyond the age of infancy, it is also apparent that parents hold gender-specific attitudes about intimacy and affectionate relationships with their children. There are a number of distinctions as to what body parts can be touched in interacting based on the gender of the child and the gender of the parent. "Too much" touching, especially by boys, causes discomfort for many adults (Roberts, Kline, & Gagnon, 1978).

Even by 18 to 24 months, infants have been observed to display a variety of forms of direct prosocial activity such as helping and comforting peers, siblings, and parents (Johnson, 1982). Gesell and Ilg (1946) indicate that children 3-and-a-half years old are interested in marriage and marrying and may propose to their parents and others of either sex. They use the expression "I love" frequently and begin to show an interest in babies, wanting to have one in their family. They like to look at and touch adults, especially mothers and babies.

Children up to 3 years of age may show no marked distinction between the sexes in play with peers. Some of the play with peers may be sexual if children of this age are left together unsupervised with nothing else that interests them more. Young children appear to prefer sex play with peers rather than with persons of older ages (Constantine & Martinson, 1981). It is a way of relating to others and can be enjoyable, providing coercion is not used. Child development experts generally believe that peer sex play is normal and is generally a harmless growing-up experience. Interest in sex play is episodic (Ilg & Ames, 1955), and may include embracing, stroking and caressing, kissing, and touching the genitals (Spiro, 1958).

Bell (1902) divided manifestations of "the emotion of love between the sexes" into two stages. The first stage included children from three to eight years old and was characterized by "hugging, kissing, lifting each other, scuffling, sitting close to each other, confessions to each other and excluding others, grief at being separated, giving of gifts, extending courtesies to each other that are withheld from others, making sacrifices such as giving up desired things or foregoing pleasures, jealousies, etc." Moll (1913) also divided childhood into two phases, the first of which ended at age 7. The first phase was more social (that is, less sexual) than the period from 8 years old and up.

PREADOLESCENCE

In older literature, preadolescence was defined as ages 8 through 12, and referred to as a period of anticipation and growth, with diminished sexual activity and interest (e.g. "latency"). It now appears that this concept was overstressed, a product of Freud's relegation of children's sexual life to fantasy. It has become apparent in more recent research that most children do not cease sexual development, interest, and behavior from ages 5 to 10, but, rather, cease to share their interest with adults and are less frequently observed, even though the behaviors continue. This may be due to adult messages of discomfort, denial, repression, and prohibition, but is also likely influenced by a sense of modesty and privacy, which develops for most children around age 5.

Awareness of the self as a sexual being and of others as potential intimate and erotic partners is very real for most preadolescents. Even in a sexually restrictive society, sexual-erotic responses and encounters occur more commonly than previously acknowledged. Children go through stages of interpersonal sexual involvement, in both fantasy and actuality, during the preadolescent years, and the likelihood of same-sex or opposite sex partners is largely a matter of opportunity prior to puberty. Children do sexual things with their peers/playmates/friends and it is with the onset of puberty that it begins to matter which "special" friend it is. Sexual interactions generally become more discriminating during puberty: both person-specific and gender-specific. The sexual, psychological, and social changes that begin during these years continue to mature during adolescence and are essential to the transition to full adult sexual functioning.

Many preadolescent children experience increased sexual interest as the changes of puberty begin to occur. The biological sexual changes—appearance of pubic hair, development of breasts, wet dreams, and so on—can be awesome to the child, who is often not sure how to react to such phenomena. Biological puberty for humans (announced by the beginning of menarche in girls and by the capacity for ejaculation in boys), begins between the ages of 8 and 15, varying in timing and rate for each child and differently for boys and girls.

However, it is apparent that the onset of puberty has changed during the last century. Whereas the average age of menarche for girls was around 14 to 15 in the early 1900s, and 13 in the 1950s, it is now under 10 for girls and only slightly older for boys. Many possible influences in the earlier onset of puberty have been investigated, with the most widely considered being the exposure to artificial estrogen in the environment: a by-product of the manufacture of plastics. Most recently, discoveries of increased toxic exposure resulting from heating and/or freezing plastics has raised concerns of additional unrecognized risks. Endocrinologists and toxicologists have seen a shift in concerns from cancer effects to reproductive and pubertal effects related to toxins in the environment (Sanghavi, 2006). The onset of puberty has been one year earlier with each generation since the 1950s, which is when plastics were first introduced (Ryan 2003).

PROBLEMATIC EROTICIZATION AND HYPER-SEXUALITY

Child-parent intimate interactions in the United States are heavily circumscribed by social norms. In early infancy, society accepts that mother-infant interaction is close, intimate, permissive, and highly sensual. As the child grows, the relationship moves further along the continuum toward role- and gender-based relationships (Douvan, 1977), and the parent represents a more demanding authoritative structure. Sensory and sexual interactions are repressed, and the child is not expected to engage in these behaviors until later in life.

Although there is still not societal agreement about what constitutes reasonable sexual behavior in childhood, there is a universal norm that infants and children should not be sexually abused or exploited. It is generally agreed that adult and child sexual involvement is fraught with the greatest dangers for the child. Full eroti-cization of the relationship between a parent and child is possible, given the interactive opportunity and emotional access to each other (Rorty, 1972; Rosenfeld, 1976). Although intimacy occurs in normative child-parent encounters, it may also occur in erotically charged parent-child encounters. Sexualized attention (Haynes-Seman & Krugman, 1989) and sexual stimulation such as fondling, caressing, and masturbation are more common in erotic parent-child encounters; physical involve-ment to the point of coitus and the use of physical force are less common (Constantine & Martinson, 1981). Erotic interactions that are seductive, exploitive, coercive, or manipulative and serve to use the child's sexual developmental behavior to meet the parent's needs have negative ramifications for a child, and are now defined as abuse.

Concentrating on the sexual dimension of family intimacy and affection, Finkelhor (1978) categorized families as sex positive or sex negative, and high-sexualized or low-sexualized. According to Finkelhor, family sexuality has at least three dimensions: a family's attitude toward sexuality (family culture); the actual eroticization of family relationships; and the family's respect for personal boundaries. In sex-positive families, children receive accurate information about sex, are given positive attitudes about their bodies, and are shown physical affection. In sex-negative families, sex and discussions about sex are loaded with anxiety and taboos. In high-sexualized families, members use one another as objects in their role playing. Each member tries to test out his or her powers of attraction and adequacy on the others. Low-sexualized families discourage sexual role playing and posturing from occurring inside the family. Regarding personal boundaries, one interpretation of clear boundaries is a family in which the privacy of each family member is respected. In such families, there is likely to be a clear differentiation of what the sex roles are between adults and children. In families with poor personal boundaries, family members intrude on one another, and childhood sexuality is not clearly distinguished from adult sexuality.

Similarly, Gilgun (1988) described a "non-normative sexual environment" in the home as one of the differentiating factors among boys who had been sexually abused either becoming or not becoming sexual offenders as adults. The two extremes definitive of her "non-normative" status were an absence or denial of all sexuality, or a highly sexualized environment. Bolton, Morris, and MacEachron (1989) also looked at sexuality in the environment and family and described "the abuse of sexuality" along a continuum having a negative effect on learning.

Cases of unusual or problematic sexualization support the appetitional theory of sexual motivation; that is, that motives are learned in association with affective experience. Hyper-sexuality is different from the norm by its interference in other aspects of development and functioning. For the hyper-sexual child, a host of acts may serve as sexual stimuli. Many children calm or amuse themselves by masturbat-ing in private; the hyper-sexual child is more likely to masturbate at times when others are present or other activities require their attention. They may also be more insistent in attempts to engage playmates in sexual activity and make advances toward others (Yates, 1978). Highly sexualized children can be uncommonly erotic, easily aroused, highly sexually motivated, and readily orgasmic. They may be easily aroused by a variety of circumstances and may not be able to discriminate erotic from nonerotic relationships. Being readily orgasmic, they may also maintain a high level of arousal without orgasm, and appear to find sexual activity eminently pleasurable. "In fact, erotic expressions may be so gratifying that it is difficult to find comparable rewards to reinforce socially acceptable behavior" (Yates, 1978).

Hyper-sexuality can also be a symptom of or a product of a variety of psychiatric disorders described in the DSM. Anxiety, depression, underachievement, somatic complaints, and self-defeating behavior patterns may all increase the need for compensatory reconciliation. However, the eroticization process may also be entirely independent of emotional disturbances, trauma, or neglect. Children's sexualization and sexual behaviors fall along a wide continuum from less to more, and normality is not easily defined.

Being affectionate is not the same as being eroticized, and being eroticized is not pathological in and of itself. Erotic activity can have either adaptive or maladaptive potential, "depending on the child's flexibility and appreciation of reality" (Yates, 1978). It cannot be assumed that sexual activity in childhood is a sign of either victimization or pathology. To do so does a great disservice to children. Numerous researchers have studied the effects of sexual experiences on children (see Ryan & Associates, 1998), and Constantine and Martinson's (1981) study concluded, "The more negative outcomes are associated with ignorance of sexuality; with negative attitudes towards sex; with tense situations; with force, brutality, or coercion; or with unsupportive, uncommunicative, or judgmental adult reactions."

Early erotic behavior by itself does not damage the child. In some families or cultures it may set them apart and create conflict or anxiety in relationships, and of course, the risks of being sexually active can be similar or even magnified for less informed or more vulnerable persons. Yet in another culture or another era, there might be no problem. But from a purely theoretical or practical standpoint, it is clear that a major consequence of overt sexual experience in childhood is an increase in the specificity of acts that the child learns to perform in satisfying sexual needs. It can follow that there might be an increase in desire to perform such sexual acts and a greater degree of frustration when the acts are prevented from occurring (Sears, Macoby, & Levine, 1957). Early eroticized sexual experiences may contribute to increased activity, which in turn may be in conflict with parental or community admonitions to abstain. From a developmental perspective, a competency may be learned at a teachable moment, even though the experience or the competency may be judged morally or even legally wrong by others. Often the learning and behaviors may be clearly within the range of normal human sexuality, but may occur in the wrong time or place, developmentally or experientially, creating a problem for the child where none would exist in another time or place.

SEXUAL BEHAVIORS IN CHILDHOOD AND ADOLESCENCE

Children go through stages of intimate erotic involvement in relationships that may or may not be characterized by overtly sexual behavior. In some communities, it is acceptable for children to begin these stages in preadolescence or earlier; in others they may be discouraged until puberty or later. The child begins by forming attachments, or "crushes," on persons outside the family. The love feeling is expressed to the other person in forms that depend on age, sexual and social maturity, and the permissiveness of the adults who supervise the child's behavior. Erotic involvement may first appear in the form of roughhouse love play (hitting a boy, pulling a girl's hair), writing notes, inviting the other to a party, or simply walking home together. If the other person responds to this attention, the two may enter into the first of what often becomes, through adolescence, a series of close relationships with peers. These relationships provide a set of learning experiences, such as learning how to kiss, how to dance, how to talk to a potential sexual partner, as well as how to fondle and caress. The process of learning these skills is often exciting and dramatic, but it can also be painful and embarrassing.

A U.S. Office of Education Survey conducted in 1958 (Lewis, 1958) supported the observation that boys and girls do not appear to feel a need to separate from each other during preadolescence. In schools, some dating begins as early as the fourth grade, and youth in grades four through six frequently asked for activities that would allow both boys and girls to participate. Boys groomed themselves (some beginning in the fourth grade), carried a comb and used it, washed their hands voluntarily, and occasionally wore a tie. Girls wore lipstick and nail polish and groomed their hair. A few children wore "going steady" rings. Broderick and Fowler's (1961) studies revealed that the majority of children in each primary grade claimed to have a sweetheart, and most of these children expected reciprocation. In the fifth grade, nearly 45% of the boys and 36% of the girls claimed to have had dating experience. By the seventh grade, nearly 70% of the boys and 53% of the girls claimed to have had at least one date. Some experience with kissing was common at these ages.

Broderick and Fowler (1961), and later Ruppel (1979), reported a pyramidally structured set of stages of social heterosexual maturation. This more-or-less orderly pattern or progression is discernible during the preadolescent years, and success or failure in each step appears to have consequences for more advanced stages of heterosexual development. Each stage is not an absolute prerequisite to the next, but the stages are closely interrelated. The beginning point seems to be in the child's attitude, with the most advanced stage for preadolescents being going out on a date. The steps or stages they delineated in the process of heterosexual development are desire to marry someone, having a certain girlfriend or boyfriend, having been in love, preferring a companion of the opposite sex over one of the same sex or no companion at all when going to a movie, and having begun to date.

Between 1960 and 1990 there was a marked trend toward greater heterosexual experience of preadolescents with their peers in the United States, as compared with studies in the 1920s and 1930s, at which time preadolescent boys seemed generally disinterested in sex and only covertly interested in girls. Most recently, the combination of earlier puberty and greater sexual stimuli in the environment has contributed to much earlier signs of sexuality among very young children. Ironically, the same adults who find it reasonable to dress and groom toddlers and very young children in "sexualized" fashions become alarmed when children and adolescents subsequently exhibit sexualized behaviors and interests. The incongruence of a highly sexualized culture and adult demands for abstinence during childhood and adolescence is a matter of curiosity and interest to sociologists, and a source of confusion for children.

At each age of preadolescence, prepubertal boys report more sexual activity of every kind than do girls (Broderick & Fowler, 1961). Differences in reported incidence of heterosexual activity for boys and girls just prior to puberty may depend in part on the increased restraints that are placed on girls by their parents as the girls approach puberty—restraints that girls often resent after a carefree childhood (Martinson, 1973). Adults tend to start restricting opposite sex contact prior to puberty much more for girls than boys, leaving girls with more opportunity for same-sex intimacy and exploration than with opposite-sex peers. Additionally, the female subculture does not advocate sexual activity for girls as the male subculture does for boys. Although few of the girls report a pattern of frequent or regular sexual activity prior to puberty, it is not possible to know to what extent girls may be reticent to self-report these behaviors. Retrospective reports from adults consistently indicate more female activity in childhood than is reported in interviews with children (Cavanaugh-Johnson, 1998; Ryan, Miyoshi, Metzner, Krugman, & Fryer, 1996).

Whereas male homophobia may sometimes be an inhibitor of same-sex contact behaviors among boys, girls are more likely to explore both same-sex and opposite-sex activities. Boys' same-sex activities often include group masturbation where several boys are together, touching themselves but not each other, whereas mutual masturbation (each touching the other) may be less frequent. Opposite-sex experiences for young boys may sometimes occur with somewhat older girls who tutor or exploit them, more than with age-mates who may be viewed as more intimidating to them. Similarly, girls may also have their first sexual experience with a somewhat older boy. Such experiences are often defined as "statutory rape" but are developmentally not unusual when consensual and not coerced (Child Trends, 2002). Adolescent females have only recently been held accountable for child abuse when involving significantly younger boys in sexual activity.

Friedrich et al. (1992); Friedrich, Fisher, Broughton, Houston, and Shafran (1998); Friedrich et al. (2001); Gil and Johnson (1993); Fitzpatrick, Deechan, and Jennings (1995); Larsson and Svedin (2002a; 2002b) and Maticka-Tyndale (2001) report on adult observations of children's sexual behaviors and juvenile self-reports, while Ryan, Miyoshi, and Krugman (1988); and Cavanaugh-Johnson (1998) have reported on adult recollections of childhood experience and behavior. These and other sources confirm that children do continue to engage in both autoerotic behaviors and sexual interactions with peers throughout childhood. Girls may be somewhat more active than in previous generations, although it is not possible to separate changes such as less secrecy and less parental denial from actual changes in behavior. Some differences seem likely in light of the much greater exposure of children to sexual stimuli in the culture when comparing studies from the 1940s, 1960s, and 1980s; however, the most significant change in the sexual behaviors of children and adolescents has been in the frequency and circumstances of oral genital contact (CDC, 2002; Matika-Tyndale, 2001).

Masturbation is more common in preadolescent boys than is heterosexual experience. Erection occurs more quickly in preadolescent boys than it does in adult males, and the capacity to achieve repeated orgasms in limited periods of time exceeds the corresponding capacity of teenage boys, who in turn are more capable of repeated orgasms than adult males are. The incidence is never precisely known, although Ramsey (1943) indicated that masturbation occurs at some time in the sexual histories of nearly all males. In collecting data and clinical interviews, it is often apparent that males do not define self-stimulation as "masturbation" until it results in ejaculation; 75% report their first experience as occurring between the ages of 10 and 16.

Masturbation is often viewed as more of a male behavior and considered less common for girls; however, differences in self-reports to investigators may account for much of this as girls tend to be more modest and also have less permission to be sexual or talk about sexuality as compared to boys. In addition, both accurate and slang terminology for male masturbation is more common, whereas even language to describe female masturbatory behaviors is discouraged. However, adult females do recall sexual behavior alone and with peers in childhood (Ryan et al., 1996).

In recent studies, rates of solitary sexual behaviors have been of less interest as the onset of sexual interactions have been studied more, partly in relation to increased definition of abusive interactions, and especially due to increased rates of sexually transmitted diseases and unwanted pregnancies. The resurgence of "abstinence only" priorities among adults, though sometimes intended as protective, may contribute to confusion in the sexual knowledge and values of youth. Current trends in adolescent sexual activity seem to be both regressive and accelerated. On the one hand, casual sexual interactions ("friends with benefits" or "hooking up"), along with increases in young people defining themselves as "bisexual" (on the basis of interactions with both same-sex and opposite-sex peers), seem to parallel earlier developmental patterns of prepubescent sexual activity with playmates rather than romantic relations. Teens report that sexual activity with friends is less complicated than within committed love relationships.

On the other hand, rates of oral and anal sexual contact have increased both before and after puberty, corresponding with increased STDs among young people. Studies have shown confusion in youthful definitions of "abstinence" and "virginity" in regards to oral and anal sexual activities. Whereas only 5.8% and 11.9% of adolescents believe that an individual is still "virgin" or "abstinent" after intercourse, 70.6% and 33.4% believe virginity and abstinence are maintained in spite of oral genital contact (Bersamin, Fisher, Walker, Hill, & Grube, 2007). Youth also underestimate the risk of transmitting disease in oral and anal activity, so are less frequently using condoms for oral and anal activity, even though the rate of condom use in casual relationship intercourse exceeds that of committed relationships (Houston, 2007).

Oral sex has been more openly discussed in North America in this generation but is often viewed as not violating pledges of faithfulness or abstinence, and is often perceived as less risky than intercourse. Increases in STDs are particularly concerning. Whereas previous generations were often dissuaded from anal and oral genital contact by hygienic perceptions, today's youth seem more willing to explore the behavior and experience its reinforcements.

Social, cultural, and economic influences may affect sexual behavior somewhat, but it is apparent that children have always been sexual and continue to be sexual. In some ways, it may be most surprising to note that the differences are not greater than they appear to be despite differing norms and exposure now as compared to 50 years ago. This may provide some evidence that childhood sexuality is primarily affected by internal biology and developmental processes more than external influences.

UNDERSTANDING AND DIFFERENTIATING SEXUAL BEHAVIOR

A number of authors have described reasons why various sexual behaviors might be considered a problem in childhood (Bonner, Walker, & Berliner, 1996; Friedrich et al., 2001; Johnson, 1991, 1998; Johnson & Doonan, 2005; Silovsky & Niec, 2002). Much of the data regarding prepubescent children in North America comes from parental reports of what they observe, which is likely to be incomplete. Using multiple sources of information, Ryan et al. (1988) described the range of behavior in terms of what appears developmentally expected (that is, frequently observed and not usually problematic) along a continuum of concern to those posing greatest risk (see Figures 4.1 and 4.2). A subsequent review of the most recent research shows little

No		Authority		Coercion		Physical Force	
___ Pressure	___	Manipulation	___	Threats	___	Threat of Harm	___
		Trickery		Bribes		Violence	

Figure 4.1   Range of Coercion

Label and React	$\longrightarrow$	Monitor	$\longrightarrow$	Confront and Prohibit	$\longrightarrow$	Monitor	$\longrightarrow$	Evaluate for Report or Referral

Figure 4.2   Range of Response

change in these behaviors, with the only significant change being in the oral genital contact previously discussed (Ryan, 2000).

Along with considering the behavior, it is stressed that behavior cannot be evaluated out of context. The importance of evaluating the nature of interactions and relationships was discussed in Chapter 1 in relation to defining abusive behaviors. Although the risks associated with some behaviors lead adults to caution adolescents against them, it is not reasonable to pathologize or stigmatize youth for normal human behaviors. The developmental dilemma that ensues from early sexual maturation along with delayed socioeconomic maturity is very real and children need to be understood and educated to cope with the incongruity of what was once a brief transitional period of development (adolescence), now lasting at least a decade. Adults need to recognize the many reasons people engage in sexual behaviors across the life span and become able to differentiate the reasons behavior might be a problem, as well as when it is not. (See Figures 4.3 and 4.4.)

Exploration/Curiosity
(What's This All About? Self/Others)
Imitation/Learning
(See/Do/Practice/Teach)
Sensation Seeking
(Arousing When Bored/Calming When Stressed)
Reinforcement: Feels Good
(Arousal, Orgasm, Tension Reduction)
Pleasure: Self/Other
(Relationship, Intimacy, Friendship, Love)
∗∗∗ **Reproduction** ∗∗∗
(from Puberty to Mid-Life)
Compensation/Improvement
(Feel Better, Do Better, Regain Self Image/Control)
Anger/Retaliation
(Get Back at Others, Make Others Feel Hurt/Angry)

Figure 4.3   Motivation for Sexual Behavior (Reasons Why Human Beings Want to Do Sexual Things)

Sexual Behavior Might be a Problem for Many Reasons:

It might be a problem for the person who is doing it . . .
because it puts the person at risk in some way:
health, reproduction, exploitation, stigma, lowers self image
It might be a problem for others . . .
because it makes them uncomfortable; violates norms, standards, or values; breaks
rules or regulations.
OR, **it might be a problem because it is abusive and/or illegal . . .**

Figure 4.4   Sexual Behavior: Is it a problem? If so, what kind of problem?

Of all the potential motivations, only the use of sexual behavior to express anger or cause harm would *always* be a problem. Yet any of the motives could become problematic in the wrong time or place, or if the behavior is putting the child at risk in some way or interfering in other aspects of life. While acknowledging all the legitimate concerns associated with children and adolescents being "sexually active," differentiating the reasons behaviors are a problem is key in providing reasonable responses.

In societies where they are permitted to do so, children increase rather than decrease their sexual activities during preadolescence. Sexual encounters first include genital auto-stimulation and mutual masturbation with the same-sex and opposite-sex peers, but with increasing age, they are characterized by increased intimacy and attempts at heterosexual intercourse. By the time children reach puberty in sexually permissive societies, their expressions of sexuality consist predominantly of the accepted adult form of heterosexual intercourse, and continue to follow this pattern across the life span (Ford & Beach, 1951).

First attempts at intercourse are not unusual between the ages of 10 and 14. Kinsey, Pomeroy, and Martin (1948) found that by age 12, at least one boy in every four or five had tried to copulate with a female. Kinsey also found lower levels of sexual activity among boys who later attended college, as compared to boys who did not finish high school.

Broderick and Fowler (1961) found some racial differences in the pattern of heterosexual development, with the most striking differences between black and white children noted during preadolescence, ages 10 to 13. Black children, especially boys, exhibited higher rates of heterosexual interaction at ages 12 and 13 than did white children.

Before assuming differences of race or educational aspirations are the source of such differences, it is important to remember that even very young children will engage in sexual behaviors more when bored and lacking stimulation. Economic differences and stresses are more likely contributors to rates of sexual behavior than race or education. When people of any age have the resources to engage in a wide range of pleasurable and interesting pursuits, the rate of sexual activity will be less than among those with fewer opportunities. Similarly, in times of extreme stress, the compensatory function of sexual intimacy and tension reduction increases rates of sexual behavior as well. This has been evident even among highly educated, majority populations by "baby booms" correlating with times of economic depression or the stresses of disasters or war.

In recent data, overall rates of sexual activity among young people do not appear dramatically different from previous generations, in spite of perceptual differences (Hampton, McWatters, Jeffrey, & Smith, 2005). Although rates of particular behaviors may vary slightly over time, it is apparent that the range of human sexual behaviors is relatively predictable and stable. Unfortunately, much of the research regarding child and adolescent sexual behaviors in North America is conducted in exploring risks and problems. Studies of sexually transmitted disease, unwanted pregnancy, sexual victimization, exploitation, abuse perpetration, statutory crimes, sexual harassment, child pornography, and so forth, often produce statistics that alarm and confuse (Alan Guttmacher Institute, 2004; Boyce, Doherty, Fortin, & MacKinnon, 2003; CDC, 2002; Henshaw, 1998). Whereas Kinsey and others in the 1940s studied infant and child sexual development, S. Janus and C. Janus (1993) only briefly mention child-hood sexuality in what was hailed as one of the biggest studies since Kinsey. Sexologists have much less opportunity to report on healthy sexual development and normative behaviors of children and youth in this culture, and more balanced views continue to come more from cross-cultural sources.

That infants and small children have the physiological capacity for sexual response, that they are curious about their bodies and the bodies of others, and that they are attracted to intimate behaviors and interaction with others has been established. With modeling, encouragement, and education, there appears to be no need for a cessation of sensory and sexual activity from first discovery through childhood and adolescence. The capacity for sexual response is very much shaped by experience; thus, the teachable moment may help children learn from their experiences and develop healthy sexual functioning or may leave the child to their own devices to make sense of sexuality.

Whereas a child in the 1950s might not receive helpful information or education about sexuality because of adults' discomfort with sexuality, unless something traumatic or deviant occurred, most children muddled through exploration and learning with friends and eventually became at least moderately successful in their sexuality. In today's world, children are exposed to so many conflicting and incomprehensible messages and images that the risks to normative learning and experience are much greater. The need for adults to be more proactive in not only protecting, but also validating and correcting learning, is clear. To respond reason-ably, in a goal-oriented manner, it is useful for adults to be thoughtful and objective, rather than reacting from a state of discomfort. Recognizing the dramatic shifts in the normality of some behaviors, which occurs between childhood and adolescence, along with the absence of guidance and sex education for children, it becomes understandable why pubescent youth are "at risk" to be misinformed, confused, and might be at risk to engage in problematic behaviors.

REFERENCES

Ainsworth, M. D. (1964). Patterns of attachment behavior shown by the infant in interaction with his mother. *Merrill-Palmer Quarterly, 10*, 51–58.

Alan Guttmacher Institute. (2004). *U.S. teenage pregnancy statistics with comparative statistics for women aged 20–24*. New York: Author.

Ames, L. B. (1966). Children's stories. *Genetic Psychology Monographs, 73*, 337–396.

Bell, S. (1902). A. preliminary study of the emotion of love between the sexes. *American Journal of Psychology, 12*, 325–354.

Bersamin, M., Fisher, D., Walker, S., Hill, D., & Grube, J. (2007). Defining virginity and abstinence: Adolescents' interpretations of sexual behaviors. *Journal of Adolescent Health, 41*, 182–188.

Blackman, N. (1980). Pleasure and touching: Their significance in the development of the preschool child—An exploratory study. *Childhood and Sexuality: Proceedings of the International Symposium*, 175–202.

Bolton, F., Morris, C., & MacEachron, A. (1989). *Males at risk*. Thousand Oaks, CA: Sage.

Bonner, B., Walker, E., & Berliner, L. (1996). *Children with sexual behavior problems: Research based treatment*. Paper presented at the Eleventh International Congress on Child Abuse and Neglect, Dublin, Ireland.

Boyce, W., Doherty, M., Fortin, C., & MacKinnon, D. (2003). *Canadian youth, sexual health and HIV/AIDS study: Factors influencing knowledge, attitudes and behaviors*. Toronto, ON: Council of Ministers of Education.

Broderick, C. B., & Fowler, S. E. (1961). New patterns of relationships between the sexes among pre-adolescents. *Marriage and Family Living, 23*, 27–30.

Bruijn, P., Burrie, I., & van Wel, F. (2006). A risky boundary: Unwanted sexual behavior among youth. *Journal of Sexual Aggression, 12*, 81–96.

Burr, W., Leigh, G. K., Day, R. D., & Constantine, J. (1979). Symbolic interaction and the family. In W. Burr, R. Hill, F. Nye, & I. Reiss (Eds.), *Contemporary theories about the family* (pp. 43–111). New York: The Free Press.

Calderone, M. (1983, May–June). Fetal erection and its message to us. *Sex Education and Information Council of the United States* (Report).

Cavanaugh-Johnson, T. (1998). *A retrospective study of the childhood sexual behaviors of Swedish and American children*. International Congress On Child Abuse and Neglect: Auckland, New Zealand, September.

Centers for Disease Control and Prevention. (2002). Trends in sexual risk behaviors among high school students—United States, 1991–2001. *Morbidity and mortality Weekly Report, 51*, 856–859.

Child Trends. (2002). *National Survey on Family Growth*. Washington, DC: United States Department of Human and Health Services.

Clark-Stewart, K. A. (1973). Interactions between mothers and young children: Characteristics and consequences. *Monographs of the Society for Research in Child Development, 38*, (P 6-7, Serial No. 153).

Conn, J. H., & Kanner, L. (1940). Spontaneous erections in early childhood. *The Journal of Pediatrics, 16*, 336–340.

Constantine, L. L., & Martinson, F. M. (1981). *Children and sex: New findings, new perspectives*. Boston: Little, Brown.

Dillon, M. S. (1934). Attitudes in children toward their own bodies and those of other children. *Child Development, 5*, 165–167.

Douvan, E. (1977). Interpersonal relations: Some questions and observations. In G. Levinger & H. L. Raush (Eds.), *Close relationships: Perspectives on the meaning of intimacy* (pp. 17–32). Amherst: University of Massachusetts Press.

Finkelhor, D. (1978). Psychological culture and family factors in incest and family sexual abuse. *Journal of Marriage and the Family, 4*, 41–49.

Fitzpatrick, P., Deechan, A., & Jennings, S. (1995). Children's sexual behavior and knowledge: A community study. *Irish Journal of Psychological Medicine, 12*, 87–91.

Ford, C. S., & Beach, F. A. (1951). *Patterns of sexual behaviors*. New York: HarperCollins.

Freud, S. (1938). *The basic writings of Sigmund Freud* (A. A. Brill, Trans. and Ed.). New York: Modern Library.

Friedrich, W., Grambsch, P., Damon, L., Koverola, C., Wolfe, V., Hewitt, S., et al. (1992). The child sexual behavior inventory: Normative and clinical comparison. *Psychological Assessment, 4*, 303–311.

Friedrich, W., Gerber, P. N., Koplin, B., Davis, M., Giese, J., Mykelbust, C., et al. (2001). Multimodal assessment of dissociation in adolescents: Inpatients and juvenile sex offenders. *Sexual Abuse: Journal of Research and Treatment, 13,* 167–177.

Friedrich, W. N., Fisher, J., Broughton, D., Houston, M., & Shafran, C. R. (1998). Normative sexual behavior in children: A contemporary sample. *Pediatrics, 7,* 54–59.

Gadpaille, W. J. (1975). Adolescent sexuality—A challenge to psychiatrists. *Journal of American Academy of Psychoanalysis, 3,* 163–177.

Galenson, E., & Riophe, H. (1974). The emergence of genital awareness during the second year of life. In R. C. Friedman, R. M. Richart, R. L. Van de Wiele (Eds.), *Sex differences in behavior* (pp. 32–38). New York: John Wiley & Sons.

Gardner, R. A. (1969). Sexual fantasies in childhood. *Medical Aspects of Human Sexuality, 3,* 121, 125, 127–128, 132–134.

Gesell, A., & Ilg, F. (1946). *The child from five to ten.* New York: HarperCollins.

Gil, E., & Johnson, T. (1993). *Sexualized children.* Rockville, MD: Launch Press.

Gilgun, J. (1988). *Factors which block the development of sexually abusive behavior in adults abused as children.* Paper presented at the National Conference on Male Victims and Offenders, Minneapolis, Minnesota.

Goldman, R. I., & Goldman, L. D. G. (1982). *Children's sexual thinking.* London: Routledge and Kegan Paul.

Halverson, H. M. (1938). Genital and sphincter behavior of the male infant. *Journal of Genetic Psychology, 56,* 383–388.

Hampton, M. R., McWatters, B., Jeffrey, B., & Smith, P. (2005). Influence of teens' perceptions of parental disapproval and peer behavior on their initiation of sexual intercourse. *The Canadian Journal of Human Sexuality, 14.* 22-SEP-2005, online edition @ access.com.

Harris, P. L., Cassel, T. Z., & Bamborough, P. (1974). Tracking by young infants. *British Journal of Psychology, 65,* 345–349.

Hattendorf, K. W. (1932). A. study of the questions of young children concerning sex: A phase of an experimental approach to parent education. *Journal of Social Psychology, 3,* 37–65.

Haynes-Seman, C., & Krugman, R. (1989). Sexualized attention: Normal interaction or precursor to sexual abuse? *American Journal of Orthopsychiatry, 59,* 238–245.

Hendrick, I. (1942). Instinct and the ego during infancy. *Psychoanalytic Quarterly, 11,* 33–58.

Henshaw, S. K. (1998). Unintended pregnancy in the United States. *Family Planning Perspectives, 30,* 24–29, 46.

Honig, A. S. (1982). Pro-social development in children. *Young Children, 37,* 51–62.

Houston, A. M. (2007). Anal intercourse and condom use patterns in "main" and "casual" sexual relationships. *Journal of Pediatric Adolescent Gynecology, 20,* 299–304.

Hurlock, E. B. (1950). *Child development.* New York: McGraw-Hill.

Ilg, F. L., & Ames, L. B. (1955). *Child behavior.* New York: Dell.

Janus, S., & Janus, C. (1993). *The Janus Report on Sexual Behavior.* New York: John Wiley & Sons.

Johnson, D. B. (1982). Altruistic behavior and the development of the self in infants. *Merrill-Palmer Quarterly, 28,* 379–388.

Johnson, T. C. (1991). *Understanding the sexual behaviors of young children.* SIECUS (Sexuality Information and Education Council of the United States) Report, August/September.

Johnson, T. C. (1998). *Helping children with sexual behavior problems—A guidebook for parents and substitute caregivers.* Self-published booklet.

Johnson, T. C., & Doonan, R. (2005). Children, twelve and younger, with sexual behavior problems: What we know in 2005 that we didn't know in 1985. In R. Longo & D. Prescott (Eds.), *Current perspectives: Working with sexually aggressive youth and youth with sexual behavior problems* (pp. 79–118). Brandon, VT: Safer Society Press.

Kanner, L. (1939). Infantile sexuality. *Journal of Pediatrics, 4,* 583–608.

Kinsey, A. C., Pomeroy, W. B., & Martin, C. E. (1948). *Sexual behavior in the human male.* Philadelphia: Saunders.

Kinsey, A. C. (1953). *Sexual behavior in the human female*. Philadelphia: Saunders.

Klaus, H. M., & Kennell, J. H. (1976). *Maternal-infant bonding*. St. Louis: Mosby-Year Book.

Langworthy, O. R. (1933). Development of behavior patterns and myelinization of the nervous system in the human fetus and infant. *Contributions to Embryology, 24*, 1–57.

Larsson, I., & Svedin, C. G. (2002a). Sexual experiences in childhood: Young adults' recollections. *Archives of Sexual Behavior, 31*, 263–273.

Larsson, I., & Svedin, C. G. (2002b). Teachers' and parents' reports on 3- to 6-year old children's sexual behavior—a comparison. *Child Abuse and Neglect, 26*, 247–266.

Lee, J. A. (1980). The politics of child sexuality. In *Childhood and sexuality* (pp. 56–70). Montreal: Editions Etudes Vivantes.

Levine, M. L. (1957). Pediatric observations on masturbation in children. *Psychoanalytic Study of the Child, 6*, 117–124.

Levinger, G. (1977). Reviewing the close relationship. In G. Levinger & H. L. Raush (Eds.), *Close relationships: Perspectives on the meaning of intimacy* (pp. 137–161). Amherst: University of Massachusetts Press.

Lewis, G. M. (1958). *Educating children in grades 4, 5, and 6*. Washington, DC: U.S. Office of Education, Department of Health, Education, and Welfare.

Lewis, W. C. (1965). Coital movements in the first year of life: Earliest anlage of genital love? *International Journal of Psychoanalysis, 46*, 372–374.

Martinson, F. M. (1973). *Infant and child sexuality: A sociological perspective*. St. Peter, MN: Book Mark.

Maticka-Tyndale, E. (2001). Sexual health and Canadian youth: How do we measure up? *The Canadian Journal of Human Sexuality, 10*, 1–17.

Moll, A. (1913). *The sexual life of the child*. New York: Macmillan.

Montague, A. (1978). *Touching: The human significance of the skin*. New York: HarperCollins.

Newton, M., & Newton, M. (1967). Psychologic aspects of lactation. *New England Journal of Medicine, 272*, 1179–1197.

Pines, M. (1982). Baby you're incredible. *Psychology Today, 16*, 48–53.

Pitcher, E. G., & Prelinger, E. (1963). *Children tell stories: An analysis of fantasy*. Madison, CT: International Universities Press.

Pouillet, T. (1883). *Etude médico-psychologique sur uonanisme chez homme*. Paris: Delahaye et Lecrosnier.

Ramsey, G. V. (1943). The sexual development of boys. *American Journal of Psychology, 56*, 217.

Riophe, H., & Galenson, E. (1981). *Infantile origins of sexual identity*. New York: International Universities Press.

Roberts, E. J., Kline, D., & Gagnon, J. (1978). *Family life and sexual learning: A study of the role of parents in the sexual learning of children*. Cambridge, MA: Population Education.

Rorty, A. O. (1972). Some social uses of the forbidden. *Psychoanalytic Review, 58*, 497–510.

Rosenfeld, A. A. (1976). Sexual misuse and the family. *Victimology: An International Journal, 2*, 226–235.

Rossi, A. (1978). A. biosocial perspective on parenting. *Daedalus, 106*, 1–31.

Ruppel, H. J. (1979). *Socio-sexual development among preadolescents*. Paper presented at the International Symposium on Childhood and Sexuality, University of Quebec, Montreal, Canada.

Ryan, G. (2000). Childhood sexuality: A decade of study. *Child Abuse and Neglect, 24*, 33–61.

Ryan, G. (2003). *Primary, secondary & tertiary perpetration prevention in childhood and adolescence*. Kempe Trainer Training Curriculum.

Ryan, G., and Associates (1998). *The web of meaning: A developmental-contextual approach in treatment of sexual abuse*. Brandon, VT: Safer Society Press.

Ryan, G., & Blum, J. (1993). *Childhood sexuality: A guide for parents*. Denver, CO: Kempe Center.

Ryan, G., Blum, J., Sandau-Christopher, D., Law, S., Weber, F., Sundine, C., et al. (1988). *Understanding and responding to the sexual behavior of children: Trainer's manual.* Denver, CO: Kempe National Centre, University of Colorado, School of Medicine.

Ryan, G., Miyoshi, T., & Krugman, R. (1988). *Early childhood experience of professionals working in child abuse.* Seventeenth Annual Symposium on Child Abuse and Neglect, Keystone, Colorado.

Ryan, G., Miyoshi, T. J., Metzner, J., Krugman, R. D., & Fryer, G. E. (1996). Trends in a national sample of juvenile sex offenders. *Journal of the American Academy of Child and Adolescent Psychiatry, 35,* 17–25.

Sanghavi, D. (2006, October 17). Preschool puberty, and a search for the causes. *New York Times.*

Schvaneveldt, J. D., Frye, M., & Ostler, R. (1970). Concepts of "badness" and "goodness" of parents as perceived by nursery school children. *Family Coordinator, 19,* 98–103.

Sears, R. R., Maccoby, E. E., & Levine, E. H. (1957). *Patterns of child rearing.* Evanston, IL: Row, Peterson.

Silovsky, J. F., & Niec, L. (2002). Characteristics of young children with sexual behavior problems: A pilot study. *Child Maltreatment, 7,* 187–197.

Spiro, M. (1958). *Children of the kibbutz.* Cambridge, MA: Harvard University Press.

Spitz, R. A., & Wolf, K. N. (1946). Anaclitic depression. *Psychoanalytic Study of the Child, 2,* 313–342.

Yates, A. (1978). *Sex without shame: Encouraging the child's healthy sexual development.* New York: Morrow.

CHAPTER 5

Deviancy

Development Gone Wrong

BRANDT R. STEELE and GAIL RYAN

D EVIANCY IN ITS broadest sense refers to any quality, conduct, or thought that significantly diverges from a standard or norm. Deviancy may be determined by the laws, customs, or standards of any group and may refer to appearances, behavior, or beliefs. Society's concern with deviancy follows a continuum that often correlates with the impact of the deviancy.

Overall, divergent or nonconforming appearances are of little concern to society as a whole, and they may be tolerated as harmless or even valued within some subcultures. Modes of dress, customs, music, and language, for instance, may deviate from the norm in order to distinguish one subgroup from another and consequently act as descriptors of individual or group identity. Negative connotations may come to be attached to appearances because of the deviant's concurrent behavior or because of the perceptions of the beholder. Teenage fads, the homeless derelict, the bag lady, or the "biker" may conjure up fear or revulsion in others; the negative connotation is not based solely on the appearances of these individuals but also stems from the values and experience of those who judge them. For some, the appearance of the uniformed police, the three-piece suit, or the cleric's collar may inspire similar fears or disgust for entirely different reasons. When the only deviant quality in a known individual is appearance, however, it is rarely of major social concern.

Deviant thinking may be valued or shunned. Creative or innovative thinking has been valued for its contribution to invention, science, art, and progress. Divergent beliefs have been defended throughout history as a right, and democracies have sought to accommodate thinking along a wide spectrum. Thought control has been labeled "brainwashing," and the lack of independent thought may be perceived as boring or even inhuman. The human intellect is inherently dependent on the ability to reason: to think differently in different situations and thereby to be deviant from other species.

It is one's behavior that has an impact on society and colors the evaluation of deviancy. Deviant behavior that benefits others by enhancing or improving the environment or the quality of life is valued; deviant behavior that has a negative or harmful impact on the self, others, or the environment is problematic. Every sphere of human behavior can demonstrate deviancy. In this chapter, we are concerned with deviant sexual behavior and the cognitive deviancy that supports or allows one to abuse or exploit others sexually.

Sexual deviance, like all other divergent qualities, may be valued or problematic. Being more "sexy" or sensual is considered an asset in most cultures, either openly or covertly. Sexual activity beyond the norm is often coveted, and extremes of sexual prowess are valued. Sexuality may become problematic if the deviancy is promiscuity, frigidity, or impotence, but the impact of these qualities for the most part is personal and of little concern to the fiber of society. Bizarre sexual thoughts are protected as one's right and may even be promoted, as in pornography and sexually explicit entertainment. It is sexually deviant behavior that has a negative impact on others—rape, assault, child abuse, harassment—that has drawn the attention of society as its incidence and prevalence has become known. Perverse sexual behaviors that misuse, debase, and corrupt others are considered negatively deviant and are therefore made illegal because of their impact. Cultural norms dictate where, when, and with whom sexual interactions are permitted or prohibited. In most modern cultures, sexual violence, sex without consent, incestuous relations, and child molestation are prohibited by custom and law.

Deviancy is identifiable because it stands out as abnormal. In an orderly society, differences that violate standards of behavior surprise and bewilder. It is assumed that all human development follows a similar course that will produce a predictable pattern of growth and result in similar, acceptable characteristics. When occurrences blatantly violate these expectations, the questions that ultimately arise are "Why?" and "How?" Why did this happen? How can this occur? Where did this aberration come from?

In exploring the development of sexually deviant behaviors, both the norms of sexuality and the range of what is developmentally possible must be understood. Chapter 4 has defined the range and progression of sexual development that may be seen in humans. The development of sexuality is shaped by cultural norms, familial and societal messages, and life experiences.

In many cultures, sexual behaviors in infancy and early childhood are repressed by parental and societal messages that deny, discourage, or punish displays of sexuality prior to puberty. "Latency" has long been considered a period of child development during which sexual issues diminish, and yet experience and research both counter that assumption. Sexuality prior to puberty may be effectively suppressed or it may be kept secret, but it is not naturally dormant or latent. Societal taboos, however, often prohibit any overt sexuality in children. Puberty and adolescence have been recognized as sexually active periods of development, but many cultures have sought to delay or repress sexual interactions prior to achievement of adult status. The child who is known to be sexual with self or others and the adolescent who defies repression have often been labeled deviant or promiscuous.

In recent years, recognition of women's rights and the "discovery" of child molestation have brought social concern to focus on sexual exploitation. Rape and child sexual abuse have been reported throughout centuries of history, and in many cultures sexual exploitation of women, children, and adolescents was the norm. Negative impacts were often minimized or denied, and blame was often placed on victims more than offenders. Historically, sexual exploitation was seen as an interactional deviancy rather than a clear-cut crime. Rape was viewed as an interaction between a provocative female and an impulsive male, incest was considered a family problem, and hands-off behaviors such as voyeurism or exhibitionism were considered "victimless" crimes perpetrated by "sick" individuals. The social outcry against the sexual abuse of children has prompted tremendous change in societal perceptions, and a new view of sexual exploitation has evolved that holds offenders personally responsible for sexually abusive behaviors. Most recently, the sexual harassment of vulnerable persons has been added to the societal definition of sexual exploitation, particularly in schools and workplaces. Sexual language or advances that cause subordinates or peers to feel uncomfortable may now result in students being suspended or expelled and sometimes legally charged due to harassment.

The capacity for sexual urges is inborn, but the ways in which sexuality is expressed are learned. Deviant sexual behavior is therefore a product of the environment, and its prevention lies in our understanding its origins. Work with sexually abusive youth offers a unique opportunity to explore the early manifestations of sexually exploitive behavior. Our hypothesis is that the origin of these behaviors lies in early childhood experience. The interaction of various factors is not always apparent in explaining why an individual manifests sexual deviancy rather than some other dysfunction, but it is usually possible in the exploration of the sexually abusive person's early life experience to see those factors that create the risk of major dysfunctions in intimate relationships.

Many child molesters, like other persons who maltreat children, have a history of significant family disruption, neglect, or abuse in their earlier years. We do not adequately know why some children who have been maltreated in early life grow up with persistent emotional problems, others become physical abusers of their own children, some become neglectful caretakers, and others become sexually abusive; at the same time, many grow up with relatively little dysfunction (Ryan et al., 1993). What seems to be the most pervasive common element in those who maltreat children is the feeling of not having been adequately cared for or loved in the emotional sense; the mother or primary caregiver did not provide a good enough holding environment for the child to develop a solid, cohesive sense of a worthwhile self.

Similarly, the child who experiences significant family disruption, especially in the preverbal years, is failed by the environment. The child who experiences loss is left with an empty and yearning dependency; a wish for love, care, and respect; and an identification with the uncaring or absent parent. Such persons, as they grow up, are constantly searching in their interactions with other people for something that will assuage the emptiness and provide satisfaction of the need for self-enhancement. The particular way in which the growing and grown-up child chooses to try to resolve earlier traumatic experiences seems to be related to a large degree on other events in the child's life. The exposure to various forms of intrafamilial violence seems likely to predispose the child to become a physical abuser, while pervasive disregard and emotional neglect is more likely to lead to a depressive, withdrawn adult who may neglect a child or may create a failure-to-thrive syndrome. Similarly, exposure to developmentally incomprehensible sexual stimuli or sexual trauma, especially the experience of being sexually abused as a child, may alter the child's development and suggest sexual behavior as a means to solve inner turmoil in later years. It is well recognized that many abusers experienced some form of abuse in their earlier years. Sexual trauma may occur as early as the first and second years of life, although it is more common between ages 6 and 12.

Widom (1995) and Williams (1995) found that only 6.5% and 14%, respectively, of sexually abused children had been arrested for sexual offenses at the twenty-year follow-up. In these studies, physically abused children appeared to be at equal risk and neglected children at even higher risk than sexually abused children for arrest for sexual offenses. These results support the growing recognition in the field that a broad definition of maltreatment is more salient than the variable of sexual victimization alone in understanding why individuals become sexually abusive (Hunter, 1996).

In exploring the development of sexually abusive behaviors, three main threads of development can be traced that appear relevant to pedophilic behavior: an empty yearning for intimacy or negative sense of self, left over from early disregard or disruptions in care; a lack of empathic modeling; and the sexualization of attempts to overcome inner conflict and satisfy nonsexual needs. Case material helps to clarify these hypotheses.

CASE 1: REGRESSION IN TIMES OF STRESS

Nineteen-year-old Robert was picked up by the police for molesting a little girl. During the course of the investigation, it developed that he had molested at least ten or twelve little girls around the age of four over the past year. He found his victims by hanging around housing projects where lonely children were often wandering around without adult supervision. He would talk to the child, walk to a secluded spot, expose himself, and have the little girl look at his erect penis and touch it after he asked her, "Do you want to see something neat?" There were no attempts at genital manipulation of the victims or any request for fellatio. In one later episode, he ejaculated while putting his penis between the girl's legs. He confessed to authorities and expressed his strong sense of embarrassment, shame, and guilt, being quite aware that what he had done was unacceptable both socially and legally. At the same time, he was aware that there was some element in his thinking that led him to believe in some way that his "playing" with the little girls was perfectly okay and that nobody had ever told him that such activities were wrong.

Robert was born when his mother was 16. Siblings from two or three different fathers had been given up for adoption. The man Robert calls his father was a stepfather who adopted him after marrying his mother when Robert was still a baby. They divorced when Robert was 7. He does not know what the trouble was but remembers some arguments and thinks that his father was much more serious and his mother much more frivolous. Since that time, his father has remarried a "nice woman" and has had two other children. His mother has been married twice and has had several other liaisons. Robert says his mother changes her man about every three years. Robert always assumed that there was a lot of sexual activity going on, but does not have a clear memory of actually witnessing any. Robert always felt the desire for a good father and never seemed to have any trouble with his stepfathers. He has had yearly visits with his father, but never a "good enough" relationship.

During his school years, Robert, with his mother and her current man, changed residences several times, to different countries and states. This meant many changes in Robert's schools, and he often felt like a stranger. He usually was treated as the "new kid" and sometimes was physically bullied. He never fought back, but became a very glib "salesman," and used his experiences to build up colorful stories of where he had been and what he had done. These gained him a certain amount of respect and acceptance, and he felt superior when he was believed.

During his childhood, Robert felt strongly that his mother did not really care about him. She never wanted to hear about any of the problems he was having and made all the household moves, which led to his problems in school, without consulting him or listening to his objections. He did not feel emotionally close to his mother, but did feel some necessity to make sure she was not upset: "She fed me and cared for me. She expected me to work and care for myself." He felt the lack of a father to turn to for guidance and support.

Over a period of several months from age 4 to 5, Robert had a close friendship with a same-aged neighbor, Jenny. He and Jenny often stayed overnight at one or the other's home, slept together, and engaged in a great deal of sex play, looking at and fondling each other's genitals. He recalls saying to her, "Want to see something neat?" and enjoying what he felt was her liking and approval. None of the parents interfered with or disapproved of these activities, and Robert assumed they were all right. Although Jenny and Robert occasionally saw each other during their school years, they never had further sexual activity. Robert still recalls the relationship with pleasure.

At 14, Robert was given the choice of living with a recently divorced stepfather and being under his control, living with his mother with no money, or being independent and earning his own keep. He took the last route with some moral support and a pat on the back, but no money from his mother. He found a job and paid his mother room and board for a few months until he moved out to his own quarters at the age of 15. He has been independent since that time, going to school and being self-supporting.

After his extensive sexual activity with the little girl at age four to five, he had no further sexual experience with girls until age 14. At that time, he met a girl two years older and went steady with her for eight months. They had sexual intercourse about twice a week, with occasional oral activity. He found her very pleasurable and was slightly upset briefly after she ended the relationship. Two months later, he met a girl his own age, Annie, with whom he quickly developed a relationship. He was still living at home, and he and Annie would spend the night either there or at her home. Both sets of parents seemed to accept this relationship. When he left home to be on his own, Annie moved in with him, and they lived together for nearly three years.

Robert believes his interest in younger girls began when he was living with Annie and wonders if it was possibly the excitement of thinking of something different or forbidden. It was not related to lack of sexual activity with Annie. If he did not have sex with her, he would masturbate with the fantasy of having sex with some other girl he had seen, usually of his own age but occasionally of somewhat younger girls. He would also look at magazine pictures, which he described as dirty pictures of women (nudity). He does not describe any hard pornography (sexually explicit, exploitative, or involving children).

The relationship with Annie finally deteriorated when he found out that she was also going out with other boys, and she told him she was through with him. They broke up, and Annie moved out. Robert was devastated, feeling rejected by an unsympathetic, uncaring female, but he was not aware of or able to express any anger.

It was while feeling lonely and depressed over the loss of Annie that he first acted on a pedophilic impulse: seeking out a 4-year-old girl and exposing himself to her. He repeated this behavior, despite feeling very scared, but thought he could control it and kept telling himself that each time was the last.

When he was arrested, Robert confessed freely to the police and prosecutors, expressing a clear sense of guilt and a great deal of remorse. He was convicted, his sentence was suspended, and he was placed on probation with the condition that he get psychiatric treatment. He began therapy in an atmosphere of gratitude for what role the therapist had in keeping him from having to face the terrors of jail. He appreciated having an outside organizing influence in his life, as well as feeling that someone was taking an interest in him and could help him guide his life more effectively.

Recurrent themes during therapy related to feelings that his mother had never really cared deeply about him or his welfare in any meaningful sense, and she had never responded to his deeper feelings. Neither his mother nor his father had ever talked to him about sexual matters or sexual behaviors, and he took their lack of concern about his behavior as a little boy as approval. Looking back, he thought that his sexual interaction with 4-year-old Jenny in his preschool years was largely an attempt to resolve the feeling that his mother did not care. Jenny had expressed admiration in what he had to show her, and he experienced a sense of positive regard in the relationship.

As an adult, Robert developed his childhood expertise as a salesman, selling high-class china, crystal, and cutlery to families. Subsequently, it was when he failed to sell his wares to women that he would sometimes have an impulse to look for a little girl again. He did not act on these impulses during treatment and began to get in touch with the depth of his own neediness. He was aware that in some sense he had followed his mother's pattern of solving life's disappointments by sexual activity. In his dating activities, he had a tendency to become involved with lonely young women who were in some sort of difficulty, finding it easier to talk with them than with men or independent women. These young women responded to his concern for their troubles and his caring attitude. He became aware that he was not sure of his own masculinity and had worried that he might have homosexual tendencies. He gradually worked toward having a more adult relationship with a woman rather than rescuing the less mature girls he had been dating.

Robert was quite capable in his work and received awards for being a top salesman, but he became aware that it was not what he really wanted to do in life. He realized that he might never be able to satisfy his needs through material gains. He also became aware that the type of work he was doing was reflective of his old pattern of trying to get recognition and acceptance by showing off something "really neat" and hoping for validation. His customers' failure to buy recreated the old feelings of desertion and disregard he had felt with his mother, and his pattern was to seek sexualized methods to restore his self-esteem.

When Robert's father suddenly asked Robert to come to work with him at a good salary, Robert was entranced and excited. His father was at last offering to be the longed-for provider. Robert left treatment abruptly, before he and his therapist had discussed the new situation realistically. He sent a happy "everything is fine" letter to the therapist after a month, followed soon after by a note that things were not working out as well as he had hoped for and that he had moved from his father's home. The therapist heard nothing further, and a letter sent to him went unanswered. Three years later, a message from a defense attorney in a distant state revealed that he had been arrested for molesting another 4-year-old girl. Details have not been made available.

Robert's life history was rather benign, and yet it demonstrates the suggested hypothesis that a lack of empathic modeling, an unfulfilled yearning for a sense of attachment and intimacy, and sexualized models of compensation may support the development of sexual deviancy.

The following case is from the other end of the spectrum and pictures the development of sexual deviance during the course of an extremely chaotic, atypical life.

CASE 2: PERVASIVE SEXUAL DEVIANCE

Warren, charged with sexually molesting his own children as well as other young boys, was referred by social services for evaluation and possible treatment. He was a small, slender young man with dark horn-rimmed glasses. Although tense and embarrassed, he was trying to be cooperative and agreeable (reminding one of a furtive, obliging little gnome).

He is not sure of his age, either 27 or 29. There is no original birth certificate, and although he obtained a copy that says he is 29, he believes this certificate is really for an older brother who died. As far as he knows, his mother gave him away sometime during his second or third year, accompanied by a short note that read, "Please take good care of John," with no last name or signature. He was placed in foster care and remembers being called John for several years, but sometime around the age of 10, his foster parents changed his name to Warren and gave him their last name. He had been told that a few months after his mother gave him away, she was sent to jail for seven years because she had given her older son a 48-ounce bottle of beer and the child had died. He says, "I don't know if I had a father."

Warren's earliest memories relate to the time just before he was abandoned by his mother. He recalls lying alone on an attic floor, bleeding from the rectum after having a glass rod inserted into him. He also recalls a man trying to penetrate him rectally with his penis, a man's penis in his mouth, and being made to hold onto a man's penis. He tends to merge these memories into a single idea of all three things happening at one time. He also recalls lying on his back and having a menstruating woman sit on him with her vulva in his face. He became nauseated and vomited. He remembers playing outdoors without any clothes on, sleeping on a sofa, and playing with rats. He has been told that when he was placed with his foster parents, he had rat bites, measles, and rickets. It seems quite possible that these are the memories of a later age and that he was really older than two or three when he was placed in foster care. Attempts to corroborate these facts through social service records in the state where he grew up were fruitless.

Warren felt that his new foster home was wonderful: a nice, warm house with food, clothing, and a bed and caring, kind people. This paradise did not endure. After about six months, Warren got into a squabble with the neighbor boy, who hit him over the head with a branch, and he came home crying. His foster father was very angry with him and said if he was going to act like a girl, he would be dressed like a girl. Warren objected, but his foster father stripped him, hit him, dressed him in girls' clothes, and put him out in the yard. Other children saw him and made fun of him. Although he had not started school at the time, the children who saw him then remembered the incident later and ridiculed him throughout his school years.

He had thoughts of running away but never did. The father periodically dressed Warren in girls' clothes in the home, would talk to him about how he would go to the toilet, take down his pants, and urinate; the father would also reach up under the dress Warren was wearing and fondle his genitals. Soon Warren became aware that the foster father was also sexually molesting an older sister in the home who was the mother's child by a previous marriage.

When Warren was 5 or 6, his foster father began having Warren and the sister come early in the morning to a restaurant he owned and do general cleaning work. They would then go to school and come back to the restaurant after school to work again until 7:00 P.M. before they could go home. The foster father was strict and demanding and often beat Warren with his fists or a belt if he did not work hard enough. Both the sexual molestation and physical punishment continued until Warren was about 12 or 14. At that time, the sister had hit the father on the head with a flower pot, and a year later Warren had a fistfight in which the father was knocked down. Following this incident, the abuse and molestation stopped. The foster father never really talked to Warren again except to say hello or goodbye and would often go into another room when Warren came in the house. Warren has felt that there was nobody really close to him or who cared about him during all those early years except possibly the sister, with whom he shared feelings about the abuse when they sat and cried together.

One of the interesting things about Warren's memories is that he can never recall the father physically abusing him when he was dressed in girls' clothes. He had a feeling of safety at such times. The sexual fondling had progressed to include some oral-genital contact but never any anal intercourse. Warren also observed the activity between the father and the sister in which the father would pull up her dress, fondle her, put fingers in her vagina, and then have alternating fellatio and cunnilingus. Warren also recalled some fuzzy memories of sexual activity between him and his sister, carried out at the father's insistence. He remembers mostly being frightened about this because the father would say, "Do it or get your ass kicked."

Warren remembers being curious about sex; he liked a little girl next door who was about age 3, and they looked at each other's genitals. He also liked to look at older girls and indicated he maintained some level of visual and possible tactile contact with girls until he was about 8 or 10. Although he has vague recollections of sexual activity with the sister, he describes his first intercourse as being with a girl during his adolescence and says, "It did not work out very well."

Warren's foster mother is conspicuous by her absence in his life story. He describes her only as being somewhat more mellow but never interfering in any way with his stepfather's abuse of him or the sister. She is only a vague presence in the background; there was no indication of any close relationship.

Warren graduated from high school with a C average and started working. He was rather shy, a loner, and a workaholic. He worked in a factory as a spray painter, teamed up with a young woman. They hardly spoke to each other for six months, but then began talking and eventually dated. After two or three months, they developed a sexual relationship and got married because "we both needed someone to hold on to." Sexual activity with his wife became comfortable and pleasurable. His wife brought with her a young boy from a previous marriage, and they had a daughter when the boy was about 4 years old.

Periodically throughout the marriage, Warren would dress in female clothing in the privacy of the home. His cross-dressing distressed his wife somewhat because she said the clothing made him look too feminine. She later decided that she did not mind because Warren seemed to feel much more secure when he was dressed that way. This sense of security seemed to be a derivative of his having felt safe because his father never beat him when he was dressed as a girl during childhood. In addition to the cross-dressing behavior, Warren used articles of female clothing as a sort of fetish. He loved the soft, silky texture of undergarments and even when not wearing them would hold them when he masturbated. At times he would wear a complete female outfit—not only underclothes but dress, stockings, and shoes. He never used any makeup.

During masturbation, from puberty to the present, Warren has had fantasies about women, usually involving straightforward intercourse, rarely any oral activity, and never any anal activity. He occasionally saw magazines like *Playboy* and had fantasies about the naked women pictured in it. He describes himself as having a strong sex urge, and says, "I don't seem to get enough sex." This is particularly referring to the present, although it also has reference to the past. He has masturbated a great deal for many years, apparently since the time the activity with his father stopped. He still either wears girls' clothing or has female garments to hold onto or to look at while masturbating. Sometimes he masturbates five to six times a day, other times only once a week. During the activity, he has a repetitive fantasy: "thinking of the kind of lady I'd like to have sex with." His ideal lady is "5 feet, 7 inches tall; weighs around 120 or 130; has firm breasts, a nice spinal curve, narrow waist and expanded hips; is either naked or dressed, but preferably wears something soft like a negligee. She is never either younger or older than 23. The colors of her hair and eyes make no difference. She knows just what to do in all kinds of activity, everything from back rubbing to oral activity, intercourse or whatever, according to her mood. She can both give and take." He denies having fantasies about children, either boys or girls.

Warren is very unsure of his identity. He wonders if he is genetically more female than male and really a female in a male body. Because of this sense that he might be female, he has wondered about homosexuality, although he has never had the desire to make love with a man. He tried once out of curiosity to have a homosexual relationship and fondled a man. This man wanted him to perform fellatio; he refused. He felt no interest in the relationship. He is also puzzled by his attraction to children, particularly to his own stepson. He feels that there is something in the back of his head that says, "Do as I did when I was a kid." He also feels he has two characters within him: one that pushes forward, the other that holds back. One is grown up, the other more childlike. He feels as if sometimes he goes back to being 7 years old, then comes back to the present and hates himself.

Warren is not quite clear about how many children he has molested. Besides his stepson and daughter, he tells specifically of another boy and two girls and vaguely indicates that there may have been others. He describes the extra-familial children as being wandering, alone, bereft, and looking for someone to care for them and love them. Apparently the sexual activity with his stepson began when the boy was about seven. It started with fondling and then progressed to include mutual masturbation and fellatio. Warren believes the son wanted him to manipulate the boy's genitals but the son never wanted to do as much for Warren. The son would often demand some reward for performing the activity for his stepfather. Warren says the son did not seem to mind when Warren put girls' clothes on him or object to the sexual activity associated with it, but he would get angry if his father pulled him away from some other activity that he was enjoying to undertake these sexual activities. Sometimes Warren dressed in girls' clothes to be sexual with the son, and sometimes he put the girls' clothes on the boy, but never had both of them dressed as females during sexual activities. Similar activities occurred with the neighbor boy, a friend of the stepson, who came over to visit with Warren when the stepson was away. The activity with his daughter, including looking and touching and possibly some oral activity, began when she was about 4. He had done physical care of his daughter when she was younger but did not like to change diapers and did not seem to be aware of any sexual interest in her until later.

In the rest of his life, Warren was a rather quiet, unsociable person with few friends, but quite devoted to duty and hard work. He was in the army for several years, working as a mechanic. He received many commendations for excellent, careful work and was promoted several times. He brought these documents to show the therapist with a great sense of pride, as if to demonstrate he really was somebody worthwhile.

While on probation, Warren worked rather faithfully at several jobs in the restaurant business, sometimes quitting because he was treated rudely and abusively by superiors, and sometimes quitting because others did not keep up the high standards of cleanliness that he tried to maintain. He also worked as an assistant manager in a cheap men's rooming house in return for free rent. As a hobby, he worked at designing women's dresses, using his excellent talent as a draftsman. Occasionally he would get material, cut the dresses out, and have them sewn up by one of his girlfriends. Women admired his work. He did develop a few rather tentative friendships with women and occasionally had some sexual activity. He continued to masturbate occasionally. He did not report any interest in or fantasies about children. His wife was divorcing him, and he was under court order not to see his children.

At the beginning of treatment, one possibility, in view of his statements of his intense, irresistible sex drive, was to put him on antiandrogenic hormone treatments. After about the third session, however, he reported that his sex drive was becoming an insignificant part of his life. He intimated that therapy was his first experience in life of somebody seeming to care for him and about him and that this was a very rewarding situation. Although it is impossible to prove, it seemed as if the experience of someone's empathizing with his life troubles and talking with him about his feelings and desires diminished his drive to use sexuality to maintain esteem and identity. He lived alone, gradually trying to improve his work situation and developing a few social relationships, but disappeared after two years in treatment. Efforts to find other support groups had been fruitless.

The life histories of these two men are remarkably different in outward details—Robert was never physically or sexually assaulted; Warren was severely sexually and physically abused—yet both ended up exhibiting paraphilias including child molesting behaviors, and there are common themes in both histories. Both had the perception of not being cared about or respected in the earliest years, with the accompanying yearning for basic regard to build some sense of self-esteem and bolster an inadequate, fragmented identity. Early sexual activities, in addition to providing solutions for developmentally expected sexual curiosity and pleasure, became the available substitute for the missing empathic care and protection. Normal dependency issues became sexualized. In his repetitive sex play with Jenny, Robert found a replacement for the prevailing feelings of his mother's lack of empathy and involvement. His mother took effective though perfunctory care of his physical needs but left his emotional needs unfulfilled. His father figures were inadequate and distant. Jenny "rescued" him from an emotional wasteland. He remembers her warmly, and their relationship provided the pattern for pedophilic behavior whenever Robert felt bereft, unloved, and rejected by adult women in later life. He would have fantasies about a girl when he felt rejected during his therapy, but these were controlled by deterring thoughts of how wrong it was, how the girl would be hurt by it, and, especially, a strong fear of jail.

Warren, despite the sexual abuse in infancy, developed in later childhood an unconscious amalgamation combining sexuality, cross-dressing, and the sense of safety. Although the foster father was physically and sexually abusive, he was also the one who had rescued young Warren from the previous horrors and was kind and gentle when he dressed Warren in girls' clothes and sexually stimulated him. As an adult parent, Warren felt he could somehow prove himself loving and lovable by recreating his foster father's pattern of sexual activity with children. His unsureness of gender identity remained a source of confusion and unusual behavior. The apparent lack of fantasy about sex with children is unusual in view of his behavior, but he may have effectively blocked all sexual fantasies involving children in order to avoid the horrifying memories of his own early abuse and abandonment. He had no good models in his experience of being parented to guide him in adequate parenting of his own children. The intensity of Warren's fantasies about a very specific adult female figure may reflect his fantasy of what he himself could be as an idealized sexual woman as much as it was a picture of a sexual object, the projection of himself as the loving and lovable female person.

Treatment was not successful for either Robert or Warren; their patterns of trying to solve deep-seated, lifelong problems were not adequately changed. This is not surprising in Warren's case. His personality disorders were severe and could not be changed in a short time, and legal and social controls were inadequate to complete treatment. It would be surprising if he did not offend again. Robert, on the other hand, had many ego strengths and adaptive abilities. Yet the failure of the hoped-for love of a caring father appears to have revived the old sense of emptiness and the pattern of relieving it by sexual expression that had been established at age 4. He had seemed to be an ideal candidate for treatment, but the old behaviors had the strength to take control again.

In the adult cases presented here, the adult manifestations of deviancy and the developmental history were explored retrospectively. In the following juvenile cases, the history is closer at hand and development is still unfolding.

CASE 3: SEXUALLY ABUSIVE BEHAVIOR IN CHILDHOOD

Eight-year-old Billy was referred for evaluation after causing serious genital injury to his 5-year-old sister. Adopted at age 5, Billy's new parents had been told that he came from a "very dysfunctional family where there might have been some incest." Within weeks following his placement, Billy revealed to the adoptive parents graphic accounts of sexual intercourse between his mother and grandfather, as well as his own sexual abuse by them both.

Billy's new parents struggled to create a new life for him, but his relationships in the family were polarized from the beginning. His interactions with his father were distant and somewhat fearful, he was defiant and violent toward his mother, and he seemed to tolerate closeness only with the younger sister, who was medically disabled and developmentally delayed. The sister began complaining about Billy's touching during the first year, and the mother's attempts to limit his behavior and protect the younger child from his sexual advances escalated his anger and violence toward the mother.

A mental health worker enlisted to treat Billy was able to confirm the multi-generational incest and dysfunction in the family of origin, including Billy's failure to thrive in infancy. Billy arrived at the child abuse center for evaluation with the appearance of a small, bereft waif and a history of sexually abusing numerous children and assaulting his mother with a baseball bat. He showed little distress for himself, no appreciation of the harm he had caused others, and no defense for his behavior. Billy was a perfect image of the empty objectification he had experienced in an unempathic, sexualized world.

Treatment is still in progress. Billy's prognosis is poor, but his youth and the intensity of intervention are enhanced by his adoptive parents' continued commitment to him.

CASE 4: SEXUALLY ABUSIVE BEHAVIOR DURING PUBERTY

Mickey, age 12, was referred for treatment after molesting a 4-year-old neighbor. Placed for adoption at age 6, Mickey had lost his parents and siblings at age 4. Mickey remembers his family of origin in idealized terms, although he reports knowing he was too young to be of any value except when caring for his younger sibling. He remembers fishing alone and wonders if his family looked for him or missed him when he was lost.

Within weeks of his placement, his new mother was concerned about his sexualized behaviors and enlisted counseling to help manage his behavior with the other children in the home. The healthy preplacement environment of the adoptive home became characterized by suspicion, and Mickey was never able to attach to the females in the home (or they to him).

After Mickey was removed from the adoptive home and placed in residential treatment, he finally revealed that he had been sodomized by an older boy in a preadoptive orphan asylum when he was 5. Although he appeared capable of some empathy for himself and others, his ability to trust was minimal, and his sexual confusion was evident in conflicting fears and desires, including homophobic and homosexual incidents. His primary arousal to older women was accompanied by shame and revulsion in response to heterosexual fantasies. He was able to acknowledge his loneliness and sadness and his feeling that he did not know who he was, either sexually or personally. Multiple losses and betrayals made attachment and trust with adults difficult, and suspicion and lack of a worthwhile identity brought little depth to relationships with peers. Mickey's most enjoyable intimacy was with younger children, whom he was quite good at engaging, and he seemed to turn to them specifically when feeling rejected by peers. His deviant sexual behaviors were somewhat random manifestations in all his relationships with peers and adults as well as younger children.

Mickey was relinquished and is alone in the world again. He was believed to be at high risk for numerous dysfunctions, but his risk of molesting was moderated by his greater capacity to anticipate its harmfulness to others and its consequences for himself.

He was discharged from treatment at age 15 and placed in a long-term foster placement with a single man whom he liked and appeared to trust. At age 25, Mickey reported that he had not been sexually abusive again but that he had been arrested once for a group burglary while drinking with friends. He felt that he had fallen into a pattern of substance abuse, which was a factor in his making poor choices about peers and behavior. He indicated that he would consider seeking counseling for this. The foster father whom he had gone to live with at age 15 continued to provide housing and a sense of family, which improved the prognosis for Mickey.

CASE 5: SEXUALLY ABUSIVE BEHAVIOR IN ADOLESCENCE

Chuck was arrested at age 14 for the molestation of several cousins and his sister. Upon interrogation, he revealed that he had been sodomized by an older cousin when he was about six years old, although later, in view of his cousin's anger and denial, he became ambivalent as to whether this had really occurred or was "just a dream."

Chuck was the second of six children, born at a time when his mother's first marriage was both abusive and breaking up. His older brother and younger siblings appeared to have satisfactory relationships with their mother, but Chuck's mother stated she had "always felt different" about him and "never felt as close to him" as to the other children. Chuck had felt this difference, and he and his mother seemed to experience a distorted intimacy only around shared feelings of fear and guilt. His mother reported that Chuck had "always been a problem" and "never been trustworthy," acting up and being in trouble perpetually from age six. Lying, stealing, intimidating his siblings, and incidents that caused his mother to feel like a failure were common occurrences, although he was well-liked by peers and had good social skills. The first-grade teacher had reported unusual sexual components in his artwork at age six. Chuck had been discovered trying to sodomize a younger sibling at that time and had gone to counseling for a brief period.

Chuck had felt set apart and different much of his life. His mother's preoccupation with a bad marriage at the time of his birth may have impaired her availability to him and precluded empathic care. Although he had no conscious memory of his natural father, there seemed to be some covert implication that he was like his father: untrustworthy, criminal, and a source of fear for his mother. He had never felt allowed to inquire about that father, and he felt some obscure sense of loss that he described as "an empty place," relative to his perceived abandonment or rejection by his father. In addition to his reported experience of sodomy at age 6, he remembered learning about sex by eavesdropping when an older brother and his friends discussed sexual matters in the home.

Chuck showed little genuine affect and was quite unaware of the feelings of self or others. He had difficulty maintaining eye contact with adults and reported feeling very helpless and small, especially with his mother. Although his sexual abuse of boys was quite aggressive, his perception of the long-term molesting relationship he had with one female cousin was that it was a loving and intimate experience, and she agreed. In every molestation, however—and also in subsequent peer relationships—his victims were related to a fierce protector whom he feared: his mother, a very scary uncle, a crazy gun-toting boyfriend, and so forth. It is possible that the experience of fear in his exploitive sexual relationships made him feel more alive and somehow connected him to that "missing part," which was the father figure whom his mother had feared.

Chuck's family was very involved and invested in treatment. Chuck completed treatment successfully and returned home for about one year before going away to college. While away, he was somewhat delinquent and was suspended from college due to grades. After a year or two on his own, he returned to his hometown with a girlfriend and was doing well at follow-up when he was 24 years old.

CASE 6: SIBLING INCEST

Jay, age 14, was referred for treatment following disclosure of a long-term incestuous relationship with his younger sister. Jay had lots of family: a natural father, a mother and a stepfather, grandparents, and siblings. His natural father and stepfather were recovering alcoholics, but everyone else appeared quite functional. The pervasive qualities in this family seemed to be distance and defense. Family members met financial and physical needs without any emotional connection. His mother was frequently absent due to business commitments, and his sister spent much of her childhood with relatives. In this case, it was the victim, Jay's sister, who had been set apart and different, with chronic patterns of acting out that may have filled some of the emotional void for all the family members. Although Jay was clearly exploiting the power in their relationship, his sister was easy prey, and both seemed to experience some intimacy in the relationship, although there did not appear to be much capacity for empathy.

After completing treatment, Jay will be sent away to boarding school, where he will be further disconnected from the family he yearns for and will likely engineer failure in the new school in order to return home. No legal constraints are in place to prevent his removal from treatment.

All of these cases demonstrate the common themes of emptiness, lack of empathic experience, and sexualized patterns of coping that are characteristic of sexual offenders. And yet every theme represented in the developmental history of these individuals is also reported by many persons who do not manifest sexual deviance or sexually abuse others.

In normal development, a child's dependency needs for empathic care, closeness, intimacy, and a sense of self follow a separate line from that of sexuality, although the two coexist and in some ways interact. The two lines of development are related but not merged. Throughout the life cycle of healthy persons, sexuality and intimacy can be expressed together or separately. Intimacy may occur in relationships that are not sexual, and sexuality can be expressed without intimacy. Ideally, both occur together in romantic relationships and can be enjoyed together, although they do not replace each other. For some people, however, there may be a merging of the two desires or drives during childhood, with sexuality being used to replace the ability to be truly empathic and intimate and to establish a sense of self and identity. Such merging is never truly successful and is never totally satisfying. It cannot replace the deficits of early childhood and has been referred to as counterfeit.

We are not suggesting that sexual activity per se in childhood leads to a fixation on children as sexual objects. Cultures in which there is free and open sexual activity all through childhood do not have any appreciable incidence of pedophilia. It is the incomprehensible or traumatic sexual exploitation of children who are seeking love and care that creates the false equation. The merging of sexuality and one's sense of self may lead to pedophilia and the repetition in adult life of identification with the kind of experience endured in childhood. Pedophilic behavior in both adolescent and adult life may be the attempt to satisfy through sexual activity the emptiness and yearning left over from the bleak early years. This is but one variation of the use of sexuality for nonsexual purposes that is also seen in rape (when sexuality is used to express hatred and hostility) and in the more commonly observed phenomena that many people enter sexual relationships or activity to satisfy more deeply felt needs for loving care and touching. As Warren said, it is important to have "someone to hold on to." Sexually exploitative behaviors reflect a basic inability to be empathic, appreciative of, and caring for another human being, a deficit that is a residue from early years of unempathic care.

REFERENCES

Hunter, J. (1996). *Working with children and adolescents who sexually abuse children*. Paper presented at the Eleventh International Congress on Child Abuse and Neglect, Dublin, Ireland.

Ryan, G., Lindstrom, B., Knight, L., Arnold, L., Yager, J., Bilbrey, C., et al. (1993). *Treatment of sexual abuse in the context of whole life experience*. Presentation at the Twenty-First Child Abuse and Neglect (CAN) Symposium, Keystone, Colorado.

Widom, C. (1995). *Victims of child sexual abuse: Later criminal consequences*. Washington, DC: U.S. Department of Justice, National Institute of Justice.

Williams, L. (1995). *Juvenile and adult offending behavior and other outcomes in the cohort of sexually abused boys: Twenty years later*. Philadelphia: Joseph J. Peters Institute.

CHAPTER 6

Typology Research

Refining Our Understanding of a Diverse Population

TOM LEVERSEE

THE JUVENILE FIELD has used primarily descriptive, actuarial, and taxonomic research methods to study the risk of juveniles initiating and continuing sexually abusive behavior and to differentiate subtypes among youth who sexually offend. The diversity of the juvenile population has been increasingly clear from the earliest studies to the present. Juveniles who commit sexual offenses differ in a wide range of characteristics including types of offending behaviors, history of child maltreatment, social and interpersonal skills and relationships, sexual knowledge and experiences, academic and cognitive functioning, and mental health issues (Righthand & Welch, 2002). Although some female juveniles are identified as perpetrating sexual offenses, the vast majority of research has studied male adolescents. The diversity that exists in the population of sexually abusive youth has supported the need for differential treatment and supervision. The diversity challenges the field's ability to test various interventions and to compare treatment outcomes.

Historically, it was assumed that sexually abusive youth were significantly different from other at-risk or delinquent adolescents and that these differences required specialized treatment programs. The higher rates of nonsexual recidivism as well as evidence of the diverse developmental and dynamic factors associated with individual differences and similarity in groups of sexually abusive youth has challenged this assumption. The integration of theory and research now calls for more holistic and comprehensive treatment plans targeting both sexual and nonsexual conduct problems, as well as other risk factors.

O'Brien and Bera (1986) developed an early classification of sexually abusive youth based on factors such as personality, victim age, family functioning, general delinquency, and sexual history. This clinically-based classification proved to be quite valuable in assessment and treatment planning and set the foundation for subsequent empirical research. Knight and Prentky (1993) found that factors such as low social competence and high rates of impulsivity and antisocial behavior differentiated adult sex offenders who began offending as juveniles from those who had not. More recently, research has made significant progress toward the development of classification systems with implications for etiology, developmental course, prognosis, and treatment (Hunter, 2006, 2008; Hunter, Figueredo, Malamuth, & Becker, 2003; Miner, 2008; Richardson, Kelly, Bhate, & Graham, 2004; Worling, 2001). Typology research has differentiated subtypes of youth based on personality characteristics, social and interpersonal skills, patterns of offending, and etiology. Such research offers an essential conceptual and empirical foundation for understanding the diversity that exists among juveniles who commit sexual offenses, illuminating static and dynamic risk factors and personality characteristics associated with the onset and maintenance of maladaptive sexual and nonsexual behavior. The differential identification and understanding of these factors now provides the foundation for treatment and supervision interventions that are individualized and sensitive to subtype-specific characteristics.

Convergence in the typology research increasingly supports a differentiation between those sexually abusive youth with psychosocial deficits and internalizing symptoms and those who manifest a broader range of delinquent conduct problems and manifest primarily externalizing symptoms (Hunter et al. 2003; Hunter, 2006, 2008; Miner, 2008; Richardson et al., 2004; Worling, 2001). Typologies also include the small subset of these adolescents who are characterized by pedophilic interests, and any of the subtypes could be compromised by a serious co-occurring psychiatric disorder.

Before discussing the author's synthesis of the typology research, it is important to discuss the limitations of the application of this research. Although there is some notable convergence in the research, there are no empirically validated typologies of juveniles who have committed sexual offenses. The subtypes should be viewed as models as opposed to discrete categories. There is a great deal of diversity within the different subtypes, and youth may manifest characteristics of more than one subtype. While typology research illuminates the diversity of this population, it can be misapplied in adopting a "cookie cutter, one-size-fits-all" approach to the treatment and supervision of each subtype. Finally, the synthesis of the typology research presented here is not sufficient to explain all of the individualized developmental and dynamic risk factors associated with sexual offending, individual strengths and protective factors, or individual treatment and supervision needs.

PSYCHOSOCIAL DEFICITS

Becker (1988) described the youth whose impaired social and interpersonal skills contribute to the molestation of younger children for sexual gratification and social interaction. Hunter, Figueredo, Malamuth, and Becker (2003) and Miner, Robinson, Knight, Berg, Swinburne-Romine, and Netland (2010) clarify specific characteristics that differentiate youth who choose child victims versus those who offend against peers/adults.

Hunter et al. (2003) and Hunter (2006, 2008) describe the "socially impaired-anxious and depressed" youth who engages in transient sexual offending predominately against children. The sexual offending of these youth is seen as a form of adolescent experimentation and compensation for psychosocial deficits that impair the development of healthy peer relationships. These adolescents typically lack the self-confidence and social skills to attract and engage same-age peers. Hunter and colleagues' (2003) clinical interpretation is that the sexual offending of these youth "reflects compensatory social behavior and an attempt to satisfy unmet intimacy needs"(p. 42). Hence, these youth may engage in sexual behavior to meet nonsexual needs.

Deficits in psychosocial functioning are frequently associated with depression and anxiety (Hunter et al., 2003). This may include social anxiety, as these youth tend to perceive themselves as socially inadequate and expect to be ridiculed and rejected by peers (Hunter, 2006). Social anxiety may result in feelings of apprehension and avoidance of social/sexual contact with same-age peers. A sense of social alienation may manifest in both dependency on adults and a preference for the company of young children.

Utilizing an attachment framework, Miner et al. (2010) found that adolescents who sexually offend against children to meet their intimacy needs do so not only because of a desire for interpersonal closeness but also because of a fear of rejection. These youth perceive themselves as socially isolated, expect peer rejection, and manifest increased anxiety in their interactions with same-age peers. They may feel inadequate as males and experience alienation from opposite gender peers, as evidenced by significantly higher anxiety with same-age girls. They may also experience a preoccupation with sexuality.

Richardson et al. (2004) described a taxonomy based on personality pattern scale scores from the Millon Adolescent Clinical Inventory (MACI) (T. Millon, D. Millon, & Davis, 1993). Worling (2001) described a personality-based typology using scores from the California Psychological Inventory (Gough, 1987). Their results did not indicate any strong link between specific profiles and victim selection based on age. However, their findings were congruent with Hunter et al. (2003) and Miner et al. (2010) in delineating subtypes of youth characterized by psychosocial deficits. Richardson et al. (2004) described the "submissive" subtype as passively dependent on others, excessively compliant with rules, deferring to authority, and subsuming his needs to the wishes of others. These youth were found to manifest highly significant levels of social or generalized anxiety and to present with mood disturbance rather than disruptive behavior disorders. Richardson et al. (2004) suggest this subtype is similar to Worling's (2001) Overcontrolled/Reserved group. Worling described these youth as cautious to interact with others and tending to keep their feelings to themselves. They may initiate offending behaviors, in part, as a result of their shy and rigid interpersonal orientation, resulting in limited access to intimate relationships with peers.

The largest subgroup delineated by Richardson et al. (2004) was the "dysthymic/inhibited" youth. This youth may be socially withdrawn and isolated, apathetic, and lacking in motivation to socialize with peers. He is likely to be moderately or severely depressed, likely to experience a sense of failure in relationship with peers, and present with a lack of self-confidence and social anxiety. Richardson and colleagues (2004) suggest this subgroup is similar to Worling's (2001) Unusual/Isolated group. Worling (2001) describes these youth as emotionally disturbed and insecure and as characterized by a peculiar presentation and social isolation. These youths' awkward personality features may inhibit their ability to develop and maintain healthy and intimate relationships with consenting peers.

The social histories of youth characterized by psychosocial deficits supports their lack of social confidence, feelings of social inadequacy, depression, social anxiety, and avoidance (Leversee, 2008). These youth frequently report significant and pervasive experiences of peer rejection and isolation. Deficits in self-esteem and social competence are reflected in negative schemas for self and relationships. These include self schema such as, "I'm a loser . . . ugly . . . worthless" and relational schema such as, "nobody likes me . . . I'm a reject . . . no girl my own age will go out with me." The emotions associated with these beliefs include rejected, unloved, insecure, inadequate, lonely, and sad. These youth report that engaging younger children in sexual behavior is associated with experiencing feelings of acceptance, emotional connection, and safety, feelings that are lacking in relationships with same-age peers. These cognitive-emotional processes illuminate the dynamics and mechanisms associated with their sexual offending.

GENERAL DELINQUENCY AND CONDUCT PROBLEMS

Moffitt's (1993) Developmental Taxonomy that differentiates Adolescent-Limited and Life-Course Persistent Antisocial Behavior has been very useful in understanding and intervening in generalized delinquency and conduct problems. Timing and duration are the defining features in Moffitt's taxonomy.

Moffitt describes the behavior of the Life-Course Persistent youth as stable and persistent with these youth, essentially engaging in delinquent behavior of one form or another at every stage of their lives. The causal factors have their origins in childhood. The types of behavior may change as age and social circumstances alter opportunities (i.e., from hitting and biting in childhood to robbery and rape in adolescence) but the coherence of delinquent personality traits and behavior are likely to continue into adulthood. Life-Course Persistent youth constitute only 5 to 6% of juveniles who engage in delinquent behavior.

In contrast, the Adolescent-Limited youth's delinquent behavior is characterized as temporary and situational (Moffitt, 1993). The delinquent behavior emerges during adolescence. Finding that the majority of adolescents engage in some type of delinquent behavior, Moffitt asserts that adolescent-limited delinquent behavior is more normal than abnormal. The majority of these youth discontinue delinquent behavior prior to adulthood as prosocial styles become more rewarding. This subtype constitutes the majority of adolescents who engage in delinquent behavior.

Similarly, Hunter and associates (2003) and Hunter (2006, 2008) identified a subgroup of sexually offending youth, described as Life-Course Persistent, characterized by lifestyle delinquency. These youth have a broader range of nonsexual delinquency, an early onset of conduct problems, and are more likely to sexually offend against peers and adults with more violent forms of coercion.

Life-Course Persistent youth are characterized by traits such as egotistical-antagonistic and hostile masculinity, aggressively seeking interpersonal dominance and justifying aggression toward females based on perceptions that females are exploitive and rejecting. Hostile masculinity is further defined as a constellation of beliefs that a masculine identity involves power, risk-taking, toughness, dominance, aggressiveness, honor defending, competitiveness, and impersonal sexuality (Miner et al., 2010), and viewing females in a negative and pejorative manner supportive of rape myths (Hunter, 2009). This may translate into the use of more gratuitous violence in their sexual offenses.

The etiological factors associated with this subtype include the highest incidence of physical abuse by father/stepfather and the highest exposure to male modeled antisocial behavior, including domestic violence and male relative substance abuse (Hunter et al., 2003; Hunter, 2006, 2008).

Miner (2008) also found few differences between those youth who had sexually offended against peers/adults and nonsexual delinquents, and found that both groups were likely to have dismissive attachment styles characterized by an avoidance of intimacy, devaluation of relationships, and striving to maintain autonomy.

Richardson et al. (2004) also identified an Antisocial subtype, described as the closest to a pure conduct disorder. As such, they are indifferent to the feelings and welfare of other people and frequently disregard social rules, the rights of others, and the consequences of their actions. They may be impulsive, self-indulgent, and excessive in the expression of their emotions and desires. This subtype does not appear to meet the diagnostic criteria for significant psychopathology or mental health difficulties. Elevated scores on the Family Discord Expressed Concerns scale reflect a very negative view of family life associated with parental rejection and intrafamilial conflict. Richardson and colleagues (2004) suggest that this subtype resembles Worling's Confident/Aggressive group.

Richardson et al. (2004) also describe a Dysthymic/Negativistic group, which manifests both internalizing and externalizing symptoms, although the externalizing symptoms are predominant. These youth present a very negative self-perception and low self-esteem, dysthymic mood that may be chronic and incapacitating, and are deficient in their capacity for self-control. These youth may be willing to intimidate others and have strong feelings of resentment about limitations. They may be indifferent to the feelings and rights of other people and have low self-confidence in relation to peers. High scores on the Family Discord scale indicate distress about family relationships. Richardson and colleagues suggest this subgroup resembles Worling's Antisocial/Impulsive group. Worling (2001) described the Antisocial/Impulsive youth as likely to have a propensity for rule violations and their sexual offending, at least initially, being more a result of this factor than deviant sexual arousal. In addition, descriptors of this subgroup may include anxious, unhappy, and rebellious.

Sexually abusive youth who are more generally delinquent often present with a higher degree of anger and are more likely to have a documented and self-reported history of impulsive and assaultive behavior, authority problems, fighting, and use of drugs and alcohol (Leversee, 2008). Their patterns of nonsexual delinquency and conduct problems often have an earlier onset and are much more extensive and pervasive than their sexual offending. Regarding the onset of sexually abusive behavior, Burton and Meezan (2004) hypothesize that, "sexual offending and rule breaking is a logical progression when they become developmentally focused on their sexuality— they see no reason not to break the rules, and have been taught that rule breaking is a way to fulfill their desires"(p. 51). Consistent with the research on juvenile delinquency, these youth are more likely to manifest delinquent attitudes, values, beliefs, and cognitive-emotional states as well as association with delinquent peers (Latessa, 2005). Identified schemas include: "If I want something, I'll take it"; "Nobody can tell me what to do . . . I'm my own boss"; "No one is going to disrespect me." For those youth who manifest hostile masculinity, examples include: "Females are objects . . . there to pleasure males"; "All women are b****** and whores"; "She was just a slut and deserved it"; "She wanted it." Emotions associated with these cognitive-emotional processes include anger, powerlessness, and vengefulness.

Hunter (2008) identified the "Adolescent Onset-Experimenters" and described the sexual offending of some youth as a transient form of adolescent experimentation. Although they may resemble the Life-Course Persistent youth in their victim choice and pattern of alcohol and drug use, they are less delinquent and have not been exposed to high levels of violence and substance abuse. They are generally less psychosocially and psychosexually disturbed than other subgroups. This subgroup has fewer victims than Hunter's other five subgroups and is comparable to Richardson et al.'s (2004) "Normal" prototype, described as presenting with relatively minor personality difficulties as compared to the other groups. In this subgroup, none of the Expressed Concerns or Clinical Syndrome scales on the MACI were clinically significant.

PEDOPHILIC INTERESTS

Becker (1988) found that whereas many adolescents who had sexually offended had a wide spectrum of sexual interest and arousal, there were some who showed a well-established pattern associated with sexually deviant stimuli. Hunter and associates (2003) also conclude that adolescent arousal is usually quite fluid, although there is a small subset of juveniles who target children and may have a more fixated interest, indicative of early onset pedophilia. The sexual offenses of these youth are thought to be motivated by deviant sexual arousal and interest in prepubescent children. The most fixated sexual arousal in adolescents is found in those who target young male children exclusively, specifically when penetration is involved (Hunter, 1999). In general, the sexual arousal and interest of adolescents appears more fluid and changeable than adult sex offenders and relate less directly to their patterns of offending behavior.

Hunter (2008) found those youth with pedophilic interests could also be differentiated by antisocial versus nonantisocial orientation. The "Pedophilic Interests/Antisocial" youth show many of the characteristics of the "Life-Course Persistent" youth and may need more of an adult lifetime management model. The "Pedophilic/Non-Antisocial" youth do not appear to be pervasively delinquent and their prognosis may be favorable. They may benefit from specialized cognitive behavioral and pharmacological treatments, including arousal reconditioning.

CO-OCCURRING MENTAL DISORDER

Many youth in these subtypes also experience mental health problems, particularly mood and anxiety symptoms and substance use problems. It is essential to identify and treat more pervasive developmental delays, neurological problems, significant substance abuse, mood instability, depression, suicidal ideation, trauma related anxiety, and disorders of thinking or reality testing, as well as the sexual offending.

Becker (1988) described adolescents who are compromised by a psychiatric condition, which interferes with the ability to regulate and inhibit aggressive and sexual impulses. Kavoussi, Kaplan, and Becker (1988) found in an outpatient sample of sexually abusive youth that 20% had some symptoms of adjustment disorder with depressed mood and close to 7% had Attention-Deficit Hyperactivity Disorder (ADHD). Becker, Kaplan, Tenke, and Tartaglini (1991) found that 42% of the youth experienced major depressive symptoms as measured by the Beck Depression Inventory. In a sample of 9- to 14-year-old boys with sexual behavior problems, Shaw et al. (1993) found that 50% had an anxiety disorder and 35% suffered from a mood disorder. Cavanaugh, Pimenthal, and Prentky (2008) studied a sample of 667 boys involved with social services, the vast majority of whom had engaged in hands-on sexualized behaviors. Almost all of the youth came from "highly dysfunctional" families and had experienced a high degree of physical, psychological, and sexual abuse as well as neglect. The authors found that 66.7% had ADHD, 55.6% had post-traumatic stress disorder, and 49.9% had a mood disorder. Approximately one-quarter used drugs and about one-fifth consumed alcohol. In sexually abused youth, Finkelhor (1987) identified behavioral manifestations of traumatic sexualization, including sexual preoccupations and compulsive, precocious, and aggressive sexual behaviors. Similar characteristics may be found in sexually abusive youth. Dailey (1996) also identified youth whose obsessive-compulsive disorders appear to drive paraphilic behaviors.

Significant advances in science have studied the impacts of neglect and trauma on the brain. Teicher et al. (2003) describe child maltreatment as promoting an alternative neural pathway that may enhance the emergence of psychiatric illness and behavioral problems. The exposure to high levels of stress hormones associated with child maltreatment causes the brain to develop along a stress-response pathway. The functional consequences of these stress-related effects on the brain may impact the control of aggressive, oral, and sexual behaviors, the formation and recollection of emotional memory, the learning of nonverbal motor patterns, the triggering of the fight-or-flight response, and the development of post-traumatic stress disorder. This evolving knowledge about the brain also has implications for the power of experiences and interventions to change an individual's adaptive functioning. Vance (2001) states, "The current understanding of the neurobiology of learning suggests that repeatedly experiencing highly rewarding or positive emotional stimuli, or practicing effective coping behaviors, will result in long-term potentiation of these neural circuits" (p. 67).

RECIDIVISM

Recidivism research with juveniles has contradicted the old assumption that "once a sex offender, always a sex offender." Alexander (1999) analyzed the follow-up data from eight studies totaling over 1,000 juveniles who participated in offense-specific treatment in a variety of settings. Combined recidivism rates for all youth were 7.1% in a three- to five-year follow-up. A more recent meta-analysis ($n = 2,986$, 2,604 known male) of published and unpublished data from nine studies on treatment effectiveness found recidivism rates with or without treatment were quite low (Reitzel & Carbonell, 2006):

- Sexual, 12.53%
- Nonsexual violent, 24.73%
- Nonsexual nonviolent, 28.51%
- Unspecified nonsexual, 20.40%

Youth who participated in treatment had a sexual recidivism rate of 7.37% while youth in the control group had a sexual recidivism rate of 18.98%.

Caldwell (2007) compared the recidivism patterns of a cohort of 249 delinquents who had committed sexual offenses and 1,780 nonsexual offending delinquents who were released from secured custody over a two- and one-half-year period. The prevalence of new sexual offense charges during the five-year follow-up period was 6.8% for those with previous sexual offenses, compared to 5.7% for the nonsexual offenders, a nonsignificant difference. Similar to the previous meta-analysis, the

% Reoffending—Up to 20-Year Follow-Up

	Treatment	Comparison
Sexual	9%	21%
Nonsexual violent	22%	39%
Nonviolent	28%	52%
Any	38%	57%

Figure 6.1   20-Year Follow-Up Data

sexually offending juveniles were much more likely to have been charged with nonsexual reoffenses than a sexual offense. It is important to note that 85% of the new sexual offenses in the follow-up period were accounted for by the previously non-sex-offending delinquents.

Worling, Litteljohn, and Bookalam (2010) reported the results of a 20-year prospective follow-up study of specialized treatment. The study compared 58 adolescents who participated in specialized individual, group, and family treatment with a comparison group of 90 adolescents who were in assessment only or dropped out of or refused treatment. The percent of reoffending in up to a 20-year follow-up. (This is depicted in Figure 6.1.)

CONCLUSION

Recidivism research as well as evidence of the differential developmental and dynamic risk factors associated with the different subtypes of sexually abusive youth offers a foundation for understanding the diversity that exists among juveniles who commit sexual offenses, illuminating static and dynamic risk factors and personality characteristics associated with the onset and maintenance of maladaptive sexual and nonsexual behavior. The differential identification and understanding of these factors now provides the foundation for treatment and supervision interventions that are individualized and sensitive to the subtype-specific characteristics.

REFERENCES

Alexander, M. (1999). Sexual offender treatment efficacy revisited. *Sexual Abuse: Journal of Research and Treatment, 11*, 101–116.

Becker, J. V. (1988). Adolescent sex offenders. *Behavior Therapy, 11*, 185–187.

Becker, J. V., Kaplan, M. S., Tenke, C. E., & Tartaglini, A. (1991). The incidence of depressive symptomatology in juvenile sex offenders with a history of abuse. *Child Abuse and Neglect, 15*, 531–536.

Burton, D. L., & Meezan, W. (2004). Revisiting recent research on social learning theory as an etiological proposition for sexually abusive male adolescents. *Journal of Evidence Based Social Work, 1*, 41–80.

Caldwell, M. F. (2007). Sexual offense adjudication and sexual recidivism among juvenile offenders. *Behavioral Science, 19*, 107–113. (Online issue.)

Cavanaugh, D. J., Pimenthal, A., & Prentky, R. (2008). A descriptive study of sexually abusive boys and girls—externalizing behaviors. In B. K. Schwartz (Ed.), *The sex offender: Offender evaluation and program strategies, volume VI* (pp. 12-1 to 12-21, Kingston, NJ: Civic Research Institute).

Dailey, L. (1996). *Adjunctive biological treatments with sexually abusive youth.* Paper presented at the Twelfth Annual Conference of the National Adolescent Perpetration Network, Minneapolis, Minnesota.

Finkelhor, D. (1987). The trauma of sexual abuse. *Journal of Interpersonal Violence, 2,* 348–366.

Gough, H. G. (1987). *California Psychological Inventory: Administrator's Guide.* Palo Alto, CA: Consulting Psychologists Press.

Hunter, J. A. (1999). *Understanding juvenile sexual offending behavior: Emerging research, treatment approaches and management practices.* Washington, DC: Center for Sex Offender Management, U.S. Department of Justice.

Hunter, J. A. (2006). *Understanding sexually abusive youth: New research and clinical directions.* Broomfield, CO: Colorado Department of Human Services, sponsored training.

Hunter, J. A. (2008). *Understanding sexually abusive youth: New research and clinical directions.* Ft. Collins, CO: Colorado Child and Adolescent Mental Health Conference.

Hunter, J. A. (2009). The sexual crimes of juveniles. In R. R. Hazelwood & A. W. Burgess (Eds.), *Practical aspects of rape investigation: A multidisciplinary approach.* Boca Raton, FL: CRC Press.

Hunter, J. A., Figueredo, A. J., Malamuth, N. M., & Becker, J. V. (2003). Juvenile sex offenders: Toward the development of a typology. *Sexual Abuse: A Journal of Research and Treatment, 15,* 27–48.

Kavoussi, R. J., Kaplan, M., & Becker, J. V. (1988). Psychiatric diagnoses in adolescent sexual offenders. *Journal of the American Child Adolescent Psychiatry, 27,* 241–243.

Knight, R. A., & Prentky, R. A. (1993). Exploring characteristics for classifying juvenile sex offenders. In H. E. Barbaree, W. L. Marshall, & S. M. Hudson (Eds.), *The juvenile sex offender* (pp. 45–83). New York: Guilford.

Latessa, E. J. (2005). *What works and what doesn't in reducing recidivism: The principles of effective intervention.* Colorado Division of Youth Corrections Provider Council Conference, Vail.

Leversee, T. (2008). Providing differential treatment and supervision to the diverse population of sexually abusive youth. In B. Schwartz (Ed.), *The Sex Offender, Volume 6* (pp. 14-1 to 14-13). Kingston, NJ: Civic Research Institute, Inc.

Millon, T., Millon, D., & Davis, R. (1993). *Millon Adolescent Clinical Inventory Manual.* Minneapolis, MN: National Computer Systems.

Miner, M. (2008). *What attachment theory tells us about unique risks for adolescent boys to sexually offend.* Portland: National Adolescent Perpetration Network Conference.

Miner, M. H., Robinson, B. E., Knight, R. A., Berg, D., Swinburne-Romine, R., & Netland, J. (2010). Understanding sexual perpetration against children: Effects of attachment style, interpersonal involvement, and hypersexuality. *Sexual Abuse: A Journal of Research and Treatment, 22*(1): 58–77.

Moffitt, T. (1993). Adolescence-Limited and Life-Course Persistent Antisocial Behavior: A developmental taxonomy. *Psychology Review, 100,* 674–701.

O'Brien, M., & Bera, W. (1986). Adolescent sexual offenders: A descriptive typology. *Preventing Sexual Abuse, 1,* 85–89.

Reitzel, L. R., & Carbonell, J. L. (2006). The effectiveness of sexual offender treatment for juveniles as measured by recidivism: A meta-analysis. *Journal of Sexual Abuse, 13,* 281–294.

Richardson, G., Kelly, T. P., Bhate, S. R., & Graham, F. (2004). Personality-based classification derived from the Personality Pattern scales from the Millon Adolescent Clinical Inventory (MACI). *British Journal of Clinical Psychology, 43,* 258–298.

Righthand, S., & Welch, C. (2002). Juveniles who have sexually offended: An introduction. *The Prevention Researcher, 9,* 1–4.

Shaw, J., Campo-Bowen, A. E., Applegate, B., Perez, D., Antoine, L. B., Hart, E. L., et al. (1993). Young boys who commit serious sexual offenses: Demographics, psychometrics, and phenomenology. *The Bulletin of the American Academy of Psychiatry and the Law, 21,* 399–408.

Teicher, M., Anderson, S. L., Polcari, A., Anderson, C. M., Navalta, C. P., & Kim, D. M. (2003). The neurobiological consequences of early stress and childhood maltreatment. *Neuroscience and Behavioral Reviews, 27,* 33–44.

Vance, J. E. (2001). Neurobiological mechanisms of psychosocial resiliency. In G. M. Richman & M. W. Fraser (Eds.), *The context of youth violence: Resilience, risk, and protection* (p. 67). Westport, CT: Prager.

Worling, J. R. (2001). Personality-based typology of adolescent male sexual offenders: Differences in recidivism rates, victim selection characteristics, and personal victimization histories. *Sexual Abuse: A Journal of Research and Treatment, 13,* 149–166.

Worling, J. R., Litteljohn, D., & Bookalam, D. (2010). 20-year prospective follow-up study of specialized treatment for adolescents who sexually offended. *Behavioral Sciences and the Law, 28,* 46–57.

CHAPTER 7

Static, Stable, and Dynamic Factors Relevant to Abusive Behaviors*

GAIL RYAN

"Abuse is Abuse, and abuse is the problem!"

I N TRYING TO imagine why one individual becomes a sexual abuser while another with similar experiences does not, it is necessary to conceptualize the interaction of experiences and perceptions, both positive and negative, to recognize strengths and health as well as deficits and deviance. On the one hand, there are the experiences illustrated in the developmental history, and on the other, there are the available models for interpreting and coping with those experiences. The first may be weighted with trauma and deficits or with good care and assets. The other may present a limited repertoire of coping behaviors, failed relationships, and dysfunctional experience, or successful relationships, effective coping skills, and developmental competency. The early life experience may be weighted with either adaptive or maladaptive models of coping, problem solving, and intimacy (Ryan et al., 1993; Ryan and Associates, 1998; Steele, 1987; Steele & Ryan, 1991).

It has become apparent over three decades of research and clinical work that, for most juveniles, sexually abusive behavior is much more related to their capacity to be abusive than some sexually deviant condition. Although a small minority do have problematic sexual interests or arousal, most are sexually interested in a range of diverse sexual stimuli and many have normative or nonproblematic sexual interests, as well as those that have caused harm. Chapters 4 and 5 have addressed both normative and deviant sexual development. But it is the abusive interaction that defines sexual abuse.

* The ideas contained in this chapter were first presented at the National Sexual Violence Prevention Conference in Dallas, Texas, March 2000, sponsored by Center for Disease Control. They were subsequently presented at the Positive Outcomes Conference in Manchester, England, July 2000. The author is indebted to many colleagues who have shared in the study of these issues over a span of 25 years, including members of the Kempe Study Group, the National Adolescent Perpetration Network, the Kempe Center, and the Kempe Foundation.

People exhibit a wide range of abusive behaviors across the life span, and such behaviors are not always recognized as "abuse" but can be defined by the risk of harm to self, others, or property. Children are not always held accountable for abusive behaviors: the child who throws the doll against the wall; the playground bully; or the siblings who hit or denigrate each other. Such behaviors are often excused as "normal" because they are so commonly observed. Yet these behaviors are abusive, and when chronic and resistant to change, may eventually result in referrals for clinical services and/or in legal charges as the child is eventually held culpable for behaviors that violate the law or cause harm to self, others, or property.

During the 1980s, the sexually abusive behavior of children and adolescents, as well as headlines regarding incidents of extreme aggression and violence by juveniles, attracted enormous publicity along with a growing awareness of the incidence and prevalence of child sexual abuse. In the community, the courts, human services, and the mental health field, sexual abuse has been viewed as categorically different from other harmful or abusive behaviors, and both those who offend and those victimized have been studied in terms of the sexual meaning (Ryan et al., 1988; Ryan, 2000). However, as clinical work and research have illuminated the development and correction of sexually abusive behavior in childhood and adolescence, it has become apparent that there is tremendous crossover in the etiological risk factors, as well as the dynamics and treatment of a wide spectrum of abusive behaviors (Ryan, 1989, 1998, 1999; Weissberg, 1982). It is the abusive nature of sexual abuse that differentiates sexually abusive behavior from other sexual behavior. It is the capacity to be abusive (to risk harm) that is the necessary precondition for all types of abusive behaviors.

Research on prediction of sexual recidivism by adults (Hanson, 2000; Prentky, Lee, Knight, & Cerce, 1997; Quinsey, 1995; Quinsey, Khanna, & Malcolm, 1998) uses actuarial methods to identify "risk factors" that are *overrepresented* in the history of those who are known to have this particular problem, *as compared to the general population*. Actuarial models are used by insurance companies to predict which clients are at greatest "risk" of a problem and subsequently charge more on "at risk" policies. For example, insurers find that 16-year-old boys are at greater risk to have accidents than any other subgroup of drivers. However, they *cannot* identify which 16-year-old will actually have an accident, or when it will happen. Similarly, actuarial research can identify risk factors relevant to sexual offending.

The Static 99 (Hanson, 2000) typifies models that isolate factors most predictive of sexual recidivism over time by adults (regardless of treatment status). Actuarial risk assessment tools can now predict which adults are most likely to *continue* sexual offending, with or without treatment, even though they cannot say which individual actually will or when it will happen. The most reliable predictors are *static* or unchangeable and do not require extensive developmental history to identify. Similarly, researchers describe tentative models predicting recidivism by juveniles (Epperson, Ralston, Fowers, & DeWitt, 2005; Knight & Prentky, 1993; Prentky & Righthand, 2001; Worling & Curwen, 2000). But actuarial models can be discouraging for treatment providers, parole boards, and clients because the retrospective factors found to predict greater risk of recidivism cannot be changed (Quinsey, 1995). In many studies of human behavior, the best predictor of future behavior is past behavior, and no intervention erases the past. Defining *dynamic* variables relevant to the actual occurrence of recidivism (see Gendreau, Little, & Goggin, 1996; Hanson & Harris, 2000) has been added to the research agenda, enabling interventionists to target *changeable* variables to improve outcomes (Hanson & Harris, 2000, rev. 2002; Quinsey, Khanna, & Malcolm, 1998).

In the 1980s, many researchers reported historical characteristics that were over-represented in those who sexually offend, contributing to the development of hypotheses relevant to the etiology or *initiation* of sexual offending. In the past 20 years, the ongoing research has focused primarily on the identification of risk factors for *continuation* or sexual offense recidivism by those already known to have offended. This shift was apparent in a meta-analysis conducted by the Centers for Disease Control, Division of Violence Prevention between 2001 and 2005 (Whitaker et al., 2008). In searching the most recent decade of empirical research for validation of hypotheses regarding risk factors for the initiation of sexual offending, it was found that many of the previously hypothesized early life variables are no longer being reported at all (as present or absent) in studies of adults who sexually offend.

Risk factors contributing to the onset of juvenile sexual offending will be child-hood variables preceding the initiation of a first offense, and research on juveniles is much more limited. Nonetheless, retrospective and prospective studies of many different populations identify factors that may be relevant to the *risk* of children initiating behaviors that are abusive to themselves, others, and/or property. By studying those who are included in groups with different types of behavioral disorders, as well as the general population of persons who do well, it is possible to identify both risks and assets relevant to human functioning. Overrepresented factors then inform identification of "at-risk" groups as well as the protective factors that might moderate risks.

Research emerging from the juvenile field has demonstrated many encouraging findings: (a) Sexually abusive youths are less at risk of sexual offense recidivism than nonsexual reoffense; (b) juveniles reoffend sexually less often than adult sex offenders, and even less after treatment (Alexander, 1999; Bourduin, Henggeler, Blaske, & Stein, 1990; Reitzel & Carbonell, 2006; Vandiver, 2005; Worling, 2000); and (c) only a small portion of juveniles who sexually offend have deviant sexual interests and/or arousal patterns (Hunter, 1996, 1999; Hunter & Becker, 1994). Such findings dispel the myths that were common assumptions in the 1980s, when it was expected that the sexual offenses of youth were reflections of sexual deviance and that youth offending as adolescents would be at high risk to become adult sexual offenders without intense interventions. Vandiver (2005) reports sexual recidivism of juveniles as adults was 4.3%, while more than half had been rearrested for a nonsexual offense.

Because it is now known that most juveniles who sexually offend are more like other delinquents than like adult sex offenders, it is reasonable to expect that many of the same risk factors contribute to the risk of delinquency, juvenile sexual offending, and other behavioral disorders (see Chapter 6). It also follows that juveniles identified due to nonsexual delinquency may be at risk for sexual offending, which provides an opportunity for secondary prevention before they do.

Risk factors for humans may be associated with heritable characteristics or prenatal insults that affect fetal development and the condition at birth. Others may occur as a product of failures in early care or developmental differences, and some may result from exposure and events in the person's early life experience (Ryan and Associates, 1998). It is apparent that risk factors do not operate in isolation, but interact in ways that may be moderated or exacerbated by other variables, either negative risks or positive assets. None of the correlations identified to date are directly causally related, for better or worse, to the specific risk of sexual offending.

However, awareness of the range and interaction of various types of risk factors now informs an understanding that some children are at greater risk than others to initiate and continue behaviors that pose a risk of harm to self or others. This knowledge informs opportunities for primary and secondary prevention, as well as the identification of early manifestations of abusive behaviors that may benefit from tertiary interventions (Ryan, 2004).

As was illustrated in Chapter 3, many theories regarding the etiology of sexual offending support a "victim-to-victimizer" hypothesis, recognizing both an overrepresentation of victimization in the history of those who sexually offend, and the impact of victimization on developmental processes, learning, reinforcement, and, (in the case of sexual abuse), sexuality (Cicchetti, 1987; Gilgun, 1990). When adults have been abused or neglected as children some experience sexual dysfunction, others develop nonsexual dysfunctions, and others have no dysfunction later in life (Widom & Williams, 1996). In studying many of the dysfunctional behaviors that pose a risk of harm, many appear to occur in repetitive patterns that may be representative of a common defensive strategy, which for some, acts to protect and contribute to recovery, but for others, becomes overgeneralized and dysfunctional over time (Ryan, 1989).

Both theorists and researchers had hypothesized that some combination of variables descriptive of: (a) the child's own experience of sexual abuse; (b) the process of discovery/disclosure; and/or (c) the subsequent reactions/interventions would be explanatory and thus predictive of eventual adult outcomes. However, after decades of study, it is apparent that although sexual victimization is overrepresented in both clinical and criminal justice populations, it is not explanatory of dysfunction or offending, nor is it uniquely powerful in predicting outcomes (Becker & Murphy, 1998; Burton, Nesmith, & Badten, 1997; Hanson & Bussiere, 1998; Hanson & Slater, 1988; Hindman, 1989; Hunter & Figueredo, 2000; Knight & Prentky, 1993; Prentky et al., 1989; Ryan and Associates, 1998; Schwartz, 2005; Seghorn, Prentky, & Boucher, 1987).

Many negative factors can be found in the history of those who are abusive and in the history of those who do not abuse. No one factor, or combination of factors, has been identified as uniquely present in the history of only those who sexually offend. Not all who sexually offend have experienced sexual victimization (Ryan, 1989). Childhood neglect, physical abuse, and witnessing family violence precede sexual offending even more often than sexual victimization (Widom & Williams, 1996). It is also apparent that many children who have experienced sexual abuse recover without long-term damage or dysfunction, even without treatment (Rind, Tromovitch, & Bauserman, 1998). Steele concludes: "It is not the bad things that happen to you in life . . . it is one's ability to *cope* with whatever happens to you!" (p. 62) (Steele, quoted in Ryan and Associates, 1998).

Hindman (1989) found, in her study of adults who had been abused as children, that the variations most relevant to their adult outcomes were not found in the "facts," but in the individual's *perception* of their experiences. More recently, Burton (2003); Burton, Miller, & Shill (2002); and Miner (2008) have similarly concluded that *qualitative* factors are more linked to the outcome of sexual offending than the fact of being sexually abused. One's perception of the relationship and its meaning may contribute to the experience in ways that distinguish those who go on to offend and those who do not. Perceptions are the product of developmental processes that accommodate and assimilate new information and experience into one's view of themselves, relationships, and the world. This is the *phenomena* that supports a developmental-contextual understanding of individual differences, and our understanding that no one fact or theory explains the etiology of sexual offending or other disordered behavior.

Specific to the outcomes for sexually abused children, Abel, Jones, Gabriel, & Harlow (2009) describe a window of opportunity of a few years (between the time a boy is sexually abused and the time he is most at risk to begin offending) when secondary prevention work might be able to moderate risk. However, although there is some support for the power of validating, protective, and supportive responses in moderating subsequent symptoms (following the disclosure of child sexual abuse), there is little evidence linking long-term outcomes to *treatment* of child victims, for better or worse (Rind, Tromovitch, & Bauserman, 1998). The resilience of human beings has been studied for many years (Cichetti, 1987; Egeland, Elizabeth, & Sroufe, 1993; Gilgun, 1990; Rutter, 1987; Sroufe, Allen, & Kreutzer, 1990; Werner, 1993) and identifies many risks and assets that affect human development and behavior. The finding that many abused children go on to recover and do well is cause for optimism that protective factors can be identified, which increase positive outcomes (Seghorn, 1998, personal communication). Pairing risk management with health promotion is a feature of many newer models throughout the child development and developmental psychopathology literature.

Combining offense-specific theories with developmental, contextual, and ecological theories (Donovan & McIntyre, 1990; Scales & Leffert, 1998; Strayhorn, 1988), a new set of hypotheses have developed and been described in the literature (Burton, 2003; Burton & Meezan, 2004; Calder, 2002; Miner & Crimmins, 1997; Rich, 2003; Ryan and Associates, 1998). One hypothesis regarding the outcomes of abused children is that the developmental status (relative competency) and prior life experience of the child (context) are likely to be more predictive of outcomes than any combination of variables descriptive of the victimizing events (Ryan et al., 1998). The most powerful variables may be related to who the child was at the time of the abuse experience, and what beliefs, skills, strategies, and/or resources were available to them to cope with the experience (Steele, 1987). A developmental, contextual, and ecological model encompasses the complexity of all these variables.

Figure 7.1 illustrates the primary domains (within which there could be both risk and protective factors) as the child grows and develops, accommodates and assimilates experiences, and is exposed to the world. Identifying specific risks and deficits in each domain could become an endless task, but the complexity of potentially relevant variables underscores the diversity of human beings and the need for comprehensive, individualized assessment and differential treatment plans to capture and address individual differences. While the typology research described in Chapter 6 differentiates various subgroups, until random controlled trials demonstrate the efficacy of different interventions with each subgroup, best practice will continue to rely on individualized assessment.

Research and clinical work on many types of juvenile behavior problems now incorporates both risks and assets into models for assessment, prediction, and prevention. Whitaker (1990) incorporated developmental competencies into programming for violent and sexually aggressive youth, and Bremer (1992, 1998) introduced a protective factors model that has been widely used by law enforcement and juvenile probation for initial risk management decisions. The National Task Force on Juvenile Sexual Offending (1993) recommended differential diagnosis and

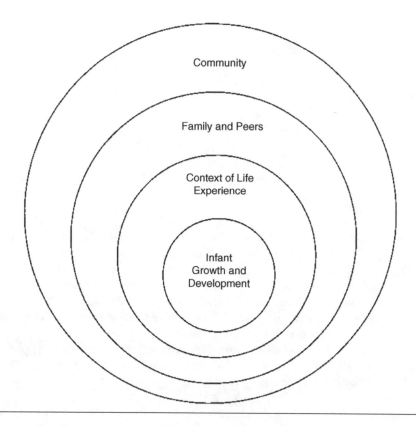

Figure 7.1   The Developmental, Contextual, and Ecological Pond

the inclusion of developmental assessment in evaluating sexually abusive youth. Gilgun's Clinical Assessment Package for Risks and Strengths (CASPARS) (1996, 1998); Rasmussen, Burton, and Christopherson (1992); Rasmussen (1999); Rich's Juvenile Risk Assessment Tool (JRAT) (2000, 2006); Griffin, Beech, Print, Bradshaw, and Quayle (2008); Collie, Ward, Ayland, and West (2007); and Worling and Curwen (2000) all consider both risk and protective factors in models designed for tracking the ongoing assessment of progress over time in treatment programs (see Figure 7.2). Gilgun's model drives home the point that it is the balance of risks and assets that is most relevant to outcomes. That a youth with high risks but also high in assets may do better over time than one with few risks but also low in assets. It is the high risk and low asset youth who is likely to have the worst outcome.

The evolution toward models that are designed to balance risk reduction with health promotion began in the juvenile field of work with sexual offending in the early 1990s and, by 1995, it was suggested that the juvenile field might have something to contribute to the adult field (Ryan, 1995, 1999). Current juvenile models are now paralleled by developments in the adult field (such as the "Good Lives" model), which offers additional support for approaches that focus more on health and current/future functioning, and less on the deviance of past behavior, which cannot be changed (Ward, 2002; Ward & Gannon, 2006; Yates & Ward, 2008). Recently, some juvenile models reflect the same principles and are congruent

Low Risk Low Asset	Low Risk High Asset
High Risk Low Asset	High Risk High Asset

Figure 7.2   Balance of Risks and Assets (Gilgun, 1996, 1998)

with other evolving juvenile models (Ayland & West, 2006; Collie, Ward, Ayland, & West, 2007; O'Callaghan, 2004; Print & O'Callaghan, 2004).

Research identifying static versus dynamic risk factors has further advanced our ability to build relevant, empirically-based models for clinical assessment and treatment. For example, Prentky, Harris, Frizell, and Righthand (2000) describe *historical* variables indicative of juvenile recidivism. These include: prior charges for sexual offenses; predatory behavior; sexual preoccupation; duration of sexually abusive history; caregiver instability; arrest before age 16; school behavior problems; suspension or expulsion from school; diagnosis of conduct disorder; multiple types of sexual offenses; impulsivity; and alcohol or drug use by either the youth or parent (Prentky, Harris, Frizzell, & Righthand, 2000).

The cessation of offending, predatory behavior, disordered conduct, school misbehavior, and drug/alcohol use are obvious and immediate treatment goals, but the cessation of such behaviors will still not erase their presence in the history of the youth. At the same time, the history of sexual preoccupation, impulsivity, and caregiver instability may be more stable or chronic factors, likely continuing to be characteristic of this youth and his relationships across the life span. There are also ongoing goals to address in the treatment, aftercare, and relapse prevention plans for the particular youth.

Similarly, the factors described by Hanson (2000) and Hanson and Morton-Bourgon (2007) as unchangeable risk factors in the history of adult offenders also suggest some immediate goals in treating juveniles to prevent the development and/ or maintenance of those factors before becoming adults. For example, Hanson describes sexual deviance, range of victims, persistence of offending, and antisocial personality as high risk factors for the adult who offends, but the developmental trajectory and reinforcement of these factors might be changed by successful treatment for juveniles.

Fortunately, Hunter and Figueredo (2000) report that plethysmography research indicates that the sexually abusive behavior of juveniles is not always associated with deviant sexual arousal. Nonetheless, the minority of sexually abusive youth who do have problematic arousal, a range of victims, and persistent offending after early intervention are likely to continue to be higher risk, as compared to youth who do not have those characteristics. For such youth, intensive targeted interventions to assess the weight of deviant or problematic arousal and, when indicated, to undertake arousal reconditioning, may be indicated. For those who have conduct disorder traits associated with the development of antisocial personality, cognitive work to change callous, irresponsible, and criminal thinking patterns and the beliefs and attitudes supportive of hyper-masculinity, sexual exploitation, and abusive behaviors would clearly be indicated (Malamuth, 1986; Yochelson & Samenow, 1977).

The most changeable factors are in the dynamics associated with the occurrence of abusive behaviors and those dynamics should be definable not only in the history of offending, but also in the current functioning of the youth. In the beginning, subsequent offending was the obvious measure of treatment "failure" (recidivism). Successful completion of programs based on length of times in treatment was often guided by the external mandate for treatment. Completion of particular lessons or modules used a more psychoeducational model measuring learning and retention, but did not offer evidence of internal or behavioral change. Defining measures of successful treatment in terms of observable changes in current functioning is a more recent development, and varies in different models from being primarily related to abuse/offense-specific treatment issues (such as taking responsibility for past behavior and expressing victim empathy) to more comprehensive holistic human functioning in the present (such as emotional regulation, impulse management, successful coping skills, etc.). Measuring progress on the basis of dynamic factors addresses present and future risk factors that are changeable rather than focusing exclusively on historical deviance that cannot be changed.

Prentky, Harris, Frizzell, and Righthand (2000) describe the reduction of dynamic risks primarily in terms of what might be observable in treatment sessions, and to a lesser extent in the ecological domains of family and community: accepting responsibility; internal motivation to change; understanding patterns associated with behavior; showing empathy and remorse; absence of cognitive distortions; anger management; stability in home and school; support systems; and quality of peer relationships. Gilgun (1998) describes markers of protective factors related to emotional expressiveness, family relationships, peer relationships, sexuality, and family "embeddedness" in the community. In a very detailed treatment model for adolescents, Rich (2000, 2006) charts 109 factors related to responsibility, relationships, cognitive functioning, social skills, comorbid psychiatric disorders, substance abuse, antisocial behaviors, family, environment, and work on past experiences. Oneal, Burns, Kahn, Rich, and Worling (2008) chart progress on sexual behavior, healthy sexuality, social competency, cognitions/attitudes supportive of sexual abuse, victim awareness, emotional and behavioral regulation, risk prevention awareness, and positive family caregiver dynamics. Righthand et al. (2005) consider motivation to change, sexual interests and drive, social skills, personal maltreatment history, victim impact/empathy, attitudes/beliefs, emotion/impulse management, positive/stable self-image, responsible behavior, family relationships/supports, peer relationships/supports, community supports, and risk management. Griffin, Beech, Print, Bradshaw, and Quayle (2008) describe concerns and strengths. Several of these progress scales allow for bimodal ratings, which can indicate presence or absence of the need/dynamic, degree of need, and more or less progress on meeting the need or changing the dynamic. Many of the variables embedded in these models intersect or appear in numerous models, thus increasing confidence in their relevance.

The most comprehensive models use dynamic factors as markers of functioning that reflect the following important aspects.

- Developmental competence (demonstrating skills for successful functioning)
- Their perceptual experience of the world, relationships, and self (as reflected in thoughts, beliefs, attitudes)
- Characteristics of the family, peer group, community, and culture in which they have lived and will continue to live

In a goal-oriented approach, tipping the balance of risks and assets in each domain so that the positives outweigh the negatives supports optimal outcomes. One's ability to cope with whatever life brings is dependent on moderating the ongoing influence of static and stable risks while decreasing dynamic risk and increasing health. Comprehensive and individualized assessment and treatment must address the complexity of human experience and functioning, without being overwhelmed by it.

Treatment interventions must aim to decrease dynamic risks and increase protective factors while reducing the effects of static and stable factors. Identifying relevant elements in each domain, which can be observed in the daily circumstances and functioning of the individual, measures progress over the course of treatment in acquiring the dynamic assets to offset the risks. By thinking first about the factors that relate to all human functioning (see Table 7.1), and then those that might specifically relate to more or less risk for abusive behavior, a framework for conceptualizing static, stable, and dynamic risks and assets emerges.

Defining static factors as retrospective/historical variables, we know that these factors cannot be changed because we cannot relive history. What can be changed is the influence of the past on the present. Such factors might include: the condition at birth, permanent disabilities, family of origin, and early life experience.

Stable factors might be defined as life spanning or chronic (that is, likely to continue to influence functioning), but might include characteristics that can be either moderated or exacerbated in how they affect one's functioning. Such factors might include temperament, intellectual potential, physical attributes, and inherited neurological characteristics.

Finally, dynamic factors might be defined as those factors that change from day to day, or at least are changeable. Specifically, dynamic factors would include situational, cognitive, emotional, and behavioral factors that will differ over time (for better or worse) and may be managed or coped with (for better or worse) throughout the individual's life, and on a daily basis.

All three types of risk factors (static, stable, and dynamic) will affect and be affected by developmental, contextual, and ecological factors. And for each factor

Table 7.1
Factors Relevant to Human Functioning (For Better or Worse)

Static (Historical/ Unchangeable)	Stable (Life Spanning/Less Changeable)	Dynamic (Change/Manage/ Moderate)
Condition at birth	Temperament	Situations
Permanent disability	Intellectual potential	Thoughts
Family of origin/culture	Heritable neurological characteristics	Feelings
Early life experience	Physical attributes	Behaviors

Table 7.2
Static Risks and Assets

Risks	Assets
_ Prenatal insults	_ Prenatal care
_ Premature/traumatic birth	_ Normative birth
_ Unempathic care	_ Empathic care
_ Caregiver loss/disruption	_ Consistent caregivers
_ Trust failure	_ Trustworthy relationship
_ Disordered attachment	_ Secure attachment
_ Dysfunctional modeling	_ Normal growth/development
_ Witness domestic violence	_ Functional modeling
_ Abuse, neglect, FTT, trauma	_ Nurturance and protection

that creates a risk, there is some corresponding factor that would moderate risk (assets).

Risks and assets relevant to the likelihood of sexually abusive behavior begin prior to birth and continue to accumulate (see Table 7.2).

Although the developmental-contextual model acknowledges the infinite number of variables that may differ for individuals, some factors seem most relevant to the risk of abusive behaviors specifically, or to the risk of dysfunction generally. Risk factors that affect the condition at birth might include genetic abnormalities; fetal exposure to drugs, alcohol, or disease; inborn disabilities; and premature or traumatic birth. The condition at birth describes all that the infant brings with them, which will profoundly affect their experience of the world, relationships, and self. Risk factors may cause the infant to be chronically distressed and hard to care for, increasing the risk of breakdown in their ability to communicate their needs and emotions and jeopardize the process of attachment and bonding between the child and caregiver. The distress of sick, premature, or low birth weight babies has been a dilemma described in neonatology (Goldson, Fitch, Wendell, & Knapp, 1978), as well as the effects of prenatal exposure to drugs and alcohol (Baumbach, 2000).

Upon arrival, the infant is dependent upon caregivers in the family of origin to read their cues and provide care and nurturance to meet their needs (sensitive parenting). If the caregiver is not consistently empathic (that is, providing for the infant's needs either sporadically and/or without regard for the infant's cues), the infants may learn to disregard their internal cues and become unable to identify and communicate their needs and emotions effectively. The lack of empathic care precludes the infant's natural acquisition of empathic recognition for self and others (Landry & Peters, 1992). Disruption of the caregiver relationship (whether through omission or commission of the caregiver), further jeopardizes the infant's emerging interpersonal skills and sense of self (Steele, 1987). The infant fails to achieve basic trust and internalizes a negative internal model for future relationships (Ainsworth, 1985; Bowlby, 1985).

The family into which the child is born is not only the source of many factors affecting the condition at birth and early caregiving, but also provides the child's first experience of the world. For better or worse, every characteristic of the family has an effect on the child: control/helplessness; competence/failure; functional/dysfunctional; safe/

vulnerable; protection/harm; support/deprivation; embeddedness/isolation in the community; and so forth.

The stresses on the family and their strategies for coping become the model for the child's earliest beliefs. The family of origin creates the ecological "pond" within which the child grows; as the child matures, the pond widens to include peer, community, and cultural influences. This ecological pond may be the source of both risks and assets.

The physiological effects of early care can also be profound. Research on early brain development (Karr-Morse & Wiley, 1997) has demonstrated that the infant's brain is growing in "use dependent" ways; that is, the functions that are most active increase growth in some areas while underused areas fail to grow. The infant using his/her brain to hold and process knowledge about the world may be developing hypersensitivities to some cues and fail to develop at all in other areas (Siegel, 1999). Severe neglect can be seen in the absence of brain growth and activity in some areas (Karr-Morse & Wiley, 1997), while fear responses can overdevelop hyper-vigilance and defensive brain functions (Knopp & Benson, 1996; Van der Kolk, 1987). When experiences occur in an organized and predictable manner, the brain grows in an organized way, but chaotic and unpredictable experiences create chaos in the brain.

Factors arising from early life experiences include both risks and assets for all children and this history (both positive and negative) is carried into future functioning and relationships. Children who lack the internal and/or external assets necessary to successfully cope with adverse experiences may become deviant or dysfunctional as a result of developmental failures that distort and shape their accommodation and assimilation of experience and exposure. When children are victims of abuse, neglect, or trauma they may either accept or reject all or parts of the experience as congruent or incongruent in the context of their view of themselves, the world, and relationships.

Very often, in the face of helplessness, the child takes on a sense of responsibility for the behavior of others and imagines that they have caused (or failed to prevent) their own victimization, that they are unworthy of care and protection, or deserving of the harm they experience. This misattribution of responsibility distorts the locus of control. Believing oneself responsible for the behavior of others lessens one's sense of personal responsibility and contributes to a dysfunctional coping style in which the child seeks to regain a sense of control by controlling others, or to compensate for unmet needs with whatever self-gratifying substitutions are available to them (Ryan, 1989).

Stable risk factors (see Table 7.3), which may be relevant to the risk of dysfunctional behaviors, might include such things as difficult temperament, low intellect or learning difficulties, negative internal working model, heritable psychiatric disorders, and/or chronic PTSD reactivity. Temperament traits are usually described as either easy or difficult. "Difficultness" is often defined in terms of how difficult certain characteristics may be for other people to deal with (Thomas & Chess, 1977). Therefore, temperament traits may be viewed as either risks or assets, depending upon the particular family, community, or culture a child arrives in. A lack of fit, when the child's temperament does not meet the expectations of the family or community, can contribute to chronic conflicts and negative interactions that affect the child's self-esteem and relationships (Turecki, 1985). However, the person most affected by temperament is the person him/herself. Some traits contribute to irritability and discontent to such a degree that the child is at risk of chronic stress and thus, dysfunctional coping. It is thought that temperament traits remain

Table 7.3
Stable Risks and Assets

Risks	Assets
_ Difficult temperament traits	_ Easy/adaptive temperament
_ Low functioning/DD/learning disability	_ Average–high intelligence (IQ)
_ Negative internal working model (self and others)	_ Positive internal working model (self and others)
_ Heritable psychiatric disorders; attention deficit disorder	_ Normative physical and neurological functioning
_ Chronic PTSD reactivity	

somewhat stable across the life span, although their effects can be moderated or exacerbated by many factors (Thomas & Chess, 1977; Turecki, 1985).

Physical attributes (such as gender, appearance, or stature) can similarly affect the child in terms of a lack of fit, when the child does not meet the expectations of the parents or is not viewed positively by others. Discontent with one's physical attributes can also affect self-esteem and contribute to the child's risk of dysfunctional coping in general, and specifically affect sexual risk-taking and self-destructive behavior. Intellectual potential (IQ) is also thought to remain somewhat stable across the life span, although brain growth, stimulation, and learning disabilities can each affect intellectual functioning. As previously stated, the influence of environment and care on brain growth is now known to be profound (Karr-Morse & Wiley, 1997), and it is likely that further research will contribute additional insight regarding cognitive functioning and the propensity for problems with both sexuality and aggression. It is apparent, however, that one's ability to learn, process information, recognize internal states, and cognitively and verbally articulate their needs, emotions, and thoughts is very relevant to successful human functioning.

Intellectual functioning can be further affected by some psychiatric disorders, which can cause emotional reactivity, cognitive confusion, delusions, rapid or sluggish thought processing, attention deficits, or intrusive thoughts or images. Some psychiatric disorders are overrepresented in many samples of sexually abusive youth. Becker, Kaplan, Tenke, and Tartaglini (1991); Dailey (1996); Cavazos (2000); and Kavoussi, Kaplan, and Becker (1998) have described the co-occurrence of mood disorders, attention disorders, obsessive-compulsive disorders, and post traumatic stress disorder in work with sexually abusive youth. The relationship between co-occurring disorders and the risk of abusive behaviors and/or sexual deviance is not always clear and is not thought to be causal, but it is apparent that both psychological and neurological functioning may exacerbate the dysfunctional patterns associated with sexual and aggressive behaviors. We also know that brain functioning can be altered by traumatic events, causing either acute or chronic reactivity. When brain functioning has been permanently altered by trauma (Van der Kolk, 1987), or in the case of neurologically-based disorders that are inherited, these disorders are likely to remain somewhat constant across the life span. Co-occurring psychiatric disorders may contribute to the risk of dysfunctional or abusive behaviors in two ways. One is to contribute to the symptoms that precede the behavior (increase emotional or cognitive stress) and the other is to benefit from and be reinforced by the neuro-chemical reactions generated by some behaviors ("self-medicating" effects). The

Table 7.4

Dynamic Risks: Global and Circumstantial

Global Risks (Long-Term)	Circumstantial Risks (Daily)
Foreseeable in life span	*Specific/fluctuating daily*
_ Constant/expected stressors	_ Current/unexpected stressors (conflict or emotional trigger)
_ Unresolved emotional issues	_ Perceived threat/vulnerability
_ Unsafe environment/persons	_ Lowered self-esteem/efficacy
_ Injury/illness	_ Negative expectations
_ Temporary disabilities	_ Isolation/lack of support
_ Lack of opportunity/support	_ Projection/externalizing
_ Change/loss	_ Mood dysregulation: anger, depression, anxiety
_ Failed relationships	_ Abusive memory/fantasy
_ Access to vulnerable persons	_ Lowered inhibitions
	_ Access to vulnerable persons
	_ Rationalization, justification

effect of psychiatric disorders can be significantly moderated by effective treatment or may exacerbate risk when untreated.

Dynamic risks and assets are those that may fluctuate from day to day and over time and are, therefore, most changeable. By observing daily functioning, it is possible to see the characteristic patterns of situations, thoughts, feelings, and behaviors that precede and follow abusive behaviors. Recognition of this common pattern has been used to target interventions, which will interrupt the progression toward abusive behavior (Lane, 1997; Ryan & Blum, 1993; Ryan, Lane, Davis, & Isaac, 1987; Way & Spieker, 1997). It is possible to identify foreseeable stressors across the life span, consciously desensitize emotionally laden issues, and develop risk moderating skills. Such strategies can address life events known to be stressful to most human beings (global), as well as those that may be very personal and unique to the individual. For example, times of transition or loss are likely to be stressful for most people; whereas the infancy of one's own child or the death of a grandparent might be uniquely stressful for a person who was abused or neglected as an infant or whose primary attachment was to the grandparent. One's ability to anticipate and prepare for both common and unique foreseeable stress is the basis for good risk management after treatment. It is also possible (and entirely normal) to think through one's plans for the day and the immediate future in order to anticipate and plan for possible risks or stressors, and to make informed choices about and preparation for such circumstances. Table 7.4 depicts examples of both global and circumstantial dynamic risk factors that might be particularly relevant to the risk of being overwhelmed, and employing dysfunctional defensive strategies.

ARTICULATING SUCCESSFUL OUTCOMES

Despite recognition of the heterogeneous characteristics of this population, many treatment programs initially required all youth referred for sexual offending to complete the same treatment. Success was often defined in terms of tasks, modules, topics, or time limits. Yet there is no evidence that a particular length of time, number

Table 7.5
Dynamic Assets Relevant to Decreased Risk

_ Consistently defines all abuse (self, others, property)

_ Acknowledges risk (and uses foresight and planning)

_ Consistently recognizes/interrupts cycle (no later than the first thought of an abusive solution)

_ Demonstrates new coping skills (when stressed)

_ Demonstrates empathy (recognizes and responds to cues of self and others)

_ Accurate attributions of responsibility (takes responsibility for own behavior, does not try to control behavior of others)

_ Able to manage frustration and unfavorable events (anger management and self-protection)

_ Rejects abusive thoughts as dissonant (incongruent with self-image)

of assignments, or specific intervention is either indicated for every youth or indicative of changes specifically relevant to decreased risk of sexual offending.

Completion of treatment should provide observable evidence in current functioning that demonstrates a decreased risk of abusive behavior and an increased likelihood of healthy, successful functioning. These can be described as the "dynamic assets," which counter the dynamic risks, previously described, and can be used as observable measures of progress over time, tipping the balance of dynamic risks with greater protective assets (see Table 7.5). Observable outcomes should address the most common issues of offending. Some are specifically relevant to the risk of juveniles continuing to be abusive to themselves, others, or property (Ryan 1997), and others provide evidence-based support for successful human functioning (Scales & Leffert, 1998; Strayhorn, 1988).

EVIDENCE OF DECREASED RISK

Many youth arrive in treatment, adjudicated and court ordered, but do not know why what they did was "abusive." Despite the pervasiveness of maltreatment in many of their lives, they have often not defined their own experiences of victimization as abuse, either. *Consistently defining all abuse* is a marker of recognition and vigilance, making it less likely that individuals might unwittingly engage in, or be victims of, abuse without defining it as such.

Many youth have experienced anxiety about the consequences and/or meaning of their behavior but have explained away its meaning and dismissed its importance to quell the anxiety, and reach a state of calm by promising themselves (and/or others) that the behavior will not reoccur. Mastering the definition of abuse makes clear the attribution of responsibility relevant to all forms of abuse and increases recognition before the behavior occurs. This culpability increases personal responsibility and decreases the capacity for defensive denial.

For many abusive youth, dysfunctional coping strategies developed initially as a temporarily adaptive response to stressors they did not have the skills or support to deal with earlier in life. When surrounded by dysfunctional modeling, many have not had functional solutions to choose. *Recognizing dysfunctional patterns* and mastering the skills to interrupt the progression before harmful behaviors occur can be demonstrated consistently by defining abuse, rejecting it, and choosing new coping strategies. *Interrupting the defensive pattern no later than the first thought of an abusive behavior* prevents the continued reinforcement of dysfunctional patterns and *demonstrates new coping skills and choices* when experiencing stress.

Acknowledging risks associated with abuse occurring in one's daily life supports the continued *use of foresight and planning* for success and safety across the life span.

Foreseeing stress in daily life is so common among functional people that using risk management strategies is second nature, having had role models who were insightful and organized in controlling and managing stress. But planning and preparation to be successful each day are skills acquired over time; mastery of self-management contributes to the internal locus of control, thus decreasing the risk of defensive reactions, as well as the misattribution of responsibility, which was previously described as a common factor in abusive dynamics.

Making accurate attributions of responsibility for behavior manifests in daily functioning and can also be observed. Taking personal responsibility for one's own behavior (without externalizing or blaming others), as well as not accepting or trying to assume control of others, and not internalizing guilt for things beyond the individual's control demonstrate this outcome.

Empathic reactions to the cues of self and others that are indicative of needs and emotions can also be observed in daily functioning. As previously stated, empathy involves skills acquired as a result of sensitive parenting (Landry & Peters, 1992). The lack of empathic recognition and responses is one of the most common deficits in all abusers. Empathy deficits associated with abusive behaviors can result from the failure to recognize cues of distress or discomfort in others, misinterpretation of such cues, or not caring about the discomfort or distress. Although the deficit may be different, the consistent demonstration of empathic recognition and responses will be observable evidence of the capacity and skills to be empathic.

Judging behavior without judging oneself or others is related to decreased tolerance for abuse in one's life. Ideally, *rejecting abusive thoughts as dissonant* with one's view of self demonstrates the acquisition of a nonabusive self-image/identity. This is of critical importance (and a great source of hope) for youth who have not yet completed the developmental task of identity formation.

EVIDENCE OF INCREASED HEALTH

Avoiding dysfunctional responses and rejecting abusive alternatives is likely to be most successful (and generalize across the life span best) when one has more positive alternatives and is able to function successfully in their daily lives. Balancing risk reduction with health promotion is the goal (see Table 7.6). Specifically, one's ability to create psychologically safe, empathic relationships may be one of the most protective factors in decreasing the risk of interpersonal abuse. Prosocial relationship skills, and especially one's ability to establish intimacy, closeness, and trustworthiness in relationships, support confidence in the value of safety in relationships. A positive self-image is reliant on mastery of the developmental skills that enable individuals to be separate and independent, while a sense of personal competency supports both personal responsibility and optimism. The ability to resolve conflicts and make reasonable decisions is reliant on assertiveness and tolerance, as well as one's ability to forgive the failures of others, and to negotiate and compromise cooperatively.

It is especially important to counter the deviant reinforcements of abusive behaviors with healthy pleasures. One's ability to relax and play, to celebrate

Table 7.6
Dynamic Assets Relevant to Increased Health

_ Prosocial relationship skills (closeness, trust, and trustworthiness)

_ Positive self-image (able to separate, independent, competent)

_ Able to resolve conflicts and make decisions (assertive, tolerant, forgiving, cooperative; able to negotiate and compromise)

_ Celebrates good and experiences pleasure (able to relax and play)

_ Works/struggles to achieve delayed gratification (persistent pursuit of goal, submission to reasonable authority)

_ Able to think and communicate effectively (rational cognitive processing; adequate verbal skills; able to concentrate)

_ Prosocial peers

_ Family and/or community support system

_ Adaptive sense of purpose and future

goodness and success, and to experience pleasure directly counter the risk of reliance on deviant or harmful solutions to compensate or feel better in times of stress. Being able to think clearly, process experiences without distortion, and effectively communicate contribute to an internal sense of control and decrease externalizing behavior. Anger management and self-protection go hand in hand with one's ability to tolerate frustration, to make accurate attributions of responsibility in unfavorable circumstances, and to recognize what they do have control of and what they do not. The willingness to struggle to achieve delayed gratification, to pursue goals without distraction or discouragement, and to be able to pursue one's own goals within the parameters set by reasonable authorities are characteristics of successful prosocial functioning. Finally, an adaptive and realistic sense of purpose, and the ability to foresee and anticipate success in the future support continued motivation to avoid abusive behaviors.

CONCLUSIONS

Understanding and differentiating static, stable, and dynamic factors suggests many hypotheses that require additional research to further refine and validate the balancing roles of risks and assets associated with the development, initiation, and maintenance of abusive behaviors. In addition to the deficits and dysfunction most commonly associated with abusive behaviors, individualized assessment often reveals uniquely personal risks and/or deficits that require specific treatment or risk management strategies for the individual who has been abusive. Working to achieve mastery of those outcomes relevant to decreasing the risk of abusive behavior and dysfunction, while seeking progress on the development of skills associated with successful human functioning, promises to tip the balance from risks to protective factors.

"Offense specific" interventions sometimes require balancing the needs and best interests of the individual with those of the community, and it has been evident that well-intentioned interventions can sometimes cause unintended consequences that create new risks (Berliner, 1998; Chaffin & Bonner, 1998; Dishion, McCord, & Poulin, 1999). However, achieving the observable assets suggested here will not cause harm to anyone and might be considered successful outcomes for all children, even if they have not been considered at-risk or identified because of abusive behaviors. In the end, the goal of perpetration prevention and intervention with all youth is always to help them be successful while insisting they not be abusive.

REFERENCES

Abel, G. G., Jones, C. D., Gabriel, W., & Harlow, N. (2009). A boy's experience of child sexual abuse: Factors that increase his risk of developing sexually abusive behavior. Submitted for publication, *Child Abuse and Neglect*.

Ainsworth, M. D. S. (1985). Attachments across the lifespan. *Bulletin of New York Academy of Medicine, 61*, 792–812.

Alexander, M. (1999). Sexual offender treatment efficacy revisited. *Sexual Abuse: Journal of Research and Treatment, 11*, 101–116.

Ayland, L., & West, B. (2006). The Good Way model: A strengths based approach for working with young people, especially those with intellectual difficulties, who have sexually abusive behavior. *Journal of Sexual Aggression, 12*, 189–201.

Baumbach, J. (2000). *When making it simpler isn't so simple: Adaptations to meet the treatment needs of sexually abusive youth with fetal alcohol syndrome.* Presentation at the 15th National Conference of the National Adolescent Perpetration Network, Denver, Colorado.

Becker, J. V., Kaplan, M. S., Tenke, C. E., & Tartaglini, A. (1991). The incidence of depressive symptomatology in juvenile sex offenders with a history of abuse. *Child Abuse and Neglect, 15*, 531–536.

Becker, J. V., & Murphy, W. (1998). What we know and do not know about assessing and treating sex offenders. *Psychology, Public Policy and Law, 4*, 116–137.

Berliner, L. (1998). Juvenile sex offenders: Should they be treated differently? *Journal of Interpersonal Violence, 13*, 645–646.

Borduin, C. M., Henggeler, S. W., Blaske, D. M., & Stein, R. (1990). Multisystemic treatment of adolescent sexual offenders. *International Journal of Offender Therapy and Comparative Criminology, 34*, 105–113.

Bowlby, J. (1985). Violence in the family as a function of the attachment system. *American Journal of Psychoanalysis, 44*, 9–27.

Bremer, J. (1992). Serious juvenile sex offenders: Treatment and long term follow-up. *Psychiatric Annals, 22*, 326–332.

Bremer, J. (1998). Challenges in the assessment and treatment of sexually abusive youth. *Irish Journal of Psychology, 19*, 82–92.

Burton, D. L. (2003). The relationship between the sexual victimization of and the subsequent sexual abuse of male adolescents. *Child and Adolescent Social Work Journal, 20*, 277–296.

Burton, D. L., & Meezan, W. (2004). Revisiting recent research on social learning theory as an etiological proposition for sexually abusive male adolescents. *Journal of Evidence Based Social Work, 1*, 41–80.

Burton, D. L., Miller, D., & Shill, C. (2002). A social learning theory comparison of the sexual victimization of adolescent sexual offenders and nonsexual offending male delinquents. *Child Abuse and Neglect, 26*, 893–907.

Burton, D. L., Nesmith, A. A., & Badten, L. (1997). Clinician's views on sexually aggressive children and their families: A theoretical exploration. *Child Abuse and Neglect, 21*, 157–170.

Calder, M. C. (2002). *Young people who sexually abuse: Building the evidence base for your practice.* Dorset, England: Russell House Publishing.

Cavazos, E. (2000). *Dual diagnosis and medication options for sexually abusive youth.* Presentation at the 15th National Conference of National Adolescent Perpetration Network, Denver, Colorado.

Chaffin, M., & Bonner, B. (1998). Don't shoot, we're your children: Have we gone too far in our response to adolescents and children with sexual behavior problems? *Child Maltreatment, 3,* 314–316.

Cicchetti, D. (1987). Developmental psychopathology in infancy: Illustrations from the study of maltreated youngsters. *Journal of Consulting and Clinical Psychology, 55,* 837–845.

Collie, R., Ward, T., Ayland, L., & West, B. (2007). The good lives model of rehabilitation: Reducing risks and promoting strengths with adolescent sexual offenders. In M. C. Calder (Ed.), *Working with children and young people who sexually abuse: Taking the field forward* (pp. 53–64). Lyme Regis, Dorset: Russell House Publishing.

Dailey, L. (1996). *Biomedical treatments with sexually abusive youth.* Presentation at the Twelfth National Conference of National Adolescent Perpetration Network, Minneapolis, Minnesota.

Dishion, T., McCord, J., & Poulin, F. (1999). When interventions harm: Peer groups and problem behavior. *American Psychologist, 54,* 755–764.

Donovan, D., & McIntyre, D. (1990). *Healing the hurt child: A developmental contextual model.* New York: Norton.

Egeland, B., Elizabeth, C., & Sroufe, L. A. (1993). Resilience as process. *Development and Psychopathology, 5,* 159–174.

Epperson, D. L., Ralston, C. A., Fowers, D., & DeWitt, J. (2005). *Optimal predictors of juvenile sexual recidivism in a large scale study of Utah adolescents who have offended sexually.* Denver, CO: National Adolescent Perpetration Network Conference.

Gendreau, P., Little, T., & Goggin, C. (1996). A meta-analysis of the predictors of adult offender recidivism: What works! *Criminology, 34,* 575–608.

Gilgun, J. (1990). Factors mediating the effects of childhood maltreatment. In M. Hunter (Ed.), *The sexually abused male: Prevalence, impact and treatment* (pp. 177–190). Lexington, MA: Lexington Books.

Gilgun, J. (1996). Human development and adversity in ecological perspective. *Families in Society, 77,* 395–402; 459–476.

Gilgun, J. (1998). CASPARS: Clinical instruments for assessing client assets and risks in mental health practice. *Medical Journal of Allina, 7,* 1.

Goldson, E., Fitch, M. J., Wendell, T. A., & Knapp, G. (1978). Child abuse: Its relationship to birthweight, Apgar Score, and developmental testing. *American Journal of Disabled Children, 132,* 790–793.

Griffin, H. L., Beech, A., Print, B., Bradshaw, H., & Quayle, J. (2008). The development and initial testing of the AIM2 framework to assess risk and strengths in young people who sexually offend. *Journal of Sexual Aggression, 14,* 211–225.

Hanson, R. K. (2000). *Static 99.* Beaverton, OR: Association for Treatment of Sexual Abusers.

Hanson, R. K., & Bussiere, M. T. (1998). Predicting relapse: A meta-analysis of sexual offender recidivism studies. *Journal of Consulting and Clinical Psychology, 66,* 348–362.

Hanson, R. K., & Harris, A. (2000; Rev 2002). *Sex Offender Need Assessment Rating (SONAR): A method for measuring change in risk levels.* Correctional Service Canada: National Sexual Offender Programs-Assessment Manual. (Revised 2002).

Hanson, R. K., & Morton-Bourgon, K. E. (2007). *The accuracy of recidivism risk assessments for sexual offenders: A meta-analysis.* Canada: Public Safety and Emergency Preparedness Canada and Department of Justice Canada.

Hanson, R. K., & Slater, S. (1988). Sexual victimization in the history of sexual abusers: A review. *Annals of Sex Research, 1,* 485–499.

Hindman, J. (1989). *Just before dawn.* Oregon: Alexandria Press.

Hunter, J. (1999). *Understanding juvenile sexual offending behavior: Emerging research, treatment approaches and management.* Silver Spring, NY: Centre for Sex Offender Management.

Hunter, J. A. (1996). *Working with children and adolescents who sexually abuse children.* Paper presented at the 11th International Congress on Child Abuse and Neglect, Dublin, Ireland.

Hunter, J. A., & Becker, J. (1994). The role of deviant arousal in juvenile sexual offending: Etiology, evaluation and treatment. *Criminal Justice and Behavior, 21*, 132–149.

Hunter, J. A., & Figueredo, A. (2000). The influence of personality and history of sexual victimization in the prediction of juvenile perpetrated child molestation. *Behavior Modification, 24*, 241–263.

Karr-Morse, R., & Wiley, M. (1997). *Ghosts from the nursery: Tracing the roots of violence.* New York: Grove Atlantic.

Kavoussi, R., Kaplan, M., & Becker, J. (1988). Psychiatric diagnoses in adolescent sex offenders. *Journal of Child and Adolescent Psychiatry, 27*, 241–243.

Knight, R. A., & Prentky, R. A. (1993). Exploring characteristics for classifying juvenile sex offenders. In H. E. Barbaree, W. L. Marshall, & S. M. Hudson (Eds.), *The juvenile sex offender* (pp. 45–83). New York: Guilford Press.

Knopp, F., & Benson, A. (1996). *A primer on the complexities of traumatic memory.* Brandon, VT: Safer Society Press.

Landry, S., & Peters, R. D. (1992). Toward understanding of a developmental paradigm for aggressive conduct problems during the preschool years. In R. D. Peters, R. McMahon, & V. Quinsey (Eds.), *Aggression and violence throughout the life span* (pp. 1–30). Newbury Park, CA: Sage.

Lane, S. (1997). The sexual abuse cycle. In G. Ryan, & S. Lane (Eds.), *Juvenile Sexual Offending: Causes, Consequences and Correction*, 2nd ed. (pp. 77–121). San Francisco: Jossey-Bass.

Malamuth, N. (1986). Predictors of naturalistic sexual aggression. *Journal of Personality and Social Psychology, 50*, 953–962.

Miner, M. (2008). *What attachment theory tells us about unique risks for adolescent boys to sexually offend.* Portland: National Adolescent Perpetration Network Conference.

Miner, M. H., & Crimmins, C. L. S. (1997). Adolescent sex offenders—Issues of etiology and risk factors. In B. K. Schwartz & H. R. Cellini (Eds.), *The sex offender: New insights, treatment innovations, and legal developments, Volume II* (pp. 9-1 to 9-15). Kingston, NJ: Civic Research Institute, Inc.

National Task Force on Juvenile Sexual Offending. (1993). The revised report. *Juvenile and Family Court Journal, 44*, 1–120.

O'Callaghan, D. (2004). Adolescents with intellectual disabilities who sexually harm: Intervention design and implementation. In G. O'Reilly, W. L. Marshall, A. Carr, & R. C. Beckett (Eds.), *The handbook of clinical intervention with young people who sexually abuse* (pp. 345–368). Hove, East Sussex: Brunner-Routledge.

Oneal, B. J., Burns, L. G., Kahn, T. J., Rich, P., & Worling, J. R. (2008). Treatment progress inventory for youth who sexually abuse (TPI-ASA). *Sexual Abuse: A Journal of Research and Treatment, 20*, 161–187.

Prentky, R., & Righthand, S. (2001). *Juvenile sex offender assessment protocol—II (J-SOAP-11).* Colorado: Office of Juvenile Justice and Delinquency Prevention.

Prentky, R., Knight, R., Sims-Knight, J. E., Straus, H., Rokous, F., and Cerce, D. D. (1989). Developmental antecedents of sexual aggression. *Development and Psychopathology, 1*, 153–169.

Prentky, R. A., Lee, A. F. S., Knight, R. A., & Cerce, D. (1997). Recidivism rates among child molesters and rapists: A methodological analysis. *Law and Human Behavior, 21*, 635–659.

Prentky, R., Harris, B., Frizell, K., & Righthand, S. (2000). An actuarial procedure for assessing risk with juvenile sex offenders. *Sexual Abuse: Journal of Research and Treatment, 12*, 71–94.

Print, B., & O'Callaghan, D. (2004). Essentials of an effective treatment program for sexually abusive adolescents: Offense specific treatment tasks. In G. O'Reilly, W. L. Marshall, A. Carr, & R. C. Beckett (Eds.), *The handbook of clinical intervention with young people who sexually abuse* (pp. 237–274). Hove, East Sussex: Brunner-Routledge.

Quinsey, V. (1995). *Actuarial prediction of sexual dangerousness.* Paper presented at the Fourteenth ATSA Conference, New Orleans, Louisiana.

Quinsey, V., Khanna, A., & Malcolm, B. (1998). A. retrospective evaluation of the regional treatment centre sex offender treatment program. *Journal of Interpersonal Violence, 13*, 621–644.

Rasmussen, L. (1999). The trauma outcome process: An integrated model for guiding clinical practice with children with sexually abusive behavior problems. *Journal of Child Sexual Abuse, 8*, 3–33.

Rasmussen, L., Burton, J., & Christopherson, B. (1992). Precursors to offending and trauma outcome process in sexually reactive children. *Journal of Child Sexual Abuse, 1*, 33–48.

Reitzel, L. R., & Carbonell, J. L. (2006). The effectiveness of sexual offender treatment for juveniles as measured by recidivism: A meta-analysis. *Sexual Abuse: A Journal of Research and Treatment, 18*, 401–421.

Rich, P. (2000). *Stetson School: Juvenile sexual offender risk for re-offending assessment*. Barre, MA: Stetson School. Unpublished manuscript.

Rich, P. (2003). *Understanding, assessing, and rehabilitating juvenile sexual offenders*. Hoboken, NJ: John Wiley & Sons.

Rich, P. (2006). *Attachment and sexual offending: Understanding and applying attachment theory to the treatment of juvenile sexual offenders*. Hoboken, NJ: John Wiley & Sons.

Righthand, S., Prentky, R., Knight, R., Carpenter, E., Hecker, J. E., & Nagel, D. (2005). Factor structure and validation of the Juvenile Offender Assessment Protocol (J-SOAP). *Sexual Abuse: A Journal of Research and Treatment, 17*, 13–30.

Rind, B., Tromovitch, P., & Bauserman, R. (1998). A. meta-analytic examination of assumed properties of child sexual abuse using college samples. *American Psychological Bulletin, 124*, 22–53.

Rutter, M. (1987). Psychosocial resilience and protective mechanisms. *American Journal of Orthopsychiatry, 57*, 316–331.

Ryan, G. (1989). Victim to victimizer: Rethinking victim treatment. *Journal of Interpersonal Violence, 4*, 325–341.

Ryan, G. (1995). *Treatment of sexually abusive youth: The evolving consensus*. Paper presented at the International Experts Conference, Utrecht, Netherlands.

Ryan, G. (1997). The sexual abuser. In M. Helfer, R. Dempe, & D. Krugman (Eds.), *The battered child* (5th ed.). Chicago: University of Chicago Press.

Ryan, G. (1998). The relevance of early life experience to the behavior of sexually abusive youth. *The Irish Journal of Psychology, 19*, 32–48.

Ryan, G. (1999). The treatment of sexually abusive youth: The evolving consensus. *Journal of Interpersonal Violence, 14*, 422–436.

Ryan, G. (2000). *Static, stable, and dynamic risks and assets relevant to the prevention and treatment of abusive behavior*. Poster presentation: First National Sexual Violence Prevention Conference; Dallas, Texas.

Ryan, G. (2004). Preventing violence and trauma in the next generation. *Journal of Interpersonal Violence, 20*, 132–141.

Ryan, G., and Associates. (1998). *The web of meaning: A developmental-contextual approach in treatment of sexual abuse*. Brandon, VT: Safer Society Press.

Ryan, G., & Blum, J. (1993). *Childhood sexuality: A guide for parents*. Denver, CO: Kempe National Center.

Ryan, G., Blum, J., Sandau-Christopher, D., Law, S., Weber, F., Sundine, C., et al. (1988). *Understanding and responding to the sexual behavior of children: Trainer's manual*. Denver, CO: Kempe National Center, University of Colorado, School of Medicine.

Ryan, G., Lane, S., Davis, J., & Isaac, C. (1987). Juvenile sexual offenders: Development and correction. *Child Abuse and Neglect, 3*, 385–395.

Ryan, G., Lindstrom, B., Knight, L., Arnold, L., Yager, J., Bilbrey, C., et al. (1993). Treatment of sexual abuse in the context of whole life experience. Paper presented at the Twenty-first Annual Child Abuse and Neglect Symposium, Keystone, Colorado.

Scales, P., & Leffert, N. (1998). *Developmental assets: A synthesis of the scientific research on adolescent development.* Minnesota, MN: Search Institute.

Schwartz, B. K. (2005). The sex offender: Trends and developments. *Correctional Mental Health Report, 7,* 49–64.

Seghorn, T. K., Prentky, R. A., & Boucher, R. J. (1987). Childhood sexual abuse in the lives of sexually aggressive offenders. *Journal of the American Academy of Child and Adolescent Psychiatry, 2,* 262–267.

Siegel, D. J. (1999). *The developing mind: Toward a neurobiology of interpersonal experience.* New York: Guilford Press.

Sroufe, L., Allen, B. E., & Kreutzer, T. (1990). The fate of early experience following developmental change: Longitudinal approaches to individual adaptation in childhood. *Child Development, 61,* 1363–1373.

Steele, B. F. (1987). Abuse and neglect in the earliest years: Groundwork for vulnerability. *Zero to Three, 7,* 14–15.

Steele, B. F., & Ryan, G. (1991). Deviancy: Development gone wrong. In G. D. Ryan & S. L. Lane (Eds.), *Juvenile sexual offending: Causes, consequences, and correction* (pp. 83–101). San Francisco: New Lexington Press.

Strayhorn, J. M. (1988). *The competent child. An approach to psychotherapy and preventive mental health.* New York: Guilford Press.

Thomas, A., & Chess, S. (1977). *Temperament and development.* New York: Brunner/Mazel.

Turecki, S. (1985). *The difficult child.* New York: Bantam Books.

Van der Kolk, B. A. (Ed.). (1987). *Psychological trauma.* Washington, DC: American Psychiatric Press.

Vandiver, D. M. (2005). A prospective analysis of juvenile male sex offenders: Characteristics and recidivism rates as adults. *Journal of Interpersonal Violence, 21,* 673–688.

Ward, T. (2002). Good lives and the rehabilitation of offenders: Promises and problems. *Aggression and Violent Behavior, 7,* 513–528.

Ward, T., & Gannon, T. A. (2006). Rehabilitation, etiology, and self-regulation: The comprehensive good lives model of treatment for sexual offenders. *Aggression and Violent Behavior, 11,* 77–94.

Way, I., & Spieker, S. (1997). *The cycle of offense.* Notre Dame, IN: Jalice Publishers.

Weissberg, M. (1982). *Dangerous secrets: Maladaptive responses to stress.* New York: Norton.

Werner, E. E. (1993). Risk, resilience and recovery: Perspectives from the Kauai Longitudinal Study. *Development and Psychopathology, 4,* 503–515.

Whitaker, D., Lea, B., Hanson, R. K., Baker, C. K., McMahon, P. M., Ryan, G., et al. (2008). Risk factors for the perpetration of child sexual abuse: A review and meta-analysis. *Child Abuse and Neglect: The International Journal, 32,* 529–548.

Widom, C. S., & Williams, L. (1996). *Cycle of sexual abuse. Research inconclusive about whether child victims become adult abusers.* Report to House of Representatives, Committee of Judiciary, Subcommittee on Crime. General Accounting Office, Washington, DC.

Worling, J. R., & Curwen, T. (2000). Adolescent sexual offender recidivism: Success of specialized treatment and implications for risk prediction. *Child Abuse and Neglect, 24,* 965–982.

Yates, P., & Ward, T. (2008). Good lives, self-regulation, and risk management: An integrated model of sexual offender assessment and treatment. *Sexual Abuse in Australia and New Zealand, 1,* 2–19.

Yochelson, S., & Samenow, S. (1977). *The criminal personality.* New York: Jason Aronson Publishers.

CHAPTER 8

Patterns of Affect and Cognition
Dynamics Associated With Behavior*

GAIL RYAN

You can't have a thought without a feeling, or a feeling without a thought.

COGNITIVE AND EMOTIONAL capacities are distinguishing characteristics of humans. The capacity for complex emotion and forethought, the ability to think through plans and make choices about behavior, the potential to use past experience to inform interpretation and learning, and the uniqueness of each individual are all components in human functioning. It is the interaction of emotions and needs, memory and cognition, and conscious and unconscious learning that define the dynamics surrounding (preceding and following) behavior.

Behavior is driven by the brain and the brain is informed by the affective cues of the body. Emotions and needs signal the brain, conscious and unconscious cognitive processes interpret the body's signals, and behaviors follow. When behavior occurs without forethought it is considered an involuntary reflex. Impulsive behaviors that seem to occur without forethought are sometimes perceived to be beyond conscious control, but even reflexes and impulses are responding to instructions from the brain.

In studying behavior, theorists have considered the etiology, the initiation, and the continuity of behaviors over time, as well as the risks and benefits. Theories of etiology of sexual offending were explored in Chapter 3 in the interest of understanding the complexity of potentially relevant variables that might help to explain behavioral differences. Chapters 4 and 5 looked specifically at developmental and contextual processes of youth that help to explain the uniqueness of every individual. Chapter 6 began to differentiate critical characteristics relevant to the particular behavior of sexual offending, and Chapter 7 outlined a model for thinking about human functioning, for better or worse. All of this helps to explain the "who" and the "why" or "why not" of behavioral differences. But, as was stated, it is the dynamic variables associated with behavior that are involved in daily functioning that are

---

*Some information published in the Sexual Abuse Cycle chapters in previous editions (1991, 1997) has been moved to this chapter to facilitate exploration of patterns.

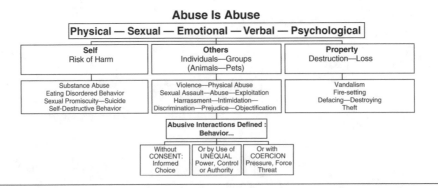

Figure 8.1   The "Abuse Is Abuse" Concept

most relevant to the "when" and "how" of behavior, and that are ultimately most flexible and changeable. In the interest of foreseeing and preventing dysfunctional behavior, and supporting successful behavior, it is necessary to consider all of these domains.

The 1980s was a decade of specialization in work on behavioral disorders. Each behavioral disorder was studied in isolation of other behaviors. Almost without exception, the behavioral disorders that bring people into treatment involve behaviors which, in moderation or in another context, are not necessarily problematic in and of themselves, but become problematic when overgeneralized. Most of the behavioral disorders, as well as delinquent behaviors that bring youth into either clinical or correctional settings, are now defined as abusive to self, others, or property in the "Abuse Is Abuse" concept (see Figure 8.1).

Substance abuse, eating disorders, sexual addictions, fire-setting, and destructive behaviors, including physical, sexual, verbal, and emotional abuse, are behaviors that with sufficient repetition and intensity create a risk of harm and are diagnosed as "behavioral disorders." Behaviors that provide some reinforcement or temporary relief are more likely to be repeated than behaviors that do not. What may initially be an adaptive response to stress may be repeated to deal with subsequent stresses. Reinforcement of imitated or imagined behaviors creates a "learning" experience. It is the brain that dictates behavior and the brain is shaped by experience.

In work with a variety of behavioral disorders, many theorists and researchers have described patterns of situations, thoughts, and feelings that seem to precede and follow particular behaviors. Identifying "thinking errors" (Yochelson & Samenow, 1976), or "hyper-masculine" attitudes/beliefs (Mosher & Sirkin, 1984) that support and justify abusive behavior has been a common tenet in offense-specific treatment programs (Freeman-Longo, Bird, Stevenson, & Fiske, 1995; Knopp, Rosenberg, & Stevenson, 1986; National Task Force on Juvenile Sexual Offending, 1988). By recognizing precursors that occur prior to a problematic behavior, an opportunity exists for the person to stop themselves, change their thinking, and choose some other behavior. For persons motivated to avoid a particular behavior that they have viewed (out of context) as being out of their conscious control, recognition of precursors puts them back in control of their reactions, and they can be held accountable for continuing to think and behave in the problematic manner or experience the rewards of avoiding the behaviors.

Weissberg (1982) described a wide range of problematic behaviors as "mal-adaptive responses to stress" and demonstrated a common pattern within which those behaviors occur. The abusive nature of behaviors such as incest, domestic violence, child abuse, alcoholism, and self-destructive/suicidal behaviors was also apparent. The commonality across all forms of abusive and disordered behavior is not only in the harm or risk of harm, but also in the dynamic patterns within which these behaviors occur. Weissberg conceptualized that when unusual stress interrupts normal functioning, some people respond with an adaptive coping strategy, whereas others do not. It may be that for some, the adaptive skills have never been learned, and for others it may be that denial of the stressor fails to evoke the adaptive coping response. Whatever the failure, without an adaptive strategy the person becomes overwhelmed and disorganized, and may develop physical, psychological, or somatic symptoms and maladaptive coping strategies (Weissberg, 1982).

In work with sexually abusive behaviors, Lane and Zamora (1978), Freeman-Longo and Bays (1988), and Wolfe (1985) began using "cycles" to depict common patterns associated with sexual offending. The first pattern was referred to as a "rape cycle" and was a reflection of what Lane and Zamora (1984) observed or heard from the violent youth they treated in a secure residential facility. Over time, very similar patterns were recognized in relation to the broader spectrum of sexual offenses (Lane, 1991, 1997; Ryan, Lane, Davis, & Isaac, 1987). Subsequently, studying the dynamics associated with other dysfunctional behaviors, similar patterns seemed to relate to many repetitive behaviors that were harmful to self, others, or property, including violence, substance abuse, eating disorders, fire-setting, sexual promiscuity, and so forth (Ryan, 1989).

In the late 1980s and the early 1990s, other clinicians observed similar patterns and offense components that were also indicative of a cycle, and over the years many clinicians have modified or adapted the cycle in different clinical settings, with various populations, and in relation to a broad spectrum of behavioral disorders (Gray, 1996; Johnson, 1989; Kahn, 1990; Lane, 1985, 1991b; Lowe [personal communication to Sandy Lane regarding the Oak Specialized Counseling Program, Preston School of Industry, California Youth Authority, 1984]; MacFarlane & Cunningham, 1996; O'Connor & Esteve, 1994; Ross, 1993; Ryan, 1989; Ryan, 1993; Ryan & Blum, 1993; Ryan, Lane, Davis, & Isaac, 1987; Stickrod, 1988; Turner, 1994).

By the 1990s the concept of a cycle was being used in the majority of "offense-specific" programs, national and international. In 2002, the Safer Society Press reported that more than 80% of all programs surveyed used the concepts of a "pre-assault/assault cycle" (McGrath, Cummings, & Burchard, 2003). There are now so many adaptations, representing clinicians' and clients' personal understanding and articulation of individual and subgroup differences in relation to the concept, that complete citations are no longer possible.

In the absence of a validated theoretical base, early clinicians relied on clinical experience and observation to develop treatment programs and strategies. The concept of the "sexual abuse cycle" has not been empirically validated, but research has confirmed various elements of the concept (see Gilgun [1988], Marshall & Barbaree [1984], and Prentky et al. [1989] re: developmental history; Fagan & Wexler [1988]; Fehrenbach, Smith, Monastersky, & Deisher [1986], and Gilgun & Connor [1989] re: isolation and loneliness; Hunter & Santos [1990] on deviant arousal; Becker, Hunter, Stein, & Kaplan [1989] re: fantasy and arousal; Marshall [1993] re: intimacy deficits and attachment styles; and Kaufman, Wallace, Johnson, & Reeder [1995] re: modus operandi).

Studies exploring the frequency and relationship of conflict, vulnerable emotions (such as loneliness and humiliation), and subsequent anger have seemed to validate the association between negative affective states and sexual fantasies, as well as with masturbation while fantasizing about abusive sexual behaviors (McKibben, Proulx, & Lusignan, 1994; Proulx, McGibbon, & Lusignan, 1996). Pithers, Kashima, Cumming, Beal, & Buell (1988) had previously reported that anger preceded abusive sexual behaviors. Ward, Louden, Hudson, and Marshall (1994) have explored the emotional dysphoria (negative affect) that is apparent in the affective components of the sexual abuse cycle. Cortoni, Anderson, and Looman (1999) studied locus of control and coping styles of adults who sexually offend, and Cortoni and Marshall (2001) explored "sex as a coping mechanism and its relationship to juvenile sexual history and intimacy" (p. 27).

Most recently, recognizing developmental deficits (the absence of skills for more successful functioning) and differences in the perceptual experience and exposure of individuals, which contribute to the thoughts and choices reflected in the pattern, continues to add confidence in many of the elements and dynamics represented in cycle concepts. At the same time, some assumptions have changed and concepts have been refined over time.

ADAPTIVE AND MALADAPTIVE "CYCLES"

A basic pattern can be recognized that represents a very common human response to stress (see Figure 8.2). Humans are endowed with defense mechanisms that protect the body and the psyche from harm. When humans experience stress it is adaptive that defense mechanisms prevent them from being so overwhelmed that they are unable to cope. In the defensive mode, the question is essentially: "What can I do to feel better, and get back a sense of control?" Sometimes the answer is completely compensatory, all about feeling better. Other times it is more about control: "What can I do to retaliate (against someone I perceive to be the source of this stress), or to make someone else feel as bad as I do?" (the "misery loves company" solution). The "fantasy solution" may be to do something functional or dysfunctional.

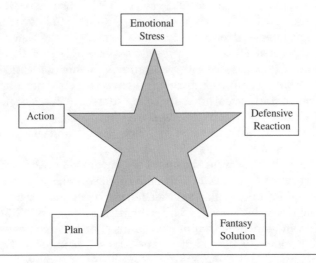

Figure 8.2   Common Human Adaptive Response to Stress

In a defensive mode, it is not particularly unusual that the first thought may be extreme, and in many instances to do something that would cause harm in some way.

For example: driving on the interstate highway, another driver cuts in and causes feelings of vulnerability. Defenses rise, and the first thought might be to swear, "flip-off" the other driver, or even to chase and cut them off like they just did. In extreme cases, some drivers actually pursue and assault the other driver ("road rage"). Functional persons will usually reject such thoughts and resist the defensive reaction by using coping skills such as depersonalizing the other driver's behavior, calming themselves with a deep breath, and resuming normal driving. Many reject the thought of verbally or physically abusing the other driver because such thoughts are incongruent with the person's self-image ("I am not an abusive person"; "I am better than that"). However, if the person's beliefs and self-image support abuse, verbal abuse, name calling, or threats, intimidation and aggression may not be dissonant. In addition, if role models have taught externalizing and retaliatory reactions, and especially if the person lacks cognitive and affective coping skills, the risk of acting on those first defensive reactions increases.

Similarly, a conflict with a co-worker may raise one's defenses, and if unresolved when leaving work, the person driving home may ruminate on the conflict: projecting, externalizing, thinking negative thoughts ("that person is such a jerk . . . they always do this . . . they stab you in the back . . . can't trust them"). Feeling unable to cope with all that, the person thinks: "What I really need is a chocolate éclair." Buying and eating an éclair works. Feeling better, the person relaxes and pushes the conflict out of mind. Whether the chocolate éclair was a functional, self-nurturing behavior or a dysfunctional avoidant response will depend on what happens next at work. If the person returns to work and talks to the co-worker to resolve the conflict, or goes to a supervisor and asks for help resolving the conflict, or at least talks to a peer and gets validation that the person really is a jerk and it's not their fault (depersonalizing the other's behavior), then the chocolate éclair may have been a functional coping response. On the other hand, if the person returns to work and avoids the person/ problem, is preoccupied with a sense of vulnerability, believes the person is out to get them, and eventually is eating 12 chocolate éclairs each night, or begins plotting some aggressive, retaliatory action against the other person, then it is easy to see how easily the overgeneralization of what was initially adaptive and harmless can become dysfunctional and abusive (to self or others).

Thus the pattern reflects a very common human response to stress, and many persons do (in times of overwhelming stress) have thoughts of doing something that would be harmful if acted out. Therefore the question is: *What stops nonabusive people from acting on abusive thoughts? And what enables others to act on abusive thoughts?* As was suggested in Chapter 7, it is likely that the answers will be different for different individuals, and it is likely to be a combination of risks and deficits, or protective assets.

Knowing that the imagined solution might be functional or dysfunctional, persons who have the knowledge and skills to use functional coping strategies, and who recognize the risk of the abusive thought, have options that make it easier to reject the imagined solution that poses a risk of harm. Whereas for many of the abusive youth, every model they have about dealing with stress involves some type of risky behavior. So the absence of functional coping skills might be the deficit, whereas beliefs, attitudes, and perceptions supportive of abuse and exposure to abusive role models might be the risk factors.

The fantasy solution may be either functional or dysfunctional, and might initially be harmless, but pose a risk of harm over time. The fantasy (that first thought) becomes a plan when it takes on the "who, what, where, when, and how" details; and when the plan has been developed, then the only thing left is the decision to act (or not act) when an opportunity occurs.

If the imagined behavior works (the person feels better or feels vindicated), that reinforcement increases the likelihood of that particular behavior being repeated in future times of stress. Although it appears to "work," the pattern becomes dysfunctional when overgeneralized because it never addresses the stress that initially overwhelmed the person and is not replaced with learning and using functional coping skills. Therefore, in the next time of stress, the person is no more able to cope than before, and may actually become more reactive to the same or similar stress over time. Aggressive or self-destructive behaviors may provide temporary relief in the form of physical tension reduction ("acting out" to relieve the stress), just as sexual behaviors provide temporary gratification and tension reduction, but the behaviors do not actually address the stress. It is an avoidant, defensive reaction.

Recognizing how common this pattern is was not immediate. Because it was initially noticed in trying to understand behavioral disorders, the dysfunctional or pathological aspects were a focus. Studying the relationship between adverse experiences in childhood and dysfunctional outcomes in adults has helped illuminate common characteristics of the cognitions and emotional issues that can exacerbate the defensive pattern relative to dysfunctional outcomes (see Figure 8.3).

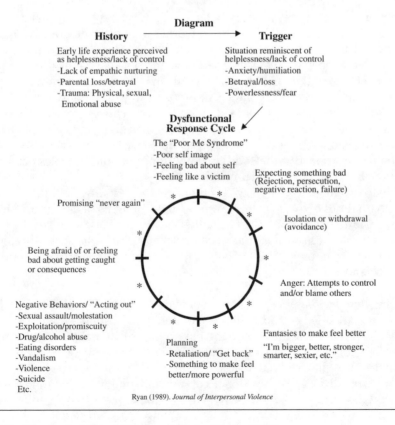

Figure 8.3   The Dysfunctional Response Cycle (Ryan, 1989)

A child's understanding of adverse experiences might initially be informed by those responsible for the adversity, and the dysfunctional pattern evident in their current functioning might represent the defensive strategy that helped them survive at that time, in the absence of the skills and support that might have mediated adversity in a more useful way.

The repeating pattern in which many abusive behaviors occur is referred to as dysfunctional, but can be observed in situations when any person experiences stress that threatens to overwhelm their ability to cope. Sometimes the stress is purely circumstantial when a current situation creates overwhelming emotion. It is also observed that the emotional response to something in the present often brings up unexpressed/unresolved emotional issues from the past. Both positive and negative experiences create memories that shape our expectations and the emotional associations connected to those memories. It is often the "emotional baggage" from the past, more than the current stressor, which overwhelms the ability to cope and activates a defensive strategy (Rasmussen, Burton, & Christopherson, 1992; Ryan, 1989).

Many of the youth who have sexually offended have experienced some type of maltreatment or adversity earlier in childhood: abuse, neglect, trauma, loss, and frightening or incomprehensible experiences. Very often, when those things occur early in life and a child does not have the skills for coping, the knowledge for understanding, or the support of a protective caregiver, the child may use defenses that push the vulnerable feelings out of sight.

When something later "triggers" an *emotional reaction* that is reminiscent of those past emotions, the emotion from the past gets brought up into the present as if it all belongs in the current reaction (Rasmussen, Burton, & Christopherson, 1992; Ryan, 1989). This results in what appears to others to be an "overreaction," and it may be hard for others to understand what it was in the present that warranted such an extreme emotional response.

For example, holidays can be stressful for everyone. Impending changes in the usual routines, preparations for new events, and anticipation of surprises and unknown outcomes can all trigger strong emotions. For many, an approaching holiday may bring excitement and joyful anticipation, along with the stress of change, because history has loaded the emotional baggage with positive memories and emotions. However, if history has included negative outcomes: the disappointment of broken promises, failed expectations, unexpected losses, and threatening, confusing, or harmful experiences, the emotional baggage may be loaded with negative memories and emotions. For many children from deprived or unsafe environments holidays may have been times when adults failed to fulfill promises and children were forgotten; with relatives drinking too much, family feuds erupting, and arguments escalating into fighting and domestic violence. For those youth, the smell of cookies baking or turkey roasting brings up a flood of anxiety in stark contrast to the positive associations other youth may have. As the holiday approaches, with decorations and preparations, cues of emotional tension are apparent. One might assume everyone is experiencing the excitement of positive anticipation, but for some the tension may be the anxiety associated with negative expectations. Everyone around the youth is excited, yet the youth is anxious; it seems that others do not recognize the impending threats the youth foresees. The youth feels unprotected and vulnerable, exhibiting emotional reactivity and defensive posturing that seems incongruent to others, but may be quite rational and reasonable for the youth.

When feeling stressed or vulnerable, it is not uncommon to have negative thoughts about oneself or others: "Nobody likes me . . . I never do anything right . . . I can never feel happy . . . nothing ever works out . . . can't trust anyone . . . people are such jerks." *Expecting negative* outcomes creates a sense of *hopelessness* and feelings of *helplessness* and incompetence. Expecting the worst, some youth essentially behave in such a way as to control being rejected or failing by way of obnoxious, repulsive behaviors. Others simply shut down or shut out interaction with others, either physically separating themselves (running away, leaving the room) or figuratively separating themselves by refusing to engage with others. Either way, the effect is to be *isolated* and alone, ruminating on the vulnerability and hopelessness that they wish to avoid.

At some point the defenses shift from internalizing to *projecting and externalizing*, shifting the negative appraisal from self to others, so the responsibility or "blame" for the negative feelings is projected onto others. Externalizing further enhances the defensive strategy by generating and justifying *anger*, covering over the vulnerable feelings. In order to create the energy for fight or flight, which is produced by anger, some youth will provoke, threaten, or argue to engage others in *power struggles* that increase the build-up of adrenaline that makes them feel powerful. Some show anger by yelling or throwing things. Others provoke anger in other people. Although for many, anger feels safer than being vulnerable, it is still a negative feeling, so the person may begin to imagine, *"What can I do to feel better? How can I get back a sense of control?"*

Imagining creates a *"fantasy solution."* Sometimes the image is of solutions that work; other times the fantasy is harmful. If the imagined solution is to do something that could be harmful to self, others, or property, it becomes an *"abusive plan."* Many things might deter a person from acting on an abusive fantasy when it occurs. As was previously stated, those who recognize the potential harm may reject the thought and use some other strategy to feel better or get back a sense of control. Calming and self-talk are very basic human skills that often relieve stress and interrupt the progression of a dysfunctional pattern; however, for some those skills have not been acquired. Babies are not born knowing how to soothe themselves; they learn self-soothing by being soothed by the caregiver. Similarly, self-talk reflects cognitive perceptions, beliefs, and attitudes, which are the product of life experience. Coping styles are learned, for better and for worse.

When all pumped up with tension or anger, the need to get rid of all that energy and tension often leads to "acting out" in some way. Many youth believe they can get rid of anxiety or anger by acting it out because it gets rid of the physical tension, but it is only a *"temporary solution."* The vulnerable emotions under the anger are still there, ready to overwhelm again. Abusive behaviors create new problems and do not do anything to change the stressful feelings that triggered the beginning of the cycle. But if the *"solution"* is abusive, and doesn't address the stress, why does it provide relief? If the coping style is dysfunctional, causes harm, and even brings on negative consequences, why does it reoccur? Cycles repeat because some part of the pattern is *"reinforcing."* That means it feels good at the time.

Sometimes the good feelings from engaging in a behavior that has some physical or psychological reward last a few minutes. Sometimes the good feeling lasts longer. But when the good feeling is over, if the behavior was a problem, there is a new *anxiety* regarding potential consequences. Sometimes the person feels bad about what they did, or they realize that they have hurt themselves or others, or they find that they have damaged something they care about. Worrying about what will happen as a result of the behavior, they may try to hide what they did; they may *promise* themselves or others that they will never do that behavior again, or they may pretend it never happened. This is recognized as the aftermath of many different problematic/risky behaviors: substance abuse, eating disorders, sexual promiscuity, vandalism, and so forth. Defenses come up again to try to calm the new anxiety; and by *minimizing, rationalizing, justifying,* or *denying* the person becomes able to believe that everything is "Okay," to believe they are not a bad person, to believe they won't get caught, or to believe that nothing bad will happen. This allows the person to return to their normal level of functioning until something else brings up those stressful feelings again! In subsequent times of stress, the memory of past behavior that felt good or provided relief before increases the risk of thinking of and deciding to use a similar behavioral response.

RELEVANCE OF CYCLES IN ASSESSMENT AND TREATMENT OF SEXUAL OFFENDING

The concept of a cycle can be used specifically to identify and address the antecedents, components, patterns, and progression of sexually abusive behavior. The framework depicts commonalities observed and reported by numerous sexually abusive youth and by therapists providing offense-specific treatment for juveniles who have sexually offended. When the cycle is personalized, the thoughts, circumstances, characteristics, reactions, feelings, and behaviors will vary from youth to youth, yet the commonalities will still be evident (Lane, 1997).

Historically, in work with juveniles who have sexually offended, the "cycle" was seen exclusively as a "sexual abuse cycle" (Kahn, 1990, 1999; Lane, 1991a, 1994; Lane & Zamora, 1978, 1984; Ryan, Lane, Davis, & Isaac, 1987; Way & Spieker, 1997; and others). The same basic patterns represented in the sexual abuse cycle were also noticed in relation to the sexually abusive behaviors of prepubescent children (All red & Burns, 1997; Cunningham & MacFarlane, 1996; Isaac, 1986), and similarly, it was used in treating adults, in combination with Relapse Prevention models, which are generally depicted as more linear patterns or "chains" of thoughts and behaviors, but focus less on emotional components (Bays, Freeman-Longo, & Hildebran, 1990; Carich & Mussack, 2001; Freeman-Longo & Bays, 1988). The concept of cycles has been helpful for therapists and clients by providing a framework to see what situations, thoughts, feelings, and behaviors have preceded and followed sexual offenses for each individual (Bruinsma, 2000; Lane, 1994; Speese, 2000; Warren & Know, 2000).

References to cycles in the literature have almost always included the caution that not every person will demonstrate exactly the same pattern, that some of the elements defined within the model will be more characteristic in some and other elements more evident in others. For example, Lane stated, "It is seldom that a youth will progress through the cycle a step at a time, start to finish, nor does a sexual offense occur every time" (1997, p. 80). Similarly, Way and Spieker state: "One must recognize that for some adolescents, the steps of the cycle are clearly defined; others skip steps or move quickly through them" (1997, p. 33). Nonetheless, the concept has sometimes been misunderstood and misused like a cookie cutter or a mold, insisting that every youth in treatment describe exactly the pattern that the therapist expects to see.

Every person is unique and the concept of patterns must be individualized to be relevant and useful in understanding each individual. In the field today, there are many different interpretations, models, and terminology used to describe the basic pattern of a cycle. There are likely as many versions as people who use them correctly, adapting the terminology to be most relevant to the clients they treat. What remains constant is the recognition by most therapists that in order to prevent further offending, one must first understand the situations, thoughts, and feelings that have contributed to or supported the behavior in the past.

"HIGH RISK" CYCLES

It is now most useful to see these patterns in relation to overall functioning. Recognizing that the cycle represents a very common pattern that can be observed in all people, more or less, of how they respond to stress in their daily lives, it is no longer seen as evidence of deviance. The cycle represents a defensive coping style that protects people from being so overwhelmed that they are unable to cope, and the resulting behavior can be either: functional or dysfunctional, sexual or nonsexual, abusive or nonabusive. Many mistaken assumptions about the sexual offending of youth have been corrected by this broader understanding.

The cycle can be used for risk management by relating it to the "risk" associated with overgeneralizing defenses and avoiding rather than dealing with stress. A youth who becomes aware of the thinking, affective reactions, and behaviors represented in the cycle is then able to identify the particular stressors and typical coping styles that have contributed to their abusive behaviors (see Figure 8.4). The stressful issues and coping deficits will be different for different youth, but to view these behaviors out of context does little to differentiate the needs of individual clients and does not guide treatment planning toward more successful functioning.

Looking specifically at the history of sexual offending, it is now understood that for some youth, the first thought of doing something sexual was actually quite normal, but it was in translating the fantasy into a plan that it developed into a sexually abusive interaction. Sometimes the plan was shaped by impediments to more normative sexual activity (e.g., lack of skills or opportunity to be sexual with a desired age-mate), and the sexual offense was influenced by access and opportunity to be sexual with an unequal or nonconsenting person. Other times the sexual thoughts may have brought up memories of the youth's own experience of sexual victimization, which then shaped the plan into a reenactment, taking the role of the aggressor. Sometimes the fantasy was to do something abusive to retaliate against some perceived wrong, and it became a plan to do something sexual to be abusive.

Looking back through the developmental history, as well as observing current interactions/behaviors, it is possible to see whether the pattern of the cycle is pervasive in how the youth deals with stress, or not; and how often it results in abusive behaviors as compared to some more functional or benign solution. It is also possible to observe changes in their pattern over time, even when there is no opportunity for any sexual behavior or offending.

By identifying risk factors specifically relevant to the likelihood of a particular person being overwhelmed by stress and getting into the defensive patterns associated with abusive behaviors, it is possible to develop preventive interventions to

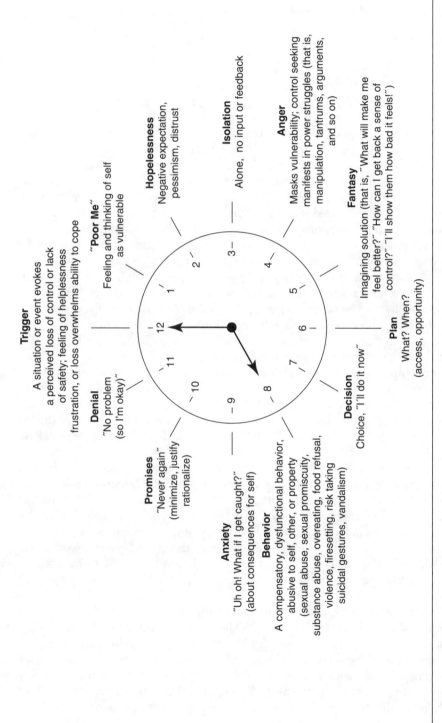

Trigger
A situation or event evokes
a perceived loss of control or lack
of safety; feeling of helplessness
frustration, or loss overwhelms ability to cope

"Poor Me"
Feeling and thinking of self
as vulnerable

Hopelessness
Negative expectation,
pessimism, distrust

Isolation
Alone, no input or feedback

Anger
Masks vulnerability; control seeking
manifests in power struggles (that is,
manipulation, tantrums, arguments,
and so on)

Fantasy
Imagining solution (that is, "What will make me
feel better?" "How can I get back a sense of
control?" "I'll show them how bad it feels!")

Plan
What? When?
(access, opportunity)

Decision
Choice, "I'll do it now"

Behavior
A compensatory, dysfunctional behavior,
abusive to self, other, or property
(sexual abuse, sexual promiscuity,
substance abuse, overeating, food refusal,
violence, firesetting, risk taking
suicidal gestures, vandalism)

Anxiety
"Uh oh! What if I get caught?"
(about consequences for self)

Promises
"Never again"
(minimize, justify
rationalize)

Denial
"No problem
(so I'm okay)"

Figure 8.4 The "High Risk" Cycle

111

Universal Goals

- Communication: Expressing thoughts, feelings, and needs (using words instead of behavior)
- Empathy: Emotional recognition, expression, and response (to cues of self and others)
- Accountability: Personal responsibility (accurate attributions re own and others' behavior)

Figure 8.5 Universal Goals

avoid, decrease, desensitize, replace, or manage those stressors. Some risks are associated with emotionally charged issues or memories and may benefit from psychotherapy to make conscious, desensitize, and integrate old emotional issues, moderating their continued effects on current functioning. Some risks are associated with cognitive beliefs or perceptions, which can benefit from education, conscious rethinking, and cognitive restructuring. Some are related to true vulnerabilities resulting from either external circumstances or internal deficits that create a sense of helplessness and vulnerability and can benefit from changes in the ecological pond or the development of increased skills and competencies.

Some deficits seem to be common factors for many who are abusive. First is the failure of communication: not necessarily poor verbal skills, but deficits in effective reciprocal communication regarding emotions and needs. Secondly, is the mis-attribution of responsibility (projecting/externalizing responsibility for one's own behavior while feeling responsible for the behavior of others), along with the empathy deficits that can be failure to perceive or failing to care about the discomfort or distress of others. These deficits were discussed in Chapter 7 and continue to draw attention from many different perspectives as "Universal Goals" (see Figure 8.5) relevant to reducing risks and supporting health.

The relationship of the dynamic risk factors described in Chapter 7 to elements that manifest specifically in abusive cycles should also be apparent (Lane, 1997; Ryan et al., 1998; Ryan, Lane, Davis, & Isaac, 1987; Way & Spiker, 1997). Those dynamic risk factors are congruent with many of the dynamic factors identified in treatment models by others in the field (Gilgun, 1998; Hanson, 2000; Prentky, Harris, Frizell, & Righthand, 2000; Rich, 2003).

The use of concepts and models, such as the "abuse is abuse" concept, cycles, and the universal goals provides a framework to explore and the language to describe issues relevant to treatment. The concepts do not replace individualized, differential assessment to discover the needs that shape treatment planning and inform the supervision and care of individual youth. Like every other aspect of these problems, individual differences can be explored in relation to these concepts to make sense of how the sexual offending occurred as well as what work needs to be done in treatment to decrease risk of continuing. Treatment will be discussed in Chapters 17 and 18.

The notion that abusive behavior does not occur randomly, without an opportunity for choice, implies hope for its control. Although the youth may initially state that they acted on impulse and without forethought (so the pattern is irrelevant), if they cannot become able to recognize a moment of choice— the decision to act—they would remain a danger, requiring external controls to protect the community. Over time they become able to see patterns and recognize the sense of self-control that comes with being able to foresee risk and make conscious choices to moderate those risks. Self-control is the goal of treatment, and the reward of change is to be successful without being abusive.

REFERENCES

Allred, T., & Burns, G. (1997). *Stop! Just for kids—for kids with sexual touching problems by kids with sexual touching problems*. Orwell, VT: Safer Society Press.

Bays, L., Freeman-Longo, R. E., & Hildebran, D. (1990). *How can I stop? Breaking my deviant cycle: A guided workbook for clients in treatment*. Brandon, VT: Safer Society Press.

Becker, J., Hunter, J. A., Stein, R. M., & Kaplan, M. S. (1989). Factors associated with erection in adolescent sex offenders. *Journal of Psychopathology and Behavioral Assessment, 11*, 353–362.

Bruinsma, F. (2000). *The sexual offense as an inadequate means of coping with stress*. Presentation at the 15th Annual NAPN Conference, Denver, Colorado.

Carich, M. S., & Mussack, S. E. (2001). *Handbook for sexual abuser assessment and treatment*. Brandon, VT: Safer Society Press.

Cortoni, F., & Marshall, W. (2001). Sex as a coping strategy and its relationship in juvenile sexual history and intimacy in sexual offenders. *Sexual Abuse: A Journal of Research and Treatment, 13*, 27–43.

Cortoni, F., Anderson, D., & Looman, J. (1999). *Locus of control and coping in sexual offenders*. Association for the Treatment of Sexual Abusers (ATSA) conference, Orlando, Florida.

Cunningham, C., & MacFarlane, K. (1996). *When children abuse: Group treatment strategies for children with impulse control problems*. Brandon, VT: Safer Society Press.

Fagan, J., & Wexler, S. (1988). Explanations of sexual assault among violent delinquents. *Journal of Adolescent Research, 58*, 281–291.

Fehrenbach, P., Smith, W., Monastersky, C., & Deisher, R. W. (1986). Adolescent sexual offenders: Offender and offense characteristics. *Journal of Orthopsychiatry, 56*, 225–233.

Freeman-Longo, R. E., & Bays, L. (1988). *Who am I and why am I in treatment?* Orwell, VT: Safer Society Press.

Freeman-Longo, R. E., Bird, S., Stevenson, W. F., & Fiske, J. A. (1995). *1994 nationwide survey of treatment programs and models: Serving abuse reactive children, adolescent and adult sex offenders*. Brandon, VT: Safer Society Press.

Gilgun, J. (1988). *Factors which block the development of sexually abusive behavior in adults abused as children*. Paper presented at the National Conference on Male Victims and Offenders: Controversies in Treatment, Minneapolis, Minnesota.

Gilgun, J. (1998). CASPARS: Clinical instruments for assessing client assets and risks in mental health practice. *Medical Journal of Allina 7*, 1.

Gilgun, J., & Connor, T. (1989). *Isolation and the adult male perpetrator of child sexual abuse*. Unpublished manuscript.

Gray, A. (1996). Juvenile fire-setters. In K. MacFarlane & C. Cunningham (Eds.), *Treatment strategies for obsessive compulsive behavior problems* (p. 194). Brandon, VT: Safer Society Press.

Hanson, R. K. (2000). *Static 99*. Beaverton, OR: Association for Treatment of Sexual Abusers.

Hunter, J., & Santos, D. (1990). Use of specialized cognitive-behavioral therapies in the treatment of adolescent sexual offenders. *Journal of Offender Therapy and Comparative Criminology, 34*, 239–248.

Isaac, C. (1986). *Identification and interruption of sexually offending behaviors in prepubescent children*. Paper presented at the Sixteenth Annual Child Abuse and Neglect Symposium, Keystone, Colorado.

Johnson, S. (1989). *Branching out: The tree cycle*. Paper presented at the Fourth National Adolescent Perpetrator Network Meeting, Keystone, Colorado.

Kahn, T. J. (1990). *Pathways: A guided workbook for youth beginning treatment*. Orwell, VT: Safer Society Press.

Kahn, T. J. (1999). *Roadmaps to recovery*, 2nd ed. Orwell, VT: Safer Society Press.

Kaufman, K. L., Wallace, A. M., Johnson, C. F., & Reeder, M. L. (1995). Comparing female and male perpetrators' modus operandi. *Journal of Interpersonal Violence, 10*, 322–333.

Knopp, F. H., Rosenberg, J., & Stevenson, W. (1986). *Report on nationwide survey of juvenile and adult sex-offender treatment programs and providers.* Orwell, VT: Safer Society Press.

Lane, S. (1985). *Treatment issues.* Presentation at the Fourteenth Annual Child Abuse and Neglect Symposium, Keystone, Colorado.

Lane, S. (1991a). The sexual abuse cycle. In G. Ryan & S. Lane (Eds.), *Juvenile sexual offending: Causes, consequences and correction* (pp. 103–141). Lexington, MA: Lexington Books.

Lane, S. (1991b). *Offense cycle: Adaptations to delinquent behavior.* Presentation to the Michigan Association of Children's Alliances, Detroit, Michigan.

Lane, S. (1994). *The cycle. Interchange: Cooperative newsletter of the National Adolescent Perpetrator Network.* C. Henry Kempe National Center for the Prevention and Treatment of Child Abuse and Neglect, Denver, Colorado, June.

Lane, S. (1997). The sexual abuse cycle. In G. Ryan & S. Lane (Eds.), *Juvenile sexual offending: Causes, consequences and correction,* 2nd ed. (pp. 77–121). San Francisco: Jossey-Bass.

Lane, S., & Zamora, P. (1978). *Syllabus materials from in-service training on adolescent sex offenders, Closed Adolescent Treatment Center, Division of Youth Services, Denver, Colorado.* Unpublished manuscript.

Lane, S., & Zamora, P. (1984). A method for treating the adolescent sex offender. In R. Mathias, P. Demuro, & R. Allinson (Eds.), *Violent juvenile offenders.* (pp. 347–363). San Francisco: National Council on Crime and Delinquency.

MacFarlane, K., & Cunningham, C. (1996). *Treatment strategies for obsessive compulsive behavior problems.* Brandon, VT: Safer Society Press.

Marshall, W. L. (1993). The role of attachments, intimacy and loneliness in the etiology and maintenance of sexual offending. *Sexual and Marital Therapy, 8*, 109–121.

Marshall, W. L., & Barbaree, H. (1984). A behavioral view of rape. *International Journal of Law and Psychiatry, 7*, 51–77.

McGrath, R. J., Cummings, G., & Burchard, B. (2003). *Current practices and trends in sexual abuse management: The Safer Society 2002 national survey.* Brandon, VT: Safer Society Foundation.

McKibben, A., Proulx, J., & Lusignan, R. (1994). Relationships between conflict, affect and deviant sexual behaviors in rapists and pedophiles. *Behavior Research and Therapy, 32*, 571–575.

Mosher, D. L., & Sirkin, M. (1984). Measuring a macho personality constellation. *Journal of Research in Personality, 18*, 150–163.

National Task Force on Juvenile Sexual Offending. (1988). Preliminary report. *Juvenile and Family Court Journal, 39*, 8, 13, 10–20, 26, 46, 36–37.

O'Connor, B., & Esteve, J. (1994). Poster session presented at the Tenth National Conference of the National Adolescent Perpetrators Network, Denver, Colorado.

Pithers, W. D., Kashima, K. M., Cumming, G. F., Beal, L. S., & Buell, M. M. (1998). Relapse prevention of sexual aggression. In R. A. Prentky & L. L. Quincey (Eds.), *Human sexual aggression: Current perspectives* (pp. 244–260). New York: New York Academy of Sciences.

Prentky, R., Knight, R., Sims-Knight, J. E., Straus, H., Rokous, F., & Cerce, D. D. (1989). *Developmental antecedents of sexual aggression.* Paper presented at the Fourth National Adolescent Perpetrator Network Meeting, Keystone, Colorado.

Prentky, R., Harris, B., Frizell, K., & Righthand, S. (2000). An actuarial procedure for assessing risk with juvenile sex offenders. *Sexual Abuse: Journal of Research and Treatment, 12*, 71–94.

Proulx, J., McGibbon, A., & Lusignan, R. (1996). Relationships between affective components and sexual behaviors in sexual aggressors. *Sexual Abuse: A Journal of Research and Treatment, 8*, 279–290.

Rasmussen, L., Burton, J., & Christopherson, B. (1992). Precursors to offending and trauma outcome process in sexually reactive children. *Journal of Child Sexual Abuse, 1*, 33–48.

Rich, P. (2003). *Understanding, assessing, and rehabilitating juvenile sexual offenders.* Hoboken, NJ: John Wiley & Sons.

Ross, J. (1993). Poster session presented at the Ninth National Conference of the National Adolescent Perpetrator Network, Lake Tahoe, Nevada.

Ryan, G. (1989). Victim to victimizer: Rethinking victim treatment. *Journal of Interpersonal Violence, 4*, 325–341.

Ryan, G. (1993). *Concurrent psychiatric disorders.* Paper presented at the Annual Conference of National Adolescent Perpetrator Network, Lake Tahoe, Nevada.

Ryan, G., and Associates (1998). *The web of meaning: A developmental-contextual approach in treatment of sexual abuse.* Brandon, VT: Safer Society Press

Ryan, G., & Blum, J. (1993). *Childhood sexuality: A guide for parents.* Denver, CO: Kempe Center.

Ryan, G., Lane, S., Davis, J., & Isaac, C. (1987). Juvenile sexual offenders: Development and correction. *Child Abuse and Neglect, 3*, 385–395.

Speese, C. (2000). *Are moral dilemmas and story telling a therapeutic silver bullet for juvenile sexual offending?* Presentation at the 20th Annual National Adolescent Perpetration Network (NAPN) Conference, Denver, Colorado.

Stickrod, A. (1988). *Preventing sexual abuse through treating juvenile sexual offenders.* Proceedings of the Adolescent Sex Offender's Symposium, Salt Lake City, Utah.

Turner, R. (1994). *Treating violent juvenile sex offenders.* Paper presented at the 10th National Conference of the NAPN, Denver, Colorado.

Ward, T., Louden, K., Hudson, S. M., & Marshall, W. L. (1994). A descriptive model of the offense chain for child molesters. Paper presented at the 13th Association for the Treatment of Sexual Abusers (ATSA) Conference, San Francisco, California.

Warren, K., & Know, K. (2000). Offense cycles, thresholds and bifurcations: Applying dynamical systems theory to the behaviors of adolescent sex offenders. *Journal of Social Services Research, 27*, 1–27.

Way, I., & Spieker, S. (1997). *The cycle of offense: A framework for treating adolescent sexual offenders.* Notre Dame, IN: Jalice Publishers.

Weissberg, M. (1982). *Dangerous secrets: Maladaptive responses to stress.* New York: Norton.

Wolfe, S. (1985). A model of sexual aggression and addiction. *Victimology, 10*, 359–374.

Wood, C. (2006). *The assault cycle as a central framework for treatment.* Presentation at the 21st NAPN conference, Atlanta, Georgia.

Yochelson, S., & Samenow, S. (1976). *The criminal personality.* New York: Jason Aronson Publishers.

CHAPTER 9

Habituated Patterns

The Sexual Abuse Cycle

SANDY LANE and GAIL RYAN

T HE SEXUAL ABUSE cycle described herein was developed in the mid-1970s at the Closed Adolescent Treatment Center, Colorado Division of Youth Services (see Chapter 8; Lane & Zamora, 1978, 1982, 1984) as a treatment method to work with youth who were incarcerated for violent, sexually abusive behaviors. The initial "rape cycle" was based on a synthesis of behavioral observations and self-reports by the youth during their two- to four-year commitment to the facility and depicted commonalities among those youth. Information was gathered from observations of daily behavior and interactions, personal journal entries describing their perceptions and reactions to various situations, self-reports of ongoing thoughts and urges to engage in sexual abuse behavior, and their retrospective descriptions of abusive behaviors and the associated thoughts and feelings.

Although each youth had unique and individual perceptions, motivations, rationalizations, and circumstances pertaining to their own abusive behaviors and life history, there appeared to be commonalities related to behavioral elements, cognitive and affective aspects, and gratification related to the behavior, as well as a somewhat predictable pattern antecedent to the sexually abusive behaviors. It appeared that the patterns represented in the sexual abuse cycle involved a maladaptive or dysfunctional coping response that was repetitive and generally consistent for each youth.

Subsequent models of the sexual abuse cycle (see Chapter 8) have been modified in part for youth who exhibit less habituated patterns or engage in sexual abuse behaviors that do not involve excessive aggression or violence. During the past 30 years, there has been a significant change in societal perceptions about sexually abusive behavior. A broader understanding of abusive behavior and increased recognition of the consequences of such behavior to victims has resulted in less tolerance for abuse in our society, resulting in more comprehensive education for police departments, clinicians, educators, and attorneys. The field has begun to be defined by research (see Chapter 6), youth entering treatment are presenting with less habituated patterns, community-based treatment is more readily available, and individual treatment needs are being identified more specifically (see Chapter 7). Yet, remarkably, the basic sexual abuse cycle concepts continue to be useful in conceptualizing the multiple factors and the complex processes that reportedly may occur as part of the commission of a sexual offense.

This cycle was developed in a juvenile correctional treatment facility. At that time there were limited community treatment models available and a paucity of literature about treating offenders. Societal views often held the victim accountable for being sexually abused and there were inconsistent efforts to identify and arrest perpetrators. Most youth who were apprehended and convicted were incarcerated and viewed as aberrant, but many already had extensive offense histories and patterns that were habituated. Consequently, the initial cycle represented the process at its most extreme and the descriptive language, which now sounds harsh and disturbing, was language that was familiar to correctional staff.

The cycle of a youth entering treatment today is likely to look quite different. The youth may now be discovered and referred earlier in their engagement in these behaviors; thus, they will not exhibit such habituated patterns. Youth treated in a community-based treatment facility will be less likely to exhibit violent behavior or aggressive thinking. When the cycle is personalized the thoughts, circumstances, characteristics, reactions, feelings, and behavior vary widely from youth to youth, yet the commonalities related to coping styles, offense components, and predictable individualized patterns continue to be evident (see discussion in Chapter 8).

The cycle must be personalized to be relevant and helpful to the individual and to inform treatment plans. The youth who is aware of his or her own thinking, affective reactions, and behaviors can develop different ways to cope with stress or problematic situations and eliminate abusive behavior as an option. It is a misuse of the construct to try to make the client's problem fit into any rigid definition or articulation of the cycle. By studying in detail the patterns that can be associated with sexual offenses, these authors do not intend to suggest that every assumption or aspect will be relevant to every client. It is very clear from the research to date that youth who commit sexual offenses are not all the same: not all of them have the beliefs and attitudes described as supportive of abuse, or hyper-masculinity, or antisocial behaviors; not all have power-based motives; not all have "thinking errors"; and not all have deviant sexual interests or arousal. The evidence is also clear that not all are at risk to continue offending (see Chapters 6 and 12).

Personalizing the cycle assists both the youth and the therapist in identifying emotionally charged issues, maladaptive coping patterns, distorted thinking, competency deficits, affective states, the progression of the cycle, and specific offense behavior variables. Interventions can then address the abusive behavior pattern, along with other treatment needs. Many "abuse-specific" interventions, and some "offense-specific" treatment strategies will be relevant for all of these youth, but individual treatment needs will differ. Interventions must be tailored for each particular youth. Some may need more assistance to change misperceptions or misattributions about others' behaviors, while others may have significant developmental deficits, trauma symptoms, or attachment issues. Many also need to develop social competencies, relationship and intimacy skills, address trauma issues and family dilemmas, correct misperceptions of motivations, needs, and emotions of others, and develop more accurate and positive self-perceptions.

OVERVIEW OF THE SEXUAL ABUSE CYCLE

The cycle is a construct representing cognitive, affective, and behavioral progressions occurring antecedent to, during, and subsequent to abusive behavior. It is descriptive of a process and is neither a causal representation, nor a proposed etiology. It is represented as a cycle because of the risk of repetition if the process becomes habitual, and because previous abuse incidents often parallel and reinforce subsequent abusive patterns. Chapter 8 described some history and basic elements of behavioral cycles that might occur naturally and adaptively, maladaptively, or even abusively (see Chapter 8 for an overview of cycle progression). The sequential response appears compensatory in that it counters perceptions of inadequacy and helplessness and reduces anxiety. As a coping mechanism, it is maladaptive because it is only a temporary measure and does not address or resolve the initial stress.

Movement through the cycle results in compensatory thoughts and anxiety reduction, but the progression is not always consistent for individuals or among various youth. It is seldom that a youth progresses through the cycle one step at a time, start to finish, nor does a sexual offense occur each time the youth is "in the cycle." Progression in the cycle will go only as far as is needed to experience some relief or improved perception, and progression to the next stage may not occur until the first stopping point no longer relieves the stress. Interruptions or delays in the cycle might be called plateaus. In response to repeated triggers, the youth may progress to the same plateau several times and not move on to the next plateau until the current stage fails to relieve anxiety and negative expectations. The stress may seem to dissipate temporarily, but in fact it accumulates over time.

The rate of progression through the cycle also varies among youth, depending on the strength of coping responses, individual reactivity, impulsivity, anxiety, frustration, tolerance, and associated thought processes. It does seem, however, that the more frequently the maladaptive response style is used, the faster the rate of progression tends to become. The more habituated the coping response depicted in the cycle becomes, the less tolerance the individual seems to have for precipitating events or stresses, progressing further in each subsequent response. Many youth move quickly to the negative anticipation or control-seeking stages of the cycle, where they experience some temporary relief. It also appears that the more the youth relies on this type of coping, the less drive there is to develop other coping strategies and competencies. Focusing on the immediate gratification associated with the offense behavior, there is less motivation to struggle with anxiety and inhibit the behavior.

BASIC ASSUMPTIONS UNDERLYING THE SEXUAL ABUSE CYCLE

Many variables contribute to or support sexually abusive behaviors. The assumptions reflect commonalities reported by many sexually abusive youth, but are only theoretical, and many details reflect established, habituated patterns. Research continues to validate, clarify, and correct these assumptions (see Chapter 8), which are all considered equally significant and are not listed here in order of importance.

Sexual Abuse   Any sexual behavior that lacks consent and involves violation, exploitation, manipulation, trickery, coercion, or force of another is considered sexually abusive and may result in varying impacts to the victim. The behaviors involved in an offense may be a sexualized expression of nonsexual needs at the expense of another individual (compensatory motives), the expression of sexual needs in an abusive manner ("something sexual will make me feel better"), or incidental to the opportunity to act out in any manner. Abusive behaviors are not viewed as impulsive acts; rather, there is some antecedent thought or period of contemplation before behavior occurs.

Control Seeking Essentially the cycle represents a control seeking coping style in an effort to reduce anxiety, provide a sense of well-being or positive self-regard, or evoke a sense of mastery by controlling another person, the situation, or the environment. For some youth, sexual abuse is a sexualized expression of power, control, and competence, as either power-based thinking or behavior may be equally gratifying to the individual. The misuse of power is thought to counter the sense of powerlessness associated with vulnerable feelings. The youth seems to experience internal perceptions of adequacy, superiority, dominance, strength, empowerment, mastery, excitement, or a sense of control, which provides a sense of being in control or of being "okay."

The beliefs are illusory in that the expectation of being able to control another or one's environment is unrealistic and the misuse of power does not really improve one's adequacy. A control-seeking or power-based response does not solve problems, resolve issues, demonstrate competencies, or contribute positively to relationships or interactions. However, this type of response style is easily habituated because of reinforcements associated with the illusion of power and control, and over time, may be used in lieu of more effective skills.

Nonsexual expressions of power may be interpersonal (yelling, hitting, manipulating others, overcompliance), or solitary (punching the wall, slamming doors, pouting, walking away from a situation). Control-seeking behaviors may be expressed overtly or covertly, in a passive, aggressive, or passive-aggressive manner.

Some degree of control appears to be present in all sexually abusive behavior. At the least, the youth may experience a feeling of empowerment or mastery by directing the incident and thus controlling a situation. In some incidents, a youth may experience a sense of dominance by gaining the cooperation of a child or an improved sense of self because a child victim accepts their authority. In other situations, successfully surprising, enticing, or setting up a person to be victimized may induce feelings of competency, control, or empowerment. A youth who engages in forcible sexual behaviors, expressions of anger, or sadistic behaviors as part of an offense exhibits a more aggressive form of power or control. It is important to realize, however, that these behaviors provide a sense of control or a perception of being powerful in reaction to feeling powerless. Many sexually abusive youth present as vulnerable, exhibiting a victim stance that reflects their sense of helplessness. Their sense of being powerless may stem from a belief that they should be able to control their environment in order to be safe.

Compensatory Aspects Many youth report temporarily experiencing an improved sense of well-being and self-esteem when they engage in behaviors that restore their sense of control; committing a sexual offense can provide a sense of gratification or well-being. When contemplating, anticipating, committing, or recalling an offense, internal experiences may include thrill, excitement, sexual arousal, risk-taking, superiority, or empowerment due to getting away with something. The experience can be so sufficiently pleasurable and self-enhancing that anxiety-provoking thoughts present prior to the behavior may be temporarily diminished. Additional reinforcement may be associated with the sexual aspect of the behavior.

The need for a compensatory experience appears to be evoked by feelings of helplessness or lack of control antecedent to the abusive behavior. The youth may feel unable to control what happens, feels powerless, and lacks sufficient psychological resources to cope. Natural defense mechanisms may include reaction formation, compensation, suppression, and repression. Engaging in control-seeking or dominating behaviors gives the youth the impression of being effective and in control, and that the precipitating event has been resolved, is less significant, or is under control. Yochelson and Samenow (1976) described these type of beliefs as "thinking errors."

The cycle begins with the emotional reaction to an event, an interaction, or stimuli. The precipitating emotional trigger is usually one of vulnerability: feeling helpless, powerless, controlled, or out of control. Events that may elicit feelings of powerlessness include abandonment or perceived abandonment, physical abuse, sexual victimization, rejection, change, humiliation, loss, alienation, refusal, debasement, control, embarrassment, or betrayal. When the occurrence of such events is interpreted as a loss of control, the youth feels unsafe and the need for a defensive response arises from feeling vulnerable. Some youth report that either their current triggers, or those occurring prior to their abusive behaviors, are reminiscent of historical problems or situations that elicited nearly intolerable feelings of helplessness and have remained unresolved. Over time, a youth may be able to identify groups of similar precursor events or interactions that typically trigger the onset of their defensive reaction and progression through the cycle. The following example concerns a youth who exhibits sensitivity to triggers that involve loss.

> When Dan was 4 years old, his grandfather died while the two of them were taking a nap. Dan, too young to understand death, felt scared and a sense of loss, believing that he had done something wrong that made his grandfather go away. When Dan was 9 years old, his parents divorced, and his mother was granted custody of him; he felt sad, helpless, scared, and a sense of loss and again believed that he was responsible, this time for his father's leaving home. Later in life when he experienced any kind of loss—when his friend moved away, his girlfriend broke up with him, he lost a job—he thought it was his fault and had similar thoughts and feelings. As time went on, he would become anxious if he lost anything—even if he misplaced his keys or papers at school.

The use of power-based behaviors or thoughts to define individual success, strengthen self-esteem, measure adequacy, or resolve interpersonal disputes is widely supported in our culture. Society tends to promote attitudes such as: "Don't get mad, get even," "Take care of number one," "Revenge is sweet." The use of sexual thoughts or behaviors to boost self-esteem, reduce tension, or provide an image of adequacy, is similarly supported by cultural messages. Some youth may believe, "If I am sexual, I am macho," or "Sex will solve my problems." These beliefs, and the perceived societal sanction for them, may support compensatory and power-based sexual thoughts and behaviors.

Arousal Aspects Sexual excitement or arousal is described by some youth as occurring not only during a sexual abuse incident but also during antecedent contemplation, preparation, and subsequent recall of abusive incidents. Sexual behaviors are reinforcing and preferences are strengthened by experiences of intimacy, arousal, orgasm, and tension reduction. This is true of sexually abusive behavior as well. Arousal and orgasm are both psychologically and physiologically pleasurable and are therefore self-reinforcing. Urges to initiate abusive sexual behaviors may intensify or become more frequent as arousal increases.

Arousal can be strengthened and sexual interest shaped by masturbatory behaviors associated with sexual fantasies. McGuire, Carlyle, and Young (1965) suggest that sexual interest is strengthened most by masturbatory fantasies, partly because individuals typically engage in sexual fantasies more frequently than the actual behaviors. Some youth report either engaging in masturbatory fantasies or experiencing sexual excitement when contemplating or specifically imagining offense behaviors. Marshall (1979) and Abel and Blanchard (1974) suggest that masturbation to deviant fantasies may occur antecedent to sexually aggressive behavior. Some youth report strengthened arousal associated with thoughts and behaviors as they engage in masturbatory fantasies of offending or memories of past victimization. Although many adolescents who sexually abuse also engage in nonabusive sexual fantasy and behaviors, they may be at risk for strengthening the arousal and interest associated with sexually abusive behaviors to the extent that normative arousal and activity could be diminished or precluded.

Elements of sexual arousal are unique for each individual and may develop from a wide variety and combination of cognitions, sensory experiences, and behaviors. Some youth report that they experience stronger arousal to anticipatory thoughts and to their recall of offense behaviors than they experience during the sexual abuse incident. Other youth describe a rush or some degree of excitement, thrill, and arousal associated with risk-taking that enhances anticipatory excitement. For others, it may be anticipation of closeness, pleasure, acceptance, or intimacy that increases anticipatory excitement. For still others, the expectation of dominance, control of another, acting out of anger, or infliction of pain may increase antecedent arousal or excitement.

If the youth experiences arousal associated with sexual abuse fantasies or behaviors it may contribute to the compensatory process, as sexual arousal can be soothing and increase positive self-regard. It is possible that self-soothing through sexual stimulation was learned early and may now be a habituated response when distressed or anxious (Money, 1986; see Chapter 4). For others, using sexual stimulation to counter boredom may be equally habituated. Many different thoughts may become associated with abuse-related arousal: memories of past sexual experiences, fantasy of imagined behaviors, or thoughts about sexual information in the culture. Repetition of abusive thoughts and arousing behavior may support an eventual pairing, and these associations may become conditioned as the patterns are repeated. For some, abuse thoughts may have become paired with arousal in the context of the youth's own victimization and the memories of victimization may intrude whenever they feel sexually aroused, or they may become aroused by thoughts of victimization. One of the most insidious effects of sexual abuse for both victims and perpetrators may be in the conflicting thoughts and feelings that can result from the pairing of abusive experiences, nonsexual needs, and sexual feelings (Ryan, 1989).

Early in the work with sexually abusive youth, it was expected that their abusive sexual behaviors were a reflection of deviant sexual preferences and arousal patterns, similar to adults who sexually offend. This assumption has not been confirmed and it is now expected that it is a small minority who actually have sexually deviant arousal. Some youth do experience deviant arousal that can be as strong as that of adult offenders, although the patterns may be less ingrained and less exclusive. Research confirms the presence of what might be thought of as pedophilic interests and arousal problems in some youth as early as age ten, particularly in boys with multiple male child victims (Becker, Hunter, Stein, & Kaplan, 1989; Becker, Stein, Kaplan, & Cunningham-Rathner, 1992; Hunter & Santos, 1990).

Seto, Lalumiere, and Blanchard (2000) validated the use of plethysmography with adolescents in correlating sexual victim history with phallometric response. However, research now suggests that a majority of youth (both those who have offended and young adults who have not) tend to be sexually interested and aroused, more or less, to a wide range of sexual stimuli (Malamuth, Sockloskie, Koss, & Tanaka, 1991; Seto, Murphy, Page, & Ennis, 2003).

In laboratory assessments (using plethysmography), Kaemingk, Koselka, Becker, and Kaplan (1995) demonstrated that younger adolescents had erectile responses to a greater number of stimuli than older adolescents and adults and suggested that one possible explanation may relate to less ability to modulate or inhibit erectile responses at a young age because frontal lobe development is incomplete. In addition, Hunter and Goodwin (1992) indicated that younger sexually abusive youth tend to have more difficulty learning to control abuse-related sexual arousal. Overall, adolescents tend to be less discriminating than older adults, prompting one expert in the field to comment: "Kids are turned on to everything from cool breezes to fire hydrants!" (Bengis, personal communication, 2009).

From a purely theoretical perspective, assumptions regarding juvenile arousal must always be cautious, as there is no known data representing "norms" for arousal in childhood and adolescence. It is quite likely that some youth will appear to have arousal when they engage in sexual behavior with prepubescent children. However, if one's only experiences of sexual interaction have been prior to puberty, it must be considered that it may be natural to have arousal to similar interactions over the next few years. Just as human development follows a pattern of "growth and regression, growth and regression," development of sexuality may also go forward and back as youth strive to master more mature aspects but also return to more familiar aspects previously learned. Theorists and practitioners must be very cautious in evaluating arousal issues outside of a developmental-contextual framework.

Cognitive Aspects A variety of cognitions, frequently referred to as "cognitive distortions" or "thinking errors," have been described in sexual abuse cycles. Some thoughts contribute to or support criminal or antisocial behavior (Yochelson & Samenow, 1976) in that they justify, rationalize, or provide the youth with a way of thinking that sexually abusive behavior is reasonable or justified. Other cognitions, developed through the life experience of the youth, reflect beliefs, perceptions, motivations, assumptions, conclusions, expectations, and fears about self, others, or the world. The emotional reactions that trigger the sexual abuse cycle are often exacerbated by cognitive perceptions. If events or stimuli are interpreted as a threat to the youth's sense of safety or control, or when the youth lacks adequate coping skills to handle a situation, progression into the cycle may be initiated. If the youth were able to reexamine thoughts and depersonalize the meaning of others' behavior, they might feel less need for a compensatory or control-seeking response.

Over time the need to differentiate cognitive "distortions" from developmental and contextual realities has become clearer. Often the individual's interpretation or experience of the triggering event may appear erroneous or extreme to others, but in the context of that youth's life experience, their reaction and beliefs may be quite rational. Historically, attention was paid to identifying and "correcting" thoughts, which support abusive, irresponsible, or antisocial behavior in some programs. There is now more recognition of the need to create some new experience of self, others, relationships, and the world to provide a rational basis for changing the beliefs and thought processes of the youth.

Yochelson and Samenow (1976) identified 52 patterns of thought—which they called "thinking errors"—that contribute to or support criminal or antisocial behavior. Berenson (in Knopp, 1982) described several of these as typically present in youth who sexually offend:

- Victim stance; "I can't" attitude
- Lack of concept of injury to others
- Failure to put oneself in the place of others
- Lack of effort
- Refusal to accept obligation
- No concept of trust
- Unrealistic expectations
- Attitude of ownership
- Irresponsible decision making
- Failure to plan ahead or think long range
- Flawed definition of success and failure
- Fear of being put down
- Refusal to acknowledge fear
- Anger used to control others
- Power thrust
- Pride or refusal to back down

These beliefs reflect an overgeneralization of defensive strategies that allow some youth to seek control over others, feel entitled to impose sexual interaction on others, objectify and depersonalize others, and believe that their behavior is warranted and reasonable. Unfortunately, as problematic as these beliefs may be for some youth, their experience and learning may have been shaped by the modeling of others as well as their own experience, so it may be a mistake to think of these only as "distortions" or "errors."

In the context of the cycle some thoughts specifically justify, rationalize, or support the behavior (Abel & Blanchard, 1974; Becker & Kaplan, 1993; Berenson, 1987). Other thoughts may allow a youth to believe a victim is willing or wants to engage in the abusive behavior. Some thoughts shape a perception of the victim as obligated to meet the needs of the perpetrator, while other thoughts construe the behavior as helpful or desired. Still other thoughts allow the youth to objectify or depersonalize the victim, disregarding their human needs and emotions. These thoughts may occur during contemplation, planning, or setting up an offense, as well as subsequent to the offense, allowing the youth to feel comfortable about their behavior.

Cognitions that allow cycle progression are those thoughts the youth develops in response to their life experiences. During childhood experience of traumatic events or confusing experiences, the child strives to interpret and understand what has happened and may develop negative self-perceptions that become the basis for triggers or events that initiate cycle progression (see Chapters 7 and 8). If a child has concluded that bad things happen because of their bad behavior or character, these conclusions become negative self-perceptions that affirm the congruence of abusive behavior in the context of their experience.

Although there are common patterns of thought that support and contribute to the cycle and to abusive behaviors, the development of specific beliefs is unique for each individual. With repetition, the individual's thoughts become ingrained and develop into patterns of thinking that support a habitual response to many situations. The thoughts become more automatic as they occur more frequently, initially only in similar situations but later generalized to a broader range of situations. When the thinking becomes ingrained and habituated through repetition, the cycle can become more rapid and abusive behaviors may occur more frequently.

Compulsive or Addictive-Like Aspects Some sexually abusive youth demonstrate impulse-control deficits and some report that the urges to engage in abusive sexual behaviors are difficult to deny or manage. Those youth describe repetitive cycles and repeated offenses despite their decision to control or cease their sexually abusive behaviors. Delaying gratification and controlling impulses are developmental skills acquired over time.

Some youth who exhibit habituated offense patterns report increases in the frequency and intensity of urges over time. Others have indicated that the internal sense of excitement and control, as well as the associated arousal, seemed to diminish with repetition, so they added new elements of risk, used more power, or added more sexual behaviors to subsequent fantasies or offenses in order to maintain the same level of gratification.

Both sexual and nonsexual control-seeking thoughts and behaviors may provide a sense of pleasure or relieve some negative internal state. The behavior patterns are experienced positively and are thus reinforced and likely to be repeated. If the youth develops a repetitive pattern, it may gradually become the favored, and eventually habitual, response to specific emotions or situations. Because the response is mal-adaptive and does not truly resolve problems, negative internal states return, and the response pattern reoccurs in an effort to reestablish a sense of well-being. The temporary effect of these efforts becomes ineffective, resulting in more frequent, and possibly more intense, anxiety, and the process continues to be repeated. Concurrently the individual's tolerance for stress diminishes, and the compensatory process occurs more frequently. There is a tendency to strive less and less for more effective solutions, exacerbating the lack of competency and limiting development of more functional skills.

Although the behavior patterns reflected in the sexual abuse cycle are not necessarily compulsions or addictions, there can be a compulsive quality to the urges reported by some youth. The need to increase the intensity of some aspects of the behavior can take on an addictive-like quality. Freeman-Longo (1982) and Carnes (1983) both indicated that because there are psychological and physiological re-inforcements in sexually aggressive behavior, it may become an addictive disorder. There are many unanswered questions regarding compulsive or addictive aspects. Some of the reinforcement of the behavior may include sexual arousal, thrill, risk-taking, empowerment, anticipation, pleasure, and self-gratifying perceptions. There may also be physiological, biochemical, and neurological processes associated with the habituation of sexually abusive behaviors. Compulsive/addictive history and characteristics are relevant to understanding some individuals.

COMPONENTS OF HABITUATED SEXUAL ABUSE CYCLES

A comprehensive, in-depth understanding of the more habituated cycles of chronic/ repetitive offending can be useful in foreseeing and addressing future risks during treatment and in aftercare plans. The cycle provides a framework for assessing the treatment needs of the youth. By developing an awareness of precursors and cues that indicate progression through various stages of the cycle, clinicians can assist the youth with learning to recognize and interrupt the pattern. The therapist can also identify potential issues (historical or trauma) that influence current functioning. When the youth understand their own personalized cycle and the patterns associated with their own abusive behaviors, they become able to develop strategies to cope with problems more effectively and control abusive behavior. For some youth, this is a welcome relief and provides hope for the future when they have perceived their behavior as unpredictable and, therefore, out of control.

The following cycle was developed for educational purposes and describes aspects of offense behavior provided by a wide range of youth. It is intended to assist in developing an awareness of potential issues. It is unlikely that any one youth would present with all (or even many) of the elements described herein.

The following list and subsections provide explanations of recognizing, understanding, and exploring three phases of the cycle:

1. *The precipitating phase:* The initial cognitive and affective reaction to some current stressor and relevant historical issues; and the defensive reaction: a sense of helplessness, dread, or hopelessness; and attempts to avoid the issue.
2. *The compensatory phase:* The attempts to compensate by engaging in nonsexual and sexual control-seeking thoughts and behaviors.
3. *The integration phase:* Efforts to assimilate the abusive behavior without self-deprecation, culminating in suppression, which allows the youth to deny that the behavior was a problem or any risk of future recurrence.

THE PRECIPITATING PHASE

During the precipitating phase the youth is reacting to something. Essentially events are neutral; it is the meaning the youth attaches to them that dictates the affective and behavioral response. The initial interpretation of any situation, interaction, or event is based on the conclusions/beliefs the individual has about the world. Each youth has the choice of reacting to a problem as something to solve or something to avoid. Healthy responses include being aware of internal affective reactions, thinking clearly and accurately about the problem, and using a variety of social competencies and resources to cope with or solve the problem.

The response depicted in the precipitating phase of the cycle is maladaptive and unhealthy. The meaning of the problem may be distorted, based on the individual's perception. In one sequence of distorted perceptions, the youth concludes they are at risk in some way, being treated unfairly, unable to cope, inadequate, and so forth. The assumption that follows is to expect similar or worse circumstances and outcomes. Attempts to avoid the issues, negative thoughts, and feelings may lead to isolating or withdrawing from others (see Figure 9.1). At times, any individual may initially respond to a situation in this way, but eventually, most recognize and interrupt the process or arrive at an effective, non-abusive plan.

In early progressions through the cycle, the process may unfold quite slowly. The cognitions may be based in adaptive defenses that developed during early childhood or may reflect the beliefs and defensive coping styles of others who have served as role models. If the distorted or inaccurate perception becomes a habitual way of interpreting certain types of events, the process can become automatic and the initial

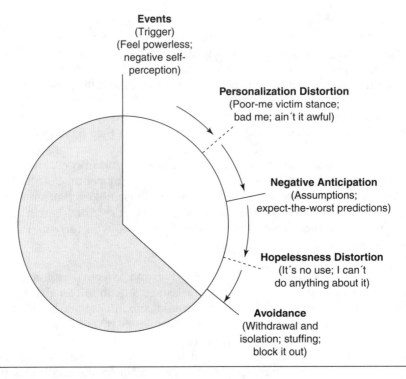

Figure 9.1   The Precipitating Phase of the Sexual Abuse Cycle
Source: Reprinted by permission of RSA, Inc.

phase can move so rapidly that the youth has little conscious awareness of its elements. Some youth entering treatment indicate that they had no problems prior to their referring behavior.

Stressors/Triggers   A wide range of stressors can trigger the sexual abuse cycle. Each individual has idiosyncratic perceptions of meaning, based on basic beliefs, life experience, and perceptions, and the nature of the stress will vary significantly from youth to youth. The reported stressors often evoke feelings of helplessness or lack of control, associated with a sense of perceived abandonment, incompetence, and vulnerability.

Helplessness is the feeling of being overwhelmed and being unable to cope. Feelings of helplessness underlie many uncomfortable feelings and traumatic experiences and may be associated with such cognitions as, "I ought to be able to prevent this from happening," "I should be able to make them feel like I want them to," "I should get what I want," or "I should know what to do"— all self-talk indicating failure. Feelings and thoughts are inextricably intertwined (see Chapter 8), so it is not always apparent whether the vulnerable feelings precede the negative expectations, or vice versa. Feeling helpless is intolerable to many people, so the defensive reaction is to deny it or mask it with anger. When it is masked with anger, the prevailing cognitions relate to win-lose, dog-eat-dog perception, and the power thrusts and struggles are preferable to the vulnerable feeling. Similarly, the pessimism of the negative thoughts changes to optimism of aggressive thoughts, with the hope of feeling better.

When the perceptions or conclusions about the original, or historical, event continue, the juvenile may suppress the issues to decrease anxiety. Subsequently there seems to be an increased sensitivity to any situation or event that is reminiscent of the original event (Lane & Zamora, 1984; Ryan, 1989). The reaction to the more current event may appear to be out of proportion to the situation because the youth is reacting to an accumulation of internal responses to past and current situations. The youth may manage the associated anxiety through the sense of control, empower-ment, or temporary relief experienced in the maladaptive cycle. If the cycle becomes repetitive, the oversensitive response may be generalized to an increased variety of situations, and there may be less tolerance for any type of situation that evokes feelings of powerlessness.

Consider a young child who observes the father being physically abusive to the mother. The child is afraid of losing the mother and feels vulnerable, then tries to intervene but is shoved out of the way. The child feels helpless and frightened and may later conclude, "I should have stopped him and protected my mom. I'm weak because I did nothing. I'm a failure. If I'm not strong enough, Mom gets hurt, and I'm not good enough." The conclusions are based on imagining that the child should be able to control the father, so it is the child's fault that mom got hurt. This is clearly not a reasonable expectation, but it makes the child feel less vulnerable, because it imagines the child able to defend rather than helpless. It is the "misattribution of responsibility" that supports the belief in controlling others. Subsequent events beyond control of the youth may trigger similar feelings of weakness, inadequacy, and vulnerability. Over time, when the youth is challenged or criticized similar feelings and conclusions may be evoked, and the defense against these thoughts and feelings is to exert control in other ways.

Frequently reported events that elicit feelings of helplessness include: parental divorce; death of a significant person or pet; loss; change in environment; sexual, physical, or emotional abuse; family violence or dysfunction; rejection; public humili-ation; ridicule; betrayal; and awareness of family members' involvement in deviant sexual behaviors. It is likely that attachment issues and the style of parenting expe-rienced as a young child are also significant historical factors that the youth may not be consciously aware of. Some youth report that loneliness or boredom triggers their cycle and that they find it intolerable to feel nothing when nothing is going on. This is a type of zero state that may result from years of defensive strategies that have effectively blocked emotions, for better and for worse. These experiences are not causal to sexual abuse behavior, but they are the stimuli for the child's development of coping styles.

Many risk factors that may contribute to the development of sexually abusive behaviors (see Chapters 3 and 5) and those same factors often correlate with the historical issues that are most emotionally charged or have shaped the cognitions that contribute to the pattern of offending. Distressing or incomprehensible sexual experiences; exposure to sexual behaviors of other family members, including fetish behaviors, pornographic involvement, or molestation; poor sexual boundaries in the home such as excessive nudity, parental sexual dysfunction, sexualized interactions with family members, or exposure to explicit, overstimulating, or incomprehensible sexual information have been reported. Those who have been sexually victimized have often failed to resolve, or at times even to define or acknowledge, the experience.

Events or situations that triggered the cycle prior to the youth's first offense and current triggers are not necessarily the same; sensitivies may change over time as they become more habituated. Typical triggers can be moving, feeling put down or challenged, entering a new school, poor grades, being told no, rejection by a friend or a romantic liaison, parental conflicts and restrictions, criticism, parental remarriage, embarrassment, losing a game, a friend moving away, feeling unaccepted, feeling that one cannot measure up, authority conflicts, and skill deficits. As tolerance lessens, even more innocuous situations may trigger similar stress: Being asked to wait, differing opinions, seeing someone laugh or stare, failing to be acknowledged, not getting one's way, being ignored, or feeling bored can be triggers for the cycle. The common theme is a lack of tolerance for feelings of helplessness and distorted conclusions about adequacy.

The Personalization Distortion   Some types of thinking are particularly evident in the progression of the cycle. The first is relevant to locus of control and "misattribution of responsibility" and strengthens the youth's sense of vulnerability, powerlessness, and inadequacy. Personalization means taking things personally that are not in fact personal. When the youth personalizes things that they have no control over, it contributes to a victim stance perception, or what has been referred to as the "poor me syndrome."

Assuming responsibility for events due to some perceived deficit, attributing negative and hurtful motivations to others, perceiving others' behavior as a personal affront or attack, believing one is a victim because of the event, focusing on inconvenience, believing it is not fair—all of these thoughts affirm the youth's worldview. The affective response may be feeling guilty, ashamed, frustrated, hurt, helpless, sad, angry, controlled, persecuted, betrayed, inadequate, or embarrassed. There is a sense of unease and anxiety associated with thinking everything going on around them is personal.

Consider a child whose parents divorce, and the custodial parent moves to the opposite side of town. The child experiences multiple losses: both parents being present all the time, predictability and familiarity, their peer group, neighborhood, house, room, and so forth. The child thinks, "They don't care about me. It's not fair. They're messing with me. I don't count. If only I had cleaned up my room. I trusted them. I didn't get a say in this." If the child does not successfully cope with the change, future changes may become triggers due to the emotionally charged experience of change being associated with loss. Over time, even minor disruptions in routine may be seen as having the same meaning as the historical situation and evoke similar feelings of powerlessness and thoughts of not being important.

By personalizing, the youth may perceive a threat and feel unable to protect. If the adolescent believes that being competent and safe depends on being able to stop or control external events, adequacy is continually questioned, a negative self-concept increases, and the youth fails to recognize the capacity for internal control. If such misattributions are not corrected, the youth may ruminate about the events, feelings of victimization and helplessness may increase, and the cycle may progress to the next stage as thinking begins to generalize.

Negative Anticipation   The human capacity to learn from past experience can be an asset or a curse. People expect that many things in the future will be similar to the past, and this expectation is the basis for accommodation and assimilation of new experiences. For those youth whose past has been perceived as negative, hurtful, or threatening, negative expectations are quite rational, even though what they have learned contributes to a sense of hopelessness and dysfunctional coping.

The youth tend to view situations as black or white, inflexible, and overwhelming, with limited options, explanations, or outcomes. The process is one of generalization, often appearing to "make mountains out of molehills," and negative predictions become the expectation. Increased anxiety and feelings of dread, apprehension, helplessness, inadequacy, and hopelessness naturally increase the need for defenses, yet the youth may feel incapacitated, depressed, and incompetent.

Statements reflecting thoughts in this stage of the cycle include words such as *always* and *never*. The predictions and assumptions are absolute and unyielding. Although the cognitions are overgeneralizing, to the youth they are solid beliefs based on the evidence they have. For example, the child whose parents are divorcing worries about the move and begins to think, "I'll never make friends over there. She'll never let me see my dad. I'll never see my old friends. Dad will never have a place for me. There will be nothing to do. They will never care about my needs." All the thoughts about the separation increase anxiety, tension, and depression. If the youth fails to communicate, does not resolve these issues, or challenge the negative assumptions, the risk of progression in the cycle increases.

The Hopelessness Distortion   Convinced that the future will be worse and feeling unable to prevent it increases hopelessness, depression, or increased anxiety. Thoughts in this stage of the cycle include: "I can't do anything," "I can't handle this," "I can't face it," and "Maybe it will go away if I don't think about it." Feelings of helplessness and incompetence may accompany increased dependency or protection-seeking behaviors, such as clinging to try to avoid loss, and the youth may exhibit a decreased tolerance for conflict or challenges.

For example, a child watches television after school instead of doing chores. When the mother gets home, she scolds and says the child is grounded. This means the child cannot go to the mall with friends. Thoughts might be: "She doesn't let me to do anything. She doesn't want me to have friends. She doesn't care about me. No matter how hard I try, I can't please her." Generalization may lead to "never" thoughts: "I can never please her. She'll never be satisfied. She'll never let me do anything. Why should I even try? It's no use, nothing ever changes."

Beliefs are the product of accumulated experiences. For some youth, negative expectations and hopelessness are based in reality and may not be distorted at all because they have such developmental deficits that they lack the skills to achieve a better outcome. If the youth has never succeeded in making friends, pleasing mom, or feeling good about themselves, the sense of hopelessness may be justified. The source of beliefs must be evaluated to determine whether the sense of hopelessness is rational or a distortion, which guides intervention.

Avoidance   First attempts to cope with negative thoughts and feelings may be to push them away, blot them out or bury them, withdraw, isolate, or avoid thinking about it. Any relief that comes from avoidance, however, is temporary, and negative thoughts and feelings continue to intrude. Instead of being able to escape the negative self-perceptions, fears, and anxiety, the youth typically ruminates about problems, self-perceived shortcomings, or negative motivations attributed to others' behaviors.

Commonly described avoidance behaviors include increased sleeping, substance abuse, spending more time alone in one's room, not answering the phone, giving excuses to avoid activities, playing video games, listening to loud music, wearing earphones to avoid interaction with others, and solitary activities like daydreaming, reading, or doing hobbies alone. Some effectively isolate by behaving in ways that irritate others to the extent that they avoid the youth.

An example of progression through the first phase of the cycle might be as shown in the following.

As the teacher is handing back the math test, she says, "Willie, you have the worst score on this test; you must not pay attention in class." Willie feels embarrassed and begins to think, "Everyone knows how dumb I am. The teacher hates me. She's trying to make me look bad." Looking around the class, he notices everyone staring at him, some are snickering. He thinks, "They're going to make fun of me because I'm dumb. I won't have friends anymore. The teacher won't ever give me a chance. My parents are going to yell, I'll be grounded for a long time." Willie stares at his desk during the rest of the class and doesn't talk to anyone. He decides he won't go with his friends after school because they will tease him, and he assumes they wouldn't want to be seen with a stupid person.

After class, he races out and doesn't respond to his best friends. He heads to his locker and decides not to take his math book, thinking, "It's no use. I won't understand it anyway." He walks home by a different route than usual and goes straight to his room at home. He turns on a video game and plays until his mother calls him to dinner. During the weekend, he spends a lot of time alone and doesn't talk much to his family. He takes a long, solitary bicycle ride and then goes fishing, also alone. He feels more and more lonely. Over the weekend, the picture of his teacher saying he's stupid pops into his mind constantly, but he keeps trying to push the thoughts away. When he can't, he thinks about how unfair she has been to him, and he dreads going to math class next week because she'll do it again. He decides he can sit in the back and keep his mouth shut so she won't notice him, and he'll call in sick the next time there is a test.

Because Willie doesn't counter his negative anticipation with anything positive, hopeless thinking and helpless feelings continue and there may be further withdrawal. Avoidance and ruminating become less effective and are gradually replaced with anger defenses.

THE COMPENSATORY PHASE

Elements of both sexualized and nonsexualized expressions of control seeking and dominance may be depicted in the compensatory phase of the cycle (see Figure 9.2). Power-based thoughts and behaviors provide a sense of mastery, empowerment, and excitement that compensate for feelings of inadequacy and helplessness. The youth may lash out at others (retaliation) or believe they are entitled to feel better (compensation).

The compensatory phase begins with projecting and externalizing: blaming others for the perceived stress. As the perception shifts from assumptions of a negative self to assumptions of negative others, anger increases and is expressed in power-based behaviors such as lying, arguing, vandalism, theft, and so forth. The gratification that comes with feeling more powerful is effective but temporary, and the youth may continue to seek further gratification if he remains in the cycle. Thoughts and fantasizing may initially meet that need, but may also evolve into a plan to engage in behaviors imagined to provide even greater gratification. Setting up the opportunity to act on that plan sometimes involves a complex set of thoughts, behaviors, and reactions.

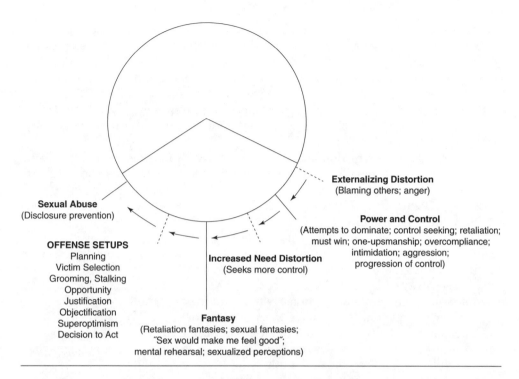

Figure 9.2 The Compensatory Phase of the Sexual Abuse Cycle
Source: Reprinted by permission of RSA, Inc.

The rate of progression in this phase can vary considerably. A youth whose response pattern is more habituated may move more quickly to nonsexualized control-seeking behaviors and more gradually toward an abusive sexual behavior. At times some youth engage in "blitz behaviors," rapidly and frequently progressing to an offense. The speed of this pattern may be driven by the significance of the precipitating issues and the degree of internal distress, may be related to general impulsivity, or to the level of comfort or relief achieved in other parts of the cycle. The control-seeking behaviors and the nature of solutions they consider will differ for each youth.

The Externalizing Distortion Ruminating about the perceived situation increases frustration. Anger is generated and justified by blaming others for causing the vulnerable feelings, to avoid the internal sense of powerlessness and inadequacy. As outrage builds, thinking about some form of retaliation or one-upmanship becomes more likely: "It's their fault I am feeling this way"; "If it weren't for them I'd be fine"; "They had no right to do this to me"; and "They'll be sorry for this." The youth may begin to develop fantasies that involve retaliation, humiliation of others, one-upmanship, or even self-harming behaviors to make others feel badly for their mistreatment.

Power and Control The first observable compensatory response may be angry affect or control-seeking behaviors. Juveniles who engage others in power struggles may feel a sense of superiority, authority, or control. A sense of adequacy and empowerment may come from dominating or controlling others and the youth may view such behaviors as a necessary or reasonable defense. Anger may mask feelings of helplessness or vulnerability, so engaging others in some conflict feels safer than being vulnerable. Control-seeking behaviors may be expressed aggressively, passively, or passive-aggressively, generating physical arousal with adrenaline and a sense of entitlement and superiority. Misuse of power may involve efforts to dominate, retaliate, or control others; pushing buttons or provoking; using loopholes to exploit; or sarcasm to belittle.

For example, the progression may be to isolate (refuse to come to dinner), create power struggles with mom (argue about the volume of the radio), or to fantasize about some compensatory or retaliatory solution (doing something sexual would make me feel better, or I could really get back at mom if I steal money from her purse and sneak out to the mall).

Control-seeking behaviors may include: arguing, slamming doors, walking out of a confrontation, having the last word, pressing one's point, not following directions, a victim-stance response, derogatory statements, ignoring others, substance abuse (either to get away with something or to oppose laws, rules, or parental expectations), obsequious or overcompliant reactions, lying, breaking rules, failing to do what was requested, manipulation, doing things one's own way or on one's own terms, tricking someone, not completing homework or failing to turn it in, intimidation, paybacks, belittling, threats, fighting, oppositional behaviors, superior stance, bragging, being critical, challenging others, or setting others up to get in trouble.

Associated thoughts might include: "I showed them. I put them in their place"; "Now he knows not to mess with me"; and "I'm really something." The affect may be angry, arrogant, or resentful.

Consider progress in this stage:

Willie was angry at his teacher and he dreaded going to class the next day. He began picking on his younger sister by hiding her favorite toy and refusing to let her watch her regular television show. When his mom reminded him to take out the trash, he told her to wait. He later decided that his mother was being unfair by expecting him to do everything. He thought, "She can just do it herself," and went to his room. On the way to school the next morning, he called his friend George "fatso." He was thinking that would teach him not to make fun of Willie or call him stupid. In his math class, he ignored the teacher's offer to give him help after school and did not turn in his homework. He sat in the back of the classroom and threw spit wads at some of the teacher's favorite students. He called one of the boys who answered a question a cheater. When he walked out of class he thought, "I'm better than all of the smart kids in that class. She was wrong to front me off."

The sense of empowerment that results from many initial control-seeking behaviors may be brief, lasting from a few minutes to a day, because they are more like "power-jabs" than full-out "power-thrusts." The more habituated the response patterns are, the briefer the positive effects from the power struggles, but the youth may fail to realize that these expressions of power are essentially ineffective. Because the behaviors do not really resolve issues, the juvenile is still faced with self-doubt, vulnerable feelings, and negative assumptions. As anxiety increases, progression in the cycle continues.

The Increased Need Distortion   Because the misuse of power does not create an enduring sense of control, anxiety returns, and the perceived need for control or a need for continued gratification may occur. Most youth are unaware of the process but may recognize a need to feel better and think of more dramatic or more aggressive control-seeking behaviors.

Consider the following: Progressing further in the cycle, Willie may imagine more harmful solutions. He may decide skipping school is the only way to avoid failure in class and ridicule from friends, so truancy becomes an issue. While skipping school, the only interactions he has in the neighborhood are with children too young to be in school, and the opportunity develops that a sexual offense could occur.

Fantasy The sequence of thoughts, or fantasies, about what to do to feel better may be nonsexualized or sexualized. As stated in Chapter 8, contemplating sexually abusive behaviors is not always where the first fantasy begins.

Control-seeking fantasies might include: being in charge of the school, the family, or others; being a star; risk-taking; being sneaky or scaring people; beating someone up; being the most popular person around; property damage; being perfect; making someone beg for forgiveness; being a millionaire; or torturing animals or people. Thoughts may include: "They'd be really sorry if I did that"; "That would really show them"; "They don't even know what I'm thinking"; or "I bet they'd never mess with me again." Affect may be exuberant or smug.

Nonsexualized control-seeking fantasies can be elaborations of previous power-based behaviors, gradually involving more expressions of anger or control, and may include themes of retaliation, humiliation, or aggression and may involve violence that appears to be out of proportion to the situation. Some fantasies may be violent and aggressive and only incidentally use sexual behaviors as an expression of that aggression. Some youth who later commit sexual offenses are coercive in some way in order to accomplish the sexual interaction, while some youth may use extremes of force and violence beyond what is necessary to complete the offense.

At some point, the thoughts begin to involve sexual behaviors. Some youth report switching to sexual fantasies when they realize they cannot do things they have imagined. Sexuality is ever-present and potentially rewarding so there is at least always the option of something sexual. Thinking of sexual matters, arousal becomes a factor in the experience, providing gratification even before the behavior occurs. Other youth report they simply began thinking that sex would make them feel better. The thoughts appear nearly automatic for habituated youth.

For some, sexual thoughts involve normative fantasies but ones that are not achievable. For example, the youth who fantasizes about being sexual with a girl in class may realize that she will not even talk to him, so developing a sexual relationship is unlikely. Another example is the youth who thinks of doing something sexual with his girlfriend, but remembers he is grounded. When impediments cause a normative thought to be rejected, the questions become: "So who can I do it with? When and where can I do it? And will I have the courage to do it then?"

Thinking about how to actually achieve what they have been thinking about shapes the fantasy into a plan that identifies *who, what, when, where,* and *how,* a plan that may become abusive in some way. The youth may think: "Since the girl won't even talk to me, I will just grab her when I get the chance and show her how I feel"; or the youth who is grounded may think: "It would serve my parents right if I do something sexual with my brother, because they wouldn't let me go out with my girlfriend."

In other instances, the thought of doing something sexual might bring up memories of past sexual victimization, and the youth might think: "I'll do the sexual things that were done to me." A youth who has angry thoughts might think "I'll get back at my mom by doing something sexual to my sister," or "I'll grab that girl and show her who's boss."

Whatever the first thought involves, the fantasy that leads to an initial offense cannot be assumed to have consciously been a sexually abusive or deviant thought, nor can subsequent offenses be assumed to involve initial thoughts of sexually offending. But once offending occurs, subsequent thoughts and fantasies are likely to be influenced by that perpetration experience. The risk of additional sexual offenses increases with each offense because those memories become potential components to be included in subsequent fantasies.

If the offense is not discovered, the effect of the past sexual offense continues to be compensatory as the youth thinks of the sense of control and/or gratification associated with the behavior and enjoys the additional thrill of "getting away with it." Fantasies may be brief, partial thought fragments, or may be elaborate and detailed. Some youth may spend hours or days in deep contemplation while others may act impulsively. But the fantasies that occur in the sexual abuse cycle serve a compensatory or retaliatory function that at the least disregards the needs of others, and in many cases, involves the misuse of power to do something sexual, and/or the misuse of sexual behavior to meet nonsexual needs.

Some sexual fantasies may initially appear quite normal, but closer examination may indicate that an element of control, dominance, or power is involved. Such fantasies might include being the most sexually desirable peer; being a "super stud" or "hottie"; being so irresistible that the most desirable person in school cannot help but be attracted; perfect sexual performance; or being sexual with a famous person. More concerning fantasies might include bondage or sadistic behaviors; having an insatiable sex partner; being sexual in public or precarious places; or engaging in humiliating sexual behaviors.

The youth who is having a lot of sexual fantasies may exhibit increased sexual preoccupation. They may make more sexual comments than usual, tell more sexual jokes, collect or hoard pornography or erotica, and engage in more masturbatory activity. They may exhibit increased sexual cues, sexualize other's behavior, misinterpret nonsexual cues, and objectify others by focusing on sexual body parts, staring, violating boundaries, or invading privacy.

Thinking of themselves as engaging in sexual behaviors enhances self-image as potent, adequate, desirable, and in control. Physical arousal and psychological pleasure reinforce sexualized thoughts of controlling and being powerful so the sexual fantasies become more gratifying than nonsexualized power-based thoughts and may lead to the use of similar fantasies in the future as a preferred way to reduce internal discomfort.

If the youth recognizes that the sexual fantasies are not attainable, the sense of an increased need for control remains and further jeopardizes self-image. The drive to identify sexual thoughts that continue to provide gratification may lead to more daring ideas, trying to imagine possible alternatives to engage in some kind of sexual behavior, how to create an opportunity to realize the fantasy, and figuring out who is most likely to cooperate.

As a youth begins to contemplate sexually abusive behavior, there is a "what if?" or "I wonder what it would be like?" quality. Some youth report that when they initially think of some type of sexually abusive behavior and experience arousal, they reject the idea based on values or internal sanctions against such behavior. They do not believe it would be right, or believe they would be in trouble. But if the thoughts reoccur and become arousing, the youth may masturbate to the ideas even while continuing to reject the idea. Continuing to pair abusive thoughts with sexual arousal may contribute to the development of deviant arousal and increase the likelihood of thinking errors developing to make the fantasy seem more possible or reasonable. Arousal and orgasm enhance a sense of well-being that may counter inhibition and may strengthen and reinforce sexual interests that were previously rejected. Due to the compensatory anxiety reduction and a perception of being in control, the youth may minimize the thought as not a problem because "it's only a fantasy, I'm not actually doing it."

With repetition, the sense of excitement and gratification may decrease over time, and the youth begin to add elements to their fantasies to maintain the earlier levels of excitement and gratification: additional sexual behaviors, increased elements of control, or improved ways of making the behavior possible. Some youth feel uncomfortable with these fantasies and try to repress them, and after actually offending may deny previous thoughts, believing the idea just popped into their head. Others may continue to refine their fantasy until they arrive at an ideal scenario and then repeat it many times. A few youth report engaging in an ideal fantasy in a compulsive manner, masturbating so vigorously that they cause penile irritation or injury. For others, the fantasies and subsequent behaviors are rigid and ritualized and change very little over time. Some report a somewhat fixated scenario, often a recreation of their own memory of being victimized, but see themselves in the role of the aggressor in their fantasy. The repetition and refinement of the fantasies becomes a mental rehearsal for later behavior.

For example:

> As Manuel rides his bike to football practice, he is steaming at his coach for scheduling a scrimmage on a Saturday and spoiling his chance to go to the mall with his friends. He had been so mad when his coach called that he had slammed the telephone down. While he was riding, he deliberately splashed gutter water on some little kid, and when he got to practice, he was sullen and talked back to the coach once. He was thinking of telling the coach what he really thought of him, getting the entire team to go on strike if there were any more Saturday practices, and deliberately giving the ball to the other team. The more he thought of these things, the better he felt. He began to think of trying some of them but realized he would get benched and lose his starting position. He starts thinking about cutting the coach's brake lines on his precious van, or blowing up his house to show him he shouldn't mess with other people's plans, but as he thinks of it, he isn't sure what lines to cut or where to buy dynamite. Besides, he'd be in a jam if there wasn't a coach for his team.

After practice, while he is riding home, he begins to think about the girl down the street. He wishes she'd notice him; he could show her a good time. He knows where his parents keep an X-rated movie; if he could get her to watch it, she'd probably like it so much she'd kiss him. Maybe she'd even let him touch her breast. Then he remembers she has an older boyfriend who would beat him up if he even tried. He remembers the coach has two little girls. He starts thinking, "I bet he'd be sorry if something happened to those girls. I could offer to baby sit for him and touch them and he wouldn't even know how bad I got him. But if they told, I could get in a lot of trouble. I could tell them if they ever told I'd shave their heads. Besides, they'd probably like it if I touched their privates. I bet I could even get them to suck me."

As Manual entertains these thoughts over the next few days, he is aroused and even masturbates once. About a week later, he decides that what he is thinking is sick and that he would never really try something like that because he'd be in a lot of trouble. He'd probably end up in some prison built just for perverts. A couple of weeks later, his friend sneaks a centerfold into practice, and all the guys ogle the picture. On his way home that night, he sees a woman walking alone on the bike path. He looks at her breasts and wonders if they look like the picture he saw. That evening he thinks that if he could find someone like her, only a little bit smaller, he could grab her breast and get away with it. He'd never be identified, and who would believe a kid would do something like that anyway? That night he thinks of trying it, masturbates, and has the best orgasm he has ever had. He thinks about grabbing her crotch and wonders what a lady's pubic hair feels like.

As the weeks go on, he imagines grabbing a lady and taking her to a bush where he could make her give him a blow job. Sometimes he imagines her thinking he is a stud and wanting to teach him all about sex. He begins to wonder if he really could pull it off. He can imagine how great he would feel. He begins to think of where he could do it. One time on the way home from practice, he even stopped by a bush and thought about the lady and got very aroused. He began to think of what kind of person he'd pick. He decides to watch for someone who isn't too alert and is small enough to handle—maybe someone who is kind of heavy so he can outrun her if he has to. He knows he'd never really do it, but he needs to have a real lady to picture when he thinks about it.

Offense Setups Through a series of thoughts and behaviors, the youth's fantasy becomes a plan, a victim is selected and objectified, the possibility of successfully engaging in the behavior is evaluated, an opportunity is developed or exploited, the behaviors are rationalized and justified, a belief in capability is reinforced, and a decision is made to engage in the behavior. Throughout the process, the youth may feel a sense of thrill, empowerment, anticipation, and, for some, sexual arousal. Youths who have engaged in previous sexually abusive behaviors may move rapidly through this stage. It can seem difficult for the youth to stop the behavior during this stage due to the experience of internal gratification.

Planning Planning refines the details of the fantasy, becoming the *"how."* The original scheme, or fantasy, becomes more explicit and is modified based on situational aspects. Sometimes the plan is completed as the offense evolves, and sometimes well before the offense. For some, the plans are elaborate and detailed, and for others merely a vague outline of what they would like to do. The youth may become increasingly excited about the anticipated outcomes and continue to feel a sense of empowerment and mastery.

It is difficult for a youth to acknowledge having planned an abusive behavior. It sounds worse if it was not an impulsive act, and the implications of premeditation may increase the need to deny planning. Most sexually abusive behaviors occur in an area that allows the behavior to succeed, and there are elements of secrecy involved, suggesting the likelihood of some degree of planning. Actually, the youth would be more dangerous if an offense actually occurred without even thinking about it.

Refining a plan might include strategies to increase victim cooperation, identify the most promising opportunity, and decide what to do during the offense. Planning may include predicting the victim's thoughts and behaviors, as well as anticipating the pleasurable experience. When a youth is thinking about an offense, he is in control and believes that how he hopes and imagines it is how it will actually be when he does it.

Juveniles who engage in repeated sexual abuse behaviors indicate that their offenses become less exciting or fulfilling over time. They tend to refine their plans to maintain excitement by introducing more intrusive sexual behaviors, manipulating the victim to agree to more sophisticated behaviors, adding to the amount of control or coercion involved, increasing the elements of risk, adding punitive aspects, choosing a new locale, or introducing rituals. Many offenders maintain elements of their original modus operandi, to which these elements are added.

Victim Selection   The *"who"* of a sexual fantasy may be determined by imagining a vulnerable person who can be exploited in an abusive fantasy, or a person likely to comply with a sexual behavior. Sometimes the choice may be based simply on availability, or it may be a person the youth believes deserves to be abused. The motivation shapes the fantasy, and may be based on the youth's perception of vulnerable characteristics that can be exploited or manipulated to engage in a sexual abuse behavior. A youth is less likely to abuse someone he does not believe he can control, and it is often someone the youth already knows and has some relationship with.

Sometimes, choosing a victim may be specific to particular age, gender, personality traits, physical features, or interpersonal qualities congruent with the youth's fantasy. The youth may approach someone outspoken, who makes him feel looked up to, or he may target a quiet child who might be less likely to tell. Some youth choose a prepubescent child because the skin is soft and lacks pubic hair, an elderly victim who is less likely to struggle, or a peer who appears naive enough to not understand what is happening. Some youth have an idiosyncratic set of criteria for the type of victims selected, while others may be less discriminating and more opportunistic.

Some rapes and hands-off offenses will involve strangers, and when the victim is a stranger, the youth may take advantage of an opportunity that presents itself, someone who matches a fantasy, or may stalk the victim. However, the majority of victims are known to the youth, with nearly half being younger children living in the same household. Sexual offenses involving similar age peers are most often acquaintances. When the victim is known, the youth may have developed a relationship or interaction specifically targeting a potential victim and then identify ways to complete the offense.

Cruising, or searching for a victim or an opportunity, is sometimes characteristic of youth who expose, peep, rape, molest young children, or make obscene telephone calls. When a youth is cruising the search is for someone perceived as vulnerable, someone who might react in the way fantasized, someone in a location where the behavior may occur undetected, or someone who meets idiosyncratic victim criteria. Some youth may cruise for a locale, then watch for a potential victim to appear. Still others may join an organization or get a job (for example, the boy scouts, a youth group, food delivery to the elderly, or telephone solicitation) in order to gain access to potential victims.

One youth described programming his telephone to dial sequential numbers until he heard a younger female respond with irritation. He then called that number repeatedly to make obscene telephone calls. He believed that because he could "make the victim angry," he was controlling her. Some youth who expose report choosing "housewife" types or teenage girls because they assume these victims are less likely to report the experience, while others report choosing young children because the anticipated response is fascination and curiosity. Some youth who rape describe looking for someone who is isolated or lacks access to assistance.

When a victim has been selected, the youth's fantasies involve a quality of ownership of the victim and expectations that the victim will behave or react in the manner fantasized. If the potential victim is known to the youth and behaves differently than expected, expressions of anger or efforts to exert nonsexual control may occur.

Access and Opportunity Watching, studying, observing, setting up, planning, arranging, or creating access and opportunity to offend are part of the *"where and when."* Traditionally, the words "grooming" and "stalking" have been used in descriptions of this stage of the cycle but the terms have often been misunderstood or overgeneralized to all of a youth's interactions or relationships. Not every interaction, behavior, or relationship that occurs in the life of a youth who has sexually abused (even a habitual offender) relates to the abuse pattern or the cycle. Part of treatment assists the youth in identifying effective, prosocial interactions and differentiating them from unhealthy patterns.

During this portion of the cycle the youth is identifying the location or situation that provides the best possibility for committing the sexual abuse behavior, the most potential for victim compliance or cooperation, and the youth's own readiness to engage in the behavior. Each youth has an idiosyncratic view of what they perceive to be the ideal opportunity. Some will only offend in specific situations, others may take advantage of any opportunity that arises and still others may develop access and opportunity. For some, the tendency is to seek similar criteria from offense to offense.

Opportunity may include both a location that is secluded or private, and a vulnerable person. A youth might volunteer to baby-sit or supervise younger children on a school outing to develop both access and opportunity to molest a child. Other youth might cruise an amusement park or a bike path to look for a potential opportunity or scheme to lure a vulnerable person to an isolated site. Still other youth may find themselves in an interaction where a vulnerable person unwittingly creates an opportunity. The youth may also study and learn about a potential victim's habits and routines. Whether the potential victim is a stranger or someone known to them, the youth may follow them, gain access to a living situation through surreptitious means, watch and study the person over an extended period of time, identifying the most likely situation or timing to successfully offend. In a home situation, the youth may violate boundaries and observe parental routines, establish patterns, and identify situations where molesting a younger child can occur. The objectification process, which enables the youth to create the relationships and opportunities to offend, may strengthen cognitions of entitlement.

If a power differential is not already apparent in age, size, or intellect, it may be established while creating an opportunity to offend. The youth relies on the perception of a power differential in order to control the situation. Power differential can involve a lack of equal knowledge, awareness, strength, experience, status, authority or even money. Young males who commit acquaintance rape may set up a peer with expensive gifts or activities, overtly or covertly expressing expectations of obligation. Controlling behaviors and criticism may also create a sense of vulnerability that is later exploited.

"Grooming" refers to the process of checking out responses to intrusive behaviors, directives, or boundary violations, or to establishing a level of comfort with the potential victim. "Stalking" refers to the process of observing a potential victim to identify lifestyle patterns, habits, and situations where the potential victim might be most vulnerable. What differentiates these behaviors from other interactions is the motivation and intent being to create the opportunity to offend.

Youth who molest younger children might develop a special relationship involving trust or closeness; establish authority by directing the child to do things or by baby-sitting, acting as a mentor, tutor, or advisor to the child; pay the child for doing favors; "accidentally" touch genitals during horseplay or wrestling; or be aggressive or threatening in nonsexual situations to make the child afraid (and more willing to comply) to avoid being harmed. Some youth who engage in hands-off behaviors may set up a person to be more fearful (the desired reaction) with threatening notes or calls.

In setting up the situation to offend, deception may lessen resistance to, discomfort with, or awareness of the impending offense. A person who questions an invasive touch may be disarmed or confused by insistence that it was unintentional. The youth may later use the same event to induce guilt by pointing out that the person did not question it previously. The youth may rationalize that the person did not mind the invasive touch, or maybe liked it, and thus would like, or not object to, more specific and overt sexual behaviors. In this way, setting up the situation and relationship may also increase the youth's own comfort with the imagined sexual behavior, over-coming doubts or inhibitions.

Readiness to engage in an offense will vary considerably among youth. Some will decide to commit an offense and work to develop the opportunity over a long period of time. Others may experience a strong urge to engage in the behavior and act almost immediately with little forethought. Some youth entertain a fantasy, reject the thoughts as improbable or too risky, then find themselves in a situation where the behavior could be easily accomplished and capitalize on the opportunity. Still other youths may prepare themselves through use of pornography or pictures that have sexual meaning to them and then use a situation that is usually available as the opportunity. Many youth report engaging in some rehearsal, trying out or practicing elements of the anticipated offense to increase success or maximize opportunity.

If an external deterrent prevents or delays access and opportunity, some youth feel frustrated and escalate efforts to engage, while others may feel irritated and act out in some other way. (Planned deterrents can be a component of treatment.) As the pattern habituates, a youth may take more risks, engaging in behaviors when adults are nearby but not in the same room or in public places with minimal cover. Sometimes a greater degree of risk may indicate the youth has normalized the behavior.

Justification Justifying or rationalizing supports the youth's decision to sexually abuse. The youth may be aware that the imagined behavior would not be approved of by others, although juveniles may not realize it is illegal. But if the notion that controlling others is accepted, and the youth feels entitled, the thrill of contemplating something forbidden may be exciting and empowering. Although the thoughts may be distorted, they may be necessary precursors for the youth to overcome or erode internal prohibitions against the behavior and make it seem reasonable and congru-ent with self-image. As offending becomes habituated, the process becomes more automatic. These perceptions are not always temporary and may be difficult to correct in habituated patterns. Even youth who challenged and rejected such justifications in treatment indicate that one of the first things that happens over time is a resumption of their belief in the justifications they had originally developed.

Justification may involve reinterpreting or redefining the behavior as not abusive, attributing positive motivations, viewing victims as willing to participate, or perceiving people as deserving to be abused. Reinterpreting the offense might include, "I'm only teaching him sex so he'll know . . . "; "This isn't abuse; it's fun"; and "It's not abuse because I didn't use my penis, just my finger." Thoughts that attribute positive motivations may include, "I'm only showing how much I care"; "I need to practice what I learned in sex education so I don't look dumb"; and "I just showed them pictures."

Examples of distorting the victim's willingness to engage in the behaviors include, "She loves me and wants to be close to me"; "She knows sitting on my lap arouses me so she must want to have sex with me"; and "He agreed to spend the night with me so he knows what I want." Thoughts that view the victim as deserving might include, "She's dressed all sexy and is obviously asking for it"; "She's a bitch; she deserved it"; and "It happened to me, so it should happen to him."

Objectifying and depersonalizing thoughts also support the justification/rationalization process. Some youth objectify all females or children during this stage. They may be intrusive, violate boundaries or privacy, make demeaning sexual comments, disregard closed bathroom or bedroom doors, look down blouses, pull someone's pants down, attribute sexual motives to others, make catcalls, or tell sexual jokes.

Super-Optimism and the Decision to Act   Super-optimism is a strong belief that one can do what one wants, attain the desired outcome, and avoid detection, interference, or consequences. This process is the *"when"* aspect of the cycle. Overestimating one's abilities contributes to a sense of euphoria, confidence, and power. Typical thoughts might include, "I'm so slick"; "Nothing can stop me now"; and "I get away with everything. No one can catch me."

The belief in success assumes that, if caught, the youth will not experience significant consequences, or if there are consequences, the youth will handle them easily. In this stage, internal prohibitions and potential deterrents are disregarded, cause-and-effect thinking erodes, and the focus is on anticipated compensatory aspects. The decision to act occurs immediately prior to the behavior and can involve a variety of factors. Some youth prefer to view their offense behavior as having "just happened" and may initially deny any conscious decision to actually sexually abuse someone.

An adrenalin rush may occur just prior to the offense: rapid heartbeat, heightened awareness, intense focus, and increased alertness. Affective reactions of excitement, thrill, risk, boldness, and adventure may be associated with the sensation. Some youth experience sexual arousal when fantasizing and setting up an offense and report increased arousal as the time to act nears, contributing to the urge for immediate gratification.

Some youth report substance use contributing to the final decision. Although initially blaming the influence of drugs or alcohol for their behavior, most eventually realize that their decision to use was designed to reduce inhibitions and get the nerve to commit the act, or to increase enjoyment and reduce the sense of personal responsibility. Anxiety, fear, and awareness of consequences are outweighed by the powerful and exhilarating feelings the youth has just before an offense. Most youth report some type of self-statement such as, "I might as well go for it; there won't be a better opportunity."

Consider Theo's experience:

Theo has been fantasizing about exposing himself. He thinks, "It seems kind of weird, but I wonder what it would be like to be naked outdoors. I could feel the sun better. It can't be too weird, I've heard of people who like to moon girls. It would be fun to try it in the park by my house. If I ever tried it, no one would ever have to know." A few days later as he walks through the park, he sees a girl who is two years behind him in school. He thinks, "She looks like someone who would get off on a thrill. The way she's dressed, she'd appreciate seeing a little skin." He blushes and feels embarrassed as he walks home.

During the next week, he thinks more about the girl and wonders how her face would look if he jumped out of a bush naked. He thinks, "She'd be startled, but then she'd say, 'What a hunk.' Maybe she'd want to touch me. I wouldn't want to date a girl like her—too cheap." He starts walking home through the park. Each day he sees her walk home by the creek, but usually she is with a bunch of friends. He'd never do it in front of a lot of people; he'd be too embarrassed. One weekend he walks down by the creek to see what it is like. He finds a big tree he could hide behind if he ever really wanted to do it. Later that week he even hid behind the tree while the girl and her friends walked by, and they never even knew he was there. He thinks, "This could work; too bad I'm too chicken to try it." About a week later he sees the girl enter the park by herself. He gets excited and thinks, "This could be it. She looks lonely; she could probably use a lift. I know how to cheer her up." He feels aroused, and he imagines how seeing him nude will make her feel better. He runs down to the tree and decides to give it a try.

Sexual Abuse Behavior Sexual behaviors that occur without consent, exploiting unequal power, or by way of coercion are abuse. The sexually abusive youth may use tricks, bribes, manipulation, pressure, threats, or force to gain compliance and may experience a sense of empowerment, mastery, and excitement when engaging in sexual abuse behavior.

Sexually abusive behaviors include exposing (flashing); voyeurism (peeping); frottage (rubbing one's genitals against another's body); obscene telephone calls, notes, or instant messages; grabbing sexual body parts; simulating intercourse; genital fondling; oral-genital or oral-anal contact; vaginal or anal penetration via digital, penile, or object insertion; inflicting pain during sexual behaviors; taking pornographic pictures; exposing a child to sexually explicit materials or incomprehensible sexual information; sexual harassment; or sexual contact with animals.

Some youth report more than one type of sexual behavior during the development of their offense behavior patterns. Some youth who engage in child molestation behaviors report prior experience with voyeurism, exhibitionism, and displaying sexually explicit materials to children before they first touched a child. Some youth report offenses of voyeurism, obscene calls, breaking and entering, stealing underwear, or frottage prior to their first rape. A progression of offense behaviors may occur when the youth adds elements to maintain previous levels of excitement, risk, thrill, or arousal. Developing additional sexual interests or experiencing high levels of arousal may also be factors.

The experience of arousal while offending varies among these youth, just as it would among people engaging in normative behaviors. Some report a loss of arousal, erectile dysfunction, or difficulty maintaining an erection or ejaculating. Other youth report remaining aroused throughout the offense. There may be greater arousal prior to the offense, and the youth may masturbate immediately before initiating the offense. Others describe higher levels of arousal subsequent to the offense and may masturbate during review or recall of the incident.

Thoughts during offending also vary greatly. Some youth indicate disappointment or anger because it is not the way they had anticipated. Some congratulate themselves for having planned well. Some maintain a distorted perception of the victim's pleasure about being involved. Others report not being aware of thinking at all, but do recall a surge of adrenalin and arousal. Some report having a backup plan in mind in case the victim struggled or was difficult to control.

The style of the offense also varies. Some intend to inflict pain and might taunt or hit the victim. Others may perceive the interaction as romantic so offer affection or reassurance. Some intend to express anger as part of the offense, so may verbalize and act out anger. Some carry a weapon that they may or may not use during the offense. If a weapon is used, the youth may show it to elicit fear or compliance or use it to harm the victim. Some incidents may involve a ritual or a fetish behavior. The youth may wear certain clothing for each offense, request specific behaviors on the part of each victim, inflict mutilation or punishment that is consistent to each offense, or take a trophy, or souvenir, from each victim. Fetish behaviors involving clothing, urination, defecation, or cross-dressing might be part of an abusive ritual for the youth. Behaviors that the youth considers arousing, amusing, or lucky may be part of the behavior style.

Typically, something will be said or done to prevent disclosure during or immediately after the offense. There are often higher levels of coercion used to keep the secret than were necessary to carry out the offense. Threats or playing on a sense of guilt, loyalty, or victim blaming are common. For example: "If you tell anyone, I'll be in big trouble"; "Keep this a secret, or your family will be hurt"; "Let's keep this a special secret between us"; "Don't tell, what you did would really upset your mom"; or "Nobody will believe you if you tell." Offenses against strangers may involve some sort of disguise, such as a mask or a hat, to prevent being identified. Some rapists have forced victims to shower or douche to eliminate evidence.

The effect of justifications and distortions seem to diminish toward the end of the offense, so anxiety regarding consequences may start right away. Some wonder why they are doing it, others think it is wrong, and still others worry about being caught. They attempt to reassure themselves by thinking again of their justifications, or they direct some anger or frustration toward the victim, as Cassie did.

Cassie was excited when she came to babysit. She couldn't wait for the parents to leave because tonight was the night. After she told the older boy it was okay for him to play outside until dark, she told the younger boy, Nathan, not to be upset because they would do something special. She turned the TV to a cable movie that had some sexual scenes in it and pulled Nathan next to her on the couch. When the couple on the screen kissed, she said, "I bet your girlfriend would like it if you knew how to kiss like that." He grinned, and she asked him if he had ever learned how. When he said no, she offered to teach him so that he could make his girlfriend happy. He looked eager, so she told him how to kiss and offered to let him practice on her so he could get it just right. She put her tongue in his mouth and told him to do that back to her. She put his hand on her breast and told him how to rub and squeeze it. Then she told him his girlfriend would probably touch his penis and offered to show him how. She began touching his penis over his clothes before he could answer her. As she pulled his pants down, she was explaining about how much girls preferred to touch a bare penis. She continued to touch him and then put her mouth on his penis. Then she told him that he always had to return the favor if he wanted to be popular with the girls. She took her pants off and showed him how to rub her genitalia, then pulled his head down and told him to stick his tongue in her vagina. When he resisted, she told him he better do it or she would tell his mom about the extra cookies he had taken last time she babysat. He started crying, but he did it. Then she masturbated while she held him close and made him watch her. When she was done, she used a mean voice and told him that if he ever told, she would go to his classroom, and for show-and-tell, she would describe how he wet his bed every night.

THE INTEGRATION PHASE

Following the offense, the youth must assimilate and integrate the experience of sexually abusing someone into their understanding of themselves and the world. The good feelings of the offense may last a few minutes or much longer, but when the excitement, thrill, and arousal diminish, the youth may attempt to recapture a feeling of adequacy and satisfaction. Despite thinking the offense was a success, fear of getting caught and potential consequences are part of the post-offense experience. The youth may also begin to experience some ambivalence about what he has done. Hindsight raises doubts that threaten the sense of adequacy, control, and empowerment. Struggling internally to manage the anxiety, defenses work again to control and suppress the anxiety (see Figure 9.3).

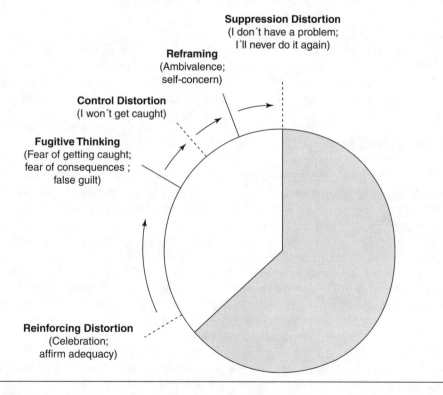

Figure 9.3   The Integration Phase of the Sexual Abuse Cycle
Source: Reprinted by permission of RSA, Inc.

The Reinforcing Distortion   The youth may question why the act did not measure up to the fantasies and expectations. Maintaining a feeling of being in control requires self-reassurance and strengthening the justifications that allowed the youth to engage in the behavior. For some, celebrating their success may suppress anxiety. The youth is convinced that if there were mistakes, he was not at fault. Typical thoughts include, "I pulled it off, I really turned her on"; "I sure made her pay"; and "He liked it, I could tell."

Fugitive Thinking   Despite self-reassurance, thoughts and concerns about getting caught arise. There may be doubt about whether the victim will tell or there may be some regret for committing the behavior. Knowing offending is something that others view as wrong and thinking about interpersonal consequences creates anxiety, even if the youth is not feeling bad about himself. Typical thoughts may include, "What if she tells? I could get into trouble"; "My friends will call me names"; "Could I go to prison?"; and "I'll be grounded for life." The more habituated youth may move through this stage rapidly as previously developed justifications and distortions have become firmly held beliefs. For youth who have less habituated patterns, there may be significant anxiety related to self-image.

In trying to suppress the anxiety, many youth make emotional bargains with themselves, such as: "If I don't get caught I'll never do it again"; or "If I do it again, I deserve to be caught"; and "If I get away with it this time, I'll go to church with my mom Sunday." Interestingly, some youth indicate they only worry for a few days. If they have not been reported by then, they believe they are safe.

The Control Distortion   If the youth becomes convinced that the victim has not or will not disclose the abuse, it seems to strengthen beliefs about controlling others. Not being caught reaffirms the distortions that support the behavior: the victim enjoyed or deserved the offense; likes, trusts, or fears the youth; no one would believe it, and so forth. Thoughts that reinforce the sense of control might include, "I really scared her, so she won't dare tell"; "He promised he wouldn't tell so I'm okay"; "I don't have to worry; who'd believe a five-year-old over me?"; and "Why sweat it? She won't even remember what I look like."

Reframing   As fears of discovery diminish, the youth may still be left with some ambivalence about himself and the incident, alternating between self-doubt and criticism or self-praise and reassurance. The internal conflict can cause additional anxiety and negative self appraisal. Some wonder if they are "weirdos" or perverts— if they are as bad as the "creeps" they hear about on the news. Those with prior offenses, who had promised themselves they would never do it again, may doubt their ability to control themselves, questioning their ability to deny their urges and feeling controlled by the compulsive quality of their behavior. There may be thoughts such as, "I shouldn't have done it," which more likely relates to potential consequences than victim harm. Although they do not typically show extensive concern about the impact to the victim, some do perceive that it was hurtful.

The Denial Defense   The final stage in the sexual abuse cycle allows the youth to enhance sense of self and suppress anxiety. Self-talk is about controlling behavior rather than being driven by urges. Self-doubts are countered with thoughts about being a good person, unlike criminals and perverts, and able to control oneself and one's destiny.

Minimization, projection, and intellectualization make it possible to think that the incident is really not a problem so self-doubts have no basis. Thoughts characteristic of this distortion include, "It's no big deal; I'm in control"; "I'll just stop doing this, and I won't have to worry about it"; "I'm not weird; I care about them and I was gentle"; "I'll never do it again"; and "I'm okay; I don't have to worry." Eventually, convinced the behavior is not a problem, or that it won't be because it will never happen again, denial protects the self and the youth can believe they are okay. This makes it possible to return to a normal level of functioning.

Despite the youth's suppression of anxiety and concerns, nothing has actually addressed the issues or the original sense of powerlessness and inadequacy that overwhelmed them, so the youth may be even more vulnerable to subsequent interactions or situations that may elicit similar perceptions. There may be increased defensiveness and protection of the self, resulting in sensitivity and misinterpretation of more types of situations. Because of the gratification experienced with the compensatory response style, it is likely the pattern will repeat the next time something overwhelms the youth's ability to cope.

CONCLUSION

As has been suggested in previous chapters, the pattern is not always pathological, and the impediments to more functional and less harmful choices may be static, stable, or dynamic. Deficits in developmental skills or ecological resources, psychiatric disorders or learning disabilities, or trauma effects from early life may all factor into the development of defensive strategies and become problematic. Youth can be helped to modify cognitions, arousal, and coping styles that have supported abusive behaviors in the past as well as those that might increase risk in the future. By recognizing signs of a progression toward abusive behaviors in current functioning, it becomes possible to develop interventions to interrupt the pattern.

In working with sexually abusive youth, therapists need to consider each youth's unique characteristics. Therapists can use the sexual abuse cycle to explore the situations, thoughts, feelings, and behaviors relevant to past offenses, and to develop an understanding of patterns with the individual; however, looking for common characteristics does not suggest they are always present. For some, the simpler cycles illustrated in Chapter 8 may be most relevant to past offenses, while for others, many aspects of the more habituated sexual abuse cycle may be recognized. It is in knowing what to look for that the cycle offers opportunities for good diagnostics and both prevention and intervention.

REFERENCES

Abel, G., & Blanchard, E. (1974). The role of fantasy in the treatment of sexual deviation. *Archives of General Psychiatry, 30*, 467–475.

Becker, J., Hunter, J. A., Stein, R. M., & Kaplan, M. S. (1989). Factors associated with erection in adolescent sex offenders. *Journal of Psychopathology and Behavioral Assessment, 11*(4), 353–362.

Becker, J. V., and Kaplan, M. S. (1993). Cognitive-behavioral treatment of the juvenile sex offender. In H. E. Barbaree, W. L. Marshall, & S. M. Hudson (Eds.), *The juvenile sex offender* (pp. 264–277). New York: Guilford Press.

Becker, J., Stein, R. M., Kaplan, M. S., & Cunningham-Rathner, J. (1992). Erection response characteristics of adolescent sex offenders. *Annals of Sex Research, 5*, 81–86.

Berenson, D. (1987). *Outline of the thinking errors approach*. Unpublished manuscript.

Carnes, P. (1983). *Out of the shadows: Understanding sexual addiction*. Minneapolis, MN: Comp Care Publications.

Freeman-Longo, R. E. (1982). Sexual learning and experience among adolescent sexual offenders. *International Journal of Offender Therapy and Comparative Criminology, 26*(2), 235–241.

Hunter, J., & Goodwin, D. (1992). The clinical utility of satiation therapy with juvenile sexual offenders: Variations and efficacy. *Annals of Sex Research, 5,* 71–80.

Hunter, J., & Santos, D. (1990). Use of specialized cognitive-behavioral therapies in the treatment of adolescent sexual offenders. *Journal of Offender Therapy and Comparative Criminology, 34,* 239–248.

Kaemingk, K., Koselka, M., Becker, J. V., & Kaplan, M. S. (1995). Age and adolescent sexual offender arousal. *Sexual Abuse: A Journal of Research and Treatment, 7,* 249–257.

Knopp, F. H. (1982). *Remedial intervention in adolescent sex offenses: Nine program descriptions.* Orwell, VT: Safer Society Press.

Lane, S., & Zamora, P. (1978). *Syllabus materials from inservice training on adolescent sex offenders.* Closed Adolescent Treatment Center, Division of Youth Services: Denver, CO. Unpublished document.

Lane, S., & Zamora, P. (1982). *Working with juvenile sex offenders.* Presentation at the National Conference on Sexual Aggression, Denver, CO.

Lane, S., & Zamora, P. (1984). A method for treating the adolescent sex offender. In R. Mathias, P. Demuro, & R. Allinson (Eds.), *Violent juvenile offenders* (pp. 347–354). San Francisco, CA: National Council on Crime and Delinquency.

Malamuth, N., Sockloskie, R., Koss, M., & Tanaka, J. (1991). The characteristics of aggressors against women: Testing a model using a national sample of college students. *Journal of Consulting and Clinical Psychology, 59,* 670–681.

Marshall, W. L. (1979). Satiation therapy: Procedure for reducing deviant sexual arousal. *Journal of Applied Behavioral Analysis, 12,* 10–22.

McGuire, R. J., Carlyle, J. M., & Young, B. G. (1965). Sexual deviations as conditional behavior: A hypothesis. *Behavior Research and Therapy, 2,* 185–190.

Money, J. (1986). *Love maps.* New York: Irvington Publishers.

Ryan, G. (1989). Victim to victimizer: Rethinking victim treatment. *Journal of Interpersonal Violence, 4*(3), 325–341.

Seto, M. C., Lalumiere, M. L., & Blanchard, R. (2000). The discriminative validity of a phallometric test for pedophilic interests among adolescent sex offenders against children. *Psychological Assessment, 12,* 319–327.

Seto, M. C., Murphy, W. D., Page, J., & Ennis, L. (2003). Detecting anomalous sexual interests among juvenile sex offenders. In R. A. Prentky, E. S. Janus, & M. C. Seto (Eds.), *Annals of the New York Academy of Sciences, vol. 189: Understanding and managing sexually coercive behavior* (pp. 118–130). New York: New York Academy of Sciences.

Yochelson, S., & Samenow, S. (1976). *The criminal personality.* Northvale, NJ: Aronson.

CHAPTER 10

The Families of Sexually Abusive Youth

GAIL RYAN

EXPLORING THEORIES AND research regarding the development of sexuality, deviance, and dysfunction suggests that many risk factors converge within the juvenile's early life experience. The family's role in shaping the beliefs and behavior patterns of its children is recognized as a primary influence in child development. It is within this earliest holding environment that the infant's view of the world and basic assumptions are formed. The early caregivers may enhance or hamper the child's growth and development either overtly or covertly. As the child's world expands and experiences broaden, extra-familial influences impact development and continue to shape the individual's beliefs and behavior, but the infant's earliest experience remains the core and is thought to be the source of the internal working model for future relationships.

Some theorists, such as Yochelson and Samenow (1976), disregard infant experiences and family influences in the development of the irresponsible patterns that support criminal behavior. Their view is based on observation of discrepant outcomes among siblings raised in the same family. The notion that having criminal and noncriminal children emerge from the same family negates the role and influence of early life fails to recognize the unique experience and individuality of each child. Siblings are not identical at birth, and each child is born into circumstances and expectations that are unique (Klaus & Kennell, 1976). Although external factors may remain somewhat constant, personal and internal circumstances do not. The most dysfunctional or inadequate family may produce a very successful child, while a family that appears more adequate and functional may raise a very deviant child. Each dyadic relationship within the family is unique, and each child's needs and perceptions are personal.

An infinite number of variables may be relevant to abusive behaviors. Research to date suggests some hypotheses regarding specific risk factors for the development of sexually abusive behavior: a nonnormative sexual environment in the home (Gilgun, 1988); sexualized models of compensation or coping (Cortoni & Marshall, 2001; Lane, 1991; Ryan, 1989); the experiences of sexual victimization, humiliation, or trauma

(Burton, 2003; Freeman-Longo, 1982; Miner & Crimmins, 1997; Prentky et al., 1989); traumatic sexualization (Finkelhor, 1986); abuse, neglect, and witnessing domestic violence (Widom & Williams, 1996); living in unsafe environments, combined with a lack of empathic care (Steele, 1987); early parental loss (Ryan, 1987); inconsistent care (Prentky et al., 1989); and the lack of a confidant in childhood (Gilgun, 1988). In prospective studies of child abuse victims, Widom (1996) and Williams (1995) found that physically abused and neglected children were even more at risk to manifest sexually abusive behaviors than sexually abused children. Hunter (1996) suggests that all forms of maltreatment represent a risk of abusive outcomes; and Burton (2003) and Miner and Crimmons (1997) state that particular aspects of victimization increase the risk of subsequent offending. These factors point either inclusively or exclusively to early childhood experience and parental influences. The dysfunctional cycle (Ryan, 1989) points specifically to factors reminiscent of earlier life experience as well as cognitive behavioral patterns that reflect mal-adaptive coping styles. Many of these issues were discussed in earlier chapters. The author does not suggest that parents are directly causal, but rather that circum-stances, experiences, and parental models in the early life environment may allow or support the development of sexual deviance or fail to develop the empathy and inhibitions that prevent exploitative behavior.

This chapter describes some of the common characteristics of families of sexually abusive youth and explores the potential of family involvement in treatment. Chapter 20 will address strategies to assess and treat the family.

RESEARCH

Family variables in 1,000 cases of sexually abusive youth referred to specialized treatment programs were described by the Uniform Data Collection System of the National Adolescent Perpetration Network at the Kempe Center in Denver. This database reported parental loss in 57% of cases and described overrepresentations of family variables and dysfunctions that are likely to have an impact on child development. Parental violence was reported by 28% and over half of those juveniles had witnessed spousal abuse. Substance abuse is reported for 27% of the mothers and 43% of the fathers. Only 27.8% of the juveniles were living with both natural parents at the time of their offense, even though most were living in households with two parental figures. The evaluating clinicians rated family functioning as "below average," "inappropriate," or "dysfunctional" in 86% of their caseload (Ryan, 1988; Ryan, Miyoshi, Metzner, Krugman, & Fryer, 1996).

Lankester and Meyer (1986, 1988), reporting on the families of 153 sexually abusive youth seen at the University of Washington in Seattle, found that 64% of family members had been physically or sexually abused as children. They urge that families be assessed for the "meaning of the sex offense behavior" within the context of the family dynamics and structure. They suggest dynamic distinctions between chaotic and rigid families and structural distinctions in single-parent and blended families. Kaplan, Becker, and Cunningham-Rathner (1988) describe the parents of 27 male adolescent incest perpetrators from the New York City ghettos and reported that these parents underreport the physical and sexual abuse of their sons, were often victims of abuse in their own childhood, and denied the incestuous behavior of their sons. Smith and Israel (1987), studying the family characteristics of 25 sibling incest perpetrators, describe distant, inaccessible parents; parental stimulation of the sexual climate in the home; and family secrets, especially extramarital affairs.

O'Brien (1989) noted important similarities and differences in family characteristics when comparing sibling incest perpetrators, juvenile extra-familial child molesters, and juveniles who assault peers or adults. In his study, over half of the families in all three groups reported substance abuse. Mothers of the sibling incest perpetrators were significantly more likely to have been victims of sexual abuse than the mothers in the two other groups. Sexual abuse (in addition to current juvenile offending) was more common in the incestuous families than the other two groups (22.4% of sibling incest group). Physical abuse was most prevalent in the incestuous group (61.2%), somewhat less in the extra-familial molester group (44.69%), and even less in the nonchild perpetrator group (36.8%). Case managers (using Beaver's levels of family functioning as a guide) rated less than 14% of the families in the study "healthy," with 52.5% of the incestuous group, 45.5% of the extra-familial group, and 34.5% of the nonchild perpetrator group rated "severely disturbed" (O'Brien, 1989).

Murray (1996) explored the relationship between natural fathers and their sons in a sample of 18 sexually abusive youths and found evidence of strained relationships lacking in warmth, closeness, and nurturing. He notes that many sexually abusive youths have no relationship at all with their natural fathers—often having never met them and sometimes not even knowing their name. Kobayashi, Sales, Becker, Figueredo, & Kaplan (1995) examined perceived parental deviance and parent-child bonding. The quality of modeling, relationships, and the child's perception of what is normal are all affected by deviance and criminality in parental figures.

Research is seriously deficient concerning the role of family variables, as is evaluation of the impact of family therapy in the treatment of sexually abusive youths. There is no evidence of direct causation on a one-to-one basis but rather a cluster of factors that appear to play some role. Further empirical research is needed in order to distinguish whether family variables increase the risk of sexually deviant development and which variables are most relevant to successful treatment outcomes. There is, however, a wealth of published information that describes incestuous family dynamics (Finkelhor, 1986) and clinical experience provides a basis for describing similarities and differences among the families of sexually abusive youth. There is also literature relevant to intervention within the families of chronically delinquent youth (Elliot, 1998), and family violence (Straus, 1990). Many theorists have contributed to the conceptualization of distinctive variables among families. This chapter addresses only the relevance of family dynamics that seem to accompany or be relevant to juvenile sexual offending. Sexual risk factors may be present within the family (such as nonnormative sexual environment or multigenerational incest), and help to understand why some youth might have been more inclined to develop sexual behavior problems rather than, or in addition to, other dysfunctional behaviors. However, the exploration and understanding of the family system is often less related to the development of sexual deviance and more related to the tolerance of abusive, nonempathic attitudes and interactions and patterns of coercive or abusive interaction and maladaptive coping.

A CONCEPTUAL TYPOLOGY

The family system includes the beliefs and expectations of its members and is the holding environment for the developing child. Conte (1986), in his critical analysis of the family system's approach to the problem of sexual abuse, stated that the system "describes function but is not causal" (p. 132). The literature on incest describes family dynamics that are common to the problem of sexual abuse in general. Some dynamics may relate to the developmental history of individuals who become victims or perpetrators, some relate to the roles and interactions that become internal working models for future relationships, and some relate to the system that allows or supports the occurrence of sexually deviant experience or behavior. Maladaptive coping styles are often multigenerational.

Just as dysfunction is often studied more than successful functioning, family characteristics and dynamics are also explored in the search to explain the problem, rather than a search to explain the absence of the problem. There is a growing body of literature describing family and parental variables that support healthy growth and development and successful functioning. Assessment and description of important aspects of the families of juveniles who sexually offend will benefit from attention to the strengths and successes as well as the malfunction. To date, the family and parental strengths research has recognized broad categories and global factors that correlate with children being more or less successful. (For example, research can show children whose families eat meals together tend to be more successful, or children who watch less television do better than peers who watch more.)

Research cited in Chapters 4 and 7 captured some of the risks and assets of parenting and the child's experience of care and interaction in the family. However, in evaluation and treatment planning, it is often the problematic characteristics that are the focus. Clinicians are trained to identify and address problems, not the absence of problems. It is important to note, that although the following discussion of common characteristics and subgroup differences focuses on problematic factors, not all families will exhibit problems warranting treatment and many can be valuable assets in the work with the youth. Most will need education and support dealing with the discovery that their child has sexually abused someone, but just as the state of the art for treating the youth relies on individualized, differential diagnosis and treatment planning, the same is true of the family system.

COMMON FAMILY CHARACTERISTICS

Some common characteristics of the families of sexually abusive youths are ineffective communication and emotional impoverishment; lack of emotional recognition, expression, and responses; dangerous secrets; distorted or disordered attachments; misattributions; and a history of disruptions in care and function. The role of the juvenile who offends has often been to act as a receptacle for negative feelings in the family (especially shame, guilt, and anxiety), and the sexual abuse may become the presenting symptom in a long history of acting-out behaviors.

Some family members show no affect at all—only stone faces that avoid eye contact or carry a blank gaze. Sometimes one or more family members show extreme affect unreasonable or out of context to the situation at hand (such as a perpetual smile and chuckle without depth or relevance or hysterical reactions out of proportion to the most minor difficulties). In both extremes, the family is not emotionally supportive or nourishing; feelings have been denied, suppressed, or distorted until family members have few meaningful labels for emotions. Affective cues may be either absent or incongruent, making it difficult to assess how others are feeling.

The juvenile's behavior reflects the myths, secrets, and beliefs of the family that have served to mediate, elicit, rationalize, or suppress various behaviors in the family members. Faulty beliefs and incorrect information have not been subjected to validation and correction because of the denial of feelings and the secrecy surrounding behavioral dysfunctions. The secrets that fester within these families are often pervasive and may span generations. The proverbial skeletons in the closet include more than just sexual abuse. Denial may have protected many forms of dysfunction, including substance abuse; physical, sexual, and emotional abuse; criminal records; mental illness; physical infirmities; and social, marital, and vocational failures. Not only are these secrets kept within the family, they are kept from the family itself. It is not only extra-familial judgment that is feared but also the secret itself. The family is often superstitious and rigid in the belief that the secrets will be more painful and powerful if they are acknowledged or discussed. The family believes the secrets are dangerous not in the keeping but in the telling.

Although the degree of attachment in the parent-child relationship may vary tremendously, the attachments that exist within the family are often distorted. Negative attachments result from role reversals, sexualized attention (Haynes-Seman & Krugman, 1989), and bonds that are rooted in negative, shared emotions. Intimacy may be misrepresented, tending to be exploitative rather than giving and sharing. Negative attachments may reflect the parents' own childhood dysfunctions or the current fearful affective state. Attachment alone fails to describe family function. It is the quality of attachment that becomes the issue.

Disruptions in care may result from family crisis, illness, hospitalization, incarceration, out-of-home placement, divorce, abandonment, or death. Foster placements and adoption, as well as extended care by various relatives, are common. Maternal stress and depressive episodes in the early years, as well as paternal absence, are characteristic of instability and interruptions that affect family function. The resulting infant perception may well be one of chaos and isolation rather than connection and control. The juvenile's ability to form empathic relationships is hampered by affective parental neglect or insensitive care-giving. (The issue of empathic development was discussed in Chapter 7.)

Other patterns frequently identifiable in the families of sexually abusive youth include sexualized problem solving or compensation, objectification and exploitation, and the pairing of intimacy and aggression. Sexualized models of coping may be a risk factor; and Smith and Israel (1987) have reported high rates of extramarital sexual relations in the families of sibling incest. Objectification refers to the depersonalization of individuals (being treated as an object, used to gratify the needs of others) and relates to the chronic exploitation of family members. Sexual objectification may be supported by exposure to or use of pornographic materials in the home. Exploitation may also relate to the imposition of roles, including role reversals, in order to meet the needs of the family. Intimacy and aggression are confused in the occurrence of physical abuse in the home, whether spouse abuse or child abuse.

These common characteristics in family structure and function relate to many of the families throughout the following typological conceptualization. Of course, not every sexually abusive youth's family fits any discrete category. Every family has its own unique history of strengths and weaknesses that can be discovered over the course of time. Nevertheless, some distinctions that may have implications relative to the origins and the correction of sexual abuse patterns may be made more clearly and can be useful in guiding the therapist's exploration of the client's history. These dynamics are not limited to incest families but seem to be present in many instances of extra-familial child molestation, rape, and hands-off offense cases as well. Research is needed to further distinguish the significant variables.

THE EXPLOITATIVE OR COERCIVE FAMILY

In the exploitative family, there is no unconditional love. Parents use their children to meet their own needs and may have very unrealistic expectations for their offspring. These expectations may be negative (the child is expected to be bad and fail) or extreme (the child is pushed to excel toward very high standards or expected to do things beyond their ability). Children's experience in the exploitative family is that they are cared for only to the extent that they are able to meet the needs of others. Because their validation is external, they fail to develop an internal sense of self-worth and instead develop a belief in an external locus of control. Objectification may be exaggerated into ownership thinking, and parents may view family members as property. The juvenile experiences that relationships are bartered: Every act of nurturance has its price. Needs are met through the manipulation of others, not as a result of communication and caring, and empathic interaction is rare. The risk of externalizing behaviors and compensatory control-seeking is clear.

Coercive styles of parenting and family interactions have been examined and described in the literature on family violence. Coercive styles are often characteristic of the exploitive family system, and must be identified and defined as contributing to the juvenile's learning coercive styles as a normal model of interacting and getting one's needs met. Coercion goes beyond the barter and deserve factors to add the threat of something bad happening as well as the absence of what is good.

THE RIGID OR ENMESHED FAMILY

Some families are secretive and socially isolated. The home is buttressed against intrusion, and there is very little social support or system contact. Family members collude in reassuring each other that they do not need or want extra-familial contacts—that the family is self-sufficient. As one mother conceptualized enmeshment, "We feed off of one another." Inquiries, investigations, and interventions are experienced as intrusive.

The rigid family often has many secrets and taboos, which are quite binding and serve to protect the family system. Enmeshment clouds the boundaries and roles of family members. Parent-child relationships may be symbiotic, with separation and individuation issues very confused. The driving force seems to be extreme insecurity and codependency. Family members fear abandonment and believe changes and disclosures will literally tear the family apart.

Lankester and Meyer (1986) describe "almost no overt expression of affection" in these families. Moreover, mothers may become overly involved with the son in order to achieve emotional intimacy, and the repressed father may implicitly accept the son's aggressive behavior. In single-mother households, mother and son may maintain a codependency that produces a constant anxiousness. The sexual offense in some cases may represent an attempt by the son to create distance in the mother-son relationship (Lankester & Meyer, 1986) and overcome the rigid controls. These are often homes that seethe with anxiety, and intrusion from the outside threatens to send everything flying out of control. Parents may impose rigid controls at home in an effort to hold everyone together because they feel helpless in relationships outside the family. Locus of control is extremely externalized, and extra-familial occurrences are blamed on the fates. The juvenile may connect anxiety to intimacy and perceive nonanxious periods as boring and intolerable. The youth's ability to enjoy relaxation may be very limited, and the absence of anxiety may reduce them to the "zero state," which Yochelson and Samenow (1976) note is a characteristic of criminal persons. Such a state is intolerable because the void of affect portends annihilation or death. For some, the anxiety associated with the risk of consequences for negative behavior may be a normalizing or reinforcing state rather than a deterrent.

THE CHAOTIC OR DISENGAGED FAMILY

The multiproblem family often has a long history of chronic dysfunctions and perpetual crises. The chaotic qualities are often related to extreme immaturity as well as poor life skills. Parents set an example of acting-out behaviors that are reflected in the children's own dysfunctional coping. These families may lack attachments, and family members appear unconnected. Affectionate expressions and relationships tend to be shallow and indiscriminate, and attachments are insecure or avoidant, placing members at risk for dangerous and exploitative encounters outside the family as well. Co-addictive patterns contribute to ineffective interventions within the family, and disengagement may leave children bereft and adrift, without the secure base of healthy attachments. Supervision is often poor, and there is little expectation of order or control. In describing this type of family, Lankester and Meyer (1986) point out, "Generational boundaries and members' personal space are not respected . . . intrusiveness and lack of privacy are the norm . . . parents are grossly dysfunctional . . . [the child] is thrust into the role of parent . . . dysfunctional modeling . . . no negative sanctions."

In a chaotic or disengaged family, the juvenile's experience may create anxiety because of the inconsistency and lack of structure, and the offense may represent an attempt to connect in a relationship perceived as controllable. Ritualization may create a structure in the abusive behavior or relationship that is reassuring to the young perpetrator, and the secrecy may be perceived as a welcome boundary around the youth.

THE "PERFECT" FAMILY

The "perfect" family initially looks functional. The youth's sexually abusive behavior appears to be an aberration in an otherwise ideal family. The marriage, living arrangements, and work history are stable, with parents in traditional patriarchal roles: career fathers and "apple pie" mothers with good social skills and community involvement. The children are succeeding in school, although they may have identified learning disabilities and require some tutoring. Parents are genuinely concerned about their juvenile's problem and appear cooperative with authorities.

No family, however, can be perfect. Over time, assessment reveals that the initial appearance is an image that lacks quality and depth. Family members are invested in maintaining the "perfect" image, and each member plays out his or her assigned role with consistent dedication. Underlying the image of bliss and contentment is an intense fear of family breakdown. Nonverbal collusion exists that denies dissonance in the family, and a convenient amnesia wipes away unpleasant realities. Communication regarding emotionally charged issues is suppressed, and problem solving is dealt with at a superficial behavioral level. The roots of the family system are often the parents' own survival of an inadequate, abusive, or deprived childhood, which they have consciously vowed to overcome. These are parents who have tried very hard to do right, feel tremendous guilt and responsibility, and are adamant in their defense of their current family.

The appearance of cooperation and compliance in arranging treatment for the sexually abusive youth meets a stone wall of resistance to actually working in treatment; control issues are paramount. Yet often this family eventually becomes able to overcome its distrust and engage in a meaningful exploration of change. These are families who are initially resentful of the intrusive implications inherent in family therapy but often emerge from treatment with positive feelings. The sexually abusive youth has fulfilled the role of facilitating a necessary (though feared) period of growth for the family.

THE PREVIOUSLY ADEQUATE FAMILY

Another family system that presents for treatment of sexually abusive youth is a blended family where, through marriage or adoption, a previously adequate family has become dysfunctional because of new dynamics. Lankester and Meyer (1986) note the dynamics of blended families wherein "older children perceive themselves losing status [and] jealousy or anger gets acted out" on the younger children. Perlmutter, Engel, and Sager (1982) have also considered "loosened sexual boundaries in remarried families" (p. 90), citing the lack of biological and developmental ties, as well as the sexual atmosphere during the new couple's romance, as factors that may increase risk of sexual behavior among children in the household. Although these families' histories are unremarkable and the juvenile's sexual problems may have originated outside the current family system, the family arrives in treatment severely damaged and distressed. The defense mechanisms that protect individuals from the pain of chronic family problems may be lacking, and family trust and function have often been severely affected by the discovery of the youth's sexually abusive behavior. These families are sometimes the hardest to engage in family therapy because they fail to acknowledge the impact of the juvenile's dysfunction on other family members. Adoptive parents are often the "walking wounded," who feel tremendous guilt in their failure to prevent or correct the problem behavior and are at risk for relinquishment, abandonment, or family dissolution if they cannot be engaged in the treatment process. The previously adequate family can be torn apart by the betrayal and distrust that are inherent in sexual abuse.

IMPLICATIONS OF THE TYPOLOGY

Understanding as much as possible about the family of origin of the youth is important to his or her therapy. Conte (1986) had suggested assessment of the pathology of individuals within the family, the pathology of interactions within the family, and the pathology of extra-familial systems. Thus, a distinction evolves among those variables that may be causal (contributing to development or generation of the problem), supportive (allowing or maintaining the problem), or consequential (resultant or reactive to the problem). The causal variables may be most basic to the change process, the supportive variables most relevant to relapse prevention, and the consequential variables most pressing in crisis interventions. As theory and practice have evolved, one would now also be advised to assess the strengths of individuals, interactions, and the systems surrounding the family.

Although this typology has focused on the dysfunctional elements within the families of sexually abusive youth, the strengths are evident as well. Intense family loyalty is often a characteristic that can be mobilized on behalf of the juvenile in order to facilitate the treatment process. Defensive characteristics are evidence of the commitment of these families to protect family members and to survive the problems they face. The parents' own history may reveal severe abuse or adversity, and the strengths that have brought them through painful experiences may serve them now and be mobilized in the current crisis.

The parents' own survivorship may be the basis for hope in times that seem hopeless. The family's genuine concern often motivates its members to explore painful issues, and many are willing to participate in treatment. The juvenile's treatment is enhanced by tapping into the family's strengths and resources.

The disclosure of sexual perpetration by a son or daughter impacts the whole family. Parents who have consciously or unconsciously harbored concerns about their child's sexualized behavior have their worst fears confirmed. Parents who have successfully denied the child's progression into sexual deviance or other dysfunctions are shocked and dismayed, feeling a complete sense of helplessness relative to the discovery of the perceived aberration. The family dynamics that accompany the development of the behavior problem are often multigenerational, and the disclosure confronts the parents' denial of victimization and dysfunction in their own life experience. Families may initially shelter siblings from the painful disclosure in an effort to protect them; nevertheless, other children most assuredly feel the anxiety and secrecy surrounding the parents and perpetrator in the family. Siblings' fear of the unknown can be more harmful than knowing what has occurred.

Initial disclosures often only partially describe the extent and duration of the abuse. Sibling victims of the disclosed offending must wait to see if the bad things that the abusive sibling had threatened them with will actually occur, and non-disclosing sibling victims remain anxious about the possible discovery of their own victimization. The extreme reactions and overwhelming consequences of partial disclosure fuel the fear of further disclosures within the family. Typological characteristics are often revealed in the observation of the family's response to the crisis at hand.

THE POTENTIAL ROLE OF THE FAMILY IN THE JUVENILE'S TREATMENT

Four significant areas of the sexually abusive youth's treatment may be enhanced by family involvement: the family is a rich source of developmental history, may be a primary source of supervision, may be able to support the juvenile's treatment and the maintenance of change, and may be capable of making alterations in the family structure and function that facilitate change and reduce risk situations for the juvenile. The full engagement and optimal work of the family in all of these areas may improve the prognosis of successful treatment and minimize risk. However, even less than full cooperation and minimal involvement of the family can be beneficial in facilitating understanding and change in the juvenile (Thomas, 1988). (Comprehensive family treatment is described in Chapter 20.)

DEVELOPMENTAL HISTORY

The abusive youth's developmental history provides a good basis for identifying his or her beliefs and assumptions, as well as sensitive risk factors, and thus helps to provide the phenomenological understanding of the sexually abusive youth. Although it is possible to identify beliefs that support problematic behaviors through self-report or the inference from observation, many juveniles have difficulty articulating their thoughts and have poor writing and communication skills, so the identification of thinking patterns can be slow and arduous. The youth's difficulty in articulating thoughts is compounded by patterns of denial and a reluctance to report thoughts that are associated with painful or shameful memories or events. Some of the most illuminating keys to understanding the juvenile's view of the world may lie in preverbal memories or unspoken family beliefs, which are most difficult to define because they were experienced without language and may be recorded in perceptions and feelings that the youth has never been consciously aware of.

When the family of origin is available and can be engaged in a thorough report of the juvenile's infancy and early childhood, as well as the circumstances in the family during those years, a wealth of information becomes available that may offer clues to the present and the past. Understanding in three major areas is facilitated: the client's view of the world, developmental deficits, and the origins of sensitive feelings and evidence in their experience that may support their beliefs. Much of the important developmental information may appear irrelevant to the current behavior problem and is reported by the family either in avoidance of the perceived problem areas or in annoyance or boredom with the therapist's apparently rambling investigation.

Worldview The juvenile's view of the world has evolved from birth and is the basis for both conscious and unconscious decision making. This worldview is often a combination of the infant's experience and the parents' own views. The child who is born into a nurturing and trustworthy home experiences the world as a logical and empathic place wherein struggles are rewarded, consequences are consistent, and needs are satisfied through communication, perseverance, and patience. It may not be as important that the caregiver succeeds in meeting every need of the infant as that the infant perceives the caregiver's appreciation of and concern for the infant's needs and his or her willingness to struggle with the infant to achieve adequate communication and care. However, the infant who is born into crisis or confusion, whose needs are not appreciated, and whose struggle to communicate needs meets with inconsistent responses, a lack of regard, or painful consequences experiences the world as incomprehensible and uncontrollable, learns that struggles are not rewarded, and comes to believe that he must take what he needs without regard from others. The infant who achieves trust and empathy may later be betrayed, but the view of the world remains more functional than the infant whose worldview lacks basic trust and empathy.

Developmental Deficits Lack of trust and the inability to recognize, express, and respond to cues of emotions and needs are developmental deficits that originate in infancy and may be revealed in the family's reports of circumstances surrounding the juvenile's birth. Many sexual abuse issues and developmental deficits are related to the preoperational stages of development, which are difficult for the juvenile to recall. The control-seeking function of the sexual abuse cycle may relate to issues of autonomy and control that are reminiscent of the toddler's association of genital shame regarding diapering, toilet training, and early sexual expression or to control issues related to feeding, bathing, and independence. Autonomy and competency are affected by separation and individuation issues, and the preschool years contain the early experiences of role taking, fantasy, and rule making or breaking. The origins of control issues may become apparent, as in the case of the 12-year-old whose mother proudly reported that as an infant, he had been prevented from walking until she had returned from a long hospitalization so she would not miss his first steps. She reported this as evidence of their closeness, but the toddler's perception can be imagined: bound (rather than bonded) to the parent in order to meet the parent's needs.

Origins of Cognitive and Emotional Associations   Patterns of thought and shared emotions may be revealed in every interaction with the juvenile and his family. Distortions, rationalization, denial, and unrealistic expectations have been described as common family characteristics and may be revealed as chronic patterns of shared beliefs among family members. Beliefs about power, sexuality, relationships, and coping may be accessible to the therapist, as well as the patterns of distorted thinking that support abusive behavior. Especially important may be the shared emotions within the family, which often describe the nature of attachments for better or worse. These shared emotions may be negative feelings, such as fear, shame, or guilt, that the family has experienced as closeness and may explain a subconscious secondary gain in the negative feelings associated with offending. The child whose early need to feel connected to others has been met within an environment of negative shared emotions may be reinforced rather than deterred by the guilt and shame associated with early abusive behaviors.

Implications of Developmental History   Efficient gathering of developmental clues can contribute to the treatment process by identifying patterns of thought and emotional reactions that previously defied explanation. The juvenile who has felt a lack of control can achieve tremendous relief from the knowledge that there are identifiable explanations for how he arrived at his current situation. The therapist becomes able to form hypotheses regarding how an infant or child might have perceived or been affected by things in the history, and how those things might contribute to understanding current functioning. The youth's faith in the therapist increases when correlations and explanations are forthcoming, even when he does not fully understand the concepts or rationale of the associations. Although no developmental antecedent can be allowed to excuse or rationalize abuse of others, the therapist's ability to imagine the early life experiences of the juvenile is a powerful demonstration of empathy, and by enabling the youth to apply empathy to their own situation, the therapist may help them develop and find empathy for others.

For example: Inquiring of mom about her discovery that she was pregnant with this child might reveal whether this child was planned or unplanned, and welcome or unwelcome when he arrived. Hearing the parents' hopes and expectations, and whether they were fulfilled or not, may suggest a good fit or not. Inquiring about what kind of baby he was will reveal whether those memories are positive or negative, thus informing hypotheses about parental bonding, expectations, and perceptions of the child. Inquiring about the circumstances of the parents when the youth was a baby can reveal stressors that may have affected their availability, demeanor, and so forth. In addition, asking the youth what stories they have been told about themselves when they were born, and as a baby, also reveals important perceptions.

The cognitive restructuring required to break the dysfunctional cycle pattern is inherently dependent on the definition of the beliefs and assumptions that arise from the client's view of the world. Although the thinking that allows or supports sexual abuse can be identified and confronted on the basis of expert definition (Berenson, 1987; Yochelson & Samenow, 1976), the process of change is made easier when the client is helped to see the origin of the thinking pattern. It is often possible to acknowledge that the defensive processes may have been temporarily adaptive, protective, or rational in origin but that generalization to subsequent functioning has become maladaptive and dysfunctional.

When developmental delays can be understood intellectually, the feelings of shame and incompetence can be addressed by direct intervention. Failure to achieve autonomy and the control issues subsequent to that failure may be more accessible to change when their origins become clear. The youth who understands the childhood dilemmas that prevented successful mastery and maturation may now be much more open to acknowledgment and disclosure and more amenable to corrective exercises and resolution, cognitive restructuring, and acceptance of accountability for more responsible functioning.

The toddler's intimidation or the preschooler's inability to find functional and trustworthy role models need not continue to control the adolescent's functioning. Negative attention seeking; intimacy through fear, dominance, or shame; sexualized compensation; and dysfunctional patterns of adaptation and coping are more easily addressed when self-understanding allows empathy and acceptance rather than continued defense. Fantasies and compensatory thinking become less shameful when the youth understands early learning processes and is given credit for survival in earlier adversity.

The developmental history helps to unravel the defenses and mysteries of the individual and focuses treatment more rapidly on the trigger issues and deficits. The therapist's understanding of the child's dilemmas in the family of origin simulta- neously reveals that family's own difficult circumstances and dilemmas, facilitating the engagement of parents in the change process.

Supervision

The imperative thing the juvenile needs from their parents is supervision. It is not reasonable for the youth to remain in the community without adult supervision. The need to remove juveniles from the home during treatment and their subsequent return is sometimes dependent on the family's ability or inability to provide adequate supervision. The National Task Force on Juvenile Sexual Offending (1998, 1993) stressed that intrafamilial sexual abuse should always result in some period of removal of the abusive child in order to provide physical and psychological safety for any victim(s) in the home and to avoid assigning a *watchdog* role to the parents, which can further erode existing levels of trust within the family. However, for the youth who has sexually abused outside the home and is in outpatient treatment, or the juvenile returning home from any treatment or correctional placement, the need for parental supervision is clear. Therapists, teachers, and probation and parole officers cannot fully monitor the juvenile's activities in the community. Parents have the maximum opportunity to supervise and monitor their child.

The family's inability to recognize the juvenile's behavior is often the first obstacle to adequate supervision (Thomas, 1988). The juvenile's abusive patterns have often developed in an environment that failed to acknowledge problem behaviors at all or perceived the patterns to be normal. Lack of definition and denial of coercive and abusive patterns is a common characteristic, although families sometimes report underlying concerns of long-standing duration. Even in families that have recognized early behaviors as problematic, minimization or ineffective interventions have often characterized parental responses. Just as victims should not be expected to believe that disclosure and entry into treatment will protect them from further abuse (Ryan, 1989), therapists must not assume adequate supervision will be forthcoming in the home following disclosure.

Parents must be educated to see and recognize the juvenile's behavior—not only the overtly abusive acts but the antecedent indicators of risk or progression. The family's ability and motivation to provide adequate supervision are improved by their involvement in the juvenile's treatment. Parental perceptions of sexual abuse are often as clouded by distorted beliefs and ignorance as the youth's own perception. Hopelessness and helplessness contribute to the parental perception that the sexual offense is an aberration that occurred without warning and is beyond prediction, comprehension, or control.

In order to protect both the abusive youth and the community from the consequences of additional abuse, the parents must be motivated and educated. Specific instructions must be given and enforced to ensure that apparently unrelated decisions do not increase risk or fail to recognize relapse cues. The parents must be taught how to supervise without any presumptions, or it is likely that the environmental factors that have either supported or allowed sexual abuse will remain unchanged.

When the youth's perpetration is first discovered, there is no reason to believe that similar behavior might not reoccur. Therefore, the youth's access to past and potential victims is a major concern and must be specifically prohibited, *until there is evidence of decreased risk*. It is important that the youth and family understand that early restrictions will be changing as they participate in treatment, and equally important for case management to continually reassess restrictions in order to modify them as needed.

It is not unusual for the parent who knows one child has been sexually abused to leave the abusive youth alone with (or even in charge of) another child. For example: A 14-year-old male who had molested his 12-year-old sister for two years was encouraged to continue bathing the 4-year-old sibling at bedtime. In another case, the 12-year-old had molested a 4-year-old sibling and was sent to live with relatives who had a 4-year-old child of their own. In some cases, the youth who molests children has been viewed as "very good" with young children or having "special" relationships with many children.

Both victim and nonvictim children may be attached to the youth who abused them and may express feelings of loss when access is curtailed; nevertheless, all of the abusive youth's access to significantly younger children should be restricted initially. Even interactions with children in view of the parents cannot be recommended until there is some progress in treatment indicating (a) the victim's sense of safety; (b) decreased risk of the abusive youth experiencing sexual thoughts, fantasy, or arousal when with past victims; (c) some clarification between the two children including redefinition of rules, boundaries, and secrecy; and (d) evidence of adequate and active supervision by parents.

Covert levels of exploitation, coercion, and sexualization are often pervasive in many relationships of the sexually abusive youth. Until the juvenile and the parents are both educated to see and change antecedent patterns, even peer relations must be supervised differently. Parents must be cautioned against assuming their child's interest in more "acceptable" sexual activity (such as opposite-sex peers) is automatically a sign of progress. Concrete rules must be set up for the parents regarding the juvenile's access and contact with vulnerable people, and detailed reporting of activities and situations must be encouraged.

The clear definition and articulation of how supervision of youth who are known to have been sexually abusive should be done has been an enormous help in the field. The Colorado State Standards for Management and Treatment of Juveniles who have committed sexual offenses (2002) defined "Informed Supervision" and require it for all juveniles adjudicated for, or in the custody of the state with a known history of sexually abusive behaviors. The concept of "Informed Supervision" has subsequently been implemented in many other states where it is not required by law but has been very useful (see Chapter 15).

Access and exposure to sexually explicit materials is another aspect that requires supervision. Many juveniles have access to pornography within their own home and the culture is full of sexually explicit materials. Popular music, media, movies, and the Internet are permeated with sexual messages and images, many of them glorifying incest, rape, sexual violence, and sadomasochism. Parents Music Resource Center (1988) had already been working to make parents aware of the prevalence of these messages in the late 1980s, and levels of exposure have continued to increase dramatically. Television, even prime-time programming, is a source of exposure to violent and sexual messages (National Coalition on Television Violence, 1988) and research has demonstrated increases in behaviors following children's observation of them in media. Sexually explicit content on the Internet is a concern as well (Laws, 1996) and, although parents may have heard about the risks of children being approached by potential perpetrators by e-mail, texting, or in chat rooms, it is not unusual for parents to be completely unaware of their children's access and exposure to sexually explicit materials in their own home. It is important to be specific about monitoring in order to establish whether such materials have contributed to the juvenile's concept of sexuality and their sexual arousal. Education and communication with the juvenile and the parents is needed.

Ideally, the supervisory role of parents includes monitoring and open communication with all the adults involved with the child in treatment and school, as well as other activities. Communication with collateral sources of information (for example, teachers and caseworkers) can be used to verify the validity of parental reports. Patterns of irresponsible behavior may be so pervasive that parents are desensitized and unable to recognize many signs of concern. Engaging parents in learning to supervise and to collaborate with other adults to meet these needs is a critical first step with the family.

PARTICIPATION IN THE JUVENILE'S TREATMENT

The third potential role of parental involvement is support for the juvenile's treatment. Some families are unable to support treatment at all, and if they completely deny the need for or sabotage the juvenile's participation, legal interventions or out-of-home placement may be necessary. However, families who can acknowledge the juvenile's need to get help and make changes, even minimal ones, can be educated in specific and nonthreatening ways to encourage the juvenile's participation in treatment and to help maintain the changes that are made.

Finally, some families will participate in family treatment with the juvenile in order to be actively involved in changes within the family structure and function that support the juvenile's treatment, decrease stress, and moderate risk factors within the home environment. The parents' willingness to take responsibility for their own issues and to do whatever is indicated to meet the needs of their child sets an example for the youth and supports the goals of enhanced communication, empathic interactions, and personal responsibility.

FAMILY: ABSENT, IMPOSSIBLE, OR AMENABLE

Every juvenile enters treatment with a family history. Whether absent, distant, functional, or dysfunctional, family issues must be addressed, and the therapist must assess the potential for family involvement. For some sexually abusive youth, family involvement appears unlikely because of absence. The situations of juveniles who have been disowned or abandoned, have been placed outside their community for treatment or incarceration, or have lost their parents due to other circumstances appear to preclude family involvement in the treatment process. Creative thinking about what is needed from families, however, may reveal alternate sources and methods.

A family orientation is crucial in terms of the client's place in the human family (Thomas, 1988). The juvenile's developmental history may be available from extended family members, such as older siblings or grandparents, and it may be obtained through correspondence with distant relatives or previous caregivers. Absent or distant parents may be willing to provide a biography of the juvenile or respond to specific questions by mail or telephone. Every source of information may offer different perspectives and pieces of understanding that complement or contradict each other. Collateral sources can be cross-checked, and diverse opinions help to identify sources of distortion and confusion for the youth.

Current caregivers can be vital observers and informants and may be educated to spot trigger situations and antecedents that are a part of the juvenile's dysfunctional cycle. These caregivers must be educated for supervision of the sexually abusive youth and may be engaged in supporting and reinforcing participation in treatment and positive change. For the juvenile who will return to a distant family, creative involvement is imperative and may include marathon family therapy weekends, conference calls, or additional family therapy in the home community. For the juvenile who has lost his family or will not be returning home, developmental history provides a basis for dealing with the dysfunction and the losses of the past as well as future familial relationships.

For some sexually abusive youth, an "impossible" family may be even more difficult than an absent or distant one. The "impossible" family is often chaotic and has manifold problem areas, frequently involving a multigenerational history of interpersonal violence and sexual abuse. The family may be absent or distant or painfully present, sabotaging treatment overtly and/or covertly. Family denial, rationalization, and distortions may be pervasive, and the family may feel threatened and intruded on by the disclosure of the juvenile's sexual offense. Although they may be willing to share developmental perceptions, these families may never be even minimally supportive in the treatment of the youth. Many times these juveniles are unable to become engaged in treatment or participate in meaningful change until they are removed from the family's influence. In some cases, the family's refusal to allow or support change makes it impossible for the juvenile to return home.

Most frustrating of all are the cases where it is not possible to remove a juvenile from a family that discourages involvement in treatment or contributes to the risk of further abusive functioning. In difficult family dilemmas, therapists should seek the help of attorneys in the field, who can communicate an understanding to the court of the detrimental effect a particular family will have on the juvenile's treatment and eventual rehabilitation. In many of these situations, therapists can only document the problems and communicate their concerns to the courts and to the juvenile.

Expectations for change must be realistic. In some cases, the juvenile is able to participate in treatment in spite of family resistance, and the therapist can be direct in acknowledging the dilemma and supporting the juvenile's personal strengths. The therapist's ability to establish a consistent, dependable relationship may enable the juvenile to trust and confide, benefiting from the treatment experience by seeing that there are other ways to view the world that are different from those previously learned in the family. It must be recognized that working in treatment to help the youth define and reject abusive history in the family may jeopardize their relationships in that family and may be experienced as extremely dangerous or as a loss of the family's love and support. In many instances the youth can be helped to accept the dilemmas or inadequacy of the family and become able to moderate the risks for themselves without feeling they must reject family ties entirely.

The amenable families are those who are able to go beyond providing history and supervision to support the juvenile's treatment and participate in meaningful family therapy as well. Chapter 20 will explore the involvement of families in crisis intervention, assessment, family therapy, reconstruction, transition, and aftercare. Crisis intervention and family assessment are immediate needs with every juvenile referral. The needs, potential, and prognosis for family involvement in therapy are not immediately apparent but emerge over time in response to early interactions with the family.

A family orientation is both possible and desirable in approaching every case (Thomas, 1988). Each piece of understanding that becomes available from family contacts must be appreciated for its contribution to the therapist's work with the juvenile.

REFERENCES

Berenson, D. (1987). Choice, thinking and responsibility: Implications for the treatment of the sex offender. In G. Ryan (Ed.) *Interchange: Newsletter of the National Adolescent Perpetrator Network.* Denver, CO: Kempe National Center.

Burton, D. L. (2003). Male adolescents: Sexual victimization and subsequent sexual abuse. *Child and Adolescent Social Work Journal, 29*(4), 277–296.

Colorado Sex Offender Management Board (CSOMB). (2002). *Standards and guidelines for the evaluation, assessment, treatment, and supervision of juveniles who have committed sexual offenses.* Colorado Department of Public Safety, Division of Criminal Justice.

Conte, J. (1986). Sexual abuse and the family: A critical analysis. In T. Trepper and M. Barrett (Eds.), *Treating incest: A multimodal systems perspective.* New York: Hawthorn Press.

Cortoni, F., & Marshall, W. (2001). Sex as a coping strategy and its relationship in juvenile sexual history and intimacy in sexual offenders. *Sexual Abuse: A Journal of Research and Treatment, 13*(1), 27–43.

Elliot, D. S. (Series Ed.). (1998). *Blueprints for violence prevention.* Boulder, CO: University of Colorado, Center for the Study and Prevention of Violence.

Finkelhor, D. (Ed.). (1986). *Sourcebook on child sexual abuse.* Thousand Oaks, CA: Sage.

Freeman-Longo, R. E. (1982). *Child molestation: The offender and the assault.* Proceedings of the 112th Annual Congress of Correction, Toronto, Canada: American Correctional Association.

Gilgun, J. (1988). *Factors which block the development of sexually abusive behavior in adults abused as children.* Paper presented at the National Conference on Male Victims and Offenders, Minneapolis, MN.

Haynes-Seman, C., & Krugman, R. (1989). Sexualized attention: Normal interaction or precursor to sexual abuse? *American Journal of Orthopsychiatry, 59*(2), 238–245.

Hunter, J. (1996, November). *The juvenile offender: Different challenges and approaches.* Paper presented at the National Summit: Promoting Public Safety Through Management of Sex Offenders in the Community, Office of Justice, Washington, DC.

Kaplan, M. S., Becker, J. V., & Cunningham-Rathner, J. (1988). Characteristics of parents of adolescent incest perpetrators: Preliminary findings. *Journal of Family Violence, 3*(3), 183–191.

Klaus, H. M., & Kennell, J. H. (1976). *Maternal-infant bonding.* St. Louis, MO: Mosby-Year Book.

Kobayashi, J., Sales, B. D., Becker, J. V., Figueredo, A. J., & Kaplan, M. S. (1995). Perceived parental deviance, parent-child bonding, child abuse, and child sexual aggression. *Sexual Abuse: A Journal of Research and Treatment 7*(1), 25–44.

Lane, S. (1991). The sexual abuse cycle. In G. Ryan & S. Lane (Eds.), *Juvenile Sexual Offending: Causes, Consequences and Correction* (pp. 103–141). Lexington, MA: Lexington Books.

Lankester, D., & Meyer, B. (1986). *Relationship of family structure to sex offense behavior.* Paper presented at the First National Conference on Juvenile Sexual Offending: Minneapolis, MN.

Lankester, D., & Meyer, B. (1988). Sex gone wrong: Adolescent sex offenders and their families. *Family Therapy Networker, 12,* 43–45, 86–90.

Laws, R. (1996). Panel moderated at the 16th Association for the Treatment of Sexual Abuser (ATSA) Conference, Chicago, IL.

Miner, M. H., & Crimmins, C. L. S. (1997). Adolescent sex offenders—Issues of etiology and risk factors. In B. K. Schwartz & H. R. Cellini (Eds.), *The sex offender: New insights, treatment innovations, and legal developments, volume II* (pp. 9-1 to–9-15). Kingston, NJ: Civic Research Institute, Inc.

Murray, M. (1996, August). *Exploratory study of the relationship between national fathers and their sons in cases of adolescent sexual offenders.* Paper presented at the Eleventh International Congress on Child Abuse and Neglect, Dublin, Ireland.

National Coalition on Television Violence. (1989). [Data sheet]. *NCTV News,* 10.

National Task Force on Juvenile Sexual Offending. (1988). Preliminary report. *Juvenile and Family Court Journal, 39*(2), 1–67.

National Task Force on Juvenile Sexual Offending. (1993). Revised report. *Juvenile and Family Court Journal, 44*(4), 1–120.

O'Brien, M. (1989). *Sibling incest.* Brandon, VT: Safer Society Press.

Parents Music Resource Center. (1988). *Rising to the challenge* [Videotape]. Alexandria, VA: Author.

Perlmutter, L., Engel, T., & Sager, C. (1982). The incest taboo: Loosened sexual boundaries in remarried families. *Journal of Sex and Marital Therapy, 8*(2), 83–96.

Prentky, R., Knight, R. A., Sims-Knight, J., Straus, F., Rokous, F., & Cerce, D. (1989). Developmental antecedents of sexual aggression. *Development and Psychopathology, 1,* 153–169.

Ryan, G. (1987). Getting at the facts. *Interchange: Newsletter of the National Adolescent Perpetrator Network*. Denver, CO: Kempe National Center.

Ryan, G. (1988). *The juvenile sexual offender: A question of diagnosis*. Presentation of unpublished data at the National Symposium on Child Victimization, Anaheim, CA.

Ryan, G. (1989). Victim to victimizer: Rethinking victim treatment. *Journal of Interpersonal Violence*, 4(3), 325–341.

Ryan, G., Miyoshi, T. J., Metzner, J. L., Krugman, R. D., & Fryer, G. E. (1996). Trends in a national sample of sexually abusive youth. *Journal of the American Academy of Child and Adolescent Psychiatry*, 35(1), 17–25.

Smith, H., & Israel, E. (1987). Sibling incest: A study of the dynamics of 25 cases. *Child Abuse and Neglect*, 11(2), 101–108.

Steele, B. F. (1987). Abuse and neglect in the earliest years: Groundwork for vulnerability. *Zero to Three*, 7(4), 14–15.

Straus, M. A. (1990). Family violence. In the *NCFR Presidential Report, 2001: Preparing families for the future* (pp. 26–27). Minneapolis, MN: National Council on Family Relations.

Thomas, J. (1988). *Multifamily group work with juvenile sexual offenders*. Paper presented at the National Training Conference, Long Beach, CA.

Widom, C. S. (1996). Childhood sexual abuse and its criminal consequences. *Society*, 33(4), 47–53.

Widom, C. S., & Williams, L. (1996). *Cycle of sexual abuse. Research inconclusive about whether child victims become adult abusers*. Report to House of Representatives, Committee of Judiciary, Subcommittee on Crime. Washington, DC: General Accounting Office.

Williams, L. M. (1995). *Juvenile and adult offending behavior and other outcomes in a cohort of sexually abused boys: Twenty years later*. Philadelphia, PA: Joseph J. Peters Institute.

Yochelson, S., & Samenow, S. (1976). *The criminal personality* (vol. 1). Northvale, NJ: Aronson.

PART THREE

CONSEQUENCES OF JUVENILE SEXUAL OFFENDING

CHAPTER 11

Consequences for Those Victimized and Those Who Offend

GAIL RYAN

S EXUAL ABUSE IS problematic not because of the sexual behavior per se, but because of the abusive nature of the interaction. Although the impact of the behavior is not what defines abuse, the impact is what causes the concern. The consequences of sexual abuse for those involved encompass the immediate qualities of the experience, the short-term effects, and the long-term sequelae. The occurrence of sexual abuse can trigger a sequence of subsequent problems for both the victimized and the youth who perpetrates the abuse. This chapter examines the perceptual experience and impact of the event itself at a personal level for both, and also for the families of each. A subsequent chapter will explore the consequences of the system's intervention and the legal jeopardy related to these behaviors.

THE EXPERIENCE OF SEXUAL VICTIMIZATION

The experience of any victimization is that of helplessness (Hiroto, 1974). For the sexual abuse victim, the experience is particularly intrusive because of the violation of both body privacy and the psychic self. However, sexual abuse does not occur in a vacuum; the experience, impact, and sequelae are affected by all that has gone before and everything that follows. The nature of the victimization only partially defines the victim's experience (Briere, 1992; Hindman, 1989). A full understanding of the experience considers each victim's own perception at a personal level.

Variables affecting the victim's experience include virtually every experience and perception of the individual since birth and the impact of the experience will differ on that basis, as well as in the many variables of subsequent life experience (Ryan et al., 1989; Ryan and Associates, 1998). An important caution, therefore, is that it cannot be assumed that every victim's experience is the same or that the impact or outcome will be the same. This has become apparent, although not always acknowledged, in the assessment of victims at the point of disclosure, as well as in consideration of intervention and long-term outcomes (Rind, Tromovitch, & Bauserman, 1998; Widom & Williams, 1996).

Although assumptions about each individual's experience cannot be made, the range of factors documented in the literature alert us to areas of consideration. These become important in discussions with youth in treatment regarding the impact of their abusive behaviors, as well as any victimization in their own life experience.

VULNERABILITIES TO ABUSE

Some sexual victimization occurs in the context of an entirely random victim selection. Many rapes of adults are perpetrated by assailants unknown to the victim, a small percentage of child molestations are committed by strangers, and many of the hands-off abuses occur somewhat randomly. However, most child sexual abuse and many acquaintance rapes occur within relationships that have either revealed or created some vulnerability in the victim. Preexisting conditions of neglect, parental loss, inferior self-image, and lack of nurturance may make potential victims, especially child victims, vulnerable to the advances of sexual perpetrators. When the youth's advances fulfill an "emotional need for nurturance" (Summit, 1983), the victims are vulnerable because resistance or disclosure will cost the victim a relationship that is meeting some emotional need. These *secondary gains* have been reported in some victims' experience, but it should also be recognized that such secondary gains are only as powerful as the needs of the victim.

PRIOR LIFE EXPERIENCE

Vulnerability is based on earlier life experiences, but many other factors also affect the impact of the experience. The degree to which the victimization is dissonant with the individual's view of the world may affect the level of trauma, as well as the method of coping. The victim who has experienced the world as a safe, empathic place may be more traumatized by but less accepting of the abuse than a victim whose worldview lacks safety. Similarly, the existing repertoire of coping mechanisms may vary in accord with past coping models and experiences. Coping styles may range from denial and disassociation to problem solving and resolution. Passivity and assertiveness, distorted or rational belief systems, and empathic or exploitative patterns may all be preexisting qualities—products of early life experience.

BETRAYAL

Sexual victimization is often perpetrated by someone whom the victim trusts, and the betrayal of that confidence is paramount. The level of trauma in the experience of sexual abuse may also relate to prior life views in the perception of betrayal as dissonant or expected. The basic development of trust or distrust emphasized in infant development contributes to the quality of all relationships, and the victim's level of trust in the exploited relationship affects the perception of betrayal. The victim whose prior experiences have been a trade-off of exploit-and-be-exploited may experience less betrayal in the sexual victimization than the victim who has believed the world is a safe, trustworthy place. The sexually abusive youth's lack of regard for the victim's needs (Steele, 1986; Willock, 1983) will be perceived in the context of earlier experiences of empathy or disregard.

THE RELATIONSHIP

The relationship that exists prior to the sexual abuse is not always easily definable. Although it has been assumed that the closer the relationship (such as family versus acquaintance) the greater the impact of the betrayal, it is the victim's perception of trust and dependency in the relationship that must be considered. The father who has been emotionally absent or distant, nonempathic, and inconsistent has a very different relationship with the child than does the older cousin who has always catered to and doted on the child. Assumptions about impact on the basis of relationship must therefore be approached from the perception of the victim.

DEVELOPMENTAL STAGES

Another area that is thought to relate to the child's experience of sexual abuse is that of developmental stage. Not only is the experience deviant, but the developmental stage of the victim may vary according to age and in terms of success or failure in earlier developmental tasks (Conte, 1985). The experience of victimization or trauma can create a developmental crisis that may arrest future development or trigger regression to an earlier developmental phase. The assault is not only on the body of the child but also on basic trust and worldview. Development of interpersonal relationships is almost certain to be adversely affected, and the child's subsequent development may be distorted.

SEXUALITY

Abuse combined with sexuality can produce an experience of "traumatic sexualization" (Conte & Browne, 1985; Finkelhor, 1986) and may be incomprehensible to a child (Summit, 1983). Concepts of sexuality relate to genitalia, arousal, and relationship. Sexual victimization may include genital injury or the perception of injury. Children who have been penetrated often believe their bodies are subsequently different from those of other children or permanently damaged. This "damaged goods" syndrome may lower self-esteem, devalue the sense of self, and discourage self-protection in the future. At the same time, sexual arousal may be present in any sexual interaction, and the resultant confusion may lead victims to perceive themselves as guilty and stigmatized (Conte, 1985). For the victim who experiences pleasure in either the physical closeness of hugging and petting or in the sexual arousal associated with the sexual abuse behavior, the subsequent pairing of fear, guilt, pain, and pleasure must be accommodated at a cognitive level. The victim's thinking is likely to incorporate the perpetrator's own explanations, rationalizations, and projection of blame or responsibility to the victim, and the risk of deviant sexual development is increased. The victim who experiences arousal without pain (as part of the abuse) is even more likely to accept a personal stigmatization, and the victim who experiences pain from the sexual behavior without arousal may pair the behavior with aggression.

GENDER ISSUES

For the male victim who is sexually abused by a male, the issue of homosexuality may arise. The male victim may conclude that the experience causes or defines him to be homosexual. The opposite conclusion may result in an extreme homophobia that impairs future same-sex relationships (Breer, 1987). The male victim may deny his arousal in the abuse or translate himself into the role of aggressor. When males are sexually exploited by a female, they are likely to attribute responsibility to themselves and may not perceive themselves a victim until later in life.

The female victim may perceive her sexuality as tarnished or perverted. Her acceptance of guilt and responsibility may lead her to interpret her victimization as deserved and lead to increased risk of further abuse, promiscuity, or self-degradation. She may feel that her virginity is forever gone and that she is therefore undeserving of nonexploitative sexual relationships in the future. For the smaller proportion of female victims who are sexually abused by a female perpetrator, confusion regarding homo-sexuality may also arise.

SECRECY

One of the most pervasively common elements in the experience of sexual victim-ization may be that of secrecy, and it is the factor that supports the helplessness of the victim and the power of the abuser. Secrecy isolates the victim (Finkelhor, 1986), separates the experience from the mainstream of life, and prevents validation of the nature of the experience. As long as the abuse remains secret, the victim is unable to express feelings or seek verification of perceptions. The secret protects the sexually abusive youth, and the victims are often led to believe that it protects them as well. In the isolation imposed by the secret, distortions and rationalizations may be the victim's only source of interpretation for the experience, and the secret gains power over time as the abuse continues.

ACCOMMODATION

The victim's experience of sexual abuse must be reconciled with his or her view of self and of the world. Summit (1983) has addressed the child victim's dilemma as the "child sexual abuse accommodation" syndrome, a concept that bridges the span from experience through disclosure. When the secret has bound the victim in a helpless complicity, disclosure may be delayed indefinitely. Even when the victim discloses the abuse, the accusation may be so tentative and exploratory as to be unconvincing. Victims may "test" the reality of the outside world and find that the immediate response is much like they had been warned. When disclosure triggers a sequence of embarrassment, disbelief, or trouble, victims sometimes retract state-ments in order to escape the impact and stigma of the family and/or system's response. The victim whose disclosure is not believed, or for whom the results of disclosure are ineffective in providing safety and protection from further abuse, is recaptured by the power of the perpetrator and left even more helpless. Even when the victim's disclosure is believed and intervention takes place, the victim's removal from the home, loss of relationship with the perpetrator, and intrusive interviews with strangers may seem a high price to pay for protection from the unwanted sexual experience.

THE SHORT-TERM IMPACT OF SEXUAL ABUSE

For the victim, emotional reactions, psychological functioning, and behavioral changes demonstrate methods of coping. In reactions to trauma and stress, males are more inclined to externalize reactions while females tend to internalize. These styles are thought to be a product of sex role modeling and socialization, which teaches females to manifest emotions and males to deny them. In reacting to sexual abuse, the female victim is more likely to internalize the experience, feeling somehow personally responsible, guilty, and deserving of abuse. Male victims, on the other hand, are more likely to externalize the experience: discounting negative feelings, depersonalizing the abuse, and identifying with the aggressor (Summit, 1983). The female victim may appear more sad, depressed, and anxious, while male victims often appear more angry, distrustful, and aggressive.

The immediate need for victims is to protect themselves from negative aspects of the abuse. Physical injuries must be repaired and those without visible injury often seek reassurance from a doctor that their body is intact. All the perceptions discussed in different experiences of victimization must be interpreted, accepted, or rejected in relation to the victim's sense of self and view of the world. To protect themselves from confusion or the meaning of the abuse, the immediate style of coping is often denial. Dissociation, blocking the memory, imagining that nothing occurred (that it was only a dream), or minimizing the exploitative or sexual nature of the interaction, are all effective forms of denial that protect the victim from being overwhelmed by the experience (Conte, 1988).

The second need for victims in coping is to regain what was lost. Experiencing powerlessness as a loss of control, one must either accept helplessness or master it. One of the immediate reactions is retaliatory thinking, which is often modeled or reinforced by others who discover the abuse. Upon discovery of abuse, uninvolved family members as well as those involved in the systems that intervene are often consumed by their own anger and the betrayal of their own basic trust in people, and they may model retaliation as a means of coping. The victim's own inclination to "get back" is thus supported by the parent who expresses the desire to incarcerate, castrate, or kill the perpetrator (Ryan, 1989).

Observations of children who have been sexually abused often include reports of acting-out behaviors (Friedrich, Urquiza, & Bielke, 1986). Acting-out behaviors may represent attempts to master the experience of helplessness by seeking control in subsequent situations (Ryan, 1984). The cognitive processes that accompany acting-out behaviors may reflect the distortions the victim was exposed to in the course of the abuse.

The victim who acts out continued helplessness may appear "tempting" to others with seductive behavior, or may engage in behavior that puts him or her at risk of injury or further abuse, may be displaying a "learned helplessness." That profile of powerlessness may actually be a very empowering mechanism for the victim by (a) reassuring the victim that he or she was truly unable to prevent the abuse and is therefore guiltless, or (b) coping with the fear of abuse by controlling its occurrence, thereby avoiding the sense of betrayal in future situations. The "delusions" of persecution noted in the literature (Adams-Tucker, 1980) may therefore actually be "illusions" supportive of the victim's coping style. The victim who acts out aggressively, on the other hand, may be attempting to master rather than accommodate the experience of helplessness and betrayal. Risk taking, fighting, and perpetration may be attempts to regain the power and control lost in the experience of abuse and can be viewed as control mechanisms (Ryan, Lane, Davis, & Isaac, 1987).

In either method of coping (continued helplessness or control seeking), the thinking that supports the reaction reflects the patterns of thinking associated with abuse. Short-term aberrations of thought and behavior may serve to protect the victim from being overwhelmed by the experience and are therefore temporarily adaptive methods of coping (Conte, 1988). However, failure to resolve the issues rationally may lead to lifelong patterns of thought and behavior that support dysfunctions or abuse (Ryan, 1989).

Not every victim's perception of sexual victimization is the same, and the process of adaptation, accommodation, and coping will be different for each individual. Resolution is also unique and intervention requires differential diagnosis and treatment to be meaningful. Terr (1983, 1985) and others (Finkelhor, 1986; Perry, 2006; Van der Kolk, 1986) have studied the traumatic nature of victimization, which for some creates a subsequent posttraumatic stress syndrome. Posttraumatic stress symptoms can be particularly resistant to resolution, as they seem to seek control by freezing the experience: reenacting the experience in fantasy or behavior that is increasingly elaborate, ritualistic, and secretive and becomes more rigid over time. This condition or syndrome may exist for years and jeopardize long-term mental health.

LONG-TERM SEQUELAE OF SEXUAL ABUSE

Adolescent and adult survivors of childhood sexual abuse are overrepresented in many dysfunctional populations. The long-term impacts are apparent in the subsequent miseries perpetuated in the victim's own life, as well as that which is perpetrated on others.

SEXUAL DYSFUNCTIONS

Many sexual dysfunctions may result from confusing, premature, or traumatic sexual experience. Hyper-sexual dysfunctions may include promiscuity, sexual addictions, compulsive masturbation, or elevated or deviant arousal patterns. Sadistic or masochistic characteristics may manifest in either consensual or exploitative relationships and are frequently present in the dynamics of prostitution and marital difficulties. Hypo-sexual dysfunctions may include inhibited desire or arousal and manifest in frigidity, impotence, or sexual aversions, which can also become dynamics in marital difficulties. Victimless fetishes too, such as cross-dressing, may relate to the impacts of childhood sexual abuse.

SOMATIC COMPLAINTS AND ANXIETY

The pervasive fears and helplessness (Sanford, 1987; Weiss, Rogers, Darwin, & Dutton, 1955) inherent in the experience of abuse may manifest across the life span and, in combination with the "damaged-goods" perception previously described, may lead to somatic complaints and nonspecific anxiety. Somatic disorders may represent hyper-vigilance of one's physical condition, while anxiety relates to loss of trust and betrayal, contributing to distrust of the environment and uneasiness in interpersonal relationships. In the extreme, these characteristics may make it impossible for survivors ever to feel entirely well or completely comfortable.

AFFECTIVE DISORDERS AND SUICIDE RISK

Chronic feelings of fear and anxiety may contribute to feelings of depression and a profound sense of hopelessness. In childhood, these qualities may manifest in either sadness and worry, or hyperactivity and attention deficits. With maturity, depressive disorders increase the risk of self-destructive behaviors and suicidal ideation. Self-destruction may relate to a control-seeking cycle, with suicide representing the ultimate control.

SUBSTANCE USE AND ABUSE

The dynamics and thinking patterns present in the abuse of alcohol or drugs may relate to either a self-medication of somatic or depressive conditions or an escape from hyper-vigilance and anxiety in order to feel more relaxed. In either case, the substance use may represent the same control-seeking cycle as other behavioral disorders, whereby the user feels isolated and separate from others and imagines that substance use will result in feeling better. This pattern of seeking external sources of control in order to feel less helpless is supported by the same patterns of thinking observed in the sexual abuse cycle (Ryan, 1989).

EATING DISORDERS

Extreme food behaviors have long been observed in abused, neglected, and deprived populations (Ryan, 1978). Treatment of eating disorders has pointed to the addictive properties as well as the control-seeking qualities of such conditions as anorexia and bulimia. The search for autonomy and body control is manifest in these binge-and-purge behaviors, and eating disorders have been associated with childhood sexual abuse by Oppenheimer, Howells, Palmer, and Challoner (1985) and others. When these disorders appear in adolescent or adult survivors, the same control-seeking cycle earlier related to sexual abuse, suicide, and substance abuse may apply, and similar thinking patterns and developmental deficits support the disorder. The eating disorders of sexual abuse survivors may extend into the next generation when nonorganic failure to thrive is manifest in the infants of some mothers who were victims of incest (Haynes-Seman, 1987). The betrayal of nurturance may explain such mothers' inability to feed their infants successfully, or the feeding interaction may manifest the power and control issues raised by sexual abuse.

COMMUNICATION, LEARNING, AND RELATIONSHIPS

Failures of communication and learning are observed in sexually abused children seen in special education and learning-disabled groups (Blum & Gray 1987; Conte, 1985). These problems significantly alter functioning and subsequent feelings of competency. Interpersonal relationships and self-image are often fragile or ambivalent. Failed marriages, parent-child conflicts, and an inability to maintain close friendships may characterize adult experiences, and intimacy may always be difficult. Communication failures hamper treatment as well as relationships, and every new experience may be perceived with distrust.

THE VICTIM'S FAMILY

Many of the issues and reactions for the parents and siblings of sexual abuse victims are similar to those of the victim. The violation of a family member violates the family as well. Betrayal of trust, intrusion, and retaliatory thinking may resonate throughout the family system. Family members' coping styles are often cast from the same mold as the victim's, and thus, denial, dissonance, accommodation, and reactive behaviors are potentially similar.

For the family that has previously experienced intrafamilial sexual abuse (incest) in the current or previous generations, the disclosure of the child's abuse may be less traumatic and more a fulfillment of the expected or the feared. For the family that experiences extra-familial sexual abuse of the child, the disclosure may be so dissonant that its validity is denied or be so traumatic that family function fails.

The family is affected by the discovery of abuse, and their subsequent reactions create additional impacts for the victim. Disbelief and inadequate protection add to the victim's original confusion and validate the threats and distortions of the offender. Belief and subsequent protection supports the victim's disclosure but at the same time acknowledges the legitimate helplessness of the victim and the family's original failure to protect. The family's sense of violation and confusion mirror the victim's own confusion and require family interventions.

PERPETRATING SEXUAL OFFENSES

In order for treatment to address the individual issues related to the youth perpetrating sexual offenses, it is necessary to understand the motivation and reinforcement of the sexually abusive behavior. This necessitates exploration of what the youth's experience of perpetrating has been. It is also important to understand the immediate and long-term impacts of that experience. Implementation of corrective relevant interventions is dependent on understanding the individual who is being treated, their past experience, and future risk factors associated with their interpersonal interactions, relationships, and sexual behavior.

BEING SEXUALLY ABUSIVE

Whether it was child molestation, rape, or more covert assaults, sexually abusive behavior sets the youth apart from the norms of the culture and peers. Deviancy carries its own stigma, and the sexually abusive youth's self-image is affected by his/ her evaluation of the behavior. The values of the culture are known and assert themselves in defining the behavior as aberrant. In spite of rationalizations, the youth learns to keep thoughts and behavior hidden in order to avoid consequences, but the secrecy fails to defend against the fear and guilt that intrude on self-image.

FANTASY

It is not always clear at what point the fantasy or thought of sexual behavior occurred within the individual in relation to the first sexual offense. However, it is the author's firm belief that interactive sexual behavior does not occur without thought. Before considering the role of fantasy for the individual client, it is imperative to underscore several ideas suggested in previous chapters:

1. The first thought of doing something sexual may have been to do something that was not abusive, and many factors might influence the eventual plan to actually act in an abusive manner.

2. Other times the fantasy may have been to do something abusive/aggressive to act out anger, and many factors might influence the eventual plan, which is to do something sexually abusive.
3. The thought process prior to a first offense might have been very different from the thoughts leading to later or repetitive offenses.
4. Some youth may move very quickly from the thought of doing something sexual, without much forethought, while others might engage in extensive fantasy and planning before acting.

With these differences in mind, exploration of the individual's thoughts will reveal many important aspects of their experience.

Sexual feelings are present even in the preverbal infant. It is possible to imagine that the thought processes accompanying those earliest experiences of sexuality would likely be self-centered: "My body has feelings." As the child begins to individuate, thoughts of interactive sexual behavior become possible. In a nurturing environment, caregivers shape the child's perceptions of human interaction by modeling empathic interactions and limit the child's early imitative role-taking and behavior in line with cultural norms.

A young child growing up in a nonnormative sexual environment—one that is rigid, coercive, and condemning; avoidant or absent of interaction and sexuality; oversexualized; or sexually abusive (Bolton, Morris, & MacEachron, 1989; Gilgun, 1988a; Haynes-Seman, 1987; Haynes-Seman & Krugman, 1989)—may process early sexual feelings through a nonnormative view and experience them as aberrant, evil, overwhelming, painful, frightening, or incomprehensible. If early sexualized behavior was encouraged by caregivers as cute or novel, discouraged by severe punishment, exploited by a perpetrator, or was a reenactment of early abusive experiences, the child's perceptions may be extremely confusing. Initial offenses may seem normal ("just something we all did") or aberrant ("I must be different from other kids"). At some point, however, whether by others' labeling the behavior directly or by the youth's own growing awareness of cultural norms, meaning becomes attached to deviant behaviors.

Individuals who seek counseling to deal with troublesome sexual thoughts afford some appreciation of the self-doubt and confusion that may accompany deviant thoughts even in the absence of behavioral manifestations. The presence of deviant sexual fantasies may isolate the individual from the mainstream, recognizing a unique quality of thoughts. In some cases, the individual may experience repetitive shifts: from feeling superior and excited imagining the experience of the sexual fantasy, to a zero state when realizing it is unlikely the fantasy will be accomplished; from feeling immensely capable to feeling utterly hopeless. Such shifts create anxiety and internal conflict. The fantasy preceding a first sexual assault may seem routine, exhilarating, or troubling to the individual in the light of its dissonance or consistency with the youth's sense of self and view of the world.

Whether experiential or observational, the origins of deviant sexual fantasy are the first element present in the experience of being sexually abusive. The risk factors described relative to the etiology of sexually abusing involve the mind and the body, and the thoughts that accompany early experience move the individual toward the manifest behavior. The fantasy that occurs prior to sexually abusive behavior may be the compensatory thinking that imagines a solution to unmet needs or an expression of angry, aggressive thoughts, but are a product of life experience, and it is the youth's perception and accommodation of the past that shapes sexual fantasy and allows or inhibits behavior. For some individuals who have experienced sexual victimization or trauma, fantasies may be replicating that earlier experience, and the initial abusive behaviors may mirror their own victimization (Freeman-Longo, 1982). For others, arousal may be associated with more normative fantasies that appear unfeasible or inaccessible and rationalizations or distortions work to alter the thoughts into a plan for abusive behaviors.

THE FIRST OCCURRENCE OF SEXUALLY ABUSIVE BEHAVIOR

The first occurrence of sexually abusive behavior may be accompanied by anxiety or fear, arising from the sense that the behavior is "wrong" or might result in negative consequences. However, anxiety may be overcome by a sense of entitlement or defensive strategies. Arousal and excitement may temporarily subdue fear and depersonalize/objectify the victim. Thoughts are for self, and immediacy foils the inhibitions that might normally preclude such behavior. Implementing the plan and experiencing the behavior, a sense of empowerment and control may emerge. Physiological arousal and satisfaction are powerful experiences that counter the youth's prior sense of helplessness and neediness.

In moving from the realm of fantasy to the actual behavior, some youth report experiencing fulfillment or a sense of mastery. Others report perceptions of a lack of control over the behavior: "It just happened." It is sometimes unclear whether this report is a conscious minimization of responsibility or an inability to remember the thought process and choices that preceded the behavior. Despite the temporary reinforcement, the good feelings associated with the physical pleasure and the sense of competence or power do not last and the youth is now at risk to repeat the behavior, attempting to reexperience the pleasure.

SUBSEQUENT OCCURRENCES OF THE BEHAVIOR

Over time, a narcissistic or egocentric orientation and the ability to objectify others may become generalized and increase isolation and interpersonal alienation in other aspects of the youth's life. As sexually abusive behaviors recur over time, the youth may sense confusion as new patterns of arousal become reinforced and, for some, the behaviors seem to assume a compulsive quality. Over time, the arousal associated with abusive behaviors may become a predominant interest, outweigh normative interest and arousal, and leave the youth increasingly dissatisfied or bored with previously pleasurable experiences or with what peers enjoy. The compulsive quality is experienced as being beyond the control of the youth and becomes yet another factor that contributes to poor self-concept, helplessness, and anxiety.

Failure to suppress the thoughts and resist the behavior has a further impact on the sense of self, and the fantasies may become more intrusive, distracting the youth from previously satisfying pastimes. Thinking patterns become altered in order to accommodate the behavior and may succeed in suppressing normal inhibitions even more. For some, the frequency and intensity of arousal may progress over time into an addictive pattern (Carnes, 1983). Behavior that initially empowered the youth may seem overpowering and unmanageable. Increasingly elaborate plans and rituals may develop to defend the youth against a feared loss of control. For others, the powerful aspects of abusing become self-perpetuating, rationalizing retaliatory and abusive behavior.

A distinctive differentiation may emerge between the more aggressive youth whose beliefs support criminal values, the more compulsive youth whose beliefs support paraphilia behaviors, and the youth who lacks the skills to create more normative relationships. Yet despite individual differences, all three are characterized by the depersonalization of the victim, personalization of the behavior, and patterns of thinking that allow and support continuing to offend (Yochelson & Samenow, 1976). The youth must be able to overlook the discomfort or distress they cause others in their attempts to stabilize their own emotional disequilibrium, but the behavior in turn "contributes to the core feelings of inadequacy and worthlessness . . . increasing hypersensitivity and [subsequent] emotional disequilibrium" (p. 224) (Gilgun, 1988b). At the same time, separation of affect and intellect divide the sense of self (Gilgun, 1988b).

THE SHORT-TERM IMPACT

Early occurrences are often followed by a surge of anxiety. As described in the patterned cycle, thoughts following sexual abuse may be of consequences for self or a temporary feeling of guilt that the behavior failed to promote an enduring sense of control and well-being. In the absence of a confidant (Gilgun & Connor, 1990), there is no external source for validation or correction of thoughts or behavior.

Fears of discovery and consequences produce an immediate anxiety, as the implications of the occurrence attack the youth's self-image. The immediate effects include a perception of powerlessness due to the confusion—"Am I a pervert?," "Am I homosexual?," "Can I control this aspect of myself?"—that accompanies attempts to accommodate this newly manifest view of self.

In the short term, declarations of reform ("I won't do this again") attempt to suppress and deny the meaning and problematic nature of the behavior, but as it reoccurs, the youth must assimilate the deviant self into their self-image. Isolation prevents normal learning and the development of interaction with age-mates and fosters shame regarding the thoughts and behavior (Gilgun & Connor, 1990).

THE LONG-TERM IMPACT

Prior to discovery, the fear of disclosure may be overwhelming, and the youth's efforts to protect the secret may be extreme. Preoccupation with offending may interfere with other areas of functioning, the victim relationship may take precedence over all other relationships, and the youth's self-image is under constant self-scrutiny. Over time, as the sexually abusive youth assimilates the role of perpetrator into their sense of self, justification of the behavior becomes routine. Even so, an awareness that others do not share those beliefs alienates the youth further from nonexploitative relationships, and offending may become an all-encompassing identity.

As the process continues, the youth is increasingly isolated, expending energy in maintaining the identity and becoming more closed to input or learning that is dissonant with the abusive lifestyle. They feel increasingly empty inside, viewing everything through the filter of who has control in any situation, and striving to be in that position. Lacking alternative internal resources to rely on, except to seek an expression of greater power, dealing with stress by being abusive may become more and more pervasive. Gilgun and Connor (1990) describe intrapersonal, interpersonal, and existential isolation as significant and pervasive in the life span of adult sexual abusers. This isolation contributes to the diminished likelihood of self-correction of the offending behaviors over time.

Some sexually abusive youth report the belief that they are "more sexual" than normal people, a rationalization in which some sense of a lack of control over the behavior is evident. Others define their whole life experience in terms of sexual abuse, and their identity as that of an unprotected victim and a rejected victimizer. One 14-year-old described his past as follows:

Age 3	Sexually abused by brother
Age 5	Sexually abused little sister—(removed from home)
Age 7	Sexually abused by foster brother/physical abuse by foster father
Age 8	Sexually abused younger child in the home—(sent to a new foster home)
Age 10	Called a liar and sex offender by foster parents
Age 11	Sexually abused foster parents' grandchild—(sent to a secure facility)
Age 12	Called a "baby raper" by older sex offenders in treatment group
Age 13	Sexually assaulted a younger peer on a pass
Age 14	Sent to a residential "sex offender" program

At 17, it was still difficult to elicit any reports from this young man of any life history or personal characteristics not associated with sexual abuse.

Following disclosure or discovery, the young person's initial fear of consequences often proves to have been an underestimation, and the youth may be devastated to learn the extent of his consequences. Many juveniles have little concept that the sexually abusive behavior is actually illegal and have not anticipated the public embarrassment and intrusion that may follow (Metzner & Ryan, 1995). Police investigation and formal court proceedings, removal from home to residential treatment or incarceration, probation, restrictions, registration and restitution may represent a far greater intrusion into his life than his worst expectations (see Chapter 12). At the same time, the consequences the youth might have anticipated—shame, guilt, stigma, parental disapproval, threats, punishment, and victim recriminations—are occurring as well, so they feel impacts on many levels simultaneously.

As one 12-year-old stated, "I knew it was wrong and that I would be in trouble . . . I always got in trouble for any sexual behavior . . . but I never knew it was illegal . . . I didn't know the police would come . . . I thought I'd be grounded . . . I never imagined my parents would kick me out. I lost my family."

For those who enter treatment, the treatment process can be long, time-consuming, and uncomfortable. Yet even treatment does not complete the consequences. The public believes there is no "cure," so the youth will always be a suspect when a sexual offense occurs in the vicinity. Many youth are subject to long-term registry and public notification (Freeman-Longo, 1996). Although some youth may pose such a risk to community safety that such measures seem justified, the laws fail to discriminate among youth based on differential diagnosis or treatment outcomes. The implications in terms of stigma and impediments to returning to a more normative course of development are clear. For some, the hopelessness of past circumstances stretches out before them endlessly into the future.

THE YOUTH'S FAMILY

The disclosure of sexual abuse may be dissonant or congruent within the abuser's family, just as it was for the victim's family. The dissonance of the occurrence supports shock and denial, whereas the family that has a history of sexual abuse may be defensive but less surprised. In many cases, the family of the sexually abusive youth has had an underlying sense of some problem prior to the discovery of a sexual offense, but the disclosure often exceeds their worst fears. Regardless of its history and experience, the family is hit by the disclosure and subsequent intrusion into the home. Fear related to the meaning of the disclosure and its implication for the home environment is accompanied by the anxiety relative to the immediate consequences for their child. Often parents were also not aware of the laws governing their child's sexual behavior, nor the legal consequences of sexual offenses.

For families experiencing intrafamilial sexual abuse, ambivalent feelings for the victims and the perpetrator create confusion. The need to protect the victim may hang in the balance along with the need to defend the abuser. The family's dilemma is exacerbated by the anger and betrayal associated with such a breach of trust.

For the family whose child has been abusive outside the family, denial may prevent their acceptance of the facts or minimize the seriousness of the behavior. They may be at risk to engage in retaliatory actions against those making the allegations, or they may expend tremendous resources in the defense of their child. As the reality becomes clear, however, their fear of consequences and the implications for the home environment are similar to other parents' reactions to such a disclosure.

Parents are often frustrated in attempts to obtain treatment for their child and may be forced into financial burdens that stress the family even more. It is important that families acknowledge the impact of sexual abuse by a family member on the other members of the family in order to receive help for everyone.

IMPLICATIONS OF UNDERSTANDING PERSONAL CONSEQUENCES

Although many survivors do very well, and most youth who have committed sexual offenses do not continue to offend as adults, the consequences of sexual victimization and perpetration can include a potential for infinite miseries across the life span. The experience may alter the course of subsequent development and jeopardize future relationships. Multiple dysfunctions may result from a failure to cope effectively, and sexual deviancy may reappear in many forms. When the victim takes on the role of victimizing others, the intergenerational cycle of abuse is perpetuated by a cycle of maladaptive coping.

Comprehension of the victim's experience of sexual abuse has many implications in the treatment of sexually abusive youth. Empathic understanding is imperative to prevention of further abuse and is relevant to those the youth has abused, as well as their own history of victimization. In addition to dealing with the impact of their own abusive behaviors, sexually abusive youth who have also been victimized may require treatment to address those issues as well. In exploration of the victim-to-victimizer transition, parallel issues and characteristics have been identified in relation to victimization and perpetration of sexual abuse. These parallels (Ryan, 1989; Ryan & Associates, 1998) have implications in relation to both treatment and prevention.

An important distinction can be drawn in defining the issues of sexual abuse separate from the ways in which the issues become characterized in the personality of the individual or manifest in behavior, either immediately or over time (Ryan, 1989). If the issues inherent in the experience of abuse are helplessness, depersonalization, misattributions of responsibility, and betrayal, then treatment of sexual abuse must address the issues rather than focus on characteristics or behavior.

Chapter 12 will describe the legal consequences for youth who sexually offend. In the legal system, (from reporting to arrest to release, in court, in investigations, in child protection, in sentencing, probation, parole, registration, and record keeping) the "facts" are important. However, in treatment, it is perception that defines the issues, and perceptions are the product of experience. Describing the experiences of individuals on the basis of commonalities among those involved with sexual abuse helps define variables of concern as they relate to the experience and subsequent impacts of abuse. The therapist's ability to identify cues indicative of these experiences and to form reasonable hypotheses for each person about what their experience might have been becomes the basis for empathic interactions in the therapeutic relationship and facilitates discovery of those issues most relevant to each individual (Yager, Knight, Arnold, & Kempe, 1998).

Approaching clients in a didactic mode, educating them regarding commonalities experienced by others in their position, gives voice to issues that might be hard for them to recognize, describe, introduce, or own in conversations in treatment. Describing these experiences to them assures them from the outset that (a) they are not as alone and unique in this problem as they may have believed; (b) the therapist "knows" this problem in a way that prevents denial of the issues; and (c) there may be hope for self-understanding and change (Yochelson & Samenow, 1976).

REFERENCES

Adams-Tucker, C. (1980). *Sex abused children: Pathology and clinical traits.* Paper presented at the Annual Meeting of American Psychiatric Association, San Francisco, CA.

Blum, J., & Gray, S. (1987). *Strategies for communicating with young children.* Paper presented at the 16th Annual Child Abuse and Neglect Symposium, Keystone, CO.

Bolton, F., Morris, C., & MacEachron, A. (1989). *Males at risk.* Thousand Oaks, CA: Sage.

Breer, W. (1987). *The adolescent molester.* Springfield, IL: Thomas.

Briere, J. (1992). *Child abuse trauma.* Thousand Oaks, CA: Sage.

Carnes, P. (1983). *Out of the shadows: Understanding sexual addiction.* Minneapolis, MN: CompCare Publications.

Conte, J. (1985). The effects of sexual victimization on children: A critique and suggestions for future research. *Victimology: The International Journal, 10,* 110–130.

Conte, J. (1988). *The effects of sexual abuse on the child victim and its treatment.* Paper presented at the 4th National Symposium on Child Sexual Abuse, Huntsville, AL.

Conte, J., & Browne, A. (1985). The traumatic impact of child sexual abuse: A conceptualization. *American Journal of Orthopsychiatry, 55*(4), 530–541.

Finkelhor, D. (1986). Initial and long-term effects: A review of the research. In D. Finkelhor (Ed.), *Sourcebook on child sexual abuse* (pp. 143–179). Thousand Oaks, CA: Sage.

Freeman-Longo, R. (1982). Sexual learning and experience among adolescent sexual offenders. *International Journal of Offender Therapy and Comparative Criminology, 26*(3), 235–241.

Freeman-Longo, R. (1996). Feel good legislation: Prevention or calamity? *Child Abuse and Neglect: The International Journal, 20*(2), 95–101.

Friedrich, W. N., Urquiza, A., & Bielke, R. (1986). Behavioral problems in sexually abused young children. *Journal of Pediatric Psychology, 11*(2), 47–57.

Gilgun, J. (1988a). *Factors which block the development of sexually abusive behavior in adults abused as children*. Paper presented at National Conference on Male Victims and Offenders, Minneapolis, MN.

Gilgun, J. (1988b). Self-centeredness and the adult perpetrator of child sexual abuse. *Comparative Family Therapy, 10*(4), 216–234.

Gilgun, J., & Connor, T. (1990). *Isolation and the adult male perpetrator of child sexual abuse*. In A. L. Horton, B. L. Johnson, L. M. Roundy, & D. Williams (Eds.), *The incest perpetrator: A family member no one wants to treat* (pp. 74–87). Thousand Oaks, CA: Sage.

Haynes-Seman, C. (1987). *Impact of sexualized attention on the preverbal child*. Paper presented at the 16th Annual Child Abuse and Neglect Symposium: Keystone, CO.

Haynes-Seman, C., & Krugman, R. (1989). Sexualized attention: Normal interaction or precursor to sexual abuse? *American Journal of Orthopsychiatry, 59*, 238–245.

Hindman, J. (1989). *Just before dawn*. Oregon: Alexandria Press.

Hiroto, D. (1974). Locus of control and learned helplessness. *Journal of Experimental Psychology, X*, 1022.

Metzner, J., & Ryan, G. (1995). Sexual abuse perpetration. In G. Sholevar (Ed.), *Conduct disorders in children and adolescents* (pp. 119–146). Washington, DC: American Psychiatric Press.

Oppenheimer, R., Howells, K., Palmer, R., & Challoner, D. (1985). *Adverse sexual experience and clinical eating disorders: A preliminary description*. Unpublished manuscript, University of Leicester, England.

Perry, B. (2006). Applying principles of neurodevelopment to clinical work with maltreated and traumatized children. In N. B. Webb (Ed.), *Working with traumatized youth in child welfare* (pp. 27–52). New York: Guilford Press.

Rind, B., Tromovitch, P., & Bauserman, R. (1998). A meta-analytic examination of assumed properties of child sexual abuse using college samples. *American Psychological Bulletin, 124*(1), 22–53.

Ryan, G. (1978). Extreme food behavior in abusive families. *Child Abuse and Neglect: The International Journal, 2*, 117–122.

Ryan, G. (1984). The child abuse connection. *Interchange: Newsletter of the National Adolescent Perpetrator Network*. Denver, CO: Kempe National Center.

Ryan, G. (1989). Victim to victimizer: Rethinking victim treatment. *Journal of Interpersonal Violence, 4*(3), 325–341.

Ryan, G., and Associates. (1998). *The web of meaning: A developmental-contextual approach in treatment of sexual abuse*. Brandon, VT: Safer Society Press.

Ryan, G., Lane, S., Davis, J., & Isaac, C. (1987). Juvenile sexual offenders: Development and correction. *Child Abuse and Neglect: The International Journal, 11*(3), 385–395.

Ryan, G., Lindstrom, B., Knight, L., Arnold, L., Yager, J., Bilbrey, C., et al. (1989). *Sexual abuse in the context of whole life experience*. Paper presented at the 18th National Symposium on Child Abuse and Neglect, Keystone, CO.

Sanford, L. (1987). Pervasive fears in victims of sexual abuse: A clinician's observations. *Preventing Sexual Abuse, 2*(2), 3–5.

Steele, B. F. (1986). Lasting effects of childhood sexual abuse. *Child Abuse and Neglect: The International Journal, 10*(2), 283–291.

Summit, R. (1983). The child sexual abuse accommodation syndrome. *Child Abuse and Neglect: The International Journal, 7*(2), 177–193.

Terr, L. (1983). Chowchilla revisited: The effects of psychic trauma four years after a schoolbus kidnapping. *American Journal of Psychiatry, 140*, 1543–1550.

Terr, L. (1985). Therapy and psychic trauma: A preliminary report. In C. Schaefer & K. O'Connor (Eds.), *Handbook of play therapy* (pp. 308–319). New York: John Wiley & Sons.

Van der Kolk, B. (1986). *Psychological trauma*. Washington, DC: American Psychiatric Press.

Weiss, J., Rogers, E., Darwin, M., & Dutton, C. (1955). A study of girl sex victims. *Psychiatric Quarterly, 29*(1), 1–27.

Widom, C. S., & Williams, L. (1996). *Cycle of sexual abuse. Research inconclusive about whether child victims become adult abusers.* Report to House of Representatives, Committee of Judiciary, Subcommittee on Crime. Washington, DC: General Accounting Office.

Willock, B. (1983). Play therapy with the aggressive, acting out child. In C. Schaefer & K. O'Connor (Eds.), *Handbook of play therapy* (pp. 386–411). New York: John Wiley & Sons.

Yager, J., Knight, L., Arnold, L., & Kempe, R. (1998). The process of discovery. In Ryan, G., et al. (Ed.), *The web of meaning.* Brandon, VT: Safer Society Press.

Yochelson, S., & Samenow, S. (1976). *The criminal personality (vol. 1).* Northvale, NJ: Aronson.

CHAPTER 12

Juvenile Justice, Legislative, and Policy Responses to Juvenile Sexual Offenses

CHRISTOPHER LOBANOV-ROSTOVSKY

Prior to the 1980s, the general societal response to juveniles who had committed sexual offenses was based on viewing the behavior as curiosity and experimentation, minimizing the severity of the behavior with a "boys will be boys" attitude (Becker, Cunningham-Rathner, & Kaplan, 1986; Ryan, Miyoshi, Metzner, Krugman, & Fryer, 1996). Common perceptions were that these juveniles were not normal, mainstream youth, but had either some sort of cognitive disability or mental health impairment, or were the products of some parental deficiency such as an unfit environment, poverty, or broken homes (Burt, 1944; Doshay, 1943; Kanner, 1948; Maclay, 1960; Wagonner & Boyd, 1941). In addition, many of the juveniles identified as sexual offenders prior to the 1980s were what would today be described as status offenders, who were charged with immorality offenses related to homosexuality, promiscuity, or sexual contact with adults (Atcheson & Williams, 1954; Markey, 1950). Given this paradigm for juveniles who commit sexual offenses, the earliest recommended policy responses were one of two extremes: either institutionalize the juvenile, or do nothing, believing the problem would self-correct (Atcheson & Williams, 1954; Markey, 1950).

THE 1980S: A RADICAL SHIFT IN RESPONSE

Historical responses to juveniles who committed sexual offenses were inextricably altered by retrospective research on adult sex offenders in the 1980s that indicated as many as half of adult sex offenders reported that the onset of their sexual offending began when they were adolescents (Abel, Mittelman, & Becker, 1985; Freeman-Longo, 1978; Longo & Groth, 1983). This finding led professionals in the field to raise the alarm about juveniles who committed sexual offenses, and encouraged a stronger systemic response and new policies including legal accountability, prosecution, mandatory treatment, and increased supervision (Leversee & Pearson, 2001). Many treating adults advocated for earlier intervention in adolescence, believing youth would be more "changeable" (Knopp, 1984). Professionals believed that court

183

supervision and treatment were necessary to prevent subsequent adult sexual offending.

The National Adolescent Perpetration Network (NAPN) was born out of the effort to prevent future sexual offending by juveniles. The National Task Force on Juvenile Sexual Offending subsequently published two "consensus" reports: *Preliminary Report* (1988), and *Revised Report* (1993). The 1993 report identified 387 "assumptions" representing the task force consensus about intervention, including statements supporting a multisystemic response.

The response that evolved in the 1980s typically consisted of adjudicating the youth delinquent in juvenile court or placing them on a diversion program in lieu of adjudication, requiring legal supervision for a limited period of time by juvenile probation officers, and requiring them to attend "offense-specific" treatment. Initially probation officers were not well trained in the management of youth who committed sexual offenses, and treatment programs typically relied on "one-size-treats-all" models modifying components used in adult sex offender treatment at that time. Without available research specific to these youth and driven by the belief that sexual offending recidivism was very high, there was a significant increase in offense-specific juvenile treatment programs during the 1980s and 1990s. Treatment and supervision was typically longer than was provided to other delinquents and long-term "relapse prevention" plans were considered imperative.

As earlier chapters have indicated, due to subsequent developments in the field including research now available and newer juvenile models, professionals now operate on remarkably different assumptions and many earlier misconceptions have been invalidated and corrected over time (Hunter, 1996, 1999; Ryan, 1998, 1999, 2000b; Ryan & Lane, 1997). While intentions in the 1980s were well-meaning, there has been a pendulum effect in that early efforts to increase awareness and do something to prevent juveniles continuing to offend have contributed to increasingly punitive systemic responses to juveniles who have committed sexual offenses during the last decade (Letourneau & Miner, 2005; Leversee & Pearson, 2001; Ryan, 1997).

Community pressures to "get tough on" juvenile violence and crime as a whole, which followed several highly publicized atrocities committed by juveniles in the 1990s, have become increasingly focused on juvenile sexual offenses. Despite a long tradition of confidentiality in the juvenile justice system and the juvenile courts' founding premise that most juvenile delinquency is not inevitably predictive of adult criminality (Empey, 1982; Gendreau & Ross, 1987; National Council of Juvenile and Family Court Judges, 1984), the community's belief that there is "no cure" for sexual offending has led to public identification of these youth.

THE 1990S: THE ONSET OF FEDERAL MANAGEMENT OF JUVENILES WHO COMMIT SEX OFFENSES

The 1990s saw the federal government become involved in legislative and policy responses to sexual offending in the United States. At the federal level, a series of landmark legislative pieces directly and indirectly shaped the response to adults and juveniles who commit sexual offenses. The Jacob Wetterling Crimes Against Children and Sexually Violent Offender Registration Act (Wetterling Act, 1994) required states to begin registering certain sexual offenders with law enforcement agencies. This law was soon followed by a series of amendments to the Act, including Megan's Law (1996), which required states to allow public access to information on certain sexual offenders, and the Campus Sex Crimes Prevention Act (2000), which required states to make information on sex offenders available to colleges and universities.

It should be noted that no legislative input was sought from organizations that directly address juvenile sexual offending, such as the National Adolescent Perpetration Network (NAPN) or the Association for the Treatment of Sexual Abusers (ATSA), prior to passing those pieces of legislation (Leversee & Pearson, 2001). While the Wetterling Act and its subsequent amendments did not specifically require states to register juveniles who committed sexual offenses (unless the juvenile was tried and convicted as an adult), its "floor, not a ceiling" philosophy allowed states to go above the minimum requirements of the Act, and therefore did not prohibit inclusion of juveniles in registration and notification schemes. As a result, many states began to require registration and notification for juveniles who were adjudicated delinquent for sexual offenses. Such approaches have further reinforced the view that juveniles who commit sexual offenses are the same as adult sex offenders and have high rates of recidivism—two myths specifically disproven in scientific literature (see Chapter 6).

By 2009, nearly three-fourths (36) of states required some form of registration for juveniles who commit sexual offenses (Terry & Furlong, 2004), and approximately one-third (17) required some type of community notification regarding those registered juveniles (Justice Policy Institute, 2008). The federal government's role in legislative and policy responses to juveniles in the 1990s led to assertions that the response to juvenile delinquency in general (Steinberg, 2009; Steinberg & Scott, 2003), and to juvenile sexual offending specifically, has gone too far (Chaffin & Bonner, 1998; Ryan, 2000a; Weinrott, 1996).

THE NEW MILLENNIUM OF 2000: CONTINUATION OF PUNITIVE RESPONSES TO JUVENILE SEXUAL OFFENDING

In the most recent decade, United States legislative and policy responses to juvenile sexual offenses, as with adult sexual offenders, have continued on an increasingly punitive path. Trends in adult sex offender management that developed in the 1980s and 1990s have been applied equally to juveniles, including provisions for civil commitment of juveniles at the end of their sentences in Pennsylvania, and even limits on where juveniles registered for sexual offenses can live based on residency restrictions and/or municipal zoning ordinances (Leversee & Pearson, 2001). These policies increase the youth's risk of stigmatization, peer rejection, and isolation from families and home communities, factors that research suggests aggravate rather than mitigate subsequent risk (Leversee & Pearson, 2001).

Most recently, the federal government in the United States has taken the extraordinary step of legislating registration and public notification for all persons who have committed sexual offenses, *including many juveniles*, in the sweeping Adam Walsh "Child Protection and Safety" Act of 2006 (AWA). For the first time, the federal government has now mandated that states must include youth ages 14 and older who commit an "aggravated sexual assault" in their registration and notification system. As a result, states are now required to publicly label juveniles as "sex offenders."

The AWA requires states to place certain offenders on the public Internet registry, actively notify the public via e-mail of their presence in the community, registering not only their home address, but also school and work addresses as well. The Tier categories of offenses (intended to designate levels of seriousness and risk) captures many juvenile offenses, and some juveniles must continue to register with law enforcement *once every three months for life*. This is despite the fact that the risk factors considered by the Tier System are based primarily on offense of conviction/adjudication classification, and do not reflect the low rates of sexual recidivism by the juveniles (Alexander, 1999; Worling & Curwen, 2000).

The effect of such provisions significantly inhibits the ability of these youth to reintegrate successfully back into their communities and often impacts their victims and families as well, fracturing relationships and stigmatizing families (Prescott & Levenson, 2007). School districts across the country have had to decide how to handle juvenile registration and notification information, often limiting dissemination of such information based on concerns for the confidentiality of the juvenile's school records, while balancing their responsibility for the safety of other students (Walker, 2008). Probation and treatment providers have included school personnel in training and team decision making in order to create reasonable protections for both the youth who offended and the school's students. Under AWA, schools will no longer have discretion in making informed and individualized decisions, as confidentiality is eliminated.

Further, the AWA requires retroactive application of the registration and notification system to all those previously adjudicated with a sexual offense who subsequently come back into the legal system, either as a juvenile or adult, based on any criminal charge, sexual or otherwise. Retroactivity will lead to newly registering many juveniles who were not previously subject to registration, given that research has consistently found that the juveniles who are rearrested later are more likely to have committed a nonsexual offense than sexual reoffending (Reitzel & Carbonell, 2006). The AWA does provide for juveniles who are subject to lifetime registration to be released from such registration after 25 years if they keep a "clean record." However, the provisions of a "clean record" include no probation revocations during the course of supervision and no subsequent delinquent adjudications or criminal convictions. Not only will such a completely "clean" record prove challenging for some of these youth, but such requirements have no relationship to their risk of sexually offending in the community, which is the premise behind the AWA.

2010: RETHINKING SYSTEMIC RESPONSES: WHAT DOES THE RESEARCH SUGGEST?

Over the past century, the response to juveniles who have committed sexual offenses has swung from one extreme to the other in a pendulum-like effect (Leversee & Pearson, 2001; Ryan, 1997). Early systemic responses to this problem alternated between marginalizing some as not like other youth (deviant) and removing them from society to institutions, or viewing them as normal boys in need of no response. Over the past 25 years, the systemic response has evolved to viewing these juveniles as the same as adult sex offenders and the line between the response to adults and juveniles has largely disappeared. Sex offenders are currently viewed as "compulsive, progressive, and incurable" regardless of age (Chaffin, Letourneau, & Silovsky, 2002, p. 205). The punitive nature of the public and policymakers' response has been based on three beliefs that have been shown to be untrue (Letourneau & Miner, 2005):

- There is an epidemic of juvenile sexual offending.
  FACT: There is no evidence to suggest that juveniles sexually offend any more frequently now than in previous generations. In fact, the overall rate of child

sexual abuse in the United States has declined over the past 25 years (Finkelhor & Jones, 2008).
- Juveniles have more in common with adult sex offenders than other juvenile delinquents.
    FACT: Every significant study of juveniles who have committed sexual offenses has found that most are more at risk for delinquency than for adult sexual offending (Caldwell, 2007; Epperson, Ralston, Fowers, DeWitt, & Gore, 2006; Letourneau & Armstrong, 2008; Worling & Curwen, 2000).
- Juveniles have a high risk of reoffending.
    FACT: Even adult recidivism rates are much lower than most believe, and juvenile recidivism is even lower. The range of sexual recidivism in most samples of juveniles is 4–20%.

There are a variety of ways in which crime statistics are measured, including the Federal Bureau of Investigation Uniform Crime Report (UCR), Bureau of Justice Statistics National Crime Victim Survey (NCSV), and the United States Department of Justice National Incidence Studies of Missing, Abducted, Runaway, and Thrownaway Children (NISMART). These sources suggest that juvenile sexual offending has maintained a fairly steady rate over the past 20 years: 10–30% of all sexual offenses in the United States, depending upon the type of measures used (Federal Bureau of Investigation, 2001; Finkelhor, Hammer, & Sedlak, 2008; U.S. Department of Justice, 2000). The notion of a new and growing epidemic of juvenile sexual offending is not supported by the facts.

Research also shows that most juveniles do not go on to be charged with or convicted of other sexual offenses, with rates of recidivism typically between 4–20% (Alexander, 1999; Epperson, Ralston, Fowers, DeWitt, & Gore, 2006; Reitzel & Carbonell, 2006; Vandiver, 2006; Worling & Curwen, 2000). In addition, as has been already noted, most juveniles who are rearrested later have engaged in nonsexual delinquency, with rates of nonsexual recidivism typically ranging from 20–50% (Reitzel & Carbonell, 2006; Vandiver, 2006; Worling & Curwen, 2000). The body of research to date about juveniles who have committed sexual offenses clearly contradicts the beliefs that have driven legislation and policy (Letourneau & Miner, 2005; Zimring, 2004).

Parallel to more punitive legislative and policy trends, treatment providers, supervising officers, researchers, and others have questioned these approaches, and have been urging caution to not overrespond (Prescott & Levenson, 2007). The goal of policy and law should be to minimize risk and increase community safety, while providing the opportunity for rehabilitation and ensuring the rights and welfare of these youth (Leversee & Pearson, 2001). The pendulum must now center on earlier interventions to reduce the risks of juvenile sexual offenses. A different legislative and policy response is needed in that it is now known that most are not destined to become adult sex offenders. Unfortunately, there are often considerable gaps between new discoveries in science and beliefs in the community.

As has been discussed in previous chapters, typology research has clarified that juveniles who commit sexual offenses are not a homogenous group. Some are at high risk for future sexual offending, as was feared in the 1980s, and need high levels of treatment and management, but many do not need such an intensive systemic response. Like other delinquents, many have significant psychosocial deficits or co-occurring mental health needs that benefit from rehabilitative approaches

(Hunter, 2008). One-size-fits-all adult sex offender management legislation and policy is clearly not warranted for juveniles to prevent future sexual recidivism. Unnecessarily wasting resources and placing punitive measures on juveniles when such measures are not needed is poor public policy. While higher-risk delinquents warrant intensive services, lower-risk juveniles are better served by low intensity programming with an emphasis on successful reintegration into normalizing life-styles (Andrews & Bonta, 2003). Ironically, similar conclusions are emerging in research with adult sex offenders (Hanson, 2006).

In one comparison study, the outcomes of a group of juveniles who had committed sexual offenses was compared to a group of juveniles who committed nonsexual offenses (Total $N = 2,029$). The results indicated no significant difference in the rate of subsequent sexual offending over a five-year follow-up period between the two groups of juveniles. In addition, of the 54 homicides committed by the sample group, none were committed by the juveniles who had previous sexual offenses (Caldwell, 2007). This finding is significant given the public's perception and fear of predatory sex offenders who kidnap, sexually assault, and murder children. While none of the murders in the sample were of this nature, this research does suggest that the public's fear of and response to juveniles who commit sexual offenses may not be significantly enhancing community safety.

Finally, in a birth cohort study from Racine, Wisconsin, 8.5% of males with juvenile sex police contacts offended sexually as adults, while 6.2% of males with any nonsexual juvenile police contacts offended sexually as adults. There was no significant statistical difference between the two groups in terms of future adult sexual offending, supporting the researchers' conclusion that targeting only juveniles who are known to have committed sexual offenses for intervention misses 90% of those who will in fact commit sexual offenses as adults, and mistakenly targets 90% of those who had sexually offended as juveniles as potential adult sex offenders. It was noted that the best predictor of adult sex offending behavior in the sample was the frequency of police contact by a juvenile, regardless of whether the contact was for a sex offense or not (Zimring, Piquero, & Jennings, 2007).

2010: RESHAPING SYSTEMIC RESPONSES—USING RESEARCH TO INFORM POLICY AND LAW

Given the apparent similarities between the majority of juveniles who commit sexual offenses and juveniles who commit nonsexual delinquent acts, legislation and policy responses consistent with broader juvenile justice paradigms appear indicated. The juvenile justice system was originally created to provide protection for juveniles and an opportunity for rehabilitation. Current brain research supports the distinction between adult and juvenile behavior, in that brain development is not complete until the twenties, suggesting that juveniles are much more changeable over time than older persons (Sowell, Thompson, Holmes, Jernigan, & Toga, 1999).

Historically, the juvenile court was created as an intermediate intervention between parental authority and adult criminal sanctions. The juvenile court's intent was to act "en loco parentae" ("in the place of a kind and just parent") in the absence or breakdown of parental care and/or control of the child. The juvenile court's role was to be that of guardian, providing guidance and discipline for rehabilitation. However, the traditional juvenile court system had assumed complete control over juveniles without regard for due process or legal representation.

In the late 1960s and 1970s, the lack of legal protection for the rights of juveniles became a heightened concern. Legislative and policy responses developed new standards for juvenile courts to balance the protection of juveniles from intrusive legal procedures. During this time, labeling theorists also began to identify that the legal processing of juveniles contributed to future delinquent and criminal behavior by labeling them delinquent or criminal. As a result, the juvenile justice system developed nonlabeling and decriminalizing responses wherever possible. "Status offenses" were defined as behaviors that were not illegal for adults but required intervention and rehabilitation, and other minor infractions were at times referred to "diversion" programs to avoid the court process, while more serious offenses were "adjudicated" delinquent but not classified as criminal convictions in an attempt to give the juvenile the opportunity for rehabilitation without being labeled a criminal.

Additional safeguards were built into the juvenile justice system, including the right to confidentiality, the adjudicatory rather than conviction process, and differential record keeping. Given that juveniles were viewed as being in need of protection and rehabilitation, they were still not afforded the same due process rights as adults, such as the right to a jury trial, under the premise that they did not need as many protections in a nonpunitive, protective system.

Unfortunately, erosion has occurred in the juvenile justice system over the past 20 years, not just in the response to juvenile sexual offenses, but for all juveniles adjudicated delinquent (Howell, 2003). More than 90% of states have made recent substantive changes to their criminal and juvenile laws. Such reforms have included: changes in juvenile court waivers for juveniles to be tried as adults; stricter sentencing guidelines; less confidentiality in juvenile records; and specifically for juveniles who commit sexual offenses, registration, and community notification requirements (Center for Sex Offender Management [CSOM], 1999). Coffey (2006) observed that sealing juvenile delinquency records once the juvenile becomes an adult is no longer a central component of the juvenile and criminal justice system.

Significant increases in the number of juveniles being waived over to adult court in the past 20 years include a 71% increase between 1985 and 1994 (Prescott & Levenson, 2007; Syzmanski, 1998). The age by which a juvenile may be waived to adult court has also been lowered in more than half the states, with 40% of states now having no minimum age at which a juvenile may be tried as an adult (CSOM, 1999). In addition, juveniles who are waived to adult court are more likely to serve a minimum correctional sentence as a result (Redding, 2008; Sickmund, Snyder, & Poe-Yamagata, 1997), are less likely to receive treatment (ATSA, 2000), and are more likely to recidivate (Letourneau & Miner, 2005; Redding, 2008). Finally, more than 20% of states now permit public juvenile hearings with no restrictions (CSOM, 1999).

As these changes have evolved in the juvenile justice system, scientific advances in research relevant to growth and development and brain functioning have led professionals to question juvenile culpability (Steinberg, 2009; Steinberg & Scott, 2003) and whether juveniles have the capacity to understand a criminal case, to properly consult an attorney, and to make sound decisions regarding possible plea bargains and defense (Grisso, 1997).

Specific to juveniles who have committed sexual offenses, a recent South Dakota Supreme Court decision (2008 SD 108) highlighted the conflict between due process and punitive measures by ruling that a juvenile should not be on the public Internet sex offender registry without being afforded the same rights as adult sex offenders. It was noted that adult sex offenders were able to get a suspended imposition of sentence, but juveniles were not afforded a similar right. The South Dakota Supreme Court ruled that, given juveniles are not afforded the same due process rights as adults, to subject them to the same legal response is unconstitutional (Associated Press, 2008).

Unlike the Wetterling Act and Megan's Law, the Adam Walsh Child Protection and Safety Act requires states to create registration and notification systems equally for juveniles and adults. Therefore, juveniles are subject to the same legislative and policy responses as adult sex offenders without being afforded the same level of rights. As a result, the consequences for juveniles who have committed sexual offenses appear worse than those for adult sex offenders.

Initially, the proposed guidelines for implementation of the AWA made no distinction at all between juveniles who have committed sexual offenses and adult sex offenders. However, after much commentary from stakeholders, the final guide-lines made several changes, including use of the Tier III designation for juveniles to be placed on the public Internet sex offender registry and deleting the victim age requirement for Tier III juveniles (i.e., adult sex offenders are Tier III if the victim is under the age of 12), which would have disproportionately placed juveniles in a higher Tier by virtue of the fact of both they and their victims being younger. Despite these modifications, more than two-thirds of states have significant discrepancies between their current juvenile registration and notification systems (if any), and the requirements of AWA, and many states have indicated concern about complying with the AWA legislation as a result (Harris & Lobanov-Rostovsky, 2009).

Although the federal government, as upheld by the United States Supreme Court (*Smith v. Doe*, 538 U.S. 84 [2003]), characterizes registration and notification as a "civil regulatory response" rather than a "punitive response," it has been found by several state Supreme Courts (e.g., Alaska Supreme Court No. S-12150, 2008; Maine Judicial Supreme Court 2007 ME 139) that the requirements of such a system are punitive, and therefore violate due process rights in their retroactive application. If registration and notification do have a punitive aspect for juveniles, there may be an iatrogenic effect on juveniles (Letourneau & Miner, 2005). Public registration has been designed to reduce recidivism and the time needed to detect recidivism (United States Department of Justice, 2007; Zimring, 2004). However, a meta-analysis of 177 research studies from 1958–2002 ($n = 442,471$ criminal offenders) determined that punitive approaches (i.e., prison and intermediate sanctions) in the absence of rehabilitation do not reduce recidivism (Smith, Goggin, & Gendreau, 2002), a policy outcome supported by others (Andrews & Bonta, 2003; Aos, Miller, & Drake, 2006). If registration and notification are truly quasi-punitive measures designed to deter future sexual offending, there is no research to suggest that such a punitive approach will be effective in reducing recidivism.

Further, research does suggest that confrontational styles of intervention lead to poorer treatment outcomes (Marshall, Anderson, & Fernandez, 1999). Legislative and policy responses to juveniles who have committed sexual offenses appear to co-opt such a style.

In surveys of judges, 75–92% indicate concerns about placing juveniles on public registries depending on the specific survey question asked (Bumby, Talbot, & West, 2006). As a result, it is possible that judges may change their behavior to reassert their influence over registration decisions (Letourneau, Bandyopadhyay, Sinha, & Arm-strong, 2009a). In addition, it was found that prosecutors also appear to modify their charging behavior to "protect" many younger juveniles and those with fewer or no prior offenses from possible lifetime registration charges following enactment of this law. In studying trends in prosecution, there was also a 22% reduction in the odds of overall prosecution, suggesting that the policy of registering juveniles may actually undermine the identification (and by proxy treatment and supervision) of juveniles who commit sexual offenses (Letourneau, Bandyopadhyay, Sinha, & Armstrong, 2009b), a finding also noted in New Jersey in response to lifetime registration requirements (CSOM, 2001; Freeman-Longo, 2001; Leversee & Pearson, 2001).

TARGETING THE BAD APPLES: CONCENTRATING RESOURCES TO BE MOST PRODUCTIVE

While there are concerns about the current legislative and policy responses for juveniles who have committed sexual offenses, it must be remembered that there is a small percentage of the juveniles who sexually offend who, due to levels of risk and/or lack of motivation to change, do need be treated like adult sex offenders. Ideally, the most resources for management and treatment interventions would be invested in those who will pose the greatest risk over time. The problem lies in identifying those at highest risk, given the limits of risk prediction with juveniles that is associated with the fluid and changeable state of young people who are growing, developing, and changing at such a rapid rate as is apparent in adolescence. In addition, research suggests that clinicians and management professionals tend to overestimate the level of risk with these youth, probably in fear of not accurately predicting a recidivist and another person being victimized (Schram, Milloy, & Rowe, 1991). Thus, policies and interventions end up targeting broader ranges of risk than might be most productive in attempting to ensure that no recidivist is missed. Until empirically validated factors clarify *with certainty* which youth will in fact continue to offend sexually as adults, systemic policies should continue to provide opportunities for rehabilitation of juveniles who have sexually offended.

CURRENT POLICIES

Over the past decade, many state and federal laws and policies for sex offender management were designed for adults but have been applied to juveniles (Chaffin, 2008). To date, there is no evidence to suggest that registration and notification is effective in reducing recidivism for juveniles who have committed sexual offenses (ATSA, 2000; Letourneau & Armstrong, 2008; Trivits & Repucci, 2002). There have been some recent general outcome studies on adult sex offenders trying to determine the effectiveness of registration and notification, with mixed results; however, there have been only two studies specifically evaluating juvenile registration and notification of juveniles, both conducted in South Carolina where registration and notification of juveniles is currently required. One study compared the recidivism rate over a four-year follow-up for 111 juveniles, who were subject to registration and notification between January 1995 and January 2005, to a matched group of 111 juveniles who were not subject to registration and notification. The results indicated an overall 1% sexual recidivism rate (two youth rearrested for sexual offenses) for all of the juveniles in the study, with both recidivism events committed by juveniles who were subject to registration and notification, and none by the group of juveniles not subject to registration and notification. The recidivism rates between the two groups (nonregistration and nonnotification) were not statistically significant, and the researchers note the common problem related to the low base rate for sexual recidivism in developing statistically significant findings (Letourneau & Armstrong, 2008). In addition, there was no significant statistical difference in recidivism involving nonsexual offenses against persons between the registration and notification group and the comparison group, but the registration and notification group was more likely to commit new offenses that were not crimes against persons (Letourneau & Armstrong, 2008).

In a second study, 1,275 male juveniles who committed sex offenses in South Carolina were reviewed, 574 of whom were required to register. In a nine-year follow-up, 7.5% of the overall sample was charged with a subsequent sex offense while 2.5% were adjudicated on a sexual offense. The overall sample was responsible for 148 assault charges and 561 other-offense charges. The findings did not provide any support for registration as a deterrent for juveniles who have sexually offended to reoffend less, given the nonsignificant difference in recidivism between the registration and notification group, and the nonregistration and nonnotification group (Letourneau, Bandyopadhyay, Sinha, & Armstrong, 2009b). It was noted that registration did appear to predict other-offense charges, but the researchers hypothesize a surveillance effect in that those who register may be more highly monitored, and therefore detected and charged at a higher rate for nonsexual delinquency and crime.

In summary, there is no empirical support for the use of registration and notification of juveniles who have sexually offended as a deterrent. Despite this finding, it is estimated that 18,721 (3%) of the 624,020 registered sex offenders in the United States are juveniles who have committed sexual offenses, although there is no specific data on the number of registered juveniles (Letourneau and colleagues, 2009b). If all states do enact the AWA, tens of thousands of additional juveniles will be required to be placed on the public Internet registry (Chaffin, 2008).

The consequences of such a policy have been described as, This has the "potential to steer attention and resources away from assisting victims and preventing future abuse" (Prescott & Levenson, 2000, p. 5). Registration and notification diverts funds from "necessary entities such as victim's advocate offices, rape crisis centers, and shelters for women and children seeking refuge from abusers" (Prescott & Levenson, 2007, p. 5). In addition, decreases in reporting of offenses by the families and victims of juveniles has been noted in two states (Colorado and New Jersey) and attributed to fears of the impact of public registration on juveniles (CSOM, 2001; Freeman-Longo, 2001; Leversee & Pearson, 2001). The idea of registration and notification provides a false sense of security for the public, while overinclusive registries make it difficult for anyone to determine the actual level of risk posed by any given registrant (Justice Policy Institute, 2008). The end result of registration and notification may actually increase denial and a return to minimization of juvenile sexual offending in order to avoid legal consequences that are perceived to be unjust (Leversee & Pearson, 2001).

REASONABLE APPROACHES FOR THE FUTURE

Systemic responses to juveniles who commit sexual offenses must consider specific needs and risks of each individual rather than a cookie-cutter approach. Treatment, supervision, and management decisions based on the needs and risks of the specific juvenile can be determined by multidisciplinary teams of specially trained professionals working with the youth and family in a collaborative manner. The use of multidisciplinary teams and individualized intervention plans have been the norm in other realms of child protection, social work, and child welfare, and have been effective in very diverse cases. Policies that allow the collaborative team flexibility and discretion, rather than rigidly prescribing a single approach, are most able to meet the needs of individuals and families. Including treatment providers, supervising officers, caseworkers, school personnel, attorneys, caregivers, and other significant adults involved with the juvenile to form a collaborative team demonstrates many of qualities relevant to the etiology of the problem. When adults take seriously their responsibility to meet the needs of youth, while holding the youth responsible for their own behaviors, the intervention parallels the goals of treatment: empathic recognition and responses, and personal responsibility.

Many states have developed policy groups and management boards made up of key stakeholders to guide sex offender laws and policy, develop treatment and supervision standards, and define criteria for specialization and expertise of treatment providers and probation services (Lobanov-Rostovsky, 2008). Such groups give individual stakeholders and agencies an opportunity to join forces and present a unified consensus and voice. In addition, such groups signify expertise, guiding policymakers and legislators to consult those most knowledgeable about the problem in making recommendations and decisions about policy and law.

Juveniles who commit sexual offenses are not the same as adult sex offenders, and legal and policy responses should not treat them as such. There is an extensive body of literature to highlight the negative impact of labeling on juveniles with delinquent behaviors, and given the apparent similarities between many juveniles who commit sexual offenses and juveniles who commit nonsexual offenses, the labeling concern is the same. Registration and notification are inherently labeling, and efforts should be taken to limit the exposure of juvenile registration information with notification being done "conscientiously, cautiously, and selectively" (ATSA, 2000). Many have suggested that juveniles be subject to community notification only in the most extreme cases (ATSA, 2000; Ryan, 2000a), if at all (Letourneau, Bandyopadhyay, Sinha, & Armstrong, 2009b). Further, if a juvenile is required to register there should be judicial discretion to relieve them of that requirement when developmental progress, risk reduction, and subsequent behavior records provide evidence of change, rather than the original charge continuing to dictate registration (Letourneau and colleagues, 2009b). Normal development and maturation moderates many of the risks associated with delinquent behavior in adolescence, including sexually abusive behavior, and should not be impeded unless there is evidence of risk to community safety (Ryan & Lane, 1997).

The juvenile justice system is designed to provide certain protections for juveniles and ensure access to rehabilitation where the juvenile is amenable, while limiting a juvenile's access to certain due process features as a trade-off. Juveniles who have committed sexual offenses should be afforded the same protections and rights to rehabilitation as other youth, provided community safety can be adequately addressed (ATSA, 2000). Juveniles should not be subjected to adult-level requirements or responsibilities without being afforded adult due process rights, and should be addressed at the juvenile court level unless the severity of the crime and empirically validated risk factors dictate a transfer to adult court.

Legislation and policy responses for juvenile sexual offending should draw on what is shown to be effective via research (evidence-based or empirically supported). Addressing juvenile behavior as part of a larger family and community system has shown promise (e.g., Multi-Systemic Therapy [MST]; Borduin and Schaeffer, 2002) in this regard for some juveniles in certain settings. As has been suggested in other chapters, the approach for youth should support normal, healthy lifestyles and assist with the development of prosocial skills and support. An adequate continuum of care (see Chapter 14) needs to ensure that a juvenile can receive treatment and supervision services relevant to their needs and maintain community connectedness, while protecting the community. Policies that limit access to treatment across the continuum of care (i.e., zoning ordinances restricting where juveniles who have sexually offended can live or with whom they can live) are counterproductive.

In summary, public policy and law must balance sanctions designed to enhance community safety and punish criminal acts, with providing interventions that enhance the prognosis for youth to be successful, productive members of that community.

REFERENCES

Abel, G. G., Mittelman, M. S., & Becker, J. V. (1985). Sexual offenders: Results of assessment and recommendations for treatment. In M. H. Ben-Aron, S. J. Hucker, & C. D. Webster (Eds.), *Clinical criminology: The assessment and treatment of criminal behavior* (pp. 191–206). Toronto: M and M Graphics.

Alexander, M. (1999). Sex offender treatment efficacy revisited. *Sexual Abuse: A Journal of Research and Treatment, 11*(2), 101–116.

Andrews, D. A., & Bonta, J. (2003). *The psychology of criminal conduct* (3rd ed.) Cincinnati, OH: Anderson.

Aos, S., Miller, M., & Drake, E. (2006). *Evidence-based adult corrections programs: What works and what does not.* Olympia, WA: Washington State Institute for Public Policy.

Associated Press. (2008). *South Dakota: Sex-offender law.* Published by the Associated Press, November 6.

Association for the Treatment of Sexual Abusers (ATSA). (2000). *The effective legal management of juvenile sexual offenders.* Adopted by the ATSA Board of Directors on March 11, 2000, from http://www.atsa.com/ppjuvenile.html

Atcheson, J. D., & Williams, D. C. (1954). A. study of juvenile sex offenders. *American Journal of Psychiatry, III*, 366–370.

Becker, J. V., Cunningham-Rathner, J., & Kaplan, M. F. (1986). Adolescent sexual offenders: Demographics, criminal sexual histories, and recommendations for reducing future offenses. *International Journal of Interpersonal Violence, 4*, 431–445.

Borduin, C. M., & Schaeffer, C. M. (2002). Multisystemic treatment of juvenile sexual offenders: A progress report. *Journal of Psychology and Human Sexuality, 13*, 25–42.

Bumby, K. M., Talbot, T. B., & West, R. (2006). *System challenges and substantive needs regarding juvenile sex offenders: A summary of perspectives from the bench.* Presentation at the 25th annual Conference of the Association for the Treatment of Sexual Abusers, Chicago, IL.

Burt, Sir C. L. (1944). *The young delinquent* (4th ed.). Bickley: University of London Press.

Caldwell, M. (2007). Sexual offense adjudication and sexual recidivism among juvenile offenders. *Sexual Abuse: A Journal of Research and Treatment, 19*(2), 107–113.

Center for Sex Offender Management (CSOM). (1999). *Understanding juvenile sexual offending behavior: Emerging research, treatment approaches and management practices.* Silver Spring, MD: Author. From http://www.csom.org

Center for Sex Offender Management (CSOM). (2001). *Community notification and education.* Silver Spring, MD: Author. From http://www.csom.org

Chaffin, M. (2008). Our minds are made up: Don't confuse us with the facts. *Child Maltreatment, 13*, 110–121.

Chaffin, M., & Bonner, B. (1998). Don't shoot, we're your children: Have we gone too far in our response to adolescent sexual abusers and children with sexual behavior problems? *Child Maltreatment: Journal of the American Professional Society on the Abuse of Children, 3*(4), 314–316.

Chaffin, M., Letourneau, E., & Silovsky, J. F. (2002). Adults, adolescents, and children who sexually abuse children: A developmental perspective. In J. E. B. Myers & L. Berliner (Eds.), *The APSAC handbook on child maltreatment* (2nd ed.) (pp. 205–232). Thousand Oaks, CA: Sage.

Coffey, P. (2006). Forensic issues in evaluating juvenile sex offenders. In D. S. Prescott (Ed.), *Risk assessment of youth who have sexually abused: Theory, controversy, and emerging strategies* (pp. 118–169). Oklahoma City, OK: Wood'N'Barnes.

Doshay, L. J. (1943). *The boy sex offender and his later career.* New York: Grune and Stratton.

Empey, L. T. (1982). *American delinquency: Its meaning and construction.* Florence, KY: Dorsey Press.

Epperson, D. L., Ralston, C. A., Fowers, D., DeWitt, J., & Gore, K. S. (2006). Actuarial risk assessment with juveniles who offend sexually: Development of the juvenile sexual offense recidivism risk assessment tool—II. In D. S. Prescott (Ed.), *Risk assessment of youth who have sexually abused: Theory, controversy, and emerging strategies* (pp. 118–169). Oklahoma City, OK: Wood'N'Barnes.

Federal Bureau of Investigation (FBI). (2001). *Crime in the United States, 1999: Uniform crime reports.* Washington, DC: U.S. Department of Justice.

Finkelhor, D., Hammer, H., & Sedlak, A. J. (2008). *Sexually assaulted children: National estimates and characteristics.* National Incidence Studies of Missing, Abducted, Runaway, and Thrown-away Children: Office of Justice Programs.

Finkelhor, D., & Jones, L. M. (2008). *Updated trends in child maltreatment 2006.* Crimes Against Children Research Center. Washington, DC: U.S. Department of Justice, Office of Justice Programs, Office of Juvenile Justice and Delinquency Prevention.

Freeman-Longo, R. E. (1978). *Child molestation: The offender and the assault.* 112th Annual Congress of Correction, Toronto, Canada.

Freeman-Longo, R. E. (2001). *Revisiting Megan's Law and sex offender registration.* Unpublished manuscript.

Gendreau, P., & Ross, R. (1987). Revivication of rehabilitation: Evidence from the 1980s. *Justice Quarterly, 4*(3), 349–407.

Grisso, T. (1997). The competence of adolescents as trial defendants. *Psychology, Public Policy, and Law, 3,* 3–32.

Hanson, R. K. (2006). *What works: The principles of effective interventions with offenders.* Presentation at the 25th Annual Conference of the Association for Treatment of Sexual Abusers, Chicago, IL.

Harris, A., & Lobanov-Rostovsky, C. (2009). SORNA: A view from the states, part I. *Sex Offender Law Report, 10*(2), 17–32.

Howell, J. C. (2003). *Preventing and reducing juvenile delinquency: A comprehensive framework.* Thousand Oaks, CA: Sage.

Hunter, J. A. (1996). *Working with children and adolescents who sexually abuse children.* Paper presented at the 11th International Congress on Child Abuse and Neglect, Dublin, Ireland.

Hunter, J. A. (1999). *Understanding juvenile sexual offending behavior: Emerging research, treatment approaches and management practices.* Silver Spring, NY: Center for Sex Offender Management.

Hunter, J. A. (2008). *Understanding sexually abusive youth: New research and clinical directions.* Ft. Collins: Colorado Child and Adolescent Mental Health Conference.

Justice Policy Institute. (2008). *Registering harm: How sex offense registries fail youth and communities.* From http://www.Justicepolicy.org

Kanner, L. (1948). *Child psychiatry.* Oxford: Blackwell Publications.

Knopp, F. H. (1984). *Retraining adult sex offenders: Methods and models.* Orwell, VT: Safer Society Press.

Letourneau, E. J., & Armstrong, K. S. (2008). Recidivism rates for registered and nonregistered juvenile sexual offenders. *Sexual Abuse: A Journal of Research and Treatment*, 20(4), 393–408.

Letourneau, E. J., Bandyopadhyay, D., Sinha, D., & Armstrong, K. (2009a). Effects of sex offender registration policies on juvenile justice decision making. *Sexual Abuse: A Journal of Research and Treatment*, 21, 149–165.

Letourneau, E. J., Bandyopadhyay, D., Sinha, D., & Armstrong, K. (2009b). The influence of sex offender registration on juvenile sexual recidivism. *Criminal Justice Policy Review*, 20, 136–153.

Letourneau, E. J., & Miner, M. H. (2005). Juvenile sex offenders: A case against the legal and clinical status quo. *Sexual Abuse: A Journal of Research and Treatment*, 17(3), 293–312.

Leversee, T., & Pearson, C. (2001). Eliminating the pendulum effect: A balanced approach to the assessment, treatment, and management of sexually abusive youth. *Journal of the Center for Families, Children, and the Courts*, 3, 45–57.

Lobanov-Rostovsky, C. (2008). Sex offender treatment/management policy groups. *ATSA Forum, XIX* (3).

Longo, R. E., & Groth, A. N. (1983). Juvenile sexual offenses in the histories of adult rapists and child molesters. *International Journal of Offender Therapy and Comparative Criminology*, 27(2), 150–155.

Maclay, D. T. (1960). Boys who commit sexual misdemeanors. *British Medical Journal*, 16 (January), 186–190.

Markey, O. B. (1950). A. study of aggressive sex misbehavior in adolescents brought to juvenile court. *American Journal of Orthopsychiatry*, 20, 719–731.

Marshall, W. L., Anderson, D. A., & Fernandez, Y. (1999). *Cognitive behavioral treatment of sexual offenders*. New York: John Wiley & Sons.

National Adolescent Perpetrator Network (NAPN). (1988). Preliminary report from the National Task Force on Juvenile Sexual Offending. *Juvenile and Family Court Journal*, 39(2), 1–67.

National Adolescent Perpetrator Network (NAPN). (1993). The revised report from the National Task Force on Juvenile Sexual Offending. *Juvenile and Family Court Journal*, 44(4), 1–120.

National Council of Juvenile and Family Court Judges. (1984). The juvenile court and serious offenders (special issue). *Juvenile and Family Court Journal*, 44(4), 1–121.

Prescott, D., & Levenson, J. (2007). Youth who have sexually abused: Registration, recidivism, and risk. *ATSA Forum, XIX* (2).

Redding, R. E. (2008). *Juvenile transfer laws: An effective deterrent to juvenile delinquency?* Washington, DC: Office of Juvenile Justice and Delinquency Prevention Bulletin.

Reitzel, L. R., & Carbonell, J. L. (2006). The effectiveness of sexual offender treatment for juveniles as measured by recidivism: A meta-analysis. *Sexual Abuse: A Journal of Research and Treatment*, 18(4), 401–421.

Ryan, G. (1997). Similarities and differences of sexually abusive adults and juveniles. *Interchange: NAPN Newsletter*. Denver, CO: Kempe National Centre, University of Colorado Health Sciences Centre, March 1–5.

Ryan, G. (1998). What's so special about specialized treatment? (Invited commentary). *Journal of Interpersonal Violence*, 13(5), 647–652.

Ryan, G. (1999). The treatment of sexually abusive youth: The evolving consensus. *Journal of Interpersonal Violence*, 14(4), 422–436.

Ryan, G. (2000a). *Overcoming our own denial: Are we willing to change when new evidence challenges old assumptions?*15th Annual NAPN Conference, Weaving a Tapestry, Denver, CO.

Ryan, G. (2000b). Static, stable and dynamic risks and assets relevant to the prevention and treatment of abusive behavior. *Poster presentation, First National Sexual Violence Prevention Conference, Dallas, TX.*

Ryan, G., & Lane, S. (Eds.). (1997). *Juvenile sexual offending: Causes, consequences, and correction.* San Francisco, CA: Jossey-Bass Publishers.

Ryan, G., Miyoshi, T. J., Metzner, J. L., Krugman, R. D., & Fryer, G. E. (1996). Trends in a national sample of sexually abusive youth. *Journal of American Academy of Child and Adolescent Psychiatry, 35*(1), 17–25.

Schram, D. D., Milloy, C. D., & Rowe, W. E. (1991). *Juvenile sex offenders: A follow-up study of reoffense behavior.* Olympia, WA: Washington State Institute for Public Policy.

Sickmund, M., Snyder, H. N., & Poe-Yamagata, E. (1997). *Juvenile offenders and victims: 1997 update on violence.* Washington, DC: Office of Juvenile Justice and Delinquency Prevention.

Smith, P., Goggin, C., & Gendreau, P. (2002). *The effects of prison sentences and intermediate sanctions on recidivism: General effects and individual differences.* Solicitor General of Canada's Office. From http://www.sgc.gc.ca.

Sowell, E. R., Thompson, P. M., Holmes, C. J., Jernigan, T. L., & Toga, A. W. (1999). In vivo evidence for post-adolescent brain maturation in frontal and striatal regions. *Nature Neuroscience, 2*(10), 859–861.

Steinberg, L. (2009). Adolescent development and juvenile justice. *Annual Review of Clinical Psychology, 5,* 47–73. From http://www.clinpsy.annualreviews.org.

Steinberg, L., & Scott, E. (2003). Less guilty by reason of adolescence: Developmental immaturity, diminished responsibility, and the juvenile death penalty. *American Psychologist, 58*(12), 4–5.

Szymanski, L., & National Center for Juvenile Justice. (1998). *Frequent questions and answers.* National Center for Juvenile Justice. (Available from the National Center for Juvenile Justice, 710 Fifth Avenue, Pittsburgh, PA 15219.)

Terry, K. J., & Furlong, J. S. (2004). *Sex offender registration and community notification: A Megan's Law sourcebook.* Kingston, NJ: Civic Research Institute.

Trivits, L. C., & Repucci, N. D. (2002). Application of Megan's Law to juveniles. *American Psychologist, 57,* 690–704.

United States Department of Justice, Bureau of Justice Statistics. (2000). *National crime victimization survey, 1992–1998.* Machine-readable data file. Ann Arbor, MI: Inter-University Consortium for Political and Social Research. National Archive of Criminal Justice Data.

United States Department of Justice. (2007). *The national guidelines for sex offender registration and notification—proposed guidelines, May 2007.* From http://www.ojp.usdoj/smart/proposed.

Vandiver, D. M. (2006). A prospective analysis of juvenile male sex offenders: Characteristics and recidivism rates as adults. *Journal of Interpersonal Violence, 21,* 673–688.

Wagonner, R. W., & Boyd, D. A. (1941). Juvenile aberrant sexual behavior. *American Journal of Orthopsychiatry, 11,* 275–292.

Walker, M. (2008). No details about sex offenders enrolled in Des Moines schools. *Des Moines Iowa Register,* November 17.

Weinrott, M. (1996). *Juvenile sexual aggression: A critical review.* Boulder, CO: University of Colorado, Institute for Behavioral Sciences, Center for the Study and Prevention of Violence.

Worling, J. R., & Curwen, T. (2000). Adolescent sexual offender recidivism: Success of specialized treatment and implications for risk prediction. *Child Abuse and Neglect, 24*(7), 965–982.

Zimring, F. E. (2004). *An American travesty: Legal responses to adolescent sexual offending.* Chicago: University of Chicago Press.

Zimring, F. E., Piquero, A. R., & Jennings, W. G. (2007). Sexual delinquency in Racine: Does early sex offending predict later sex offending in youth and young adulthood? *Criminology and Public Policy, 6*(3), 507–534.

PART FOUR

CORRECTION: DIFFERENTIAL INTERVENTIONS

CHAPTER 13

Comprehensive and Individualized Evaluation and Ongoing Assessment

TOM LEVERSEE

T HE DEVELOPMENTAL/CONTEXTUAL FRAMEWORK of adolescent development supports comprehensive and individualized evaluation and ongoing assessment of risks, assets, and protective factors across multiple domains of development (cognitive, social/emotional, moral, physical, and language) and interactions with multiple microsystems (family, peer group, school, and neighborhood). Evaluation and ongoing assessment is an ongoing, dynamic process that occurs throughout the youth's involvement with juvenile justice and treatment providers.

This chapter differentiates the initial comprehensive "sex offense specific" or "psychosexual" evaluation and the ongoing assessment of risk, treatment and supervision needs, and progress over time. The initial evaluation is typically conducted by a specially trained clinician, and the ongoing assessment is typically conducted by a multidisciplinary team (MDT) as part of the case management process.

The National Task Force on Juvenile Sexual Offending (1993) differentiated five distinct purposes of evaluation and assessment:

Phase 1: Pretrial (investigative)
Phase 2: Presentence (dangerousness, risk, placement, and prognosis)
Phase 3: Postadjudication clinical assessment (treatment needs and modality)
Phase 4: Prerelease and termination of treatment (community safety, successful application of treatment tools)
Phase 5: Monitoring and follow-up (ongoing treatment needs, life adjustment)

Comprehensive evaluation is an essential prerequisite to the formulation of an individualized and thorough treatment plan. Offense-specific evaluations serve many purposes (Bonner, Marx, Thompson, & Michaelson, 1998; CSOMB, 2002; Epperson, Fowers, & DeWitt, 2005; Rich, 2009):

- Exploration of the nature, development, history and trajectory of sexually abusive and nonsexual conduct problems.

- Assessment of risk relevant to whether the youth can reasonably be treated in the community or a more restrictive setting.
- Recommendations for risk management and supervision.
- Estimates of treatment length and intensity, placement needs, and treatment modalities.
- Placement needs and relevance of segregation of lower risk and higher risk youth.
- Assessment of strengths and assets/protective factors, and deficits; static and dynamic risk factors; and specific treatment needs.
- Identification of individual differences, potential impediments to treatment.
- Estimates of the youth and family's amenability to treatment.

Presentence reports and offense-specific evaluations cannot determine guilt or innocence or investigate additional or undisclosed sex crimes. The purpose of presentence reports is to provide judges with information to inform disposition orders, such as probation with special conditions, a period of incarceration, and/or specialized treatment (Bumby & Talbot, 2007; Lane, 1997).

FRAMEWORK AND GUIDING PRINCIPLES

The core principles of Risk, Need, and Responsivity provide a useful framework for evaluation and treatment planning within juvenile justice systems (Andrews, Bonta, & Hoge, 1990; Bumby & Talbot, 2007). These principles ensure that assessment processes guide treatment and supervision plans.

The risk principle supports matching the levels of treatment/service to the risk level of the youth. Empirically-based risk instruments and risk factors, discussed following, are utilized to estimate levels of risk and to guide decisions related to the intensity and duration of treatment and supervision. This allows limited resources to be focused both on the youth who need the most and lower risk youth to receive less restrictive and less intensive interventions.

The "need" principle identifies specific targets of treatment and supervision that will have the greatest impact on reducing ongoing risk. Empirically guided risk assessment instruments, typology research, and research on risk and protective factors associated with resilience provide important empirical information on factors associated with risk reduction and increased health. The "need" is to change or moderate stable or chronic factors and acute dynamics that exacerbate the youth's behavior or impede success. The need principle informs disposition by matching youth to interventions that meet their needs.

"Responsivity" informs service delivery and improves amenability by providing treatment and supervision interventions in a style and mode that is consistent with the ability and learning style of the youth. Responsivity factors include motivation and readiness, intellectual functioning, learning style or disabilities, co-occurring psychiatric disorders, patterns of behavior, developmental issues, personality, anger/hostility, cultural factors, and religious beliefs (Andrews, Bonta, & Hoge, 1990).

OVERVIEW OF METHODOLOGY AND PROTOCOL

There has been an evolving consensus supporting the need to balance community safety and to promote these youths' positive development in a systematic manner

(CSOMB, 2002; Mulvey & Iselen, 2008; National Task Force on Juvenile Sexual Offending, 1993; Prescott & Longo, 2006; Ryan, 1997). Evaluation of risk and amenability to treatment uses a combination of actuarial and clinical methods. Actuarial methods rate and group individuals according to the likelihood of a specific event happening in the future. They are consistent and systematic methods that provide straightforward estimates of future behavior based solely on what is known about groups of individuals.

Actuarial methods focus primarily on static, historical factors and rely less on dynamic, changeable factors such as self-regulation or social competence (Hanson & Harris, 2000, 2001; Prentky & Knight, 1991; Quinsey, 1995; Worling, 2000). There are a number of actuarial scales for the prediction of adult sex offender recidivism, but to date there are no empirically validated risk prediction instruments for juveniles (Bumby & Talbot, 2007).

The clinical approach provides an opinion about the likelihood of future events by constructing a coherent picture of how characteristics of the individual and different circumstances increase or decrease the chances they will happen. The accuracy of clinical judgment alone in predicting the risk of sexual recidivism is only slightly above chance levels (Hanson, 2000). However, clinical approaches provide complex assessments based on what is known about an individual and inform the objectives of differential diagnosis and individualized care.

"Functional analysis" is an example of a clinical tool that assesses the offense pathway that is characteristic of the offending pattern of an individual (Beech, Fisher, & Thornton, 2003). Functional analysis identifies the antecedent thoughts and feelings, behaviors, and consequences of offending, which is congruent with the concept of the sexual abuse cycle. In practice, actuarial and clinical methods are merged into a comprehensive evaluation that informs subsequent recommendations. This has been referred to as "structured clinical judgment" (Mulvey & Iselen, 2008) and described as "empirically informed assessment" (Rich, 2007) or "an expert's opinion, systematically guided by research and empirical findings" (Packard, 2006).

Research on the varied, complex, and multidetermined nature of sexual offending has continued to validate the need for more comprehensive individualized assessments and treatment planning, which was foreshadowed in the 1990s (National Task Force on Juvenile Sexual Offending, 1993; Righthand & Welch, 2001; Ryan 1995, 1999; Ryan & Lane, 1997b). A comprehensive evaluation protocol is necessary in order to develop relevant treatment and supervision plans. In addition to sexual deviance and other risk related variables, global issues related to responsivity, and overall wellness and functioning comprise a "comprehensive evaluation" (CSOMB, 2002; Lane, 1997).

So many domains of functioning require assessment that putting together a jigsaw puzzle with hundreds of pieces is an apt metaphor for conducting a comprehensive evaluation and distilling the relevant information into a report. Regardless of thoroughness, experience, and skills of the evaluator, there are always going to be pieces missing because of incomplete information, imperfect instruments, evaluator limitations, and the evolving knowledge in this field. With children and adolescents, growth and development are constantly changing the factors that necessitate continuous ongoing assessment.

Comprehensive offense-specific or psychosexual evaluations consider content in many domains (CSOMB, 2002; Lane, 1997; National Task Force on Juvenile Sexual Offending, 1993; Rich, 2009):

- Developmental and family history
- Social history, relationships, and social functioning
- Educational and intellectual functioning
- Personality, psychiatric disorders, mental health
- Developmental competencies
- Biological and neurological vulnerabilities
- Sexual experience, interests, and arousal
- Delinquency and conduct/behavioral history
- History of offending and risk assessment
- Current individual risks, assets, and functioning
- Current family risks, assets, and functioning
- Parental cooperation and amenability to treatment
- School, community, and cultural risks and protective factors

The evaluator forms diagnostic impressions and makes recommendations on the basis of all available information. Information is gathered regarding static (historic and unchangeable) and dynamic (variable and potentially changeable) factors, with attention to stable or chronic factors that will continue to affect functioning (Ryan, 2000, 2007; Worling & Curwen, 2001; Worling & Langstrom, 2006). The evaluator's job is to identify strengths and assets, protective factors, risks, and deficits in each domain. Individual factors cannot be evaluated in isolation and out of context.

The methods of data collection used to inform the initial assessment include clinical and sexual history interviews, screening instruments, psychological and educational tests, specialized measures, behavioral observation, and reviews of previous case records and reports. Information is gathered from multiple sources including the youth and parents, police reports and victim statements, court and probation reports, child protection and social services records, family members, educators, residential staff, and/or other mental health professionals who are familiar with the youth and family (National Task Force on Juvenile Sexual Offending, 1988, 1993; Rich, 2009; Ryan & Lane, 1991, 1997a; Worling & Curwen, 2001; Worling & Langstrom, 2006).

The dynamic and evolving nature of adolescent development complicates the discussion of assessment methods. The instability and impulsivity of youth contributes to inconsistencies, increasing one's sense of trying to evaluate a moving target (Mulvey & Iselen, 2008; Prescott, 2004). Challenges include the evolving sexuality, the degree of persistence of abusive and delinquent behaviors across time, and the adolescent's dependency on and interaction with family, school, and community. Prescott (2004, pp. 93–94) suggests: "Those assessing risk for sexual reoffense among youth may wish to consider to what extent the individual's personality, sense of identity, attitudes, and beliefs are fully formed. More difficult still is the evolving understanding of brain development and plasticity" (Siegel 1999).

GUIDELINES FOR EVALUATORS

Evaluators must be specially trained for the offense-specific aspects of the assessment while traditional clinical training informs the assessment of many domains. When any domain or aspect needing assessment falls outside the evaluators' areas of expertise, referral for supplemental evaluation may be required.

Even in court-ordered evaluations, evaluators must act within the ethics of their professions and with regard for basic human rights and the juvenile's legal rights. Consent of parent or guardian and assent of juveniles is still a necessary precondition for many aspects of the assessment process, and the limits of a waiver of confidentiality must be made clear. The purpose of the evaluation, how it will be used, and who it will be shared with must be explained.

Evaluators should be aware of the strengths and limitations of any instruments they use, and be trained and/or supervised in their use. The uncertainty of prediction in human functioning is apparent and exacerbated by the instability of adolescence, so risk predictions and amenability measures may miss the mark. Therefore, assumptions stated in the initial evaluation should speak to variables that are unknown as well as those apparent.

Clinical interviews and review of auxiliary documents can also be missing or misrepresent important information. Earlier reports by other professionals may now be invalid or irrelevant, in light of new evidence from science or new developments with the individual youth or family. It is also completely natural that these youth, and often parents or others who care about them, might deny, minimize, or misrepresent the nature or extent of problems for reasons associated with the implications and potential consequences of the youth's behavior.

Evaluators must be aware that reports written regarding juveniles who have sexually offended are often not held confidential, by design, and the community often believes those who sexually offend cannot change, despite scientific evidence to the contrary. Evaluators must be conscious of the profound effects such reports can have in the long term. Worling (2000) goes so far as to state that assessments of juveniles should be written in disappearing ink because any report more than six months old may be obsolete, due to the rapid changes of youth. Statements can often be framed as "may," "might," "likely," or "possible" rather than being set in stone, and recommendations can be stated as the "opinion" or "the strong recommendation" of this evaluator, based on what is currently known.

As was apparent in earlier chapters, the evaluator needs to identify what the evidence of change needs to be before recommended levels of supervision or restrictions change, in order to assure that others do not assume that what is recommended at the beginning is needed indefinitely or "for life."

Recommendations should be based on the youth's level of risk and needs rather than on available resources (National Task Force on Juvenile Sexual Offending, 1993). When resources are not available to provide what is recommended, alternatives can be suggested, with the caveat that such alternatives may not have the optimal outcome. (For example: "If the recommended intensity of treatment is not an option, a less intensive course of treatment is likely to extend the duration of services for this case"; or "Inability to remove the youth from the home may jeopardize the sense of safety for the victim in the home"; or "If an alternative classroom is not available, this youth will require higher levels of supervision than peers in the school setting.")

Finally, it must always be stated that it is not the role of evaluation to establish innocence or guilt. The initial evaluation is typically conducted postdisposition and presentence. If there is an admission of guilt and/or there is a voluntary request by the juvenile with the consent of a parent/guardian, evaluations may be done prior to or in the absence of the filing of charges or adjudication (CSOMB, 2002).

INTERVIEWING AND INTERACTING WITH THE YOUTH

The sex offense-specific evaluation includes psychosocial and sexual history interviewing. Using the information gathered from the record review and collateral contacts as a foundation, the evaluator conducts a structured clinical interview focusing on the broad content areas previously discussed. The evaluation protocol and the structured interview guide could be described as the science of the evaluation, and the experience, skills, and practice wisdom of the interviewer could be described as the art. As in any type of clinical encounter, the nature and outcome of the interview is dependent on factors related to the interviewer, the youth, and the therapeutic relationship. In Chapter 16, Powell describes the therapist's interpersonal skills of empathy, warmth, unconditional positive regard, and genuineness as creating an environment in which youth are more receptive to interventions. Rich (2009) identifies evaluator skill variables as preparation, timing, sensitivity, awareness of cues and nuances, flexibility, directing, clarifying, tracking and a non-judgmental approach. Structured interview guides provide specific questions and areas of focus, but the youth's verbal, behavioral, and emotional responses guide what should or should not be pursued at each moment.

Lambie and McCarthy (2004) described the following strategies for interviewing sexually abusive youth:

- Establish rapport
- Show respect
- Express concern
- Provide information
- Create a facilitative environment in which there are opportunities for honesty
- Establish credibility and control of the interview
- Ask open-ended questions
- Anticipate embarrassment and defenses
- Predict and challenge cognitive distortions
- Expect and work with denial
- Allow juveniles to tell their story
- Use reframing statements
- Allow face-saving maneuvers
- Take care in expressing personal emotions

McGrath (1990, p. 511) describes the unique dynamics associated with the sexual history interview:

> (Under) defenses of denial and minimization are often feelings of shame, confusion, and inadequacy. It is unlikely (the youth has ever felt) someone could understand deviant urges and behaviors. The evaluator who can communicate understanding about the (youth's) private sexual life is therefore in a powerful position to create an atmosphere in which the (youth) can discuss the problem. The goal is to let the (youth) know they are not alone and that the evaluator is knowledgeable about these experiences.

Jenkins (1990) suggested "inviting" youth to imagine being responsible, and stressed the importance of recognizing and capitalizing on their innate sense of "justice."

Motivational interviewing (Miller & Rollnick, 2002) is useful in assessing the youth's willingness and motivation to change (Schladale, 2008). Motivational interviewing is designed to enhance the intrinsic motivation to change by illuminating ambivalence. The general principles are to develop discrepancies, express empathy, amplify ambivalence, roll with resistance, and support self-efficacy. For example, a youth could be asked to rate his motivation to stop offending, his confidence in his ability to change, why he would not rate himself higher, how he might go about changing, what obstacle he might encounter, and how he foresees overcoming these obstacles.

The clinician can gather valuable information by observing the youth's resistance, denial, defensiveness, or manifestations of anxiety (Lane, 1997). Defensive reactions may illustrate the misattribution of responsibility. Lane went on to state:

> *Confronting a discrepancy between the victim's account and the youth's version allows assessment of his response to criticism and disagreement, as well as the degree of responsibility he is taking for his own behavior. . . . Discrepancies that remain after probing and encouragement can be articulated and identified as areas that will become clearer in treatment. . . . Asking for information in several different ways, particularly when the youth is not acknowledging some aspect, helps to assess denial issues. (p. 224)*

MENTAL STATUS

Whether it is approached as a structured component or integrated into the general interview, the youth's mental status contributes important information to diagnostic impressions and treatment recommendations. Traditional mental status screening includes appearance and behavior; speech, mood, and affect; stream of thought; thought content; orientation to time and place; concentration; memory; judgment, insight, abstraction; suicidal ideation; and homicidal ideation.

Evaluating the degree of stability of co-occurring psychiatric disorders currently being treated with psychotherapy and/or pharmacological treatment, as well as screening for undiagnosed, misdiagnosed, or untreated disorders is also critical. These can be important factors affecting amenability to treatment and initial and long-term recommendations for treatment.

DEVELOPMENTAL/FAMILY/SOCIAL HISTORY

The static or historical component of the evaluation seeks to explore and begin to understand the juvenile's development as it relates to risks and protective factors and developmental competence in the cognitive, social/emotional, moral, physical, and language domains. As described in Chapter 6, development is explored in the context of the interaction between the youth and the microsystems of family, peer group, school, and community. This provides a lens for reviewing a child's history to understand how earlier experiences have influenced the child's development and contributed to current problems (Davies, 2004). Lane (1997) states that, "understanding how the youth's development contributed to current beliefs, the capacity for attachment and intimacy, coping styles, competency to relate to others effectively, and life experiences the youth was exposed to is critical in identifying the issues that underlie the sexually abusive behaviors and developing effective treatment approaches" (p. 248). The evaluator can begin to identify cognitive-emotional processes that include the relational and self-schemas, social norms, and social information processing patterns that underlie abusive and maladaptive patterns of behavior (Dodge & Pettit, 2003).

Chapter 7 provides guidance in the exploration and identification of static assets and protective factors that include prenatal care, normative birth, empathic care, consistent caregiver, and secure attachment, as well as static risk factors such as biological predispositions, abuse and neglect, loss and disruptions of care, and so forth (Dodge & Pettit, 2003; Moffitt, 1993; Ryan & Lane, 1997a).

The youth's social history is explored to identify risk factors relevant to the Psychosocial Deficit or Delinquent Lifestyle subtypes discussed in Chapter 6. Risk factors include rejection by prosocial peers, social competency deficits and social isolation, association with younger children, association with delinquent peers, and isolation from prosocial peers (Hunter, Figueredo, Malamuth, & Becker, 2003; Latessa, 2005; Worling & Langstrom, 2006).

EDUCATIONAL AND INTELLECTUAL FUNCTIONING

Evaluating cognitive/intellectual functioning includes assessing intelligence, learning disabilities, memory and learning abilities, and neuropsychological problems. The youth's past academic achievement and functioning is explored with a focus on educational successes, failures, and problems. The overall goal is to determine strengths or the extent of cognitive impairment and also to determine fit for treatment (Bonner, Marx, Thompson, & Michaelson, 1998). This may also illuminate issues related to responsivity to treatment.

Examples of intelligence and educational testing include:

- The Wechsler Adult Intelligence Scale-III (WAIS-III): provides verbal, performance, and full-scale IQ for individuals age 16 and older
- The Wechsler Intelligence Scale for Children (WISC-III): provides verbal, performance, and full-scale IQ for children ages 5 to 15
- Woodcock-Johnson Psychoeducational Battery Revised

PERSONALITY, PSYCHIATRIC DISORDERS, AND MENTAL HEALTH

A variety of symptoms and characteristics may influence sexual acting out, non-sexual conduct problems, and other maladaptive behavioral patterns. Evaluators must assess the presence of pervasive, serious, or long-standing psychological problems; history of psychiatric hospitalization; outpatient treatment; past evaluations; family history of mental illness, substance abuse, or criminality; and level of social adjustment/maturity (National Task Force on Juvenile Sexual Offending, 1993; Ryan & Lane, 1997b).

Instruments such as psychological and neuropsychological tests and nonpsychometric questionnaires may be utilized to identify and measure interests, attitudes, and functioning.

DEVELOPMENTAL COMPETENCE

Developmental competence is assessed in the cognitive, social/emotional, moral, physical, and language domains. Developmental competence is defined as having the skills for successful human functioning at each age or stage. These include skills for daily living, socialization, communication, motor skills, resiliency, self-esteem/self-concept, and self-mastery/self-efficacy. Developmental competence is relatively stable in that once learned, skills are not forgotten; however, developmental delays and deficits can significantly impede success, and when addressed, are critical components in the capacity for change (CSOMB, 2002).

Many developmental models address essentially the same basic areas of human functioning. Strayhorn (1988) identified 62 specific skills needed for success in nine areas of functioning:

1. Closeness, trust, relationship building
2. Handling separation and independence
3. Handling joint decisions and interpersonal conflict
4. Dealing with frustration and unfavorable events
5. Celebrating good things, feeling pleasure
6. Working for delayed gratification
7. Relaxing, playing
8. Cognitive processing through words, symbols, images
9. An adaptive sense of direction and purpose

Assessing developmental competencies helps to define what skills and capacities to target in treatment planning and to plan treatment activities congruent with the youth's cognitive functioning and language development. Significant skill deficits or delays, indicative of missed development, may require "therapeutic care" as described in Chapter 15. It also supports more realistic expectations about the goals of treatment when the assessment shows significant deficits that will impede the treatment process (Davies, 2004).

CURRENT INDIVIDUAL FUNCTIONING

Developmental competence is seen as more stable, while current functioning is viewed as dynamic and constantly changing. Current functioning is affected by developmental competence, but is also affected by factors such as stress, choices, illness/health, internal/external factors, and opportunity. An important factor in ongoing assessment is to what degree are internal and external risk factors present and how successfully is the juvenile managing these risk factors. Dynamic circumstantial risk factors and dynamic risk factors that are foreseeable in the life span provide a useful framework for recognizing current risks (see Chapter 7).

Current functioning may look good because of no stress or strong defenses, or behavioral compliance in a very structured setting (good functioning in this case may cover up lack of skills). Current functioning can also look worse as the youth pushes forward, trying new things, letting defenses down, taking a chance, getting in touch with emotions, and so forth, with behavior getting worse before things get better, when working on difficult issues (Ryan, Yager, Sobicinski, & Metzner, 2002).

CURRENT FAMILY FUNCTIONING

Current family functioning is a factor in determining a juvenile's suitability for outpatient treatment and/or readiness for transition back into the community after residential treatment. Evaluation and ongoing assessment consider the family's response to youth's sexual offense (denial or minimization versus realistic appraisal of the offense and support of accountability) and the degree to which the family is willing and able to provide informed supervision, and/or the support necessary for community-based treatment, home visits from a residential setting, or a return home from custody.

Instability where the youth lives considers household members (caregivers, their partners, or the juvenile's siblings) involvement in: substance abuse; frequent changes in sexual partners; poor boundaries; pornography; family violence and/or child neglect; adult criminality in the home; psychiatric problems; economic stress; lack of structure; lack of engagement; inconsistent/harsh/abusive punishment; frequently relocating the family's home; and dishonesty.

Stability might be reflected in the current status of the marriage, communication between family members, openness about family issues, emotional expressiveness, support systems, healthy sexual attitudes, intimacy, consistent discipline, family honesty, cohesive relationships (emotional bonding and individual autonomy of family members), adaptability (capacity of the family unit to adjust in response to stress), emotional expressiveness, conflict resolution, and problem solving (Bremer & O'Brien, 1996; Prentky & Righthand, 2003; Ross & Loss, 1991).

ASSESSING ABUSIVE DYNAMICS

Chapter 8 detailed the need to address all types of abusive behaviors and the common dynamics associated with their occurrence. As previously stated, for most juveniles sexual offenses are much more a reflection of their capacity to be abusive than an indication of sexual deviance, per se. Defining all the ways in which youth have been abusive to themselves, others, and property allows the evaluator to discern how pervasively abusive the youth might be, or whether the abusive incident(s) were uncharacteristic of the youth's usual functioning.

Many of these youth have been abusive to themselves and others in many ways for a long time, but were never held accountable until the behavior was sexual. Many also had no idea the behavior was illegal, or what the consequences might be, and do not have any idea why it is defined as "abuse." For some, their choice of sexually abusive behavior was more a product of opportunity than by design; while others had many thoughts of sexual offending before the opportunity occurred.

The cycle may be used to guide the exploration of antecedent situations, thoughts, and feelings preceding the offending, facilitating the discovery of when the youth first thought of doing something sexual, whether the motivation was more compensatory or retaliatory, whether the function of the act was to "feel better" or to "get back" at someone, and how much forethought and planning preceded the decision to act. The more the evaluator is able to understand the antecedent patterns, the more their recommendations can address relevant factors in terms of both supervision and treatment needs.

SEXUAL EVALUATION

The sexual evaluation is done to understand the developmental and etiological factors related to sexual development and the development of sexually abusive behavior; to understand to what degree, if any, deviant sexual interests are present;

and to understand to what degree distorted thinking, sexual values and attitudes, or lack of sexual knowledge contributed to engaging in sexually abusive behavior (Lane, 1997).

Evaluation of sexual history must consider experience in context and clearly differentiate illegal and abusive sexual behaviors from more normative behaviors. Knowing a youth has sexually offended, evaluators and treatment providers subsequently exploring the whole sexual history often assume all previous sexual behavior was abusive. Failure to educate and differentiate all the many reasons sexual behaviors of children and adolescents are problematic and prohibited, even when the behaviors are not illegal or abusive, results in reporting higher numbers of victims and adjusting estimates of risk incorrectly.

As illuminated in Chapter 4, childhood sexuality is not a pathological condition and the ways in which people behave sexually are learned products of life experience and exposure. Motivation for sexual behavior may be exploratory, imitative, reactionary, compensatory, or retaliatory. Evaluating sexual history must be much more than simply listing incidents and behaviors out of context. Evaluating sexual interactions must always define the presence or absence of consent, equality, and coercion; whether the behavior was an illegal act, whether the child was legally culpable at that time, antecedent thoughts, emotions, stressors, and motivation. The evaluator's responsibility is to discover factors that influenced how, when, what, and who were involved when the actual behavior occurred.

As previously described, sexual interests and arousal in childhood and adolescence are diverse and fluid, reflecting developmental and experiential differences, so any "snapshot" of behavior out of context may be misleading (Abel & Emmerick, 2005; Hunter, 1999; Prentky, 2001; Worling, 2000). The adolescent's pattern of offending behavior may be more influenced by access, opportunity, and the impediments to more normative consensual activities and less a reflection of sexual arousal and interests per se. Exploring antecedents often reveals that the first thoughts of doing something sexual prior to a first offense reflect normative sexual interest (doing something sexual) and the subsequent behavior was influenced by factors of access and opportunity to actually engage in any sexual activity. For some, thoughts of past victimization led to reenactment, identifying with the aggressor in attempts to overcome or make sense of their own victimization.

Sexual history includes the range of behaviors, sexual development, sources of sex education, consensual sexual experiences, sexual apprehension/confidence, exposure to sexual stimuli/use of pornography, sexual victimization, masturbatory behaviors, and the memories, thoughts, and fantasies accompanying the experience of arousal and behavior. When incidents of abuse have been clearly defined, either abuse of or abuse by the youth, the characteristics of the two, victim profile and perpetrator profile, can be utilized in illuminating interpersonal variables associated with the abusive pattern of the youth. Motivation and intent do not define abuse but are relevant to the evaluation of the nature of sexual and aggressive aspects of the offending (Lane, 1997).

The empirically-based sexual variables related to risk assessment include (Epperson, Ralston, Fowers, & DeWitt, 2005b; Prentky & Righthand, 2003; Rich, 2009; Worling & Curwen, 2001):

- Number of adjudications for sex offenses
- Number of sexual abuse victims

- Male child victims
- Any sexual assault of a stranger
- Indiscriminate choice of victims
- Duration of sex offense history
- Abusive sexual interests (significantly younger children, violence)
- Sexualized aggression
- Obsessive sexual interests/preoccupation with sexual thoughts
- Thoughts, beliefs, and attitudes supportive of sexual offending
- Unwillingness to change problematic sexual interests/attitudes
- Sexually abuse the same victim two or more times
- Diverse sexual-assault behaviors
- Continuing to sexually offend while under any form of supervision during investigation of prior offenses for which they were eventually adjudicated
- Any felony-level sex offense (charged or adjudicated) committed in a public place
- Patterns of deception or grooming in sex offenses that were charged or adjudicated
- Previous diagnosis of paraphilia

It is important to note that the only changes in the sexual factors influencing the level of risk would be new disclosure of past sexual offenses and/or new sexual offenses occurring after the initial evaluation. Nothing done in treatment will ever erase the historical sexual offenses, so the static risk assessment will never decrease. A youth found to be "high risk" based on these historical variables will continue to score as "high risk" on them forever, even though research is clear in the fact that most do not in fact continue to be high risk. Therefore, reassessing risk later must consider relevant changes in the present.

In addition to those variables relevant to risk of recidivism measures, the clinical interview also explores the following variables that will be relevant in treatment (Lane, 1997; Rich, 2009):

- Victims' gender, age range, and relationship; how and why particular victims were selected; and how victims were persuaded to cooperate, comply, and not disclose
- Types of sexual contact; actual behaviors
- Duration and progression of sexual offense history over time
- Elements that may have predisposed or desensitized the youth to the sexually abusive behavior such as mental rehearsal, sexual fantasies, use of pornography, or previous sexual victimization
- Degree of planning and time spent in the preassault pattern
- Verbal threats, physical force, or sexualized aggression
- Circumstances under which the sexually abusive behavior was discovered
- Evidence of the youth stopping/desisting sexually abusing without being discovered, and, if so, why
- Motivation for engaging in the sexually abusive behavior, the role and function it played, and the perception of needs met
- The relationship between the sexually abusive behavior and recent or remote stressors, such as personal victimization or maltreatment, losses, rejections, or narcissistic injuries
- Involvement in other sexual paraphilias, including duration and frequency

As previously discussed, a minority of sexually abusive youth actually have significantly established deviant sexual interest and arousal patterns. Deviant sexual arousal is more clearly established or "fixated" as a motivation in adult sexual offending, particularly as it relates to pedophilia. A small subset of juveniles who offend against children may represent an early onset pedophilia. The highest levels of deviant sexual arousal are found in juveniles who exclusively target young male children, specifically when penetration is involved (Hunter & Becker, 1994; Marshall, Barbaree, & Eccles, 1991). In general, the sexual arousal patterns of juveniles who sexually offend appear more diverse, fluid, and changeable than those of adult sex offenders, and are less directly related to their patterns of offending behavior (Hunter & Becker, 1994; Hunter, Goodwin, & Becker, 1994).

Specific measures of sexual interests and arousal may also be used in assessments. Methods may include penile plethysmography (PPG) and viewing time procedures. Plethysmography is a laboratory assessment of sexual arousal. Sexual interest measures include card sorts, questionnaires, and viewing time procedures. All of these measure the relative level of interest or arousal to different sexual cues.

Research indicates that the relationship between measured arousal and past offenses is weaker in adolescents who have sexually offended in comparison to adult sex offenders (Hunter & Becker, 1994), and plethysmography is not recommended prior to age 14. Use of physiological arousal assessments in the treatment process will be discussed in a later chapter, but it is rarely indicated for use in the initial evaluation. Measures of sexual interest may be included in initial evaluations.

The Multiphasic Sex Inventory II J is a 559-item self-report questionnaire that measures the psychosexual characteristics of sexually abusive juveniles. The MSI II J consists of a social sexual history and 36 clinical/behavioral scales and indices and can be useful in providing information differentiating subtypes of youth identified in the typologies. The "Heterosexual Inadequacies" and "Emotional Neediness" scales identify youth whose psychosocial deficits and anxiety about making social/sexual contact with same age peers are contributing factors to their engaging in sexually abusive behavior. Reflecting the compensatory aspect of the Psychosocial Deficits subtype, these scales distinguish youth who are "affection starved" and "emotionally needy" and who are likely to associate the need for affection and feelings of loneliness with sexual desires. Responses on the "Body Image" and "Asocial (Loner) Type" scales also provide diagnostic information. The "Conduct Disorder" and "Sex Deviance" scales and indices may be useful in differentiating the Delinquent Lifestyle and the Pedophilic Interest subtypes (Leversee, 2007).

In some states, polygraphy is also used in initial or ongoing assessment. The polygraph measures physiological changes in reaction to whatever question is being asked (e.g., respiration, blood pressure, and heart rate). Although the polygraph is not actually a "lie detector," significant reactions are often believed to be associated with deception. Accuracy may be affected by false negatives or false positives, but the technique essentially coerces people to tell more than they would otherwise disclose, most often in preparing to be tested. Polygraphy is sometimes used to verify the completeness of sexual history disclosures, to rule out specific concerns, and/or to encourage and verify compliance with supervision conditions.

ASSESSMENT OF RISK

There are a number of widely used actuarial risk assessment instruments for adult sex offenders, including the Sex Offender Risk Assessment Guide (SORAG) (Quinsey, Rice, & Harris, 1995); the Rapid Risk Assessment of Sexual Offense Recidivism (RRASOR) (Hanson, 1997); the Minnesota Sex Offender Screening Tool–Revised (MnSOST-R) (Epperson, Kaul, & Hesselton, 1998; Epperson, Kaul, Huot, et al., 2000); and the STATIC-99 (Hanson & Thornton, 1999, 2000).

Although there are no current actuarial risk assessment tools for juveniles, empirically-based instruments include the Juvenile Sex Offender Assessment Protocol II (J-SOAP II) (Prentky & Righthand, 2003); the Estimate of Risk of Adolescent Sex Offender Recidivism (ERASOR) (Worling & Curwen, 2001); the Juvenile Sexual Offense Recidivism Assessment Tool-II (JSORRAT-II) (Epperson, Ralston, Fowers, & DeWitt, 2005b); the Multidimensional Inventory of Development, Sex, and Aggression (MIDSA) (Knight, 2004); the Multiplex Empirically Guided Inventory of Ecological Aggregates for Assessing Sexually Abusive Adolescents and Children (MEGA) (Miccio-Fonesca & Rasmussen, 2006); the Juvenile Risk Assessment Tool (J-RAT) (Rich, 2003, 2007); and the Risk Assessment Matrix (RAM) (Christodoulides, Richardson, Graham, Kennedy, & Kelly, 2005). Research is ongoing in the development of the JSORRAT-II as a possible actuarial instrument.

Without empirical validation of these tools there are no rules for how to weight and combine risk factors in an overall assessment of risk (Epperson, Ralston, Fowers, & DeWitt, 2005a). The final determination of risk is based on the judgment of the evaluator. Robert Prentky (2001) stated that, "instruments that are still in the incubator are being used to make profoundly important decisions that impact people's liberty." Evaluation reports should state that there are no empirically validated risk assessment instruments for juveniles and that estimates of risk for future reoffending are limited and qualified (Prentky & Righthand, 2001; Worling & Langstrom, 2006).

Worling and Langstrom (2006) reviewed the research and categorized risk factors for sexual recidivism according to the amount of evidence that supports them:

- Empirically-supported risk factors—deviant sexual interest, prior legal sanctions for sexual offending, sexual offending against more than one victim, sexual offending against a stranger victim, social isolation, and uncompleted offense-specific treatment.
- Promising risk factors (limited empirical support)—problematic parent-adolescent relationships and attitudes supportive of sexual offending.
- Possible risk factors (lack empirical support)—high-stress family environment, impulsivity, antisocial interpersonal orientation, interpersonal aggression, negative peer associations, sexual preoccupation, sexual offending against a male victim, sexual offending against a child, threats, violence, or weapons in sexual offense, and an environment supporting offending.
- Unlikely risk factors—adolescent's own history of sexual victimization, history of nonsexual offending, sexual offending involving penetration, denial of sexual offending, and low victim empathy.

As previously stated, it is incumbent that evaluation and ongoing assessment processes are cognizant of and address the broad range of abusive and delinquent behaviors. As discussed in Chapter 6, juveniles who have sexually offended have higher rates of nonsexual recidivism. Typology research discussed in Chapter 6 identified a subtype of adolescents whose sexual offending is a part of a broader range of nonsexual conduct problems and delinquency. Timing and duration are important, with the degree of stability and persistence of conduct/delinquent history differentiating the life course persistent from the adolescent limited delinquent (Moffitt, 1993).

Factors related to nonsexual delinquent recidivism among sexually offending juveniles are different from those associated with sexual recidivism (Langstrom, 2002; Langstrom & Grann, 2000; Worling & Curwen, 2000). These factors have been identified as: early onset conduct disorder; number of previous convictions for any offense; prior violent conviction; characteristics associated with adult antisocial personality; sexual offense related variables such as use of threats or weapons, death threats, and causing physical injury to the victim; lower socioeconomic status; hostility; and aggression.

The Impulsive/Antisocial scale of the J-SOAP II (Prentky & Righthand, 2003) identifies the historical risk factors related to general delinquency and conduct/ behavioral problems as pervasive anger, school behavior problems, history of conduct disorder before the age of 10, delinquent behavior between the ages of 10 and 17, charges or arrests before the age of 16, legally charged offenses, and physical assault history and/or exposure to family violence. Latessa (2005) identifies the salient dynamic risk factors for general delinquency as: antisocial/procriminal attitudes, values, beliefs, and cognitive-emotional states; and presence of procriminal associates and absence of anticriminal others. Sociocultural factors associated with general delinquency and youth violence include disadvantaged ecological niches that are characterized by resource scarcity, concentrated disadvantage, and dangerous neighborhoods (Guerra & Williams, 2006). Parent interviews, elementary school records, and the Child Behavior Checklist (CBCL) (Achenbach, 1991) can provide valuable information as to the timing and duration of conduct problems, differentiating childhood versus adolescent onset of delinquency.

AMENABILITY TO TREATMENT

Amenability refers to the youth's ability, willingness, and motivation to engage in treatment. Motivation is a critical element of Responsivity. It is important in treatment planning to identify strengths and assets that enhance the potential success of treatment and to identify areas of individual functioning (cognitive, social, emotional, psychological, etc.) and attitudinal factors that may inhibit successful engagement in treatment. Evaluators consider whether there is a desire to avoid sexually abusive behavior and fantasies and to instead satisfy needs in a healthy, nonabusive manner; how bothered the youth is by the behavior, thoughts, and urges; and the degree to which the youth views the offenses as problematic.

Factors that can affect amenability include (Lane, 1997; Prentky & Righthand, 2003):

- Cognitive ability and intellectual capacity
- Willingness and motivation to enroll in treatment
- The accuracy of attributions of responsibility versus denial, projection, externalization

- The extent to which the behavior patterns or associated cognitions are considered normal, accepted, and ingrained
- The presence of concurrent psychiatric disorders
- Negative perceptions of treatment

Internal motivation for change may be the degree to which the youth truly experiences sexual offending as out of character and appears to have a genuine desire to change his behavior and avoid recurrences. This is often an advantage with youth, in that they are not comfortable with what they may perceive to be deviant behavior, do not want to be thought of as a sex offender, and are not yet successfully defended against such perceptions.

Some family variables are also related to the youth's amenability for treatment:

- The safety and cooperativeness of the family environment.
- The family's response to the youth's sexual offense (denial or minimization versus realistic appraisal of the offense, and rejecting the behavior without rejecting the youth).
- The willingness and ability of the family to support the treatment process of the youth, to engage in family therapy as indicated, and allow family secrets to be told.

It is not reasonable to expect youth to engage in treatment, disclose sensitive history, and make dramatic changes in themselves, if the family actively sabotages their efforts. Sometimes it becomes imperative to separate the youth from the family in order for them to make the necessary changes; and other times, the youth cannot change until some significant "other" gives them permission to live differently than family traditions dictate. For some, the therapeutic relationship becomes that significant other. For others, a mentor or peer or teacher might be.

ASSESSMENT OF ASSETS AND PROTECTIVE FACTORS

Chapter 7 discussed the resiliency of youth, the role of protective factors in mitigating risk, and the evolution of the field toward models that balance risk reduction with health promotion. Assessment, treatment planning, and risk management strive to identify and enhance protective factors in the youth and the environment that moderate risk by reducing stress, providing opportunities for growth, strengthening coping capacities, and mobilizing adults to meet the needs of youth (Davies, 2004; Prescott, 2004; Ryan, Yager, Sobicinski, & Metzner, 2002).

Bremer (1991, 1998, 2001); Gilgun (1988, 1998); and Whittaker (1986, 1990 [personal communication]) were some of the earliest practitioners focusing on resiliency factors in working with sexually abusive youth. By 1993, the National Task Force recommended more effort be focused on developmental skills to capitalize on the opportunities for rapid growth and change of youth. Health promotion has increased dramatically as juvenile models have replaced the modified adult models of the 1980s.

The Protective Factors Scale (PFS) (Bremer, 1998, 2001) focuses on identifying and building on strengths of the youth, family, and community. The PFS was initially designed to evaluate the adequacy of placement orders for treatment, and a pilot study indicated that the PFS did predict at what levels in the continuum of care different youth were most likely to successfully complete treatment. The PFS provides a "snapshot" of risk and protective factors (which can be easily recognized by professionals not trained in clinical assessment) early in the pretrial phase, and the Protective Factors Scale has been widely used by juvenile probation departments to inform initial decisions regarding detaining juveniles following arrest or releasing them to parents, as well as subsequent supervision and assessment issues.

The Clinical Assessment Package for Risks and Strengths (CASPARS) (Gilgun, 1998, 1999) considers emotional expressiveness, family relationships, peer relationships, sexuality, and family embeddedness in the community. The CASPARS, developed for clinical assessment of needs and change over time with prepubescent boys, uses bimodal ratings to track needs and positive change on the variables in each scale and to support ongoing assessment and treatment goals.

The Community Stability/Adjustment scale on the J-SOAP II (Prentky & Righthand, 2003) assesses risks and protective factors related to the stability of the current living situation, stability in school, and evidence of a positive support network. Support systems may include: apparently supportive family members, extended families, foster families; friends; and members of the multidisciplinary team, such as therapists, probation officers, and caseworkers. Protective factors may also include participation in organized after-school sports and activities and involvement in church-related functions.

The inclusion of the environmental/ecological assets in these models parallels work in child development, developmental psychopathology, and delinquency research, capitalizing on the role of adults in the family, schools, and community. These adults who essentially "surround" the child are resources not available to those working with adults in the way they are present and responsible for youth. The balancing of risks and assets evolved into models such as Ryan detailed in Chapter 7, identifying static, stable, and dynamic risks and assets that can guide evaluation and ongoing assessment.

REPORTING DIAGNOSTIC IMPRESSIONS

Creating a coherent picture based on the evaluation of all the domains described is the "art" of the evaluator. The evaluator essentially speculates on the meaning of the data and articulates their clinical formulation. The report discusses the evaluator's understanding of the nature, development, history, and trajectory of sexually abusive and other nonsexual conduct problems and speculates on the influence of past and present factors in shaping the youth's thinking, attitudes, behaviors, and interactions. Typology related information is identified, including the youth's subtype and associated clinical characteristics, motivation and intent, cognitive-emotional processes, and dynamic risk factors.

Diagnostic impressions should be supported by the reasoning used to reach the impression and based on information that has been detailed in reporting specific findings in each domain. Information that does not support conclusions should be discussed and areas of uncertainty stated (McGrath, 1993).

ONGOING ASSESSMENT

Multidisciplinary teams must use ongoing assessment to revise risk management and treatment needs and supervision plans over time. Ongoing assessment continues to be comprehensive and uses collaboration and observations of all the adults involved. Whereas risk *prediction* must use static, reliable factors that do not change over time, risk *management* addresses dynamic factors that are sensitive to change within a narrower time frame (CSOMB, 2002; Packard, 2006; Quinsey, 1995; Ryan, 1997; Ryan, Yager, Sobicinski, & Metzner, 2002). The overall goals of risk reduction and risk management require measuring treatment outcomes and their resulting impact on risk (Epperson, Ralston, Fowers, & DeWitt, 2005a).

The ongoing assessment of risks and needs must be responsive to the developmental changes and, at times, unstable life circumstances of adolescence. Risk is not static and may change, sometimes dramatically, in brief periods of time. Chapter 7 outlined stable or chronic risk factors that are likely to continue to pose a risk across the life span for the individual, and differentiated dynamic risk factors as either "global" or "circumstantial." Global dynamic risk refers to life events that are known to be stressful to human beings in general, as well as foreseeable future stress points that are personal and unique to the individual. Circumstantial dynamic risks refers to situations, thoughts, emotions, and behaviors that can change from day to day and may account for changes in risk from day to day. Ryan suggests that stable or chronic and global risks are relevant to long-term planning toward the end of treatment, informing relevant "relapse prevention" strategies and aftercare plans.

The "static, stable, dynamic" model (see Chapter 7) draws from a wide range of research on children and human beings as a whole, as well as that specific to juvenile sexual offending, to integrate current knowledge into a cohesive model that supports risk reduction and health promotion ideals (Ryan, 2000).

In the research specific to juvenile sexual offending, others have referred to dynamic factors as either "chronic" or "acute." Chronic dynamic factors for youth have been identified as social competency deficits and social isolation, poor parent-child relationships, antisocial values and behaviors, impulsivity, and noncompliance with treatment (Hunter, Figueredo, Malamuth, & Becker, 2003; Longo & Prescott, 2006; Worling & Langstrom, 2006). Acute dynamic factors are current stressors and are addressed in modification of the duration and intensity of supervision and management strategies (Bumby & Talbot, 2007).

Ongoing assessment considers both risks and assets and is the source of evidence of change over time. It is the ongoing assessment that measures treatment progress and supports changes in treatment and supervision plans. Ryan's model defines successful completion of treatment as "mastery of dynamic assets associated with decreased risk and progress on those indicative of increased health" (see Chapter 7). The JRAT (Rich, 2007) was similarly influenced by the earlier risk and asset models, and was designed to increase consistency and accuracy across multiple clinicians in tracking needs and progress over the course of treatment.

Structured models designed for reassessment of risk and progress over time include the dynamic scales of the J-SOAP II (Prentky & Righthand, 2003); the MIDSA (Knight, 2004); the MEGA (Miccio-Fonseca & Rasmussen, 2006); the Juvenile Sex Offense Specific Needs and Progress Scale (Righthand, 2005); and the Treatment Progress Inventory for Adolescents who Sexually Abuse (TPI-ASA) (Oneal, Burns, Kahn, Rich, & Worling, 2008). The TPI-ASA (Oneal and colleagues, 2008) domains include inappropriate sexual behavior, healthy sexuality, social competency, cognitions supportive of sexual abuse, attitudes supportive of sexual abuse, victim awareness, affective/behavioral regulation, risk prevention awareness, and positive family caregiver dynamics.

CONCLUSION

The diversity in the population of juveniles who have committed sexual offenses supports the need for comprehensive individualized evaluation and ongoing assessment. The initial evaluation can provide a significant foundation for understanding the nature, development, history, and trajectory of sexually abusive and other nonsexual conduct problems and address the youth's unique placement, treatment, and supervision needs. The dynamic and evolving nature of adolescent development creates special opportunities and challenges as treatment providers and other multidisciplinary team members seek to find the right balance between risk management, risk reduction, and health promotion.

REFERENCES

Abel, G., & Emmerick, R. (2005). *The sexual misconduct of five thousand adolescent males.* Presentation at the 20th Annual Conference of the National Adolescent Perpetration Network, Denver, Colorado.

Achenbach, T. M. (1991). *Manual for child behavior checklist/4-18 and 1991 profile.* Burlington, VT: University of Vermont, Department of Psychiatry.

Andrews, D. A., Bonta, J., & Hoge, R. D. (1990). Classification for effective rehabilitation: Rediscovering psychology. *Criminal Justice and Behavior, 17,* 19–52.

Beech, A. R., Fisher, D. D., & Thornton, D. (2003). Risk assessment of sex offenders. *Professional Psychology: Research and Practice, 34*(4), 339–352.

Bonner, B. L., Marx, B. P., Thompson, J. M., & Michaelson, P. (1998). Assessment of adolescent sexual offenders. *Child Maltreatment, 3*(4), 374–383.

Bremer, J. F. (1991). Intervention with the juvenile sex offender. *Human Systems: The Journal of Systemic Consultation and Management, 22*(6), 235–246. (V2N3–4 Annals).

Bremer, J. F. (1998). Challenges in the assessment and treatment of sexually abusive youth. *Irish Journal of Psychology, 19*(1), 82–92.

Bremer, J. F. (2001). *The protective factors scale: Assessing youth with sexual concerns.* Plenary address at the 16th Annual National Adolescent Perpetration Network, Kansas City, KS.

Bremer, J. F., & O'Brien, M. (1996). *Court dispositional assessments and treatment outcomes: Directions for success.* Presented at the 15th Annual Association for the Treatment of Sexual Abusers Conference, Chicago, IL.

Bumby, K., & Talbot, T. (2007). *The importance of assessment in sex offender management: An overview of key principles and practices.* Silver Spring, MD: Center for Sex Offender Management.

Christodoulides, T. E., Richardson, G., Graham, F., Kennedy, P. J., & Kelly, T. P. (2005). Risk assessment with adolescent sex offenders. *Journal of Sexual Aggression, 11,* 37–48.

Colorado Sex Offender Management Board (CSOMB). (2002). *Standards and guidelines for the evaluation, assessment, treatment, and supervision of juveniles who have committed sexual offenses.* Colorado Department of Public Safety, Division of Criminal Justice.

Davies, D. (2004). *Child development: A practitioner's guide* (2nd ed.). New York: Guilford Press.

Dodge, K. A., & Pettit, G. S. (2003). A biopsychosocial model of the development of chronic conduct problems in adolescence. *Developmental Psychology, 39*(2), 349–371.

Epperson, D. L., Kaul, J. D., & Hesselton, D. (1998, October). *Final report for the development of the Minnesota Sex Offender Screening Tool-Revised (MnSOST-R).* Presentation at the 17th Annual Research and Treatment Conference of the Association for the Treatment of Sexual Abusers, Vancouver, British Columbia, Canada.

Epperson, D. L., Kaul, J. D., Huot, S. J., Hesselton, D., Alexander, W., & Goldman, R. (2000, November). *Cross-validation of the Minnesota Sex Offender Screening Tool-Revised*

(MnSOST-R). Paper presented at the 19th Annual Conference of the Association for the Treatment of Sexual Abusers, San Diego, CA.

Epperson, D. L., Fowers, D., & DeWitt, J. (2005). *Predictors of sexual recidivism in large scale study of Utah adolescents*. Denver, CO: National Adolescent Perpetration Network Conference.

Epperson, D. L., Ralston, C. A., Fowers, D., & DeWitt, J. (2005a). Actuarial risk assessment with juveniles who sexually offend: Development of the Juvenile Sexual Recidivism Risk Assessment Tool-II (J-SORRAT-II). (pp. 118–169). In D. S. Prescott (Ed.), *Risk assessment of youth who have sexually abused: Theory, controversy, and emerging strategies* (pp. 118–169). Oklahoma City, OK: Woods 'N' Barnes.

Epperson, D. L., Ralston, C. A., Fowers, D., & DeWitt, J. (2005b). *Juvenile Sexual Offense Recidivism Risk Assessment Tool- II (JSORRAT- II)*. Utah State Juvenile Justice Services.

Gilgun, J. (1988). *Factors which block the development of sexually abusive behavior in adults abused as children*. Presented at the National conference on Male Victims and Offenders, Minneapolis, MN.

Gilgun, J. F. (1998). CASPARS: Clinical instruments for assessing client assets and risk in mental health practice. *The Medical Journal of Allina, 7*, 1.

Gilgun, J. F. (1999). CASPARS: Clinical assessment instruments that measure strengths and risks in children and families. In M. C. Calder (Ed.), *Working with young people who sexually abuse: New pieces of the jigsaw puzzle* (pp. 48–58). Lyme Regis: Russell House Publishing.

Guerra, N. G., & Williams, K. R. (2006). Ethnicity, youth violence, and the ecology of development. In N. Guerra & E. Smith (Eds.), *Preventing youth violence in a multicultural society* (pp. 17–45). Washington, DC: American Psychological Association.

Hanson, R. K. (1997). *The development of a brief actuarial risk scale for sexual offense recidivism*. (User Report 97-04). Ottawa, Canada: Department of Solicitor General of Canada.

Hanson, R. K. (2000). *Risk assessment*. Beaverton, OR: Association for the Treatment of Sexual Abusers.

Hanson, R. K., & Harris, A. (2000; rev. 2002). *Sex Offender Need Assessment Rating (SONAR): A method for measuring change in risk levels*. Correctional Service Canada: National Sexual Offender Programs—Assessment Manual.

Hanson, R. K., & Harris, A. J. R. (2001). A structured approach to evaluating change among sexual offenders. *Sexual Abuse: A Journal of Research and Treatment, 13*, 105–122.

Hanson, R. K., & Thornton, D. (1999). *Static 99: Improving actuarial risk assessments for sex offenders*. Ottawa, Canada: Department of Solicitor General of Canada.

Hanson, R. K., & Thornton, D. (2000). Improving risk assessments for sex offenders: A comparison of three actuarial scales. *Law & Human Behavior, 24*, 119–136.

Hunter, J. A. (1999). *Understanding juvenile sexual offending behavior: Emerging research, treatment approaches and management practices*. Silver Spring, MD: Center for Sex Offender Management.

Hunter, J. A., & Becker, J. V. (1994). The role of deviant arousal in juvenile sexual offending etiology, evaluation and treatment. *Criminal Justice and Behavior, 21*(1), 132–149.

Hunter, J. A., Figueredo, A. J., Malamuth, N. M., & Becker, J. V. (2003). Juvenile sex offenders: Toward the development of a typology. *Sexual Abuse: A Journal of Research and Treatment, 15*(1), 27–48.

Hunter, J. A., Goodwin, D. W., & Becker, J. V. (1994). The relationship between phallometrically measured deviant sexual arousal and clinical characteristics in juvenile sexual offenders. *Behavioral Research and Therapy, 32*(5), 533–538.

Jenkins, A. (1990). *Invitations to responsibility: The therapeutic engagement of men who are violent & abusive*. Adelaide, South Australia: Dulwich Centre Publications.

Knight, R. A. (2004, September). *Assessing youth who sexually abuse using the MIDSA*. Presentation at the 9th International Conference on Family Violence, San Diego, CA.

Lambie, I., & McCarthy, J. (2004). Interviewing strategies with sexually abusive youth. In R. Geffner, K. C. Franey, T. G. Arnold, & R. Falconer (Eds.), *Identifying and treating youth who sexually offend: Current approaches, techniques, and research* (pp. 107–123). Binghampton, NY: Hayworth Press.

Lane, S. (1997). Assessment of sexually abusive youth. In G. Ryan & S. Lane (Eds.), *Juvenile sexual offending: Causes, consequences, and corrections* (pp. 219–263). San Francisco, CA: Jossey-Bass.

Langstrom, N. (2002). Long-term follow-up of criminal recidivism in young sex offenders: Temporal patterns and risk factors. *Psychology, Crime and Law, 8,* 41–58.

Langstrom, N., & Grann, M. (2000). Risk for criminal recidivism among young sex offenders. *Journal of Interpersonal Violence, 15*(8), 855–871.

Latessa, E. J. (2005). *What works and what doesn't in reducing recidivism: The principles of effective intervention.* Colorado Division of Youth Corrections Provider Council Conference, Vail, CO.

Leversee, T. (2007). Using typologies to individualize the assessment, treatment and supervision of sexually abusive youth. In M. Calder (Ed.), *Children and young people who sexually abuse: Taking the field forward* (pp. 38–52). Lyme Regis, Dorset: Russell House Publishing.

Longo, R. E., & Prescott, D. S. (2006). Current perspective: Working with young people who sexually abuse. In R. E. Longo & D. S. Prescott (Eds.), *Current perspectives: Working with sexually aggressive youth and youth with sexual behavior problems,* (pp. 45–61). Holyoke, MA: NEARI Press.

Marshall, W. L., Barbaree, H. E., & Eccles, A. (1991). Early onset and deviant sexuality in child molesters. *Journal of Interpersonal Violence, 6,* 323–336.

McGrath, R. J. (1990). Assessment of sexual aggressors: Practical clinical interviewing strategies. *Journal of Interpersonal Violence, 5*(4), 507–519.

McGrath, R. J. (1993). Preparing psychosexual evaluations of sex offenders: Strategies for practitioners. *Journal of Offender Rehabilitation, 20*(1/2), 139–158.

Miccio-Fonseca, L. C., & Rasmussen, L. A. (2006). *Multiplex empirically guided inventory of ecological aggregates for assessing sexually abusive adolescents and children-MEGA: Professional manual.* San Diego, CA: Author.

Miller, W. R., & Rollnick, S. (2002). *Motivational interviewing: Preparing people for change* (2nd ed.). New York: Guilford Press.

Moffitt, T. (1993). Adolescence-limited and life-course persistent antisocial behavior: A developmental taxonomy. *Psychology Review, 100*(4), 674–701.

Mulvey, E. P., & Iselen, A. R. (2008). Improving professional judgments of risk and amenability in juvenile justice. *Project Muse: The Future of Children, 18*(2), 35–57. From http://www.futureofchildren.org

National Task Force on Juvenile Sexual Offending. (1988). Preliminary report. *Juvenile and Family Court Journal, 39*(2), 1–67.

National Task Force on Juvenile Sexual Offending, National Adolescent Perpetration Network. (1993). The revised report from the National Task Force on Juvenile Sexual Offending. *Juvenile and Family Court Journal, 44*(4), 1–120.

Oneal, B. J., Burns, L. G., Kahn, T. J., Rich, P., & Worling, J. R. (2008). The Treatment Progress Inventory for Adolescents who Sexually Abuse (TPI-ASA). *Sexual Abuse: A Journal of Research and Treatment, 20*(2), 161–187.

Packard, R. L. (2006). *Risk assessment: Theory and application.* Sex Offender Management Board, Division of Criminal Justice conference, Winter Park, CO.

Prentky, R. A. (2001). *Assessing actuarial and dynamic risk with sexually abusive youth.* National Adolescent Perpetration Network Conference, Kansas City, KS.

Prentky, R. A., & Knight, R. A. (1991). Identifying critical dimensions for discriminating among rapists. *Journal of Consulting Clinical Psychology, 59*(5), 643–661.

Prentky, R. A., & Righthand, S. (2001). *Juvenile Sex Offender Assessment Protocol—II (J-SOAP-11).* Colorado: Office of Juvenile Justice and Delinquency Prevention.

Prentky, R. A., & Righthand, S. (2003). *Juvenile Sex Offender Assessment Protocol: Manual.* Washington, DC: Office of Juvenile Justice and Delinquency Prevention.

Prescott, D. S. (2004). Emerging strategies for risk assessment of sexually abusive youth: Theory, controversy, and practice. *Journal of Child Sexual Abuse,* 13(3), 4, 83–105.

Prescott, D. S., & Longo, R. E. (2006). Current perspectives: Working with young people who sexually abuse. In R. E. Longo & D. S. Prescott (Eds.), *Current perspectives: Working with sexually aggressive youth & youth with sexual behavior problems* (pp. 45–61). Holyoke, MA: NEARI Press Publishers.

Quinsey, V. (1995). *Actuarial prediction of sexual dangerousness.* Paper presented at the 14th Association for the Treatment of Sexual Abusers (ATSA) Conference, New Orleans, LA.

Quinsey, V. L., Rice, M. E., & Harris, G. T. (1995). Actuarial prediction of sexual recidivism. *Journal of Interpersonal Violence,* 10, 85–105.

Rich, P. (2003). *Understanding, assessing, and rehabilitating juvenile sexual offenders.* Hoboken, NJ: John Wiley & Sons.

Rich, P. (2007). *The Juvenile Risk Assessment Tool (J-RAT).* Barre, MA: Stetson School. From http://www.stetsonschool.org/clinicalmaterials/assessmenttools/assessmenttools.html.

Rich, P. (2009). *Juvenile sexual offenders: A comprehensive guide to risk evaluation.* Hoboken, NJ: John Wiley & Sons.

Righthand, S. (2005). *Juvenile sex offense specific needs and progress scale.* From http://www.csom.org/ref/JSOProgressScale/pdf

Righthand, S., & Welch, C. (2001). *Juveniles who have sexually offended.* Washington, DC: Office of Juvenile Justice and Delinquency Prevention.

Ross, J., & Loss, P. (1991). Assessment of the juvenile sex offender. In G. Ryan & S. Lane (Eds.), *Juvenile sexual offending: Causes, consequences, and correction* (1st ed.) (pp. 199–251). Lanham, MD: Lexington Books.

Ryan, G. (1995). *Treatment of sexually abusive youth: The evolving consensus.* Paper presented at the International Experts Conference, Utrecht, Netherlands.

Ryan, G. (1997). Creating an "abuse-specific milieu." In G. Ryan & S. Lane (Eds.), *Juvenile sexual offending: Causes, consequences, and corrections* (pp. 404–416). San Francisco: Jossey-Bass.

Ryan, G. (1999). The treatment of sexually abusive youth: The evolving consensus. *Journal of Interpersonal Violence,* 14(4), 422–436.

Ryan, G. (2000). *Static, stable and dynamic risks and assets relevant to the prevention and treatment of abusive behavior.* Poster presentation, First National Sexual Violence Prevention Conference, Dallas, TX.

Ryan, G. (2007). Static, stable and dynamic risks and assets relevant to the prevention and treatment of abusive behavior. In M. Calder (Ed.), *Children and young people who sexually abuse: Taking the field forward* (pp. 161–176). United Kingdom: Russell House Co.

Ryan, G., & Lane, S. (Eds.). (1991). *Juvenile sexual offending: Causes, consequences and correction* (1st ed.). Lanham, MD: Lexington Books.

Ryan, G., & Lane, S. (1997a). Integrating theory and method. In G. Ryan & S. Lane (Eds.), *Juvenile sexual offending: Causes, consequences, and corrections* (pp. 267–321). San Francisco: Jossey-Bass.

Ryan, G., & Lane, S. (Eds.). (1997b). *Juvenile sexual offending: Causes, consequences, and correction* (2nd ed.). Los Angeles, CA: Jossey-Bass.

Ryan, G., Yager, J., Sobicinski, M., & Metzner, J. (2002). *Informed supervision and therapeutic care for juveniles who commit sexual offenses.* Kempe Trainer Training Curriculum.

Schladale, J. (2008). Empirically driven assessment of juvenile sex offenders. In B. K. Schwartz (Ed.), *The sex offender: Offender evaluation: Volume VI* (pp. 11-1 to 11-12). Kingston, NJ: Civic Research Institute, Inc.

Siegel, D. J. (1999). *The developing mind: Toward a neurobiology of interpersonal experience.* New York: Guilford Press.

Strayhorn, J. M. (1988). *The competent child. An approach to psychotherapy and preventive mental health.* New York: Guilford Press.

Whitaker, M. (1986). *The low-functioning client.* Paper presented at the 2nd National Training Conference, Atlanta, GA.

Worling, J. R. (2000). *Adolescent sexual offender recidivism: 10 year follow-up of specialized treatment and implications for risk prediction.* Paper presented at the 15th Annual Conference of the National Adolescent Perpetration Network, Denver, CO.

Worling, J. R., & Curwen, T. (2001). *Estimate of Risk of Adolescent Sexual Offense Recidivism (ERASOR). Version 2.0.* Toronto, Canada: Safe-T Program, Thistletown Regional Centre for Children and Adolescents, Ontario Ministry of Community and Social Services.

Worling, J. R., & Langstrom, N. (2006). Risk of sexual recidivism in adolescents who offend sexually: Correlates and assessment. In H. E. Barbaree & W. L. Marshall (Eds.), *The juvenile sex offender* (2nd ed.) (pp. 219–247). New York: Guilford Press.

CHAPTER 14

Comprehensive Service Delivery With a Continuum of Care

STEVEN BENGIS

S TARTING IN THE mid-1980s and continuing for most of a decade, there was virtual unanimity among professionals treating sexually abusive youth that successful intervention required specialized diagnostic evaluations and specialized treatment (Bengis, 1986; Knopp, 1982, 1985). Given the consequences to innocent victims of diagnostic and treatment mistakes, many practitioners committed themselves to victim protection (many proclaimed the community as their client), legal accountability, specialized diagnosis, and "offense specific" group treatment. This approach was consistent with the consensus reached by the National Task Force on Juvenile Sexual Offending (1988, 1993).

As research has subsequently demonstrated the wide variation in diagnostic profiles of youth who abuse, the commonality between conduct disordered youth who abuse sexually and those committing other crimes, the lower than previously expected sexual recidivism rates and higher than previously thought rates of other delinquent behavior, consensus in the field has changed regarding how best to manage, treat, and intervene with juveniles. If victim protection is the highest priority, so too is the duty to "do no harm" to a youthful client, particularly as legislation has imposed often draconian consequences on ever-younger abusing youth (adult prosecutions, residency restrictions, registration, and community notification). If legal accountability continues to be necessary and desirable in many cases, the impact of recent brain-based research on juvenile culpability is now an added consideration (i.e., the frontal lobes responsible for impulse control, judgment, and planning do not fully develop until a youth is in his/her twenties). Thus prosecution in Juvenile Court, where such issues can be more carefully weighed in each case, is even more essential except in the most heinous cases.

While specialized knowledge is still paramount for practitioners, the understanding of "specialization" has become much more complex. It is no longer assumed that cognitive-behavioral therapy in groups is always the imperative intervention modality. Rather, intervention for juveniles who sexually offend now requires careful integration of a wide range of interventions, risk management strategies, and treatment techniques. Recognizing that sexual abuse is a behavior and not a diagnosis, the importance of careful individualized, differential diagnosis is essential, and a "one size fits all" approach is contraindicated. For example, the same set of facts describing an offense may have profoundly different meanings for conduct-disordered youth as opposed to those on the autism spectrum, those struggling with severe developmental deficits, or those with significant mental health diagnoses or trauma issues. The complexity of individual differences often involves combinations of the aforementioned.

Intervention can now be guided by research and evidence-based practices specifically relevant to each individual's needs. Thoughtful clinical judgment combines with a comprehensive understanding that sexual abuse occurs within the context of a "whole child." The field continues to change as new research guides the work, validating some assumptions and correcting others.

As assessment, risk management, and treatment models have evolved, the need for a comprehensive continuum of care service delivery system has remained consistent since first articulated in the early 1980s. Regardless of the chosen approach, intervention must be implemented across a carefully constructed service delivery system with a continuum of care that guarantees both a range of residential and outpatient alternatives and a consistent therapeutic approach across the treatment continuum (Bengis, 1986).

THE CONTINUUM OF CARE

A care continuum honors the varying levels of risk inherent in a juvenile population. A youth who comes to the attention of the service system early, prior to developing chronic or habituated abusive behavior patterns, and who has not used violence in his/her offenses is often treatable in outpatient settings and may be able to continue attending public school, with reasonable risk-management strategies and safety plans. Outpatient services may include individual, group, family, and/or systemic therapy approaches. Youth whose diagnostic and risk assessments reveal a longer history of sexually abusive behaviors, other abusive and delinquent behaviors, or violent sexual assaults require more secure settings. Some such youth may safely be treated in staff-secure community-based residential programs. Others may require a physically secure hospital or juvenile correctional facility. Given these wide-ranging risk and diagnostic factors, the following components comprise a well-conceived comprehensive service delivery system that should also include a continuum of care as follows.

1. Locked residential treatment facilities: hospital, treatment, and correctional facilities.
2. Unlocked, community-based staff-secure residential treatment programs.
3. Alternative community-based living environments (specialized foster care, group homes, mentor programs, supervised apartments).
4. Outpatient treatment programs, case management, and transitional services, special education day schools, and after-school programs.
5. Community-based Mental Health Services capable of providing diagnostic and risk assessments and comprehensive treatment interventions.

This same treatment service continuum should be replicated for profoundly intellectually limited clients who, because of the risks they pose and their special treatment needs, should not be integrated with more cognitively capable adolescents or with nonabusive disabled clients.

But the aforementioned continuum of services is not a *care continuum*. The latter provides both consistency of approach and a continuity of caregivers as the youth moves in and out of more or less restrictive settings. Without a care continuum, a youth who enters the system in a highly secure residential setting and moves through less restrictive residential programs (foster care, home placement, group homes, or a supervised apartment) may be confronted with a variety of treatment approaches/philosophies, intervention styles, and clinical strategies. Direct care personnel, clinicians, and teachers may change with each new placement. Such changes would be stressful for any youth, and are particularly destructive given the disruptions of care, failed relationships, and attachment problems that have contributed to these juveniles developing these behavior problems. Disruption of relationships interferes with the attachment process, may hinder the development of stable adult relationships, and may weaken the impact of otherwise well-conceived models of intervention. This sort of inconsistency is thought to contribute to recidivism in the general population of emotionally disturbed juveniles, and may be particularly risky for sexually abusive children/youth (Prentky, Harris, Frizell, & Righthand, 2000).

Even with a specialized approach that is consistently implemented over time by treatment staff whom these youth know and trust, some youth who abuse sexually experience great difficulty in freeing themselves from deeply imprinted behavior responses. These responses tend to reassert themselves when the youth is under stress or pressure, or dealing with disappointment, failure, or highly emotional encounters. To avoid regression and new abusive behavior, these youth need to have their new behaviors and new coping mechanisms reinforced over and over again in a consistent and predictable manner. If any of the service providers along the care continuum fails to support and reinforce the principles and practices of abuse-specific treatment (i.e., confronting attitudes supportive of abuse, and reinforcing accountability for current behavior), the denial, minimization, and acting-out that brought some of these adolescents into the system may resume. The consistency and predictability of approach, central elements in the treatment of these clients, can be guaranteed only when service providers at all levels of the service delivery system are committed to a common treatment philosophy. This requires cross training all the professionals who work together as multidisciplinary teams.

Thus, a comprehensive service delivery system with a continuum of care must contain the components listed previously *and* be guided by the following basic premises:

1. That each youth moving through the system be treated with a consistent approach regardless of his/her residential or outpatient placement. Although different placements might require a modification of technique, objectives, or strategies, the basic treatment orientation should remain the same.
2. That every effort be made to maintain certain staff-client-peer relationships as a youth moves from one placement to another (i.e., a youth would continue to work with the same therapist, group leader, or day program staff as he changes residential placements and moves along the continuum from secure treatment to independent living). This relationship continuity is often the most difficult

component of quality treatment given the complexities of the service-system that rarely is administered by a single agency with consistent personnel. In the absence of a single provider administering several levels of care, the continuity of relationships is often the biggest challenge facing agencies and treatment providers.

THE ECONOMICS OF A CONTINUUM OF CARE

In addition to enhancing the quality of treatment created by the development of a care continuum, there is also a compelling economic argument for its development. Without adequate step-downs, many youth remain in costly residential settings far longer than their treatment requires. By creating the various steps in the continuum, a youth need only internalize self-control to the degree required to step down to the next service level. For example, rather than having to move from a structured residential program to a home placement, a youth need only progress to the point where he/she can be treated in a less intensive (step-down) group home. With the latter as an option, a two- to three-year residential placement may, in some cases, be dramatically reduced with a concomitant significant cost savings.

On all relevant dimensions including quality treatment, relationship consistency, and economic efficiency, the development of a continuum of care is crucial to safe management and quality intervention with youth who abuse sexually. By establishing a continuum of care based on the five components, communities create the optimal conditions for meeting both their own needs and the needs of this specific client population.

HETEROGENEOUS VERSUS HOMOGENEOUS PLACEMENTS

The question of creating homogeneous versus heterogeneous placements is central to the care continuum for which the author is advocating. Can sexually abusive youth be successfully placed in programs designed to serve emotionally or behaviorally disturbed adolescents who are not known to have been sexually abusive? This question is particularly pertinent when considering the need to create new services versus the utilization of existing ones and the difficulties and ethical issues raised by attempting to site a residence specifically designed for sexually abusive youth within the community.

RESIDENTIAL SETTINGS

In addressing this question, Knopp, Rosenberg, and Stevenson (1986) had reported that "most residential programs do not provide separate cottages or quarters for sex offenders. Usually, they live in the general population, but meet in separate offense-specific groups at least once per week." Knopp and others suggested that such an arrangement might not be optimal.

With the passage of over 20 years and experience, the question of segregation versus inclusion has become much more complex. Specialized programs, especially those with a diagnostic mix of those who are sexually abusive, allow for staff to develop strong risk-management skills as well as common intervention techniques that can be consistently implemented. Such programs allow youth to address sexual issues they may be extremely reluctant to discuss with those who have not acted out in a similar manner and such programs avoid the "stigma" that other nonsexually abusive youth may apply to those who abuse sexually.

Alternatively, segregated programs may focus too intensively on sexual deviance and fail to provide enough opportunities for sexually abusive youth to experience other dimensions of themselves that are healthy and more normalizing.

In the absence of definitive research indicating the best placement for various diagnostic youth (i.e., conduct disordered versus those in the Pervasive Developmental Disorder spectrum), it may be best for programs to consider the importance of safety/risk management, treatment models for various populations, and the need for normalizing experiences, rather than a preconceived philosophy about segregation versus integration. It may be that different approaches will prove more useful with different types of youth. Most importantly, placements should not be based on behavior alone and placing youth in either segregated or integrated programs requires careful consideration of a number of variables.

Examples of successfully integrated programs include hospital-based and correctional settings and special education day-school settings. However, even in settings that are able to create sexual safety for all their clients, the issue of stigmatization of those who abuse sexually can be difficult to overcome. "Abuse specific" programming can help staff and residents see the commonalities in many clinical and correctional settings (Ryan, 1997).

Given the risk factors in mixing abusive and nonabusive youth, mixed-diagnostic residential programs should develop strict criteria and procedural guidelines to ensure the safety of all of their client populations. The principles of Informed Supervision and Therapeutic Care (see Chapter 15) are particularly useful in meeting the needs of mixed populations of special needs youth. In addition, certain categories of youth who are known to have been abusive (for example, youth who have committed serious hands-on offenses for which they have never been adjudicated, who are in denial, and who will not voluntarily agree to participate in abuse-specific treatment) may pose too high a risk for unlocked community-based integrated placements.

INTEGRATED SPECIAL EDUCATION DAY PROGRAMS

An example of a successful mixed-diagnostic program is a special education day school. Oftentimes, sexually abusive youth do well in an educational setting. Such a setting is highly structured and can limit opportunities for students to be out of sight of staff. In such a setting, many youth who abuse sexually are behaviorally compliant (that is, they can move through the school routines with relative ease without disruptively acting out), and they are often educationally advanced in comparison to other emotionally disturbed clients. Therefore, they may provide positive role models for other students in an educational setting while themselves benefiting from the normalized social interactions.

An educational environment generally focused on emotionally neutral subject matter with a highly structured setting seems to help these youths regulate their oversexualized lifestyle and preoccupation with sexual issues. Leisure time and residential environments such as bedrooms and common living areas may aggravate these issues.

Finally, school can serve as a bridge between residential placement and a return to the community for youth who will need to be able to cope with both their own sexually abusive histories and a nonabusive community population. Within the structure of the school, they can practice prosocial community behaviors and new skills, in an environment that includes male and female peers and teachers. If the staff has been specially trained to work with sexual abuse issues, they can confront any abusive or sexual behaviors and work on them immediately.

Thus, a mixed-diagnostic category day program can provide the type of structured environment suited to helping youth move along the care continuum toward more normal independent living.

Minimally, all residential, day program, and educational staff should be provided with extensive training in the management of sexual abuse issues. In addition, these programs should be provided with sufficient resources for consultation and supervision by qualified treatment specialists and for one-to-one staffing of abusive youth during initial assessment periods and times of crisis. Without such basic safeguards, the placement of sexually abusive youth in residential and other community-based programs that have not been designed to serve them raises serious legal and ethical issues should another client be sexually victimized while in treatment in these same sites (Freeman-Longo & Ryan, 1990).

The lack of adequate resources or other administrative or political realities may prevent the implementation of the entire service delivery system at any one time in every rural community, but a minimum commitment of resources allocated for training can facilitate the initiation of specialized interventions and abuse-specific evaluation and treatment planning in residential programs and outpatient clinics where personnel trained in general assessment and group treatment techniques already practice.

In the past decade, many communities have implemented standards for treatment and management of these youth. It is important for standards, policies, and programs to be continuously in touch with new advances in the field and willing to update practices.

In order to create all of the components of the care continuum, many states need only to redesign portions of their existing delivery systems. By allocating resources to training and evaluation and by mandating relevant treatment for the youth who has been sexually abusive, the sexually abusive behaviors of this client population can be addressed directly and specifically during adolescence, with a better prognosis and fewer victims.

REFERENCES

Bengis, S. (1986). *A comprehensive service delivery and a continuum of care for adolescent sexual offenders.* Orwell, VT: Safer Society Press.

Freeman-Longo, R., & Ryan, G. (1990). *Tort liability in treatment of sexually abusive juveniles. Interchange: Newsletter.* Denver, CO: National Adolescent Perpetration Network, Kempe Center.

Knopp, F. H. (1982). *Remedial intervention in adolescent sex offenders.* Orwell, VT: Safer Society Press.

Knopp, F. H. (1985). *The youthful sex offender: Rationale and goals for treatment.* Orwell, VT: Safer Society Press.

Knopp, F. H., Rosenberg, J., & Stevenson, W. (1986). *Report on nationwide survey of juvenile and adult sex-offender treatment programs and providers: 1986*. Orwell, VT: Safer Society Press.

National Task Force on Juvenile Sexual Offending. (1988). Preliminary report. *Juvenile and Family Court Journal, 39*(2), 1–67.

National Task Force on Juvenile Sexual Offending. (1993). Revised report. *Juvenile and Family Court Journal, 44*(4), 1–120.

Prentky, R., Harris, B., Frizell, K., & Righthand, S. (2000). An actuarial procedure for assessing risk with juvenile sex offenders. *Sexual Abuse: Journal of Research and Treatment, 12*(2), 71–94.

Ryan, G. (1997). Creating an "abuse-specific milieu." In G. Ryan & S. Lane (Eds.), *Juvenile sexual offending: Causes, consequences, and corrections* (pp. 404–416). San Francisco: Jossey-Bass.

CHAPTER 15

Adult Responsibilities

Abuse-Specific Supervision and Care

GAIL RYAN

> When we see kids doing "inhuman" things, maybe it's because they have not
> experienced "human" development.
>
> (Michael Whitaker, 1990)

IT IS THE responsibility of adults to provide children and youth with supervision, guidance, and support to meet the child's needs. Children known to have a history of abusive behaviors that pose a risk to themselves, others, or property need adults to supervise and care for them in ways that protect the youth from causing further harm to others or to themselves. In doing so, the adult demonstrates personal responsibility and concern for the well-being of all.

When parents or others ask the court to allow a youth who has sexually offended to stay in the community while serving time on probation and completing treatment, it is reasonable to expect that those adults take responsibility for protecting others and holding the youth responsible for complying with whatever conditions are imposed on them. Keeping the community safe initially requires high levels of supervision and external controls to moderate the risk of reoffense because until assessment and treatment demonstrate "evidence of decreased risk," it must initially be assumed that the youth may be as likely to offend today as they were on the day they previously offended. Therefore, the first condition that is usually placed on these youth is that they cooperate with high levels of adult supervision.

The need for supervision has always been apparent, more or less, in this work, but professionals have realized that a parent stating that they would "supervise" the youth did not actually ensure that they knew how to do so in a manner relevant to the risk of sexual offending. It did seem that if they had not been aware of the offending in the past, they might not recognize signs of risk in the present just because they now knew about the offense. The quality of supervision and care, for better or worse, can be an enormous asset or can exacerbate risk. Adults are not always consistent in holding children accountable for their behavior, and sometimes actually model the same patterns of thinking or dysfunction that are associated with the problematic behavior of the youth.

The most apparent differences in the treatment and management of youth who have committed sexual offenses, as compared to adult sex offender management strategies, are: (a) the developmental stage of youth; and (b) the presence of adults who are responsible for the youth. Mobilizing adults to protect the community and foster healthy development are the tenets most relevant to the supervision and care of juveniles who have sexually offended.

In child welfare and child protective services, mobilizing multidisciplinary teams (MDT) in order to bring a wide range of roles and expertise together in a process of shared responsibility and team decision making has been a widely replicated and successful approach. For all youth successful outcomes are enhanced by effective adults. In order for adults to meet the needs of youth who are in treatment for sexual offending, the adults need knowledge about the problem and knowledge about the needs of the particular youth to be effective.

In developing state standards for the management and treatment of juveniles who have committed sexual offenses, Colorado's Sex Offender Management Board (2002) included a clear articulation of what constituted relevant supervision and care for these youth. The concepts of "Informed Supervision" and "Therapeutic Care" are now requirements for these youth to be allowed to stay in, or return to, community-based homes, schools, and treatment programs in Colorado. The clear definition and articulation of relevant adult responsibilities has been useful to others in the field as well; providers in many other states have embraced the utility of these constructs. Requirements for adults to take responsibility for providing adequate supervision and care can be implemented as policy or conditions of treatment programs, child welfare, probation, or the juvenile court, even when not required by state legislation or regulations.

Clinicians and probation officers cannot be present 24 hours a day; however, there are many other adults involved in kids' lives who become critical links between the professionals and the youth. Probation officers and treatment providers cannot make informed decisions or address the special needs of each individual without good observations and information from the caregivers and teachers who spend the most time with the youth. The team must rely on other adults to carry pertinent information back and forth and to document observable changes (for better and worse) as the youth progresses through treatment.

The caregiver's input is critical in conveying what the ongoing needs and risks are that pertain to the youth's ability to do well. Adults must have knowledge about the problem and the youth in order to recognize risks and progress, monitor compliance with treatment plans, communicate relevant information to the team, intervene in specific risks, and maximize their own effectiveness with the youth. Eleven requirements define and operationalize the concept of "Informed Supervision" (CSOMB 5.711, 2002) as specifically related to reducing the risk of abusive behaviors.

"INFORMED SUPERVISION"

At least one primary caregiver must meet these criteria, but other adults can also become "informed supervisors" as needed. An "informed supervisor" is an adult who meets the following requirements:

1. Is aware of the juvenile's history of abusive and/or high risk behaviors.
2. Does not deny or minimize the youth's responsibility for, or the seriousness of, abusive behaviors.

3. Does not allow the juvenile to be in situations that provide access or opportunity for such behaviors to occur, until there is evidence of decreased risk.
4. Monitors all contact between the juvenile and "vulnerable persons," including siblings, peers, and past or potential victims.
5. Can define and recognize all types of abusive behaviors in daily functioning and in the environment. (Using the Abuse Is Abuse concept.)
6. Is aware of the dynamic patterns associated with abusive behaviors and is able to recognize such patterns in daily functioning. (Using the Cycle.)
7. Has the skills to intervene in and interrupt high-risk patterns that manifest in the youth's daily functioning. (Interrupting the Cycle.)
8. Participate in designing, implementing, and monitoring safety plans for daily activities. (Risk management.)
9. Is aware of the laws defining illegal behaviors of juveniles and relevant reporting requirements, informs children of such laws as they relate to their daily patterns of behavior, and holds children accountable for responsible and legal behavior.
10. Clearly articulates the rules governing the child's behavior in their daily lives, and holds children accountable for following the rules (including conditions of probation and/or treatment).
11. Communicates openly with the child, and with other adults involved in the child's life, making accurate observations regarding the youth's daily functioning.

Informed Supervisors:

Who:
    Primary Caregivers
    (May also be other adults)
Qualifications:
    Not deny or minimize importance of abuse
    Available, Able, and Willing
    No active criminal cases
Conditions:
    Aware of History: Sexual Offense
    Aware of Conditions: Probation; Treatment; Safety Plans
    Aware of Laws: Prevention and Accountability
    Acquires Concepts and Skills to Actively Supervise
Actions:
    Prevent Victim Contact: Except when approved by MDT
    Observe and Monitor Contact: Past Victim(s), Siblings, Vulnerable persons
    Hold Juvenile Responsible: Accountability and Consequences
    Consistently Define All Abuse: All types; All contexts
    Observe and Report Patterns and Changes in Daily functioning
    Safety Planning: Recognize risk and use risk-management strategies

By addressing all types of abusive and illegal behaviors the risk of a wide range of problems is addressed, including other delinquent behaviors, which are much more often the cause of rearrest or revocations of probation than sexual reoffending.

To be able to meet the requirements, the informed Supervisor must learn a few basic concepts and acquire the skills to do what they are expected to do. This can be accomplished by reading written materials or through training, either with a group of adults who are all learning to provide Informed Supervision, or one-on-one with a teacher, therapist, or probation officer (Ryan, Yager, Sobicinski, & Metzner, 2002). The immediate goal is to create a shared base of knowledge and language so that the Informed Supervisor is able to communicate effectively with the team and the youth and to understand what the youth will be expected to learn and do over the course of treatment. The basic concepts are the foundation for understanding the goals and outcomes of treatment and management plans.

Basic Concepts

"Abuse Is Abuse" The Ability to define all types of abuse (self, others, property) and to Differentiate Laws, Rules, Problem Behaviors and Abuse

"High Risk Cycle" Recognition of Patterns associated with abusive behavior as might be observed in daily life; and Adult Interventions to interrupt the progression, reinforcement, and habituation of such patterns

"Safety Planning" Recognition of risk, and Risk-Management Strategies

"Outcomes" Observable change showing Decreased Risk/Increased Health

The goal of the first concept is for the adult to notice, define, and model recognition of all types of abuse wherever it appears (in movies, music, the news, and history, as well as in current behaviors), and to be able to make clear distinctions between abusive behavior, illegal behavior, behavior that violates a rule, and behaviors that are a problem for other reasons (see Chapter 8). This enables the adult to communicate with other adults and the youth about risks and observations and to reinforce what the youth is learning.

The goal of the second concept is for the adults to recognize patterns associated with the risk of abusive behavior and learn how to interrupt those patterns (see Chapter 8). Long before the youth has learned about those patterns, acquired the skills to recognize and interrupt the patterns, or demonstrated the motivation and ability to consistently do so, the adult can focus attention on recognizing the first phase of the cycle and intervening there instead of focusing on punishing bad behavior after the fact. Every time the pattern is disrupted by circumstance or by design of the adult or the youth, the habituation is interrupted. With younger at-risk children it may never be expected that the child learn all this; much more of the expectations fall to adult responsibilities.

The goal of Safety Planning is to recognize risks and know how to moderate risks in planning daily activities, and to make informed decisions about the level of supervision and support the youth may need during activities. The goal of introducing Informed Supervisors to the observable outcomes that the youth will be working to demonstrate is so the adults can not only be good observers, but know what observations are important to report to the team.

By requiring (by policy, law, or a court order) at least one primary caregiver of every youth with a history of sexually abusive behaviors to acquire the knowledge and provide Informed Supervision, the requirement is not "personal." The team does not need a full evaluation before this requirement is introduced and it is not required specifically because of some problem or deficit of the particular parent or youth. This can effectively engage the parent in knowing immediately what will be expected of them to enable their youth to be in the least restrictive setting possible and to succeed in treatment.

Teaching and holding kids accountable for responsible and legal behavior are adult responsibilities. Sexual Offenses are illegal sexual behaviors; individuals can be arrested, charged, and prosecuted for illegal behaviors. The ages at which children become legally "culpable" are different in each state, some defined by statute and others by case law. The age of legal culpability is the minimum age at which children can be arrested and charged, and in the United States ranges from about 7 to 12. The minimum age tends to be somewhat older in other countries; 12 is the more common age of culpability in Europe and the United Kingdom. Many adults raising their own children or working with children in the community are not even aware of this change in children's status. It is important for adults to be made aware of and teach children this, as well as what laws are likely to be relevant to juvenile supervision conditions. Truancy, curfew violations, or trespassing on skateboards or bikes may be the violations that jeopardize conditions of probation that require "no illegal behavior."

The laws relevant to sexual behavior also include an "age of consent," below which children cannot be involved sexually with adults. The age of consent laws also differ by state in the United States and range from 14 to 18; the age is somewhat younger in other countries, where 14 to 15 is more characteristic. In many places, an age difference of more than two to four years between two juveniles may also define juvenile sexual interactions as "illegal."

Although legally culpable for their own behavior, juveniles are not considered able to give permission to an older partner to be sexual with them until a specific age, which is legally considered the "age of consent." The "age of consent" laws are also different in each state and adults must be aware of and teach children these laws. Such laws represent a community's values about human behavior, but the "age of consent" is an arbitrary legal boundary that reflects both adult denial and repression of children's sexuality and adults' legitimate concerns about the risks associated with sexual behavior. However, these laws have little to do with normal human development or functioning. As any teenager will attest, it is ironic that the law says children are "culpable" while deemed unable to "consent" to choices about their behavior.

Legal statues defining sexual offenses can be hard to decipher. In laymen's terms, the laws defining juvenile sexual offenses primarily consider six types of sexual behaviors.

Types of Illegal Sexual Behavior

Sexual contact that occurs without consent, with an unequal partner, or as a result of coercion (*Sexual abuse; Molestation*)

Sexual contact with a child by a person in a position of trust (Babysitter, Position of Authority over child; coaching, tutoring, babysitting, etc.)

Incest (Sexual contact with a family member)

Rape (Forced/violent/aggressive and usually including penetration)

Noncontact sexual offenses (Peeping, exposing, obscene calls, stalking; and making or viewing child pornography)

Sexual Harassment (Unwelcome sexual advances, words, or behavior, which cause one to feel uncomfortable or unsafe)

Sexual harassment is the only type of offense that is defined not by the person's behavior but by the victim's experience or perception, which underscores the importance of youth recognizing and responding to the cues of others (empathic recognition and response). Behavior that might be welcome flirting with one peer can be sexual harassment to another; noticing and responding to cues of discomfort or distress in others differentiates the two.

Some sexual behaviors are illegal but not abusive, while others may be abusive but not defined by law as "offenses." Abusive behaviors cause harm even if they are not illegal.

Informed supervisors must recognize illegal behavior and also be able to clearly define abusive interactions in terms of: Lack of consent, Lack of equality, and Coercion (see Chapter 1).

It is NOT the sexual behavior that defines abuse; it is the quality of the relationship and interaction. Differentiating all the reasons sexual behaviors may be a problem even if not abusive or illegal is also an adult responsibility.

As discussed in earlier chapters, research has shown that many juveniles who commit sexual offenses have also been, or are at risk to be, involved in other types of abusive, delinquent, and harmful behaviors. Treatment goals include defining and preventing a wide range of behaviors that are abusive to self, others, or property. Whether physical, sexual, verbal, emotional, or psychological, abusive behaviors seem to occur in similar patterns and those who engage in one type may be at risk to engage in other types as well. Informed Supervisors need to define, recognize, and intervene in all types of abusive behavior, and to recognize and interrupt the patterns that precede and reinforce abusive behaviors. To be able to do this, they need to learn about the "Abuse is Abuse" concept and the "cycle" (see Chapters 8 and 9).

Recognizing the risk of a wide range of problematic behaviors and using the cycle allows the Informed Supervisor to recognize and interrupt progression toward abusive behaviors before the behavior occurs. The *"high risk cycle"* represents situations, thoughts, feelings, and behaviors that interact in a predictable pattern that is a common manifestation of human defenses when stressed. An *emotional response* (in some current situation) creates stress and is referred to as the "trigger" emotion. Being overwhelmed by emotion or stress creates a sense of vulnerability, an inability to cope. The cycle begins as a coping strategy but becomes dysfunctional when overgeneralized, and avoids the actual issues.

The Informed Supervisor is taught to use the cycle to identify signs of the pattern in the daily functioning of the youth. When adults are able to see the antecedents, they have the opportunity to intervene in ways that disrupt the overgeneralization and habituation of the defensive strategy. As the adult becomes more vigilant and conscious of the situations or times the youth experiences trigger emotions or stressors, communicating those observations to the treatment providers expedites the clinical work to explore sensitive issues and emotions from the past that are continuing to create stress for the youth. At the same time, recognizing the commonalities in the occurrence of those triggers enables the Informed Supervisor and team to recognize those risks in safety planning for current activities. Simply foreseeing stress is a first step in desensitizing the youth so they do not get so overwhelmed. The Informed Supervisor is taught to recognize and interrupt cycles, and to provide anticipatory desensitization in situations known to be emotionally stressful for the youth by Safety Planning. They are also expected to actively intervene when noticing signs of stress or the cycle.

Interrupting the cycle of another

12:00: Validate the emotional *Triggers* (empathy).

1:00: Identify and articulate the *Sense of being unsafe*.

2:00: Challenge the *Hopelessness and Negative Expectations* (by teaching and practicing new skills and providing new experiences of self, others, and relationships).

3:00: Decrease *Isolation* by "being with" the youth (minimize "time outs" for youth who lack the skills to calm down, rethink, and problem solve).

4:00: Refuse to engage in the *Power* struggles; teach *nonaggressive* tension reduction and *Anger* management.

5:00: Define abusive *Fantasies* when heard, and develop new skills to increase possible *Solutions*.

As was emphasized previously (see Chapters 8 and 9), the patterns look different and progress differently for each youth, so the adult is looking for signs of these elements and is taught to respond to whatever element(s) they recognize.

Addressing the emotional baggage that gets brought up by the trigger and exploring dysfunctional behavior and experience of the past is done in clinical interventions, while the Informed Supervisor focuses on the present. By understanding risks, as well as ways to moderate risk by interrupting the cycle with more functional solutions, the adult helps the youth develop skills that support more functional coping in their daily lives. Safety Planning teaches youth to anticipate risks and use foresight and planning to prevent stress and be successful.

Successful people plan ahead and develop skills for dealing with stress and to be prepared for stress. The concept of preparing for stress is often a foreign notion for dysfunctional youth, never having seen modeling of forethought and planning. Just as it is recognized that the dysfunctional cycle is simply an overgeneralization of normal human defenses, safety planning and risk management are also very common in human functioning. Using calendars to remember commitments and looking ahead at the next day and week and preparing for meetings or appointments are examples of the things people do to be successful and are different for different people, but they are "planful," not accidental. Things as simple as getting a good night's sleep, eating a good breakfast, making a list, wearing the right clothing, and asking others for help, are all routine for many people. Reducing the risk of being overwhelmed by unexpected stress also includes foreseeing potential emotional stress.

Safety Planning

1. What are the risks? (i.e., What in the situation might be stressful and/or bring up old emotional triggers? What situations might create access to vulnerable persons where allegations might arise, or a reoffense opportunity exist?)
2. What would need to happen to moderate those risks? (i.e., What skills would the youth need to use to handle things himself? What would be needed from others [such as support or supervision]? Could parts of the plan be altered to reduce undue risk? etc.)
3. Is it possible to do the things that would moderate risk? (i.e., Does the youth have the skills needed and have they demonstrated motivation to use the skills when relevant; is the adult able to provide the support or supervision that is needed?)

Safety Planning is risk management for current activities and informs good decisions about what activities are reasonable to expect the youth to be successful doing. If the only risk considered is whether there might be an opportunity for the youth to reoffend, then safety planning is perceived as unnecessary in many activities and also suggests that the youth continues to be at risk to sexually offend whenever there is an opportunity, despite progress in treatment. However, by considering the risk of allegations, avoidance of situations that do in fact create "opportunity" is improved; expressing concern for the youth avoiding allegations demonstrates concern for the safety of all, rather than focusing exclusively on the welfare of others. Adding the risks of stress or emotional triggers addresses the risk of the youth being overwhelmed, falling back on old defensive patterns and being at heightened risk as a result, either during or after the activity. The answer to the question, "What are the risks?" is never "There aren't any." For almost every risk, adults can help identify ways to moderate the risk when committed to maximizing the youth's opportunities to participate in normalizing, health-promoting activities.

Risk management is a process, and if by the end of the process, the answers to the third question are all "yes," then the plan is probably reasonable. If the answers are "no" then the plan is probably too risky *at this time*, but the process has illuminated what the youth or others would need to be able to do for the risk moderating things to become possible. The youth and team can work toward goals to be able to do the activity in the future.

Safety plans are designed to manage risk in the least restrictive and least intrusive manner in order to maximize normalizing activities. By the end of the process, the team knows what is needed of adults, including whether or not a fully "Informed Supervisor" is needed. Many activities may require adult "supervision," but not always by an adult meeting the 11 requirements of Informed Supervision. Initially, much of the risk management is the responsibility of adults, but as the youth demonstrates the skills and motivation to manage themselves, the gradual transfer of responsibility to the youth demonstrates progress toward the goal of "self-control." Progress on the treatment "outcomes" described in previous chapters is the evidence which informs that transfer of responsibility.

Informed Supervisors are taught what safety plans are and how they are developed, and are expected to become able to help the youth construct safety plans for daily activities. It is the MDT's responsibility to support and monitor the adults' mastery of the concepts and consistency in implementing them. Some safety plans may require approval by the MDT or the probation officer, especially when representing changes in the level of adult supervision or changes in contact with victims or other vulnerable persons. Many safety plans will have common elements (such as "going to school," "using public restrooms"), but need to be readdressed to ask "what might be different in this situation, or on a particular day" and should be processed afterward to check how well the plan worked.

Safety Plans are designed to help youth be able to participate successfully and safely in activities that are good for them, by managing risks with foresight and planning. Some Safety Plans are entirely dependent on constant adult supervision and should NOT always restrict activities just because there are risks. For most youth, return to normal lifestyles in the community should be possible, and safety planning creates those opportunities. Good communication and lots of adult involvement maximize success.

Aftercare may recommend continued supervision, which parallels adult models of containment (using many external sources of oversight and control) for those youth who will remain at high risk due to static or stable risks that cannot be moderated by treatment, or for youth who might not demonstrate change over time. However, most juveniles will not need lifetime supervision if adults are patient and firm and help them develop good skills for self-control.

Many juveniles who commit sexual offenses during adolescence are not pervasively abusive or sexually deviant and can remain at home in the community on probation while participating in outpatient education and treatment programs. Others may require placements outside their home for some period of time primarily because they have sexually abused someone in their own household, without needing care beyond normal parenting. Others need more extensive treatment and corrective parenting. Informed supervision is recommended for all youth with a history of abusive behaviors, whether they are living at home or placed in alternative care. Some will need Therapeutic Care.

THERAPEUTIC CARE

The clear articulation of the caregivers' role is a strength of the Colorado State standards for sexually abusive youth. Defining the roles of adults who provide care in alternative placements (foster care, residential, or correctional) has been useful in other states and is also useful with younger and at-risk children. Therapeutic care providers have three primary roles: to protect, to nurture, and to observe. Protection is demonstrated in the struggle to achieve physical and psychological safety. Nurturance involves all the roles of parenting to help children grow and develop. Observation informs the process of ongoing assessment and treatment planning.

Rationale for Therapeutic Care

It is the responsibility of adults to provide children and youth with supervision, guidance, and support to meet the child's needs.

Therapeutic care provides corrective care and guidance, beyond what is normally expected of a parent, to assist a juvenile in addressing special needs or developmental deficits that impede successful functioning.

Therapeutic care providers address treatment goals relevant to daily behavior management, education, and increased health skills, while providing new experiences.

Therapeutic caregivers provide "informed supervision" and also:

1. Provide a physically safe environment by implementing effective behavior management techniques and consistent consequences.
2. Provide a psychologically safe environment by modeling consistency, respect, and trustworthiness.
3. Assess risks, deficits, strengths, and skills that are observable in the daily functioning of the juvenile.
4. Implement purposeful planning to help the juvenile develop new skills and to reinforce strengths.
5. Model nonaggressive and noncoercive interpersonal interactions and nonaggressive anger management.

6. Provide opportunities for the juvenile to interact with positive male and female adult and peer role models.
7. Provide opportunities to practice new coping skills and social skills.
8. Provide activities that promote positive relaxation, recreation, and play.
9. Maximize participation in "normalizing" experiences in the community.
10. Participate in team decisions with the professionals as member of the MDT.

Therapeutic caregivers act as temporary primary caregivers and must be actively involved with the MDT, where they have unique responsibilities in the decision process. Examples of therapeutic caregivers include foster parents and residential program milieu staff. Not only does the therapeutic care provider make daily decisions regarding the care and management of the youth (using safety plans and other treatment concepts), but also, these caregivers *work on the goals that are most relevant to tipping the balance of risks and assets*, helping the youth to get on with healthy development. Throughout treatment the caregiver is uniquely positioned to be the best observer of the juvenile's *progress* and *daily functioning*, as well as *noticing increased risks*.

Therapeutic Care provides care and guidance beyond normal parenting in a growing and nurturing environment, and models normative, healthy, prosocial attitudes and relationships. The primary goals are: Current safety; Daily functioning; Increased Health; and a New Experience of Self, Others, Relationship, and the World.

Successful, productive care providers must have an abundance of time, motivation, energy, and flexibility, and be essentially good-natured adults with a sense of humor and lots of patience. The first expectation of a therapeutic care provider is that they be willing to enter into a relationship with youth who are at times very hard to be with. A relationship characterized by empathy, consistency, trustworthiness, and worthy of secure attachment is needed. Providing empathic care requires flexibility to be responsive to the needs of each individual.

The therapeutic care provider first meets the 11 requirements of Informed Supervision, and in addition is responsible for creating a physically and psychologically safe environment within which it is reasonable to ask children to let down defenses, be vulnerable, and try new things. Creating a new experience of self, relationships, and the world is a big job and requires commitment far beyond simply supervising, feeding, and observing children.

Like other informed supervisors, the care provider is consistently defining all abuse, recognizing and interrupting cyclical patterns, and using safety plans to purposefully moderate risks, while trying to maximize the youth's opportunities for normative exposure and experiences. Providing opportunities for growth include all areas of human functioning.

Physical Safety is an intrinsic need for all humans; without physical safety, growth and change are not likely. It must be held apparent that bringing abusive youth into alternative care settings creates a threat to physical safety. Risk management in relation to all Abuse-specific programming will be discussed in Chapter 17, but it is the caregivers' dilemma to struggle with the daily behaviors. Physical safety means *everyone* must be safe, with no threat of physical harm to the adults or the youth.

To achieve physical safety, care providers must initially employ external sources of control to stabilize the abusive dynamics that bring these youth into special needs settings.

Physical Safety

Everyone able to be safe: No physical abuse
   External Containment/Restraints
   Adult Supervision
   Programming
   Rules and Structure
   Behavior Modification: Rewards and Consequences

When the care environment has stabilized and youth appear to be exercising better self-control so they are not blowing up or shutting down, it is then possible to work toward the psychological safety that will enable the youth to be less guarded and more open to working on painful issues and trying new things without feeling so threatened.

Briggs (1975) described the characteristics of psychological safety in relation to an infant's ability to develop basic trust. As previously described, it is not reasonable or rational for the adults or the youth to seek to establish trust with each other until there is evidence of trustworthiness. In the absence of trust, creating the sense of safety that will enable growth, development, and new experiences is necessary and can be established through the same characteristics described by Briggs:

Psychological Safety

Focused Attention
   Eye contact, active listening, avoiding distractions
Nonjudgmental
   Labeling/judging behavior, not the person
Emotional Expression
   Each expressing their own feelings, not assuming others feel the same
Empathic care
   Providing care in response to cues of emotions and needs
Celebration of differences
   Validation of unique individuality of each person
Trustworthiness
   Consistency, follow-through, and no abuse of power

Recognizing signs of the cycle indicative of emotional stress before youth shut down or heat up, *de-escalation* and *time out* are two interventions that can slow things down and give both the youth and the adult time to avert either a meltdown or an explosion.

De-escalation is all about *slowing down* and requires both *patience and silence*; being willing to *stay with* the youth without pursuing any agenda other than that of helping them calm and achieve self-control. Asking benign questions (What time was that?), and *putting things in order* (Was that before or after . . . ?), are conscious techniques to slow things down by switching the youth's thinking into the less emotional parts of the brain. Being able to remain calm, even when upset, is one of those *"new experiences"* that require developmental skills.

Use of *time out* is a very common technique in child serving settings but requires second thoughts to differentiate when it is and is not a helpful intervention. Being alone, cutting off communication with others, and thinking about whatever was upsetting, describes time out but also describes the isolation of the cycle. In use of time out, adults must consider whether the youth has the skills and the motivation to use time alone in a helpful manner or whether the youth uses that time to ruminate, project and externalize, become increasingly angry, and develop abusive fantasies and plans to retaliate against whatever or whomever they perceive is the cause of their stress. Many times youth are sent to time out without having the skills to calm themselves, think and rethink, and arrive at any nonabusive solution or plan. In such instances, minimizing time alone is in the best interest of all, when physical safety can be maintained.

De-escalation:
> Slowing down . . . silence . . . benign pursuits . . . sorting and ordering . . . modeling, calming

Time Out:
> Giving or taking space to: Calm down . . . Think . . . Rethink . . . New Solutions

Ongoing goals of the abuse-specific milieu are communication, empathy, and accountability: the ability to articulate rather than act out, the ability to participate in empathic interactions, and the accurate attribution of responsibility. These are referred to as universal goals that promote the sense of safety that enables growth and change.

The struggle to create a physically and psychologically safe environment is sometimes the hardest part of caring for youth with pervasively abusive experiences and behaviors, but when caregivers are willing to persist in their commitment to safety, eventually it becomes possible to actually create the nurturing environment within which everything else should be fun. The work of childhood is play, and it is in their play that children develop and master skills for successful functioning at each stage of development. The care provider's mission is to foster growth and development of skills for each area of human functioning: the "evidence of increased health" required for success.

Fostering Growth and Developmental Competencies

Prosocial Relationship Skills
> (Closeness, Trust, and Trustworthiness)

Positive Self-Image
> (Able to be Separate, Independent, Competent)

Able to Resolve Conflicts and Make Decisions
> (Assertive, Tolerant, Cooperative; Able to Negotiate, Compromise)

Celebrates Good and Experiences Pleasure
> (Able to Relax and Play)

Works/Struggles to Achieve Delayed Gratification
> (Persistent pursuit of goals, Submission to reasonable authority)

Able to Think and Communicate Effectively
> (Rational Cognitive Processing; Adequate Verbal Skills; Able to concentrate)

Prosocial relationships with peers
> (Attitudes and Behavior)

Family and/or Community Support System

(Able to access and ask for help)
Adaptive Sense of Purpose and Future
   (Confidence, competence, foresight, goals)

Helping kids change bad behaviors requires the development of something good to replace them, and helping kids become competent "prosocial" human beings is the best defense against and prevention of abusive behavior.

FOSTERING PROSOCIAL DEVELOPMENT

The characteristics, attitudes, and behaviors that need to be evaluated to identify positive prosocial peers and role models include:

- Successful, Functional coping when stressed
- Empathic Recognition and Responses
- Accurate attributions of Responsibility
- Open Communication
- Rejection of abusive attitudes and behavior

The need to evaluate the quality of relationships includes family members, peers, and adult role models. The care provider needs to actively monitor who the youth spends time with in order to moderate deviant exposure. Evaluating the qualities of peer relationships addresses the risk of "deviance training" among delinquent youth (delinquent peers reinforcing and increasing the risk of negative effects on each other in group settings). Children and adolescents often recreate the dynamics of sibling interaction in their relationships with peers. Caregivers, with other members of the team, can evaluate sibling and peer relationships in terms of the following characteristics.

1. Rivalry versus Conflict and Abuse Many parents say: "All kids fight" without differentiating the nature of conflicts. Rivalry arises from respectful competition for scarce resources and results in mastery, assertiveness, and identity. Conflict arises from anger and disagreement and results in anger management and conflict resolution skills. Abuse arises from a sense of inefficacy and vulnerability and results in habituation of misattributions and externalizing behavior, and physical/emotional harm and insecurity to the other.

2. Use of Power and Authority: Nurturance, Protection, Manipulation, Coercion, Abuse The inherent inequality of siblings may be exacerbated by parental expectations, family roles, neglect, dysfunction, or poor boundaries. Older children, who are cast in a parental or protector role due to circumstances, may rely on intimidation and coercion to control younger siblings and miss many normative opportunities for childhood experience and growth. Some sibling relationships are pervasively abusive, both toward each other or the one toward the other, for many years before sibling incest brings them into protective services or therapeutic care. In other sibling relationships, one is the primary nurturer and protector of the other prior to sexual contact resulting in referral. Coercive styles of interacting with siblings and peers often mirror coercive styles of parenting. A lack of empathy results from a lack of empathic experience.

3. Prosocial . . . Benign . . . Delinquent . . . "Hyper-Masculinity" . . . Antisocial Association with deviant peers is a potent risk factor for delinquency, and adult criminality in the home is even more so. Caregivers must pay close attention to attitudes supportive of irresponsible, antisocial, and/or violent, insensitive, exploitive, and abusive behaviors, knowing these attitudes reinforce the externalizing cognitions and objectification of others that allow and justify abusive behaviors. Exposure to deviant peer influences and adult role models during formative developmental stages can influence identity formation and increase habituation of dysfunctional, exploitive, coercive, and abusive patterns.

Caregivers and educators need to control peer group settings to minimize deviant peer influences. Peer associations outside school classrooms should be subject to adult supervision sufficient to provide some assessment of responsible, prosocial influences and attitudes in the peer group and relationships. Sometimes, maximizing "normal" experiences can be the biggest challenge for the caregiver who needs to make thoughtful decisions about who the youth spends time with.

"Who's your friend" is a common dilemma for all parents, and becomes critical in decision making for these youth to participate in activities with other youth. This dilemma is somewhat different for caregivers of kids living at home or in group care, but the principles of minimizing and controlling for deviant exposure and reinforcement can guide good decision making, whether deciding a youth can go out with "friends" or deciding whether two kids can be roommates, or spend unstructured time together in the living environment.

Caregivers require some minimal level of knowledge regarding peers prior to approving any activities not supervised by an adult authority (Yockley & Bulanda, 2002). Minimal information might assume that a "friend" meet the following conditions:

1. Should be willing to meet face-to-face the parental figures of their friend.
2. Has a last name, address, phone, and parent name.
3. Should be aware of their friend's probation status and relevant conditions, and support compliance.

Not everyone needs to know the nature of the youth's offense. In many situations it is sufficient for others to simply know the youth is on probation and therefore has conditions that other youth might not. In safety planning for activities it should become apparent whether or not someone else needs to know the youth had a sexual offense in their past. For example, a youth whose offending was against significantly younger children may need a friend's parent to know something about their history if the friend has younger siblings. However, teams must be thoughtful about requiring wide disclosures, which impair the youth's ability to reintegrate into their schools and communities after treatment. If safety planning concludes that a lot of potentially stigmatizing information would need to be shared due to ongoing risk, it may be better to wait until there is evidence of decreased risk before approving the activity.

Activities in the community (movies, parties, clubs, sports, etc.) may need approval by probation or the MDT, but with safety planning, such activities should be expected to be part of the normalizing activities for these youth as they demonstrate decreased risk over the course of treatment.

Comprehensive ongoing assessment is designed to identify the unique strengths and needs of each individual youth (see Chapter 13). The treatment plan is constantly changing and evolving to address the unique risks and needs of the youth based on observations of actual functioning, which changes from day to day. For some youth, many of the problems will be identified by teachers and caregivers who have daily opportunities to observe the youth, and some of the objectives will be the responsibility of therapeutic caregivers to address.

Understanding the process of treatment planning helps the caregiver recognize how their piece fits with the other components of treatment and clarifies the boundaries in terms of what work should be referred into which components. Remembering the "Goal Orientation," the caregiver refers the painful, traumatic, deviant, and dysfunctional issues into the clinical components of Individual, Group, or Family Therapy. Putting some containment around those issues allows youth to focus on present, more normative experiences and current functioning in their daily lives.

Observation is the primary source informing ongoing assessment and treatment planning. It is only through informed observations that treatment providers and the MDT can recognize the developmental context, the cues, and the changes over time that are the basis for determining treatment needs, progress, and outcomes. The observations of the caregiver that inform ongoing assessment often involve aspects of the care environment and the caregiver's role becomes apparent in relation to the objectives of the overall treatment plan (Wilson & Viar, 1996).

Caregivers can observe both skills and deficits, and consciously work to help develop missing skills. "Competency" models such as Strayhorn (1988) identify areas of functioning, and the skills within each, which human beings need for optimal success. Caregivers need to be trained and have available developmental assessment and enhancement information to do their job effectively. The evidence of increased health involves nine areas of human functioning. Strayhorn identifies skills in each area, totaling 62 "health skills," and discusses the assessment, as well as the development, of these skills into the optimal functioning adult human (Strayhorn, 1988). Pond and Brown (1996) described some youth as "developmental Swiss cheese" in that they appear in many ways to be older but are actually missing skills that a much younger child should have.

To address developmental delays and skill deficits, asking the right questions is the key to understanding and responding: the caregiver can think about problematic behaviors they observe in terms of what it might mean if a much younger child (or even an infant or toddler) were behaving in that way. Is the behavior an ineffective way of expressing needs? (Using behavior instead of words?) Is the behavior part of a defensive pattern the child uses to feel safe? (Does the environment feel safe?) Or is the behavior a sign of a skill deficit? (Has the caregiver ever observed relevant success?) How would a parent normally manage such behavior in order to assure the child's safety? Meet the need? (Increasing proximity and support? Changing levels of supervision? Changing expectations or activities?) And what developmental skills would a parent be modeling, teaching, and encouraging as they respond to a young child who behaves that way? When do children typically develop the skill for themselves in the normal developmental process? Then it becomes possible to think about what it is they are doing at that stage of development. By thinking about how children normally acquire those skills, caregivers can recreate opportunities for growth and development in the daily lives of kids.

Recreating lost early childhood opportunities and experiences in ways that are reasonable and practical for an older child allows for the natural developmental processes of growth and regression. The need is not dissimilar to the need to "re-parent parents," which has been one basic approach in treating abusive parents (Bavolek, 1984; Helfer, 1978, 1984). Mobilizing caregivers on the mission of "increased health" outcomes often requires thought, creativity, and efforts that go beyond normal parenting to recreate the nurturance that was absent earlier in life.

This is the mission of the therapeutic care provider and, within the treatment plan, encompasses their goals and objectives. For example, therapeutic care providers who notice patterns associated with problems can be trained to think systematically about what "areas of human functioning" are involved, what skills are necessary for humans to succeed in that area, and then think specifically about how children develop those skills. How would a 2-year-old develop those skills? What would a 4-year-old be doing in their play that facilitates their learning and mastering those skills?

The overall treatment plan will generally list specific problems, as well as specific goals and objectives representing the steps involved in addressing the problem. It is important for the whole team, as well as the youth and their family, to understand how each problem is relevant to the issues they are in treatment for. As stated in previous chapters, "comprehensive, developmental-contextual assessment and treatment planning" addresses the domains of abusive dynamics, sexual deviance, growth and development, co-occurring disorders, and the ecological "pond." The alternative care setting is an alternative "pond" that exposes the youth to new experiences of family, community, and relationships.

Therapeutic care plans will be subsets of goals in the larger treatment plan, and identifying skills and skill deficits is a part of the continuous ongoing process that must be informed by the caregiver's observations. The caregiver's identification of problems in current functioning must be communicated to the whole team so each member of the team can address the aspects relevant to their particular role on the team. For each problem, some of the work may be done in individual, group, or family therapy sessions, some work might best engage a teacher or the probation officer, and other work would fall in the domain of the caregiver.

For example, for a youth who is constantly in conflict with staff and peers in a group living setting or in school, the team may recognize that some relevant issues are related to past offending, some are specifically triggers from unresolved conflicts in the past, and others might be the product of the way the family models conflict resolution or fails to acknowledge conflicts. The treatment provider will work on those aspects in the clinical sessions, but the caregiver who observed the problem in current interactions is in the position to continue to observe and address skill deficits that might be relevant.

Developing Therapeutic Care Plans

Goals based on ongoing assessment of skill deficits.
  Observation: Youth provokes and is provoked by peers, and avoids participation in group activities that others enjoy.
  Possible Deficit: Youth seems unable to relax and play.
  Skills to be able to relax and play: Negotiation, creativity, humor, cooperation.
  Activities in the care environment:

_____

_____

Desired Outcome: Youth successfully engages in recreational activities with peers.

In the type of problem shown in this example, one area of human functioning involved would be interpersonal relationship skills and another is the skills related to being able to relax and play. Separating the two helps target both observations and the development of hypotheses about what might be related to "issues" and what is more related to skill deficits.

In addressing the lack of participation, the caregiver is often tempted to continue trying to engage the youth in group activities that adolescents usually enjoy, but this can become a power struggle—winding up in the caregiver feeling frustrated, perceiving themselves as failing to engage the youth, and eventually employing coercive styles to force the youth into participating—while the youth sabotages every effort by causing disturbances that wind up in consequences instead of the desired participation. By taking a step back to think about all the skills involved in participating in group activities with peers, as well as skills to successfully participate in the particular activity, the caregiver can then observe whether there is any evidence that the youth has those skills.

Think about how infants become able to play with other children. Adults first play "for" the baby, then the baby becomes interested in imitating and practicing the modeled behavior, and eventually masters the behavior. For example, the adult shakes the rattle repeatedly, eventually babies reach for and grasp the rattle and with some practice become able to rattle the rattle for themselves. A parallel process can be observed with hundreds of behaviors that the infant eventually masters. Play by the adult leads to play with the adult and then to solitary play. When infants are first in the presence of other infants, they may all play the same things but only with themselves (solitary play), without even noticing the other babies' play.

Eventually awareness of the others' play leads to what is termed "parallel play"— all the babies are playing with cars, but the cars are not on the same road, so there is no interaction. Finally, interactive play with peers can be observed after the babies have mastered the play alone, observed others engaging in the same play, and the infants begin interactive communication using facial expressions, sounds, and body language with each other. And from the moment interactive play begins, a whole new set of interpersonal skills begin to emerge.

The youth who avoids, resists, or sabotages group activities with peers may be lacking some of the skills of the toddler. The youth may not have had adults model "play" (having a nice experience with toys) or may not have had the opportunity to observe others enjoy play, or may not have had opportunities to connect at the primitive level of parallel play. It has been noted that often parents who experienced harsh or abusive punishment for making "messes" while playing as children may be unable to allow their own children to "relax and play" as well. As the caregiver of the youth goes back to the beginning and creates opportunities to model enjoying play, then offers opportunities for solitary play, they can observe whether in fact the youth does or does not demonstrate mastery in those opportunities.

Creating group activities that foster the experience of parallel activity without requiring interaction similarly creates a developmental opportunity for the youth, as well as the opportunity for adult observation of skills or skill deficits. For youth whose life experience has been filled with failures and rejection in interpersonal interactions, and a lack of positive successful experiences, the time it takes to counter the weight of the past may be even longer than it takes an infant to learn and master the same fundamental skills. However, as the caregiver identifies skills as present, creating opportunities for success using those skills provides the new experiences that challenge the hopelessness and negative expectations of the past.

The youth who has always become embroiled in conflicts with peers on the basketball court (resulting in being removed from the court) may not have had opportunities for the stepwise development of skills for ball play: exposure to many types of balls; others modeling different ways balls can be bounced, rolled, thrown, and so forth; opportunities to imitate and practice rolling, bouncing, and throwing balls; much less the hours of solitary play to master dribbling and shooting a basketball. As an adolescent, getting thrown off the court may seem preferable to revealing the lack of skills in play with peers.

Similarly, the caregiver can process and observe the skills for every area of human functioning, and identify the skill deficits that impede success. This is the job of the caregiver, and when trained to recognize the relevance of these skills in the context of the larger treatment plan, the caregiver can be encouraged and expected to work on the increased health outcomes while clinicians work on the issues associated with deviance and dysfunction.

How youth are functioning, and how well they have mastered skills for success in each aspect of the outcomes relevant to increased health, are expected to be different for different kids. Age, intellect, resources, history, and the static and stable factors account for individual differences. However, if kids do NOT have the skills to be successful, every risk weighs more heavily in the balance.

Children and adolescents who acquire the knowledge and skills to achieve observable changes in how they function are likely to do better in all ways, as well as being less at risk specifically for abusive sexual recidivism. Although some of these youth will continue to be at risk in some ways, and some will even continue to sexually offend, most become able to moderate risks and the prognosis for them is good. At the same time, for any person of any age, demonstrating the outcomes described as "relevant to decreased risk of abusive behavior" and "relevant to increased health" in their daily lives will "do no harm," and provides evidence that the youth is able to reject abuse if they choose to do so. This supports the reasonableness of these interventions.

Finally, for the caregivers who supervise and nurture youth who are court ordered into their care and must make all these changes within an involuntary relationship, it is important to accept the rational reality of their experience: Arriving in the unknown, with persons unknown; being told they must enter into a relationship with persons who not only carry the power of being the adults, but also the power of the court; being told they must follow directives and change the ways they have historically coped with stress to defend themselves from vulnerability; and being told that failure to comply will result in further judicial sanctions, it would not be rational for the youth to feel safe. The conditions of alternative care placements and involuntary treatment embody the very factors that define abusive interactions: Lack of Consent, Unequal power, and Coercion. In an involuntary relationship, the caregiver must demonstrate evidence of safety and trustworthiness before it is reasonable to expect growth and change.

The developmental task of adolescence is to develop autonomy and independence in order to separate from caregivers and become an adult (Fine, 1973). Increased adult supervision and control exacerbate natural adolescent control issues with adults.

Research has shown that along with the rapid growth and pruning in the brain, which exacerbates impulsivity and moodiness, adolescents may also misperceive negative meaning in adult facial expressions and body language as more negative or threatening than others see (Baird et al., 1999). Caregivers must be clear, objective, goal directed, and consistent, insisting on physical and psychological safety, before expecting adolescents to begin to let go of habituated defensive patterns and become open to nurturance, support, and new experiences. The caregiver cannot personalize or pathologize resistance and oppositional behaviors that are foreseeable in this process and are not a reflection of the caregiver's reality or competence.

Anticipatory Guidance for Therapeutic Caregivers

Expect Resistance and Opposition
> No one likes being controlled, and it is natural and healthy for kids to seek autonomy and independence. (Model nonabusive use of power, and avoid the power struggles.)

Expect Escalation
> Kids who have been acting out, and then are under complete control, often "explode" a few times from the stress, especially when dealing with hard issues. (Things often look worse before they get better.)

Expect Regression
Kids grow and show progress when they are feeling strong and courageous; then regress to old patterns to find comfort in the familiar when stressed. Caregiving is like managing the string of a kite in gusty winds. The caregiver must know when to let the string out, so the kite can fly, and when to pull the string in so it doesn't crash (Yockley & Bulanda, 2002).

Safety Planning is the tool for deciding how long the string can be! But also: Expect to be amazed at how many eventually do well!! (Ryan, Yager, Metzner, & Sobisinski, 2002).

The resilience of human children is incredible when they are in a safe place and required to change their behavior.[*] For some, creating that safety is a monumental task, but once achieved, growth and development become possible and humanity can emerge.

REFERENCES

Baird, A. A., Gruber, S. A., Fein, D. A., Maas, L. C., Steingard, R. J., Renshaw, P. F., et al. (1999). Functional magnetic resonance imaging of facial affect recognition in children and adolescents. *Journal of the American Academy of Child and Adolescent Psychiatry, 38*(2), 195–199.

Bavolek, S. J. (1984). An innovated program for reducing abusive parenting. *Child Resource World Review, 2*, 6–24.

Briggs, D. C. (1975). *Your child's self esteem.* New York: Doubleday.

---

[*] The author acknowledges the role of three residential programs' participation in the development of the concepts of an abuse-specific milieu that continue to form the foundation for therapeutic care: Denver Children's Home (a long-term residential program with a mixed population); Synergy at Fort Logan Mental Health Hospital (a long-term residential substance abuse program for teenagers); and Falcon Lodge at Griffith Center (a long-term "offense-specific" residential unit for sexually abusive teenagers). Jeff Metzner, Jerry Yager, and staff of the Denver Children's Home were particularly supportive in piloting these concepts during the late 1980s.

Colorado Sex Offender Management Board (CSOMB). (2002). *Standards and guidelines for the evaluation, assessment, treatment, and supervision of juveniles who have committed sexual offenses.* Colorado Department of Public Safety, Division of Criminal Justice: Author.

Fine, L. L. (1973). What's a normal adolescent? *Clinical Pediatrics, 12,* 1–10.

Helfer, R. (1978, 1984). *Childhood comes first: A crash course in childhood for adults.* Lansing, MI: Author.

Pond, A., & Brown, J. (1996). *Disclosure: Obtaining sexual histories from developmentally disabled youth.* Paper presented at the 12th Annual Conference of the National Adolescent Perpetrator Network, Minneapolis, MN.

Ryan, G., Yager, J., Metzner, J., & Sobisinski, M. (2002). *Informed supervision and therapeutic care for juveniles who commit sexual offenses.* Kempe Trainer Training Curriculum.

Strayhorn, J. M. (1988). *The competent child. An approach to psychotherapy and preventive mental health.* New York: Guilford Press.

Wilson, J., & Viar, W. (1996). Estimating length of stay: The individualized treatment plan. *Interchange: NAPN.* Denver, CO.

Yockley, J., & Bulanda, B. (2002). *Forensic foster care for youth with abusive behaviors: Social responsibility therapy in family setting.* Presented at the 17th National Adolescent Perpetration Network Annual Conference: By Leaps and Bounds, Toledo, OH.

PART FIVE

TREATMENT: INTEGRATING THEORY AND METHOD IN A GOAL-ORIENTED APPROACH

CHAPTER 16

Therapeutic Relationships and the Process of Change

KEVIN M. POWELL

YOUTH WHO ARE in treatment for sexually abusive behavior are expected to talk openly about their sexuality and behaviors. It is not uncommon for youth at the onset of assessment and treatment to feel embarrassment, shame, guilt, anger, and/or defensiveness. In order to be effective, providers must get beyond emotional responses that impede the treatment process. Establishing a therapeutic relationship enhances the youths' openness, honesty, and commitment to change.

In addition to cognitive-behavioral interventions, which have been central to sex offense-specific treatment, there are other essential variables that influence treatment outcomes. Creating a foundation to support the work of treatment requires establishing and maintaining a positive therapeutic relationship (Blanchard, 1995; Marshall et al., 2002); promoting optimism and hope regarding the youths' capacity to make positive changes; enhancing the youth's internal motivation for change; and creating the sense of safety that enables the youth to talk about difficult issues.

ESTABLISHING AND MAINTAINING A POSITIVE THERAPEUTIC RELATIONSHIP

The role of relationship seems intuitively relevant in treating interpersonal abuse issues, and in the psychotherapy literature, numerous studies have led researchers to estimate that *18% of the positive change in psychotherapy is due to factors associated with the "therapy relationship" (10%) and "therapist's qualities" (8%)*, (Hubble, Duncan, & Miller, 1999; Norcross, 2001, 2002; Norcross & Lambert, 2006). Only 5 to 8% of positive change is attributed to specific therapeutic techniques. Lambert and Barley (2001, p. 359) state, "Therapists need to remember that the development and maintenance of the therapeutic relationship is a primary curative component of therapy and that the relationship provides the context in which specific techniques exert their influence."

It is likely that the reticence to explore the role of relationship in treating those who have sexually offended has had more to do with therapists' discomfort entering into a relationship with these clients than any theoretical or empirical basis. A positive therapeutic relationship can significantly enhance a youth's engagement in the assessment and treatment process, and provides a new experience of relationship that may be quite different from others in the past.

Much of the early research on therapeutic relationships and treatment outcomes was conducted on adults; but more recently a meta-analysis of therapeutic relationship variables within youth treatment identified the following as associated with positive treatment outcomes (Karver, Handelsman, Fields, & Bickman, 2006):

1. *Therapist Direct Influence Skills* refers to the therapist actively structuring the session, and providing a clear, understandable rationale for the treatment being used.

2. *Therapist Interpersonal Skills* includes (a) *Empathy*, defined as the provider's ability to accurately sense the feelings and personal meanings that a youth is experiencing and communicate this understanding to them. (b) *Warmth and Unconditional Positive Regard*, defined as the provider's ability to express an accepting, positive attitude toward youth regardless of youths' emotional state or behavior. That is, making a distinction between a youth's abusive behaviors and their value as a human being (being nonjudgmental). (c) *Genuineness* (also referred to as Congruence or Realness), defined as the provider being themselves and not putting on a facade within the relationship. Carl Rogers identified these three interpersonal factors as "necessary and sufficient" for promoting therapeutic change (Rogers, 1957). When youth experience a provider as empathetic, accepting, and genuine, they become more trusting and open to forming a positive relationship and more receptive to treatment interventions.

3. *Youth and Parents' Willingness and Actual Participation in Treatment* describes the family's feelings of acceptance in treatment and their desire/commitment to participate, as well as their involvement, collaboration, cooperation, and engagement in therapy sessions and/or homework tasks.

4. *Therapeutic Alliance with the Youth* includes *Emotional* connection (youth's affective bond with the therapist); *Cognitive* connection (youth's hopefulness about treatment); and *Behavioral* components (youth's actual participation in treatment).

The therapist's willingness to enter into a relationship with the youth provides the foundation for exploring past and current relationships, experiencing nonabusive interactions, receiving empathic responses, and forming positive, prosocial relationships in the future. Research also reveals that positive relationships are important in settings outside the therapy session, including: School relationships with teachers (V. F. Jones & L. S. Jones, 1998; Murphy, 1999; Rogers & Renard, 1999); Home relationships with parents (Amato, 1994; Forehand & Nousiainen, 1993; Laursen & Birmingham, 2003); and relationships with mentors (Keating, Tomishima, Foster, & Alessandri, 2002; Turner & Scherman, 1996). Characteristics of the therapeutic caregiver and the therapist have much in common regarding the need to create a psychologically safe atmosphere, which enables growth and change.

SPECIFIC STRATEGIES FOR ESTABLISHING POSITIVE RELATIONSHIPS WITH YOUTH

Clinical and empirical wisdom and a treatment plan will not overcome the resistance of youth who are court ordered into treatment. Establishing and maintaining a positive, therapeutic relationship and facilitating effective communication are pre-cursors for treatment to become possible. People do not openly share themselves with others who are not trustworthy, and the issues these youth bring to treatment have created a wall of defenses that must be respected.

Strategies for creating a positive, therapeutic relationship include: (a) Being patient and understanding when youth are initially defensive about treatment or the mental health "system"; (b) Showing interest in youth by asking questions about their lives (initially excluding any focus on their sexual behavior problems); (c) Being present in the "here and now" to ensure youth have providers' full and undivided attention; (d) Maintaining a "staff to youth" ratio that gives providers the time to enter into a therapeutic relationship with youth; (e) Utilizing nonverbal behaviors, such as an open posture (without arms crossed) to communicate attentiveness and acceptance (Egan, 1998); and (f) Joining with youth by matching their interpersonal style and affective range (Minuchin, 1974, p. 128). If a provider and a youth's interpersonal style and affective range are incongruent, the youth may feel less connected and be less likely to communicate openly. For example, a youth who presents with high energy and an upbeat mood typically will not be as responsive toward a provider whose mannerisms are overly reserved and serious compared to a more active, optimistic therapist.

SPECIFIC STRATEGIES FOR ESTABLISHING POSITIVE RELATIONSHIPS WITH SIGNIFICANT OTHERS

Facilitating communication and entering into relationships with the youth's family and significant others is also essential. In addition to parents, "significant others" might be a legal guardian or alternative caregiver, extended family members, teachers, coaches, mentors, or other prosocial adults who will be present in youths' lives long after treatment has ceased. Strategies for connecting with significant others include: (a) Talking about their child's strengths and positive behaviors; (b) Giving positive feedback or compliments; (c) Asking questions that acknowledge significant others as "experts" about their child; (d) Getting significant others involved in the child's treatment activities; and (e) Asking significant others questions about their own support system to ensure they are getting enough care and assistance for themselves. The stress associated with the discovery of a youth's sexual offending can be emotionally taxing and elicit feelings of shame, guilt, anxiety, anger, sadness, and fear. Acknowledging significant others' stress and providing support can go a long way toward establishing a positive relationship.

PROMOTING OPTIMISM AND HOPE REGARDING YOUTHS' CAPACITY TO MAKE POSITIVE CHANGES

Working with youth who have sexually abused increases a provider's exposure to the darker side of human experience, including abuse, trauma, and significant mental and behavioral dysfunction. This exposure can increase a provider's risk of becoming negative and pessimistic about the youths' capacity to make positive changes in treatment. Reciprocally, it can also influence youth and their families to lose hope, and hopelessness impedes treatment progress.

There are actually neurophysiological reasons and research statistics that provide evidence to support optimism about juvenile sexually abusive and impulsive behaviors improving over time. *Enhancing optimism within youth and families, as well as within evaluators and treatment providers, can augment the effectiveness of sex offense-specific services. Instilling hope helps engage the youth and family in the treatment process. Reviewing relevant research with the youth and family at the beginning of treatment decreases their negative expectations, demystifies the therapeutic process, and increases their confidence in the therapist's expertise.*

REASON FOR OPTIMISM: MATURATION OF THE BRAIN'S PREFRONTAL CORTEX

The prefrontal cortex of the brain is located directly behind the forehead and governs our executive functions such as planning, goal setting, problem solving, judgment, attention, and impulse control. Neurological research has identified the prefrontal cortex as being one of the last regions to fully mature (Casey, Giedd, & Thomas, 2000; Diamond, 2002; Giedd et al., 1999; Luna & Sweeney, 2004; Sowell, Thompson, Holmes, Batth, Jernigan, & Toga, 1999; Sowell, Thompson, Holmes, Jernigan, & Toga, 1999; Sowell, Thompson, Tessner, & Toga, 2001; Sowell, Trauner, Garnst, & Jernigan, 2002; Spear, 2000). During adolescence, significant changes occur to this region of the brain due to the Myelination process (insulation of axons, which speeds neuronal transmission throughout the brain), and Synaptic Pruning process (elimination of unused or redundant synapses, which helps the brain operate more efficiently). *As the prefrontal cortex matures, youths' ability to regulate emotions, manage sexual impulses, and think consequentially* (Baird & Fugelsang, 2004), *can significantly improve.*

REASON FOR OPTIMISM: AS THE BRAIN MATURES, IT USES LESS OF THE EMOTIONAL REGION AND MORE OF THE EXECUTIVE FUNCTION REGION

Although more research with larger numbers and longitudinal designs are needed to clarify the maturational process of the human brain, available research suggests adolescents process emotions differently than adults at the neurological level. Studies using brain scans (functional magnetic resonance imaging [fMRI]) have found that when processing emotion (identifying emotions from people's facial expressions), adolescents have lower activity in the prefrontal region and more activity in the amygdala region compared to adults (Baird et al., 1999; Yurgelun-Todd, 1998). The amygdala is part of the limbic system and functions as a rapid response system associated with immediate, impulsive reactions, such as fear and aggression. Children and young adolescents appear to be using more of the rapid response, emotional region of the brain compared to adults. As youth develop into adulthood, the brain begins to utilize more of the prefrontal region, which can significantly improve their ability to "think before acting" and change abusive behavior patterns.

REASON FOR OPTIMISM: "NEUROPLASTICITY" OF THE BRAIN

The human brain works on a "use it or lose it" principle. The neural pathways that are being used become strong and thrive, while the pathways not used get pruned away or become less prominent (Bennett, Diamond, Krech, & Rosenzweig, 1996; Cicchetti & Tucker, 1994; Diamond, 2001; Nelson, 2003; Nelson & Bloom, 1997). This process is referred to as "neuroplasticity" and highlights the importance (on a neurological level) of youth receiving therapeutic interventions. *Treatment that encourages youth to repeatedly practice "healthy alternatives" and to avoid dysfunctional behaviors can stimulate neural pathways and wire the brain in very positive ways.* Educating youth about the effects of "neuroplasticity" can enhance youths' understanding and motivation to practice healthy, nonabusive behaviors every day.

REASON FOR OPTIMISM: DELINQUENT BEHAVIORS DRAMATICALLY DECREASE IN LATE ADOLESCENCE AND YOUNG ADULTHOOD

Statistics on the prevalence of delinquent behaviors have found that delinquency peaks at approximately age 17 and dramatically decreases in late adolescence and young adulthood (Caspi & Moffit, 1995; Hirschi & Gottfredson, 1983; Moffit, 1993). *The large majority of youth who commit delinquent acts during adolescence do not continue on this path as adults.*

REASON FOR OPTIMISM: YOUTH RECIDIVISM RATE FOR SEXUAL RE-OFFENSES IS LOW

According to the National Center on Sexual Behavior of Youth (2003), the sexual re-offense recidivism rate for youth who have committed a sexual offense is between 5 and 14%. The low base rate of recidivism is another reason to be hopeful and optimistic about youths' ability to make positive life changes. The "no cure" and "once a sex offender, always a sex offender" belief of the 1980s is *not* supported by research (Gerhold, Browne, & Beckett, 2007; Reitzel & Carbonell, 2006; Worling & Curwen, 2000). *The large majority of youth who have committed a sexual offense will not sexually reoffend in the future, and even less after treatment. This is yet another reason to remain optimistic about youth who have sexually offended.*

ENHANCING INTERNAL MOTIVATION FOR CHANGE

One of the most important ingredients for treatment success is the youth's internal motivation for change. Strategies for enhancing motivation include meeting youth's basic human needs, establishing a collaborative communication style, providing a rationale for interventions, and utilizing specific interviewing strategies.

ENHANCING MOTIVATION: MEETING BASIC HUMAN NEEDS

Maslow's Hierarchy of Needs describes five levels of need that humans are motivated to fulfill (Maslow, 1970). Maslow suggests that the most basic needs must be met before higher-level concerns can be addressed. Providing physical safety, nurturance, and psychological safety in therapeutic care were described as preconditions for growth and development (see Chapter 7). Basic human needs also affect the youth's participation in treatment and their internal motivation for change.

Physiological Needs: Life-sustaining processes, such as the need for food and water, breathing air, elimination of bodily waste, comfortable body temperature, and sleep, are very potent needs. In most situations, motivation to meet these needs takes priority over all other concerns. For example, if a reader of this chapter is feeling sleepy or the room is cold, the ability to focus on the content of what they are reading will be impeded by the internal motivation to meet the physiological need for sleep and/or warmth. The same principle holds true for youth in therapy.

Safety Needs: The need for safety requires that there is no threat of physical or emotional harm and includes the need for stability, consistency, protection, and freedom from fear, anxiety, and chaos. When youth feel physically or emotionally unsafe, their internal motivation will be focused on achieving safety and it is natural that their defenses will prepare them for fight, flight, or freeze. Under these conditions, one cannot expect youth to have the capacity to focus and comprehend higher-level concerns.

Social Needs (Belongingness and Attachment): Humans are social creatures and have a basic need to be connected to others. Social needs include the need to love and be loved, to be accepted, and to belong to a group or family. This need also includes the desire to avoid loneliness, alienation, and rejection. A common reaction for anyone who has lost a significant relationship (e.g., due to breakup, divorce, parental abandonment, or death) is to become preoccupied with the loss and struggle to concentrate on anything except the lost relationship. The same holds true for youth with sexual behavior problems who will have difficulty fully engaging in treatment if the need to feel connected and belong is not being met. Social needs can be a strong motivational force within relationships with treatment providers and family members, as well as with peers. Research shows empirical support for peer mentoring and peer tutoring services, which have been found to enhance self-esteem, improve peer relationships, and reduce problem school behaviors (Dennison, 2000; Spencer, 2006; Stenhoff & Lignugaris-Kraft, 2007). Creating these types of prosocial opportunities with peers is beneficial regardless of a youth's level of social competence, so long as they are able to experience some success and not be further rejected. Team building and icebreakers (Ragsdale & Saylor, 2007) can help facilitate these social connections among youth.

Once the most basic physiological, safety, and social needs are satisfied, humans are motivated to work toward higher-level needs to gain competence and be successful in life. These higher-level needs include "esteem and achievement needs" and "self-actualization needs."

Esteem and Achievement Needs: The *need for high self-esteem, achievement, and mastery of the environment* is identified as a higher-level need. This need includes the desire to be recognized by others and respected for personal achievements and competencies. However, self-esteem must be based on prosocial, nonabusive attributes, as opposed to their delinquent behaviors (Hughes, Cavell, & Grossman, 1997).

Self-Actualization Needs: The final and most advanced need is a youth's need for self-actualization, meaning *the need to live up to one's potential and become everything that one is capable of becoming*. Once a youth's other needs are being met, their motivation is to maximize their potential in life. As suggested in developmental models and the outcomes relevant to increased health (see Chapter 7), "an adaptive sense of future" is a goal.

It is important to note that the order and potency of Maslow's Hierarchy of Needs is not universally fixed; however, the underlying theory as it relates to fulfilling unmet needs appears to be very applicable for better understanding how to motivate youth and their families in treatment (Dunlap, 2004).

A mistake that providers sometimes make is to overlook the need to address the youth's most basic physiological, safety, and social needs before attempting interventions directed at higher-level needs. If a youth is feeling alienated or rejected by family, peers, or providers (Social Need), their capacity to focus on treatment concepts that will help them develop into prosocial adults (the Esteem and Achievement Need) can be significantly impaired. Youth cannot be expected to be internally motivated in treatment if their most basic needs are not currently being met. The same holds true when conducting an assessment. It is not uncommon for youth who have been arrested and charged with a sexual offense to feel unsafe (Safety Need) and fearful of rejection from others (Social Need). These basic unmet needs and situational stressors can result in youth exhibiting serious yet transient symptoms that can be misinterpreted by evaluators. Youth can mistakenly be classified as higher risk and possessing more pathology than is actually true.

A common goal in abuse-specific treatment is to enhance empathy for others; however, when the youth's own most basic needs are *not* being met it can impair their ability to focus on anything except their own needs. In contrast, when providers begin to assist youth in fulfilling their basic needs, it can enhance youths' capacity to focus on the needs of others (increased prosocial and empathetic behaviors). *Providers should begin each assessment and treatment session by asking themselves, "What needs are not being met for this youth and how can I help meet these needs?"*

ENHANCING MOTIVATION: ESTABLISHING A COLLABORATIVE TEAM APPROACH

"Collaboration" and "goal consensus" between the youth and providers enhances the effectiveness of treatment (Karver, Handelsman, Fields, & Bickman, 2006; Norcross, 2002). A collaborative, team approach is an effective method of engaging youth and their families in the assessment and treatment process. Rather than providers' taking on a one-sided expert role, there is a mutual exploration of what will help youth develop into healthy successful adults. Participation in this collaborative team approach includes providers, youth, parents, and anyone else involved in the youth's life. For youth who are court ordered into treatment, the "coercion" to fulfill the requirements of treatment can come from the court, while the role of the collaborative team can be to assist youth in meeting the court's requirements. This collaborative process is only possible when providers have established a positive therapeutic relationship with youth, as opposed to an authoritarian, confrontational, judgmental relationship.

ENHANCING MOTIVATION: ILLUMINATING THE "RATIONALE" FOR INTERVENTIONS

When providers attempt interventions but do not get "buy in" from youth and their families, the likelihood of a positive treatment outcome is diminished. Treatment for interpersonal issues is not like treating an infection with penicillin. The therapist cannot "change" the client, only the client's participation and resolve can bring about change. If the youth and/or parents do not understand how or why the treatment interventions are relevant to the problem they were referred to treatment for, resistance and a lack of participation may actually be quite natural. However, when given a rationale for why a certain intervention is important, they are much more likely to be engaged and internally motivated in treatment.

Helping youth and their families to be "informed consumers" about the treatment process increases their internal motivation and commitment to following through with treatment expectations. For example, a condition of treatment that the youth not masturbate when thinking about abusive fantasies may seem intrusive and over-controlling to the youth, who may think: "They can't read my thoughts, and just thinking about it isn't hurting anyone, so why should they care? They're just trying to boss me around, and adults never want kids to do anything sexual anyway." However, the youth as an informed consumer would learn that repeatedly masturbating to abusive fantasies neurologically stimulates the brain and reinforces the risk of becoming sexually aroused to abusive acts. This knowledge provides the rationale for why it is important to not continue pairing a pleasant feeling with something that gets them in trouble and causes harm to others. Helping youth develop prosocial fantasies that can help wire the brain in healthy ways (due to the neuroplasticity of the brain) then becomes a mutual goal to tip the balance from deviance to health.

ENHANCING MOTIVATION: UTILIZING SPECIFIC INTERVIEWING STRATEGIES

Motivational Interviewing (Miller & Rollnick, 2002) and the "invitational approach" of Jenkins (1990) were discussed in Chapter 13 in relation to strategies to engage the youth in the initial assessment. These interview strategies continue to be useful in creating motivation and engagement in the therapeutic relationship throughout treatment.

CONCLUSION

Establishing a treatment environment in which youth are receptive and motivated to make positive life changes is essential in any treatment process. This is particularly important when treating youth with sexual behavior problems who are typically court ordered into treatment and are often defensive and distrusting of the system. Establishing a positive therapeutic relationship is a key component to creating this type of treatment environment. Within the context of this relationship, other essential factors include the promotion of optimism regarding a youth's capacity to overcome sexual behavior problems and the enhancement of youth's internal motivation to participate in treatment. Strategies for promoting youth's optimism involve the sharing of information about neurophysiological development and research statistics. Strategies for enhancing youth's internal motivation include meeting their basic human needs, establishing a collaborative team approach, and providing a rationale for treatment interventions. Regardless of the specific modality or approach, treatment will not be effective if providers do not establish a therapeutic relationship and create the physically and psychologically safe environment in which youth will be receptive to learning, exploring, and understanding the treatment and change process.

REFERENCES

Amato, P. (1994). Father-child relations, mother-child relations, and offspring psychological well-being in adulthood. *Journal of Marriage and the Family, 56*, 1031–1042.

Baird, A. A., & Fugelsang, J. A. (2004). The emergence of consequential thought: Evidence from neuroscience. *Philosophical Transactions of the Royal Society of London Biological Sciences, 359*, 1797–1804.

Baird, A. A., Gruber, S. A., Fein, D. A., Maas, L. C., Steingard, R. J., Renshaw, P. F., et al. (1999). Functional magnetic resonance imaging of facial affect recognition in children and adolescents. *Journal of the American Academy of Child and Adolescent Psychiatry, 38*(2), 195–199.

Bennett, E. L., Diamond, M. C., Krech, D., & Rosenzweig, M. R. (1996). Chemical and anatomical plasticity of brain. *Journal of Neuropsychiatry, 8*(4), 459–470.

Blanchard, G. T. (1995). *The difficult connection: The therapeutic relationship in sex offender treatment.* Brandon, VT: Safer Society Press.

Casey, B. J., Giedd, J. N., & Thomas, K. M. (2000). Structural and functional brain development and its relation to cognitive development. *Biological Psychology, 54*, 241–257.

Caspi, A, & Moffitt, T. E. (1995). The continuity of maladaptive behavior: From description to understanding in the study of antisocial behavior. In D. Cicchetti & D. J. Cohen (Eds.), *Developmental psychopathology: Vol. 2. Risk, disorder, and adaptation* (pp. 472–511). New York: John Wiley & Sons.

Cicchetti, D., & Tucker, D. (Eds.) (1994). Special issue: Neural plasticity, sensitive periods and psychopathology. *Development and Psychopathology, 6*(4), 533–813.

Dennison, S. (2000). A win-win peer mentoring and tutoring program: A collaborative model. *The Journal of Primary Prevention, 20*(3), 161–174.

Diamond, A. (2002). Normal development of prefrontal cortex from birth to young adulthood: Cognitive functions, anatomy, and biochemistry. In D. T. Stuss & R. T. Knight (Eds.), *Principles of frontal lobe function* (pp. 466–503). New York: Oxford University Press.

Diamond, M. C. (2001). Response of the brain to enrichment. *Anais Academia Brasileria de Ciencias, 73*(2), 211–220.

Dunlap, L. L. (2004). *What all children need: Theory and application* (2nd ed.). Lanham, MD: University Press of America.

Egan, G. (1998). *The skilled helper: A problem-management approach to helping* (6th ed.). Pacific Grove, CA: Brooks/Cole Publishing.

Forehand, R., & Nousiainen, S. (1993). Maternal and paternal parenting: Critical dimensions in adolescent functioning. *Journal of Family Psychology, 7*, 213–221.

Gerhold, C. K., Browne, K. D., & Beckett, R. (2007). Predicting recidivism in adolescent sexual offenders. *Aggression and Violent Behavior, 12*, 427–438.

Giedd, J. N., Blumenthal, J., Jeffries, N. O., Castellanos, F. X., Liu, H., Zijdenbos, A., et al. (1999). Brain development during childhood and adolescence: A longitudinal MRI study. *Nature Neuroscience, 2*(10), 861–863.

Hirschi, T., & Gottfredson, M. (1983). Age and the explanation of crime. *American Journal of Sociology, 89*, 552–583.

Hubble, M. A., Duncan, B. L., & Miller, S. D. (Eds.). (1999). *The heart & soul of change: What works in therapy.* Washington, DC: American Psychological Association.

Hughes, J. N., Cavell, T. A., & Grossman, P. B. (1997). A positive view of self: Risk or protection for aggressive children? *Development and Psychopathology, 9*, 75–94.

Jenkins, A. (1990). *Invitations to responsibility: The therapeutic engagement of men who are violent & abusive.* Adelaide, South Australia: Dulwich Centre Publications.

Jones, V. F., & Jones, L. S. (1998). *Comprehensive classroom management: Creating communities of support and solving problems* (5th ed.). Needham Heights, MA: Allyn & Bacon.

Karver, M. S., Handelsman, J. B., Fields, S., & Bickman, L. (2006). Meta-analysis of therapeutic relationship variables in youth and family therapy: The evidence for different relationship variables in child and adolescent treatment outcome literature. *Clinical Psychology Review, 26*, 50–65.

Keating, L. M., Tomishima, M. A., Foster, S., & Alessandri, M. (2002). The effects of a mentoring program on at risk youth. *Adolescence, 37*(148), 717–734.

Lambert, M. J., & Barley, D. E. (2001). Research summary on the therapeutic relationship and psychotherapy outcome. *Psychotherapy: Theory, Research, Practice, Training, 38*(4), 357–361.

Laursen, E. K., & Birmingham, S. M. (2003). Caring relationships as a protective factor for at risk youth: An ethnographic study. *Families in Society, 84*(2), 240–246.

Luna, B., & Sweeney, J. (2004). The emergence of collaborative brain function: fMRI studies of the development of response inhibition. *Annuals of the New York Academy of Science, 1021*, 296–309.

Marshall, W. L., Serran, G., Moulden, H., Mulloy, R., Fernandez, Y. M., Mann, R., et al. (2002). Therapist features in sexual offender treatment: Their reliable identification and influence on behaviour change. *Clinical Psychology and Psychotherapy, 9*, 395–405.

Maslow, A. H. (1970). *Motivation and personality* (2nd ed). New York: Harper & Row.

Miller, W. R., & Rollnick, S. (2002). *Motivational interviewing: Preparing people for change* (2nd ed). New York: Guilford Press.

Minuchin, S. (1974). *Families and family therapy*. Cambridge, MA: Harvard University Press.

Moffitt, T. E. (1993). Adolescence-limited and life-course-persistent antisocial behavior: A developmental taxonomy. *Psychological Review, 100*(4), 674–701.

Murphy, J. J. (1999). Common factors of school-based change. In M. A. Hubble, B. L. Duncan, & S. D. Miller (Eds.), *The heart & soul of change: What works in therapy* (pp. 361–386). Washington, DC: American Psychological Association.

National Center on Sexual Behavior of Youth. (2003, July). Publications, *NCSBY fact sheet: What research shows about adolescent sex offenders*. From http://www.ncsby.org

Nelson, C. A. (2003). Neural development and lifelong plasticity. In R. Learner, E. Jacobs, & D. Wertlieb (Eds.), *Handbook of applied developmental science* (vol. 1). Thousand Oaks, CA: Sage.

Nelson, C. A., & Bloom, F. E. (1997). Child development and neuroscience. *Child Development, 68*, 970–987.

Norcross, J. C. (Ed.). (2001). Empirically supported therapy relationships: Conclusions & recommendations of the Division 29 task force. *Psychotherapy, 38*(4), 495–497.

Norcross, J. C. (Ed.). (2002). *Psychotherapy relationships that work*. New York: Oxford University Press.

Norcross, J. C., & Lambert, M. J. (2006). The therapy relationship. In J. C. Norcross, L. E. Beutler, & R. F. Levant (Eds.), *Evidenced-based practices in mental health: Debate and dialogue on fundamental questions* (pp. 208–218). Washington, DC: American Psychological Association.

Ragsdale, S., & Saylor, A. (2007). *Great group games: 175 boredom-busting, zero-prep team builders for all ages*. Minneapolis, MN: Search Institute.

Reitzel, L. R., & Carbonell, J. L. (2006). The effectiveness of sexual offender treatment for juveniles as measured by recidivism: A meta-analysis. *Sex Abuse, 18*(4), 401–421.

Rogers, C. R. (1957). The necessary and sufficient conditions of therapeutic personality change. *Journal of Consulting Psychology, 21*(2), 95–103.

Rogers, S., & Renard, L. (1999). Relationship-driven teaching. *Educational Leadership, 57*(1), 34–37.

Sowell, E. R., Thompson, P. M., Holmes, C. J., Batth, R., Jernigan, T. L., & Toga, A. W. (1999). Localizing age-related changes in brain structure between childhood and adolescence using statistical parametric mapping. *NeuroImage, 9*, 587–597.

Sowell, E. R., Thompson, P. M., Holmes, C. J., Jernigan, T. L., & Toga, A. W. (1999). In vivo evidence for post adolescent brain maturation in frontal and striatal regions. *Nature Neuroscience, 2*(10), 859–861.

Sowell, E. R., Thompson, P. M., Tessner, K. D., & Toga, A. W. (2001). Mapping continued brain growth and gray matter density reduction in dorsal frontal cortex: Inverse relationships during post-adolescent brain maturation. *The Journal of Neuroscience, 21*(22), 8819–8829.

Sowell, E. R., Trauner, D. A., Garnst, A., & Jernigan, T. L. (2002). Development of cortical and subcortical brain structures in childhood and adolescence: A structural MRI study. *Developmental Medicine and Child Neurology, 44*, 4–16.

Spear, L. P. (2000). The adolescent brain and age-related behavioral manifestations. *Neuroscience and Biobehavioral Reviews, 24*, 417–463.

Spencer, V. G. (2006). Peer tutoring and students with emotional or behavioral disorders: A review of the literature. *Behavioral Disorders, 31*(2), 204–222.

Stenhoff, D. M., & Lignugaris-Kraft, B. (2007). A review of the effects of peer tutoring on students with mild disabilities in secondary settings. *Council for Exceptional Children, 74*(1), 8–30.

Turner, S., & Scherman, A. (1996). Big brothers: Impact on little brothers' self-concepts and behaviors. *Adolescence, 31*(124), 875–882.

Worling, J. R., & Curwen, T. (2000). Adolescent sexual offender recidivism: Success of specialized treatment and implications for risk prediction. *Child Abuse and Neglect, 24*(7), 965–982.

Yurgelun-Todd, D. (1998, June). *Brain and psyche seminar*. Presented at the Whitehead Institute for Biomedical Research, Cambridge, MA.

CHAPTER 17

Integrating Theory and Method
Goal-Oriented Treatment

GAIL RYAN, TOM LEVERSEE, and SANDY LANE

INTEGRATING THEORY AND METHOD

The emphasis in program development for sexually abusive youth throughout the 1980s was clearly to develop treatment interventions that would specifically address the problem of sexually abusive behavior. In that decade of specialization, sexually abusive behavior was studied intensely, and offense-specific treatment strategies were developed incorporating a variety of techniques to address sexual interests and arousal, as well as the attitudes, beliefs, and thinking that support and rationalize sexual offending. Treatment approaches for sexually abusive youth were profoundly influenced by research and experience with adult sexual offenders, and many offense-specific techniques were adapted to work with younger clients. Most of the techniques that distinguish offense-specific programs from other treatment programs for juveniles originated in the work with adults, with the exception of the "sexual abuse cycle" (see Chapter 9).

The sexual abuse cycle demonstrates a specific behavioral manifestation of a compensatory response style in a general dysfunctional cycle (Lane & Zamora, 1978, 1984; Ryan, 1989; Ryan & Lane, 1991; Ryan, Lane, Davis, & Isaac, 1987). Following the conception of the original cycle depicting the pattern described by young rapists (Lane & Zamora, 1982), clinicians working in various programs have used the cycle in many ways, adapting the concept relative to a broad spectrum of sexually abusive behaviors as well as its application to other control-seeking dysfunctions (Freeman-Longo & Bays, 1989; Johnson, 1989; Lowe, 1984 [personal communication]; Ryan, 1989; Smith, 1987; Stickrod, 1988). In its broader context, sexual abuse is one of many negative behaviors that might result from a similar cognitive behavioral syndrome. Because the cycle considers situations, thoughts, feelings, and behaviors (and because of its versatility and applicability to dysfunctional patterns generally and sexually abusive patterns specifically), it has been an ideal framework for understanding behavior and eclectic approaches to treatment of sexual offending. It has been widely used in the juvenile field for more than 20 years (Freeman-Longo, Bird, Stevenson, & Fiske, 1995; McGrath, Cummings, & Burchard, 2003; National Task Force on Juvenile Sexual Offending, 1988, 1993; Rich, 2003).

Many adult programs use the concept of cycles as well (Freeman-Longo & Bays, 1988, 1989; McGrath, Cummings, & Burchard, 2003; Pithers & Gray, 1996); it is compatible with the cognitive-behavioral approaches and relapse-prevention concepts that formed the foundations of sex offender treatment, research, and practice throughout the 1980s and 1990s. The work with adults has typically focused on thoughts, fantasies, planning, deviant sexual arousal, and sexually abusive behaviors. Although the immediate precursors (stresses) and the cognitive justifications have been addressed in adult programming, there has tended to be less emphasis on the historical and affective elements depicted in the cycle model. In fact, many practitioners believed that exploration of etiological risk factors and vulnerable feelings (the elements reflected in the beginning phase of the cycle) might encourage offenders to excuse and justify their abusive behavior. Intense controversy in the 1990s focused on the pros and cons of dealing with childhood victimization in the course of offense-specific treatment, with some programs prohibiting that work entirely and others specifically limiting that work to modules separate from the offense-specific work, often at the end of the treatment process.

It is likely that a variety of factors supported the intense focus on sexual dysfunction (and the exclusion of the broader implications of the cycle). Most obvious, the sexual behavior was the reason for referral and specialized techniques dealing with sexual deviance clearly distinguished offense-specific treatment from traditional, generalist treatments. Secondly, the relative lack of scientific knowledge and techniques to treat sexual aggression and/or deviant arousal prior to the 1980s dictated a need for basic and applied research to focus on the sexual aspect of the problem. Additionally, the crimes of sexual offenders are so abhorrent for clinicians to contemplate that some resistance to compassionate understanding of the phenomenology and developmental influences was inevitable. Clinicians did not want to confront the possibility that sex offenders might be more similar to than different from other people (Marshall, 1996).

The life histories of many perpetrators are so horrendous that the temptation to avoid painful issues associated with abuse, neglect, and trauma was a parallel issue for both the therapist and the client. If the sexual arousal, fantasies, and behaviors could be addressed in isolation, a mechanistic approach could apply cognitive and behavioral interventions without going through the painful affective issues and without forming a therapeutic relationship (Blanchard, 1995).

Most people have been affected by the impacts of sexual abuse in their own lives or the lives of someone they know or care about. For decades people have struggled to understand the behavior, identify how and why such a thing could occur, grasp what really happens during sexual abuse, or come to terms with feelings of shame, guilt, and fear. Perhaps focusing on sexual deviance as the cause of the problem was, in part, a vehicle for self-reassurance, or to provide the relief (or sense of control) that ensues when one gains an understanding of a particularly puzzling and affect-laden problem.

Perhaps the juvenile field was forced to confront childhood experiences because the clients were still children, or perhaps the earlier aspects of the cycle were more apparent in interventions with youth because the sexual aspects were less habituated and the cycle moved more slowly. Or perhaps the drive to understand the developmental pathway to offending in order to develop primary and secondary prevention strategies (Gilgun, 1988; Hunter, 1996a; Prentky et al., 1989b; Ryan, 1984a, 1984b, 1989) provided the impetus for juvenile treatment providers to explore the experiential, developmental, and etiological antecedents of sexually abusive behavior. Or perhaps it was simply curiosity. In any case, work with sexually abusive youth began to contribute to a developmental-contextual understanding, which has led to important changes in therapeutic approaches (Gilgun, 1996; Ryan, 1995; Whitaker, 1987).

Research continues to support that, for most sexually abusive youth, sexual deviance is secondary to the abusive nature of the problem and that exposure to sexual deviance is less relevant than the developmental deficits and phenomenological context in terms of risk. Research discussed in earlier chapters supports the more holistic, developmental approaches that have been articulated by numerous theorists and clinicians (Bremer, 1992; Marshall, Hudson, Jones, & Fernandez, 1995; National Task Force, 1993; Rasmussen, 1999; Rich, 2003; Ryan, 2000b; Ryan et al., 1993; Ryan & Lane, 1997b; Whitaker, 1990 [personal communication]).

It is clear that each youth is a unique individual but research now delineates some critical differences in subgroups that have important implications for treatment planning and program development. Three particular subgroups were described in Chapter 6, characterized by psychosocial deficits, delinquent lifestyle, and pedophilic interests. Although some youth in each of these groups will have problems related to sexual fantasies, interests, and/or arousal (Hunter & Becker, 1994; Kaemingk, Koselka, Becker, & Kaplan, 1995), some research suggests that the beliefs, attitudes, and sexual interests of many persons in the nonoffender population are not so different from those of many sexually abusive youth (Hunter, 1996b; Malamuth, 1984; 1986; Prentky et al., 1989b).

Appreciation of the powerful reinforcers associated with sexual behavior (intimacy, arousal, orgasm, and tension reduction) helps explain why problematic sexual behaviors may become more apparent and more influential over time, thus requiring more intense interventions for more habituated patterns. Sexual deviance may be less a focus in interventions that occur earlier in the development of the behavior, and the development and reinforcement of healthy sexuality is an attainable goal for most of these youth. Differentiating among the varied reasons sexual behaviors can become problematic is a first step in differentiating the "pedophilic type interests" subgroup's sexual problem from others.

Nonetheless, assessment and treatment techniques specifically related to the sexual aspects of offending and in the cycle (sexual thoughts, fantasies, interests, arousal, and behavior) remain imperatives in treating sexually abusive youth and still distinguish the "offense-specific" components of treatment (see Chapter 18). Newer models reflect the challenge of integrating offense-specific techniques into more individualized, holistic, developmental-contextual approaches, as well as respecting the needs of various subgroups within the population.

The 1997 edition of this text outlined the need to address the unique needs of the individual and more global patterns of functioning that are the developmental and contextual phenomena within which the initiation and continuation of sexually abusive behavior occurs. The struggle has been to help clinicians integrate goal-oriented interventions and offense-specific interventions into more comprehensive approaches that support differential treatment plans. Treatment strategies must address the sexual, the abusive, and the youthful characteristics of sexually abusive youth *and* explore the developmental and contextual phenomena in order to identify both risks and assets (Gilgun, 1996; Rich, 2003; Ryan, 2000b; Ryan & Lane, 1997b). As detailed in Chapter 7, the goal is to decrease the deficits and deviance and increase health.

Treatment modalities include peer groups, individual and family therapies, psychoeducation and skill building, as well as nurturance of growth and development within the family or alternative care milieus. Evidence-based treatments now inform some aspects of the clinical work and "goal oriented" or "outcome oriented" approaches focus more on change rather than methods. A wide range of interventions may be employed differently in different programs and with different youth, but the goals remain the same for all: to be successful, and not be abusive.

Components of a Goal-Oriented Approach

The goals are self-control, competence, increased health, and decreased dysfunction (see Figure 17.1). By clarifying the roles and goals of each component, treatment planning can more easily address each component and identify what is needed from the adults who comprise the multidisciplinary team. All the adults participate in providing the initial "containment" and use safety planning to gradually transfer responsibilities to the youth as they make progress and demonstrate the skills and motivation for self-control. All adults must use the teachable moments to educate, and teachers contribute to the team's understanding of learning disabilities, styles, and teaching strategies. Care providers and parents foster growth and development relevant to increased health, and clinicians work to decrease dysfunction and address individual differences that might impede progress in the present or create chronic stressors or risks across the life span.

Treatment Outcomes: Observable Changes in Current Functioning

Treatment Outcomes are the assets relevant to decreased risk and increased health (described in Chapter 7), and progress is regularly rated in terms of what is being worked on and progress over time (see Figure 17.2). Some youth will need minimal education and counseling to be able to demonstrate these outcomes, and others may

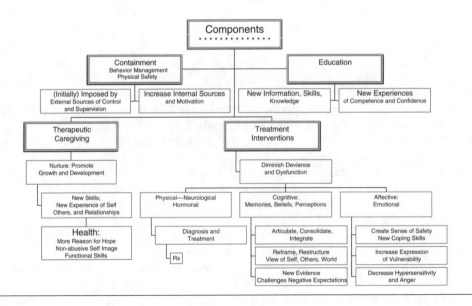

Figure 17.1   Four Components of a Goal-Oriented Approach

Treatment Outcome Summary

Name:_____

Relevant to Decreased Risk: Date:_____

_____

_____   X = Mastered   ? = Work in Progress
                            /= Significant Progress   TBA = To Be Addressed
_____

_____   • Consistently Defines All Abuse (Self, others, property)

_____   • Acknowledges Risk and Uses Foresight and Safety Planning

_____   • Consistently Recognizes/Interrupts Cycle
                              (No later than the first thought of an abusive solution)
_____
                            • Demonstrates Functional Coping Skills When Stressed
_____
                            • Demonstrates Emotional Recognition and Empathic Responses
_____   (Recognizes cues of self and others and responds)

_____   • Accurate Attributions of Responsibility
                                  (Takes responsibility for own behavior, does
_____   not try to control behavior of others)

_____   • Able to Manage Frustration and Unfavorable Events
                                  (Anger Management and Self-Protection)
_____
                            • Rejects Abusive Thoughts as Dissonant
_____   (Incongruent with self-image)

Relevant to Increased Health: * Has learned to moderate personal risks identified by ongoing
                                   assessment and is able to use aftercare plan (e.g., Family
_____   dilemmas, psychiatric disorders, sexual arousal)

_____

_____   Demonstrates:

_____   * Prosocial Relationship Skills (Able to establish Closeness,
                                        Trust, and assess Trustworthiness)
_____
                            • Positive Self-Image
_____   (Able to be Separate, Independent, Competent)

_____   • Able to Resolve Conflicts and Make Decisions
                                  (Assertive, Tolerant, Forgiving, Cooperative)
_____   (Able to Negotiate and Compromise)

_____   • Celebrates Good and Experiences Pleasure
                                  (Able to Relax and Play)
_____
                            • Seeks and Maintains Prosocial Peers
_____
                            • Able to Participate in Prosocial Activities
_____   * Identifies Family and/or Community Support System

_____   • Works/Struggles to Achieve Delayed Gratification
                                        (Persistent pursuit of goals)
_____   (Submission to reasonable authority)

_____   • Able to Think and Communicate Effectively
                                  (Rational Cognitive Processing; Adequate
                                   Verbal Skills; Able to Concentrate)
_____   • Adaptive Sense of Purpose & Future

Figure 17.2   Treatment Outcome Summary (Ryan, 2000, 2002 Rev.)

need a great deal of care and treatment to acquire the knowledge and skills and be motivated to demonstrate these changes in their daily functioning.

The good news is that children and adolescents can moderate all kinds of risks and be more successful when they have the knowledge and skills to do so and the support of knowledgeable, responsible adults. As youth participate in treatment, opportunities for new experiences include their experience of the patience and concern of the adults who comprise their team and the experience of their own ability to be successful.

CONDITIONS AFFECTING THE THERAPEUTIC RELATIONSHIP

In defining sexual abuse it has been stated that it is not the sexual behavior that defines sexually abusive behavior, but rather the abusive qualities of the interaction and the relationship. Specifically, consent, equality, and coercion are the definitive factors, and the relationship of victim and perpetrator is often characterized by coercive and exploitive patterns of interaction that demonstrate a lack of regard for the victim's needs and feelings. This lack of regard is often a reflection of the abusive youth's experience of relationships and constitutes a lack of empathy. Also, if the individual's internal working model for relationships is the basis for one's view of the world, it is apparent that the youth's earliest relationships and attachment models are profoundly relevant to the problem of abusive relationships and therefore to the treatment process. Some new or corrective experience must occur to challenge the youth's view of self, others, and relationships. Much of the resistance in treatment may be related to the therapist's attempts to change the client's view of the world (cognitive restructuring) without providing any evidence that the change is rational. To change the youth's beliefs about the nature of relationships, the clinician must be willing to provide a corrective experience; that is, to enter into a therapeutic relationship with the client (see Chapter 16). Every interaction with the sexually abusive youth provides an opportunity to model empathic relationship skills that challenge the youth's beliefs about self and others. Yet some therapists find these crimes so abhorrent that they struggle with their own feelings and may be unable to tolerate entering into a relationship with the youth (see Chapter 22 regarding the impact on interventionists).

In Chapter 16, Powell reviewed the evidence base for the power of therapeutic relationships in the change process and detailed the qualities of such relationships. Historically, cognitive-behavioral programming for many disorders, and especially sexual offending, failed to address or appreciate the role of the relationship. Blanchard (1995) provides a rich discussion of the therapeutic relationship in treatment with sexually abusive clients, a text well worth consideration. It has often been assumed that involuntary clients were "difficult," without much understanding of why that may be reasonable. The unique conditions of involuntary relationships pose particular challenges, which are present before the therapist and client even meet.

First is the issue of consent: The relationship cannot be defined as consensual because of the involuntary nature of the referral. The court-ordered client is clearly coerced by the power of the court and usually faces some negative consequence if the client fails to participate in treatment. In addition, the power of parents, caseworkers, and probation, as well as the power of the therapist as an authority and agent of the court, provides overwhelming evidence of the imbalance of power in the relationship. With these three factors—lack of consent, lack of equality, and the pressure of coercion in the relationship—there is a high risk that the youth will perceive the relationship with the therapist as potentially abusive. The discomfort is exacerbated by several other nontraditional factors, which are also present prior to entering the relationship: victim advocacy, lack of confidentiality, lack of trust, and confrontation.

Basic to our understanding of the process of offense-specific treatment is that the purpose is to prevent sexual abuse. Sexual perpetration is not a personal problem in the sense that it is a private concern of the perpetrator; it is a social and legal concern as well. It is not an isolated dysfunction that can be addressed in isolation.

VICTIM ADVOCACY

Victim advocacy drives the treatment of sexually abusive youth. Although this statement seems simple enough, its implications in treatment are complex. The National Task Force on Juvenile Sexual Offending stated in its 1993 report, "Protection of the community . . . is the highest priority of intervention in sexual offending; the community is the ultimate client" (p. 12). Although discussions of professional ethics for clinicians have subsequently altered this view somewhat, the nature of the therapeutic relationship is clearly affected, and decision making is based in the second assumption of the task force report: "Community safety takes precedence over any other consideration, and ultimately is in the best interests of the (youth)" (p. 12).

In practice, this assumption requires the therapist to consider the needs and rights of others in priority over the needs and rights of the client. Issues of victim contact, where the youth can reside, the type of treatment setting, and accountability are dictated by these concerns. These considerations are not a large step for those working in corrections, but are a giant step for those working in mental health.

Placing community protection in the forefront requires the therapist-client relationship to include monitoring and accountability. This is not entirely unwarranted and can be a powerful therapeutic lesson: the need to consider others. The therapist's demonstration of concern for victim protection and community safety parallels the goals of treatment and is congruent with the treatment process. In this light the youth's treatment is enhanced by victim advocacy as well as the immediate advantage of reducing the risk of additional offenses, which is clearly in the best interest of the client as well.

Nonetheless, therapists appreciate the role of the courts in being the source of coercion to participate in treatment, consequences of noncompliance, and accountability. By being clear that the mandate for involuntary treatment is a condition of the court, the therapists can frame their role as a helper; a professional trained and willing to struggle with them to fulfill the court's demands. The importance of keeping the coercion in the court and out of the therapeutic relationship cannot be overstated. Abuse is the problem and not the solution! The team must model the nonabusive use of power, and respect the client's lack of consent. Engagement is the responsibility of the therapist and cannot be expected to occur easily.

CONFIDENTIALITY

Confidentiality is the next issue requiring special consideration in the treatment of sexually abusive youth. Again, this concept is a small step for corrections people and a large step for traditional therapists. The National Task Force reports (1988, 1993) state, "Confidentiality cannot apply in the treatment of this population because it promotes the secrecy which supports offending" (1993, p. 37).

By requiring that the juvenile client (and parents) sign a complete waiver (or extensive releases) of confidentiality as a condition of treatment in the community, the therapist not only maximizes communication regarding the client's current functioning but also makes a clear, therapeutic statement to the client: "You must be willing to give up the secrecy that supports your problem, and you must control your behaviors." Waivers or releases allow the team to verify the juvenile's self-reports and to communicate concerns with the other adults involved in the care, education, and supervision of the youth.

Trust

Trust surfaces as the next special concern in treatment. Not surprisingly, the priority of community safety and the waiver of confidentiality are overt statements reflecting the provider's distrust of the client's behavior and self-reports. These are obvious and understandable factors, directly stemming from the referring problem. Because the youth has engaged in abusive behaviors that have hidden aspects, and has denied and minimized the harm of those behaviors in order to maintain feelings of gratification, the associated risks support distrust in these areas.

There are, however, two underlying issues that more subtly influence trust in the therapeutic relationship. The first lies within the youth: an impaired ability to trust. Many sexually abusive youth have never achieved basic trust or have experienced loss or betrayal that severely impairs their ability to trust. (See relevant discussions in Chapters 3, 5, and 7.) They may hope for someone who is trustworthy, but it is not their expectation and it is unlikely that they would risk trusting early in the therapeutic relationship. It is more likely that the youth will take a defensive or manipulative posture initially, based on their life experience.

The second underlying trust issue lies within the therapist: the desire to trust. The unconditional acceptance that is a basic element of relationship-based treatment can conflict with the need to challenge and confront the denial, minimization, and thinking of the youth who abuses. The therapist, bringing to the relationship the capacity for basic trust that the youth lacks, may be tempted to model trust in spite of the untrustworthy nature of the client. It is a mistake, however, to imagine that trust will be warranted, reciprocated, or respected. It would be irrational for the treatment provider to trust the self-control or self-report of clients who demonstrate a lack of control and rely on exerting power over others to meet their needs. The therapist may convey unconditional positive regard for the youth as an individual, but it is not reasonable to trust them until they demonstrate decreased risk.

Therefore, trust is a long-term goal in this therapy, not an immediate or necessary precondition for growth and change. The initial goal is developing a therapeutic alliance based on direct communication of expectations and goals. The client must begin to behave responsibly, control behaviors, and risk trying new behaviors before the therapist can model trust, and the client must begin to understand the nature and value of trustworthiness before the risk of trusting others is reasonable. It would be naive to imagine that a youth who has never known a trusting relationship would ever be able to trust the therapist who had so little understanding of the client as to trust (even superficially) the client who is not trustworthy. Yet most therapists have been trained to establish trust first and then do the work of treatment.

So how can the therapist create a condition that will enable growth and development and change in the absence of trust? The same conditions that enable infants to develop basic trust are the basis of trustworthiness in all relationships, as was discussed in relation to the caregiver relationship (see Chapter 15) and Maslow's "Hierarchy of Needs" (see Chapter 16). Therapists must create the sense of safety that Briggs (1975) described as the preconditions for a "psychologically safe relationship":

1. Focused attention (listening, seeing, reading cues)
2. Nonjudgmental (judging behavior separate from identity)
3. Owning feelings (personal expression of sympathy)
4. Recognition of diversity (the individual's unique developmental context)

5. Empathy (interpreting and validating cues)
6. Trustworthiness (no abuse of power, authority, faith, consistency, dependability)

In a psychologically safe relationship, the therapist is able to convey the understanding and unconditional acceptance of the youth as a worthy person, capable of change, and able to achieve control. Acceptance of person must be carefully distinguished from acceptance of thoughts, words, and behaviors. Finally, it is imperative that the therapist demonstrate his or her own trustworthiness throughout the process, never abusing the privilege and power of the therapist's role in the youth's life.

As the layers of defenses begin to be discarded and the youth begins to experience the self-confidence that accompanies more functional and responsible living, it becomes possible to experience confidence in others as well. The provider's own accountability becomes a model for the building of trusting relationships. The growth of trust in the relationship is a parallel process—a product of consistent empathic interactions and trustworthy behavior. This relationship provides the evidence to support change in the view of self, others, and the world.

Finally, the need for the therapist to challenge perceptions and beliefs rather than work from a position of unconditional acceptance is also unusual for many therapists. The court's order for "offense-specific" treatment dictates the direction and scope of treatment, and is dependent on challenging beliefs and requiring personal accountability. The locus of responsibility and change must lie within the client, who may resist giving up a behavior pattern that provides a significant sense of gratification, empowerment, and adequacy. The youth must begin to feel uncomfortable with abusive behavior if giving it up is to be reasonable. Developing empathy and personal responsibility, the client may go through periods of intense discomfort (shame, guilt, grief, and remorse) and must confront many painful issues. Feeling responsible for increasing a client's distress is an uncomfortable experience for the therapist as well, who must understand and validate the client's resistance.

Being aware of the unique conditions affecting the therapeutic relationship is imperative for the therapist to be able to monitor and manage his or her own reactions in the relationship and to be able to validate the client's experience. The resistance and defensive posturing of the youth can be viewed as rational and adaptive protective strategies. As the therapist articulates the cues that indicate the client's experience, expresses his or her own feelings, and shares thoughts about the reasons why it is hard to feel safe and comfortable in the relationship, it clarifies that the uncomfortable conditions stem from the nature of the work and not because of who the client is or who the therapist is. The therapist is modeling *communication, empathy*, and *the accurate attribution of responsibility*, the very tools necessary for creating a sense of safety and empathic interaction (Ryan et al., 1988).

There has been a tendency among practitioners to avoid the process of creating a therapeutic relationship; to look for interventions that could be applied in an educational, didactic, or impersonal fashion; and to create the illusion of safety by imposing tight structure and rules in the treatment setting. It is the authors' belief, however, that the struggle to create psychologically safe relationships (and to model the empathic responses that are missing in the youth) is an important part of treatment.

The therapist's willingness to struggle to create a sense of safety in relationships is one of the new experiences that challenges the client's view and is also directly relevant to the cycle, demonstrating that someone who feels unsafe in interaction with others can identify safe relationships and ask for help rather than isolate, and can avoid the externalized control seeking and compensatory solutions depicted in the cycle. Therapists should not be discouraged by the struggle it takes to create a relationship, but should view it as a critical component of treatment.

GOAL-ORIENTED INTERVENTIONS

The elements in the cycle manifest in diverse and unique ways by each individual. Differential diagnosis and treatment is designed to meet the specific needs of each youth, recognizing that diverse strengths and deficits will have an impact on the type of intervention required. Certainly some interventions are common to the needs of all these youth, but there are many interventions that may apply to fewer youth or situations. Goal-oriented treatment plans allow for the specificity required to provide differential treatment.

The repertoire of treatment interventions described in treating these youth has at times appeared to use a shotgun approach (doing everything that might work and hoping some of it works). In fact, each intervention does have a specific goal designed to target a specific need; however, without differential treatment planning, many programs had required the same interventions for every youth. As the health care field continues to change, the demand for more discrete and targeted treatment practices grows.

As research has begun to clarify what risks and deficits are actually relevant to the continuation of offending, identifying the goal (the youth's specific treatment needs), the process of working on the goals (specific objectives), and recognizing the desired outcome (behavioral, cognitive, affective, and/or situational changes) as a measure of progress (evidence that change has occurred), now allows providers to be more focused and efficient in the treatment process. Progress or lack thereof and the need for modification or addition of interventions are now based on the ongoing assessment of current functioning, and much less energy is focused on unchangeable aspects of history. The challenge to practitioners has been to actually individualize treatment and to identify adjunct interventions that address some of the diverse qualities identified in more comprehensive assessments.

The community's interests in providing treatment for sexually abusive youth are to stop all sexually abusive behavior, protect members of society from further victimization, and prevent other aggressive or abusive behaviors (National Task Force Report, 1993). In order to accomplish that mission, goals in the treatment process include: creating a physically and psychologically safe environment in the treatment setting; consistent modeling of communication, empathy, and accountability; consistent definition of abusive interactions; acknowledgment of risks; foresight and planning; recognition of the dysfunctional cycle; interrupting the cycle; and demonstrating changed patterns of functioning and empathy in the treatment setting and daily life. Goal-oriented interventions must address each of these areas of concern: abusive dynamics, sexual deviance, growth and development, co-occurring disorders, and environmental factors.

Treatment may occur in various settings: institutional settings, residential facilities, psychiatric hospitals, probation offices, mental health centers, schools, churches, or a private therapist's office. Offense-specific treatment typically occurs in group or individual sessions, but a considerable amount of work may occur in the youth's living environment and/or family therapy. Caregivers provide feedback to the youth about current functioning, challenge old patterns of thinking or behavior, and hold youth responsible for maintaining behavioral changes. In alternative care settings a therapeutic community or a positive peer culture may support the youth, but even outpatient treatment plans can involve many other adults. Mobilizing adults and holding them responsible for meeting the special needs of these youth was discussed in Chapter 15.

SUBTYPE DIFFERENCES IN TREATMENT

The differential developmental and dynamic factors illuminated by the typology research also provide guidance relevant to the treatment needs of individual youth (Hunter, 2001; Worling, 2001). Differences within subgroups will affect decisions regarding placements and treatment grouping. For example, a youth with "psychosocial deficits" is more likely to require therapeutic care that goes beyond normal parenting to work on increasing developmental competencies. A youth characterized by "persistent delinquent lifestyle" may be more likely to have the "deviance training" effect on lower risk youth and may need a higher level of structure and accountability initially. These youth may benefit from ecological approaches working with them in their home and community to increase effective parenting, prosocial modeling, and opportunities for exposure to prosocial peers and activities. A youth with "pedophilic type" sexual issues may pose a risk to younger or less developed boys, whereas a violent/aggressive youth might pose significant risks of physical assaults on peers.

The various characteristics definitive of each subtype are indicative of particular treatment needs. For example, knowing that the youth characterized by psychosocial deficits are more likely to have symptoms of depression than their peers suggests that the treatment plans for that subgroup will need to address the risk of depression. (This will also be a risk factor for individuals within other subgroups who have been physically abused by father figures.)

Generally, the implications for treatment planning relevant to the various subtypes will consider the following, illustrated in the next sections.

PSYCHOSOCIAL DEFICITS

Because the sexual offending of many of the youth characterized by psychosocial deficits reflects compensatory social behavior and an attempt to satisfy unmet intimacy needs, Hunter, Figueredo, Malamuth, and Becker (2003) place emphasis on the importance of addressing deficits in self-esteem, self-efficacy, and social competency. For these youth, the new experience they need is of themselves as competent people. A strengths-based approach can be useful to the process of identifying and utilizing personal strengths and talents and creating opportunities for success. Whitaker (1990, personal communication), Worling (2001), and others have recommended utilizing structured skill-building curriculums such as *Life Space Interventions* (Grskovic & Goetze, 2005), *Prism* (Wexler, 1991), and *Skillstreaming the Adolescent* (Goldstein & McGinnis, 1997), along with affectively oriented psycho-education models for skill and knowledge acquisition. Therapeutic care providers can clearly be involved with much of this work.

For these youth, it is particularly important to engage rather than exclude them from activities. Behavior management systems should use a rewards/discipline paradigm within which participants are not required to "earn" participation, but rather participation is based on safety and current functioning. That is, if the youth demonstrates the ability to participate without posing a risk to self or others they are included in every activity without having to earn participation as if it were a privilege (Whitaker, 1990).

The focus for youth characterized by psychosocial deficits is on social skills, relationship skills, and skills related to the recognition and expression of feelings. Skill-building goals could include: starting a conversation, having a conversation, joining in, and expressing feelings. Research shows that new skills can be learned through a step-by-step process that includes modeling, role-playing, feedback, and the transfer to when, where, and with whom the skill is needed (Goldstein & McGinnis, 1997). Social anxiety can be addressed by changing maladaptive self and interpersonal schemas, defining and changing the aversive habits that often work against the youth in interactions with others. Narrative techniques and visualization exercises can be a part of redefining self-image and/or negative expectations. Exposure techniques, such as taking social risks and participating in normative experiences, work to decrease social isolation and social skill deficits and increase the sense of mastery that supports cognitive and behavioral change (Hunter, 2006).

For these youth successful participation in simple activities with others provides a new experience of themselves as "likeable" and "capable." This can be supported and reinforced in extracurricular activities and relationships with positive peer mentors. Psychological safety is a necessary precondition for such youth to be willing to take social risks due to the weight of social rejection, alienation, and failures they have experienced in the past when trying to relate to others, when they did not have the skills to do so successfully.

Healthy sexuality education is a useful part of their overall skill development, with particular emphasis on relationships, courtship and dating skills, and topics including reproductive and sexual anatomy, sexual feelings, sexual decision-making, sexual values, and personal responsibility (Brown, 2000). In addition to the psychosocial deficits, compensatory patterns sometimes include sexual preoccupation, excessive masturbation, pornography, and/or other sexual paraphilias, which will be discussed in offense-specific treatment in Chapter 18.

Initially, subtype-specific grouping in the care environment as well as the treatment components may be effective in order to focus on the dynamics associated with psychosocial deficits, increase participation and openness, and minimize exposure to more delinquent youth (Dishion, McCord, & Poulin, 1999).

DELINQUENT LIFESTYLE

The youth with delinquent lifestyle characteristics are likely to have sexually offended as part of a more general pattern of delinquent behavior. They may have a wide range of abusive and aggressive acting out behaviors and may exhibit egotistical-antagonistic and/or hostile masculinity traits. Their "macho" demeanor and tendency to use intimidation and superiority to control others is indicative of the potential negative influence they may have on others. Such attitudes and patterns often reflect those of adult role models in the home or community where they live. Within the delinquent lifestyle subgroup, a range of severity from the "Adolescent Onset-Experimenters" to the "Life Course Persistent" youth further divides the group in terms of treatment and supervision needs (Hunter, 2006, 2008; Moffitt, 1993).

Youth characterized as having delinquent lifestyles who sexually offend have much in common with other delinquents and will benefit from treatment interventions effective with that population (Prentky & Righthand, 2003; Worling, 2001). Edward Latessa (2005) describes risk/need factors for juvenile delinquents as follows:

- Antisocial/procriminal attitudes, values, beliefs, and cognitive-emotional states.
- Procriminal associates and isolation from anticriminal others.
- Temperamental and personality factors conducive to criminal activity including: self-regulation deficits, weak socialization; impulsivity; restless aggressive energy; egocentrism; below average verbal intelligence; a taste for risk; and weak problem-solving skills.
- A history of conduct problems and delinquency.
- Family factors include: adult criminality in the home; psychological problems in the family of origin; low levels of affection, caring, and cohesiveness; poor parental supervision and discipline practices; and outright neglect and abuse.
- Low levels of personal educational, vocational, or financial achievement.

The care environment can pose significant challenges in achieving both physical and psychological safety and often needs strict behavioral systems. Assessment and interventions will need to consider external risk factors in the home and community associated with inadequate or coercive parenting styles, domestic violence, gang involvement, and substance abuse, as well as nonsexual delinquency such as assault, harassment, and property crimes.

Sexuality education for the more delinquent subgroup needs to stress sexual harassment, date rape and acquaintance rape, personal boundaries, consent, non-abusive sexual behavior, safe sex practices, responsible parenting, and healthy masculinity.

In institutional settings, Aggression Replacement Training (ART) (Glick, 2006; Goldstein, Glick, & Gibbs, 1998) provides a multimodal, evidence-based intervention using cognitive-behavioral approaches for aggressive and violence-prone youth (Greenwood, 2008). Three separate ten-week components run simultaneously and include social skills training, anger control training, and moral reasoning. For delinquent youth who can be treated in their own homes, Multi-Systemic Therapy (MST) has been very effective with the generally delinquent population and in a pilot study with juveniles who have committed sexual offenses (Borduin, Henggeler, Blaske, & Stein, 1990; Burton & Meezan, 2004; Henggeler, Schoenwald, Borduin, Rowland, & Cunningham, 1996).

Treatment of those youth characterized by delinquent lifestyle as well as egotistical antagonistic masculinity, interpersonal dominance, and/or hostile masculinity, will need to focus on the attitudes and beliefs that contribute to negative and pejorative views of women, rape myths, and coercive styles of interpersonal relationships. Challenging and altering belief systems will start with clearly defining abuse. Exposure to adult role modeling of healthy masculinity can also be an important step in redefining masculine identity. Opportunities for prosocial interaction and relationships may occur with alternative care providers, mentors, positive peers, and treatment providers.

PEDOPHILIC INTERESTS

Although the pedophilic interest subtype represents the smallest portion of juveniles who sexually offend, the sexual deviance poses a significant risk of recidivism. The higher risk to reoffend sexually represented by this subtype necessitates higher levels of external supervision and containment. Much more of their treatment will focus on offense-specific interventions aimed at changing or controlling deviant interests and arousal. Techniques to manage deviant sexual arousal will be discussed in the offense-specific treatment chapter. Thought stopping and covert sensitization stress increased cognitive control, and for some youth in this subgroup, more intrusive interventions may be warranted. The lack of conclusive research on interventions to address arousal problems with juveniles continues to severely impede the treatment of these youth, and deserves more attention from researchers.

Sex education for these youth will need to include very specific emphasis on the dangers of continuing to dwell on abusive fantasies, the powerful reinforcement of the problem when deviant fantasy is paired with arousal and masturbation, and sincere efforts to engage and motivate them to want to control a behavior that they find pleasurable. Clear definition of the laws and the legal consequences of child molestation are clearly imperatives.

Exploring personal history for deviant sexual experiences and influences that may be relevant, and clearly differentiating abusive from nonabusive sexual interactions is critical. Many of the youth with persistent and exclusive pedophilic interests may be referred into adult programs as they mature, and some will require lifetime management strategies. It cannot be assumed such youth are "untreatable," although it is not yet known how to most effectively treat them. Resisting problematic sexual impulses is a part of normal functioning by most people, and it is reasonable to expect that youth can acquire some methods to do so, even those who are not able to act on more normative impulses.

GOAL-ORIENTED TREATMENT PLANNING

A cursory look at examples of Goals and Objectives that might be a part of a treatment plan clearly demonstrates how much the observations of the caregiver will inform ongoing assessments and illuminate individual differences. Treatment plans evolve over time from the outline of concerns identified in the initial evaluation, becoming more discrete and targeted as individual issues are revealed. Some objectives of the overall treatment plan will be most effectively addressed in the care environment and the caregiver's role will be apparent. Other objectives will clearly be relevant to family therapy and others can more naturally be addressed in individual, group, or educational sessions (Thomas & Viar, 2005).

Ongoing Assessment: Observations of Current Functioning

1. A youth is easily frustrated and blows up when he has to wait.
2. A youth is verbally abusive to staff and peers after returning from visits with Dad.
3. A youth is highly sexualized and easily stimulated by sexual cues in the environment.

Treatment Planning

Goals based on ongoing assessment

Problem Statement: 1. Youth is easily frustrated and blows up when made to wait.

Relevance: Abusive Dynamics; Developmental Deficits

Goal: Youth will become able to manage frustration.

Objectives:

1. Youth will identify calming skills.
2. Youth will define internal cues of frustration.
3. Youth will identify hypotheses regarding triggers.
4. Youth will develop a plan to deal with frustration.
5. Youth will practice stepwise goal achievement.
6. Youth will demonstrate an ability to wait.

Outcome: Youth will demonstrate patience and work to achieve delayed gratification.

Problem Statement: 2. Youth is verbally abusive after passes with Dad.

Relevance: Abusive Dynamics; Growth and Development; Ecological Strengths/ Deficits

Goal: Youth will become able to go on pass with Dad without getting into cycle.

Objectives:

1. Youth will acknowledge pattern.
2. Youth will define abusive language.
3. Youth will share problem with Dad.
4. Youth will identify hypotheses regarding triggers on visits with Dad and Youth and Dad will work on relevant issues.
5. Youth will develop safety plans for visits and for return.
6. Youth will practice anticipatory desensitization.
7. Youth will demonstrate nonabusive emotional expression.

Outcome: Youth will return from passes without being abusive.

Problem Statement: 3. Youth is easily stimulated and uses sexualized language/ innuendo.

Relevance: Deviance; Ecological Risks

Goal: Youth will be able to interact without sexualizing nonsexual situations.

Objectives:

1. Youth will acknowledge pattern of behavior.
2. Youth will define sexual stimuli and innuendo.
3. Youth will define sexual vs. nonsexual relationships.
4. Youth will identify nonsexual activities.
5. Youth will identify nonsexual social skills.
6. Youth will participate in nonsexual activities.
7. Youth will demonstrate nonsexual emotional expression/interactions.

Outcome: Youth will enjoy activities and interactions without sexualizing (adapted from Thomas & Viar, 2005).

The objectives are the small steps toward the goal and by taking one step at a time, the work becomes more manageable. Defining and acknowledging the problem is always a first step.

The "observable outcomes" described as measures of change relevant to decreased risk and increased health will be observed in the context of daily functioning, not just in treatment sessions but in the home and school. Demonstrating those outcomes consistently throughout the day is likely a better measure of internalization of those changes than simply being on "best behavior" during clinical hours. Nonetheless, there is no evidence that any particular clinical intervention, or change in the client, will definitely prevent further offending.

It is important for the youth to understand that treatment is not a magic "fix" guaranteeing no further offenses. The therapist's responsibility is to provide the clinical interventions and support for the youth to acquire and demonstrate new knowledge and skills so they are able to avoid offending, if they choose to do so. It becomes the youth's responsibility to make the choices and use the knowledge and skills to prevent additional offending in the future.

As the youth begins to practice new skills, the adults have a responsibility to monitor closely the level of competency, expecting regression in times of stress and increasing or decreasing external supports as needed. Regression is a natural part of change and should not be punished. Just as a parent does not let go of the toddler's hand to "test" their ability to remember to not run into the street, adults cannot suddenly hold the youth accountable for using new skills until there is evidence of mastery. Continually revisiting safety plans for current activities is the basis for good monitoring and support.

"ABUSE-SPECIFIC," "OFFENSE-SPECIFIC," AND CONCURRENT TREATMENT COMPONENTS

Youth with many types of harmful behaviors can benefit from the same abuse-specific education and treatment to reduce the risk of all abusive behavior, in conjunction with treatment components specifically relevant to their other clinical needs and behavioral disorders. For those who have sexually offended, both abuse-specific and offense-specific intervention is indicated. Knowing that most youth who sexually offend are at greater risk to be arrested later for other types of harmful behaviors than for continuing to sexually offend, it is apparent that all have the capacity to be abusive. Offense-specific treatment addresses the sexual aspect of sexual offending, using interventions specifically relevant to abusive sexuality, and that are actually a discrete piece of the comprehensive treatment plan (see Chapter 18).

Using the Abuse Is Abuse concept as the common denominator, specialized interventions for all types of aggressive and destructive behaviors can be integrated into a congruent model, maximizing the use of scarce resources and strategically addressing the risk of all types of harmful behavior in the future. For example, concurrent treatment components for some might address trauma treatment, neurological interventions, substance abuse, anger management, violence and aggression, eating disorders, self-destructive behaviors, co-occurring psychiatric disorders, or family dysfunction. The abuse-specific approach is the equalizer and the bottom line; successful integration of other components relies on the adjunct components using approaches that are congruent with the concepts of the abuse-specific model.

Although there is no single evidence-based treatment for sexual offending, many of the co-occurring disorders and general delinquency do have evidence-based interventions with proven efficacy, which can and should be used in those concurrent components that are relevant to the individual case. Chapters building on the abuse-specific approach will discuss trauma treatment and some of the co-occurring disorders. Research is needed to test combinations of interventions in treating youth with multiple complex treatment needs. Therapists must continue to be cognizant of new discoveries in science and be willing to change when new knowledge challenges old assumptions (Ryan, 2000a).

ABUSE-SPECIFIC TREATMENT

Abuse-specific supervision, education, and care have been described in Chapter 15 as distinctly different from the role and goal of the clinical components. In a goal-oriented approach, issues of deviance and dysfunction (past, present, and future) can be referred into the clinical sessions in order to put some containment around those issues and free up time for youth to have more normalizing experiences.

Abuse-specific *treatment* is the clinical work that addresses the risk of harmful behaviors. Using the Abuse Is Abuse concept to define abuse of self, others, and property, and the cycle to recognize the patterns antecedent to many types of abusive behaviors, many of the "issues" that put youth at risk to be abusive and dysfunctional are emotionally laden memories and cognitive beliefs and perceptions from earlier life experiences. Helping youth to recognize, express, understand, and manage painful and confusing experiences from early childhood to the present is the largest piece of clinical work. As is true in relation to the supervision, education, and care previously described in the abuse-specific approach, many youth with a wide range of harmful behaviors have many clinical issues in common as well.

Historically, all youth who were referred for offense-specific treatment were treated in clinical sessions apart from youth with other referring problems. For some, that is still a necessary first step, when assessment or observation suggests that they pose a risk of harm to similar age peers. However, many (and almost all as they make progress through treatment), can participate in topic-related groups with other youth who are struggling with similar issues in their lives and with their families. Abuse-specific approaches can be used in mixed population settings along with concurrent offense-specific treatment.

The characteristics of abuse-specific treatment that distinguish it from other treatment approaches reflect the basic concepts described in Chapters 7 and 8: definition of all abuse; recognition of maladaptive response patterns; development of more effective coping skills; risk recognition, foresight, and planning; emotional recognition, expression, and empathic responses; and accurate attributions of responsibility. The Abuse Is Abuse concept, Cycles, and the Universal goals continue to be common denominators in every component of the work, while helping the youth develop skills for more successful functioning.

INTRODUCTION TO TREATMENT

At the outset, the rules and expectations of the treatment provider, the group, and the program must be discussed. Group rules may cover confidentiality, behavior, and participation, and should clearly define the consequences of noncompliance. Similarly, therapists must explain the limits of their own confidentiality, define their role within the group, and convey their basic expectations regarding group participation, assignments, and attendance. Programs that provide care and/or experiential or educational components may have more global expectations relative to behavior beyond the treatment group.

Initial sessions must also address the same issues that any other group therapy must. Clients—not even voluntary and motivated clients—do not arrive in treatment knowing how to use treatment. Anxiety and inexperience hamper every new client's first group experience, and for juveniles, suspicion and reluctance can be expected. The therapist may outline the goals of the program and empathize with the client's understandable anxiety. Reassurance is possible, however, as the therapist is able to reveal his or her understanding and experience relevant to the client's problems and offer encouragement that new information and understanding will be available to the client. In all fairness, the therapist must warn the youth that the treatment process can sometimes be emotionally painful and people often wish to quit, but that successfully completing treatment helps people do better. Early assignments might include clarifying why the youth are in the program, what they hope to get out of treatment, and definition of short-term and long-term goals for themselves—information that can guide the therapist's efforts to engage them.

THE TREATMENT GROUP

Housing and/or treating juveniles in groups has come under intense scrutiny in juvenile justice. The risk of youth actually learning bad behavior from other youth is apparent in the finding that the number one risk factor for the adolescent onset of delinquency is delinquent peers. It is not surprising that adolescents are influenced by peer pressure and the desire to be part of a peer group, and within juvenile correctional facilities research has documented the risk of "deviance training" (Dishion, McCord, & Poulin, 1999) (defined as lower-risk youth becoming higher risk during exposure to and association with higher-risk youth). Therapists and administrators must take seriously the weight of such research, and the temptation is to never bring delinquent youth together in group living or treatment. However, knowing that humans are social beings, seek intimacy and connection with others, and require interaction with others to survive, it may be short-sighted to simply prohibit contact with others.

What happens in groups is that sometimes one member has a negative effect on the others, or one member is negatively affected by the others. Adults have a responsibility to control for this, monitoring how the members of any group are affected by the others. Sometimes it is necessary to remove one youth who is having a negative effect on others, and to work individually to change that before they can rejoin the group. That work might focus on anger management, changing attitudes that reflect hyper-masculinity, domination or intimidation, or power-based interaction. Other times, it is necessary to remove one youth who is being negatively affected by others to work individually to become more self-aware, self-confident, assertive, and so forth.

Initially separating various subgroups of youth may be indicated, but ultimately, it must be a goal of treatment for youth to be able to be a part of groups with diverse peers without being either a negative influence on others or negatively affected by others. This is congruent with the other goals of abuse-specific treatment: to recognize and care about how one affects others, to be able to create safety in relationships, and to not be abusive or abused.

Many of the common issues associated with abusive behavior can be effectively addressed in a group setting, ideally with male and female co-therapists. A male and female co-therapy team offers modeling of healthy interactions and heterosexual relationships that are equal, nonabusive, and communicative. Group membership models and promotes relationship development and it is a safe testing ground for practicing new ways of interacting. As the youth hears others describe similar experiences and behaviors, it challenges negative self-perceptions. There is some reassurance that they are not the only one who ever had bad experiences or did bad things.

Hearing the distortions and minimizations of others, the youth begins to recognize the lack of logic and the objectifying aspects without defensiveness, before recognizing the same in themselves. Observing another youth share painful experiences or accepting constructive feedback encourages the youth to take similar risks. Youth can sometimes identify denial and minimization in each other's accounts even more quickly and accurately than the therapist can because of the similarity of their experiences. In the group process, clients manifest their unique strengths, patterns, and vulnerabilities and newer members can see that change is possible.

Truly individualized treatment should not be time limited, so "open" groups are best able to accommodate the individual differences in how long, and at what point, the youth can benefit from the group. As new members join a group, those who are further along can demonstrate their progress in their interaction with new members. Some psychoeducational groups may be more didactic and with a specific agenda be time limited, but the treatment process is less predictable.

Because progress in treatment requires that youth actually demonstrate changes in their current functioning as a condition of successful completion of treatment, there may be advantages to having less structure in the treatment group instead of more. One's ability to observe individual differences and change over time can be hampered by too many external controls.

Youth can often jump through hoops, once they decide to do so. They can:

- Follow rules when they perceive it is in their interest
- Complete assignments when there is some reward
- Learn to say what others want to hear

However, all three of the above mentioned may have little to do with their risk of continuing to be abusive. It is much more difficult to fake changes in daily functioning when required to "show" that they are consistently demonstrating the "outcomes."

The minimal rules for an abusive specific group would be:

- Not being abusive
- Not being disruptive of others' work
- Not taking peers' issues out of group
- Not losing control and either blowing up or blowing out

Of course, "not being abusive" sounds like a set up for failure since the youth are in treatment because they are abusive, but the rule means that whenever anything abusive happens in the room it is defined and worked on as a treatment issue. It is often the second rule, "not disrupting the peers' work in group," that is the biggest struggle. For many of the youth, the peers' issues are so close to their own that even hearing a peer talk about them creates anxiety by indirectly bringing up the other members' issues. Since the hard issues are the very things that are likely to trigger defenses, peers in the group will often become disruptive, abusive, or shut down just hearing another youth talk, without anyone bringing up their own issues.

The struggle to help the group tolerate the work on sensitive issues is another of the new experiences for the youth: that the therapist does not "give up" on them, and works hard to help them stay in the group without being disruptive, rather than simply removing the disruptive person. Also, it becomes apparent over time that youth who are quiet but attentive can be learning a lot, even without actively working on their individual issues. In the goal-oriented approach it is not what the therapist actually does, nor what the client actually does during treatment, it is the demonstration of the outcomes that is the measure of success.

The same techniques employed to deescalate youth in the care environment are also necessary in the treatment group. Being willing to slow down or even stop and be silent, to change the subject to something benign, or to put the emotionally charged issue on the agenda for another day, can all help maintain the group without anyone getting too upset to stay. When the same youth repeatedly disrupts the process because they cannot tolerate or are not willing to listen to the hard issues, that member might need a break from attending the group while they work on the skills they will need to manage their emotions during group, or to process their own issues, which are overwhelming their ability to cope.

Adults are often tempted to develop a long list of rules, or to keep adding rules to address every problem that occurs. Following rules is an external source of containment, and the longer the list, the more time is spent learning it and processing rule violations. Making only the rules that relate to the necessary preconditions of safety (Physical and Psychological safety) and treatment (Not preventing therapy) means the adults and youth will experience the actual process of being and functioning together. Experiencing the struggle of creating safe relationships may be as important as any other aspect of treatment.

As a sense of safety develops in the group, the clients are encouraged to report their daily experiences and provide information about themselves. Defining what is abusive and teaching the concept of cycles are didactic pieces or work that can help youth feel more at ease in that learning new information parallels the school process. Teaching information and concepts without getting personal, the therapist begins creating the language for doing the work of treatment. Hearing bits of their current experiences, the therapist can begin to point out examples of things that illustrate the concepts being taught.

By using various components and modalities with the group, the co-therapists provide each member the opportunity to explore, experience, and benefit from a wide range of ideas and types of interventions. One juvenile may prove most competent in the cognitive areas, another might make best use of behavioral interventions, and yet another could make significant affective changes. For some, educational components work to correct faulty beliefs or skill deficits, while others accept one or more specific techniques and become adept at averting themselves from their own cycle.

The experience of individuals through this group process not only exposes them to many different ways of thinking and types of intervention relevant to various issues, but also demonstrates the individuality of each member, increasing their capacity for empathy and appreciation of each individual's unique needs and competencies.

DEFINING ALL ABUSE

Juveniles arriving in treatment do not usually understand what abusive behavior is. It is important for them to hear that they will be expected to learn how to define all types of abusive behaviors. The evolution of the abuse is abuse concept was fully described in Chapter 7. Using the concept with youth who are referred for a specific harmful behavior often meets with resistance, as they protest that they are not in treatment for anything but the particular referring behavior problem. It is important to teach them not only how abuse is defined but also why it is relevant in treatment. Treatment cannot be a mystery. By explaining the relationship of various types of abuse in terms of the risk of multiple delinquent or harmful behaviors and the fact that the behaviors all occur in a similar pattern demonstrates the therapist's concern for their safety as well as the safety of others.

The therapist can make the general statement that knowing they are referred for a particular abusive behavior, it is assumed that most of them have been abusive in other ways as well, to themselves, others, and property, and that many of them have been abused as well. Behaviors are considered "self-abusive" when they pose a risk of harm to self. "Abuse of others" also poses a risk of harm, but the "risk of harm" is not what defines abusive interactions. It is the nature of the interaction and relationship that defines interpersonal abuse.

The factors that define abusive interactions are consent, equality, and coercion. Group discussion should result in correct definitions:

Consent: (a) understanding what is proposed without confusion or trickery; (b) knowing the standard for the behavior in the culture, the family, and the peer group; (c) awareness of possible consequences including stigma, punishment, pain, and disease; and (d) respect for agreement or disagreement without repercussions. It is imperative that therapist and client distinguish consent, cooperation, and compliance. *Cooperation* implies participation without regard for one's personal beliefs or desires. *Compliance* implies allowing without regard for one's personal beliefs or desires. Neither cooperation nor compliance equals consent.

Equality: Equal authority, power, and control within a relationship. Although significant age or size differentials are clearly indicators of inequality, there are many more subtle indicators of unequal power or authority: intellectual or strength differentials; knowledge and experience differentials; assertiveness, popularity, and self-image differentials; and delegated authority differentials such as big brother, baby-sitter, leader, or boss.

Coercion: Pressures—either explicit or implied—that are exerted in order to get someone else to do something that they would not otherwise agree to do. These pressures may include subtle threats such as loss of love, attention, or friendship; covert manipulation, trickery, and bribes; overt threats and peer pressure; as well as physical force and violence. Juveniles must understand the whole continuum of coercion in order to define the nature of abusive behavior.

Assignments can be given to challenge clients to define these terms and apply them to their own experiences. Subsequent group discussion will continue to refine definitions. Assignments might include defining abusive behaviors or abusive language in movies, music, or the news; identifying situations in which they consented, complied, or cooperated during a given week; or describing in detail pressures they have recognized as coercion.

As youth begin to understand the definition of abuse, they are likely to become aware of many experiences and behaviors in their history that were also abusive. New disclosures of both victimization and perpetration are common during this process. As the youth becomes aware of the elements of consent, inequalities of power, and forms of coercion, they often notice the abusive behaviors of others before recognizing their own.

When the youth has learned and understands the abuse is abuse concept and how to define abusive interactions, they can be held accountable for consistently defining all abuse in themselves and others.

Consequences, Deterrence, and Empathy

There are many reasons people might not act on abusive thoughts. The consequences of abusive behaviors will vary depending on the type of abuse. The consequences of some behaviors may be in the reaction of others, or in the harm to self, or in damage to someone or something the person cares about. Consequences for those who are abusive are sometimes imposed punishments or restrictions. Being aware of consequences for self, others, or property sometimes acts as a deterrent. Deterrence can be discussed in terms of external restraint, limited access, punishment, aversion, and sympathetic and empathic recognition and responses (see Chapters 7, 11, and 12).

External restraints may include removal from the home, placement in residential or correctional facilities, and/or limited access imposed by supervision and conditions that restrict personal freedoms. Punishment may be imposed by the family or the courts.

Aversion and empathy are internal deterrents that will be goals of the treatment process. Aversive deterrence is the result of the discomfort or anxiety a youth experiences when he is aware of the potential consequences of a behavior. For some, aversive deterrence may be the highest level achieved. Empathic deterrence is based in awareness of the harmfulness of an imagined behavior and is the highest form of deterrence. This is a long-term goal of treatment and is unlikely to occur in a meaningful sense until much later in the treatment process as the youth develops empathic skills.

It may be helpful in discussing the various levels of deterrence to relate to common learning experiences. External restraint may be demonstrated in the example of a parent putting a fence around the play area to prevent the child from running into the street. Limited access would be the parent's putting a fence around the swimming pool in order to keep the child from falling in. Learning as a result of punishment occurs not only in spanking but also in learning not to touch the hot stove as a result of being burned. Learning to stay away from skunks is the best example of aversive conditioning wherein that which initially looks cute and cuddly proves itself noxious by its odor.

These examples also demonstrate how learning situations may inadvertently teach lessons other than that which is intended or desirable. For instance, the child who must learn about hot stoves by being burned may also learn that the world is a dangerous place rather than a safe, protected environment. Similarly, the child who is spanked or beaten to deter further misbehavior may learn that physical force and violence are methods of achieving control over others. Another lesson of aversion demonstrates aversive experiences as a betrayal of one's trust in one's own perception.

Early discussions of deterrence may later be recalled in social skills training and relationship building as the group explores the ways in which they deter others from getting close enough to form friendships and achieve intimacy. At that time assignments may challenge group members to identify their own obnoxious or distancing patterns of behavior, as well as confronting these same patterns in the peer group. Self-control can be discussed in terms of deterring themselves from negative behavior, as well as not deterring others from desirable interactions. Assignments might include completing a decision matrix that identifies the positive and negative outcomes for choices they make to engage or not to engage in abusive behaviors.

RECOGNIZING CYCLES OF FUNCTIONING

From birth, every encounter is assimilated into one's unique worldview. Each individual is probably most affected by the earliest experiences during infancy and childhood, developing perceptions and beliefs about whatever is encountered. Perceptions and reactions to subsequent experiences are influenced by past experience, and incorporate all information into a continually evolving belief system. Testing the environment's ability to meet basic needs, those behaviors that elicit positive or negative responses are remembered and the child begins to develop predictions, assumptions, and expectations about self, others, and the world as well as behaviors to navigate and manipulate the environment. Developmental and learning theories rely on the universal predictability of human developmental processes.

Over time, patterns of behavior evolve and certain responses come to be associated with certain situations. At times responses are self-protective, at times behaviors are aimed at self gratification, and at times behaviors seek connections with others. If responses achieve the intended purpose, contentment and a sense of self-efficacy and control follows; if they do not, unhappiness, confusion, or a sense of helplessness may follow. Behaviors that are perceived as successful in meeting needs or goals continue. Different responses or repeated attempts at the original unsuccessful behavior may continue to be repeated as well. Beliefs, perceptions, or responses may be modified by additional or conflicting experiences but over time, beliefs, perceptions, and responses become more ingrained and may become habits. The whole process represents the uniqueness, personal characteristics, and adaptive style of the individual. Some patterns may be healthy and some may be unhealthy, but they are all part of the individual's personal style of navigating and manipulating the environment in attempts to fulfill basic needs.

The concept of the cycle (see Figure 17.3) facilitates an understanding of behavior in the context of overall functioning, both generally and specifically, and distinguishes situational, cognitive, affective, and behavioral elements. Once identified, these elements can be addressed with clinical interventions that target cognitive, behavioral, emotional, and ecological symptoms. Clinicians are trained in various models and modalities, and may use a wide array of interventions differentially with individual youth, just as they would any other client. It is not the interventions that are unique; it is being able to recognize what the elements are that require intervention.

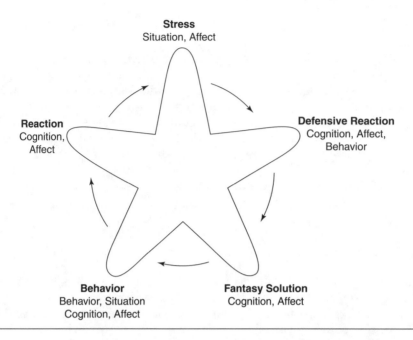

Figure 17.3 A Simplistic Adaptation of the Abuse Cycle

The cycles described in Chapters 8 and 9 represent a general style of responding that may be compensatory or retaliatory and in the event of sexually abusive behavior has involved an abusive expression of a sexual behavior.

The various elements of the cycle interact and result in the functioning observed by others. Cognitive and affective elements occur in response to, and are influenced by, situational elements, and the cumulative process influences behavioral elements, which in turn stimulate cognitive and affective elements. The various elements interact in a cyclical process that influences the youth's future experience (see Table 17.1). Treatment interventions are directed toward modifying these elements.

ELEMENTS OF THE ABUSE CYCLE: HISTORICAL, SITUATIONAL, COGNITIVE, AFFECTIVE, AND BEHAVIORAL

Historical elements are unique to each individual's development and life experience, but the origins of behavior patterns can often be traced to earlier experiences, unresolved sources of affective stress, deficits in care and coping, beliefs that influence emotional and behavioral reactions, and dysfunctional models of avoidance and compensation. Clinical work on historical elements is often aimed at making issues in the past conscious and changing coping and relationship styles.

Developmental questionnaires gather historical details from the parents' recollections, and family sessions illuminate the experiential understanding of the juvenile's life perceptions. Client and family may work together to create a family tree or geneagram that facilitates discussion of intergenerational patterns of behavior and belief systems. When family members are not available, the youth can often tell stories they heard about their history. In the context of the family, divergent perceptions of shared memories may reveal the shared emotions and define role

Table 17.1

Elements of the Abuse Cycle

Historical Elements	Cognitive Elements
Development history	View of world, basic beliefs, self-image
Early childhood attachment	Distortions, rationalizations, thinking errors
View of world, basic beliefs	Denial, minimization, overoptimism
Stressors: abuse, neglect, loss, trauma	Blaming, projection, irresponsibility
Consistency of care	Failure to consider consequences
Significant relationships	Unempathic, depersonalization, retaliatory
	Unrealistic, negative expectations
Situational Elements.	Decision making, problem solving, choice
Home, family role models	Fantasies, imagination
Peer expectations	Personalization
Structure, control, predictability	
Success, failure, expectations	*Behavioral Elements*
Relationships, events	Impulsivity, compulsivity
Supervision, opportunity	Aggression, passivity
	Control seeking, dominating
Affective Elements	Violence, exploitation, manipulation, isolation, withdrawal, avoidance
Helplessness, powerlessness, lack of control	
Degradation, humiliation, embarrassment	Sexual arousal, sexual behaviors
Abandonment, fear, distrust	Self-destructive behaviors, abusive behaviors
Guilt, blame, shame	Risk taking, thrill seeking
Victimization, persecution	Interactions, social competencies, deficits
Lack of empathy, insecure attachment, affective memories, connectedness	Addictive behaviors

expectations. A youth who creates a lifeline can use it to integrate past and present perceptions.

Most of the youth who abuse have experienced some type of maltreatment, trauma, or a lack of consistent nurturing and empathic care. These historical elements carry emotional associations and contribute to their basic beliefs and the capacities they develop to cope with the world. This emotional and cognitive baggage from the past is often the cause of stress and, although their initial coping mechanisms may have been adaptive and protective at the time, those same strategies may become maladaptive or dysfunctional over time. Children may initially mimic or learn coping strategies from those around them, but bring with them the innate human defense mechanisms that protect them when they lack the skills or support to deal with overwhelming experiences.

The interactional models that they are exposed to are incorporated into their belief system as being representative of relationships. The youth's ability to develop and their capacity to maintain relationships are based on the quality of those initial relationships with caregivers. Youth who have positive experiences may become resilient and flexible and develop a wider range of competent coping skills.

Situational elements are external events and circumstances experienced by the youth and their family, the home and community environment the youth is exposed to, the nature of the guidance and structure provided by the youth's caregivers, and the quality of role models and interactions with family members, peers, and associates.

Situational elements contribute to the development of behavior, and play a role in the onset of specific behaviors. Sensitivity to some particular trigger precipitates the onset of a response style based in life experience. Over time, situations that evoke an emotional response reminiscent of the past can bring up the old emotions as if they too belong in the present.

Observers can often recognize the signs of emotional reactivity, but may perceive it as an "overreaction" without recognizing the connection to past issues.

Some treatment interventions are geared toward assisting the youth in recognizing sensitive emotions, identifying the developmental experience that contributed to the sensitivity, and modifying the intensity of their reactions. Other interventions address situational variables that offer foresight into the times or types of situations when those emotions are most likely to come up. Anticipatory desensitization comes with foresight, as well as affording the opportunity to consciously express those emotions before being overwhelmed by them.

When the historical elements represent traumatic experiences, the youth may be so reactive that consciously working on past issues essentially retraumatizes them. The therapist must remember that what is traumatic for one may not be for another and not make assumptions about the need for trauma treatment based simply on history. For some, medication may be helpful in managing the work on emotionally charged issues. For others, Post-Traumatic Stress Disorder (PTSD) symptoms may impede the work in treatment and evidence-based trauma treatment may be needed before they can tolerate the work of offense-specific treatment.

Affective elements in the cycle are the feelings or emotions. Some of the feelings are the emotional baggage from the past that now trigger overwhelming stress. These feelings are particularly anxiety-producing or discomforting when the youth is unaware of their origin. They are vulnerable emotions the youth would prefer not to experience, although because they are familiar a youth may be accustomed to them and the defensive reaction may be so automatic and practiced that they never allow themselves to feel vulnerable. These youth may have difficulty identifying the early parts of the cycle and deny vulnerable feelings. Other youth are so accustomed to feeling vulnerable that they are very conscious of those feelings and can easily identify feelings of helplessness, but have more difficulty recognizing how they progressed to the offending.

Anger is a secondary emotion that is part of the human defense system. Vulnerable feelings are effectively blocked by angry feelings that evoke the build-up of adrenaline, which prepares for fight or flight. Some youth become angry immediately when triggered, others move toward anger in the stepwise progression of the cycle from vulnerability, to negative expectations, to isolation, and to projecting and externalizing, and the anger grows almost subconsciously. Other youth may be consciously angry about memories or feelings from the past, and still others may be angry all the time, effectively blocking awareness of past issues and vulnerable feelings. In any case, the defensive reaction decreases the anxiety or discomfort and the goal of the fantasy that develops is to feel better (a compensatory response) or more empowered (a retaliatory, "get back" response).

Other affective elements in the cycle may occur in reaction to or association with the behavioral and cognitive elements in the cycle and may be elating, comfortable, or uncomfortable. For example, the negative expectations may bring up feelings of depression or anxiety, which in turn contribute to the tendency to have negative expectations.

The intervention for emotion is always first to VALIDATE. Denial of emotions is at the core of the defensive strategy and often the youth has had many adults deny or dismiss their emotions. Becoming more aware of internal cues is a precondition to being able to recognize and interpret the cues of others. Treatment intervention is geared toward helping the youth recognize the internal cues of emotions; experience, express, and manage the feelings; and make conscious the connections past and present.

When the work on past emotions is so overwhelming that the youth cannot tolerate it, resistance to the work may indicate a need for medication to help the youth tolerate the work. When emotional reactivity impedes the youth's ability to tolerate the issues of treatment interventions to decondition anxiety and arousal levels may be indicated, which could include neurological or pharmacological interventions to calm the reactivity before the youth can succeed in other aspects of treatment.

Cognitive elements are the thoughts that interact with both emotion and behavior. Thoughts and feelings form a chain, with every thought influencing the subsequent feelings and every feeling being interpreted in subsequent thought. Similarly, thought and behavior form an interlocking path with thought driving behavior, although the process may be so rapid for some youth that they are not even aware of the thought.

Some youth deny thoughts that they perceive as shameful or to minimize their responsibility for behaviors. Very impulsive youth are often sincere when they report that they did not think about the behavior before they acted. Cognitive elements influence the development of fantasy and plans and the decision to act when the opportunity presents. Cognitive elements also include the memories, which play a role in the sensitivity of the trigger at the onset of the response pattern, and how the current trigger is perceived.

Common cognitive elements include personalizing the behavior of others; self-deprecating thoughts; assumptions and expectations; perceptions and beliefs; control-seeking and retaliatory thinking, fantasies, plans, decisions, anticipations, assessment, and interpretations. Following abusive behaviors, thoughts reflect the second defensive phase, which thinks of ways to minimize, rationalize, or justify the behavior in order to calm the anxiety related to the meaning and potential consequences of the behavior. The sequence of cognitions represented in the cycle seems to perpetuate the cycle as one type of cognition leads to the next.

Treatment intervention is geared toward recognizing thought patterns associated with current or historical triggers and modifying the perceptions that contribute to the youth's discomfort. It is in the cognitive realm that the therapist is CHALLENGING the client to think differently, which is only rational if they have evidence that supports thinking differently. Efforts are also geared toward assisting the youth in making accurate attributions of responsibility regarding their own and others' behavior, interrupting the sequence of cognitions associated with the maladaptive pattern, rejecting thoughts of abusive behavior, modifying negative assumptions and self-talk, and modifying beliefs that support the misattribution of responsibility or sanction abusive behavior, influencing decision making and managing fantasies.

Ultimately, it is in the cognitive realm that treatment offers the client both evidence to support being more hopeful, and the control they seek. The message to the youth is that there are many times that they do not have control over the situation and that they should not try to control others, but that the one thing they can always control is how they think about what is going on. Cognitive restructuring and asking for help in rethinking things are relevant tools.

Behavioral elements are the actions of the cycle. "Acting out" is a way to communicate, express, or reduce the tensions associated with emotionally charged issues. Behavior may occur in reaction to thoughts or feelings or to achieve some type of gratification. The actions in the cycle include isolating, controlling, dominating, interacting, stalking, and the abusive behavior. Qualities associated with the behaviors include impulsivity and compulsivity, risk taking and thrill seeking, aggression and passivity, violence and exploitation, and self-defeating behaviors. The youth may use power struggles to increase the anger and adrenaline, which masks the vulnerable feelings. Provoking parents or peers into arguments and fights in the past may transfer into resistance and oppositional behavior in treatment. The therapist must recognize that the dynamics of power struggles reinforce the cycle and resist the youth's provocation. Sexual arousal and masturbation fall within the behavioral realm as well and will be discussed in relation to offense-specific treatment.

THERAPEUTIC PROCESSING OF CURRENT CYCLES

It is often in the process of revealing childhood experiences that offenders are first able to access and acknowledge the feelings of vulnerability and helplessness that they have denied in their more recent experiences. It is also in relation to childhood memories that the group members are first able to express empathy for each other, and through that experience of empathic responses, become able to express some empathy for themselves as children. Cognitive, educational, and experiential techniques can then work to confront the negative reinforcers of their subsequent behaviors and challenge the underlying beliefs that have allowed them to cause harm to themselves and others.

The juvenile whose lifeline is shown in Figure 17.4 engaged in lying, stealing, and sneaky behavior from the time he was very young. His older and younger siblings had never displayed these irresponsible patterns. At the time of his birth, his mother's first marriage was disintegrating, and his father was both physically and emotionally abusive. An older sibling took on the role of nurturer and protector, and the mother dealt first with her fear and guilt relative to the bad marriage and subsequently with her fears relative to separating and becoming self-sufficient. Her issues were compounded by the guilt she felt that her children were inadequately cared for when she returned to work. She described her relationship with the client as always "different" from those she had with her other children; saying she never felt close to this child. Younger siblings born later in a subsequent marriage all seemed securely attached and mother reported good relationships with them.

Identifying the chronic pattern of misbehavior encompassed the lying, stealing, and sneaky behaviors as all being part of the abuse problem. Mother's recognition of the relationship being "different" correlated with the initial evaluation, suggesting the boy had an "anxious attachment style." Hearing accounts of the client feeling fearful of his mother's anger and guilty about her anguish over him, while hearing the mother describe her fears that this child was "like his father" and her guilt that she was not a good enough mother, the therapist realized that the shared emotions in this parent-child dyad were fear and guilt. Not surprisingly, work with the cycle revealed that one of the primary triggers for the boy was fear, and that consequently,

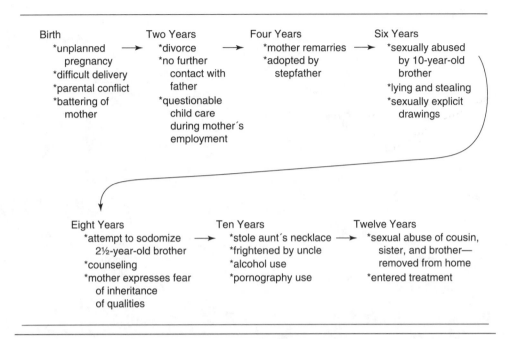

Figure 17.4   Lifeline of a Sexually Abusive Youth

the shame and anxiety following the abusive behaviors, including the sexual abuse, was actually a reinforcer, because it connected him to his mother's concern for him.

When emotional triggers and reinforcers are identified, their role in the cycle can be illustrated relative to the sexual abuse and other problem behaviors as well. This particular client described "feeling very small" whenever his mother confronted him, and that small, fearful feeling became one of his primary indicators of risk. "Feeling small" seemed to encompass the vulnerability, helplessness, and lack of importance he had experienced early in life. In family and group sessions, his body language would convey this "small" feeling as he seemed to diminish visibly when confronted. The fact that this 16-year-old was now strong, athletic, and almost 6 feet tall was part of the ironic unfolding of his self-image. As he restructured his thinking, he became able to maintain his stature and more able to own and control his responses to fear. As he experienced competency and pride, he became less at risk and more self-satisfied.

In the treatment group, consistent labels for the various points on the abuse cycle create a common language within the group that the therapist begins to relate to each client's reports of past and current functioning. As they begin to understand and define the elements of the cycle, group members begin to take on the role of identifying the cycle in the accounts of their peers, and finally they begin to see similar patterns and common characteristics in themselves. Over time, the youth understands the various concepts and labels and sees how they apply to situations, thoughts, feelings, and behavior. The cycle is used to promote understanding of past and present patterns, as well as to identify risk in the future and develop more functional response patterns. The various interventions apply to each element in the cycle. Each youth's cycle of situations, thoughts, feelings, and behaviors is unique

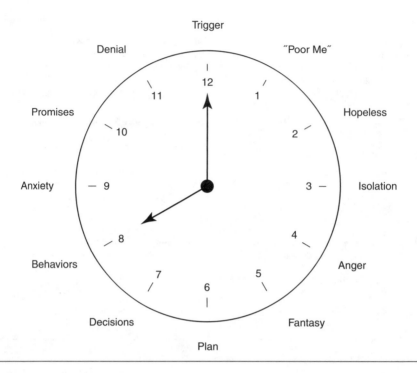

Figure 17.5   Twelve-Part Cycle

and descriptors for the elements and stages of the cycle may be simplified to suit the client's intellectual and conceptual ability, but the process of identifying predictable patterns in themselves becomes a source of self-control.

The 12-part cycle depicted in Figure 17.5 is useful in working with 10- to 18-year-old youth, because it uses very simple terms and creates an association with the face of a clock.

The group process provides a forum for defining abuse, labeling body language and affective cues, challenging nonempathic responses, sharing perceptions, and defining shameful thoughts and painful emotions such as embarrassment, sadness, humiliation, helplessness, and loss. Client-centered psychotherapy techniques aid in the identification and labeling of feelings, and the group milieu can demonstrate empathic relationships. The goal of exploring and defining the full range of emotions—both positive and negative—is to clarify for the individual the role of emotions in triggering or reinforcing behavior patterns while helping the client learn healthy aspects of experiencing and coping with feelings.

Cognitive work requires the ability to describe thoughts separate from the associated situations, feelings, and behaviors, even though they interact together in the youth's functioning. The denial, rationalizations, and distortions that are so characteristic of the abusive cycle are cognitive processes. In the group process, existential, rational emotive, Adlerian, and reality-based approaches help to access and challenge the thoughts of the youth. Many of the historic and affective techniques make important contributions to the understanding of patterns of thought and the individual's view of the world. Other cognitive interventions include visualization exercises and the psychoeducational components.

Ultimately treatment works toward self-monitoring and self-control, and the cycle is primarily a tool to facilitate communication. As the youth identifies experiences and personalizes the elements in the cycle, self-awareness identifies the red flags that characterize each individual's pattern and new knowledge and skills provide ways to interrupt the pattern. Consistent definition of all abuse increases the client's recognition of abusive thoughts. As each youth begins to identify specific situations that trigger their defenses, safety planning not only addresses the risk of opportunities to reoffend or for allegations to be made, but also models foresight and planning to prepare for predictable stressors. Situational elements are also affected by those aspects of treatment that change the individual's thoughts and behaviors in interaction with others.

When the youth identify triggers and reinforcers, their role in the cycle can be illustrated relative to the sexual abuse and other problem behaviors as well. Throughout treatment, the youth receives the message that there are many situations they cannot control; therefore, the focus of treatment is to learn to control themselves in all situations. The question is simply, "What do I have control over here?" Changing their thinking and their own behavior is the key to self-control. As the youth begin to demonstrate the skills and motivation for self-control, the responsibility for behavior management should be gradually transferred with decreases in the external controls of containment and increased opportunities for the youth to practice self-control.

CONFRONTATION

Confrontation is one of the least understood techniques in this field of treatment. Many interventions or interactions with the youth are likely to involve an element of feedback or be challenging of the youth's beliefs or behaviors. The combination of confrontation and support is most useful as it originates in a psychologically safe environment, whether the dyad of individual therapy, the family system, or the peer group. Adolescents are sometimes less resistant when challenged by their peers than in similar interactions with adults, although how they respond to confrontation by different persons can be indicative of their issues. The role of confrontation in the treatment of abusive youth is clear, but the concept is often misunderstood.

Often the confusion seems to relate to misattributions of anger, degradation, and shame to the process. The goal of confrontation is to provide feedback to help the clients be aware of the nature of their thoughts and behaviors and reach a breakthrough that illuminates their understanding of a concept, helping them to own the thought or behavior in question. It is a tool that guides and supports the client's process of change.

When confrontation is based in anger and shame and expressed through yelling, name calling, and put-downs, it may be a powerful experience that influences the client's thinking, but the change may increase defensiveness and self-protection rather than understanding by triggering the client's sense of victimization, helplessness, and poor self-image. It is the authors' belief that shame and victimization are inherent in the problem; they are not the solution. Confrontation should be a calm and rational process in a direct and purposeful progression toward an identified goal.

Confrontation by peers is likely to be abusive at times when they are all in treatment for abusive behaviors. The therapist must be vigilant in both defining abusive dynamics in the room and also in modeling gentle respectful confrontation themselves. The dynamics and distortions that allow abusive behaviors must be confronted, and the beliefs that support risk must be challenged.

It is imperative for the clinician to be aware of the client's past experiences of assault. These youth have often been battered, both verbally and physically, and frequently they expect to be maligned and threatened. The goal of confrontation is to define and challenge dishonest, irrational, or distorted thoughts and exploitive behavior. The youth needs to become uncomfortable with irresponsible thoughts or behavior, but further damage to self-image is counterproductive. Confrontation should be undertaken only to help the client's self-awareness and change process, never as a vehicle for the clinician's own anger, frustration, or vicarious control issues (Davis, 1989).

Three factors are crucial in regard to confrontations: timing, relationship, and impact. The timing of confrontation must consider the therapist's preparedness, the constraints of the treatment session, and the youth's readiness to hear the issues. If the therapist is angry or frustrated or has personalized the client's behavior, it is wise to delay a confrontation in order to clarify the youth's needs and allow the therapist to formulate a clear and rational course. Supervision or collegial discussions are useful in clarifying the goal and strategy of an anticipated confrontation. Another aspect of the time factor is that of having adequate time; effective confrontation needs to proceed without distraction and may require some follow-up time to monitor the impact and process the material with other group members. It is better to wait until a later session to begin than to be interrupted in the process. Also, if a youth is just beginning treatment, confrontation may stop with simply identifying something for future work without pushing the client to consider it at that moment.

The second factor relative to confrontation is relationship. In order to avoid the "battered client syndrome" (Davis, 1989), confrontation must convey a genuine sense of empathy and concern and provide helpful information. Coming from either the clinician or the peer group, the desired change is unlikely to occur outside a respectful and supportive relationship. Without a positive relationship, confrontation may be experienced as an assault. Care must be taken that indiscriminate confrontation does not inadvertently reflect a dynamic of scapegoating within the peer group, always remembering that "abuse is the problem, not the solution."

The effectiveness of confrontation is increased by accurate definition of the specific thoughts being confronted, sensitivity to the youth's ability to hear feedback at a particular time, and the youth's readiness or willingness to risk self-examination. This readiness is increased and the confrontation is more likely to be heard and considered if some positive feedback regarding associated thoughts is included (for example, "I think you are absolutely right about . . . but where I see a problem is. . . . ").

Finally, the impact of confrontation may well be the most important variable. The reasonable level of confrontation is determined by the impact it has on the client (Ross, 1987). Although the level may exceed what the therapist is personally comfortable with or may raise resistance in other group members, it is the impact on the person being confronted that must be used to gauge the effective level. Some youth acknowledge that they need to be pushed to do the work of treatment, while others cannot tolerate any pressure. Individual differences must be respected. A goal is for the youth's discomfort with his or her thoughts or behaviors to become sufficient to motivate the desired change. It is often immediately apparent when confrontation becomes counterproductive because the defensive reaction cuts off effective communication and learning. Acknowledging this and changing course should be consciously articulated and models empathic recognition and responses in how the therapists change their own behavior in response to the cues of the client.

The role of co-therapy is especially important when confrontation is employed. While the confronting therapist encourages the desired change, his or her attention is best focused on the youth who is being confronted in order to follow the cognitive progression and monitor the impact. The co-therapist can observe the confrontation while staying tuned in to the reactions and resistance of other group members in order to be prepared to process issues with the group. Co-therapists may also need to trade roles occasionally if a client becomes engaged in a standoff. Sometimes the observing therapist is able to comment on a standoff and suggest an alternative thought or approach, taking over to complete the desired progression when the original therapist has hit a brick wall. Some co-therapists trade off in a "good guy–bad guy" parlay wherein one confronts and the other resolves. The key word here is *trade*, so that neither therapist is cast permanently in the "bad guy" role. A combination of confrontation and nurturance is an ideal combination.

Different clients and different situations require different levels of confrontation. These levels should represent a continuum of assertiveness rather than force. The mildest confrontation may simply identify the area of concern and wonder about it, seeking clarification and understanding from the client (for example, "I hear you saying . . . I wonder if you can help me understand"). The client may achieve the desired change under the challenge of explaining himself. The moderately assertive confrontation may identify the concern and challenge more directly (e.g., "I hear. . . . That has not been my experience. How can you explain?").

In a major confrontation, the therapist again identifies the concern and confronts the denial or distortion with disparate facts (e.g., "I hear . . . and yet I know. . . ."). In this most assertive confrontation, the challenge may be for honesty more than a cognitive shift relative to the identified concern, and the therapist must convey expectations relative to the therapeutic relationship while acknowledging the youth's dilemma (as in, "We have to be honest with each other. I know that it may be difficult to believe this process is helpful"; or "You seem to be seeing it like . . . but it appears to me that. . . .").

It is important to recognize that defensiveness is a normal reaction to confrontation. When confrontation is perceived as a threat to one's self, instinct dictates flight or fight. When confrontation is unavoidable, it is natural to defend one's self. The clinician must remove the perceived threat and model nonexploitive resolution (Davis, 1989). When the client has shut down or become argumentative, nothing helpful ensues. Better to simply "sign-off" and turn to another subject or person, with an expectation of revisiting the more emotionally charged issue later.

Early confrontations in the treatment process may be related to the behavior of record and may draw on police reports and victim statements in confronting denial or minimization of past abusive behavior. Sometimes confrontation may include new information and be part of the educational process. In other instances, the process of confrontation may lead the therapist to an "aha!" experience by demonstrating a lack of knowledge or understanding by the client that requires more basic education. As treatment progresses, confrontations are often related to old patterns reappearing or the failure to generalize treatment concepts to current situations, choices, and functioning. Consider the following example.

A youth might say: "I never said a word to him. It's not my problem if he's intimidated by me." The goal is to confront the client's denial of psychological intimidation and define the coercive behavior.

THERAPIST: I would like to talk to you about group today. I noticed that John suddenly changed his report of what happened in school yesterday. My observation is that he changed his story after you stared at him.

CLIENT: I didn't stare at him. Are you telling me I can't look at someone?

THERAPIST: John was describing the fight yesterday involving your friend Marcus. I noticed that you sat up, leaned forward in your chair, and stared at John. I confronted you numerous times before you stopped. Do you remember when we were discussing pre-assault patterns in group a few weeks ago?

CLIENT: Yes.

THERAPIST: What were some of the terms we used to describe the tactics a person might use besides verbal threats and physical force to get someone to comply?

CLIENT: I don't remember.

THERAPIST: We called it emotional or psychological intimidation. We discussed how past abusive behavior, body language, or a look can be part of an abusive pattern. Do you remember now?

CLIENT: Yes.

THERAPIST: Do you remember how you and other group members shared experiences of both victimization and perpetration and talked about how it feels to be intimidated and afraid because of someone's facial expressions or body language?

CLIENT: Yes, but I don't want to talk about it.

THERAPIST: What were your thoughts and feelings about John reporting Marcus' aggressive behavior?

CLIENT: Marcus is my friend and he's going to get into trouble over this. I wanted John to shut up and mind his own business.

THERAPIST: Was it your intention to give John that message when you stared at him?

CLIENT: Maybe.

THERAPIST: Do you think that he may have felt intimidated and threatened by you and that is why he changed his story?

CLIENT: I suppose.

When the therapist is confronting the client's inadequate participation in treatment, the consequences of nonparticipation need not lie within the group but rather are presented relative to the client's being clear about the choices he is making regarding current and future conditions; that is, violation of the court orders for treatment and risk of reoffense.

LEARNING TO USE THE CYCLE

The concept of the cycle is introduced very early in treatment in a didactic framework, like an algebra formula that must be learned before it can be applied to a problem. Just as mathematical terms must be understandably defined before the equation makes sense, the elements of the cycle must also be defined. Assignments can help the juvenile learn to distinguish situations, thoughts, feelings, and behavior. These early assignments may include such activities as making lists of feelings, describing situations, reporting thoughts, and recording the behavior of others.

Clients might be instructed to observe others in a public place where they do not have knowledge of other persons' thoughts or feelings in order to clarify behavior and to notice those things we infer about thoughts and feelings on the basis of body language. Group members can analyze the incidents that the client describes to the group in order to separate the various elements.

As group members become able to distinguish these elements, their reporting of thoughts and descriptions of feelings are enhanced by writing assignments such as journal and letter writing. Cognitive and affective statements can be differentiated throughout the group process by the therapist's observations as well as direct questions. Traditional psychotherapeutic techniques can be used with a focus on the relationship of the cycle. For example:

"I hear you saying that you think. Now tell me what you feel about. . . . " or
"It sounds as if you are feeling. . . . Can you tell me what thoughts make you feel that way?"

This exchange can be followed by pointing out for the group the presence of both thoughts and feelings in the client's report. As the youth describes problems he encounters or cognitive or affective aspects, it is helpful to write those on the board to assist the group with beginning to see how the various elements of the cycle interact. It is important for the youth to begin to recognize that he exhibits parts of the cycle several times each day, and that these things are not always problematic. The "normalizing" of the pattern helps overcome resistance in the clients, and they particularly enjoy recognizing it in their parents or the therapist.

In preparation for teaching the client to use the cycle, the therapist can collect anecdotal information in group discussions that demonstrates the elements of the cycle. The therapist can use these examples of the cycle to make connections between current material and the cycle that is being discussed. A whiteboard may be helpful in illustrating the cycle for the group. For example, the therapist can say, *"Let's see if we can relate the incident Shane described in our last group to the cycle. Shane reported that he and his mother had a big fight because his stereo was too loud. But what had happened before the fight? I find that blasting one's parents with the stereo is often a power-and-control behavior, so let's see if we can make the cycle work here."* Beginning with the power-and-control behavior, the therapist helps the group recall other things Shane had said about the incident and helps Shane describe his thoughts and feelings, filling in key words and phrases in the applicable places on the figure on the whiteboard:

Situation: Mother says she does not want Shane to spend the weekend with her because she has a lot to do.
Triggers: Feeling disappointment and hurt.
Victim-stance perception: "She doesn't think I can help her."
Negative expectation: "She will never let me help her with anything."
Feeling: Rejection.
Isolation and withdrawal: Going in his room alone.
Power-and-control behaviors: Slamming door, blasting stereo, arguing with mother about the volume.
Fantasy: "Maybe I should run away."
Retaliatory thought: "Then she'll feel sorry."
Plan: None.

Further discussion can then explore how the feelings might have been expressed directly instead of through behavior (e.g., "Mom, when you say you don't want me with you, it makes me feel hurt. I'm disappointed that you don't want me to help you this weekend"), or how feelings might have been changed by restructuring thoughts (e.g., "Just because I can't help her this weekend doesn't mean I can't do something else helpful"). The implications of the fantasy for Shane and the consequences of acting on the fantasy can be discussed. Finally, the retaliatory thought can be shown to parallel the trigger feeling: that making someone else feel bad would somehow "get back" for the youth's own bad feeling.

In this illustration, the cycle did not run its full course, but the issues were not resolved. Mother and Shane fought about the volume of the stereo but did not resolve Shane's issues. This event would be considered unresolved, leaving Shane at risk to feel angry more quickly and escalate his conflicts with mom in future situations that cause him to feel disappointment or rejection. Youth can often recognize how many conflicts are repeated with parents and that eventually with enough conflict Shane might think he would be justified in actually running away. The avoidant function of the pattern is clear, that the anger and power struggles cover over the sad feelings, and with each repetition it becomes less likely that Shane's mother would recognize how he really feels.

As each aspect of the cycle is explained, clients can be given assignments to monitor thoughts, feelings, or behavior during the week and list examples of ways they exhibit the concept. A format such as Exhibit 17.1 can provide some structure. Typically, youth may spend time reflecting and recalling things but may write minimally or not at all on the actual assignments. When the group discusses each individual's assignment, the client becomes more willing to share thoughts that were not written down.

Review of homework in the group helps group members to begin recognizing their own manifestations of these elements in more depth. Requesting the group members to make note of three examples of incidents that occur during the week that elicit a feeling of helplessness or vulnerability is a first step. The group can then work on identifying the progression of thoughts and behaviors through the fantasy or planning stages. Group discussion of these assignments should always include the identification of nonaggressive solutions for coping with the situation, as well as identification of the failure of the acting-out behaviors to solve the dilemma or to make the client feel better in an enduring way.

After the group has been involved in some illustrations of the cycle, they can be challenged to begin assignments relating the cycle specifically to their own abusive behaviors. They should look back to identify what issues were occurring at the time they first started engaging in the behavior, their emotional reactions to events, and subsequent thinking.

In homogeneous groups where all the youth have the same type of abusive behavior, whether sexual offending, substance abuse, and so forth, the retrospective application of the cycle elements to the early manifestation of the behavior and how the pattern may have changed with repetition might be discussed in the group. In mixed population groups the group work might be less personal, and more detailed exploration is referred into individual or family sessions. Modeling reasonable boundaries around personal issues requires some guidance from the therapist as youth often have little understanding of personal boundaries and privacy.

Situation: _____

_____

Feelings:_____

_____

Thoughts:_____

_____

How do you feel now?	What bad thing did you expect?*
_____	_____
_____	_____
Did you get caught?*	Did you isolate?*
_____	_____
_____	_____
What did you think would happen?	What were you angry about?*
_____	_____
_____	_____
Did you hurt someone?	Power struggles:_____
Yourself?_____	_____
Property?_____	
What was your plan?*	What did you imagine to make you feel better?*
_____	_____
_____	_____
_____	_____

*What were you thinking?

Exhibit 17.1   Juvenile Group Cycle

For youth who have difficulty identifying trigger situations or events or cognitive aspects, or who have more impulsive or compulsive patterns, journal keeping may be of benefit. Keeping a daily log of any signs they notice can help the therapist and client identify patterns. Initially, the youth might be requested to describe situations that elicit feelings of helplessness, control, or anger and then to write down associated thinking. Detailing what the situation meant to the client, retaliatory thoughts, or negative expectations will begin to help the youth identify the early phases of the cycle. The youth might then be asked to include retaliatory or control behaviors and fantasies, and for those with sexual issues, to include sexual thinking.

Therapeutic journaling must be taught like other interventions. For decades people believed that venting anger got rid of it due to the physical tension reduction that follows. More recent research on anger and aggression has clearly demonstrated that the feelings of relief are short-term and the anger is actually greater in subsequent episodes. Just as youth and parents must learn that "venting" or "acting out" anger does not actually work, youth must be taught that writing pages and pages of angry abusive thoughts or problematic sexual fantasies reinforces the very patterns they are working to change. Instructions for journaling should limit angry, abusive tirades or problematic sexual fantasies to a sentence, a paragraph, or a page, and then redirect to other things.

Providing clarifying questions and feedback when reviewing the journal is critical, as the therapist must monitor what is being written. In order to minimize unintended risks it is important to limit journaling that simply reinforces abusive fantasies. Feedback should always define abusive elements in whatever the youth is writing or saying and be directed toward healthy alternatives. Psychological safety is a prerequisite for any expectation of legitimate engagement in sharing the thoughts most closely associated with sexual abuse. Initially, it is quite risky for the client to disclose thinking and can be uncomfortable for the therapist to hear or read it. The therapist can articulate the cues of discomfort and validate the reasonableness of that discomfort, while monitoring the need to redirect or process the sensitive issues that arise. It is important to respect the client's vulnerability with assignments that require disclosure of personal issues unless clear safety issues are apparent. Some youth benefit from short-term journal assignments, and others may benefit from keeping a journal throughout treatment.

Establishing the abuse-specific agenda and defining the concepts, the therapist can relate every subsequent intervention back to one or more of those concepts. Individual treatment plans will become more and more specific as the therapist ascertains more details about the risks and assets, frequency and types of abusiveness, and the developmental and contextual framework of the youth. Interventions that address the contextual phenomenology of the youth will be relevant to the client's sense of safety and expectations of self and others, and so are relevant to the early phase of the cycle. Interventions that address growth and development and increase competency are relevant to the youth's sense of self-esteem and competence and will counter negative expectations of failure and rejection, as well as providing options for more functional solutions.

Therapists, staff, teachers, and parents do well to be creative in developing interventions based on a goal orientation, and treatment providers must be prepared to articulate the relationship between the referring problem, the interventions, and the goals of treatment. Courts, social services, and managed care companies cannot be expected to understand the relevance of specific risks and assets to the referring problems without the therapist being able to explain the connections. In describing the relationship between treatment interventions and treatment goals, the primary goal is to change abusive patterns. Therefore, it is useful to think about what elements of the cycle might be affected by various interventions. Table 17.2 outlines some of those connections.

EDUCATION AND ASSIGNMENTS

Meaningful participation in the treatment process and the demonstration of understanding and change relevant to the abuse cycle are enhanced by a variety of structured, psychoeducational components. The specific components may be eclectic and are designed to develop the youth's ability to function differently and reject the avoidant patterns and abusive behaviors of the past. Treatment is not something the therapist does to the client but is designed to help the youth achieve self-control. The youth is the only one who can implement control of thoughts, expression of feelings, and functional behaviors.

Although the needs and deficits of each individual vary, some of the more common areas of treatment are presented here with suggestions of topics and assignments. Equally important are the interventions that improve social skills and competence, which can involve the caregivers. Homework assignments reinforce the educational components of treatment and can demonstrate that the client is learning things that are useful outside of treatment sessions.

Educational, psychotherapeutic, vocational, or recreational programs may be indicated to address skill deficits, psychological conditions, and competency issues

Table 17.2
Goal-Oriented Interventions for the Cycle

Historical Elements	*Cognitive Elements*
Family therapy	Phenomenological reporting, journals
Psychotherapy (person-centered, humanistic)	Cognitive restructuring
Biography, memories	Confrontation, accountability
Family tree, genograms	Thought stopping
Lifeline	Covert sensitization
Role definition	Social skills, relationship building
Situational Elements	Visualization, guided fantasies
Supervision, structure restrictions	Problem solving, decision making
Family therapy	Empathy training
Competency, self-image	Group process
Risk management, risk taking	Psychotherapy (existential, rational emotive therapy, Adlerian, and reality-based)
Temperament	Risk taking, expectations
Peer culture	Values clarification
Psychotherapy	
Affective Elements	*Behavioral Elements*
Identification and labeling	Supervision, structure, restrictions
Journaling	Positive and negative reinforcers
Group process	Logical consequences, impulse control
Psychotherapy (traditional, rational emotive)	External controls, group process
Anger management	Arousal conditioning
Empathy training	Behavior modification, social skills
	Systematic sensitization and desensitization
	Psychotherapy (reality, behavioral)

that are unique to the individual but not relevant to either the abuse-specific or offense-specific elements of treatment. Drawing on community resources to improve the client's overall functioning and competency supports the treatment process and demonstrates the therapist's concern for the client's future success.

COGNITIVE RESTRUCTURING

Cognitive restructuring is a concrete aspect of treatment that involves identifying and changing the thoughts that support or exacerbate the risk of abusive and maladaptive behaviors. Thinking errors, distortions, and expectations about self, relationships, events, the world, and so forth, must be modified and the client needs to be responsible for how behavior affects others. The youth must change patterns of thinking, decision making, attitudes, and knowledge by identifying, creating, and testing nonabusive and more adaptive ways of thinking.

Initially, many youth have very rigid beliefs and thoughts that seem very reasonable to them, but may seem distorted or extreme to others. Early in work with those who sexually offend, the concepts of thinking errors and cognitive distortions supported a lot of cognitive work aimed at changing the thinking of the client. Youth were taught to identify a long list of thoughts that would support irresponsible, illegal, and abusive behaviors, and then to change such thoughts.

As appreciation of the reality of these youths' experiences in relationships and in the world increased, it became apparent that many of their beliefs were not in fact "distortions" or "errors," but were actually either defense mechanisms or realistic appraisals of their life experience. Youth were being taught to speak differently but often had no rational or realistic basis for believing what they were taught. The more recent emphasis on providing youth with new experiences addresses the need to provide "evidence" that supports thinking differently.

The therapist must listen closely and observe in order to understand how each youth does think about or view the world. Autobiographies, lifelines, and journaling about past or present occurrences, and statements in current functioning can provide clues for the therapist about individual thinking styles and beliefs. The therapist must first recognize and validate prior life experiences that have supported the client's beliefs or created the need for cognitive defenses (such as minimization, justification, rationalization, intellectualization, and denial) before suggesting that there might be other ways to think about things. Providing evidence that contrasts with prior life experiences creates a basis for thinking differently and changing one's view of the world. Those new experiences are a product of therapeutic relationships with clinicians and caregivers, healthy development, and normalizing activities.

The basis for beliefs and attitudes, and therefore the types of thinking that need to be addressed, will be different for different youth, although there will be some commonality within the different subtypes of youth. For example, the youth with Delinquent Lifestyle characteristics are more likely to manifest some of the thoughts and beliefs that Yochelson and Samenow (1976) had identified as "criminal thinking," which supports law breaking and egocentric, manipulative patterns of thinking; whereas the youth characterized by Psychosocial Deficits may think badly of themselves and have negative expectations and self-defeating thoughts that reflect disorganized or insecure attachment styles. Youth characterized by Pedophilic interests would manifest a completely different pattern of thinking to support sexual offending as compared to youth who commit rapes or sexually harass peers.

Considering types of thinking, interventions such as exploring the moral inventory, values, knowledge and beliefs; anticipatory desensitization and preplanned coping responses; disposing of criminal thinking by reasoning; or the development of anticipatory mental strategies for changing thoughts; are all relevant cognitive interventions. Once there is evidence that the youth characterized as having a delinquent lifestyle has a basis to think differently, feedback will challenge thoughts and beliefs that indicate that the youth feels superior to others, should dominate others, and so forth, with more responsible, empathic perceptions. When the youth characterized by psychosocial deficits has acquired some new skills and experienced some success in new relationships, their negative expectations can be challenged and self-abusive thoughts be defined. Those youth with aggressive or exploitive beliefs about sexuality must know how to define abuse, become aware of victim impacts, and learn what the laws are about sexual behaviors before they can be held accountable for changing their beliefs about sexuality.

Rational emotive therapists (Ellis, 1962; and others) introduce counter thoughts through a structured process that challenges the client to identify perceptions and assumptions that contribute to or exacerbate negative feelings. The process of

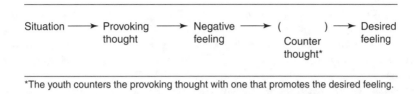

*The youth counters the provoking thought with one that promotes the desired feeling.

Figure 17.6 Cognitive Restructuring

cognitive restructuring alters affective responses by changing one's perception or thinking about the situation (see Figure 17.6).

Youth can be taught to counter the thinking that exacerbates the emotional elements of the cycle with thoughts that promote more desirable or benign feelings. As this process becomes clear to the client, expectations of actually using the technique to correct irrational and distorted thoughts can increase.

Examples of counter thoughts that often work to interrupt the cycle might include the following:

Depersonalizing other's behavior: "That person's rudeness is not about me."
Competency beliefs: "I think I can, I think I can. . . . "
Reaching out: "I can ask xxxx for help."
Control seeking: "I can't control others. What I can do differently is. . . . "
Fantasy solutions: "That would be abusive; I'm not an abusive person anymore."

Approaches that increase the client's ability to relate to others in a reciprocal way, increasing awareness of the impact of behavior on others, and developing an ability to be interdependent with others without controlling or being controlled are clearly relevant to decreasing abuse and increasing success in relationships. Learning to solve problems and make decisions that are not based on unrealistic expectations or faulty assumptions improves the client's ability to function in a way that does not involve domination of others.

Learning to interrupt thoughts that corrode or discount deterrents, cut off fear, or allow super-optimism (thinking one can get away with things) is critical to interrupting the immediate antecedents to decisions to act abusively. Critical to motivating change is some level of self-disgust or dissatisfaction with one's behavior.

It is not effective to approach the client in a punitive or angry way to motivate change, as that will challenge assumptions of superiority in some and undermine self-image in others, eliciting defensiveness in both. Instead, techniques should be directed toward rational and informative approaches that facilitate the development of open communication and learning, bringing the youth some new level of understanding of themselves (Berenson, 1987).

Empathy

Affective education is utilized to help youth learn to accurately recognize and respond to their own emotional experiences, as well as the emotions of others. Although victim empathy has not been empirically linked to the risk of sexual offense recidivism (Hanson, 2006; Worling & Lansgtrom 2006), empathic recognition and responses are important in health promotion and interpersonal functioning. A majority of programs report that work on "victim empathy" is a critical component in treatment (McGrath, Cummings, & Burchard, 2003). Many techniques have been described in the field for developing victim empathy; however, in developing research methodologies to measure empathy during the early 1990s, several controversies arose.

First was in the definition of the construct itself. Most often researchers have discussed role taking or perspective taking as markers of empathy; that is, one's ability to imagine themselves in another's place and how they might feel being there. Perspective taking is related to one's ability to be sympathetic, but is not definitive of empathic recognition and responses, which are defined here as one's ability to: *Recognize the cues of emotions and needs, Interpret the meaning of such cues,* and *Respond to validate the emotion or need.* Perspective taking is the basis for sympathetic responses, which are based in the "assumption of sameness"; imagining the feeling of another, based on one's own feeling in similar experiences. Empathy is based on the "assumption of difference"; that not everyone will feel the same, even in the same experience, but that it is possible to recognize the needs and emotions of the other by recognizing the cues of emotions and needs (Bennett, 1988). One of the critical issues for the abusive youth is the need to understand that not everyone sees or feels as he does, even in the same moment in the same place and time.

Victim awareness—increasing the youth's understanding of the negative impacts abuse can have on others—may be an important step in motivating the youth to work in treatment to change abusive patterns and to use the knowledge and skills acquired in treatment in the future. Appreciation of the negative effects of abuse must begin with validation of their own negative experiences, just as empathic recognition and responses are a product of one's own experience of empathic responses. Empathy is a critical psychological health skill and is vital to the quality of all future relationships. Empathic recognition and responses should become noticeable and observable before treatment ends. To expect less is to settle for lower-level deterrents to prevent abusive interactions, which may be less likely to generalize in future relationships.

ABUSE-SPECIFIC PROGRAMMING IN GROUP LIVING AND SPECIAL NEEDS SETTINGS

Chapter 14 (Bengis) discussed the range of settings in which sexually abusive youth might receive services and the pros and cons of those settings' segregating or integrating the sexually abusive youth from or with youth who have other referring problems. Although it is clear that some sexually abusive and some violent youth pose a danger to similar-age peers and must be segregated in settings designed to manage those risks (see Chapter 21), the majority of youth who have sexually offended do not appear to pose any greater risk to peers than do many other delinquent or acting-out adolescents. The youth who abuses smaller, vulnerable children or engages in hands-off offenses against adults or strangers is often treated in outpatient, day treatment, or mixed population settings.

The notion that all youth in special needs settings constitute an at-risk population and embody many of the risks that arise from abuse issues has grown increasingly apparent. Such settings include treatment programs that specifically address sexually abusive behaviors, violent assaultive behaviors, fire-setting, vandalism, substance abuse, eating disorders, self-injurious behaviors, suicidal behaviors, and other chronic behavioral acting out. Youth with these issues may be housed in remedial settings such as residential, group, or foster care, and schooled in special education classrooms or alternative school settings.

Sometimes it is known that youth in special needs settings have been abused, but the referral into treatment is related to current behavior problems that are not viewed as abuse-related; sometimes victimization issues are very apparent in the referral, but the risk of becoming abusive has not been recognized; sometimes youth are referred for unrelated behavior problems, and it is not known until they settle into treatment that they have also been abused or abusive.

Informed supervision and therapeutic care stress behavior management and physical safety as well as many other needs that go beyond normal parenting. An abuse-specific approach enables professionals to address risks of abusive incidents in child serving settings. Achieving "observable outcomes relevant to a decreased risk of being abusive and relevant to increased capacity for success and health" poses no risk to anyone and is likely to improve future functioning. Therefore abuse-specific programming is an asset in any special needs setting, and relevant to primary, secondary, and tertiary perpetration prevention.

PLANNING FOR SAFETY IN CHILD SERVING INSTITUTIONS

Whereas in the past, the abuse of one child by another may not have been a foreseeable risk, the current body of literature on juvenile sexual offending (as well as bullying, harassment, and/or violence) supports the need to anticipate the risk of such behavior. In addition to the risk of perpetration by juveniles previously identified as having sexually offended, it has been noted that children in out-of-home care may be at an increased risk for sexual acting out and abusive behaviors because many risk factors play a part in their being placed in alternative care.

The prevalence of abuse issues in special needs settings is sufficient in that it has been suggested that such settings must acknowledge the risk of children abusing other children while in care and must purposefully plan risk-management strategies to moderate those risks (Freeman-Longo & Ryan, 1990; National Task Force, 1993; Thomas, 1996). Negligence suits arise from a lack of purposeful planning, lack of defined policy and procedure, lack of ongoing risk assessment, and lack of adequate documentation of preventive and intervention strategies.

It is suggested that decisions relevant to policy, procedure, and practice in juvenile service settings be made in consideration of the risk of abusive behaviors, as well as the following.

1. Clearly define policy and procedure.
2. Implement team decision making.
3. Document prevention and intervention strategies.
4. Follow relevant ethics/standards of care that exist and apply.
5. Access current professional knowledge, including new practice discoveries.
6. Make relevant referrals and placements.
7. Seek consultation in difficult or unusual circumstances.
8. Exercise due care in selecting, training, and supervising all adults, including employees, volunteers, and student interns.
9. Know and follow all mandatory reporting laws.
10. Consult an attorney routinely and in cases or events that raise questions of liability or civil rights (Freeman-Longo & Ryan, 1990).

Policy and procedure should clearly define the limits of confidentiality in order to foster open communication among staff and administration and minimize the secrecy that enables abuse to occur and be undetected. Agencies must address the risks of staff abusing children, children abusing other children, and children abusing staff (Thomas, 1993, 1996). At the same time, reporting and disclosures of information must be carried out with caution and respect for the rights and safety of all involved.

Management for child serving institutions needs to examine the physical plant and staffing patterns, in addition to the policies and programming from a risk-management perspective. Staff cannot adequately supervise and protect children if they cannot see them, do not have adequate backup, or do not have the training to understand relevant risks and implement preventive strategies.

Documentation of routine care, treatment sessions, decision making, and incidents occurring during the treatment process is crucial to both daily practice and one's potential defense against suit. Documentation should include:

Incidents during treatment (or care)
Noncompliance
Less than adequate resources
System or family not following recommendations
Termination of treatment without successful completion
Continued risk factors and recommended follow-up

Routine care decisions should be a part of written policies and procedures and emergency situations requiring immediate decisions by individuals should be anticipated. Overall, team decision making (preferably multidisciplinary) regarding deviations in the course of treatment, supervision, crisis management, expulsion/termination/completion of treatment, passes, privileges, consequences, and so forth, protects both individuals and agencies from allegations of negligence. The reasonableness of decision making is strengthened by numbers and documentation (Freeman-Longo & Ryan, 1990, pp. 2–3).

Safety in child serving settings requires acknowledgment of the risks, and purposeful foresight and planning, just as the "safety planning" for activities was described in Chapter 15. As is always the case, the biggest risk is denial of risk. The need for risk-management plans should not discourage agencies serving children, as there are many ways to moderate risk, and planning for safety is a good thing for all children.

Since the Abuse Is Abuse concept addresses the risk of all types of harmful behaviors, keeping children safe is enhanced by implementation of the Informed Supervision and Abuse-Specific constructs in all child serving settings, and the concepts of Therapeutic Care can be useful in thinking about primary and secondary prevention and remediation of lesser problems in homes, as well as corrective or alternative care settings.

REFERENCES

Bennett, M. (1988). Overcoming the golden rule: Sympathy and empathy. In D. Nimmo (Ed.), *Communication yearbook* (3rd ed.) (pp. 408–422). New Brunswick, NJ: Transaction.
Berenson, D. (1987). Choice, thinking and responsibility: Implications for the treatment of the sex offender. In G. Ryan (Ed.), *Interchange* (Newsletter of the National Adolescent Perpetrator Network). Denver, CO: Kempe National Center.

Blanchard, G. (1995). *The difficult connection: The therapeutic relationship in sex offender treatment.* Orwell, VT: Safer Society Press.

Borduin, C. M., Henggeler, S. W., Blaske, D. M., & Stein, R. (1990). Multisystemic treatment of adolescent sexual offenders. *International Journal of Offender Therapy and Comparative Criminology, 34*(2), 105–113.

Bremer, J. F. (1992). Serious juvenile sex offenders: Treatment and long term follow-up. *Psychiatric Annals, 22*(6), 326–332.

Briggs, D. C. (1975). *Your child's self-esteem.* New York: Doubleday.

Brown, S. M. (2000). Healthy sexuality and the treatment of sexually abusive youth. *Siecus Report, 29*(1), 40–46.

Burton, D. L., & Meezan, W. (2004). Revisiting recent research on social learning theory as an etiological proposition for sexually abusive male adolescents. *Journal of Evidence Based Social Work, 1*, 41–80.

Davis, D. (1989). *Counseling techniques with reluctant clients: Core curriculum training manual for sex offender counselors.* Louisville, KY: Kentucky Department of Social Services.

Dishion, T. J., McCord, J., & Poulin, F. (1999). When interventions harm: Peer groups and problem behavior. *American Psychologist, 54*(9), 755–764.

Ellis, A. (1962). *Reason and emotion in psychotherapy.* Secaucus, NJ: Citadel Press.

Freeman-Longo, R. E., & Bays, L. (1988). *Who am I and why am I in treatment?* Orwell, VT: Safer Society Press.

Freeman-Longo, R., & Bays, L. (1989). *Why did I do it again?* Orwell, VT: Safer Society Press.

Freeman-Longo, R., & Ryan, G. (1990). *Tort liability in treatment of sexually abusive juveniles.* Denver, CO: *Interchange.* National Adolescent Perpetration Network, Kempe Center.

Freeman-Longo, R. E., Bird, S., Stevenson, W., & Fiske, J. (1995). *1994 nationwide survey of treatment programs and models: Serving abuse reactive children, adolescent and adult sex offenders.* Brandon, VT: Safer Society Press.

Gilgun, J. (1988). *Factors which block the development of sexually abusive behavior in adults abused as children.* Paper presented at the National Conference on Male Victims and Offenders: Controversies in Treatment, Minneapolis, MN.

Gilgun, J. (1996). Human development and adversity in ecological perspective. *Families in Society, 77*(8), 395–402, 459–476.

Glick, B. (2006). *Cognitive behavioral interventions with at-risk youth.* Kingston, NJ: Civic Research Institute.

Goldstein, A. P., Glick, B., & Gibbs, J. (1998). *Aggression replacement training— revision edition: A comprehensive intervention for aggressive youth.* Champaign, IL: Research Press.

Goldstein, A. P., & McGinnis, B. (1997). *Skillstreaming the adolescent (revised edition): New strategies and perspectives for teaching pro-social skills.* Champaign, IL: Research Press.

Greenwood, P. (2008). *Prevention and intervention programs for juvenile offenders, 18*(2). From http://www.futureofchildren.org.

Grskovic, J. A., & Goetze, H. (2005). An evaluation of the effects of life space crisis intervention on the challenging behavior of individual students. *Reclaiming Children and Youth, 13*(4), 231–235.

Hanson, R. K. (2006). *What works: The principles of effective interventions with offenders.* Presentation at the 25th Annual Conference of the Association for Treatment of Sexual Abusers, Chicago, IL.

Henggeler, S. W., Schoenwald, S. K., Borduin, C. M., Rowland, M. D., & Cunningham, P. B. (1996). *Multisystemic treatment of antisocial behavior in children and adolescents.* New York: Guilford Press.

Hunter, J. (1996a). *The juvenile offender: Different challenges and approaches.* Paper presented at the National Summit: Promoting Public Safety through Management of Sex Offenders in the Community, Office of Justice, Washington, DC.

Hunter, J. (1996b). *Understanding the impact of trauma on children: When victimization leads to victimizing.* Paper presented at the 11th International Congress on Child Abuse and Neglect, Dublin, Ireland.

Hunter, J. A. (2001). *What research tells us about this population*. Presented at the Annual National Adolescent Perpetration Network Conference, Kansas City, KS.

Hunter, J. A. (2006). *Understanding sexually abusive youth: New research and clinical directions*. Colorado Department of Human Services sponsored training, Broomfield, CO.

Hunter, J. A. (2008). *Understanding sexually abusive youth: New research and clinical directions*. Colorado Child and Adolescent Mental Health Conference, Ft. Collins, CO.

Hunter, J. A., & Becker, J. (1994). The role of deviant arousal in juvenile sexual offending etiology, evaluation and treatment. *Criminal Justice and Behavior, 21*(1), 132–149.

Hunter, J., Figueredo, A. J., Malamuth, N. M., & Becker, J. V. (2003). Juvenile sex offenders: Toward the development of a typology. *Sexual Abuse: A Journal of Research and Treatment, 15*(1), 27–48.

Johnson, S. (1989). *Branching out: The tree cycle*. Paper presented at the 4th National Adolescent Perpetrator Network Meeting, Keystone, CO.

Kaemingk, K., Koselka, M., Becker, J. V., & Kaplan, M. S. (1995). Age and adolescent sexual offender arousal. *Sexual Abuse: A Journal of Research and Treatment, 7*, 249–257.

Lane, S., & Zamora, P. (1978). Syllabus materials from in-service training on adolescent sex offenders, Closed Adolescent Treatment Center, Division of Youth Services: Denver, CO. Unpublished document.

Lane, S., & Zamora, P. (1982). *Working with juvenile sex offenders*. Presentation at the National Conference on Sexual Aggression, Denver, CO.

Lane, S., & Zamora, P. (1984). A method for treating the adolescent sex offender. In R. Mathias, P. Demuro, & R. Allinson (Eds.), *Violent juvenile offenders* (pp. 347–363). San Francisco, CA: National Council on Crime and Delinquency.

Latessa, E. J. (2005). *What works and what doesn't in reducing recidivism: The principles of effective intervention*. Vail, CO: Colorado Division of Youth Corrections Provider Council Conference.

Malamuth, N. (1984). *Pornography and sexual aggression*. New York: Academic Press.

Malamuth, N. (1986). Predictors of naturalistic sexual aggression. *Journal of Personality and Social Psychology, 50*, 953–962.

Marshall, W. (1996). The sexual offender: Monster, victim or everyman? *Sexual Abuse: A Journal of Research and Treatment, 8*(4), 317–336.

Marshall, W. L., Hudson, S. M., Jones, R., & Fernandez, Y. M. (1995). Empathy in sex offenders. *Clinical Psychology Review, 15*(2), 99–113.

McGrath, R. J., Cummings, G., & Burchard, B. (2003). *Current practices and trends in sexual abuse management: The Safer Society 2002 national survey*. Brandon, VT: Safer Society Foundation.

Moffitt, T. (1993). Adolescence-limited and life-course persistent antisocial behavior: A developmental taxonomy. *Psychology Review, 100*(4), 674–701.

National Task Force on Juvenile Sexual Offending. (1988). Preliminary report. *Juvenile and Family Court Journal, 39*(2), 1–67.

National Task Force on Juvenile Sexual Offending, National Adolescent Perpetration Network. (1993). The revised report. *Juvenile and Family Court Journal, 44*(4), 1–120.

Pithers, W., & Gray, A. (1996). Utility of relapse prevention in treatment of sexual abusers. *Sexual Abuse: A Journal of Research and Treatment, 8*(3), 223–230.

Prentky, R., Knight, R. A., Sims-Knight, J. E., Straus, J., Rokous, F., Cerce, D., et al. (1989a). *Developmental antecedents of sexual aggression*. Paper presented at the 4th National Adolescent Perpetrator Network Meeting, Keystone, CO.

Prentky, R., Knight, R. A., Sims-Knight, J. E., Straus, J., Rokous, F., Cerce, D., et al. (1989b). Developmental antecedents of sexual aggression. *Development and Psychopathology, 1*, 153–169.

Prentky, R. A., & Righthand, S. (2003). *Juvenile sex offender assessment protocol-zones: Manual*. Washington, DC: Office of Juvenile Justice and Delinquency Prevention.

Rasmussen, L. (1999). The trauma outcome process: An integrated model for guiding clinical practice with children with sexually abusive behavior problems. *Journal of Child Sexual Abuse, 8*(4), 3–33.

Rich, P. (2003). *Understanding, assessing, and rehabilitating juvenile sexual offenders*. Hoboken, NJ: John Wiley & Sons.

Rich, P. (2009). *Juvenile sexual offenders: A comprehensive guide to risk evaluation*. Hoboken, NJ: John Wiley & Sons.

Ross, J. (1987). *Treating the adolescent perpetrator*. Paper presented at the 16th National Symposium on Child Abuse and Neglect, Keystone, CO.

Ryan, G. (1984a). *Why treatment instead of incarceration?* Panel presentation at the University of Minnesota, Program in Human Sexuality, Minneapolis, MN.

Ryan, G. (1984b). The child abuse connection. *Interchange*. (Newsletter of the National Adolescent Perpetrator Network). Denver, CO: Kempe National Center.

Ryan, G. (1989). Victim to victimizer: Rethinking victim treatment. *Journal of Interpersonal Violence, 4*(3), 325–341.

Ryan, G. (1995). *The difficult client: Temperament or resistance?* Paper presented at the 11th Annual Conference of the National Adolescent Perpetrator Network, St. Louis, MO.

Ryan, G. (2000a). *Overcoming our own denial: Are we willing to change when new evidence challenges old assumptions?* 15th Annual NAPN Conference, Weaving a Tapestry, Denver, CO.

Ryan, G. (2000b). *Static, stable and dynamic risks and assets relevant to the prevention and treatment of abusive behavior*. Poster presentation, First National Sexual Violence Prevention Conference, Dallas, TX.

Ryan, G., Blum, J., Sandau-Christopher, D., Law, S., Weber, F., Sundine, C., et al. (1988). *Understanding and responding to the sexual behavior of children: Trainer's manual*. Denver, CO: Kempe National Centre, University of Colorado Health Sciences Centre.

Ryan, G., & Lane, S. (Eds.). (1991). *Juvenile sexual offending: Causes, consequences, and correction* (1st ed.)., Lexington, MA: Lexington Books.

Ryan, G., & Lane, S. (1997a). Integrating theory and method. In G. Ryan & S. Lane (Eds.), *Juvenile sexual offending: Causes, consequences, and corrections* (pp. 267–321). San Francisco: Jossey-Bass.

Ryan, G., & Lane, S. (Eds.). (1997b). *Juvenile sexual offending: Causes, consequences, and correction* (2nd ed.). Los Angeles, CA: Jossey-Bass.

Ryan, G., Lane, S., Davis, J., & Isaac, C. (1987). Juvenile sexual offenders: Development and correction. *Child Abuse and Neglect, 3*(3), 385–395.

Ryan, G., Lindstrom, B., Knight, L., Arnold, L., Yager, J., Bilbrey, C., et al. (1993). *Treatment of sexual abuse in the context of whole life experience*. Paper presented at the 21st Annual Child Abuse and Neglect Symposium, Keystone, CO.

Smith, T. (1987). *You don't have to molest that child*. Chicago, IL: National Committee for Prevention of Child Abuse.

Stickrod, A. (1988). *Preventing sexual abuse through treating juvenile sexual offenders*. Proceedings of the Adolescent Sex Offender's Symposium, Salt Lake City, UT.

Thomas, J. (1993). *Safety in residential programs*. Presentation at the 9th Annual Conference of the National Adolescent Perpetrator Network, Lake Tahoe, NV.

Thomas, J. (1996). *Safety in residential settings*. Paper presented at the 12th Annual National Adolescent Perpetrator Network, Minneapolis, MN.

Thomas, J., & Viar, W. (2005). Family reunification in sibling incest: A step by step process. In M. C. Calder (Ed.), *Children and young people who sexually abuse: New theory, research and practice developments*. Dorset: Russell House Publishing.

Wexler, D. B. (1991). *The PRISM workbook*. New York: W.W. Norton & Company.

Whitaker, M. (1987). *Behavioral goal areas: An overview of Allegheny Intensive Treatment Program*. [Brochure.] Pittsburgh, PA: Allegheny Intensive Treatment Program, Youth Services Training Center.

Worling, J. R. (2001). Personality-based typology of adolescent male sexual offenders: Differences in recidivism rates, victim selection characteristics, and personal victimization histories. *Sexual Abuse: A Journal of Research and Treatment, 13*(3), 149–166.

Worling, J. R., & Langstrom, N. (2006). Risk of sexual recidivism in adolescents who offend sexually: Correlates and assessment. In H. E. Barbaree & W. L. Marshall (Eds.), *The juvenile sex offender* (pp. 219–247) (2nd ed.). New York: Guilford Press.

Yochelson, S., & Samenow, S. (1976). *The criminal personality.* New York: Jason Aronson Publishers.

CHAPTER 18

Sexuality

The Offense-Specific Component of Treatment

GAIL RYAN, TOM LEVERSEE, and SANDY LANE

S EXUALITY IS THE component that distinguishes "offense-specific" from "abuse-specific" treatment. In the 1980s, there was an assumption that juveniles who sexually offended could not be in treatment with other clinical populations. This was partly due to the belief that sexual offenses were a product of sexual deviance and therefore represented an entirely different problem from other behavioral disorders. It was also partly due to the belief that these youth might pose a risk of sexually assaulting peers in other group settings. It was partly due to the stigma that often followed these youth, resulting in ridicule or harassment from other youth. And it may also have been partly because many therapists found the sexually abusive behaviors so abhorrent that they could not extend their work to deal with the issue.

Although it is clear that some sexually abusive and some violent youth pose a danger to similar-age peers and must be segregated in settings designed to manage those risks (see Chapter 21), the majority of youth who have sexually offended do not appear to pose any greater risk to peers than do many other delinquent or acting-out adolescents. A majority of these youth are educated and housed in the community while receiving offense-specific treatment in specialized outpatient or residential programs.

As the abuse-specific approach has demonstrated, much of the education, skills, and treatment needed for some sexually abusive youth is the same as that needed by other youth with harmful behaviors (see Chapter 17). Defining all types of abuse as abuse reduces some of the stigmatizing risks by holding all youth responsible for harmful behaviors. However, the sexual aspect of sexual offending does require assessment and treatment that differs from what might be provided to other youth without any history of sexual behavior problems.

Offense-specific components represent a discrete domain of the treatment plan and require intervention to address issues of sexuality and sexual deviance. Interventions specific to sexuality that will be discussed in this chapter include: sex education; sexual interest and identity; sexual preoccupation; fantasy and arousal patterns; masturbation; arousal assessment, suppression, and conditioning processes.

TREATMENT GROUPS

Most offense-specific treatment has been done in specialized groups with other youth who have also sexually offended. Hunter (2001) stresses that research does not support that all sexually abusive youth are in need of or will benefit from group therapy. Group may be contraindicated for some adolescents for a variety of different reasons such as developmental, intellectual, or learning difficulties as well as subtype differences (see Chapters 6 and 17). In addition, group work may be contraindicated for some youth who are easily aroused in discussions of the sexual aspects of offending (Worling, 2004).

Nonetheless, offense-specific treatment groups are still useful and efficient in addressing many of the common issues and needs specifically relevant for these youth, when they are able to be in a group without posing a risk to others. Advanced group members are able to model positive behaviors such as acceptance of responsibility and empathy. Peers can help to identify and challenge cognitive defenses such as minimization, distortion, rationalization, or denial; high-risk behaviors; and coercive dynamics.

The first session of an offense-specific treatment group typically clarifies that the focus is on the sexual nature of the youth's abusive behavior and that all members of the offense-specific group share the common issue of having been sexually abusive to someone in the past. Whether a new member is joining an existing group or a new group is forming, the youth will need to introduce themselves to each other, acknowledging their respective abuse behaviors.

When a new member joins an ongoing group, the older members can introduce themselves first and the new member last. The introduction is a first step in being responsible for their offense behavior and verifies the specific reason for them being in the group together. Preparation for this first session should be part of the initial assessment and intake process so the arriving youth is aware of the expectation of some personal disclosure in the introductions.

In communicating the expectation that the youth must control sexually abusive behaviors during treatment, it needs to be made clear from the beginning of treatment what the consequences of reoffending might be for each youth personally, in the group, and in the legal system. Definition of these potential consequences can be the basis of early assignments and be discussed in the group. Discussion of the legal definitions of sexual offenses is typically enlightening to all youth.

Many programs require at least a disclosure of the type of charges or some description of the referring abuse behavior at the first group session. Introductions do not need (nor is it advisable to encourage) full, detailed descriptions of the sexual aspects of the offense. The initial focus in offense-specific groups will not be on the sexually explicit aspects of past offenses. The introductory statement in the first group may be simply name, age, grade, and "I'm here because I sexually abused my sister," or "I'm here because I did some sexual stuff with some kids in my neighborhood."

Over the course of treatment, specific aspects of each individual's offense history will be revisited, but not before providing education, information, and language for the youth to have a basis for thinking about and talking about their offending. Prematurely pushing youth to answer questions or explain themselves can lock them into answers that may be quite misleading for the therapist and for them. Better to avoid questions until the youth has accurate information and language to participate in discussions of personal sexual history.

Research has not been done to establish the effect of exposure to deviant sexual information or stimuli on the arousal patterns of juveniles. However, as has been noted, assessments of adolescents who have sexually offended have shown that many have a wide range of sexual interests and only a few demonstrate a specific fixated interest correlating with their past behavior. For this reason, treatment providers are now very conscious of the risks of reinforcement of sexual deviance during disclosures of memories and/or fantasies of sexual abuse victimization or perpetration. Therapists need to control and minimize the exposure of youth to deviant sexual stimuli that could be triggering trauma memories for some and/or arousing others during the treatment process.

Working on detailed sexually explicit aspects of offenses is often referred into individual therapy sessions outside of a group setting, minimizing risks to other group members. Sexually explicit work in groups is now processed primarily in relation to defining and developing healthy sexuality. Group work regarding past offenses primarily focuses on defining the abusive characteristics of the relationship and/or interaction; exploring emotional triggers and cognitive, emotional, and behavioral patterns preceding and following past offenses and how those patterns may have changed over time; exploring motivations for sexually abusive behavior; and work to identify the lack of and/or to develop empathic deterrents relevant to the victim's experience.

PSYCHOEDUCATIONAL TOPICS AND THERAPEUTIC INTERVENTIONS

Topics specifically relevant to juvenile perpetration of sexual offenses comprise a significant agenda of education that is relevant and necessary for the youth to become able to explore sexual issues and make sense of their own offenses. Each area of work requires education in order to provide facts and language for the youth to reasonably understand the issues. Providing factual, impersonal information in a didactic teaching mode is also less threatening and helps group members adjust to being together in a room where sexuality and sexual offenses can be discussed. Simply desensitizing the embarrassment and discomfort they have often experienced in adults discussing sexual issues with them is a first step. Hearing objective information about offending and learning factual information about sexual abuse and offending also begins to overcome the secrecy and shame that have surrounded these issues.

Some of the more common topics taught in offense-specific treatment and the offense-specific treatment interventions are the focus of this chapter. Topics include: learning, reinforcement, and deterrence; sex education, including human sexuality, sexual development, sexual interests, motivation, fantasy and arousal, relationship and dating skills, laws, risks, and benefits of sexuality; consequences of victimization and offending; and social and cultural messages and myths. Offense-specific "treatment" includes: defining sexually abusive behavior; patterns associated with sexual offending; empathic deterrence; and physiological measures such as plethysmography (arousal conditioning and suppression) and polygraphs (disclosure and accountability); and victim clarification and reunification.

Many other types of psychoeducation may also be apparent in working with this diverse population. Correcting misinformation about human beings and the world is often necessary. Concurrent treatment, education, and care interventions are discussed elsewhere. Beliefs and information the youth has acquired that support or contribute to their offending, dysfunction, and/or impede success become topics to explore, and therapists cannot expect to know it all. It is perfectly reasonable for the clinician to validate the need for information, state that they are not sure about a topic, and reserve the topic for future discussion when they are able to bring accurate information to the group. Youth can often find information to address questions that arise on the Internet and bring this information back to the group. Curiosity and the process of learning model important skills.

In most programs, education and treatment are interwoven, with more of the early educational work gradually becoming more personal, and introducing various clinical interventions as they relate to the information and issues. Some programs begin with basic introductory education in purely psychoeducational groups and then involve youth in "advanced" or "therapy" groups where the clinical work applies what they have learned to the issues and interventions. There is no one "recipe" for treatment or programs, and what works with one group of clients may need to be done differently with the next. An advantage of the "goal-oriented" approach is that it does not prescribe HOW to do the work, but does make clear the goals that represent successful outcomes. This approach is congruent with the individualized, differential diagnosis and treatment, which is the current "state of the art." It should be expected that there will eventually be empirical evidence that certain interventions are most effective with particular subgroups, but the diversity of the population suggests that individual differences, even within various subgroups, will continue to benefit from the flexibility of informed clinical judgment, differential interventions, and a goal-oriented approach.

Going into sessions with an idea of issues and information that are next on the agenda is useful, but the therapists must be able and willing to set aside their own agendas and follow the needs of the youth. In treatment sessions, current issues often preclude work on the referring issues, as youth are preoccupied with current issues that need to be addressed in order to be available for learning and the work of treatment. Therapists must be flexible in their expectations and be prepared to combine counseling, therapeutic process, and education, using the "teachable moments" when topics are relevant and relating current issues to past issues. Holding in mind all the things that need to be taught helps the therapist recognize relevant issues and take advantage of the teachable moments, as well as being able to alternate topics when youth need a break from more emotionally charged issues. The didactic style of educating is one in which the youth is familiar with and can provide some structure around impersonal information, and the therapeutic process is dependent upon the youth acquiring the knowledge and skills to explore and understand themselves as sexual beings.

Chapter 17 has discussed the education that relates to the abusive nature of sexual offending. When youth are already in abuse-specific treatment, the basic concepts of "Abuse Is Abuse," "Cycles," "Universal Goals," "Safety Planning," and "Observable Outcomes" are already covered. If the offense-specific treatment group is the only education and treatment setting the youth will be participating in, the abuse-specific work will occur in combination with the offense-specific work. Either way, the concepts of the abuse-specific model will be used in the offense-specific work as they relate to the sexual offending. Education regarding those basic concepts is always a place to begin.

LEARNING, REINFORCEMENT, AND DETERRENCE

Sexual behaviors may be learned through direct experience or observation. (In this culture, all youth are exposed to both normative and deviant sexual information and stimuli.) All sexual behaviors are intrinsically physically reinforcing due to the experience of intimacy, arousal, orgasm, or tension reduction, powerful reinforcements that make it likely that behaviors will be repeated unless something occurs to deter repetition. The nonsexual behaviors that are defined as abusive to self, others, or property tend to become habituated or chronic as well, due to the intrinsic reinforcers associated with each. Reinforcement from physical sensations may result from the introduction of foreign substances into the body, from substances generated in the brain as a result of certain behaviors, or from the arousal and tension reduction of cycles associated with physical aggression and risk taking. In addition, psychological reinforcement results from the person's perception that the behavior in some way increases pleasure or efficacy or decreases negative factors for the individual. The more potent the physical and psychological reinforcers are, the more likely it is that the behavior will be repeated.

People may be deterred from imagined behavior by external factors: physical restraints that block opportunity; punishments, negative consequences, or negative associations that are more powerful disincentives than the perceived reinforcement of the behavior. Positive consequences associated with restraint that are perceived to be more beneficial than the behavior may also deter action. People may be deterred from behaviors that are harmful to themselves by internal cues that make clear the negative effects of the behavior. They may also be deterred from behaviors that are harmful to others by internal factors: sympathetic responses based on assumptions that others will feel as the individual does may deter behavior that is perceived as unpleasant; empathic responses, noticing the other's signs of distress and changing behavior; or empathic foresight, which predicts how behavior might affect others and avoids behavior that might be perceived as distressing to others. Empathy is believed to be the highest and most lasting deterrent for abusive behavior, when paired with accurate attributions and a sense of personal responsibility.

SEXUALITY

Basic to the process of reducing the risk of sexually exploitive behaviors is the client's need for correct sexual information, dating skills and relationship-building skills, definition and acceptance of personal sexual identity, and developing knowledge and values that support reciprocal and consensual sexual interactions. Sex education curriculums may be used, and assignments may include reading and reporting on relevant physiological and relationship aspects. Many videos relevant to sex education, dating skills, responsible sex, and acquaintance rape are available for group discussions. Values-based sex education challenges the youth to identify values regarding nonconsensual interactions, sexual fantasies, arousal patterns, masturbation, and homosexuality, all areas deserving open group discussion and examination. Many sexually abusive youth are confused about the implications of victimization and/or perpetration in defining their sexual preference and identity. Reassurance that fantasy and experience do not define the person and need not dictate future sexuality is comforting and enables more open discussion of confusion, fears, and perceptions.

As a whole, providers have been much more conscientious about addressing sexual deviance than sexual health. Conscious efforts must always be to reinforce the positive aspects of sexuality and relationships.

SEX EDUCATION

Two very basic topics that facilitate discussion and understanding of other sexual topics are learning to differentiate types of sexual behavior problems, and being aware of the wide continuum of motivations for sexual behavior. People (children, adolescents, and adults) engage in a wide range of sexual behaviors across the life span for many different reasons.

The motivations for children and adults who engage in sexual behaviors are not categorically different, although the way they manifest and are understood by the person will differ with age. From early childhood on, the basic motivations include exploration and curiosity, imitation and learning, sensation seeking, physical pleasure, intimacy and connection, compensation, improvement, and anger and retaliation. The only change in motive is that from puberty to mid-life an additional motivation may be to do sexual things in order to reproduce. Of all the possible motives, the only one that is always problematic is the last: using sexual behavior to express anger and harm others. Other motives may be problematic if they are out of balance or interfere with other areas of life, but are not problematic in and of themselves.

Motivation: Why People Do Sexual Things

Exploration/Curiosity
   (What's This All About? Self/Others)
Imitation/Learning
   (See/Try Doing/Practice/Teach Others)
Sensation Seeking
   (Arousing When Bored/Calming When Stressed)
Physical Reinforcement: Feels Good
   (Arousal, Orgasm, Tension Reduction)
Psychological Pleasure: Self plus Others
   (Relationship, Intimacy, Friendship, Love)
Compensation/Improvement
   (Feel Better, Do Better, Regain Self-Image, Competence, Control)
Anger/Retaliation
   (Get Back at Others, Make Others Feel Hurt, "Act Out" Anger)

Differentiating the many reasons why sexual behavior might be a problem is a concept that is as useful for the youth in treatment as for the adults evaluating youthful behaviors. Taking the time to articulate the reasons behavior is a problem informs reasonable responses. By asking "Is this behavior a problem?" and if so, "What kind of problem is it?," it becomes apparent that there are many reasons behaviors might be problematic or pose risks besides being illegal or abusive.

Defining what is abusive and what is illegal is a clear imperative. Equally important is recognizing all the ways sexual behavior might be a problem for the person doing it or for others. Sexual behavior is a problem if it poses a risk of harm to self: injury, disease, pregnancy, stigma, consequences, and so forth. It might also be a problem for others: violating norms or values, causing discomfort, and so forth. It is important for youth to understand the legitimate concerns adults have regarding them being sexually active.

It is equally important to address the topic of sexual fantasies and arousal early in treatment, teaching immediately the danger of continuing to dwell on abusive thoughts, especially while aroused or masturbating. Fantasy may be even more reinforcing than actual behavior (due to total control and no impediments in fantasy), which is why it is so important to interrupt the pattern preceding abusive behaviors "no later than the first abusive thought." Continuing to pair a natural, pleasurable physical state with problematic thoughts works against becoming healthy.

Along with that knowledge, it is important to talk about natural associations: that when people think of something sexual, or when they feel sexually aroused, what comes to mind may be fantasies of things they have never done, but can also be memories of experiences from the past (which could be victimization, perpetration, or more normative experiences). It should be made clear that it is expected that there will be times when the youth might have abusive sexual thoughts. However, knowing the danger of dwelling on abusive thoughts while aroused, it is important to stop those thoughts and think about or do something else. At the same time, therapists must admit that they are not mind-readers and will not know whether the youth has difficulty stopping abusive thoughts, or trouble being aroused without thinking abusive thoughts, unless they tell the therapist. If they do have trouble with that and they tell the therapist, they can be assured that there are ways to help them with that.

Sexual interest and arousal requires multiple conversations. First to define the terms:

THERAPIST: What is arousal and how does it happen?
GROUP: Getting turned on?
THERAPIST: Yes, that happens when increased blood flows to the genitals so the penis becomes engorged (erect/hard), or for girls, the vagina becomes engorged.

Sometimes, this might lead to quizzical looks or questions about female arousal:

THERAPIST: The female's vagina becomes engorged and begins secreting fluid so that if intercourse follows, the vagina will be both tight and lubricated. When intercourse occurs without the female feeling aroused, it can be painful or uncomfortable and less satisfying to both partners.
GROUP: So that's why rape hurts?

For some groups that may be all that can be taught at that time, but it was a priceless teachable moment. For other groups the topic of female arousal may need to wait for a subsequent discussion. Therapists must pay attention to the cues in the room to gauge how much information can be introduced without overwhelming the group's ability to learn without getting silly, embarrassed, or aroused. These topics will need to be revisited several times over the course of treatment.

Sexual interests will be relevant to sexual identity, orientation, and preferences, but it is important to make conscious for the youth, that adolescents are not "finished products"; that developmentally, physically, and neurologically they are still growing and changing a lot into their early twenties. Too often, teens feel pressured to figure out who they are when identity formation is only beginning. Especially for youth who have many developmental delays and have had both exposure to deviance and a lot of interruptions in nurturance and growth, it is very important to communicate to them that it is expected that they probably feel pretty confused at times about lots of things in life and that is very natural.

The natural associations created by past experiences have been discussed, but the term "sexual interest" needs to be defined:

THERAPIST: What is meant by "sexual interests"?
GROUP: What turns you on?
THERAPIST: Right. And what the research shows is that most teens and young adult males are "sexually interested" in a wide range of sexual stimuli. That is, they get "turned on," more or less, by a lot of different things. As people mature, they tend to focus increasingly on some types of stimuli and be less interested in other types, and so, for adults, the sexual partners and behaviors they choose tend to be influenced by their sexual interests and preferences. We know that for some of you, the people you have done sexual things with have been partly determined by who you had "access and opportunity" to do them with. We know that very young children will explore sexuality with their playmates, and are "interested" in exploring both genders. So kids do sexual things with their friends. Then during puberty, it begins to matter which friend it is and which gender they are. That's when kids begin to describe special feelings for a particular friend. What parents often call "puppy love." So sexual interests and preferences become more apparent over time, but many teens have not yet settled into a narrow area of focus and some continue to explore both same sex and opposite sex interactions, but eventually become entirely interested in either same sex or opposite sex partners . . . what we define as "homosexual" or "heterosexual" identity. Especially because you have had unusual or deviant experiences, we expect that a lot of you may be pretty confused about your sexuality at this point, which is okay. With treatment, you will become able to make sense of sexuality and figure these things out for yourself.

Again, the initial topic has introduced a teachable moment for the therapist to provide youth with some knowledge that will help them think about their own sexual development and experiences. Another day, the therapist might ask, *"So have you all been thinking about the question we asked before: What 'turns you on?'"*, and pursue other aspects of the topic, such as: *"For some guys it is the shape of a person's legs, for others it might be the size of boobs or the color of the eyes. For some girls, it may be a boy's appearance, for others it may be the sound of someone's voice."* In this way the research and information covered in the section of this text on theory and research informs the therapist's education of the youth.

As previously stated, an important warning in treatment is for the youth to avoid pairing abusive thoughts with arousal. Groups of teens can usually generate long lists of ways to suppress "unwanted arousal" once they understand the importance of taking control of their sexuality. Examples to stop abusive thoughts and arousal might include: think of the consequences; talk to staff or parents or peers about something completely different; change activity or place; wash hands and face; take a cold shower; go for a run; do push-ups; and so forth. Initially, when asking how a youth suppresses unwanted arousal, there is often a reaction of denial, as if all sexual arousal is good. This opens the teachable moment to confront the reality that there are times when arousal is not welcome and can cause embarrassment or discomfort, as well as times that the youth might not be sexually interested in someone who is interested in them. This in turn opens the path to discussions of dating relationships, and as is often the case, the therapist has the opportunity to follow the path from one topic to another. When time runs out before all the open topics can be discussed, making a note of the unfinished business can help the group pick back up more easily in the next session.

One concrete tool for youth to interrupt abusive thoughts and stop the associated arousal is for them to develop an "aversive scene" (all the bad things that might occur if they reoffend). This can be worked on with peers very early in treatment since they already know the consequences they have experienced and can think about what would likely be similar or different if they reoffended. The scene they develop will be also be useful later in treatment for doing covert sensitization conditioning, which will be discussed later in this chapter. Once they have written an aversive scene that takes them three minutes to read aloud, they can switch their thinking to it, as it is hard to stay aroused while describing being arrested, jailed, shunned, fearful, and so forth.

Once the youth have mastered their understanding of what constitutes consent, equality, and coercion, and developed nonabusive fantasies, substituting a nonproblematic fantasy for the abusive one and pairing it with arousal will be another goal for them.

Another concrete tool that can be taught is "Rules for Masturbation." Very often youth have been told many things NOT to do, but little about what is natural or nonproblematic to do.

Simple "rules" FOR masturbating would be:

- In a private place
- When feeling good
- While thinking caring thoughts

In this way the relevant elements are each addressed: situation, thoughts, and feelings. The goals are to teach and practice personal boundaries and privacy, to avoid use of sexuality as an avoidant, compensatory behavior when feeling bad so that it is not paired with angry or vulnerable feelings, and to avoid dwelling on negative/abusive thoughts (about self or others) while masturbating.

Masturbation, like the other topics, requires education and desensitization. It is never wise to ask, "How many of you masturbate?" as initial reactions may be unreliable and can shut down further discussion. The didactic impersonal approach, talking about how babies discover the parts of their body, discover their genitals, discover that touching them feels good, and will touch them, more or less, across the life span unless something stops them from doing so, sets the stage for the topic. Next, the therapist can suggest some reasons why some children might not engage in the behavior (adult reactions, punishment, family values, etc.) and simply state that since it is a very normal behavior it is assumed that most of the youth have masturbated, more or less, even though some may not. "Closing the door" at that point prevents peers influencing other's ability to think about what has been said in relation to their own experiences.

Subsequent discussions might explore what the youth actually remember about sexual learning in their own lives: what they first remember hearing, knowing, or doing, and so forth; who they got information from, when, and whether they actually had sex education in school or not; when they first remember being aware of arousal or an erection, and so forth. Youth often deny arousal that is not acted on, or does not produce a full erection, or masturbatory behavior and orgasms that do not include ejaculation, but ejaculation does not define arousal or orgasm, any more than ovulation would.

Talking about sexual thoughts, fantasies, and memories is clearly relevant, but again requires definition of terms. Sexual *thoughts*, *feelings*, and *behaviors* are three different things, involving three different parts of people, but all interacting.

Sexual thoughts can be of past experiences, of information, or of "fantasy." Every sexual thought can be positive or negative and might be abusive or nonabusive. Fantasy refers to thoughts of something one imagines or thinks of doing in the future, and may be to repeat past behaviors or to do something never done before. Sexual thoughts can also be simply that: thinking about sexual things without imagining doing them.

Feelings may be warm intimate feelings, could be scary or upsetting feelings, or might be angry, silly, or sad feelings. Any strong feeling can cause physical arousal that is a change in the way the body feels: tense, aggressive, or sexual. "Sexual" or "genital" arousal refers to changes in how the genitals feel.

Just as sexual behaviors can be differentiated and defined as problematic, abusive, or illegal, sexual thoughts and the feelings associated with them need to be differentiated and defined so the youth learns to reject those that are problematic. Differentiating and evaluating fantasies, thoughts, and memories, the same criteria that define problematic behaviors, can be used:

- Is it abusive? (Lack of equality, Lack of consent, or Coercive)
- Is it a problem because it puts oneself at risk in some way? (Physically, socially, etc.)
- Is it a problem for others? (Violating rules of home/family, causing others discomfort)

All these topics can be taught and discussed in group and are congruent with other goals of treatment.

Developing a "nonproblematic" sexual fantasy that they can think about when aroused is a more goal-oriented intervention than dwelling on descriptors of abusive sexual fantasies. In working on normative fantasies or scenarios, the emphasis in the group is on identifying overt abuse as well as covertly exploitive or objectifying elements of fantasy material and developing nonexploitive scenarios. Discussions of deviant material should be balanced by constant restructuring to more normative or nonproblematic thinking.

In discussing elements of fantasy, the topics might include: empathic interactions (two people both paying attention to each other's cues and behaving in ways that are pleasing to each other); relationship and dating skills (how do you create a relationship within which it is reasonable to imagine or pursue sexual interaction?, etc.); risks of sexual activity outside an ongoing relationship (it must be acknowledged that "one-night stands" are not always abusive, exploitive, or even problematic when involving two consenting persons practicing safe sex, but the reasons such relationships can be risky and less satisfying can be explored). The first risk many youth cite is that of allegations: that someone they don't know well might later accuse them of rape.

It must be recognized that arousal and subsequent masturbatory behaviors might be increased by sexual topics, and the therapist must gauge how much or little time should be spent on such topics before turning to some other subject. Therapists must be alert to hyper-sexuality (youth who are easily aroused, even by educational discussions) and be particularly vigilant for signs of reinforcement of any particular group member's prurient interest in deviant material. Clients who have not achieved understanding of the exploitive elements of fantasy or are unable or unwilling to use consensual, nondeviant fantasies should be advised to avoid masturbation for the time being in order to minimize continued reinforcement of any problematic arousal patterns and deviant sexual preferences. Some youth will need individual treatment sessions to address these issues. Those who acknowledge deviant interests or compulsive masturbation can be helped to redirect their time and energy into nonsexual activities in order to achieve a less sexualized lifestyle.

A period of abstinence can be suggested as putting a conscious stop to the deviance, with the expectation that in time, most will become able to experience more normative thoughts and arousal. Recognizing the level of stimulation and reinforcement in sexual behaviors, alternative activities during prescribed periods of abstinence or decreased sexual activity need to provide stimulation and satisfaction if they are to compete in diverting the youth from the levels of sexuality that were previously habituated.

Whereas caregivers of younger children who need to decrease habituated hypersexuality have been advised to create active diversions to engage the child in nonsexual activities, the older youth can be an active participant in figuring out alternative activities that are stimulating and satisfying enough to help them avoid/ decrease (sublimate) sexual arousal. For some youth, it is their current living environment that requires decreased sexual activity due to lack of privacy.

If a youth is not committed to changing problematic interests and avoiding associated arousal (i.e., continues to enjoy and justify thinking about being sexual with children or assaulting others), the therapist may need to exclude them from the group where those are clearly goals of the group. Such youth may benefit from individual or family sessions to explore their resistance to change, but ultimately may need to be referred back to the courts to be remanded to some higher level of containment or treatment, or to "do their time" without treatment. Such decisions should only be reached after significant efforts have been made by more than one therapist to engage the youth, and not as a result of power struggles and frustration. Clearly articulating the risks of refusing treatment for the youth in the current case, and across the life span, should be discussed as well; the return to court should include whatever information might inform alternative containment plans with the goal of community safety.

It is important that youth hear repeatedly that the goal and expectation is that most will become healthy sexual persons. Using the research discussed in earlier chapters informs every discussion, and can sometimes be specifically cited as evidence that supports the information. As the therapist demonstrates knowledge about human sexuality, understanding of the development of sexual behavior problems, and confidence in the youth's ability to change their behaviors and be healthy, the youth are reassured, and most become increasingly engaged in treatment.

SOCIETAL MESSAGES AND MYTHS

Although a focus in treatment is on identifying and restructuring the client's own knowledge and beliefs and the thinking patterns that allow and enable sexually abusive behavior, it is also important to explore the role of external systems in the development and maintenance of sexual and abusive problems. Remembering Conte's (1986) suggestion that the therapist first explore the pathology of the individual, then the pathology of the family, and then the pathology of external systems, it is important to sensitize the client to the societal messages and myths that support sexually abusive and exploitive behavior. The attitudes manifested in the peer group, the community, and the culture have been part of the client's learning process and experience, and much of what they are exposed to is not what adults actually want them to learn or do.

Awareness of pervasive influences in the culture that contribute to sexually exploitive thinking allows exploration of relevant social learning theories and the origins of attitudes and beliefs that support current myths. Socialization, stereotyping, and role expectations demonstrate the ways in which people are depersonalized and objectified. Each of these areas can be discussed in terms of the attitudes of others that have a negative impact on the client, as well as their contribution to attitudes of the client that have had a negative impact on others. For example, male socialization suggests that males are tough and able to protect themselves (therefore they are not victims), males are sexually aggressive (therefore, always willing in sexual interactions), and males are dominant (therefore, always in control of others). The client's experience has often been a contradiction of many of these myths; having been victimized or sexually confused, and made to feel helpless and out of control. At the same time, sexually aggressive behaviors are supported by these messages, yet violate the laws and customs of the culture.

Stereotypes, prejudice, and role expectations depersonalize the clients as well as the victims of sexual abuse, and contradict the need to appreciate the needs and feelings of others as unique individuals. For example, older adolescent males are stereotyped as the strongest, most virile, and most aggressive members of the community, yet young males between the ages of 15 and 24 are more often victims of both violent and personal crimes than any other segment of the community (National Criminal Justice Information and Statistics Service, 1995). The only type of crime that happens more to females than to their male age-mates are sexual crimes. The lack of protection and empathy for the male who is victimized is in direct conflict with the expectations of treatment. More globally, attitudes and myths relevant to sexual aggression include many exploitive and depersonalizing messages that support male domination, victim blaming/culpability, and deviant sexuality.

Individual attitudes and beliefs may be identified within the group's discussions or through testing instruments such as the Burt Rape Myth Acceptance Scale, Buss-Durkee Hostility Inventory, Attitudes Toward Women Scale, Phase Sexual Attitudes Questionnaire, and the Multiphasic Sexual Inventory—Juvenile. Assignments designed to identify and sensitize group members to the messages that support their attitudes may include definitions of sexually derogatory language, the portrayal of stereotypes in advertising and movies, sexual objectification in pornography and advertising, biases in news reporting, and the glorification of sexual deviance and exploitation in song lyrics and entertainment.

Youth may resist defining abuse in the music, media, and entertainment they like, so it must be made clear that the expectation is *not* that they can avoid these messages but that they become consciously *aware* of them. Understanding advertising techniques that influence behavior, such as the repetition of visual and auditory images that subconsciously influence choices in buying detergent, choosing a restaurant, or preferring a particular brand of jeans or shoes, can be generalized to acceptance of sexual myths and the subsequent risk of behavior. By challenging the client's acceptance and awareness of these messages in the cultural environment, the suggestion is made that the client can learn to control the influence that these things have rather than being subconsciously controlled by external messages.

DEFINITION OF SEXUAL ABUSE

Many sexually abusive youth arrive in treatment without clearly understanding what sexual abuse is. Although they know what behavior was involved and the legal consequences, they often have little or no understanding as to why the behavior was considered abusive. When a significant age difference or extreme force was involved, they may believe those are the only criteria for definition of abuse. Just as adults have historically been confused in the evaluation of the sexual interactions of children and the meaning of hands-off offenses, the juvenile is similarly confused. The youth are often relieved to hear that the sexual behaviors involved in the abuse are normal human behaviors (with very few exceptions). The therapist identifies the behavior but pursues the definition regarding why the interaction was abusive.

The factors that must be understood are consent, equality, and coercion. Group discussion should result in correct definitions of Consent, Equality, and Coercion. (Detailed definitions were presented in Chapters 1 and 17.) In order to fully define the exploitive nature of their behavior, the youth must know the following:

1. The elements of consent, and one's understanding of these things, are different at different ages and for different individuals. It is the similarity of understanding that defines consent in all sexual experiences.
2. How to define power differentials in relation to perceptions of authority and control in relationships.
3. Recognize the whole continuum of coercion, which represents the pressures that might bear on a person to get them to do things they would not otherwise do. The most subtle forms of coercion are not always immediately apparent.

Group discussions continue to revisit and refine these definitions over the course of treatment. Assignments can be given to challenge clients to define the terms and apply them to their own experiences: things that have happened to them as well as things they have done. Defining how they obtained the cooperation or compliance of victims; identifying situations in which they have consented, complied, or cooperated during sexual activities themselves; recognizing pressures they brought to bear on others to get them to do things; and the nature of inequalities between themselves and the victim.

Helping youth clearly define why what they did was abusive can start with simply asking: "What is your understanding of why what you did was abusive?" This is the first discussion specifically about their own offenses. In ongoing groups, members have numerous opportunities to demonstrate their mastery of these definitions as they help newer members learn them. The youth's first attempts to define the abusive elements can be expected to leave a lot to be revisited in further discussions, and each time these issues are addressed, their understanding should be enhanced.

Some youth will own right away that what they did was wrong, without being able to say why. Others will know why it was illegal, but not why it was abusive. Many will simply state: "I knew I'd be in trouble 'cause I was always in trouble for anything sexual, but I never knew it was illegal, and I don't know why they call it 'abuse.'" As the definitions evolve, many do not immediately recognize the ways in which they were unequal or coercive. Asking, "Have you thought of any other ways you had unequal power?" or "Have you thought about what your brother might have thought would happen if he refused?" will often add more to the descriptors. The therapist will be more effective in discovering the relevant indicators when they have access to victim statements from the police reports or the victim's therapist. Typically this process reduces any residual denial or minimization of the abusiveness of the behavior, and hearing other youth do the work encourages more detailed sharing.

For example, a therapist defines coercion as pressures that are brought to bear on the victim. The client states, "Well, I never threatened anybody." Gently confronting the client's denial of coercion can help him recognize the coercive dynamic.

THERAPIST:: What did you say would happen if she didn't do it?
CLIENT: Nothing.
THERAPIST: Then why do you suppose she went along?
CLIENT: I don't know.
THERAPIST: What do you think she thought would happen if she did not?
CLIENT: Maybe that I wouldn't like it.
THERAPIST: Did you say you wouldn't like it?
CLIENT: Yes.
THERAPIST: Do you think she thought you wouldn't like her?
CLIENT: Maybe.
THERAPIST: Did you say you wouldn't like her?
CLIENT: I said if she loved me she would.
THERAPIST: So do you suppose she thought you wouldn't love her if she wouldn't?
CLIENT: Maybe.
THERAPIST: You were a pretty important person to her?
CLIENT: Yeah. I was the one who always stuck up for her and did things for her. She always came to me.
THERAPIST: So, what do you think it meant to her to think you might not love her if she didn't do it?
CLIENT: I don't know.
THERAPIST: Do you think not being loved by you would be pretty bad for her?
CLIENT: Yes.
THERAPIST: So you think not loving her anymore seemed like a threat?
CLIENT: Maybe.
THERAPIST: So do you think maybe you did threaten her?
CLIENT: Yes . . .

PATTERNS ASSOCIATED WITH SEXUAL OFFENDING

As clients master the concepts of the cycle, they become more accurate with identifying the characteristics of each component for themselves. The second piece of work specifically relevant to their own sexual offending then begins: to identify possible antecedents leading up to the first thought of the fantasy, and what those first thoughts actually were, prior to their first offense. For some, the first thought was simply to do something sexual to feel better. For others the first thought may have been angry and retaliatory without even being sexual. How the first thought evolved into the plan that they actually acted on will be different for each youth. Sometimes there were impediments to acting on a normative nonproblematic sexual fantasy, and other times something they did to "act out" their anger became a sexual behavior.

The therapist can provide examples of normal sexual thoughts or fantasies and some possible impediments that might have contributed to the eventual plan being very different from the first thought. Group members who are further along can often contribute ideas too. The client is then asked to identify each element involved in contemplating, planning, or setting up the opportunity to abuse, and what coercive actions were used to gain the victim's cooperation or compliance, signs of resistance and distress that were misinterpreted or ignored, any threats or promises made to keep the victim from disclosing, and the cognitive, emotional, and behavioral aftermath.

Later the client will be asked to identify historical issues that may have affected his reactions to issues at the time of the sexual assault, as well as patterns of thinking, situations, or feelings associated with other fantasies of sexual abuse or other incidents that may have occurred. The youth is encouraged to identify the first onset of any sexually abusive thoughts or behavior, progressions in how the abusive pattern may have changed over time, and crossover behaviors (other sexual behaviors that were added to the original pattern or different types of offenses that may have occurred in either similar or different progressions).

If written assignments are given, it is important to monitor the sexual content of homework or journal work, because fantasies of sexually abusive behaviors can be very reinforcing. Written work describing sexual interactions should focus on defining abusive aspects, precursors, or victim impacts rather than sexually explicit descriptions of arousal and orgasm, which are more usefully incorporated into nonabusive fantasies describing consensual interactions.

DENIAL AND DISCLOSURE

In work with all sexual offending, there have been controversies about the two "Big Ds": denial and disclosure. Programs have often had youth write about their offenses, sometimes in great detail, with an expectation that "full disclosure" was the evidence of "accountability" (the youth accepting responsibility for their behaviors). Yet concern for the amount of time spent on deviance rather than health, and the potential for reinforcement of deviant arousal that could be a result of that focus, have always raised questions about disclosure work. The potential for additional charges to be filed as a result of new disclosures of additional offenses was another concern, often handled by reaching agreements with prosecutors to not pursue additional charges unless the new disclosures actually created a need for higher levels of intervention that could not be provided under the current circumstances (National Task Force, 1988, 1993).

With the introduction of actuarial models of research and risk assessment differentiating static unchangeable factors from those dynamics that can change, it has been very apparent that the history of sexual offenses is static and nothing done in treatment will erase the past. Therefore, if an initial risk assessment shows a youth to be "high risk" they will still be deemed high risk at the end of treatment on those measures, no matter how much they have changed or how long they have been "offense free." Therefore, if knowing about additional offending will not change the risk assessment, and if already recommending the highest levels of supervision and containment at the beginning of treatment, then knowing more has little purpose, except as specifically related to issues in treatment and victim protection.

Therefore, in thinking through the issue of disclosure work, several questions should be considered, and differential treatment will follow:

- What are the risks of disclosure work in this case: Legal, clinical, iatrogenic?
- What information is needed to do an initial risk assessment and how does it inform the supervision and treatment plans?

- What information is needed for risk to be moderated and health increased?
- How can necessary information be obtained and worked on in treatment without the peril of iatrogenic risks such as increased exposure to deviance?

Whatever history is discovered, it is critically important that therapists evaluate the nature of each sexual interaction and relationship before concluding that every sexual contact in the youth's history is another offense. This has been a frequently observed problem in the field and contributes to inaccurate data as well as confusion for the youth and unreasonable responses in the system. Becker, Cunningham-Rathner, and Kaplan (1986) found that many juveniles who had committed sexual offenses had previously or concurrently also had more normative experiences. The only way to differentiate the history is to do the work of talking through the nature of each relationship and the quality of interactions. For youth with extensive histories who are already considered high risk and beginning interventions at the highest levels, this may not be the best use of clinical hours, although clearly some discussion of the sexual history is relevant and necessary.

It is actually the lower-risk youth, who appear least at risk and will begin intervention at lower levels of supervision, where detailed history and careful evaluation of each sexual contact may be more useful to either verify the low risk or increase knowledge of risk factors. In either case, thinking about what is actually needed and being thoughtful about how it is collected are responsibilities of therapists and evaluators.

In terms of both risk assessment and treatment planning, the information needed is most often less than the "full sexual history disclosure" that has been thought of in this work, and is likely to be somewhat different with different youth, but the basics seem to include:

Ages, genders, and relationships of those victimized (Sibling/relative, known, or stranger)
Youth's age at the time of the offenses
Range of behaviors and approximate numbers of offenses
Methods of engagement (Elaborate planning vs. opportunistic)
Nature of the interaction (Lack of Consent, Unequal power, Coercion)
Nature of the prior relationship (positive/negative)
Forms of coercion to engage, or to prevent disclosure/discovery
Failure of empathic deterrence (Distress cues not noticed, misinterpreted, ignored)
Other types of abusive behaviors in same relationship
Pervasiveness of abusive patterns of youth (other types of abusive behaviors)
Contextual factors (family, school, peers, etc.) prior to and at the time of the offenses

A simple form collecting this information about the first offense, the last offense, and collectively all others can be used as a "Limited Disclosure" assignment, providing evidence of the youth's accountability. (The youth cannot be expected to take responsibility for and know all these things until each aspect has been addressed with the education and process of treatment to inform accurate reporting.) Such an assignment can strategically limit the details to be focused on and can specifically instruct the youth to stop working on it if they experience arousal, and to go back to it later after interrupting the arousal state. In many instances, the facts suggested here are sufficient to inform the risk assessment tools, and individual issues may suggest additional areas for clinical exploration.

Example of a Limited Disclosure Assignment

First Offense:

　Age at that time: *12*

　Age and relationship of victim: *My sister was 7*

　Location where offense happened: *Basement family room*

　Specific sexual behaviors: *Looking at and touching her genitals*

　Coercion: *Told her big girls do this and that she was a baby if she wouldn't*

　Coercion to keep the incident secret: *Told her mom would be mad at us*

　Signs of confusion or distress: *She seemed nervous*

Last Offense:

　Age: *14*

　Age and relationship of victim: *My sister was 9*

　Location: *My bedroom*

　Sexual behaviors not previously mentioned:

　　Put my finger in her vagina

　　Tried to put my penis in her butt

　Coercion: *Bribed her with my Game-boy*

　Coercion to keep the secret: *Told her we would be in trouble*

　Signs of confusion or distress: *She was embarrassed and cried one time*

All other offenses between first and last:

　Other Locations: *always at our house*

　Approximately how many incidents between first and last times: *5 or 6*

　Other sexual behaviors not previously mentioned:

　　Masturbating and showing her how I ejaculate

　　Rubbed her genitals

　Other tools of coercion: *Bribed her one time saying I would play with her after*

　Age(s) and relationship(s) of other victims: *My cousin when he was 8. One time, when he spent the night, I showed him how to masturbate by doing it with him. We each touched ourselves but not each other.*

DENIAL

The second of the "Big Ds" in this work is denial. Treatment of juveniles or adolescents, who completely deny the referring offense, continues to be one of the most controversial issues in the field. For years the prevailing opinion was that complete denial was reason to refuse to provide offense-specific treatment, with some primarily concerned that there was no "accountability" and others stating that if the person denies the problem you could not ethically say you were treating them. A number of considerations have clouded that assumption:

- Meta-analysis of research on juveniles has found denial to be an unlikely risk factor for sexual recidivism (Worling & Langstrom, 2006).
- The evolving understanding of the denial that is part of human defense mechanisms, and some understanding of the protective function that unconscious denial can serve. It has been hypothesized that some mechanisms that result in denial (i.e., guilt, embarrassment, etc.) may also actually reduce

the odds of reoffending. Purely intuitive thinking supports questioning why someone would continue to deny a behavior in spite of consequences resulting from the denial. Simplistically, thinking that one would not deny something unless it was incongruent with their values.

- Another consideration is that for some juveniles, admitting would constitute having to choose to give up their family, in cases where the parent(s) cannot accept the reality of what the youth has done, and have vowed that if it were true, they would abandon the youth. For some of those parents, their own unresolved issues from childhood victimization are so tied into their denial of what has now transpired with their own child, that it would take years of involuntary treatment with the whole family to attempt repair of all the complex issues.
- Especially more recently, due to the severe legal penalties that can be incurred, attorneys representing the youth may advise against "confessions." And of course, it must be acknowledged that some might actually be innocent, despite a court's finding of guilt.
- Another consideration arises in thinking about treatment of other disorders that people deny, whether physical, behavioral, or mental, that there are actually many disorders that people deny yet receive treatment for.
- Many providers had eventually developed "pre-treatment" interventions essentially designed to try to help "deniers" give up the denial with support from peers, education, and encouragement, some with success, and others still never admitting.
- Many providers offered a time-limited involvement during which various coercive techniques, including legal sanctions and polygraph testing, were used to try to "break through" denial.
- And a few providers did accept court ordered deniers into separate groups where they offered treatment for many of the issues without acknowledgment of the act.

At one point, those working with deniers were severely chastised by others in the field, but more recently, the long-term actuarial research on adults indicated that denial was actually not predictive of recidivism (Hanson & Morton-Bourgon, 2005). In spite of many possible explanations for those findings, that finding did seem to contradict earlier assumptions that denial was necessarily a high risk factor. In addition, one study has subsequently been published that did show a reduction in recidivism for deniers who did participate in treatment (Maletzky & MacFarland, 1995).

At this point in time, for juveniles, it seems reasonable that many programs still require that the youth be admitting that something sexual occurred and they were present, to agree to treat them in offense-specific treatment with other youth. Nonetheless, with a court order for treatment and the severe legal consequences for youth who do not get treatment, abuse-specific treatment and the goal-oriented approach do provide a framework within which these authors can suggest a strategy for treatment providers to follow when a referred youth completely denies involvement in an adjudicated offense.

Essentially, the treatment provider could agree to: (a) provide abuse-specific treatment, work to achieve the same "observable outcomes" previously discussed; and (b) address "perpetration prevention" through education. This would not be defined as offense-specific and some offense-specific treatment interventions would not be used. This would still require the youth's assent to participate in treatment. In addition to the abuse-specific education and treatment described in Chapter 17, perpetration prevention education would include:

1. Education regarding the laws relevant to sexual behavior and legal consequences of sexual offending.
2. Definition of sexually abusive interactions (lack of consent, unequal power or authority, coercion).
3. Education regarding the range of possible impacts/consequences for victims of sexual abuse, initially and over time.
4. Explore interpersonal relationship history, including the youth's relationship with the alleged victim, including issues of: attachment, empathy, coercive styles, and so forth.
5. Explore the youth's own history of victimization, loss, trauma, and so forth.
6. Educate regarding how people respond to stress (human defenses) and the function of denial.
7. Evaluate overall functioning/dysfunction, to define other types of abusive behavior.
8. Educate about healthy sexuality, relationship skills, and so forth.
9. Teach what is known about juveniles who do sexually offend, including the low base rate of recidivism.
10. Teach risk management (safety planning) in terms of the need to avoid any situations in which further allegations might occur.

As the work evolves, the therapist might occasionally ask things like:

"If you did do what was alleged, what would that mean to you?
If you did do it, what would admitting it say about you?
What do you think would happen if you did admit?
What would you expect others to say?
Can you see any reasons, looking back, why these allegations came up?
Are there things you would like to know about juveniles who sexually abuse younger children (or sexually assault others)?"

In this way, the therapist can keep opening the door in case the juvenile does in fact reach a point of admitting, but does not force the issue. Doing this work provides an extended evaluation of whether this youth does demonstrate a lot of abusive or dysfunctional dynamics, and other aspects of the youth that might be risk factors for general delinquency, sexual abuse, or other risk behaviors.

If the youth does become able to demonstrate the "observable outcomes relevant to decreased risk and increased health," the report to the court should be clear that the treatment was not specific to the alleged offending but has addressed the overall functioning and risk of being abusive in general.

VICTIM AWARENESS, EMPATHY, AND SYMPATHY

The process of developing an awareness of how sexually abusive behaviors affect others is critical to countering the beliefs, attitudes, and distortions that support, allow, or rationalize abusive behavior. Education again precedes work on the youth's own offenses. Videos and books regarding child victims and adult survivors may be used to broaden the group's appreciation of the impact of sexual abuse. The youth's own experiences of victimization can also be a source of understanding.

Early work related to victim awareness may include assignments requiring the youth to learn and think about immediate, short-term, and long-term changes that could be consequences for victims of sexual abuse. Understanding the aversive consequences of their offenses for those they sexually abused is a part of the work to increase empathic and sympathetic deterrence. Information about survivor issues might come from reading materials, videos, or actually meeting with adults who have survived childhood sexual abuse. The hope is that understanding the impact of sexual victimization will motivate the youth to work in treatment and ultimately to appreciate the feelings of others.

In some groups, the victimization in the lives of the youth is so pervasive that the group can be a source of both support and confrontation from peers in relation to how their behaviors may have affected others. Discussion of victimization issues can also trigger PTSD symptoms for some youth. The uniqueness of every individual's thoughts, perceptions, and emotions must be understood in relation to victimization, and the consequences may also be uniquely shaped by the individual's view of themselves and relationships and the world. Prior life experiences and coping skills affect the victim's perceptions and experience as well as the subsequent accommodation and assimilation of victimization (see Chapter 11). As individual differences are discussed, the need to recognize cues of others becomes increasingly apparent.

The range of possibilities of how different victims might perceive, understand, and be affected by abuse is probably infinite. For some an abusive experience may be perceived as a betrayal of one's trust in one's own perceptions as well as betrayal of trust in others, when a relationship appears to be good and then proves to be exploitive. For others abuse can be a traumatic experience in which the perception is one of total helplessness and a lack of control, contributing to a pervasive sense of unpredictable danger. It is imperative that the youth explore the range of possible effects without making assumptions that they can now know how the victim feels when they did not at the time they were with them.

Direct knowledge of victim impacts can also inform discussions. It is often possible for therapists to obtain victim statements and in many cases it is useful for the therapist, in communication with the therapist or parent who knows the person who was abused, to invite correspondence expressing thoughts, questions, and emotions. Such correspondence should only be through the therapists and shared in therapy sessions.

Having provided general information and defined general impacts, the third piece of work that is specific to the youth's own offenses is to explore the lack of empathic deterrence when they offended. It is critical to personalize the victim as a human being: validating the victim's right to safety and privacy; using only first names; and challenging expressions, such as "my victim," that objectify or assert ownership of victims.

Whereas victim awareness work may ask the youth to imagine what the victim was feeling or to describe the ways abuse experiences may continue to affect people in future relationships, victim empathy work will ask the youth: "What signs did you see in the other person that might be indicators of how they were feeling? What cues did you miss? Or what cues did you misinterpret?" Similarly, youth can be helped to develop empathy for self and others by getting in touch with their own cues. Questions like, "What was your body telling you? What was your heart feeling?" can help the person recognize their own cues.

By the end of treatment, many youth can engage in a process of "clarification" with the person they offended; increasing their awareness of victim issues prepares them for that, as well as contributing to their capacity for sympathy and empathy in future relationships. Sibling clarification and reunification will be discussed later in this chapter.

Victim-perpetrator sessions—with the specific victim when the victim is in the family and reunification is a goal, or when such sessions are requested by a victim therapist for a third-party offense—can be useful, but they must be carefully prepared for and must always be responsive to the victim's need for such a session. Many times a very specific need may be addressed by receiving letters and helping the youth respond in a helpful way. For example, a younger sibling who is preoccupied with their fear that the youth blames them or is mad at them can be reassured by a letter from their sibling simply stating that the younger child was not at fault and there is no anger. This can occur long before the youth is actually ready to sit with the victim in clarification sessions.

CONTROLLING AROUSAL

All of the work in treatment is relevant to avoidance or interruption of future dysfunctional cycles, but a few interventions very specifically address arousal. Covert sensitization and conditioning techniques are used to decrease deviant arousal, and cognitive restructuring techniques are used to correct the thoughts, attitudes, beliefs, justifications, and rationalizations that supported or allowed their sexual offense behavior. Either can be introduced as soon as clients have applied the cycle to their situation or have identified the thinking that supports sexual offending and the immediate antecedents occurring prior to the sexual abuse.

Sexual arousal and masturbation are often associated with cognitive elements of anticipation and contemplation, and sexual arousal is integral to the sexual aspect of sexual offense behavior. Treatment is geared toward assisting the youth in defining, decreasing, or managing the arousal that is associated with the sexually abusive behavior, in order to prevent reinforcement of sexual deviance. The National Task Force on Juvenile Sexual Offending (1988) made the following assumption: "If arousal patterns indicate significant or fixated interest in deviant and/or criminal sexual behaviors, it is in (the juvenile's) best interest to change or control his arousal" (p. 46). A similar statement was repeated in the 1993 revised report (p. 80).

Covert sensitization is a self-conducted technique that develops uncomfortable associations with thoughts, fantasy, or behavior that has occurred immediately antecedent to the youth's offense behavior. The process is designed to interrupt the pleasurable association and anticipation that previously reinforced the pattern. Several potential effects can be beneficial, including: earlier recognition of the first abusive sexual thought; improved impulse control or decision making; decreased frequency or strength of sexually abusive thoughts or fantasy; decreased frequency or intensity of arousal to abusive thoughts; and an improved sense of self-control. Although most research substantiating the effectiveness of this technique has been related to work with adult offenders (Abel et al., 1984; Quinsey & Marshall, 1983), research by Hunter and Santos (1990); Becker, Cunningham-Rathner, and Kaplan (1986); Faniff and Becker (2005); and Aylwin, Reddon, and Burke (2005) describe the effective use of this technique with adolescents.

Although it is clear that not all youth have difficulty with recurring sexually abusive thoughts or arousal, it is reasonable to presume that this could be a risk. Continuing to experience abuse-related arousal is a significant risk factor for recidivism, yet talking with therapists about problematic sexual fantasies and arousal can also be quite difficult for some youth. Completing the covert sensitization intervention should not pose any risk of harm *when done correctly*, even if a youth does not need the intervention; all the work done in preparation for the conditioning process is relevant to other treatment goals. For these reasons many programs do require some work on this assignment for all the youth. Youth with recurring sexually abusive thoughts associated with their arousal may later state that they felt a benefit from completing the entire conditioning protocol, even if they were not forthcoming in discussing the problem with the therapist, before doing the assignment.

The youth is taught to mentally pair the pattern of a personally typical precipitating phase of the cycle ending with the first thought of a sexually abusive fantasy with aversive consequences through a structured sequence. The youth may be expected to record sessions on audiotape or to complete the assignments in the treatment setting (Ryan & Lane, 1997). Because fantasies of sexually abusive behaviors could be very reinforcing, it is again cautioned that this assignment should not include detailed descriptions of sexual offense fantasy or behaviors.

Clinicians who use covert sensitization techniques must initially educate the youth regarding the expected outcomes and effects (talking about the potential risks if they continue to have abusive thoughts and/or arousal) and how, for those who do have trouble with that, this conditioning process can help. It is important to state that, even though not all of them have trouble avoiding those thoughts, it is one factor that would be such a big risk that it is a good idea for all of them to address that risk. Again, talking about the research that supports the technique, the therapist can state:

> Although this does not always work for everyone, the research shows that for some the conditioning process does significantly decrease either the frequency or intensity of either the thoughts or the arousal associated with sexual offending.

The scenes developed by the youth are the "high risk" or precipitating scene, the aversive scene, and the rewards-of-change scene. The precipitating scene is a one- to two-minute scene describing the sequence of thoughts and behaviors occurring immediately antecedent to the client's first thought of sexually acting out, and stops at that thought.

The writing of the aversive scene was described earlier in this chapter. In the conditioning process, the aversive scene picks up at the point where the thought of sexually abusive behavior occurred, and without describing specific sexual behavior, simply states that they reoffended. The aversive scene is a description of strongly aversive personal and social consequences that could occur as a result of reoffending and must be at least three minutes long when read aloud. During this scene, the client makes three to four references as to why these aversive consequences are occurring (perhaps because of their abusive sexual thoughts or sexually abusive behaviors). This strengthens the pairing of the consequences with the precipitating thoughts and behaviors.

The client then switches to the rewards-of-change scene, which is a one- to two-minute description of what they do instead of acting out the abusive thought, and throughout the scene, the youth makes reference to the positive things that now occur being possible because of no longer engaging in sexually abusive behaviors and being in control of sexual thoughts and behaviors.

Assignments will include developing the three scenes, written in first person/present tense and identifying the most aversive consequences of reoffending: *"I am really scared . . . the police are here . . . I am standing in court . . . "* (etc.), and the most rewarding outcomes that the youth can imagine if they do not: *"My mom tells me she is proud of me . . . I feel good because I don't abuse anymore."* The high risk or precipitating scene must be general enough to be relevant to a variety of times in the foreseeable future and contains the basic elements of the youth's cycle up to the first abusive thought: *"I am having a horrible day . . . (this and that) happened at school or work . . . I am feeling terrible; it isn't fair . . . I start to think about doing something sexual to my sister when I get home. (Stop).* The first scene ends with the abusive thought. As mentioned earlier in this chapter, the aversive scene can be written early in treatment and becomes a concrete tool for those youth who need to stop abusive thoughts and/or arousal. The youth are instructed to repeat the aversive scene to themselves to interrupt unwanted thoughts or arousal.

Writing the precipitating scene will be done second because it requires the youth to have learned about the cycle and understand their own patterns that could lead up to a compensatory or retaliatory sexual thought. And the change scene cannot be written until the youth has begun to demonstrate some new ways of coping and interrupting their own cycle. The change scene is strengthened as youth begin to experience their ability to change and identify positive goals for the future. Writing the scenes can be quite difficult for some youth, but they can have lots of help from peers in the group, parents, staff, and therapists. The expectation is that they draft a scene, bring it to read in group, get feedback and ideas from others, rewrite, and so forth, until it is the approved length and includes the necessary elements. When all three scenes are complete, they can begin the conditioning process using the scenes they have written.

According to research by Abel et al. (1984), the most effective results of the conditioning process are obtained when 4 hours of this technique are completed in 20-minute segments. Therefore, it is recommended that the juvenile complete twelve 20-minute segments, at a rate of not more than four per week. The conditioning technique is not useful if it is not done correctly and the client needs to complete the required number of sessions, so the most efficacious process is to record the sessions on audiotape.

A typical protocol would include repeating three to four sets of the three scenes for a 20-minute session. Some youth may not have a private place at home to make the recordings without interruption and might need to come early or stay late at the treatment agency to complete the conditioning tapes. The therapist must check the tapes, carefully at first, and then spot check them for continued compliance with the process. The client is provided feedback regarding how well they follow the protocol, and the audiotapes are destroyed after use.

Although the work on covert sensitization takes a lot of time, everything the time is spent on is relevant to the other goals of treatment, so the time is well spent, and completion of the assignment is a milestone in treatment.

It is unclear how many youth might be dissuaded from offending if they simply thought about the consequences before they did it. Repetition of the aversive scene is akin to writing 100 times on the blackboard "I will not chew gum in class!" Many of the kids who were younger and lower risk have said they did not know all the bad things that would happen—just thought they would be "in trouble." Youth who continue to acknowledge problems with deviant thoughts and arousal after completion of the conditioning process might benefit from the following:

1. Plethysmography assessment of their patterns to establish a baseline.
2. An additional covert sensitization protocol repeating the recitation of their precipitating, aversive, and reward scenes into a tape recorder several times per week for a few weeks.

3. Self-monitoring and reporting of the patterns they notice in themselves in a journal. Many in the field have raised the concern regarding the use of fantasy logs focusing on deviant thoughts due to the potential reinforcement of deviance (Aylwin, Reddon, & Burke, 2005; Faniff & Becker, 2005), so using journals or logs must be explained clearly. If the youth is able to recognize that a fantasy is problematic, the goal is to stop thinking about it and either do something unrelated or switch to a healthy fantasy.
4. Plethysmography assessment at the end of six months in which they are directed to suppress arousal to the problematic cues. (Some will do this with mental repetition of the aversive scene.) The results can then be compared to the baseline plethysmography and if there is no change, some other interventions should be explored.

Additional arousal conditioning techniques might include fantasy management to develop nonabusive, arousing sexual fantasies; thought-stopping techniques to interrupt deviant fantasy; or aversive conditioning. While covert sensitization can be used for virtually all youth who have sexually offended, more intrusive or experimental conditioning techniques, developed primarily in work with adults, may be useful for those few who really do need more.

In more recent developments, Hunter and Lexier (1998) cite reports on the use of Selective Serotonin Reuptake Inhibitors (SSRIs) in the treatment of paraphilias. These pharmaceuticals are typically prescribed as antidepressant and anti-obsessional agents but have been utilized with juveniles who commit sexual offenses due to side effects that include suppression of sexual desire and delayed ejaculation. Similar to the more extreme conditioning techniques discussed, there is not enough known about the effectiveness of SSRIs or about the types of juveniles with whom they may be effective, although research continues relevant to these types of interventions.

One form of arousal conditioning intervention from the adult field is satiation. Satiation techniques have been used in some programs with juveniles to decrease the client's arousal to deviant behaviors and stimuli. The satiation procedure is based on an extinction model designed to eliminate the erotic aspects through boredom. Most programs that include satiation techniques use Abel's protocol (Abel et al., 1984). Essentially, the process involves repeating the deviant fantasy for specified periods of time until it becomes boring. The repetition may be accompanied by masturbation or may consist of only verbal repetition. Each satiation session typically lasts for 1 hour and consists of one 5- to 10-minute scene describing consensual activity with an appropriate-aged partner, followed by 50 to 55 minutes of repeating a specific, arousing component of a deviant sexual behavior. Approximately six to eight sessions are required for beneficial results. This technique has not been popular in the field because of parental resistance, difficulty in monitoring, and limited research.

Satiation therapy, arousal conditioning, and vicarious sensitization are among the more controversial techniques designed to reduce deviant arousal or to increase sexual interest. These techniques have been used sparingly due to the inconsistent empirical data on their efficacy as well as questions as to the appropriateness of techniques that expose youth to physically or emotionally aversive stimuli or that involve masturbation (Hunter & Goodwin, 1992; National Task Force, 1993). Behavioral conditioning with noxious olfactory stimuli such as ammonia is similarly controversial, although it has been effective in reducing unwanted arousal for some juveniles. The National Task Force on Juvenile Sexual Offending (1993) recommends that aversive conditioning with ammonia only be used in laboratory settings if self-administered by the juvenile and with assent/consent from the juvenile, parent, and referring authority.

The National Task Force (1993) also stated: "When there is a reason to suspect a continuing problem with thoughts and arousal that appears indicative of a sexual deviance problem, either by history (e.g., multiple male child victims), by observation of the youth, or by self reports, physiological testing may be indicated, as the more intrusive techniques are considered somewhat experimental and require careful monitoring" (pp. 88–89).

PHYSIOLOGICAL TESTING OF JUVENILES: PLETHYSMOGRAPHY AND POLYGRAPHY

Somewhat like the two "Big Ds" of Denial and Disclosure work, the two "Big Ps" involving physiological testing have also been somewhat controversial in work with juveniles. A position statement drafted for the National Task Force in 2001 and reviewed without revision by Ryan in 2009 has been adapted in the following section.

Two types of physiological measures that have been used, more or less, in treatment and supervision of youth who have sexually offended are plethysmography and polygraphy. Both are sometimes controversial and neither is used by all providers. There is no research to date to show that such measures specifically reduce the risk of future offending, or to support their use indiscriminately with all juveniles who have committed sexual offenses. Like every other intervention, physiological measures may provide information that is useful in the treatment process and/or the supervision and monitoring process for some youth when used thoughtfully in the context of individualized interventions.

Physiological measures are, by design, somewhat intrusive measures, and may be perceived as coercive techniques used to extract information from the juvenile that they are either unwilling or unable to describe verbally. Coercion is a quality inherent in the problem of abuse and should be minimized in treating abuse issues. Therefore, physiological measures should be used thoughtfully, and with respect for the youth's willingness to assent. The purpose should be clearly stated in relation to the individual youth, and based on needs identified by the ongoing assessment process.

Prior to the youth's assent to submit to physiological testing, the technology and process of the testing should be thoroughly explained, and the potential relevance of the procedure to the juvenile's treatment and/or supervision should be explained. No juvenile should be tested without the full, informed consent of the parent or legal guardian and the informed assent of the juvenile. The potential consequences of both compliance and noncompliance with the procedure should be fully explained, including legal consequences when such procedures are included in court orders.

While acknowledging the potentially intrusive nature of physiological testing, such testing should not be withheld when clinically indicated, or when used as a part of monitoring, which enables the juvenile to benefit from lower levels of containment or higher degrees of freedom. Juveniles often experience the verbal discussion of many topics inherent in treatment of sexual disorders, victimization, and/or perpetration issues as intrusive. Some experience the physiological measures as less intrusive than prolonged discussions of embarrassing or painful issues. Others might experience distress or discomfort. Individual differences should guide the treatment plan.

The juvenile's understanding, experience, and perceptions should be assessed throughout the introduction and administration of physiological testing, and such procedures should be discontinued if there are indications of undue distress or unintended consequences for the juvenile. Physiological assessments should not be used alone, or exclusively, as the sole basis for treatment or management decisions, but can sometimes provide useful information to the ongoing assessment in an expedient manner.

Technicians must be qualified and specially trained in use of these techniques with juveniles, and must follow ethical and professional standards relevant to the technique and the standards of professional associations such as ATSA and APA.

Plethysmography

Plethysmography is a laboratory assessment of sexual arousal patterns that can provide the youth and treatment provider with valuable information about the individual's sexuality. Plethysmography is a physiological measure that records changes in penile tumescence (increase in the circumference of the penis) and detumescence (decrease in the circumference of the penis) occurring in response to a variety of sexual stimulus (Davis, 1988).

The stimulus materials used vary. Originally, in the 1970s and 1980s, all stimuli were visual pictures. Concerns about use of pornographic images, some of which would be illegal to possess, led to development of auditory stimuli, which were found to be even more discriminating. In use with juveniles, ATSA had recommended use of auditory stimulus materials and that clients be at least 14 years of age. There has always been some controversy regarding the potential iatrogenic risks of juveniles being exposed to deviant stimuli; however, Becker, Hunter, Stein, and Kaplan (1989) and Hunter and Santos (1990) cite the use of auditory stimulus material that were specifically developed for the assessment of adolescents, and some newer systems use benign clothed pictures of people of different ages, developmental stages, and gender.

The assessment measures the differential response of the individual to the variety of sexual stimuli presented in order to identify the client's arousal and interest patterns (such as prepubescent children versus similar age peers and forceful versus consenting sexual behaviors). Levels of penile tumescence are used to understand to what degree the subject is interested in deviant versus nonproblematic sexual behaviors or partners and to understand the client's arousal pattern so that specific interventions can be applied to alter or manage problematic sexual arousal patterns (Davis, 1988).

Research has not been done to assess the arousal patterns of juveniles in the general population, so there is no "normative" data for adolescents. Research using samples of college age males has shown that even as older teens and young adults, many males in this culture experience a wide range of sexual interests. The limited research using plethysmography with juveniles is at least partly due to ethical concerns regarding what is perceived to be an intrusive procedure and exposure of minors to sexual stimuli.

There is some research to support that juveniles who have sexually abused multiple male children may have specific interests in prepubescent males, whereas those who abuse female children may not be specifically interested in prepubescent children (Hunter, Goodwin, & Becker, 1994; Murphy, DiLillo, Haynes, & Steere, 2001; Seto, Lalumiere, & Blanchard, 2000). Nonetheless, Becker, Hunter, Goodwin, Kaplan, and Martinez (1992) found that sustained interest in prepubescent females may also demonstrate other forms of problematic interest.

The connection between denial and decreased responding does suggest that some juveniles may be able to successfully suppress unwanted arousal even without specific treatment interventions (Becker & colleagues, 1992). Kaemingk, Koselka, Becker, and Kaplan (1995) found that younger juveniles were more responsive to a wider range of cue categories than older youth. There have also been mixed results as to whether some youth who have experienced child sexual abuse themselves may respond more indiscriminately to stimuli (Faniff & Becker, 2005). Even with the research that has been done with juveniles who have sexually offended, without adolescent "norms" for arousal it is premature to consider plethysmography valid or reliable as an assessment of "deviant" sexual arousal in juveniles (Faniff & Becker, 2005).

It is clear that not all youth who sexually offend have problematic sexual interests and arousal; however, there is support for the use of plethysmography with some juveniles. Individualized treatment planning should always inform differences in treatment interventions related to arousal. Hunter and Lexier (1998) question the advisability of exposing juveniles to stimuli involving children, and Becker and Harris (2004) suggest that plethysmography may be most indicated for older adolescents who have targeted multiple male children. Ongoing research such as Burton and Meezan (2004); Abel, Jones, Gabriel, and Harlow (2009); and Miner and colleagues (2010) continues to illuminate factors that may be indicators of adolescent arousal and interest in prepubescent male children.

Potential uses of juvenile plethysmography assessment include the following:

1. To compare the juvenile's relative physiological arousal to their own self-report in order to assess their self-awareness and enhance their understanding of their own sexuality.
2. To compare the individual's relative physiological arousal to different types of sexual stimuli (i.e., different behaviors, in the context of different types of relationships, and/or with different ages of partners).
3. To compare the juvenile's patterns of arousal over time in order to discern change (i.e., to measure increased arousal to nonproblematic stimuli and/or decreased arousal to problematic stimuli).
4. To assess the effectiveness of conditioning processes and/or suppression techniques the juvenile has worked on in treatment (i.e., to measure the juvenile's ability to suppress unwanted arousal).
5. To carefully control the administration of and monitor the effects of more intrusive conditioning techniques (such as olfactory conditioning). Such techniques are rarely indicated but should not be ruled out for juveniles who continue to experience problematic arousal associated with high-risk behaviors, and who are requesting treatment to address such.

Physiological assessment of arousal using plethysmography must only be done in a laboratory setting by operators trained and following relevant ethical and professional standards, including from ATSA. Technicians should have training specific to use of these instruments with juveniles.

POLYGRAPHY

Polygraphy measures a person's physiological responses/reactions when asked questions about relevant issues. Physiological reactions such as skin temperature, heart rate, respiration, and so forth are believed to be an indication of emotional responses that may be indicative of significant issues associated with the questions being posed, and may be related to denial, secrecy, deception, or involuntary or unconscious internal reactions. Polygraph tests are often referred to as "lie detectors" but may or may not be indicative of conscious deception. Polygraph testing can be used to measure physiological responses to questions regarding past or present behavior, and may be specific to certain topics or issues.

Polygraphy has been widely used as a tool in the assessment, treatment, and management of adult sexual offenders in the community, but is much less widely used with juveniles. Research specific to its use with juveniles who are known to have committed sexual offenses has shown that it does have a coercive effect in motivating some juveniles to disclose more information than they had previously disclosed, but there is no research directly correlating "more information" about past offending with better or different treatment outcomes, and some in the field recommend that it not be utilized at all with juveniles (Faniff & Becker, 2005; National Research Council, 2003).

The potential risks of using polygraphy to encourage or coerce more complete disclosures of past sexual offenses include the risk that work done in preparation for "full sexual history" or "full sexual offense history" might increase the reinforcement of problematic sexual arousal associated with thoughts of past sexual offenses. Therefore, care should be taken when using polygraphy to gain more disclosure of offense-specific information, to minimize the focus on sexual material that might be sexually arousing, and to direct the focus to discrete factual information that is clinically relevant to risk assessment, such as the range of behaviors, the numbers and types of victims, and the duration and frequency of sexual offending. Questions about undisclosed sexual offenses and/or sexually abusive behaviors cannot be reasonably posed until the juvenile has demonstrated an understanding of how to define illegal and abusive behaviors.

The specific disclosure questions that may be particularly relevant to treatment and management decisions would be those specific to sexual contact with younger siblings in the household, and those specific to identification of past victims. The results of polygraph testing can reassure parents and the community that they have tried to obtain the most complete information relevant to the protection of other children.

Polygraphy can also be used for purposes of monitoring, in order to encourage the juvenile to comply with, and then to measure reactions to questions regarding compliance with, conditions of probation, treatment, supervision, safety plans, and/or relapse prevention plans. Such use is superfluous when the juvenile is in higher levels of care where they are constantly observed by staff that monitor such compliance. However, some juveniles are able to remain at home, or move to a lower level of care when polygraph monitoring is in place. In such circumstances, the cost/benefit ratio for both the juvenile and the system is clear.

Polygraph test results for juveniles should be reported as "significantly reactive" or "not significantly reactive," and the assessment of the significance of such reactions becomes an area for treatment to explore with the juvenile in order to understand why the juvenile reacts to the question, topic, or issue. The results of polygraph tests, or the juvenile's compliance or refusal to comply with requests for polygraph testing, should not be used alone in making treatment and/or supervision decisions, but may be useful in some ways with some juveniles.

VICTIM-CENTERED CLARIFICATION AND REUNIFICATION
IN CASES OF SIBLING INCEST

When youth have sexually abused siblings, families and therapists face a number of dilemmas. More than 40% of child sexual abuse perpetrated by juveniles involves children living in the same households (Snyder & Sickmund, 2008). The expedient disposition may appear to be that such youth be removed from the home and never returned; however, the reality is not so simple. Even those juveniles who emancipate outside the family do eventually return to have sporadic or ongoing contact with family members as adults. Sibling relationships are not expendable, and can continue to be a source of either risks or assets across the life span. Therefore it is the responsibility of the therapist to direct the processes of clarification and reunification.

Family therapy (see Chapter 20) may include many aspects of the family system, functioning, and history that are relevant to the youth's past, present, and future issues, development, and functioning, but are not specifically related to the youth's sexual offense history. The issues of clarification are clearly offense-specific issues, and clarification should be considered in every case, as it addresses the needs of victims. Similarly, reunification with family members can be an issue in many cases when youth have been separated by circumstance or by design while in treatment, but in cases of sibling incest, reunification is an offense-specific issue. In sibling cases, decisions to reunify can only be made following the process of clarification, and the preparation for reunification must be "victim-centered."

Clarification is a process designed to benefit the victim in understanding and coping with what has happened. The essential elements of clarification are:

- To invite the victim to express feelings and/or ask questions related to the abuse.
- To communicate to the victim the clear attribution of the abuser's responsibility.
- To explain what is being done to prevent further offending; treatment, supervision.
- To assess the potential for further interaction to be beneficial or detrimental.
- To develop safety plans for further contact or condition to prevent future contact.

Meeting for face-to-face clarification is a goal when the two expect to have ongoing contact in the future, but may be preceded by correspondence long before either is ready to meet. In cases where further contact is not expected, clarification may be only through correspondence. Clarification correspondence is only through the youth's therapist and the therapist working with the person who was abused (or a parent or other advocate, in the absence of a therapist).

The goal of clarification is always to moderate potential negative sequelae for the victim by minimizing potential dysfunctional coping strategies such as: feeling responsible ("victim blaming"); repressing memories or emotions; guilt or shame; fear, distrust, and hyper-vigilance; and cognitive confusion. By making clear the victim's lack of culpability and responsibility, the attribution of responsibility to the youth who abused them allows recognition that the victim was not the one with a problem. The impacts on them and any subsequent problems may be moderated by that understanding.

Victim's needs in treatment and in clarification are unique, and individualized assessment is needed before decisions about clarification can be made. It cannot be assumed that every victim requires extensive treatment, and the victim may be ready to meet long before the youth who abused them is ready. The therapist will need some evidence of decreased risk before arranging a complete clarification process, but by inviting correspondence in the beginning, some of the victim's needs can often be addressed quite specifically before a meeting is warranted.

For example, a young child may be afraid that the youth who abused them is mad at them for telling, or may think it is their fault the abuse happened. Receiving a letter with those questions, the therapist is often able to facilitate the youth responding in writing to address those questions. Often the question is, "Why did you do it?" or "Why me?," and the youth may be able to state that they do not know the answers but that they are in treatment to figure that out and to learn to not do it anymore.

It can be reassuring to the victim to know that they are not the one who has to figure out why the abuse happened. Waiting for the youth to be ready to meet is easier when there is communication regarding progress, although, especially in family cases, the other family members are often impatient for the youth to be ready. When the youth is not cooperating in responding to victim correspondence, it becomes the responsibility of their therapist to communicate that they are working with the youth but the youth is not yet able to answer their questions.

Writing to express feelings does not require an immediate response but informs the youth's work in terms of victim awareness and empathy. It is often expected that the youth express remorse, apologize, and seek "forgiveness," but it is important to make clear that these are not a part of early communications. It may be reasonable that remorse and apologies are goals by the end of treatment, but will not be meaningful until the youth has done the work of treatment to understand what they have done, and demonstrates their commitment to change. It is important that the therapist take responsibility for the restriction on apologies and forgiveness in the beginning. Too often, families are eager to put the abuse behind them and rush to forgive and forget before there is evidence of decreased risk. (See Chapters 10 and 20 for more information regarding work with families.)

MILIEU STAFF AND OFFENSE-SPECIFIC PROGRAMMING

Milieu staff working with sexually abusive youth should be highly trained in safety planning and vigilant supervision, as well as the concepts of Abuse Is Abuse, the cycle, the universal goals, and developmental competence. Training must be reinforced with encouragement, support, and supervision, and staff must be accountable for implementing abuse-specific interventions in their interactions in the milieu.

The abuse-specific milieu model has several advantages for staff in segregated offense-specific programming. First, it offers a more holistic approach, viewing the youth as whole human beings rather than "sex offenders." Second, it keeps the focus on the abuse issues but without the constant vicarious exposure of staff and peers to the deviance and trauma of abuse. Third, it helps to provide some containment around the issues that escalate the youth's acting out by labeling and referring the manifestations of the cycle back into the clinical components of treatment. For example, when staff intervene in an escalating abuse cycle, they may identify important clues about triggers, cognitive distortions, or fantasy material. However, the issue is referred to the clinical components. For example: *"Saul, I noticed that you were kind of shut down right before you blew up at Pete. It might be helpful to talk to your group today about what kind of thoughts you were having,"* or *"Sara, I noticed you had a strong reaction when we walked past the stairwell. You might want to look at what that trigger was when you go to group today."* The fourth advantage is the clear distinction of role boundaries between direct care staff and clinicians and the reduced risk of burnout from chronic exposure to deviance.

The abuse-specific milieu also has many advantages for mixed population settings. By relating a single model to the dysfunctions of all the youth, staff and peers can see their similarities and avoid stigmatizing some behaviors as "worse" than others. The goal orientation of safety and growth meets the needs of all youth, and promoting communication, empathy, and responsibility represents universal goals for healthy, empathic relationships. For staff, the containment of deviant exposure in the milieu and the heterogeneity of a mixed population reduce the high risks of burnout associated with offense-specific work.

CONCLUSION

As previously stated, the offense-specific work that is uniquely relevant to the history of sexual offending is a discrete part of the treatment plan, and can be incorporated with the abuse-specific work, or addressed in adjunct individual, family, or group therapy. For some youth, the sexual issues involved in their offending are a large part of treatment; for many, the offending was much more related to their capacity to be abusive, or impediments to more functional behaviors. The individualized treatment plan should reflect both abuse-specific and offense-specific components.

REFERENCES

Abel, G., Gore, D., Holland, C., Camp, N., Becker, J., & Rathner, J. (1984). *The treatment of child molesters: A Manual.* Unpublished manuscript.

Abel, G. G., Jones, C. D., Gabriel, W., & Harlow, N. (2009). *A boy's experience of child sexual abuse: Factors that increase his risk of developing sexually abusive behavior.* Submitted for publication.

Aylwin, A. S., Reddon, J. R., & Burke, A. R. (2005). Sexual fantasies of adolescent male sex offenders in residential treatment: A descriptive study. *Archives of Sexual Behavior, 34*(2), 231–239.

Becker, J. V., Cunningham-Rathner, J., & Kaplan, M. F. (1986). Adolescent sexual offenders: Demographics, criminal sexual histories, and recommendations for reducing future offenses. *Journal of Interpersonal Violence, 4,* 431–445.

Becker, J. V., & Harris, C. (2004). The psychophysiological assessment of juvenile sex offenders. In G. O'Reilly, W. L. Marshall, A. Carr, & R. C. Beckett (Eds.), *The handbook of clinical intervention with young people who sexually abuse* (pp. 191–202). New York: Psychology Press, Taylor and Francis Group.

Becker, J. V., Hunter, J. A., Goodwin, D., Kaplan, M. S., & Martinez, D. (1992). Test-retest reliability of audio taped phallometric stimuli with adolescent sex offenders. *Annals of Sex Research,* 5: 45–51.

Becker, J. V., Hunter, J. A., Stein, R. M., & Kaplan, M. S. (1989). Factors associated with erection in adolescent sex offenders. *Journal of Psychopathology and Behavioral Assessment, 11*(4), 353–362.

Burton, D. L., & Meezan, W. (2004). Revisiting recent research on social learning theory as an etiological proposition for sexually abusive male adolescents. *Journal of Evidence Based Social Work, 1,* 41–80.

Conte, J. (1986). *Sexual abuse and the family: A critical analysis.* In T. Trepper & M. Barrett (Eds.), *Treating incest: A multimodal systems perspective* (pp. 113–126). New York: Hawthorn Press.

Davis, J. (1988). *Sexual arousal and related treatment*. Presentation handout at the "What Is the Plethysmograph?" workshop, National Conference on Juvenile Sex Offenders, Long Beach, CA.

Faniff, A. M., & Becker, J. V. (2005). Specialized assessment and treatment of adolescent sexual offenders. *Aggression and Violent Behavior, 11*, 265–282.

Hanson, R. K., & Morton-Bourgon, K. E. (2005). The characteristics of persistent sexual offenders: A meta-analysis of recidivism studies. *Journal of Consulting & Clinical Psychology, 73*(6), 1154–1163.

Hunter, J. A. (2001). *What research tells us about this population*. National Adolescent Perpetration Network Conference, Kansas City, MO.

Hunter, J. A., & Goodwin, D. W. (1992). The utility of satiation therapy in the treatment of juvenile sexual offenders: Variations and efficacy. *Annals of Sex Research, 5*, 71–80.

Hunter, J. A., Goodwin, D. W., & Becker, J. V. (1994). The relationship between phallometrically measured deviant arousal and clinical characteristics in juvenile sexual offenders. *Behavioral Research and Therapy, 32*, 533–538.

Hunter, J. A., & Lexier, L. J. (1998). Ethical and legal issues in the assessment and treatment of juvenile sex offenders. *Child Maltreatment, 3*, 339–348.

Hunter, J., & Santos, D. (1990). Use of specialized cognitive-behavioral therapies in the treatment of adolescent sexual offenders. *Journal of Offender Therapy and Comparative Criminology, 34*, 239–248.

Kaemingk, K. L., Koselka, M., Becker, J. V., & Kaplan, M. S. (1995). Age and adolescent sexual offender arousal. *Sexual Abuse: A Journal of Research and Treatment, 7*, 249–257.

Maletzky, B. M., & MacFarland, B. (1995). *Treatment results in offenders who deny their crimes*. Manuscript submitted for publication. [Study cited in Maletzky, B. M. (1996). Denial of treatment or treatment of denial? *Sexual Abuse: A Journal of Research and Treatment, 8*(1), 1–5.]

Miner, M. H., Robinson, B. E., Knight, R. A., Berg, D., Swinburne-Romine, R., & Netland, J. (2010). Understanding sexual perpetration against children: Effects of attachment style, interpersonal involvement, and hypersexuality. *Sexual Abuse: A Journal of Research and Treatment 22*(1), 58–77 (March).

Murphy, W. D., DiLillo, D., Haynes, M. R., & Steere, E. (2001). An exploration of factors related to deviant sexual arousal among juvenile sex offenders. *Sexual Abuse: A Journal of Research and Treatment, 13*, 91–102.

National Criminal Justice Information and Statistics Service. (1995). *Criminal victimization in the United States*. Washington, DC: U.S. Government Printing Office.

National Research Council of the National Academies. (2003). *The polygraph and lie detection*. Washington, DC: National Academies Press.

National Task Force on Juvenile Sexual Offending. (1988). Preliminary report. *Juvenile and Family Court Journal, 39*(2), 1–67.

National Task Force on Juvenile Sexual Offending, National Adolescent Perpetration Network. (1993). The revised report. *Juvenile and Family Court Journal, 44*(4), 1–120.

Quinsey, V., & Marshall, W. (1983). Procedures for reducing inappropriate sexual arousal. In I. Stuart & J. Greer (Eds.), *The sexual aggressor* (pp. 267–292). New York: Van Nostrand Reinhold.

Ryan, G. (2009). *Physiological testing of juveniles using plethysmography and polygraphy*. Unpublished position paper. Kempe Center: Denver, CO.

Ryan, G., & Lane, S. (1997). Integrating theory and method. In G. Ryan & S. Lane (Eds.), *Juvenile sexual offending: Causes, consequences, and corrections* (pp. 267–321). San Francisco: Jossey-Bass.

Seto, M. C., Lalumiere, M. L., & Blanchard, R. (2000). The discriminate ability of phallometric test for pedophilic interest among adolescent sex offenders against children. *Psychological Assessment, 12*, 319–327.

Snyder, H. M., & Sickmund, M. (2008). *Juvenile offenders and victims: 2006 National Report.* Washington, DC: U.S. Department of Justice, Office of Justice Programs, Office of Juvenile Justice and Delinquency Prevention.

Worling, J. R. (2004). Essentials of a good intervention program for sexually abusive juveniles: Offence related treatment tasks. In G. O'Reilly, W. L. Marshall, A. Carr, & R. C. Beckett (Eds.), *The handbook of clinical intervention with young people who sexually abuse* (pp. 275–296). New York: Taylor and Francis.

Worling, J. R., & Langstrom, N. (2006). Risk of sexual recidivism in adolescents who offend sexually: Correlates and assessment. In H. E. Barbaree & W. L. Marshall (Eds.), *The juvenile sex offender* (2nd ed., pp. 219–247). New York: Guilford Press.

CHAPTER 19

Brain Development and Function

Neurology and Psychiatry in the Treatment
of Sexually Abusive Youth

TOM LEVERSEE and GAIL RYAN

IN ORDER TO appreciate and validate the unique phenomenology of each youth and the implications of differential diagnosis and treatment, the provider must not lose sight of concurrent psychiatric disorders. Chapter 6 discusses those disorders that are particularly prevalent among sexually abusive youth (that is, overrepresented in this population compared to nonclinical peers). Attention-Deficit/Hyperactivity Disorder (Predominantly Inattentive Type, Predominantly Hyperactive-Impulsive Type, and Combined Type), affective (mood) disorders (especially depression and bipolar disorders), and anxiety disorders, (particularly Post-Traumatic Stress Disorder [PTSD]) are of special note (Becker, Kaplan, Tenke, & Tartaglini, 1991; Cavanaugh, Pimenthal, & Prentky, 2008; Ryan, Miyoshi, Metzner, Krugman, & Fryer, 1996). Estimates are that a significant number of these youth (especially those with more serious and chronic behaviors) may benefit from medical-psychiatric-neurological evaluation (Dailey, 1987; Lewis, Shanok, & Pincus, 1981).

Many juveniles who initially appear unable to participate and benefit from cognitive/affective/behavioral treatments have become able to do so when underlying attention deficit, anxiety, or depressive conditions are accurately diagnosed and treated. The importance of recognizing and treating concurrent psychiatric disorders became apparent as youth who were failing in offense-specific treatment programs were eventually diagnosed and treated with psychiatric interventions (especially pharmacology) for concurrent disorders, and became able to participate and complete the offense-specific programs (Dailey, 1987; Sczechowicz, 1988).

More recently advances in neurology and psychiatry have further refined the diagnosis and treatment of co-occurring disorders using new knowledge gleaned from brain research. The brain is involved in every aspect of human growth, experience, and functioning. More has been learned about the human brain in recent decades than in all the history of mankind (Kotulak, 1996). The technology and methodology to actually study the living brain only became available in the 1970s and now contributes much greater specificity to the diagnosis and treatment of neurological and psychiatric

344

disorders. The science of the brain has informed many of the developmental, cognitive, and affective interventions described in earlier chapters.

The brain is continually developing and changing across the life span, most rapidly in the earliest years, although recent research suggests the neo-cortex is not mature until the mid-twenties. Higher cognitive processes are not fully developed in adolescence, as compared to adults, which manifests in adolescents being less efficient in cognitive processing and working memory, and impairs judgment and anticipation of consequences (Yager, 2005). Children and adolescents "appear to be using more of the rapid response, emotional region of the brain" (Powell, Chapter 16), whereas adult brain development improves the ability to think before acting, consider consequences, and to control and change behavior patterns. Understanding the role of brain development in self-regulation and cognition, Steinberg and Haskins (2008) now question the legal culpability of youth and the emotional distress and distressing behaviors of adolescents can now be better explained and treated. A fundamental understanding of the brain enhances every therapist's work.

One's genetic inheritance provides the foundation of the brain's potential, but individual experience shapes its construction, organization, and functions. Neural pathways that are used are strengthened and remain available, while unused pathways atrophy. Brain development has been described as progressing "from the bottom up," from the primitive to most complex fashion, from the brain stem and systems in the midbrain to the limbic system, concluding with the cortical areas. Table 19.1 (Creeden,

Table 19.1
Brain Development

Cortex	Cognitive and executive functioning
• Neocortex	➢ Thinking, reasoning, and cognition
↑	➢ Symbolic language
↑	➢ Conscious awareness
↑	➢ Meta-cognition
↑	➢ Planning, setting priorities, organizing thoughts, suppressing impulses, weighing the consequences of our actions
Limbic System	**Emotional processing and emotional regulation**
• Amygdala	➢ Monitor incoming stimuli and threat response
• Hippocampus	➢ Formation/recollection of emotional memory
• Thalamus	➢ Learning non-verbal motor patterns
↑	➢ Fight or flight response
↑	➢ Information exchange between mind and body
Brainstem	**Regulate Body Functions**
• Cerebellum	➢ Cardiovascular functions
	➢ Sleep cycles
	➢ Appetite
	➢ Coordination of movement

Source: Leversee (2009).

2006; Davies, 2004; Perry, 1997; Stien & Kendall, 2004) organizes this concept of brain development.

The brain stem regulates body functions, including cardiovascular functions, sleep cycles, and appetite. The brain stem region includes the cerebellum, which helps coordinate movement and a variety of social, emotional, and cognitive functions (Creeden, 2006; Stien & Kendall, 2004).

The limbic system is referred to as the emotional brain and functions as the center for processing urges, appetites, and emotions. The structures within the limbic system are seen as important in understanding the brain's response to experiences. The amygdala is involved in monitoring incoming stimuli and threat response. The amygdala may also be involved in the formation and recollection of emotional memory, the learning of nonverbal motor patterns, and the triggering of the fight or flight response (Teicher, Andersen, Polcari, Anderson, Navalta, & Kim, 2003). The hippocampus is the focal point for memory and learning, including processing conscious memory. The thalamus acts as a "relay station" for incoming stimuli, maintaining homeostasis and functioning as the main center for information exchange between the brain and the body (Creeden, 2006; Stien & Kendall, 2004).

The cortex is typically referred to as the thinking brain, where reasoning and cognition take place. The neo-cortex provides the capacity for symbolic language, conscious awareness, and metacognition, the capacity to think about our thoughts. The neo-cortex functions in planning, setting priorities, organizing thoughts, suppressing impulses, and weighing the consequences of our actions. The development of the cortex exerts a modulating influence in regulating limbic and brain stem responses (Creeden, 2006; Perry, 1997; Stien & Kendall, 2004). "With a set of sufficient motor, sensory, emotional, cognitive, and social experiences during infancy and childhood, the mature brain develops in a use-dependent fashion, a mature, humane capacity to tolerate frustration, contain impulsivity, and channel aggressive urges" (Perry, 1997, p. 129). Similarly, secure attachment supports coherent interpersonal relationships, producing the coherent neural integration within the child, which is the root of adaptive self-regulation (Siegel, 2001).

The brain is also organized into highly specialized hemispheres. The left hemisphere is specialized for perception, expression of language, and logical and analytical thought. The right hemisphere is focused on expression of emotion, particularly unpleasant emotion (Teicher and colleagues, 2003).

Brain development can be compromised by a number of biological and environmental factors, including genetic disorders, prenatal drug/alcohol exposure, prematurity, or poor nutrition (Davies, 2004). The plasticity of the child's brain makes it vulnerable to negative impacts from adverse experiences such as neglectful caregiving, abuse, trauma, and malnutrition (Perry, 2002).

Brain function contributes to understanding psychiatric and neurological disorders.

PSYCHIATRIC DISORDERS' RELATIONSHIP TO SEXUALITY AND ABUSIVE BEHAVIORS

One of the obstacles to effective integration of psychiatric and neurological interventions in work with sexually abusive youth has been differences in professional terminology used by offense-specific therapists and generalist psychiatrists. Specialist therapists must accurately communicate the symptoms that describe concurrent disorders, and diagnostic summaries from psychiatrists, must be relevant to the specialists' understanding of the youth. Language barriers can result in a breakdown in services that are critical to the youth's ability to be successful in treatment and across the life span. Maletzky (1996) explored the lack of collaboration between psychiatry and offense-specific treatment and found several factors related to poor communication. In an effort to create better communication, Ryan (1993) proposed a psychiatric view of the cycle that simplistically suggests psychiatric terms that may be relevant to different aspects of the cycle and symptomatic of the characteristics of the youth (see Table 19.2).

Some diagnosed disorders are the result of circumstance; that is, the symptoms were not present in the past, became present in reaction to some particular circumstance or event, and may dissipate over time, either with or without treatment. For example, many experience some degree of depression following the loss of a loved one. For some the depression reaches clinical levels and may benefit from therapy, but in most cases the depression lessens over time with or without treatment.

Other disorders are inherited predispositions that are actually discernable across the life span, more or less. For example, Attention-Deficit/Hyperactive Disorder (ADHD) and Bipolar disorder are found to run through families, but were not always recognized in childhood due to age differences in how the symptoms manifest. Newer, age-specific diagnostic criteria are addressing this.

Finally, some disorders are the result of circumstance but create differences in how the brain is organized and functions. This is particularly evident in some people's Post-Traumatic Stress Disorder (PTSD) symptoms, such as the veteran who still hits the ground when a car backfires many years later.

Knowledge arising from neurological and pharmaceutical research and practice in psychiatry (particularly in understanding the neurological functioning associated with symptoms such as attention-deficit/hyperactive disorders (before and after puberty), mood disorders in childhood and adolescence, obsessive-compulsive disorders, and trauma effects has improved the prognosis for some of the hardest-to-treat youth (those who have sometimes been labeled "untreatable" because professionals did not yet know how to treat them). Neurological and pharmacological interventions are now making significant advances in treating symptoms that were previously thought to be the product of permanent differences in the brain.

Clinicians and consulting psychiatrists working in specialist programs must routinely and consistently review the literature for studies including combinations of disorders, such as ADHD with Tourette's syndrome, depression combined with ADHD, or trauma symptoms combined with an inherited predisposition to depression. Pharmacological studies continue to refine medications that are more targeted and have fewer side effects, and many disorders now have evidence-based interventions that must be incorporated into the offense-specific work (Eth & Pynoos, 1985; James, 1989; Spiegel, 1993; Terr, 1990; van der Kolk, 1986).

Training for therapists has improved communication, as well as recognition and referrals for psychiatric and/or neurological evaluation. Screening for diagnostic characteristics in the patterns that manifest in behavior can expedite management of symptoms that pose an impediment in therapy. Diagnostic criteria have become increasingly age-specific and now inform more targeted pharmacological and neurological interventions.

Medication studies not only demonstrate which agents are most effective for particular disorders, but which work on particular symptoms best (for example, some medications are particularly effective in reducing intrusive fantasies, some are

Table 19.2

Psychiatric Symptomatology Associated with the Cycle

History	*Fantasy solution*
Trauma	Ruminating
Unresolved losses, rejection	Intrusive thoughts
Family history of affective disorders	Grandiosity
Family history of substance abuse	Suicidal ideation
Family history of suicide	Paraphiliac ideation
Head injuries	Homicidal ideation
School reports of attention deficit/hyperactivity disorder, learning disabilities, and so on	*Plan*
	Ritualized
Prenatal drug or alcohol exposure	Defensive
Complications at birth	
Enmeshed or intrusive parenting	*Decision*
Attachment disorders	Impulsive
Disruptions in early care	Dissociated
Developmental disability, deviance	Irrational
Trigger	*Behavior*
Flashbacks	Disordered
Flooding	Habituated
Overwhelming affect	Reinforcing
	Aggressive
Victim stance	Self-destructive
Paranoia	
Anxiety	*Anxiety*
Helplessness	Attention deficits
	Distractibility
Hopelessness	Hypervigilance
Depression	
External locus of control	*Promises*
Disorganized thinking	Grandiosity
Distortions	Magical thinking
Isolation	*Denial*
Dissociation	Amnesia
Withdrawal	Dissociated
Avoidant behavior	
Anger	
Defensiveness	
Projection	
Externalizing	
Mania	
Hysteria	

Source: Ryan (1993).

particularly helpful in reducing the affective flooding associated with PTSD triggers, some are useful in reducing disorganized thinking, and others address impulsive urges).

When medication is indicated, the intent is to moderate symptoms biochemically so the youth is able to successfully participate in treatment, not simply to sedate the client in order to stifle behavior. Monitoring medication trials for youth must provide the prescribing doctor with relevant details in order to determine when dosage needs adjustment or another medication should be tried. The need for monitoring and documentation of medication effects implies that all caregivers, therapists, and special educators need to learn what the medication is expected to change, as well as potential side effects.

Providers should have access to the most recent *Diagnostic and Statistical Manual of Mental Disorders* (DSM) and *Physician's Desk Reference* (PDR), and therapists and caregivers should ask the prescribing doctor for specific indicators of a positive or negative response (Dailey, 1996). Similarly, psychiatrists who consult on these cases enhance their role by learning about abuse-specific and offense-specific treatment in order to minimize communication barriers.

Understanding the relationship of concurrent psychiatric disorders and the dynamics associated with abuse informs differential treatment approaches. Simplistically, emotions are the fuel that powers the dynamics of the cycle and cognitions are the connectors at each step in the progression. Mood symptoms tend to exacerbate the emotional components while cognitions exacerbate the progression.

Psychiatric disorders influence the youth's way of thinking, reacting, and behaving. Some disorders may be manifest in ways that appear to be part of an abuse cycle when in fact they are not; at other times the manifestation may be triggered by the cycle progression itself. For example, a youth who has been diagnosed as dysthymic and is not sleeping well may be manifesting associated hyperactivity rather than responding to anxiety associated with his current treatment work. Another youth may be extremely upset by exploring abuse issues and experience an increase in obsessive thoughts or compensatory fantasies, trying to cope with the anxiety. Youth exhibiting increased defensiveness or irritability may be manifesting elements of the cycle, or could be experiencing symptoms of a mood disorder, or could be reacting to some PTSD symptom, or might just be hungry (blood sugar too low). As the provider becomes increasingly aware of how a youth's particular disorder interacts with the abusive dynamics of the cycle, treatment for that youth can become increasingly specific.

Some disorders, especially those associated with traumatic experience, are often resolvable if the client is able to tolerate the work, and short-term use of medications may aid the process. Some disorders appear more transitory or situational (see aforementioned) and may be more easily resolved with short-term medication and/ or counseling. Other disorders are inherited and chronic, and will require lifelong management. For the inherited disorders, pharmacological interventions are often most successful and optimal results are achieved when medication is used in combination with other therapeutic interventions.

The goals in treatment of any concurrent psychiatric disorders are:

1. To manage symptoms that might impede success in the offense program.
2. To achieve resolution of or develop a life span management perspective of effects that might impede success in relationships.
3. To achieve optimal global functioning.
4. To achieve knowledge and acceptance of those disorders that are unchangeable.

For many psychiatric disorders, there are now evidence-based treatments that are congruent adjuncts to the abuse-specific and offense-specific work. Some of the most innovative and successful advances are in treatment of post-traumatic stress disorder.

NEURODEVELOPMENTAL IMPACTS OF TRAUMA

Risk factors discussed in previous chapters enumerate many adverse experiences that are overrepresented in the population of youth referred for offense-specific treatment. Although not all adverse experience is traumatic, post-traumatic stress symptoms are quite common in many of these youth. For some the experience of abuse or abandonment is traumatic; for others, losses, chronic stress, or other adversity creates a traumatic syndrome. In healthy development, secure attachment provides a sense of security, validation and regulation of affect and arousal, promotes the expression of feelings and communication, and serves as a base for developmental exploration as well as a protective shield in times of adversity (Davies, 2004). The child who experiences adversity without protection is at risk for developmental disruption, dysfunctional coping, and cognitive confusion.

The cognitive-emotional processes and behavioral manifestations of child maltreatment and trauma are all too familiar to the professionals working with youth diagnosed with conduct disorders. One youth described his mother, *"walking out on my life . . . it's happened three to four different times."* He reported that he was left with his father and an uncle who sexually abused him at age 2-and-a-half. In describing abandonment as an emotional trigger, he stated, *"It's like a nuclear bomb . . . it's always going to happen, nothing is going to change, can't trust people . . . imagine ways to get my power back."* He reported behavioral manifestations as isolating, antisocial and destructive behaviors, lying, manipulating, and power struggles.

Youth in residential settings and foster homes describe hyper-vigilance as being *"nervous"* and *"cautious"* in group living settings, being *"very aware of my surroundings,"* and *"sleeping with my back to the wall."* One youth who had been physically abused by a male caregiver reported being triggered by external cues reminiscent of his trauma, including *"people yelling . . . invading my space . . . verbal put-downs . . . hearing loud voices."* Another youth who had experienced neglect and multiple traumas reported to the group, *"I'm on a short thread. I just wanna hit someone."*

The consequences of traumatic experiences for the developing child or adolescent are uniquely personal for each individual but may be affected by the age at which a child is first traumatized, the frequency of traumatic experience, and/or the availability (or lack) of caregivers as supportive resources (Davies, 2004; Ryan and Associates, 1998; Terr, 1990; van der Kolk, 2003; van der Kolk, McFarlane, & Weisaith, 1996). More advanced development may be a protective factor as a child becomes better able to assess, interpret, and cope with distressing events (Rutter, 1985).

The child's experience of and the meaning attributed to traumatic experiences are salient factors related to the impact of trauma and its accommodation and assimilation into the child's view of self, relationships, and the world (see Chapters 8 and 11). Symptoms of trauma may be expressed in intense psychological distress and/or physiological reactivity when exposed to internal or external cues reminiscent of an aspect of the traumatic event or exposure including: chronic hyper-arousal; hyper-vigilance; problems with self-regulation, attention, and dissociation; aggression toward self and others; physical problems, distorted self-concept, and impaired capacity to negotiate satisfactory interpersonal relationships (APA, 2000; van der Kolk, 1986, 2003).

Ryan (1989) described parallels in victimization outcomes and offending triggers and Gil and Johnson (1993) described the sexually reactive child. Finkelhor (1987) describes "traumatic sexualization" associated with some sexual abuse including sexual preoccupation, compulsive sexual behaviors, precocious sexual activity, and aggressive sexual behaviors. Traumatized youth may be likely (more than those who do not have trauma effects) to report sexual preoccupations that interfere with daily functioning such as compulsive masturbation, involvement in multiple sexual paraphilias, and, for some, extensive involvement in pornography.

TRAUMA AND THE BRAIN

Research has illuminated changes in the brain associated with trauma that affect cognitive, emotional, and behavioral patterns (Perry, 1997; van der Kolk, 1986). The neural plasticity of the brain allows it to be molded and altered by the quality of the individual's transactions with the environment, for better or worse (Nelson, 2000; Vance, 2001). Because brain growth is "experience-dependent" or "use-dependent," trauma can have neurotoxic impacts on the developing brain that compromise important neural pathways (van der Kolk, McFarlane, & Weisaith, 1996).

Teicher et al. (2003) postulates that repeated exposure to childhood maltreatment promotes an alternative neurodevelopmental pathway that may potentiate the development of psychiatric illness and behavioral dysfunction. "The brain goes through a sensitive period in post natal life in which exposure to high levels of stress hormones (corticosteroids) . . . causes the brain to develop along a stress-response pathway" in order "to survive in a malevolent stress filled world" (p. 39). This adaptive alternative pathway allows that individual to adapt to high levels of life-long stress, enabling the individual to mobilize intense fight or flight responses or react aggressively to challenge. These alterations are unnecessary and maladaptive in a more benign environment. What may appear to adults as willful, oppositional, and self-defeating behavior may have developed and be perceived by the youth as a matter of survival.

Stress-related effects on the development of the different regions of the brain include functional consequences (Teicher et al., 2003). The hippocampus has been implicated in the generation of dissociative states and plays a significant role in generalized anxiety and panic disorder as well as long-term memory and emotional regulation (Vance, 2001). Lack of development of the hippocampal region may contribute to increased language difficulties and lower verbal memory (Teicher, Andersen, Polcari, Anderson, & Navalta, 2002).

The amygdala plays a crucial role in fear conditioning and in controlling aggressive oral and sexual behaviors, as well as episodic impulsive violence. Excessive activation of the amygdala is thought to play a crucial role in the development of PTSD (Teicher et al., 2002).

Brain research has significantly improved the clinical understanding of neurological functioning, and now informs the treatment of trauma and psychiatric disorders. Creeden's (2006) summary illuminates the potential impacts of trauma on functioning as well as the implications for responsivity to treatment:

> . . . persistent levels of amygdala activation generate a kindling effect where the individual can become hypervigilant in scanning for threat cues and over-interprets

or misrepresents mildly difficult or even innocuous cues as being significantly threat-ening. This pattern of amygdala response has a variety of consequences such as general difficulties in affect regulation; problems in effectively learning from highly charged emotional situations, and applying that learning to new or novel stimulus; decreased activation of the speech center of the brain, contributing to difficulties in expressive/receptive language difficulties and auditory processing; social relational problems generated by inaccurately reading social cues; attentional problems generated by a focus on scanning the environment for threat while simultaneously dismissing infor-mation as unimportant when it is not viewed as being threat (or safety) related. (p. 398)

Teicher et al. (2003) hypothesized that early stress also has a strong effect on the degree of right-left hemispheric integration and may be associated with levels of anxiety. The impact of trauma on compromised prefrontal inhibition results in problems of the cortex effectively and adaptively processing and regulating limbic responses (Creeden, 2006). Stress-related effects on the cerebellar vermis have implications for maintenance of mental health as well as its role in mediating the response to stress.

TREATMENT OF TRAUMA

Chapter 16 (Powell) describes the neural plasticity of the brain as the basis for optimism in the potential to successfully intervene with youth. Siegel (as cited in Sykes, 2004) asserts that learning about the brain and the power of relationship to create and change neural circuits is the most important challenge the therapy field will face in years to come. In discussing the power of experiences and interventions later in life to change an individual's adaptive functioning, Vance (2001) states, "The current understanding of the neurobiology of learning suggests that repeatedly experiencing highly rewarding or positive emotional stimuli, or practicing effective coping behaviors, will result in long-term synaptic potentiation of these neural circuits" (p. 67).

Transferring this into practical application, van der Kolk, McFarlane, and Wei-saeth (1996) identifies phases in the treatment of trauma:

1. Establishing safety and predictability
2. Deconditioning and decreasing anxiety and arousal (physiological and psy-chological) level
3. Altering the way victims view themselves and their world
4. Establishing secure social relationships
5. Accumulating positive/restitutive emotional experiences

The phased model of trauma treatment emphasizes the importance of physical and psychological safety. The abuse-specific, therapeutic care environment is an essential foundation for treating traumatized youth (see Chapter 15). In an unsafe or threatening environment, youth will continue to manifest the physiological and psychological reactivity and cognitive, emotional, and behavioral patterns they perceive as necessary to survive in a "malevolent world." The degree of emotional and behavioral stability of the most traumatized youth in group settings serves as a barometer of sorts, measuring the sense of safety. In a safe environment, youth can begin learning coping skills to decrease and manage anxiety and arousal, enabling them to tolerate the work on past traumatic experiences.

Understanding the brain's reaction to trauma, neurological interventions can decrease the emotion reactivity associated with trauma: biofeedback, relaxation, meditation, and/or yoga; art, drama, and/or occupational therapy; Eye Movement Desensitization and Reprocessing (EMDR), Dialectical Behavioral Therapy (DBT), and cognitive-behavioral treatment (Creeden, 2006; Fentress, 2005; Linehan, 1993; Longo, 2009); Multimodal techniques (verbal, visual, movement, kinesthetic, music) and "whole brain" teaching in order to accommodate receptive/expressive language and auditory processing problems, and address self-regulation (Creeden, 2007).

Providing a "safe place," weighted blankets (deep pressure), and sensory rooms that are accompanied by soothing music may also be helpful (Creeden, 2005). Bergman and Pratt (2009) describe the first task in the treatment of traumatized youth as "awaken the body and connect it to the mind." The goal is to teach affect regulation and then begin narrative therapy with a focus on internal states of awareness.

Evidence-based treatments for trauma incorporate cognitive-behavioral components, exposure strategies, stress management/relaxation, and cognitive/narrative restructuring (Cohen, Berliner, & March, 2000). For children and adolescents trauma treatment often includes a parental component that parallels the child's treatment, recognizing that parents often experience the trauma effects of their children vicariously and may exacerbate the negative impacts for the child as they struggle to accept and understand what has occurred. A supportive response from caregivers is essential in moderating long-term effects for the traumatized child.

Biofeedback enables individuals to learn how to change their internal physiological activity in order to improve health and functioning. Precise instruments measure physiological activity such as brainwaves, heart function, breathing, muscle activity, and skin temperature. These instruments rapidly and accurately "feed back" information to the user. The presentation of this information—often in conjunction with changes in thinking, emotions, and behavior—supports desired physiological changes. Over time, these changes can endure without continued therapy.

Biofeedback increases self-awareness and self-monitoring by recognizing increased arousal and monitoring successful strategies and progress. Self-regulation (yoga, breathing, movement, weighted vests, and visualization) is taught in conjunction with biofeedback (Creeden, 2006; Fentress, 2005; Longo, 2009). Neurofeedback presents the user with real-time feedback on brainwave activity, as measured by sensors on the scalp, typically in the form of a video display, sound, or vibration. The aim is to provide real-time information regarding the Central Nervous System's current activity.

There is evidence that DBT (Dialectic Behavioral Therapy) can be particularly helpful treating severe and chronic multidiagnostic, difficult-to-treat patients. The four primary components of the skills training portion of DBT are core mindfulness, interpersonal effectiveness, emotional regulation, and distress tolerance. Research on DBT resulted in significant reductions with suicidal teens' symptoms, including anxiety, depression, interpersonal sensitivity, and obsessive-compulsive symptom patterns. Additional reductions were found in the problem areas of confusion about self, impulsivity, emotional dysregulation, and interpersonal difficulties (Miller, Rathus, Leigh, & Landsman, 1996).

Once youth have acquired some self-monitoring and self-regulation skills to decrease anxiety and arousal (physiological and psychological) levels, the next step is altering the way they view themselves and their world and helping them reestablish secure social relationships. The parallel issues of victimization outcomes and triggers associated with the abusive cycle demonstrate the link between past trauma and current abusive behavior in feelings such as anxiety, fear, abandonment, rejection, shame, helplessness, and powerlessness (Ryan, 1989). Van der Kolk (2004) emphasizes the importance of processing and integrating trauma memories into conscious mental frameworks.

Siegel (as cited in Sykes, 2004) states that if you can make sense of your story, you can change it. Youth seek to gain a deeper understanding by creating a coherent narrative, an autobiographical story, and utilize this coherent narrative as a retrospective journey to discover the origins of the cognitive and emotional triggers that are precursors to their offending. This insight and awareness can have a powerful impact and be a first step toward the youth being open to corrective experiences that challenge dysfunctional and abuse-supportive thinking and moderate the emotional pain/triggers.

It is not possible here to adequately review all the information on psychiatric disorders, pharmacology, and neurological interventions that might be relevant, but practitioners are encouraged to look beyond the offense-specific field to benefit from other work in progress.

REFERENCES

American Psychiatric Association. (2000). *Diagnostic and statistical manual of mental disorders: Fourth edition, text revision.* Washington, DC: Office of Publishing Operations, American Psychiatric Associations.

Becker, J. V., Kaplan, M. S., Tenke, C. E., & Tartaglini, A. (1991). The incidence of depressive symptomatology in juvenile sex offenders with a history of abuse. *Child Abuse and Neglect, 15,* 531–536.

Bergman, J., & Pratt, R. (2009). *Making a brain/trauma/attachment treatment program for young people actually work: Melbourne Australia.* Presentation to the National Adolescent Perpetration Network Conference, Tampa, FL.

Cavanaugh, D. J., Pimenthal, A., & Prentky, R. (2008). A descriptive study of sexually abusive boys and girls—Externalizing behaviors. In B. K. Schwartz (Ed.), *The sex offender: Offender evaluation and program strategies* volume VI (pp. 12-1–12-21). Kingston: Civic Research Institute.

Cohen, J. A., Berliner, L., & March, J. S. (2000). Treatment of children and adolescents. In E. B. Foa, T. M. Keane, & M. J. Friedman (Eds.), *Effective treatments for PTSD* (pp. 308–328). New York: Guilford Press.

Creeden, K. (2005). *The brain's part in juvenile sexual offending.* Presentation to the National Adolescent Perpetration Network Annual Conference, Denver, CO.

Creeden, K. (2007). *Brain functioning and dynamics involved in problematic or abusive sexual behavior.* Presentation to the Colorado Continuum Network, Denver, CO.

Creeden, K. J. (2006). Trauma and neurobiology: Considerations for the treatment of sexual behavior problems in children and adolescents. In R. E. Longo & D. S. Prescott (Eds.), *Current perspectives: Working with sexually aggressive youth and youth with sexual behavior problems* (pp. 395–418). Holyoke, MA: NEARI Press.

Dailey, L. (1987). *Utilizing psychiatric consultation: Implications of dual diagnosis.* Paper presented at the 4th National Adolescent Perpetrator Network Meeting, Keystone, CO.

Dailey, L. (1996). *Adjunctive biological treatments.* Paper presented at the 12th Annual Conference of the National Adolescent Perpetrator Network, Minneapolis, MN.

Davies, D. (2004). *Child development: A practitioner's guide* (2nd ed.). New York: Guilford Press.

Eth, S., & Pynoos, M. (1985). *Post traumatic stress disorder in children.* Washington, DC: American Psychiatric Press.

Fentress, D. (2005). *The brain's part in juvenile sexual offending.* Presentation to the National Adolescent Perpetration Network Conference, Denver, CO.

Finkelhor, D. (1987). The trauma of sexual abuse. *Journal of Interpersonal Violence, 2*(4), 348–366.

Gil, E., & Johnson, T. C. (1993). *Sexualized children: Assessment & treatment of sexualized children & children who molest.* Rockville, MD: Launch Press.

James, B. (1989). *Treating traumatized children.* San Francisco: Lexington Books.

Kotulak, R. (1996 /1997). *Inside the brain: Revolutionary discoveries of how the mind works.* Kansas City, MO: Andrews McMeel Publishing.

Lewis, D. O., Shanok, S. S., & Pincus, J. H. (1981). Juvenile male sexual assaulters: Psychiatric, neurological, psycho-educational, and abuse factors. In D. O. Lewis (Ed.), *Vulnerabilities to delinquency* (pp. 67–88). Jamaica, NY: Spectrum Publications.

Linehan, M. (1993). *Skills training manual for treating borderline personality disorder.* New York: Guilford Press.

Longo, R. E. (2009). *Trauma and its impact on the brain.* Presentation to the National Adolescent Perpetration Network Conference, Tampa, FL.

Maletzky, B. (1996). Treatment by degrees. *Sexual Abuse: A Journal of Research and Treatment, 8*(2), 83–87.

Miller, A. L., Rathus, J. H., Leigh, E., & Landsman, N. (1996). *A pilot study: Dialectical Behavior Therapy adapted for suicidal adolescents.* Poster presentation at the 1st annual meeting of the International Society for the Improvement and Teaching of Dialectical Behavior Therapy, New York, NY.

Nelson, C. A. (2000). Neural plasticity and human development: The role of early experience in sculpting memory systems. *Developmental Science, 3,* 115–136.

Perry, B. D. (1997). Incubated in terror: Neurodevelopmental factors in the "cycle of violence." In J. D. Osofsky (Ed.), *Children in a violent society* (pp. 124–149). New York: Guilford Press.

Perry, B. D. (2002). Childhood experience and the expression of genetic potential: What childhood neglect tells us about nature and nurture. *Brain and Mind, 3,* 79–100.

Ryan, G. (1989). Victim to victimizer: Rethinking victim treatment. *Journal of Interpersonal Violence, 3*(4), 325–341.

Ryan, G. (1993). *Concurrent psychiatric disorders.* Paper presented at the Annual Conference of National Adolescent Perpetrator Network, Lake Tahoe, NV.

Ryan, G., and Associates (1998). *The web of meaning: A developmental-contextual approach in treatment of sexual abuse.* Brandon, VT: Safer Society Press.

Ryan, G., Miyoshi, T. J., Metzner, J. L., Krugman, R. D., & Fryer, G. E. (1996). Trends in a national sample of sexually abusive youths. *Journal of the American Academy of Child and Adolescent Psychiatry, 35*(1), 17–25.

Rutter, M. (1985). Resilience in the face of adversity: Protective factors and resistance to psychiatric disorders. *British Journal of Psychiatry, 147,* 598–611.

Sczechowicz, E. (1988). *Residential programming for adolescent sexual offenders.* Presentation at the 5th Annual Conference of the National Adolescent Perpetrator Network, Anaheim, CA.

Siegel, D. J. (2001). Toward an interpersonal neurobiology of the developing mind: Attachment relationships, "mindsight," and neural integration. *Infant Mental Health Journal, 22,* 67–94.

Spiegel, D. (1993). *Dissociative disorders.* Lutherville, MD: Siedran Press.

Steinberg, L., & Haskins, R. (2008). *Keeping adolescents out of prison.* The Future of Children: Princeton-Brookings.

Stien, P., & Kendall, J. (2004). *Psychological trauma and the developing brain.* New York: Haworth Press.

Sykes, M. (2004). Mindsight. *Psychotherapy Networker, 28*(5) (September/October) 29–39.

Teicher, M., Andersen, S. L., Polcari, A., Anderson, C. M., & Navalta, C. P. (2002). Developmental neurobiology of childhood stress and trauma. *Psychiatric Clinics of North America, 25,* 397–426.

Teicher, M., Andersen, S. L., Polcari, A., Anderson, C. M., Navalta, C. P., & Kim, D. M. (2003). The neurobiological consequences of early stress and childhood maltreatment. *Neuroscience and Behavioral Reviews, 27,* 33–44.

Terr, L. (1990). *Too scared to cry: Psychic trauma in childhood*. New York: Harper and Row.

Vance, J. E. (2001). Neurobiological mechanisms of psychosocial resiliency. In G. M. Richman & M. W. Fraser (Eds.), *The context of youth violence: Resilience, risk, and protection*. Westport, CT: Prager.

van der Kolk, B. (1986). *Psychological trauma*. Washington, DC: American Psychiatric Press.

van der Kolk, B. (2003). The neurobiology of childhood trauma and abuse. *Child and Adolescent Psychiatric Clinics of North America, 12*, 293–317.

van der Kolk, B., McFarlane, A., & Weisaith, L. (1996). *Traumatic stress*. New York: Guilford Press.

Yager, J. B. (2005). *The brain's part in juvenile sexual offending*. Presentation to the National Adolescent Perpetration Network Annual Conference, Denver, CO.

CHAPTER 20

Family Therapy

A Critical Component in Treatment of Sexually Abusive Youth

JERRY THOMAS, IN COOPERATION WITH THE EDITORS

HISTORICALLY, MENTAL HEALTH, child welfare, juvenile justice, and education practices have always considered family involvement imperative in working with children and youth with behavior problems. The models that have evolved in treatment of sexually abusive youth originally focused primarily on the individual youth, but now recognize and emphasize the importance of family involvement and have brought into the work the wisdom of family therapy (Schladale, 2002, 2005, 2006; Thomas, 1988, 1999; Thomas & Viar, 2001, 2005). Standards for both community-based and residential treatment of sexually abusive youth indicate that the involvement of families should always be a consideration in treatment planning (ACA, 1993; Bengis et al., 1999; CSOMB, 2002; Schladale et al., 2006; Thomas, 2001).

Parents are now more often being held responsible for meeting the needs of their children, including supervision, nurturance, and support (see Chapter 15). Family treatment can identify, interrupt, and replace family patterns that may have allowed or supported abusive behaviors and increase the overall health of the family system.

FAMILIES

Although the socialization of children is an interaction over time of countless influences, personal characteristics, situational factors, and the sometimes inexplicable vagaries of life, it is generally accepted that the family and family environment are primary factors in that process. These are not the only factors, of course. There are countless other factors (sometimes multidimensional) that take place in every individual's life. However, the family and its environment represent a child's primary developmental influence and provide the context of time and space in which the other factors occur. (Ward, Hudson, Marshall, & Siegert, 1995, p. 320)

Children come into the world as part of a family, which serves as the basis of their socioemotional world and is invariably at the center of the child's life, shaping the child's emotions, beliefs, and behaviors, for better or worse. Family can be the most influential and practical support system for any youth in offense-specific treatment, and provides the (informed) supervision that supports the most "normalizing" experiences in the least restrictive manner both during and after the youth's discharge from treatment. As described in Chapter 10, parents are responsible for ensuring a safe and healthy environment for their children.

Family may be defined by its absence or presence, closeness or distance, attachment or lack of attachment; and can be functional or dysfunctional, loving or hostile, mentally healthy or unhealthy, criminal or noncriminal. Families may represent a multitude of different cultures, nationalities, and ethnicities, and may be composed in part or whole by alternative caregivers (kin or institutional staff). The composition of any given family can be two-parent or single parent, parents of the same sex, communal parents, foster parents, grandparents, extended family, and so forth. For some adolescents, organizations and professionals fill the role and provide the support that is more generally provided by families. Whatever the composition, the realities of family exist and must be addressed for each youth, and the potential for family involvement be assessed. The comprehensive assessment, evaluation, and treatment plan benefits from a family-systems perspective.

All people have a need for family for a sense of connectedness with significant others. It is not unusual to see youth in treatment create their own fantasy of family much like a small child will create an imaginary friend. This fantasy family may become so ingrained that accepting the reality of their actual family is difficult. In other cases, the youth may defend the most inadequate family to avoid being left without any family at all.

As described in Chapters 10 and 15, parents have a responsibility to meet the needs of their children. Helping parents meet these needs provides the youth with the understanding and skills needed for their own parenting roles in the future. Many families can develop the strengths that support positive outcomes for the youth.

Without some insight into the family context of the youth, treatment planning becomes a ship without a rudder. The complexity and uniqueness of each family's history underscores the need for the individualized assessment to include an evaluation of the family. Family systems fall on a continuum from healthy to pathological and from supportive to hostile, so the frequency and intensity of family work will vary greatly. Given the heterogeneity of the youth and of their families and the fact that individuals react differently to similar objective circumstances, treatment plans for each family will be unique.

The family's involvement in treatment provides the opportunity to deal with emotionally charged or cognitively confusing family issues, dysfunctions, or idiosyncrasies and to identify patterns that might support abusive behaviors. It is not realistic to expect a youth to make meaningful changes and to maintain a non-offending lifestyle within a nonsupportive or sabotaging family unit. For many youth participation by family members is a significant factor in achieving the goals of treatment, and the family's role is very similar in all aspects of the continuum of services and care (see Chapter 14).

THEORY AND RESEARCH

As the professional literature reflects, theoretical models now integrate information from a broad variety of sources and professional fields and take advantage of a more complex base of knowledge, including family systems. As such, the field is better able to account for and cope with the tremendous diversity of these youth and their families.

Theoretical models help professionals gather, process, and interpret the information that is generated by a comprehensive assessment, and the family assessment represents a critical domain. In order to consider numerous interacting psychological, social, and physiological factors, individual responsivity, pre-existing behavior patterns of the youth and their family, as well as the immediate precursors of the youth's offending behavior, evaluators need models that guide, organize, and interpret their assessment of the family system and each individual in relation to the treatment needs of the youth and the family as a whole. This organization and conceptualization constitutes the clinical "evaluation."

Current models now focus on the identification of protective factors identified in research on resiliency and assets (Benson, Blyth, Deville, & Wachs, 1997; Rutter, 1985; Werner & Smith, 1992). Bremer's Protective Factors Model (2001) was initially designed as a scale that could be used to evaluate the adequacy of supervision in relation to the youth's placement within the continuum of care early on, before a comprehensive evaluation was possible. Bremer's 10-factor measure looks at personal, social, sexual, and environmental assets of the youth. Rutter had suggested in regard to general delinquency that protective factors are important in supporting positive individual development and interaction in the family, as well as mitigating the impact of adverse life experiences.

Protective factors are critical elements of a safe environment that fosters successful growth and development. Two factors consistently identified as particularly relevant for these youth involve the family: *Caregiver Stability* and *Family Functioning*.

Rutter (1972) found that caregiver stability was a central factor in the development of healthy social orientation and the ability to conceive of another in an empathic, humanized fashion. Many researchers suggest that multiple disruptions of caregiver relationships are a strong predictor of delinquent behavior in adolescence. Hawkins, Farrington, and Catalano (1998) found that disrupted parent-child relationships were linked to subsequent violent behavior, and studies of parent-child separations prior to age 16 (Harris, Rice, & Quinsey, 1993) and prior to age 10 (Farrington, 1991) also suggest such occurrences are predictive of later violence. Disruptions in the caregiver relationship have also been indicated in the etiology of youthful sexual offending as indicative of inconsistent care (see Chapters 7 and 10) and is well documented as predictive of attachment styles and the internal working model for relationships.

The ability of children and young adults to behave in a healthy, safe, and productive fashion in the community at large has been conclusively and repeatedly linked to whatever constitutes a family in their lives. The availability of structure and support are particularly crucial (Bremer, 2001), as are consistency, communication, and parental involvement in children's lives (Benson, Blyth, Deville, & Wachs, 1997).

Research has also indicated that substance abuse, domestic violence, mental problems, and/or criminal behavior of the primary caregiver are linked to poor social, psychological, and behavioral development. Primary caregivers with these characteristics tend to be inconsistent in providing structure, support, communication, and reliable involvement in their children's lives, and may be modeling dysfunctional patterns in their daily functioning. Various characteristics of the families of youths who have sexually offended have been explored.

Smith and Israel (1987): Physically and emotionally inaccessible parents, lax parental control, secrecy, and a sexually stimulating climate associated with parental affairs.

Manocha and Mezey (1998): 25.5% of families had a "lack of sexual boundaries," 33.3% of the families kept sexually explicit materials, and 29.4% of the parents described as "uncaring."

Graves et al. (1996); Serfabi (1990): Families functioning at extremes—either disengaged or enmeshed.

Miner, Siekert, and Ackland (1997): "Chaotic" family environments.

Bagley and Shewchuk-Dann (1991); Miner et al. (1997); Morenz and Becker (1995): Prevalent instability, disorganization, and violence.

Fehrenbach, Smith, Monastersky, and Deisher (1986); Kahn and Chambers (1991); Smith and Israel (1987): Physical and/or emotional separations from one or both parents.

Ward et al. (1995): Poor quality of care; relationships often disrupted; inadequate attachments.

Miner and Crimmins (1995): Instability, disengagement, and poor attachment.

Smith and Monastersky (1986): Low level of perceived family support.

Blaske, Borduin, Henggeler, and Mann (1989): Negative patterns of communication, aggressive statements and interruptions, lack of supportive communication and dialogue.

Kobayashi, Sales, Becker, Figueredo, and Kaplan (1995); Richardson, Kelly, Bhate, and Graham (1997): Physical abuse, neglect, and witnessing family violence independently associated with sexual violence in adolescents.

Bentovin (1998); Marshall (1989): Developmental trauma resulting from rejection and/or abuse.

Bagley (1992); Browne and Falshaw (1998); Dolan, Holloway, Bailey, and Kroll (1996); Graves, Openshaw, Ascione, and Ericksen (1996); Gray, Pithers, Busconi, and Houchens (1999); Hsu and Starzynski (1990); Manocha and Mezey (1998); Pithers, Gray, Busconi, and Houchens (1998): Criminality; mental health problems; economic disadvantage; drug and alcohol abuse; and medical problems in families.

Finally, in relation to the youth's own experience of sexual victimization, Abel, Jones, Gabriel, & Harlow (2009); Hunter and Figueredo (2000); and Ryan, Miyoshi, Metzner, Krugman, and Fryer (1996) have suggested that multiple variables are relevant in understanding why some youth go on to commit sexual assaults while others do not, which include the youth's perception of relationships and familial responses upon discovery.

THE CONTINUUM OF INTERVENTION: COMMUNITY-BASED AND RESIDENTIAL TREATMENT

The majority of lower-risk youth with relatively functional families are treated as outpatients who remain in the community, live at home, and attend public schools. A smaller portion of youth must be removed from the home initially because their offenses occurred there, while others may be removed due to inadequacies in the home, and still others must be removed from their homes due to greater risk or greater needs. For higher risk youth, levels of supervision and intensity of treatment may require higher levels of care, and for higher need youth, some will benefit from therapeutic care (see Chapters 14 and 15). However, a majority of youth who sexually offend are treated in community-based programs (CSOMB, 2002; McGrath, Cummings, & Burchard, 2003).

As previously discussed (see Chapter 17), many youth who sexually offend are more like other delinquents than "sex offenders" and can be expected to benefit from evidence-based practices that have been developed for general delinquency, co-occurring disorders, substance abuse, DD, LD, and so forth. Youth with co-occurring psychiatric disorders will benefit from evidence-based practices developed in mental health services that specifically address those symptoms. The role and benefit of family involvement has been apparent in all areas of research with children and youth. The younger the child, the more dependent interventions and outcomes are on parental involvement.

Multi-Systemic Treatment (MST) is an evidence-based intervention for delinquent youth that is entirely delivered in the home with the youth's family system (Borduin, Henggeler, Blaske, & Stein, 1990). Research trials with modifications for youth who have sexually offended have also shown promise for some youth who are able to remain in their own homes with cooperative parents (Borduin et al., in preparation; Schoenwald, Borduin, & Henggeler, 1998). Although grant-funded studies of MST have been effective, replicating the model in practice has been difficult with less funding and has shown somewhat mixed results (BCMCFD, 2007; Littell, 2005).

The basic premises guiding the MST model are not new to family therapists and can be useful with families of youth who remain at home, as well as youth returning home following offense-specific treatment in residential placements; children have difficulty incorporating changes they make during treatment into the daily functioning of the family without the family's understanding and support.

While MST is a specifically defined model of intervention, family systems theory informs a wide range of systemic approaches. Family systems interventions are particularly suited to address the factors that surround the youth, for better or worse, in family, peer groups, schools, and community.

Youth who are living in foster or group homes may receive community-based treatment along with youth who remain at home in outpatient or day-treatment programs. Residential treatment programs that also house and school youth who have sexually offended have been guided by the National Residential Standards (ACA, 1993; Bengis et al., 1999; Thomas, 1996). To be licensed and accredited such programs must have comprehensive policy and procedure manuals describing interventions used by the program, how those will be carried out and by whom, and how staff is trained, supervised, and evaluated. These are standard quality control approaches and are measures used by licensure and accreditation agencies to ensure compliance with service contracts.

Whether youth are in residential or outpatient treatment, family members need to be fully informed from the beginning about the nature of the program, the rights of family members and the youth, relevant benefits and risks of interventions to be used, treatment goals and foreseeable changes expected prior to discharge, and conditions relevant to family contact and visitation, victim clarification, and/or reunification work. The role of the family in treatment, expectations regarding supervision, and the limits of confidentiality should all be discussed and verified in written consents.

All families can benefit from educational components and can learn to supervise and develop safety plans for their particular situations (see Chapter 15). Those who are invested in family therapy may address family secrets and dynamics, explore emotional "triggers," work to recognize and define roles in the family, develop new boundaries, and some make significant changes in the overall functioning of their family system. Family traditions, cultural and ethnic customs, and diversity need to be identified, respected, and accommodated to the extent that is congruent with the fundamental goals of treatment: being successful without being abusive.

At times the logistics of doing family therapy can be cumbersome and may necessitate innovative and creative strategies to accomplish the tasks (multifamily education therapy and/or support groups, therapy via technology: i.e., telephones, interactive video conferencing, computers, etc.), as well as families or therapists traveling significant distances. Some programs facilitate periodic family "weekends," which accommodate those who must travel by offering intensive schedules combining family visitation, and multiple education and treatment sessions.

THE STAGES OF FAMILY TREATMENT

The family's involvement is characterized by roughly five different stages:

Stage I occurs with the discovery of abuse, which precipitates a crisis for all families. Although painful for the family, it is an opportunity for treatment providers to form helping relationships with the family. Interventions during this period set the stage for the family's commitment and involvement in the treatment process, and establish the treatment provider's professional competency and therapeutic role as one of collaboration.

Stage II initiates the assessment, evaluation, and treatment planning that will continue throughout every stage. The initial assessment is personal, individualized, and anxiety producing for parents who often expect to be indicted or blamed in some way.

Stage III involves goal-setting and treatment. Ideally, the family is involved in the process of working with the professional team on the goals of treatment, a process that will be more or less intensive and extensive depending on the needs identified in the individualized treatment plan.

Stage IV focuses on the family's future (whatever it will be) with work on clarification, reconciliation, and reunification work.

Stage V transitions adult responsibilities from the team back to the parents, as the youth completes treatment and the family and team consider the aftercare needs of each individual and the family as a whole.

Although each family's course of treatment is unique, some issues in each of these stages are common and somewhat predictable.

Stage I: The Crisis of Disclosure

The discovery of sexual offending by a family member is a time of stress, confusion, and vulnerability for parents and other family members as well. Information, support, and directive guidance are needed. Ideally, when family therapists are available during the crisis that disclosure precipitates, family members are often more open to discussing their perceptions and feelings than they are only a short time later. During that crisis is often when they are most open to receiving help from outside sources, creating an opportunity to provide them with stability, information, and structure while assessing the family's style of functioning in times of stress.

As stated in Chapter 15, requiring the education for informed supervision of all parents has the advantage of casting providers in a helping role, initiating a didactic relationship that is less intrusive than the process of assessment and treatment planning, prepares fertile ground for the therapeutic relationship to evolve, and can instill confidence in the parents that they are working with competent professionals to meet their child's needs.

In times of crisis, it is important to focus on the crisis instead of avoiding it. Family members may be overwhelmed with emotions and may struggle to understand the abuse behavior. Remaining nonjudgmental and informative regarding the nature and dynamics of abuse behaviors and clearly articulating the foreseeable legal and systemic consequences can assist the family through the crisis as well as establishing a therapeutic relationship.

At the time the youth's behavior is disclosed, parents typically experience feelings of hopelessness, helplessness, and a loss of control over their child and their family. The stress of trying to deal with an incomprehensible behavior while interacting with numerous strangers often triggers intense defensive reactions. Parents may feel like failures, fear they will be judged or ridiculed, and exhibit self-protective defenses such as denial, minimization, and withdrawal. For others, externalizing the problem projects blame and anger onto others: their child, their spouse, or those professionals who respond. It is important to recognize the protective function of defensive reactions and not personalize parental anger during the early stages of this process.

Confrontation of denial at this time only increases defenses, while gentle didactic education and support are helpful. Providing information about the problem of adolescent sexual offending, what to anticipate in the legal, social welfare, and community systems, identifying evidence of family strengths that have gotten them through other hard times, and identifying extra-familial support systems can help the family cope and have hope for the future while increasing their acceptance of the need for family therapy.

Stage II: Assessment, Evaluation, and Treatment Planning

Assessment is the process of gathering information and applying expert knowledge in order to understand the status of a problem and the context within which the problem is occurring. Evaluation is the application of some criteria in forming judgments that inform the corrective plan. Data gathering is the obtaining of information, while observation is looking at patterns of language, nonverbal behavior, and behavior as a whole. Patterns represent behaviors that are observed repetitively over a period of time (Maddock & Larson, 1995).

A comprehensive assessment of the family system is critical in the design of treatment and supervision planning. This assessment provides the information needed to recognize static, stable and dynamic risks, assets, and issues in the family system, and guides treatment planning for family involvement. Theories of etiology, risk factor research, family systems theory, child development, mental health diagnostics, and clinical training all inform the assessment protocol. Evidence from research and clinical studies identify risk factors in family systems, and the psychosocial history of the youth and family provides basic information about family health and functioning. The family history and dynamics give the family therapist the background for developing further inquiry and an agenda for family therapy.

If the family therapist is not the same person doing the comprehensive, individualized evaluation of the youth, coordination is essential so the parents are not frustrated by duplication. The family therapist and offense-specific evaluator must work together in open communication, within a single congruent framework, and share information and reports so they are not repeating the same inquiries.

Assessment is not time limited, as observation and interpretations are not static. The therapist's understanding will evolve over time as additional information becomes available. A series of interviews provides an initial agenda while ongoing assessment will continue to shape supervision, care, and treatment plans. New data will emerge over time and the accuracy and reliability of reports and observations will change as the family's trust in the therapist grows and they begin to learn to recognize what is relevant to the abuse problem in their family.

As stated in Chapter 10, the family is first of all a source of behavioral history, and secondly the source of developmental history that informs critical domains in the individualized assessment of the youth. The family's history and traditions provide the contextual basis for understanding the youth's view of self, others, and relationships. Engaging family members in a collaborative process of discovery in the interest of understanding their child advances the goals of family therapy, supports the therapeutic relationship, and illuminates the parents' role of working with the team to help their child. In the course of describing their child's developmental history, parents reveal much about themselves, their parenting, their own childhood experiences, and their attitudes and beliefs about themselves, others, and relationships. Individual evaluators and family therapists can collaborate in recognizing each other's roles and goals to effectively share in the gathering of information.

Family assessment involves more than collecting facts. The subjective perceptions of family members, collectively and individually, are as important to understanding the family system as any objective facts, and behavioral observations are as important as verbal reports. The interpretation of data obtained in the assessment process is affected by the evaluator's professional and personal perceptions, prejudices, and beliefs, so self-awareness is critical.

Parents often balk at the suggestion that they need treatment themselves or as a family unit. It is not uncommon for the parents to refuse the idea of family therapy initially when their perception is that they are being blamed for the youth's behavior. Engaging them in the development of the treatment plan for their child is a more acceptable entrée.

Identifying the family's strengths, assets and resources—as well as their problems and shortcomings—follows the same principles of risk reduction and health promotion previously described. For example, parents with a strong marital relationship will provide each other support and comfort during this painful experience, and parents who have good verbal communication skills and a strong sense of self will be able to manage the myriad of systems involved with more ease than those who have skill deficits and emotional reactions to the issues.

Each family treatment plan is unique to a particular family and should not be a "boilerplate" or "recipe" applied indiscriminately to every family. Familial strengths and deficits influence both process and outcomes. By creating a collaborative relationship with the family, treatment providers can mobilize the natural resources of the family and create assets that will continue long after treatment ends.

Areas of interest that guide the process throughout assessment and treatment include:

Demographics: Who are the participants? What is their relationship to the youth? What is their attitude toward the events that led to treatment and the treatment process itself, including legal and social service interventions?

Family environment: To what extent are the physical, emotional, psychological, and sexual boundaries in the family blurred, rigid, nonexistent? Is there a sexualized environment in the family or a void of acknowledgment of sexuality? How is it characterized? Is there family disorganization, poor social judgment?

External and internal stress: Are there more than a normal number of intra and extrafamilial problems such as financial debt, illness, legal problems, extended family conflict? Have family resources been weakened by all of the stresses that are present? Are coping mechanisms poor or maladaptive?

Emotional deprivation: Are emotional needs for nurturance and closeness met? Are parents caring or uncaring? Is there a lack of attachment?

Family context: How is the outside world seen by the family? Is it perceived as hostile and has this family closed itself off from the world? Is there any support system in the community? Is there a culture of secrecy in the family? Is there an absence of reality checks? Empathic or coercive parenting styles, type of discipline? What are the educational, criminal, correctional, psychiatric, and medical histories of the adolescent and significant family members?

Family background: Relationship history; number of siblings by generation, developmental stage, birth orders, character of interfamilial relationships, religious environment and influences, socioeconomic stability of home(s), perceptions and expressions of sexuality, and disruptions such as single-incident violence, death, divorce, abandonment, financial hardship, legal history, long-term or forced separation of family members, and behavior problems. Evidence of physical trauma (treated and untreated), accident proneness, enuresis or encopresis, psychosomatic complaints, venereal disease, addictive or obsessive neuroses, or developmental problems.

Abuse history: Multigenerational abuse, or past victimization of the youth and/or other family members, other sexual offenses, physical or emotional violence in the home, or significant lapses of self-control or accountability (that is, addictive, obsessive, or chronic depression).

Psychological data: Have any family members received mental health services in the past? If so, what were the reasons for these services? Did they perceive benefit, help, or change as a result of these services? Has the family or any subgroup of its members ever been in family therapy or treatment programs before? Reports from former therapists or programs can provide additional perspectives of family functioning over time.

Sexuality histories: Family's perception of normal sexual development of children and of their own youth; sexual influences and role models within the family; parents' own sex education and their communication with their children regarding sexuality and personal values; sexual acting out within the family; level of comfort with the subject and specifics of sexuality; sexual relationship(s) of the parents; sexual dysfunctions in relationships; marital history and parental infidelity; family perceptions, standards, and rules regarding the youth (or any siblings) being sexually active.

Communication styles: Direct or indirect communication, verbal communication, emotional expression, thoughts expressed through behavior, misunderstandings, negative communication patterns, aggressive statements, interruptions, lack of supportive communication, expressed anger, conflict resolution styles.

Leisure time: Individual, family, community activities, isolation, and sociability.

Substance use: Medical and recreational drugs of choice within the family: prescribed or illegal; quantity and frequency of alcohol use; effects on the person and family; history of drug/alcohol treatment?

Family strengths: The ability of a youth to maintain behavioral safety in the community is enhanced by the availability of structure and support in the family or living situation. If the family is stable and the parents are active and involved the prognosis for the youth in treatment is improved.

In addition to evaluating the basic functioning and health of the family, it is important to assess the impact of the abuse and its disclosure on the family system: levels of denial or minimization, reactions, defenses, and explanations in the immediate and extended family; who knows and who does not know about the sexual abuse, and what the parents tell others about the family.

Just as the youth is expected to consistently demonstrate observable changes in their current functioning, the family should also be demonstrating changes relevant to goals they have developed for themselves. In reviewing and revising the family's treatment plan, the needs of the youth who offended, the needs of siblings, and the needs of the parents must all be considered. In the case of sibling incest the needs of those who were victimized may take precedence in some decisions. It is important to consider siblings who were not abused and not abusive as well, as they are often significantly affected by the disclosure of abuse within the family.

Family therapy needs are one domain in the comprehensive assessment and treatment plan. The treatment plan for the youth may include or refer to treatment goals developed by the family therapist with the family. The treatment team must respect the roles of each professional as they develop the overall plan. A collaborative effort gives input and information from many different perspectives and gives everyone involved a motivation to problem solve and to be invested in the outcome.

The treatment plan is simply an outline of goals, objectives necessary to meet those goals, and the "who, what, when" relevant to each goal. Treatment goals should be observable, measurable, realistic, and relevant (see Chapter 17). Jongsma, Peterson, and McInnis (1996) suggested stepwise treatment plans for families that are congruent with the process described in Chapter 15: define a problem; identify relevant family strengths; define a goal in terms of measurable change; identify specific objectives and relevant interventions and who is responsible for implementing them.

Treatment plans should not be a mystery to anyone. Openness increases trust and confidence in the process. Plans and reports should be available and useful for the youth and the family as well as professional staff, so use of professional jargon should be minimized. Some therapists write the treatment plan with the family present and use the family's terminology. Involvement of the family in developing and reviewing the treatment plan respects their role in the teams' work and gives parents a sense of understanding and being both empowered and responsible at a time when they may feel most helpless.

Treatment goals must also be achievable given the family's strengths and deficits, and the length of treatment time available to accomplish those goals. For example, if open and honest communication is a goal the objectives may be such things as learning to express opinions in a direct, nonaggressive manner; learning to manage and express vulnerable feelings without getting angry and abusive; not personalizing disagreements, and so forth.

Interventions identified in the family treatment plan will be influenced by the treatment setting and the therapist's resources. Treatment providers who are part of an extensive outpatient, residential, or inpatient program may have access to adjunctive groups that treatment providers working alone or in small programs do not. The approach the therapist uses may be dependent on the size of the program, the staff, and available resources. In many instances, community resources can be utilized to supplement the youth's offense-specific program.

The treatment plan is a working document, continually reviewed and updated to allow for changes in treatment because of progress, regression, or new discoveries. Some problems will be resolved during the course of treatment, and others will be added. Both the family and the youth must be kept informed of the identification of any new goals, and the progress or lack of progress made toward reaching established goals. During periodic reviews, the plan is reviewed and revised to reflect accomplishments as well as new issues or needs that have surfaced.

Stage III: The Family in Therapy

There are many different styles and modalities for doing family therapy that will differ depending on the variables associated with each therapist and each family. Intervening in cognitive, developmental, and behavioral dynamics may be useful for different aspects of the work and with different individuals and families. Treatment programs may offer a range of modalities including multifamily education or therapy groups, couples or parent/child dyads, individual family therapy with all or parts of the family or with extended family, parent support group, family retreats, program visits, community visits, and home visits. Individualized treatment plans can then identify which interventions and modalities are relevant for each youth and their family. For example, some families who are socially isolated will benefit from multifamily therapy group, whereas families with a background of mixed criminal and mental health issues might not.

The treatment issues within family systems where a child has sexually offended often parallel those previously described as issues for the youth. While the issues will vary depending on individual and systemic dynamics, there are some that are typical for many families.

Denial, Minimization, and Projection of Blame   The first reaction of parents to the news that their child has committed a sexual offense is usually disbelief. It is difficult for any family to believe that their child would be capable of sexually abusive acts. Parental minimization of the behavior is also common, particularly if the youth encourages and supports the parents' denial. Some parents are so upset that they would prefer to believe the youth rather than the victim so they will not have to deal with the reality of the problem.

Even when the victim is within the home, parents may find it easier to see the allegation as a "victim who is lying" than to acknowledge that their child has molested or raped someone. Another common reaction is the belief that the police, social services, or the therapist is overreacting. Because the therapist is available they may be perceived as the bearer of bad news and become the object of the family's anger and blame. The therapist can be understanding and sympathetic as denial and projection are natural defenses. The therapist must be direct and firm but never shaming or humiliating.

Participation in educational groups will give parents an opportunity to hear didactic material that is less threatening than personal information that attacks their self-esteem as parents and human beings. In parent support groups and multifamily therapy groups, parents can hear from other families who have dealt with their own denial and be supported and encouraged when they are stuck. Seeing that other parents have been similarly affected can be either helpful or counterproductive, so the therapist must control for negative influences within any group of parents.

Disclosure   As the youth makes progress in their treatment, one goal is to become able to tell their parents what happened, why it was abusive, and that he or she is responsible. The youth's acceptance of responsibility sometimes impacts the family's denial. As the youth demonstrates more open and direct communication, the parents often step up and begin to provide the support and encouragement that the youth needs. When denial remains entrenched, it becomes a dilemma that the youth must put in perspective and deal with in their treatment, recognizing that neither the youth nor the therapist can control the parent.

Abuse of Power, Powerlessness, and Empowerment   When parents feel powerless, they may either abdicate responsibility or engage in constant power struggles (with the therapist or their children) in their search for some semblance of control. The therapist must acknowledge those struggles while refusing to engage, constantly reframing their role as guide, advocate, and counselor. Making accurate attributions regarding what the parents do and do not have control over, and what they are and are not responsible for, empowers them and redirects them to proactive versus reactive.

In every interaction with the family, the therapist has the opportunity to articulate and respond to the affective cues of family members, validating the needs and feelings of each. Consistently prioritizing physical and psychological safety is as critical in family sessions as in the groups for the youths' behavior.

When parents do become engaged in the treatment process children may be initially unhappy and attempt to split the therapist and parents in order to avoid what is unknown territory. The therapist models the nonabusive use of power in their interactions and requires the same of the parents, emphasizing the parents' right to make decisions as well as their responsibility to meet their child's needs. Respecting parents' needs, the therapist helps the family identify options and reinforces positive choices. When families begin to share feelings rather than act them out, psychological safety becomes possible.

Multigenerational Abuse   The disclosure of child sexual abuse can trigger remembrance of parents' own abuse that has been blocked and is not even a part of their awareness. In some families multigenerational abuse is a norm and not thought to be unusual or damaging. For children who live in families with multigenerational abuse the dynamics are compounded. Symptoms of abuse—anger, inability to trust or bond, depression, and isolation—may be indicative of the family dynamics. Sometimes the disclosure of the abuse of a sibling may be a catalyst for the disclosure that one of the other children was also abused by one of the parents, or that one of the parents was abused by their parent. Some parents who have not dealt with their own abuse may be unable to deal with their children's abuse until they acknowledge and face their own.

It is not unusual for a parent who has been abused in the past to use the abusive youth as the target for his/her unresolved issues. Mothers may reject children who abuse, or (if the mother was abused by a sibling) she may put a son in positions that support fulfillment of her expectation that he will abuse. If disclosure indicates one or both parents have been abusive, a report must be made. Therapists must prepare every family for the necessity of this at the time of the initial referral to be able to do this without breaking therapeutic ties. Whether or not it destroys the therapeutic alliance it is necessary, not only for legal and ethical reasons, but for therapeutic accountability.

Families in which multigenerational abuse is present will require careful treatment planning and coordination with numerous therapists and agencies. All family members must be held accountable for their own behavior. Abusive incidents and failure to respect and protect each other must be acknowledged. It is sometimes necessary to refer family members to individual and/or group therapy to meet their own treatment needs, or even refer for hospitalization if family members exhibit extreme post-traumatic stress reactions. Whatever other treatment is occurring, all interventions must be congruent with the overall treatment plan.

Family Secrets Often the issues that parents do not want to talk about are the most important ones. Discrepancies in prior assessments and reports are often indicative of secrets. Secrets may be kept to prove loyalty, show power, strengthen boundaries and alliances, or protect family members from consequences or painful memories. Incest is only possible when there is a culture of secrecy. The therapist must be careful not to enter into secrets with either individual family members or the family as a whole. Releasing confidentiality within the team reduces the risk of reinforcing secrets.

Confrontation of discrepancies in what is said and what is observed in behavior, interactions, or family history may initially evoke defensive reactions. Over time, confrontation can be more specific and direct. When painful family secrets do emerge a grieving process characterized by anger, denial, acceptance, sadness, and grief is common.

Role Reversals and Personal Boundaries In families in which children are acting out, there is often evidence of role confusion. Parents and children are in constantly changing roles with one another, and role confusion can compromise parental authority and responsibility. Parents sometimes behave like children and children like parents. Children need parents to provide reasonable external controls. The development of a healthy family is dependent on intact parent-child boundaries.

When the father is distant or physically abusive, treatment strategies may focus on increasing paternal involvement and nurturing in family interactions, as well as increasing maternal support and protection. Previously undisclosed physical abuse in the home must also be reported. When the mother is enmeshed or passive, treatment strategies may focus on personal boundaries and individuation. For families that are rigid or enmeshed, having family members create a human sculpture in which each person places themselves in ways that represent the family's functioning helps them see where these alliances are and demonstrate the discomfort of entanglements.

Sex and Sexuality   Confusion about sex and sexuality is often a problem for family members. It can be particularly difficult for parents to discuss their child's sexuality, gender identity, sexual arousal, and the sexually abusive behaviors. Since the misuse and abuse of sexuality is definitive of an offense, it is necessary that sex and sexuality be discussed accurately while respecting the private nature of sexuality and the personal boundaries of each family member.

Didactic education decreases the family's anxiety about sexual topics and is often included in other components. When it is not, the family therapist may benefit from the same strategies discussed in Chapters 10, 15, and 18, and needs to be prepared for the same topics to be discussed with parents that come up with the youth in their treatment. Sex education for the parents should mirror the content of this subject for the youth so that communication can flow more easily.

Personal, cultural, and religious values influence the way individuals perceive sexuality. It is necessary to understand, respect, and support these differences as long as they are congruent with a positive view of human sexuality and nonabusive sexual behaviors. It is important for the youth to hear from their parents that it is not sexuality that is bad, but the abuse of it.

Behavior Contracts   Safety plans discussed in Chapter 15 model the use of foresight and planning to reduce risks and increase success. However, there are also rules and expectations in every home that represent the beliefs and values of the parent about behavior in their home and do not change from day to day.

Adolescents often fail to recognize the freedom represented in the opportunity to make behavioral choices, and instead define freedom as having no restrictions, no limits, and no consequences. It is important to be clear and concrete about the rules in the home, and to provide logical consequences for problematic behavior. Some families find it helpful to use a behavior contract that spells out the most important boundaries of behavior and clearly articulates both privileges and consequences associated with their behavior.

Parrish (1985) identifies advantages of using behavior contracts for families:

1. To clarify parental beliefs, values, and expectations while preventing arguments, misunderstanding, or manipulation.
2. Keeping parents from having to reiterate rules over and over again.
3. Adolescents consistently experience direct, predictable cause and effect, either positive or negative, to their behavioral choices.

A behavior contract should represent a system of discipline rather than punishment. Punishment is what a frustrated adult does to an adolescent to decrease the adult's feeling of frustration; it is rarely effective as a method of instilling values or lasting changes. Discipline, on the other hand, is feedback to the adolescent that validates or corrects their choice of behavior.

Involving parents and the youth in the development of behavior contracts increases their investment and commitment and reduces the sense of powerlessness, the abuse of power, or power struggles between the parent and the youth. Although adolescents need to be able to discuss and negotiate rules with their parents, the parents must have the final approval. When young people participate in decision making about rules and consequences, they are often quite fair and reasonable, sometimes making rules that are unreasonably difficult—in which case parents need to keep the rules realistic.

Behavior contracts can often be changed as the adolescent's behavior changes and the need for structure and feedback decreases. Modifications should not be made on the spur of the moment or in the heat of an argument. As discussed in Chapter 15, the parents work with the team to develop safety plans that should include the youth following any behavior contracts they may have at home. If terms of a contract at home conflict with the treatment plan or safety plans, or if the terms are ambiguous or unclear, the team can help to clarify. It is important that the conditions placed on these youth be congruent throughout all the systems. Informed supervision enhances this congruence.

Generally consequences should be as natural as possible and related to the behavior that violated the contract. Short-term consequences are usually more effective than long-term ones. Unending restrictions leave the adolescent hopeless and feeling as if there is nothing to lose by continuing to violate the condition of their contract.

STAGE IV: THE ULTIMATE GOALS OF FAMILY TREATMENT—RECONCILIATION AND REUNIFICATION

For the youth who has been in out of home placement and will return home to live with a sibling they previously victimized or in close proximity to any other past child victims, it is necessary to develop a step-by-step plan for contact, clarification, reunification, and reintegration into the family and the community. Successful completion of these steps is dependent on the engagement, coordination, and collaboration of the family members as well as all the professional agencies involved.

Although there are many good reasons to work toward family reunification, there are always safety concerns when past victims or other vulnerable persons are in the same household. Reunification is a process that evolves through assessment, treatment planning, family engagement, and clarification (Warsh, Pine, & Maluccio, 1994). Only after the work of clarification has occurred can an informed decision be made to proceed with reconciliation and reunification work. Permanency planning goals must often be stated to include both "return home" and "long-term placement/emancipation" alternatives until clarification work can be done.

There is often professional disagreement about when, if, and how to approach family reunification. Although it is important to preserve and restore families, it is most important to keep children safe. When these two needs conflict, decision making must always work to increase safety. However, family treatment can be useful and healing even when reunification is contraindicated or unworkable. It is important to distinguish between reconciliation and reunification. There is a continuum of family resolution that can go from grieving the loss of family to full family reunification. The goal is for all family members to lead healthy, productive lives and this may mean different things for different families. "Family members can be supported in efforts to reconcile experiences of violence and/or sexual harm without being reunified" (Schladale, 2005, p. 4).

Reunification work is a process with a range of potential outcomes determined on a case-by-case basis as the process unfolds. It is through the process of clarification and reunification work that decisions about the risks and benefits for the children involved should be addressed. Saunders and Meinig (1995) referred to this as a "family resolution" process rather than a reunification process to emphasize that family treatment is an ongoing, continuing process.

Sometimes the goal is full reunification into the family system with the youth returning home to finish growing up. However, even when a return home is deemed unfeasible or unlikely for whatever reason, it continues to be important to do the work of clarification and reunification. It must be acknowledged that for most people sibling relations continue to be important across the life span, providing a sense of continuity and support as well as being the extended family roots of future generations. Even youth who are emancipated tend to seek out their families as young adults and if it is foreseeable that family members who have been separated, including victim siblings or cousins and their parents, will likely have contact in the future, responsible teams should do the work to prepare for and ease the risks of such contacts. The involvement of victim therapists/advocates is an essential part of this process in order to assure that the victim is ready for and capable of engaging in the clarification process.

The sessions between the sexually abused and sexually abusive siblings are called clarification sessions, during which the youth gives clear and direct messages regarding their responsibility for the abuse in the past and safety in the present. When the youth accepts full responsibility for the abuse and is able to demonstrate empathy for the victim, the risk to the victim is substantially reduced. Before such a session can take place parents and other family members need to have established a strong alliance with the victim and demonstrated a clear understanding of who is responsible for the abuse. All therapists involved must determine when the two siblings are therapeutically prepared for such a session and retain the option to stop the session if blaming, shaming, intimidation, or unforeseen discomfort occurs.

By doing the work of clarification and reunification the team and family can make informed decisions regarding the appropriate level of reunification: reentry into the home, part-time supervised time in the home, less intense time together in the community, or minimal to no contact. To write off the family relationships without doing the work just because the youth is nearly grown and will not be returning to the home seems irresponsible.

Treatment and social service agencies often have policies and procedures to guide the family reunification process. However, the idiosyncrasies and complexities of each family will affect the length of time and the areas of work involved. For example, in a relatively functional family where the duration and intrusiveness of sibling incest was minimal, it may be that the youth who was abusive and the abused child will both be ready to meet for clarification in a relatively short amount of time; whereas a family plagued by multigenerational abuse and other complex problems may require a great deal of work (regardless of the nature of the sibling incest) before it is deemed reasonable to reunite the two children. On the other hand, when the abuse was long-term and/or more violent or intrusive both the child who was victimized and the sibling who abused them may not feel safe enough or ready to do clarification work at the same time.

It is not unusual for a child who has been abused to be ready to do clarification and want to get on with life considerably before the youth who abused them is ready. It is the youth with a preexisting problem who sometimes requires significant treatment, whereas the child they abused who was healthy before and has received support and validation of their experience may need minimal counseling. On the other hand, for some children who have been abused by a sibling the abuse is symptomatic of pervasive abuse and dysfunction in an unsafe environment, and the child who has now been sexually abused by a youth in their home may require significant counseling, including family therapy, before they can be expected to feel safe and protected in the home. It is important that each family and each child be evaluated to establish their individual needs, just as it is for the youth who has offended.

Family Reunification Benchmarks   There are three benchmarks in the process of family restoration: clarification of the abuse, the reconciliation of issues, and the reconstruction of the roles and boundaries of those in the family system (Thomas & Viar, 2005). The goal is for the family to provide a safe environment where the needs of each child can be met. Sometimes subsystems of the family system require intensive work, which can be time-consuming, work intensive, and emotionally draining for all involved. The commitment to do the work despite these difficulties validates the importance of family in everyone's life and is responsive to the voice of the child who often says, *"I just wanted the abuse to stop. I didn't want to lose my family."*

The first benchmark is the successful completion of face-to-face clarification session(s). Sometimes the first meeting may be with the youth and the parents before the parents feel comfortable allowing the two children to meet. In these meetings the youth expresses their understanding about the nature of their sexually abusive behavior, being clear in describing the factors that made the behavior abusive (lack of consent, unequal power, and/or coercion), as well as their understanding of how such behavior betrays the trust of family, can affect the child who was abused, and violates the law. There is an expectation that the youth be prepared to answer foreseeable questions such as "Why?" and in doing so, demonstrate that they are taking full responsibility without minimization, rationalization, or projection of blame (Bera, Yokley, Hindman, Hutchens, & McGuire, 1990; Gil, 1987).

The first step in clarification is often an exchange of letters, which provides a safe forum to express feelings and ask and answer questions. Sometimes those letters are read aloud in their first meeting as well (see Chapter 18). A goal is for the two children to be able to meet together and, after clarifying the abuse, go on to discuss changes that might now be necessary to establish a sense of safety in their relationship and in the home, if the youth returns home. Ideally both children are accompanied by their own therapist, although circumstances vary so that sometimes the parent or another advocate is present. When there is no one working with the child who was abused, the therapist treating the family may be the one attending.

The second benchmark involves resolution and reconciliation of issues. Reconciliation is dependent on the family members coming to terms with (or being able to resolve) the fact that sexual abuse has occurred in the family, and recognizing the issues and problems that may have contributed to the failure of family members to maintain healthy and safe relationships. Reconciliation may take place without reunification, but reunification cannot take place without reconciliation. Each member of the family needs to have the opportunity to express their thoughts and feelings of hurt, betrayal, and mistrust before they can move on without anger.

The third benchmark is family reunification. In childhood cases reunification is the rejoining of a family in which sexual abuse has occurred between siblings or with other children in the same household or the extended family. Reunification can only take place after the sibling who has been abusive has shown evidence of decreased risk and when the victim(s) feels safe, supported, and empowered. Parents must identify, eliminate, and repair deficits in supervision or care as well as any patterns of behavior that may have supported, encouraged, or inadvertently allowed any type of abusive behavior in the home.

Each of the benchmarks involves a series of smaller steps. For example, initial sessions are usually conducted with various subsystems within the family. As relationships between the members of each subsystem are reestablished and fortified, the various subgroups can come together. The process is sometimes more complicated and protracted with larger families, more extensive abuse, multiple perpetrators or victims, and family members with more pervasive pathology.

The foundation for reconstruction of the family is developed during the course of treatment. Early family sessions typically involve the sexually abusive youth and the parents and, as treatment progresses, consideration is given to the inclusion of other family members. Sessions that include the parents and the nonabusive siblings are helpful in assessing their readiness for the work of reconstructing the family. Such sessions provide an opportunity to share information about treatment issues and to assist the family members in dealing with unresolved feelings and concerns. Family therapy sessions that involve the entire family will be safe and productive only when the preliminary work has already been done with the various subsystems within the family.

The resolution and reconstruction phase is more difficult when the sexual abuse victim is a member of the family or when other family members have been sexually or physically abusive. Given the high number of sexually abusive youth who report experiencing abuse, it is not surprising that many have been victimized by siblings, parents, grandparents, or other relatives. In these cases, decisions have to be made regarding which family members to include and at what point in the therapeutic process.

The same concerns and principles apply with complicated family situations as with less complicated ones. Establishing basic alliances within the family, resolving problems and resistances, promoting a willingness to work together to prevent further abuse, and strengthening the sense of stability and health in the family.

Even if the youth is not able to rejoin the family or return home families can still benefit from clarifying and strengthening family bonds, sharing feelings about the abuse, grieving losses and celebrating positive changes of family members, and the redefinition of relationships. The ultimate goal of family treatment is to establish a functionally healthy family system in which further abuse is unlikely. Despite limitations, many families can overcome the obstacles or impediments to reunification if they can address pertinent feelings and issues, are provided adequate instruction and support, and have a sincere willingness to solve problems and rebuild family relationships.

Maintaining a family perspective with youth who are separated from their family of origin can help the youth prepare to create a healthy family for themselves as adults. Breaking the cycle of dysfunctional family relationships and abuse, foster families or staff and peers in group care settings can provide positive experiences and practice in a family-like constellation. Youth often report a sense of "family" in group therapy, particularly when the group is led by male and female co-therapists. Although work in group is not typically considered part of family therapy, the "family" within the group may be the only available resource for dealing with family relationship issues.

When Reunification Is Unworkable   Reconstruction cannot be accomplished with all families. At times the youth is so fixated, disturbed, or unwilling to alter his or her sexually abusive behavioral pattern that he or she cannot be safely returned to the family. In other cases, one or more of the family members is unable or unwilling to address and work through personal issues related to the abuse to allow resolution and reconstruction to occur. Similarly, the individual pathology, cognitive deficits, or abusiveness of significant family members may hinder or prevent the family environment from being a safe place for the youth.

In some cases, the treatment team recognizes that parents cannot or will not provide adequate supervision or support for the siblings, are not able or willing to develop and practice family safety plans, or cannot meet the needs of both siblings. This creates a dilemma for the youth that requires open communication and accurate attributions of responsibility. The team has a responsibility to realistically assess the reasonableness of reunification based on the work they do with the family.

Sometimes families lose the opportunity to reunify because of factors outside the control of the involved professionals. Issues involving children, families, or sexuality are socially and politically volatile, and child sexual abuse and incest involves all three. In spite of legislative mandates for family preservation, policies are often determined at the political rather than professional level and the decision to reunify or maintain the separation of a family may or may not be controlled by the treatment team. Whether the final decision about reunifying a particular family is made by qualified professionals or is a result of judicial or social policy, doing the work of family resolution and reunification supports the goals of safety and health for the family and community.

STAGE V: PREPARATION FOR DISCHARGE AND AFTERCARE SERVICES

Treatment will not always be successful and it is important to continuously evaluate the available information, from the initial assessment through the later stages of treatment, to foresee the possibility of either successful or unsuccessful termination of treatment. It is as important to have policy and planning for unsuccessful discharges as for success, and parents and youth need to be made aware of both. Sometimes youth are removed from treatment by external forces that have nothing to do with the youth or the therapist (e.g., court orders, probation or case management decisions, family circumstances, or lack of funding).

Whenever a youth terminates or is terminated from contact prior to successfully completing treatment, providers must document the reasons for termination, outline the unmet needs, and suggest alternatives for continued risk reduction. It is important to try to have some opportunity to process such discharges with the youth and family: making accurate attributions of responsibility that clarify what the treatment providers, the parents, and the youth do and do not have control over; articulating ongoing risks and dilemmas; and making recommendations regarding future needs.

Successful completion of treatment is based on specific, measurable objectives and consistent demonstration of observable changes in current functioning (see Chapter 17). As the family and youth become increasingly stable and self-sufficient, the family therapist and treatment team can gradually disengage. Treatment discharge marks the final disengagement. This is not always termination of all contact, as it is often desirable for the family therapist or team to monitor stability or offer ongoing support services. However, even when it is clear that the youth and/or family will require ongoing support, it is important to officially discharge the youth from offense-specific treatment and celebrate the successful demonstration of the outcomes relevant to decreased risk and increased health.

Aftercare refers to ongoing therapeutic support after successful completion of treatment. Aftercare plans may involve the youth, the family, treatment professionals, and/or other service agencies. The number, length, and duration of aftercare services are determined by the treatment team, which can make referrals for aftercare services in the community. Limited access and inadequate resources can be obstacles to comprehensive follow-up care. Families should be encouraged to return for help in times of stress or increased risk so that early interventions can prevent relapses. It is the parent's responsibility to ask for help; however, timely follow-up by the treatment provider increases the likelihood that parents will follow through. Sometimes a phone call is as meaningful as a face-to-face meeting. Inquiring about current conditions and expressing care and concern can reinforce positive changes, as well as remind families to continue to be vigilant.

The post-discharge environment is a powerful factor in determining the successful long-term adjustment of the youth. Family and community resources are essential in providing the structure, support, controls, and interventions to maintain the gains of treatment.

REFERENCES

Abel, G. G., Jones, C. D., Gabriel, W., & Harlow, N. (2009). *A boy's experience of child sexual abuse: Factors that increase his risk of developing sexually abusive behavior*. Submitted for publication.

American Correctional Association (ACA). (1993). *Standards for juvenile community residential facilities*. Laurel, MD: The Association.

Bagley, C. (1992). Development of an adolescent stress scale for use of school counselors. *School Psychology International, 13,* 31–49.

Bagley, C., & Shewchuk-Dann, D. (1991). Characteristics of 60 children and adolescents who have a history of sexual assault against others: Evidence from a controlled study. *Journal of Child and Youth Care, (Fall Special Issue),* 43–52.

Bengis, S., Brown, A., Freeman-Longo, R., Matsuda, B., Ross, J., Singer, K., et al. (1999). *Standards of care for youth in sex offense-specific residential programs*. National Offense-Specific Residential Standards Task Force. Holyoke, MA: NEARI Press.

Benson, P. L., Blyth, D.A., Deville, C., & Wachs, J. (1997). *Developmental assets among Seattle youth*. Minneapolis, MN: Search Institute.

Bentovin, A. (1998). Significant harm in context. In M. Adcock & R. White (Eds.), *Significant harm: Its management and outcome*. Croydon: Significant Publications.

Bera, W., Yokley, J. M., Hindman, J., Hutchens, L., & McGuire, D. (1990). *The use of victim-offender communication in the treatment of sexual abuse: Three intervention models*. Brandon, VT: Safer Society Press.

Blaske, D. M., Borduin, C. M., Henggeler, S. W., & Mann, B. J. (1989). Individual, family, and peer characteristics of adolescent sex offenders and assaultive offenders. *Developmental Psychology, 25*(5), 846–845.

Borduin, C. M., Henggeler, S. W., Blaske, D. M., & Stein, R. J. (1990). Multi-systemic treatment of adolescent sexual offenders. *International Journal of Offender Therapy and Comparative Criminology, 34,* 105–113.

Borduin, C. M., Letourneau, E. J., & Henggeler, S. H. (In preparation.) *Multisystemic treatment with juvenile sexual offenders and their families*. New York: Guilford Press.

Bremer, J. F. (2001). *The Protective Factors Scale: Assessing youth with sexual concerns*. Plenary address at the 16th annual National Adolescent Perpetration Network, Kansas City, KS.

British Columbia Ministry of Children and Family Development (BCMCFD). (2007). The latest evidence on Multi-Systemic Therapy (MST). *Children's Mental Health Research Quarterly, Spring* (Children's Behavioural Well-being), 1–3.

Browne, K., & Falshaw, L. (1998). Street children and crime in the UK: A case of abuse and neglect. *Child Abuse Review, 7*(4), 241–253.

Colorado Sex Offender Management Board (CSOMB). (2002). *Standards and guidelines for the evaluation, assessment, treatment, and supervision of juveniles who have committed sexual offenses*. Colorado Department of Public Safety, Division of Criminal Justice.

Dolan, M., Holloway, J., Bailey, S., & Kroll, L. (1996). The psychosocial characteristics of juvenile sexual offenders referred to an adolescent forensic service in the UK. *Medicine, Science, and Law, 36*, 343–352.

Farrington, D. (1991). Childhood aggression and adult violence. In D. Pepler & K. Rubin (Eds.), *The development and treatment of childhood aggression*. Hillsdale, NY: Lawrence Erlbaum Associates.

Fehrenbach, P., Smith, W., Monastersky, C., & Deisher, R. W. (1986). Adolescent sexual offenders: Offender and offense characteristics. *Journal of Orthopsychiatry, 56*, 225–233.

Gil, E. (1987). *Children who molest: A guide for parents of young sex offenders*. California: Launch Press.

Graves, R. B., Openshaw, D. K., Ascione, F. R., & Ericksen, S. L. (1996). Demographic and parental characteristics of youthful sexual offenders. *International Journal of Offender Therapy and Comparative Criminology, 40*(4), 300–317.

Gray, A. S., Pithers, W. D., Busconi, A., & Houchens, P. (1999). Developmental and etiological characteristics of children with sexual behavior problems: Treatment implications. *Child Abuse & Neglect, 23*, 601–621.

Harris, G. T., Rice, M. E., & Quinsey, V. L. (1993). Violent recidivism of mentally disordered offenders: The development of a statistical prediction instrument. *Criminal Justice and Behavior, 20*(4), 315–335.

Hawkins, J. D., Farrington, D. P., & Catalano, R. F. (1998). Reducing violence through the schools. In D. S. Elliott, B. A. Hamburg, & K. R. Williams (Eds.), *Violence in American schools: A new perspective* (pp. 188–216). Cambridge: Cambridge University Press.

Hsu, L. K. G., & Starzynski, J. (1990). Adolescent rapists and adolescent child sexual assaulters. *International Journal of Offender Therapy and Comparative Criminology, 34*(1), 23–30.

Hunter, J. A., & Figueredo, A. (2000). The influence of personality and history of sexual victimization in the prediction of juvenile perpetrated child molestation. *Behavior Modification, 24*(2), 241–263.

Jongsma, A. E., Peterson, L. M., & McInnis, W. P. (1996). *The child and adolescent psychotherapy treatment planner*. New York: John Wiley & Sons.

Kahn, T. J., & Chambers, H. J. (1991). Assessing reoffense risk with juvenile sexual offenders. *Child Welfare, 70*(3), 333–345.

Kobayashi, J., Sales, B. D., Becker, J. V., Figueredo, A. J., & Kaplan, M. S. (1995). Perceived parental deviance, parent-child bonding, child abuse, and child sexual aggression. *Sexual Abuse: A Journal of Research and Treatment, 7*(1), 25–44.

Littell, J. H. (2005). Lessons from a systematic review of effects of multisystemic therapy. *Children and Youth Services Review, 27*, 445–463.

Maddock, J. W., & Larson, N. R. (1995). *Incestuous families: An ecological approach to understanding and treatment*. New York: W.W. Norton & Company.

Manocha, K. F., & Mezey, G. (1998). British adolescents who sexually abuse: A descriptive study. *The Journal of Forensic Psychiatry, 9*(3), 588–608.

Marshall, W. L. (1989). Intimacy, loneliness, and sexual offenders. *Behavior Research and Therapy, 27*, 491–503.

McGrath, R. J., Cummings, G., & Burchard, B. (2003). *Current practices and trends in sexual abuse management: The Safer Society 2002 national survey.* Brandon, VT: Safer Society Foundation.

Miner, M. H., & Crimmins, C. L. S. (1995). Adolescent sex offenders—Issues of etiology and risk factors. In B. K. Schwartz & H. R. Cellini (Eds.), *The sex offender: New insights, treatment innovations, and legal developments: Volume II* (9-1 to 9-15). Kingston, NJ: Civic Research Institute.

Miner, M. H., Siekert, G. P., & Ackland, M. A. (1997). *Evaluation: Juvenile sex offender treatment program, Minnesota Correctional Facility—Sauk Centre: Final report—Biennium 1995–1997.* Minneapolis, MN: University of Minnesota, Department of Family Practice and Community Health, Program in Human Sexuality.

Morenz, B., and Becker, J. V. 1995. The treatment of youthful sexual offenders. *Applied and Preventive Psychology 4*(4), 247–256.

Parrish, L. (1985). *Behavioral contracting: Description and guidelines.* Unpublished manuscript.

Pithers, W. D., Gray, A., Busconi, A., & Houchens, P. (1998). Caregivers of children with sexual behavior problems: Psychological and familial functioning. *Child Abuse and Neglect, 22*(2), 129–141.

Richardson, G., Kelly, T. P., Bhate, S. R., & Graham, F. (1997). Group differences in abuser and abuse characteristics in a British sample of sexually abusive adolescents. *Sexual Abuse: A Journal of Research and Treatment, 9*(3), 239–257.

Rutter, M. (1972). Maternal deprivation reconsidered. *Journal of Psychosomatic Research, 16*(4), 241–250.

Rutter, M. (1985). Resilience in the face of adversity: Protective factors and resistance to psychiatric disorders. *British Journal of Psychiatry, 147*, 598–611.

Ryan, G., Miyoshi, T. J., Metzner, J. L., Krugman, R. D., & Fryer, G. E. (1996). Trends in a national sample of sexually abusive youths. *Journal of the American Academy of Child and Adolescent Psychiatry, 35*(1), 17–25.

Saunders, B. E., & Meinig, M. B. (1995). *Family resolution therapy: The latter stages of family therapy.* Lexington, MA: Lexington Books.

Schladale, J. (2002). *A collaborative approach for engaging families in treatment with sexually aggressive youth.* Presentation to the 7th International Conference for the Treatment of Sexual Offenders, Vienna, Austria.

Schladale, J. (2005). Rough terrain: Navigating around barriers to family involvement with youth who have caused sexual harm. *ATSA Forum, 17*(3).

Schladale, J. (2006). Family matters: The importance of engaging families in treatment with youth who have caused sexual harm. In R. Longo & D. Prescott (Eds.), *Current perspective: Working with sexually aggressive youth and youth with sexual behavior problems* (pp. 493–514). Holyoke, MA: NEARI Press.

Schladale, J., Langan, T., Barnett, P., Nunez, J., Moylan/Trigiano, J., Brown, D., et al. (2006). *Community based standards for addressing youth who have caused sexual harm.* Resolving Sexual Violence: pdf available at http://www.resourcesforresolvingviolence.com

Schoenwald, S. K., Borduin, C. M., & Henggeler, S. W. (1998). Multisystemic therapy: Changing the natural and service ecologies of adolescents and families. In M. H. Epstein, K. Kutash, & A. J. Duchnowski (Eds.), *Outcomes for children and youth with emotional and behavioral disorders and their families: Programs and evaluation best practices* (pp. 485–511). Austin, TX: PRO-ED.

Sefarbi, R. (1990). Admitters and deniers among adolescent sex offenders and their families: A preliminary study. *American Journal of Orthopsychiatry, 60*(3), 460–465.

Smith, H., & Israel, E. (1987). Sibling incest: A study of the dynamics of 25 cases. *Child Abuse and Neglect, 11*(2), 101–108.

Smith, W. R., & Monastersky, C. (1986). Assessing juvenile sexual offenders' risk for reoffending. *Criminal Justice and Behavior 13*(2): 115–140.

Thomas, J. (1988). *Multifamily group work with juvenile sexual offenders.* Paper presented at the National Training Conference, Long Beach, CA.

Thomas, J. (1996). *Safety in residential settings.* Paper presented at the 12th Annual National Adolescent Perpetrator Network, Minneapolis, MN.

Thomas, J. (1999). *Plan for family reunification when the victim and offender are siblings in the same home.* Presented at the National Adolescents Perpetrator Network Conference, Denver, CO.

Thomas, J. (2001). *Holding ourselves accountable: National standards for sex offense specific residential programs.* 2001: Paradigm.

Thomas, J., & Viar, W. (2001). Familial influences, family treatment. In S. Mussack & M. Carich (Eds.), *Handbook for sexual abuser assessment and treatment* (pp. 163–192). Brandon, VT: Safer Society Press.

Thomas, J., & Viar, W. (2005). Family reunification in sibling incest: A step by step process. In M. C. Calder (Ed.), *Children and young people who sexually abuse: New theory, research and practice developments.* Dorset: Russell House Publishing.

Ward, T., Hudson, S. M., Marshall, W. L., & Siegert, R. (1995). Attachment style and intimacy deficits in sexual offenders: A theoretical framework. *Sexual Abuse: Journal of Research and Treatment, 7*(4), 317–335.

Warsh, R., Pine, B., & Maluccio, A. (1994). *Teaching family reunification: A sourcebook.* Washington, DC: Child Welfare League of America.

Werner, E., & Smith, R. (1992). *Overcoming the odds: High-risk children from birth to adulthood.* New York: Cornell University Press.

CHAPTER 21

Special Populations

Children, Female, Developmentally Disabled, and Violent Youth

GAIL RYAN, TOM LEVERSEE, and SANDY LANE*

T HE SPECIAL POPULATIONS that are the subject of this chapter—young children, female, developmentally disabled, and violent youth—have some unique characteristics that require special consideration or modifications in treatment approaches. In the past, fewer specialized services were available for these youth or, because of their unique characteristics, the abusive nature of their sexual behaviors was sometimes minimized or discounted and at other times, elicited extreme reactions. Systemic interventions were often disproportionate to their behavior. Some viewed these youths as untreatable and others as unlikely to have actually perpetrated sexually abusive behaviors. However, it has been demonstrated that each of these populations is represented in referrals for offense-specific treatment, and are able to benefit from treatment that considers all aspects of their life experience, developmental history, and abusive behavior with the same goals of health promotion and risk reduction that guide current practice with male adolescents who have sexually offended.

In recent years, exciting developments have occurred in work with each of these populations. More specialized treatment programs are available, books and articles have been published, and some research studies are specifically relevant. These youth are now more readily identified and likely to be referred for evaluation and treatment. There are still controversies, and abusive behaviors are sometimes still minimized, misconstrued, or overreacted to, but the efforts to identify effective approaches, developmental antecedents, and program development have been ongoing. So much is still unknown about the influences of gender, experience, culture, and ecology on human sexuality that professionals must expect knowledge to continue to evolve over time in ways that may continue to change practices with subgroups such as these.

---

* Adapted from Lane and Lobanov-Rostovsky (1997).

CHILDREN WITH SEXUAL ABUSE BEHAVIOR PROBLEMS

Treatment programs working with young children with sexual abuse behavior problems began in the mid-1980s, as therapists treating older juveniles heard from adolescents and parents about abusive behaviors occurring in preschool and elementary years. Victim therapists were also recognizing sexual behavior problems in young children who had been abused (Freidrich, Urquiza, & Bielke, 1986). Some offense-specific treatment providers began offering perpetration prevention treatment for male child victims, only to find that many of the referred boys had already perpetrated offenses on other children (Isaac, 1986; Lane & Lobanov-Rostovsky, 1997). In the first group for 7- to 10-year-old male victims that Lane and Lobanov-Rostovsky (1997) described, each of the boys had already engaged in abusive behaviors toward other children and some reported the onset of those behaviors as occurring as early as ages four and five.

A survey conducted within the membership of the National Adolescent Perpetration Network (NAPN) (Rogers, 1992) elicited 25 responses from clinicians who were working with young children with sexually abusive behavior problems. Approximately half of the respondents indicated concern about social service agencies responding only to intrafamilial sexual abuse cases, and law enforcement not being trained or empowered to respond when children were too young to be arrested and charged for sexual offending. Additional dilemmas have been the failure of adults to clearly differentiate between normative and nonnormative sexual behaviors, and failure to achieve a balance of concern for victimization and perpetration issues. Although many of these dilemmas have been recognized, they have not always been addressed in a reasonable and productive manner.

Early identification and intervention efforts faced the disbelief that children so young could be sexually abusive and even, at times, that the behavior of children that young was actually sexual. Nonetheless, some very young children demonstrate a progression of sexual behavior over time, reflecting compensatory or retaliatory patterns of thoughts, feelings, and behaviors that can be quite similar in function to those of adolescents who sexually offend (Isaac, 1986; Lane & Lobanov-Rostovsky, 1997). Children are less sophisticated and may be less calculating, but the basic issues and elements are similar.

Whereas research related to differentiating between normative and nonnormative sexual behaviors prior to puberty was scarce in the 1980s (Ryan, 2000; Ryan et al., 1988), the work is now informed by a substantial body of literature describing adults' reports of observed behaviors (Friedrich, Damon, & Hewitt, 1992; Johnson, 1991). Resources have been developed to help parents and others understand and respond to the wide range of behaviors observed among prepubescent children (Gil, 1986; Johnson, 1998; Pithers, Gray, Cunningham, & Lane, 1993; Ryan, 2000; Ryan & Blum, 1994; Ryan et al., 1988).

A variety of treatment approaches have been refined, characteristics of children with sexual abuse behavior problems and their response to various treatment approaches have been described (Bonner, Walker, & Berliner, 1996; Pithers & Gray, 1998), and various etiological theories have been explored in relation to the early onset of abusive behaviors (Burton & Meezan, 2004; Gil, 1993; Miner, 2008; Ryan, 1989; Ryan, 1998; Ryan, and Associates, 1998; Ryan, 2004a). Assessment tools for children now include the Child Sexual Behavior Inventory (Friedrich et al., 1992); the Child Sexual Behavior Checklist-R (Johnson, 1992), and the MEGA (Miccio-Fonseca & Rasmussen, 2006), and typologies for children who molest have been suggested (Gray, Pithers, Busconi, & Houchens, 1997; Johnson 1993, 1995a).

Children in preschool and early elementary grades exhibit a wide range of sexual behaviors that may or may not be symptomatic of underlying needs, and may or may not be problematic. Children also sometimes exhibit a constellation of behaviors and symptoms that may be precursors of sexually abusive behaviors. Abel, Jones, Gabriel, and Harlow (2009) have suggested that for those boys who are sexually abused and later perpetrate sexual offenses, the time between their own abuse and the onset of their offending may be only a few years. Earlier identification and preventive interventions can help young children avoid the habituation of sexually abusive behavior problems.

Early childhood professionals now recognize their need for information about children's sexual behaviors and to be trained to identify and respond to those behaviors in child care settings. Particularly encouraging has been an increased use of developmental-contextual assessments and the exploration of developmental antecedents, identifying issues of disrupted or dysfunctional attachments, and variables in experience and social learning that contribute to the development of abusive behaviors (Abel, Jones, Gabriel, & Harlow, 2009; Burton & Meezan, 2004; Marshall, Hudson, & Hodkinson, 1993; Miner, 2008; Ryan, 1988; Ryan and Associates, 1998).

Although jurisdictional and budgetary constraints continue to limit some social service agencies to intrafamilial abuse intervention, there is improved awareness, identification, consideration, and intervention with reports of sexually abusive behavior by children when it occurs outside the home. Behaviors are viewed more thoughtfully and evaluated more consistently, although it continues to be a struggle to balance safety considerations with the child's developmental needs. There continue to be controversies about differentiating and labeling children with sexual behavior problems and a variety of diverse treatment approaches (Cunningham & MacFarlane, 1991; Friedrich, Davies, Feher, & Wright, 2003; Johnson & Doonan, 2005; MacFarlane & Cunningham, 1989; Miccio-Fonseca & Rasmussen, 2006; Rasmussen, 2000; Rasmussen, Burton, & Christopherson, 1990; Rich, 2003).

Much of the work continues to be fairly eclectic, as it was in the 1990s (Lane & Lobanov-Rostovsky, 1997). Treatment and assessment are based in the same basic concepts described in Chapters 15, 17, and 18: *Defining all types of abuse; recognizing skill deficits and patterns in the child's functioning; and promoting the universal goals of communication, empathy, and accurate attributions of responsibility for behavior.*

Recognition of the function of behavior informs interventions. Underlying the theoretical concept of the cycle is the belief that people initially respond to overwhelming trauma or vulnerable feelings using human defenses (Finkelhor, 1986; Porter, 1986). The development of the child's worldview, belief system, coping strategies, internal reactions, and behavior is influenced by exposure and life experience. The young child's behavior may be reactive to early childhood maltreatment or loss, a traumatic experience, some type of victimization, lack of stimulation, neglect, an unsafe or chaotic environment, disrupted relationships, inconsistent care, dysfunctional models of coping, or a lack of nurturing, empathic care. The coping style the child manifests may demonstrate functional coping or may involve a compensatory use of sexual or aggressive behavior or a misuse of power or intimacy that is expressed sexually.

THE CHILDREN

Characteristics of children with sexual behavior problems include a wide range of similarities and differences. In this text puberty represents the division between childhood and adolescence. However, puberty represents a period of developmental changes characterized by growth and regression over more than a year. Prepubescent children and post-pubescent adolescents can be more accurately described and evaluated, while the description and evaluation of pubescent children represents a fuzzy and unstable picture. Professionals must always be wary of rigid definitions and overgeneralization of what is known about children based on age alone, especially during puberty, and respect the developmental contextual differences among children of similar ages.

Much of the literature and data of the twentieth century relevant to children's sexual behavior and the treatment of sexual behavior problems has referred to "children under 12." However, the average onset of puberty has dropped from approximately 13 in the 1950s to approximately 10 at this time (see Chapter 4). The reader is cautioned to think of "children" as "prepubescent" and "adolescents" as "post-pubescent," and appreciate that during puberty, the transition is in flux.

The sexually abusive behaviors of even very young children represent the whole range of human sexual behaviors. It is not the behavior per se that defines abuse. Lane and Lobanov-Rostovsky (1997) described the behaviors of the 5- to 12-year-old boys referred to their earliest groups as including genital fondling, vaginal and anal intercourse, fellatio, attempted intercourse, "humping," cunnilingus, "french kisses," rubbing chests, digital vaginal and anal penetration, exhibitionism, voyeurism, rubbing penis against genitals, fondling buttocks, and object penetration. Over two-thirds of the victims were either siblings or nonrelated children who were visiting in the home. Of the sibling victims, about one-quarter were half- or step-siblings, and the remainder were full biological siblings. About one-third of the victims were neighbors or schoolmates. The numbers of victims varied considerably (from one to more than fifty), but most children reported involvement in three to six different abuse incidents. Over half of the behaviors involved taking advantage of an opportunity that occurred in a home when an adult was in another room, asleep, or outside. The children expressed more concern about getting to do the behavior without being interrupted than about someone finding out what they had done. The frequency of the behaviors ranged from daily to once every three or four months.

Many of the children referred for treatment due to sexual behavior problems have a history of sexual, physical, or emotional victimization, neglect, or abandonment experiences. Many have been exposed to violent, disruptive, or dysfunctional home environments. Some have concurrent psychiatric diagnoses (especially attention deficit/hyperactivity disorder, attachment disorders, PTSD, and mood disorders), learning disabilities, and medical problems. Some have also engaged in nonsexual delinquent behaviors (Lane & Lobanov-Rostovsky, 1997). Early intervention can stem the development, reinforcement, and continuation of sexually abusive behaviors.

Many of these children exhibit social competency deficits: they have difficulty with joining in, asking for help, handling failure or mistakes, apologizing, compromising, building friendships, sharing, problem solving, handling embarrassment, accepting compliments, playing with others, impulse control, empathy, intimacy, handling conflicts, making decisions, delaying gratification, anger management, or accepting "no." They tend to be socially isolated in school situations and few have any close friends (Lane & Lobanov-Rostovsky, 1997). These deficits can be addressed in group settings, which foster missing skills and provide a safe forum for children to express and overcome negative perceptions.

INTERVENTION

Offense-specific or behavior-specific interventions can often be addressed in psycho-educational support groups, although individual differences sometimes indicate more or additional needs for individual or family interventions. Abusive sexual behavior must be defined as harmful to others and to themselves and, although the child may not consciously "decide" to hurt someone, exert power over another, or coerce another child in an abusive manner, the behavioral manifestation of the child's functioning may involve an expression of sexual or nonsexual control-seeking, dominating behaviors, and a coercive style of interpersonal interaction. The power differential between children may involve contrasting levels of experience, sophistication, knowledge, age, size, authority, personality characteristics, intellectual capacity, and developmental aspects of the participants in the abuse behavior.

Holding even very young children "responsible" for abusive behaviors, and requiring such behaviors to stop, is not the same as "blaming," "shaming," or "punishing." Making accurate attributions of responsibility is directly relevant to the child's internalizing a sense of personal responsibility and competence. Making clear whose behavior is problematic and why is the goal.

A child's understanding of treatment concepts will be different than an older person's, and clinicians must modify language and concepts to facilitate accurate and comprehensible communication. For example, the concept of "cycles" requires abstract thought and younger children often are more able to recognize commonalities in their patterns of functioning when viewed as "stair-steps" rather than circles (Lane & Lobanov-Rostovsky, 1997). Figure 21.1 exemplifies one child's description of that pattern. Preventive interventions are directed at "getting off the steps" that precede sexually abusive behaviors, and the adult is more often the source of alternative solutions (see Chapter 15). With younger children, experiential activities increase their recognition and awareness of foreseeable patterns in how they behave.

Children may lack frustration tolerance and emotional recognition of vulnerable feelings like helplessness, powerlessness, abandonment, rejection, or humiliation, just as older sexually abusive youth do. The vocabulary they use to describe their perceptual and affective experiences is more simplistic and representative of their age level, but they do communicate beliefs about what they have experienced in their lives, and often express the perception that they have no control and cannot understand why these things have happened. Often they assume they are somehow responsible for things like victimization, disrupted parent-child relationships, physical violence in their homes, boundary violations, losses, neglect, frequent moves, and/or family enmeshment, as if these things result from "being bad." They personalize other's statements, feedback, and discipline and often believe others intend to harm them, make them look bad, or reject them.

Some children rely on a compensatory coping style that involves a misuse of power or control in many situations, or use sexual behaviors to meet nonsexual needs. The style of the child may be less sophisticated than that of older sexually

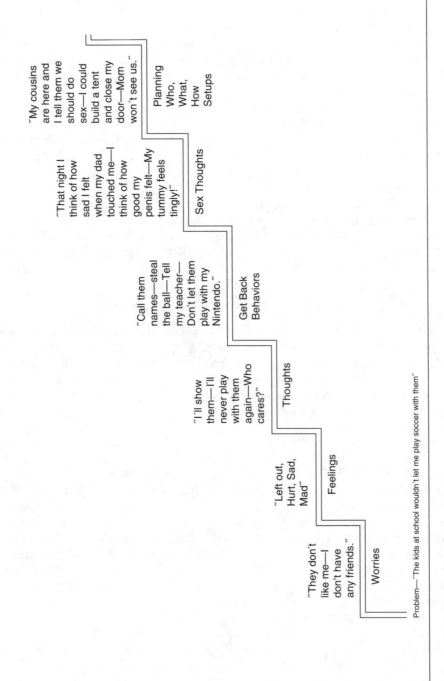

Figure 21.1 One Child's Step Cycle

385

abusive youth, but appears very similar in nature: some children are characterized by their vulnerabilities and others by their defenses against feeling vulnerable, such as needing to be first or best, cheating or changing rules in order to win, blaming others while shaming themselves, or exhibiting retaliatory and manipulative behaviors. Ultimately all children want to feel strong and safe, and sexually abusive behaviors often represent compensatory or control-seeking functions. Parents and school personnel are often caught up in the child's power-based behaviors: fighting, arguing, being disruptive, or disobeying rules. Low frustration tolerance leads to tantrums and oppositional behavior, pushing limits, hitting, whining, and provoking younger children and peers.

Sexualized behaviors or sexual preoccupation often manifest when children are confused, stressed, or angry. They also exhibit sexualized behaviors and curiosity, which are quite normative for their developmental level. They may perceive or react to benign, nonsexual situations in a sexualized manner, describe sexual experiences in ways that seem to be self-enhancing, make sexual comments, or describe sexual behaviors in a more sophisticated manner than is typical of their age or developmental level. Some report a preoccupation with sexual thoughts or masturbation, and many describe engaging in "humping" behaviors on their bed or with stuffed animals, as well as genital stimulation. During play with other children, boundary violations and intrusive touches may be observed (Lane & Lobanov-Rostovsky, 1997; Ryan, 2000).

Evaluation and Assessment of Childhood Sexual Behavior Problems

The basic concepts and process of assessment is not dissimilar to that suggested for older youth. Evaluating the nature of sexual behavior and interactions, the child's motivation and culpability regarding their behavior, developmental deficits, unmet needs, and emotionally charged or unresolved issues result in treatment plans that focus on all problematic areas and needs. Behavior is often symptomatic of the young child's inability to express needs and emotions verbally; however, the behavior is not always easily interpreted.

Differentiating between normative and nonnormative sexual behaviors of prepubescent children has been based on a variety of sources: Friedrich, Beilke, & Urquiza, 1988; Friedrich, Fisher, Broughton, Houston, & Shafran, 1991; Friedrich et al., 1992; Johnson, 1988, 1993, 1995a; Ryan, 2000; Ryan et al., 1988. However, behavior out of context can be misleading. It is imperative that evaluators of children with sexual behavior problems have a functional understanding of human sexuality, sexual development, potential motivations driving sexual behaviors of humans, and the use of sexual behavior to meet nonsexual needs or express unmet needs. In evaluating the nature of the interactions and relationships between children, it is also necessary to explore issues related to the nature of the relationship, balance of power (Isaac, 1986; Ryan et al., 1989), developmental-contextual history, family, and risk factors.

Meaningful evaluation of the sexual behaviors of young children is most successful using a process of thoughtful exploration of the behavior in context—ask first of all, "Is this behavior a problem?," and realizing that some behaviors are not a problem at all. If the evaluator (parent or professional) does recognize a problem, then ask "What kind of problem is it?" There are many reasons adults may view a child's sexual behavior as problematic and whether it is abusive and/or illegal are only two possibilities. It is useful to think systematically about whether the behavior poses some risk for the child themselves; then thinking whether it poses a problem for others; and then whether it is, in fact, abusive or illegal. Identifying the kind of problem informs more reasonable, individualized interventions, rather than responding to all sexual behaviors in the same way.

Thinking through the potential risks of a behavior identifies all the ways the behavior might be problematic for self, others, or the law. The treatment plan can then address those risks specifically, along with other needs identified by the comprehensive assessment. The same process guides educational prevention and intervention strategies with children and adult caregivers.

A comprehensive and holistic evaluation is as necessary for the young child as for older youth. The childhood onset of behavior problems can continue into adulthood if not addressed. Exploring all areas of functioning and competencies in the developmental context of the child, the evaluation should include the same domains discussed in earlier chapters for adolescents in terms of comprehensive/holistic, individualized, differential diagnosis and treatment planning (see Chapter 13).

Although the referral may be made due to sexual behavior, the child and the family often need treatment for symptoms related to unresolved issues, stressors, or deficits in functioning; family members may be referred for evaluation of concurrent psychiatric disorders, parenting education, adjunct individual or couples therapy, parent/child therapy, or family therapy.

The Adults' Role in Treating Children with Sexually Abusive Behavior Problems

Whereas older youth who are referred for treatment due to sexual offending are expected to acquire the knowledge and skills to recognize and interrupt abusive patterns of behavior and to master self-control and autonomy, younger children rely more on the adults in their lives to provide supervision, guidance, and support to meet their needs. The younger the child, the more the treatment plan must focus on involvement of caregivers. The adult's role is to validate and correct behaviors that reflect the child's learning in a goal-oriented manner, which will decrease the risk of abusive behaviors and increase the child's ability to be successful (Ryan, Yager, Sobicinski, & Metzner, 2002).

The comprehensive assessment will identify the strengths and needs of the family as they relate to the family's ability to meet the child's needs, and some children may need alternative care providers to meet special needs. Just as the evaluation of older youth must identify what the youth needs from the adults in their lives, the prepubescent child can be expected to need much more from adults, and the younger the child is, the greater portion of intervention will be provided through the caregiver. Educating and supporting caregivers in providing "informed supervision" and "therapeutic care" are even more critical for younger children. Therefore, the concepts and strategies described in Chapters 15, 17, and 18 provide a foundation for treatment planning for children with sexual behavior problems, and for the role and responsibilities of those adults.

Immediate and consistent responses shape the child's behaviors in every domain, while patient redirection and limit setting create the boundaries children need modeled in order to acquire an appreciation for personal space, privacy, and empathy. The adult's active definition of abusive behaviors and redirection toward more functional behaviors combines with the "universal goals" of increasing effective cognitive and affective communication, the experience of emotional re-cognition and empathic responses, and the accurate attribution of responsibility. The adults' responsibility to validate and correct behavior while fostering growth and development is clear.

Safety planning for children uses the same basic risk-management protocol described in Chapter 15. The concreteness and specificity of safety plans, as well as their flexibility, seem to be helpful to children and adults in avoiding ambiguity, while making informed decisions that balance the child's needs and the safety of others. The conditions of safety plans support boundaries, use adults and parents as a source of support and control, avoid stimuli that might support abusive behavior, and minimize opportunities for reoffending as well as allegations. Safety plans are continuously reviewed with the child and caregivers during treatment. Plans include supervision needs and strategies, and identify how the adults can support and assist the child who continues to express thoughts or urges to do abusive or problematic sexual behaviors.

Family involvement is both psychoeducational and therapeutic. The parents or caretakers can be required to attend educational sessions to develop an under-standing of the abuse behavior, the concepts their child will learn, protective supervision, and how to assist their child during and after treatment. These concepts are clearly articulated and the adult's role made explicit in teaching parents to be "Informed Supervisors" (see Chapter 15). Family therapy sessions dispel secrecy, model open communication, deal with current issues, address family dysfunctions, and support parents in understanding and meeting the child's needs.

Beyond the caregiver's role, much of the clinical treatment for younger children parallels work with children who have experienced similar risks and adversity such as abuse, trauma, and loss. Such issues can be addressed with evidence-based practices in the same way clinicians are trained to work with other emotionally-behaviorally disturbed clinical populations. Symptoms of depression, social isola-tion/alienation, enuresis, thoughts of drinking or using drugs, excessive fears, nightmares, communication problems, eating problems, and self-mutilation some-times require clinical intervention. Co-occurring disorders and sensitive personal issues are often addressed in individual or family therapy sessions, and/or concur-rent referrals (see Chapters 19 and 20).

SPECIALIZED TREATMENT OF SEXUALLY ABUSIVE BEHAVIOR PROBLEMS

Many of the issues specifically relevant to sexual behavior problems can be addressed in psychoeducational support groups with other children who have sexual behavior problems, and parents often benefit from parallel psychoeducational support groups with other parents.

The goals and process of treatment specifically relevant to sexually abusive behavior are actually quite similar with younger children, as has been described for adolescents. It is the language, perceptions, and thinking that will be more childish. Adapting language and concepts to children's cognitive, developmental, and learn-ing abilities is imperative in developing treatment approaches. The therapist must appreciate the concrete simplicity of children's thoughts, while recognizing symp-toms of traumatic experience, incomprehensible exposure, and developmental disruptions. However, the goals remain the same across childhood and adoles-cence: to reduce the risk of abusive behaviors and help the child be successful.

Therapeutic relationship and individualized treatment plans should still guide the process. As was true for older youth, the prerequisites for therapeutic change are first to create the physical and psychological safety that allow learning and vulnerability without defenses. Psychoeducational groups can provide support for children and the reassurance that others have similar problems.

Secrecy is often characteristic of sexual interactions and dispelling that secrecy with conversation, education, and supervision immediately creates the containment that decreases opportunities for the child to continue relying on sexual behaviors as a coping response. Initially, "rules" and the rewards and consequences of behavior modification systems may be a necessary part of the containment that provides safety for the child and others. However, just as the child tests the limits of other behaviors in different settings and circumstances, teaching rules and laws does not create a capacity for empathic interpersonal interactions across the life span. The goals must be to help the child master the knowledge and the skills that support successful functioning and relationships.

Some structure is necessary in group settings, but ideally limiting the number of rules to only those most important minimizes the risk of spending all the time dealing with rule violations. Rules might be: not hurting others, listening without interrupting others, and following directions. A certain amount of disruption must be expected and the limits that are emphasized should be carefully chosen. Responding to excessive disruptive behaviors can promote the universal goals by labeling the behavior, stating how one feels, and requesting the child to stop the behavior. Consistent expectations based on personal choice and self-control place the responsibility with the child while empowering them with internal control. Children who are not able to settle when reminded may need or benefit from modified time-out, but ideally stay in the room. Exclusion from the group room should only occur when the child poses a risk to self or others in the room, with a goal of earliest possible return.

Group treatment sessions can address specific topics related to abuse behavior, but must be flexible enough to provide the forum for processing current concerns of individual children and, especially, to allow for the interpersonal skill building many of these children need to practice. Topics that constitute the educational agenda might include:

Sex education including human sexuality and behavior
Defining abusive behavior
Learning the laws about youthful sexual behaviors
Defenses, coping, impulses, reinforcement, patterns of behavior
Behavioral, cognitive, and affective antecedents to behavior
Emotional recognition and responses
Cognitive restructuring
Foreseeable patterns (cycles or stair steps)
Sympathy, empathy, and intimacy
Consequences of abusive behaviors
Foresight and planning, risk management (safety planning)

Because so many children have short attention spans or hyperactivity, an hour-and-a-half group time can be split into segments to decrease distraction, boredom, and disruptiveness; for example: sharing something important; learning something new; playtime; wrapping up thoughts and feelings (i.e., what to take home and what to leave for next group). Nearly all topics must be revisited once or twice over the course of treatment to increase understanding and retention (Lane & Lobanov-Rostovsky, 1997).

Experiential activities and exercises should be designed to facilitate learning and make concepts memorable. Several publications suggest activities to engage and facilitate the educational components of treatment (Berliner & Rawlings, 1991; Camino, 2000; Cunningham & MacFarlane, 1991, 1996; Gray, 1991; Johnson, 1995b; Kahn, 1990, 1991; Ryan, 2004b; Webster-Stratton, 2005). Learning exercises, stories, experiential activities, role playing, puppets, art, movement, and group discussions may be used to make the concepts more meaningful and memorable. Books that are specifically relevant to discussions of the sexual issues include: *A Very Touching Book* (Hindman, 1983); *No No Seal* (Patterson, 1986); *Steps to Healthy Touching* (MacFarlane & Cunningham, 1989); and *Good Touch, Bad Touch* (Denige, 1987).

Identifying distressing developmental, traumatic, or victimization experiences that the children have in common may occur in group discussions and be referred into individual and family therapy for personal issues work. However, one of the things Lane and Lobanov-Rostovsky (1997) described in their early work was that group work on offense-specific topics can be particularly useful when past sexually abusive behavior is the referring problem and is what differentiates this setting from all others in the child's life.

Although not all children do well in groups, some of the issues they had anticipated would be hardest for the younger boys to discuss in group were the very issues the boys brought up there. For example, they found that discussions of healthy sexuality and sex education included the topics of arousal, orgasm, and sexual thoughts, and proved beneficial in clarifying misconceptions and confusion.

Lane and Lobanov-Rostovsky (1997) described children in their treatment group initiating talk about early arousal experiences and their difficulty avoiding thoughts of being sexual with other children when they experienced arousal. One group of boys had revealed that although none of them wanted to do another abuse behavior, they kept having a problem with their penis getting hard when they thought about sex, and it made them want to do sexual things with their siblings. Some of the boys had gone to extreme lengths trying to suppress unwanted arousal, such as tying strings on the penis, snapping rubber bands or running cold water on the genitals to make the hardness go away, or slapping their penis.

The boys were frustrated because nothing they had tried seemed to work, and they believed that having an erection caused their abuse behavior. Some said that they had tried masturbation to control feeling associated with arousal such as "the tingly feeling," "butterflies in the stomach," "an erection," "feeling good," "having a queasy stomach," "feeling happy," or "a penis that is sort of hard," and reported that these feelings occurred when they had "sex thoughts" or "touching thoughts" and were "near the top of the (stair) steps."

To improve impulse control a modified form of covert sensitization can be used with older children; a potential benefit associated with the technique is the reduction of the frequency or intensity of sexual urges and/or thoughts. Although the efficacy of covert sensitization has been documented with adults and adolescents, there is no known objective verification of these effects with children beyond their own self-reports, but some children are very clear in reporting the technique has helped them. The adaptation for children that has been used involves helping the children write two or three sentences that they can rely on when they think of abuse. Older children might carry the sentences with them and read them while younger children might simply remember the key elements. For example, *"Thinking about touching my sister's privates. STOP. I don't want to do this. I got in trouble last time. I felt bad. If I stop myself, I'll feel good, and my mom will be proud. When she tells me, 'Good job,' I feel good."* This type of "self-talk" can be helpful for more hypersexual or habituated children, although not all children are troubled by recurring urges.

Other aspects of their past offending that also seemed easier to discuss with other boys in a group (than one-on-one with adults) included fantasies and plans. Thoughts about sexual behavior may be memories of past experience, fantasies of future behaviors, or simply thoughts about sexual information or stimuli in the environment. Sexual thoughts may be brief thought fragments, mental images, or more detailed plans. Lane and Lobanov-Rostovsky (1997) found that most of the young children they had in treatment could describe thoughts that occurred prior to their abusive behavior. The children were not asked about fantasizing but rather about what they thought about before the abuse happened. They were then asked to show where on the stair steps the thoughts occurred.

Of the children who reported fantasies, about one-third indicated explicit sexual thoughts. Some thoughts were wondering about babies, some were related to things they had seen or heard, some were the recall of previous sexual behaviors that they had done, and some were memories of being sexually victimized by others. Slightly over half of the children who reported antecedent "fantasies" said they thought about the abuse behavior in advance. About half of those thought of what they could do, and about half thought of what they could do and who they could do it with. About one-fourth reported experiencing urges to do the behavior, about a third reported masturbation or genital self-touch during the thoughts, and a few said they thought of using sexual behaviors to get back at their parents when they were angry.

The boys also talked about how they got other children to do what they wanted, strategies or behaviors that would increase the likelihood of cooperation, and some even described testing the other child's reactions in advance. Use of threats, bribery, buttering up, tricks, playing games, pressure, force, and authority (like being bossy) were all described. Only a few described specific planning, although many acknowledged some action to create the opportunity to engage the other child, including manipulation of a parent or other responsible adult. One boy said that when he was five, he thought of doing a sexual behavior with a small child in the home, but he knew people would not like it so he got up in the middle of the night to engage in the behavior without getting caught (Lane & Lobanov-Rostovsky, 1997).

Group discussions also reveal many justifications for past sexual abuse behaviors that are not so different from older youth and often reflect common messages in the culture, as well as common defense tactics. Examples include, "She wanted me to do it," "Well, she took her clothes off first," "But my cousin asked me to do it before I did anything," "He liked it just as much as I did, so it's both our faults," "She pushed me on the bed; I don't see why everyone is mad at me," and "Well, I had to do it; I was mad at my dad."

Although young children are quite able to recognize the "steps" that led up to their offenses, they are less aware of the cyclical nature of the pattern. They attempt to come to terms with their offenses in order to lessen their bad feelings about being caught and consequently punished, but they do not see this process as part of the steps. It may be that concepts of defenses like suppression or denial are too abstract for younger children to work with; however, they can relate to the "after" thoughts and feelings of their peers.

In the group, children often benefit from help identifying and practicing ways they can seek help from parents or other adults to help them avoid urges to act on sexual thoughts, as well as sharing ideas about situations they need to walk away from, and the choices they make.

In addressing sexual behaviors with children, they must learn that many sexual behaviors are normal and good, even those that parents and others do not want them to engage in during childhood. Validating the reasonableness of adult concerns and respecting differences in parents' values and rules is imperative. Children can often understand the parallel between readiness for sexual interactions and readiness to drive a car: they know that people drive and have some idea of what it involves, but they do not really know how to drive themselves and they are not big enough to reach the pedals and still see out the window.

Emphasis is placed on understanding that sex is typically private and that respect for others involves respect for their boundaries and the issues of consent. Boundaries and privacy are specifically addressed to differentiate concepts of personal body space, boundary violations, intimacy, and invasive behaviors. Children can practice recognition and respect for personal space during activities in the group.

The stair step cycle can be used with younger children and the simple cycles introduced in Chapter 15, or Figure 21.2 (Lane & Lobanov-Rostovsky, 1997), can be used with older children. These modifications of the cycle help children become aware of the patterns of thoughts, feelings, and behaviors antecedent to their sexual abuse behavior.

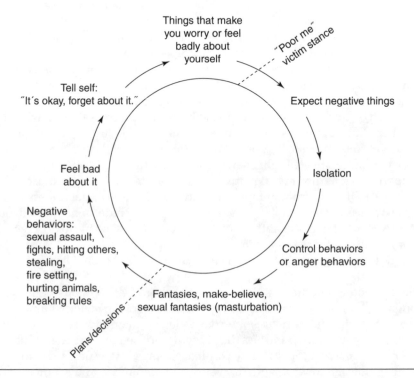

Figure 21.2   Modification of the Sexual Abuse Cycle Used with Children

Children can learn to recognize clues or signs that they are moving up the steps (or through the cycle) and develop strategies to help them interrupt the pattern. The younger children may picture themselves walking backward down the stairs, turning around and walking down the stairs toward something that is good, or jumping off the stairs. As children become able to recognize and redirect themselves, they experience a sense of competency and internalized self-control. It is a good feeling to become able to understand oneself and acquire skills that support success.

COGNITIVE AND BEHAVIORAL INTERVENTIONS

Cognitive-behavioral interventions can take advantage of school age children's gradual development of cognitive skills, including perspective taking, logical thinking, and improved understanding of cause and effect (Davies, 2004). Group work with children can employ a variety of techniques, ranging from group discussions to stories, scripts, and structured exercises, as well as feedback that interrupts and reinterprets negative expectations and abuse-supportive thinking. Recognizing what they do and do not have control over supports the accurate attribution of responsibility and relieves the need to try to control others. Identifying that uncomfortable feelings are a reaction to something in the present, they can learn to talk about the feelings and avoid negative conclusions about themselves instead of thinking something is wrong with them. Children often report that they assume they are bad when they are disciplined or receive corrective feedback at home or school, so a focus on positive characteristics, permission to make mistakes, and separating behavior from person demonstrates that they can make choices to do things they can feel good about.

Children can be encouraged to develop positive self-talk to counter negative expectations about themselves or others. As has been stated previously, it is important to be sure the child has some evidence that supports positive statements and is not just learning to talk differently. Adults, articulating strengths and positives when they are observable, create a conscious basis for changing how the child thinks of themselves and others. Defining self-abusive statements such as "I'm stupid" is as important as defining name calling and other verbal abuse of others. When the child makes statements that reflect negative assumptions about other's motives or behaviors, the thought must be countered with evidence that supports questioning the assumption.

When working on positive self-talk, older children can talk about current situations, recognize when their thinking is abusive, and practice saying something like, *"Stop. I'm telling myself I'm bad, but that's abusive. I know I am good at helping my mom"*; or, *"Stop. I'm thinking my mom hates me because she won't let me do what I want. I know that's not true because she reads to me at bedtime and tells me she loves me."* Finding alternative ways to think about things empowers children to recognize how much their thinking affects their perceptions and feelings. *"My mom thinks that would be bad for me so she's trying to help me."*

Developing problem-solving skills also increases their sense of empowerment. Helping peers identify problems, brainstorming solutions, and offering each other suggestions begins to demonstrate the value of positive interactions. Children can think through all the reasons something might be a problem by asking: *"Is the solution safe? Will it hurt anyone? Will it work? Can I do it by myself?"* Many times they rely on retaliatory solutions and are resistant to other alternatives. The children struggle most with changing things their families' model for them. When parents use similar dysfunctional strategies to try to solve problems, it should be expected that change will come slower to the child and is enhanced when family sessions work with the whole family around such changes. As children develop problem-solving skills and experience success with alternative solutions, their internal reactions create a sense of well-being that is more lasting than the temporary relief of power-seeking alternatives.

Children can identify physical and cognitive clues related to moving up the steps or through the cycle and practice new ways of reacting when they recognize the signs. For example, *a child might identify that he is angry and is moving up the steps when he is clenching his fists and getting a stomachache. He might decide to tell his mom when he recognizes these signs if he is confident she will understand and help him get out of the dysfunctional pattern.* Children can learn thought-stopping techniques that involve saying or thinking "Stop" or "No" to interrupt their thoughts and avoid contemplation of sexually abusive behaviors. They can practice cognitive self-talk to avoid abusive behaviors. Children typically describe a desire to not hurt someone or to avoid getting in trouble. Self-talk is useful early in the contemplation or planning process but has less impact as the child moves closer to doing an abuse behavior.

Masturbation is surely a relevant topic and concern. As discussed in Chapter 18, it is important for children to know that masturbation is a normal human behavior that does not cause harm, and not a sign of pathology. They can also learn "Rules for Healthy Masturbation" as well as the parents' rules regarding masturbation in their home. Too often children have learned that adults do not want them to touch their genitals and do not want them to ask questions about sexuality.

Arousal can be the "elephant in the room" that no one speaks of with children. Adult denial of sexual arousal in childhood is fueled by adults' perception that children are innocent and that innocence and sexuality are incongruent. However, the innocence of childhood sexuality is not in the absence of sexuality but in how children think about it. The pleasurable aspects of sexual arousal and behavior must be discussed to improve the children's understanding and enable them to initiate interruption or control techniques when the arousal is problematic.

Acknowledging how good arousal feels or that the abuse behaviors may have felt good for a short time validates the children's perception and helps decrease confusion and anxiety. Children must be taught about the reinforcement that occurs when behaviors are pleasurable so they can understand the importance of not dwelling on thoughts of abuse while feeling aroused or masturbating (see Chapter 18 for more detail). Adults should not assume that even preschool and early elementary children cannot understand that pleasure drives repetition and lots of examples can illustrate the concept for them: for example, "If you like the flavor of your ice cream, you are more likely to ask for the same flavor next time"; "If a particular show makes you laugh, you are more likely to watch it again tomorrow."

Encouraging children to avoid the pairing of abuse and arousal means adults must offer alternatives. The first step is to define and stop when they recognize their thoughts are abusive, but telling themselves to stop is difficult when they are feeling excited and aroused. It does not make sense to them to stop something that feels good. But children can identify substitution behaviors that help them slow the process and distract themselves, or develop more functional options to feel good.

To effectively distract the child from highly stimulating behaviors, the substitute behavior must also be stimulating and similarly meet the child's needs. For some children playing ball, riding a bicycle, or running helps sublimate sexual arousal and decreases physical tensions, while others might choose special time with family members as a source of intimacy and connectedness. For caregivers of very young children who are highly sexualized, redirecting the child to nonsexual alternatives that are also exciting can sometimes require extraordinary creativity and energy, as well as patience.

When substitute behaviors are identified it is helpful to consider potential impediments that might occur because the child may think of the substitutes quite literally. For example, one child did not use the option of playing basketball because it was too dark to see the basket, so decided it was okay to do something sexual instead. It cannot be assumed that substitute behaviors will decrease the occurrence of sexual arousal; it simply slows the progression and gives the child time to control the urges that occur.

Teaching children the "Rules FOR Masturbating" instead of all the prohibitions is actually not hard to do: In a private *place*; While *feeling* good about themselves; While *thinking* caring thoughts.

Even children whose parents disapprove or prohibit masturbation due to personal values or beliefs need to know that the parents' rule is a personal choice. The therapist must support the child abiding by the parents' rules, while acknowledging that this may be hard for some children. Sometimes in cases of highly sexualized children, parent and child must negotiate a plan for gradually decreasing such behavior, as well as identifying alternative activities the child can engage in.

Children must be encouraged to think of neutral scenes that make them feel good about themselves and specifically scenes that do not involve animals, younger children, or any coercion when they choose to masturbate. They also need to be instructed that if they begin to think of sexual abuse while masturbating, they should use the thought-stopping technique, switch scenes, or stop the masturbatory behavior and do one of their alternative activities instead. It is difficult to evaluate or monitor masturbatory behaviors because children typically hide these behaviors from their parents and caregivers. Encouraging open communication about the behavior and helping children feel comfortable talking about the times when they think about masturbating are goals, but much of the intervention is in teaching the children the things they need to know to make good choices for themselves.

Treatment issues for the child are identified in their developmental history and life experience. Working on "issues" from the past often creates more discomfort than work on current situations. Talking about painful feelings, maltreatment, neglect, or trauma is anxiety producing and can trigger PTSD symptoms. When children are engaged in working on hard issues in their treatment sessions, caregivers often report regression in their behaviors at home. Open communication between the caregiver and the therapists is imperative to meet the child's need for increased patience, support, and containment at those times.

Children often benefit from nonverbal, experiential, or play therapy to work on these issues. The use of play therapy is congruent with the school age child's utilization of the defense mechanism of displacement, projecting personal experiences and inner concerns into play and fantasy (Davies, 2004). Therapists and caregivers observing children's play must be cautioned, however, regarding the reenactment phenomena associated with PTSD, which can lead to rigid repetitious replays of traumatic experiences and might reinforce the risk of reenacting victimization experiences with other children, taking the role of the aggressor (Terr, 1985,

1990). Play therapy can be useful in articulating nonverbally what the child lacks vocabulary or permission to speak of, but is only therapeutic when it results in a new understanding of the experience.

Clinical work may occur in individual or family sessions, identifying areas of confusion and recognition about how experiences have affected the child and family, and learning new ways to handle memories and emotions. The universal goals of validating perceptions and affective reactions, articulating and reframing cognitive confusion, and developing accurate attributions of responsibility are all relevant in the clinical work.

When the child's abusive behavior occurred within the family or with neighbors, cousins, or others who may continue to have contact over time, it can be useful to have a clarifying talk with the children who were abused or affected by the child's behavior, bringing them together with the child who was abusive. Parents and each child's therapist can be included in one or more of the clarification meetings as indicated, with the focus directed toward dispelling secrecy, clarifying the reasons why the sexual interaction was abusive, identifying power inequities or coercion in the relationship (e.g., *"I'm your big brother so I shouldn't have taken advantage of you,"* or *"I bribed you with something you wanted, and that's not fair"*), and establishing future boundaries (e.g., *"A new rule will be that we do not go in each other's room,"* etc.).

As children make progress toward the outcomes relevant to increased health, they experience increased self-confidence, openness, and social success, as well as the ability to handle problems without misusing power. Their need for compensatory and avoidant strategies lessens. Caregivers' mastery of the outcomes relevant to decreased risk decreases the focus on abuse issues with the child, freeing time for normalizing, health promoting activity. By including the caregivers in risk management and the delivery of interventions throughout treatment, they are well prepared to support the transition out of treatment and to continue to reinforce treatment concepts as the child matures. Occasional return visits to the therapist are sometimes useful in maintaining the adults' skills or to resolve specific issues that might arise, but most children who have been treated early do not appear to be at any greater risk than their peers as they mature (Bonner et al., 1996; Chaffin & Bonner, 1998; Gil, 1993; Gray, 1991).

JUVENILE FEMALES WHO SEXUALLY OFFEND

Arrest data on female juveniles committing sexual offenses indicate that females account for 3% of forcible rape, 5% of other violent sex offenses, and 19% of nonviolent sex offenses handled by the juvenile courts on an annual basis. Between 1997 and 2002, the number of juvenile cases involving female sexual offending increased significantly (Snyder & Sickmund, 2006). Data from sex offender treatment programs across the country indicate that more than 250 programs provide treatment for female adolescents (McGrath, Cummings, & Burchard, 2003).

The data and the professional consensus support the conclusion that female adults and adolescents represent the minority of sexual offenders. However, Giguere and Bumby (2007) cite evidence to suggest that female sexual offending may be under-identified as compared to male offending due to societal and cultural stereotypes, professional biases, problems with research methodologies, and unique dynamics that impact victims' disclosures and reporting of these offenses. In official reports of child sexual abuse cases it is usually less than 10% perpetrated by females; however, data from adult survivors (especially male survivors) report much higher percentages. Older females initiating sexual contact with young boys has often been depicted in entertainment as harmless.

The revised report from the National Task Force on Juvenile Offending (1993) indicated that identification and reporting of female perpetrators might be inhibited by many factors. The legitimate authority and primary relationships that females have with children in our society may make it especially difficult for victims to report due to dependency needs and ambivalence in the relationship. The legitimate genital contacts females have with children as a function of child care may also increase the child victim's confusion in defining the abuse. Discovery of ongoing abuse perpetrated by females may be impeded by stereotypic views of female sexuality that support denial in potential reporters, while the easy access female caregivers have to potential victims may decrease suspicion at the same time it creates opportunity (Lane & Lobanov-Rostovsky, 1997).

The research on adolescent females who commit sexual offenses is limited as compared to males who commit sexual offenses. Most studies are descriptive in nature and characterized by small sample sizes (Frey, 2006). Therefore, the field is still in the early stages of developing assessment, treatment, and supervision protocols for girls who sexually offend (Giguere & Bumby, 2007). Research to this point has suggested a few common characteristics (N. H. Bumby & K. M. Bumby, 2004; Frey, 2006; Hunter, Becker, & Lexier, 2006; Robinson, 2006):

- A high prevalence of sexual victimization, including indications that many sexually abusive girls have been sexually victimized by more than one perpetrator.
- A high rate of nonsexual child maltreatment, including physical and emotional abuse, and instability and dysfunction within the family and home.
- Co-occurring mental health problems and psychiatric disorders, including suicidal ideation and attempts, Depression, and Post-Traumatic Stress Disorder.
- Most likely to engage in sexually abusive behavior toward young children within the family or with whom they are familiar, to target victims of either gender, and to act alone, often within the context of care-giving activities like babysitting.

The first typology suggested for juvenile females came from one published study of 67 adolescent females (Mathews, Hunter, & Vuz, 1997). The first subtype engaged in a limited number of incidents against a nonrelated child that generally involved fondling and oral sex, typically occurring within the context of babysitting. They were relatively inexperienced, naïve, and somewhat fearful with respect to sexual matters and their offending behaviors appeared to be motivated primarily by experimentation or curiosity. Histories of maltreatment, family dysfunction, and psychological difficulties were fairly limited. The second subtype was described as engaging in more extensive sexually abusive behavior. Their offending appeared to be reactive: abusing younger children in a manner that mirrored their own victimization. Although some in this subtype had emotional, psychological, and other difficulties, these issues generally were not severe. Many of these youth had adequate social skills and other personality strengths. The third subtype, which constituted approximately half of the female adolescents, engaged in more extensive and repetitive sexually abusive behaviors. These youth had much greater levels of emotional and psychological disturbance as well as significant conduct disorder, deviant sexual arousal, and impairments in attachment. Many had experienced developmental trauma (including sexual victimization) often beginning at an early age, which might account for significant difficulties with adjustment and stability.

Mathews et al. (1997) reached the following conclusion regarding risk and protective factors associated with female offending:

> Overall, the data from this study seem consistent with the authors' impression that biological and socialization factors create a higher threshold for externalization of experienced developmental trauma in females than males. In this regard, it may be that females are generally less likely than males to manifest the effects of maltreatment in the form of interpersonal aggression or violence and that females who develop such patterns of behavior are generally those who have experienced remarkably high levels of developmental trauma in the absence of environmental support for recovery and without healthy female role models. (p. 194)

More recently, Garbarino (2006) has studied the increase in general aggression among female youth, and suggests a number of hypotheses regarding the upward trend in female aggression. Cultural changes including the empowerment of women through women's rights and the extreme exposure to violence-supportive messages and images that children experience are possible factors, as well as the experience of abuse and trauma (Garbarino, 2006). In addition, the family violence literature points to coercive styles of parenting, domestic violence, and adult criminality in the home as potent risk factors for the development of aggressive and unsocialized children (Straus & Gelles, 1990).

FOUNDATIONS FOR PRACTICE

Assessment and treatment interventions with females who have committed sexual offenses were historically modeled after those utilized with male sex offenders (Giguere & Bumby, 2007; Robinson, 2006), resulting in assessment, treatment, and supervision models that were not conceptualized from a female standpoint and were not grounded and guided by knowledge and understanding of female development or socialization.

It has been suggested that female pathways to offending (Frey, 2006; Giguere & Bumby, 2007; Robinson, 2006) may manifest important differences as compared to males. Letendre (2007) identifies gender-specific developmental and relational tasks for females as being driven by a higher value, attributed to relationships and the consideration of the needs of others, greater interest in and attention to the other person, greater focus on empathic sharing, and interactions based on mutual sensitivity, receptivity, and responsibility. Gilgun (1982) describes female moral development being based on the ethics of care and relational bonds. In relation to these hypotheses, current trends among youth toward less "relationship" with sexual partners during adolescence (the "friends with benefits" phenomena) may be indications of gender changes that may signal a decrease in male/female differences.

It has been suggested that what may initially appear to be differences between males and females of all ages who sexually offend dynamically may reflect the misuse of power and coping styles reflective of differences in how males and females are socialized, more than actual differences in risk factors or pathology (Ryan, 1998). The ways in which males and females express emotion, manipulate others, and interact socially are distorted in the dynamics of offending, but the process of that distortion may actually not be much different.

For example: Cognitively, male and female beliefs and expectations are shaped by socialization, and the observer/evaluator's perspective is similarly influenced. The expectation that females require protection and that women are nurturing protectors of children affects children from birth. Females are expected to be more vulnerable, thus shaping perceptions of their victimization as more likely and more harmful than the same experiences might be for males. Males are expected to be invulnerable and more likely to pose a risk to others than to be at risk to be victimized or harmed themselves. Yet male children from birth experience more physical abuse than female children and are victims of personal crimes more often than their female age-mates across the life span. Denial of male victimization is so pervasive that perceptions of traumatic experiences may minimize or deny the impacts when the victim is male.

It has often been stated that female samples have "greater" incidence of trauma in their histories than male samples. Nonetheless, the life histories of many male adolescents who offend include tremendous victimization and trauma as well. Differences in the portion of each research sample with adverse life experiences may actually reflect denial of male victimization and/or the underreporting of less intrusive female offending. If samples were matching comparable histories or comparable offending behaviors, the levels of various risk factors might be more similar than different, based on gender.

Similarly, the male who feels vulnerable may think, "Something is wrong with me. I am supposed to be strong and invulnerable. I am expected to be in control so it is justifiable that I be sexual in a controlling manner." On the other hand, the female who feels vulnerable may think, "Of course I am vulnerable because I am female. I am helpless and have no control so I am not responsible, so it is justifiable that I am not responsible for controlling my urge to be sexual." The thoughts are different due to cultural differences in gender socialization, but the dynamic process is quite similar.

Other important differences in the dynamics or patterns of male and female offending may be products of external differences rather than differences in individual pathology. For example, the male who seeks an opportunity to be sexual with a child may have to invest heavily in gaining the child and parent's trust, whereas the female has such frequent and unquestioned access to be alone and in physical contact with children that there may very little necessity to manipulate others to gain access. Therefore the "modus operandi" of females may appear quite different while the internal factors and process may be quite similar.

Perhaps more than any other subgroup of juveniles who sexually abuse, professionals must be cautious about gender biases shaping assumptions that affect treatment and supervision of females who sexually offend. Clearly more research is needed; however, comprehensive and individualized assessment and treatment planning and continuous safety planning for risk management should help to moderate the underestimation of female risk.

Assessment

There are currently no empirically-based or validated risk-assessment instruments for sexually abusive adolescent females. The use of instruments designed for adolescent males may overestimate the relevance of specific risk factors to the female population, as well as underestimate or fail to identify factors that may be relevant (Schmidt & Pierce, 2004). Robinson (2006) has identified risk factors from the instruments designed for males that appear to correspond to females. In addition, risk factors identified in the general female delinquency literature include sexual and physical victimization, dysfunctional family, parent/child relationship difficulties, antisocial peers, academic failure, pregnancy, early onset puberty, mental health difficulties, and substance abuse (Chesney-Lind & Shelden, 2004).

Physiological assessment of arousal or interests is even more challenging with female than male juveniles. There is very little information about the role that arousal or interests play in the offense patterns and risk of reoffense for female sex offenders of any age and none regarding juveniles. Research is lacking in regard to the reliability and validity of both vaginal photo-plethysmography and viewing time measures. Photo-plethysmography is rarely used and should be considered experimental for female adolescents (Robinson, 2006). It would rarely be indicated for juveniles.

TREATMENT

In assessment and treatment of prepubescent children, gender seems to be less of an issue. It is during puberty that the quality of relationships and sexual expectations become more distinctly gender related. It is apparent that additional research is needed to explore sexual and nonsexual recidivism rates, and tools and methods for assessing re-offense risk of adolescent females. Development of evidence-based intervention methods and meaningful treatment outcome studies are needed (Schmidt & Pierce, 2004). Feminine psychology can inform the development of quality gender-responsive intervention models for female adolescents (Frey, 2006).

Gender-specific intervention must respect the feminine socialization process and the focus it places on self in relationship to others (Frey, 2006; Giguere & Bumby, 2007; Letendre, 2007; Robinson, 2006). Female treatment needs can be identified by individualized assessment and often include victimization issues, relationship development, and sexual health education (Grayston & DeLuca, 1999; Mathews et al., 1997). Robinson (2002, 2006) proposes a "relational model" that promotes healthy female identity formation, relational development, sexual efficacy, and healing reparation (for those with abuse histories). The model focuses on self, relational, social, sexual, healing, academic, and spiritual domains. Robinson further recommends that this gender-specific model consider the unique learning styles of girls regarding verbal communication skills, ability to emotionally process and empathize, process orientation, emotional expressivity, and learning through collaboration and cooperation (Grayston & DeLuca, 1999; Mathews et al., 1997).

Post-traumatic stress symptoms and co-occurring psychiatric disorders can already be treated with evidenced-based treatments. The abuse-specific aspects of treatment can reasonably address the same issues and goals, as have been previously described (see Chapter 17), with an expectation that females may manifest more self-abusive behaviors and that control seeking and sexual issues may manifest in somewhat different types of risk taking. The phenomena of females who have been sexually abused being revictimized in subsequent relationships have been apparent in the survivor literature, in spite of generally greater attention to self-protection for females.

Promiscuity and prostitution are variations of control-seeking, risk-taking, self-abusive behaviors.

The "universal" goals of communication, empathy, and accountability are as relevant for females as males, with a tendency for females to be more verbal, and somewhat more sympathetic, yet often much less accountable for their own behaviors and harm. Projecting and externalizing the locus of control is still problematic. Holding females accountable for avoiding the risk of harm to themselves as well as others parallels holding males accountable for avoiding all types of abusive behaviors. The cyclical elements of vulnerability, negative expectations, isolation, and compensatory behaviors may manifest somewhat differently in female functioning but still represent a defensive strategy.

Observation of changes in current functioning that are relevant to decreased risk and increased health can still be the measure of treatment progress. Ultimately, the goals remain the same regardless of gender: to help the youth be successful, while insisting they not be abusive.

YOUTH WITH AN INTELLECTUAL OR OTHER DEVELOPMENTAL DISABILITY

The Americans with Disabilities Act in 1990 mandates protections and accommodations for those with disabilities. Although the incidence of youth with intellectual or developmental disabilities who engage in sexually abusive behaviors is not known, it is apparent that some of these youth do engage in abusive sexual behaviors and are referred for specialized treatment. Whereas historically institutionalization or incarceration were the only interventions for repetitive sexual offenses by the developmentally disabled, there are now many offense-specific treatment professionals who provide differential assessment and treatment for this population. (Abrams & Brecht, 1996; Baker, 1996; Blasingame, 2005, 2006; Myers, 1991; O'Callahan, 2006; Pond & Brown, 1996; Stermac & Sheridan, 1993; Stoops & Baiser, 1996).

It is often the opinion of parents and others that the developmentally disabled should not engage in sexual behavior at all, resulting in repressive or punitive responses to all types of sexual behavior. Community responses can be extreme in either minimizing or overreacting to the sexual behaviors of these youth. Understanding the potential for nonproblematic as well as sexually abusive behaviors is a prerequisite in evaluating the sexual behaviors of developmentally disabled youth. The same model used throughout this text continues to guide practitioners toward reasonable interventions and determining whether a sexual behavior is problematic for the youth because it poses a risk of harm to self, is problematic for others, or is abusive or illegal is the first step.

Juveniles with developmental disabilities are sometimes judged legally culpable for their behavior and other times may be found incompetent to stand trial and not be charged with a sexual offense. These responses are not always related to the risk or harm caused by the juvenile or the level of disability. The courts' failure to hold the youth responsible can result in inadequate intervention (Blasingame, 2005; Ward, Trigler, & Pfeiffer, 2001), while charges may result in overreactive responses. Many jurisdictions have community-centered boards that provide case management services to persons with a developmental disability. Such boards may determine the eligibility of such persons, determine the needs of eligible persons, and prepare and implement long-range plans for their accommodation (refer to section 27-10.5-105, CO.R.S.). However, such boards are not always well trained on the laws or the dynamics of sexual offending, and would benefit from the same training suggested for other adults who provide informed supervision. Such boards' ability to understand and implement safety plans for these youth in the community is imperative.

Organizations that specifically work with developmentally disabled youth must develop strategies for supervision and must be creative to assist with the generalization of treatment concepts (Ryan & Lane, 1997). Many of the basics of treatment for much younger children are relevant for older youth who function at younger developmental levels than their age. As was suggested in relation to young children, the less mature the level of functioning, the more responsibility lies with adult caregivers to deliver validating and correcting interventions and master risk-management skills.

ABUSE BEHAVIORS

There are numerous similarities but also some unique differences between sexually abusive behavior of disabled and nondisabled youth. The range of behaviors, the types of sexually abusive behaviors, and the elements of the behavior appear similar, while there are some differences in the cognitive process, the context of the behaviors, and the level of sophistication (Ryan & Lane, 1997).

Data published by the Safer Society Program (Knopp & Lackey, 1987) identified 3,355 offenses committed by slightly more than 1,500 developmentally disabled adults and adolescents that included a full range of types of sexually abusive behaviors. Gilby, Wolf, and Goldberg (1989) found no significant difference between the intellectually disabled and nondisabled youth in regard to the overall frequency of sexual behavior problems. While the intellectually normal youth were more likely to offend against female victims, the intellectually disabled youth were equally likely to select male and female victims. They found greater numbers of noncontact behaviors such as exhibitionism and public masturbation among the intellectually disabled youth.

The fewer number of "consented to" sexual activities among the youth with intellectual disabilities may suggest a lack of opportunity. Once placed in residential settings these youth were more indiscriminant in their sexual activities, including being more likely to engage in both same sex and opposite sex activities. These authors hypothesized that the increased number of reported sexual problems among youth with developmental disabilities may be related to increased levels of supervision. Nonetheless, Blasingame (2009, personal communication) reports that using the Abel-Blasingame Assessment System often indicates a significant amount of crossover of victim gender and age, as well as a number of other forms of sexual misconduct that were not known to the referring parties before the assessment was completed.

Clinical observation suggests that victims are more likely to be someone the youth knows or that they have observed in their living, school, or recreational sphere. When the victim is a stranger, it is more likely to occur in situations that are part of the youth's daily routine. Choices about who they will abuse appear to be similar to that of nondisabled youth in terms of perceiving vulnerable qualities or identifying characteristics that are appealing. A significant degree of objectification of others is characteristic. The level of sophistication in planning is more similar to that exhibited by children with sexual abuse behaviors.

Offenses tend to be opportunistic, but sometimes youth with developmental disabilities describe specific attempts to isolate a victim or lure the person to a specific location. They may tend to underestimate problems that could occur, but they do report thinking about what they want to do and how to make it happen. At times they misjudge their ability to control the victim, and if the person resists, they may be equally likely to become either more aggressive or to run away and find a different person (Ryan & Lane, 1997).

There appears to be more repetition in either who they abuse or where they abuse. This may indicate somewhat less imagination and planning, and more of a repetitive process, which may become habituated. In some cases, reports of antecedent thoughts may be similar to those of nondisabled youth, but many of these youth indicate that when they start thinking of a sexual behavior they are unable to interrupt the thought. Some describe a preoccupation or perseverative thinking pattern that interferes with other activities (Ryan & Lane, 1997).

The youth do describe contemplation of their abuse behavior, elements of planning, and the associated arousal and excitement in concrete terms. Statements such as, *"I got real excited and thought I'm a pretty smart fella when I did it"* or *"I feel real big when I do it"* suggest there is a compensatory dynamic involved that is similar to that of nondisabled youth. The ways in which they justify or explain their behavior may appear ingrained and narcissistic reflecting their perceptions of what is considered normal (e.g., *"being a real man"*). They are also likely to initially deny involvement in the behaviors (Ryan & Lane, 1997).

Although there is an absence of empirically-based data, physiological assessment of arousal by plethysmography suggests that many developmentally delayed clients tend to respond with uniformly high arousal (highly aroused by all types of sexual stimuli). This would suggest that the arousal profile is not necessarily indicative of sexual arousal to the described behavior or a reflection of deviant arousal (CSOMB, 2009). Clinical observation indicates that some developmentally delayed clients have difficulty differentiating the abusive nature of some behaviors (Comte, 1988; Murphy, Coleman, & Haynes, 1983), and may respond to the sexual words and/ or to the tone of voice used rather than the content of the description. Developmentally delayed clients may also have more difficulty accurately perceiving visual stimuli (CSOMB, 2009).

CHARACTERISTICS

As has been described with other youth who sexually offend, the developmental history and life experience of many youth with developmental disabilities includes trauma, disruption of attachment bonds, and family dysfunction (Lindsay, Neilson, Morrison, & Smith, 2001; O'Callaghan, 2006; Thompson & Brown, 1998). The higher rate of sexual victimization relative to nondisabled individuals has been cited as a significant factor in the histories of youth with developmental disabilities who sexually offend (Blasingame, 2005; Lindsay et al., 2001; O'Callaghan, 2006). Familial separation due to respite or full-time substitute care contributes to the disruption of attachments. Many youth who have been in alternative care settings report exploitive and victimizing experiences by other residents or their caretakers (Ryan & Lane, 1997).

The deficit in coping skills for these youth may increase the negative impacts of adverse events. Other salient issues for youth with developmental disabilities include limited opportunities for social development, social isolation, limited sexual education, a lack of privacy, a lack of opportunity to experience normative sexual interactions with peers, specific difficulties in communication, and the impacts of specific genetic and medical factors (Gursky, 2009, personal communication; Herzog & Money, 1993; O'Callaghan, 2006; Thompson & Brown, 1998).

Developmental deficits often necessitate life management interventions that foster an external locus of control and the perception that the youth has little control over their environment and limited opportunity for choices. Although there have been efforts to inform youth of their options and acknowledge their preferences, their disabilities do pose impediments. The youth with developmental disabilities is often impulsive and less inclined to foresee potential outcomes of the choices they do make (Ryan & Lane, 1997).

Significant social competency deficits, inept interactional styles, and aversive characteristics or habits often evoke rejection or ridicule rather than acceptance by similar age peers. Many of these youth seek affirmation and acceptance by "normal" youth or exhibit a desire to be perceived as normal. Given the concreteness of their cognitive processes, they sometimes misunderstand, misinterpret, or over-emulate what they observe nondisabled youth doing, but they lack the skills to be successful. Sometimes these youth have described believing that if they are sexual they are like other youth, a perception that may also be influenced by media (Ryan & Lane, 1997).

Many youth with developmental disabilities exhibit a paucity of sexual knowledge. Denial and repression of all sexuality among caregivers of these youth has been so pervasive that only recently have there been reasonable efforts to develop effective sex education for this population. They are often not educated about birth control or safe sex nor do they exhibit familiarity with the mechanics of sexual intercourse. Information about relationships, reciprocal aspects of sexual interactions, and social-sexual norms about age, consent, or privacy may be completely absent (Gursky, 2009, personal communication; Ryan & Lane, 1997).

SPECIAL NEEDS IN TREATMENT

There can be significant variability in the functioning of youth defined as intellectually or developmentally disabled, ranging from individuals who can live independently with low levels of support to those with profound and possibly multiple impairments that require high levels of care (O'Callaghan, 2006). Most youth with developmental disabilities who are accepted for treatment in community-based and residential programs have a mild to moderate level of disability with some at least some literacy, communication, and retention skills.

Assessment and treatment interventions need to address the specific needs of this population including literacy deficits, difficulties in comprehension of complex language and concepts, possible speech and communication problems, memory deficits, deficits in sociosexual understanding, limited knowledge base, and potential for suggestibility (Blasingame, 2005; O'Callaghan, 2006).

These youths' style of thinking is usually more concrete, their information about the world may be more restricted, and their learning styles may require special approaches. Their ability to manage daily living activities, level of sophistication, and the ways they have learned to adapt to their environment must be assessed separately. These factors have a significant impact on decisions about management during treatment and the style of treatment intervention required (Ryan & Lane, 1997).

The risk of reoffense during treatment may be somewhat higher for this population, perhaps due to habituation, perseverative thinking, impulsivity, low frustration tolerance, and/or an increased need for compensatory solutions or seeking immediate gratification. When these youth are treated in community-based or residential treatment, it is important that caregivers and supervisors be thoroughly trained and aware of the youth's sexual abuse behavior characteristics and patterns. Consistent, frequent communication about the issues that arise for the youth and current treatment objectives need to occur to enhance safety for the youth and community, as well as ensure that treatment concepts are reinforced and practiced by these youth in their living situation (Ryan & Lane, 1997). Training on informed supervision and therapeutic care are particularly relevant for all the adults responsible for these youth (see Chapter 15).

When practitioners adapt offense-specific treatment concepts for this population, they must consider style of learning. Abrams and Brecht (1996) suggest using relational, repetitive, and rehearsal strategies to encourage internalization and retention. Generalizations must be taught through describing similarities and applications of various concepts. Attempts must be made to cover all aspects and avoid leaving loopholes that the youth may exploit (Ryan & Lane, 1997). Because the attention span of these youth may be shorter, concepts presented in several brief segments and reinforced by an experiential activity may be effective.

Experiential activities often link an affective component to the information, which may increase retention (Ryan & Lane, 1997). Whitaker (1986) suggests, "Present concrete information or concepts by providing an experiential presentation that is dramatic and includes powerful repetitions of information that involve descriptions or discussions of how the concept is experienced. Practice application of the concepts through role playing or games, expect application of concepts and provide feedback regarding situations the concept applies to, or assist the youth with identifying when and how to use the concept." Activities such as finger painting, drawing, puppets, anatomically correct dolls, and flash cards with different colors may be useful (Gursky, 2009, personal communication).

Care must be taken with the language that is used to explain concepts because the youth will hear information in a concrete, literal manner. For example, if one explains that some touch is unacceptable, the youth may hear, "I'm not supposed to touch anybody," and miss the implication that sexually abusive touch is being discussed. As is true for many children, the word *inappropriate* is often used to refer to sexual behaviors but is not at all definitive. Simple definitions must be explained in very concrete terms. For example, to teach the elements of consent: "How do you know whether the other person wants to do the same thing you do?" "What is the behavior?" "Could anything bad happen if you do it?" "What would your parent or friend think about the behavior?" "Is it ok to say yes or no?"

The process of providing information must be slower to give the youth time to think about what is being presented. It appears that comprehension is best when one style of presentation is used at a time, such as verbally one time and visually another. Associations with familiar objects will provide more meaning and improve retention. Such associations might involve sports concepts, traffic lights, or concrete objects (Ryan & Lane, 1997).

Developmentally disabled youth appear to benefit from the same offense-specific treatment concepts used with nondisabled youth if the presentation of the concepts is adapted to their learning style (Blasingame, 2005; Gursky, 2009, personal communication; O'Callaghan, 2006; Ryan & Lane, 1997). Sexual abuse cycle concepts are useful, but they are more easily understood if there are fewer steps and the information is presented in a linear format, such as Blasingame's (2005) "Ladder to Trouble," or representations of roadways (Kahn, 1999) or paths (Lane, 1991) with each fork in the road representing a decision point.

"Safe Plans" may be utilized to apply the relapse prevention constructs such as avoidance, escape strategies, or meeting one's needs in healthy ways instead of keeping things to oneself and climbing the ladder toward trouble. The Safe Plan could be framed as "what else could I do" to handle a problem or situation. This seems to be best done through role plays, repetition, and in vivo supported enactments (Blasingame, 2005).

Provider qualities include patience, creativity, a willingness to learn about the complexities of this population, and "trying to understand their experiences and beliefs based on their world view" (Gursky, 2009, personal communication).

OUTCOMES

It is often assumed that persons with lower levels of functioning cannot be expected to learn and practice new skills beyond concrete rules and changes based on rewards and consequences are all that can be expected. However, providers and caregivers may be underestimating the capacity of developmentally immature persons to develop the skills to be nonabusive. Remembering that humans are born with the capacity to express their needs, and that it is through the experience of sensitive/empathic care that the toddler acquires the capacity for empathic recognition and responses, it is reasonable to expect that even very low functioning youth should be able to do the same.

As has been suggested for all juveniles in treatment due to abusive behaviors, the adults' responsibility is to be patient and nurturing in order to help the child be successful at whatever stage of development they are, and at the same time, insist they not be abusive. Adults who supervise and care for youth with developmental disabilities must provide the containment and structure to preserve safety for the youth and the community while meeting the youth's needs in treatment and care.

VIOLENT YOUTH

Chapter 6 described juveniles whose sexual offending was part of a broad range of nonsexual conduct problems. A small segment of these youth constitute what has been described as hard core, violent delinquents (National Task Force on Juvenile Offending, 1993). Moffitt's (1993) seminal research identifying the Life Course Persistent delinquent, as well as Hunter's application of this construct to juveniles who have committed sexual offenses (Hunter, 2006, 2008; Hunter, Figueredo, Malamuth, & Becker, 2003) address this subgroup. For the youth defined as "life course persistent" delinquents, conduct problems and delinquent behavior have been persistent across each stage of the youth's life, beginning with the childhood onset of delinquent behavior, elementary school maladjustment, and adolescent delinquency. Life Course Persistent youth are likely to score high on the Impulsive/ Antisocial scale of the J-SOAP II, with histories that reflect pervasive anger and aggression in multiple domains including fighting, assaultive behavior, destruction of property, and possession and use of weapons.

Life course persistent youth who have engaged in sexual offending are more likely to recidivate with nonsexual delinquency than to be rearrested for subsequent sexual offenses. Research cited in Chapter 6 pointed out that the factors related to nonsexual delinquent recidivism among sexually offending juveniles are different from those associated with sexual recidivism (Langstrom, 2002; Langstrom & Grann, 2000; Worling & Curwen, 2000). These factors include:

- Early onset conduct disorder
- Number of previous convictions for any offense
- Prior violent conviction
- Psychopathy
- Antisocial personality
- Sexual offense variables such as use of threats or weapons, death threats, and/ or causing physical injury to the victim
- Lower socioeconomic status
- Hostility
- Aggression

Increased levels of force and violence may reflect the presence of hostile masculinity and the use of gratuitous and expressive aggression in the commission of sexual offense(s). Aggression toward females is justified based on perceptions that females are exploitive and rejecting, thus deserving of less respect and more abuse than males. Hostile masculinity further reflects beliefs that a masculine identity involves power, risk taking, toughness, dominance, aggressiveness, competitiveness, impersonal sexuality, and defending one's honor (Miner, Robinson, Knight, Berg, Swinburne-Romine, & Netland, 2010), as well as viewing females in a negative and pejorative manner supportive of rape myths (Hunter, 2009). These beliefs and attitudes frequently translate to covert and overt hostility and power struggles with female professionals who are working with these youth. The harm that violence can impose on victims if these youth reoffend sexually must be considered an aggravating factor in risk assessment and safety planning.

Consistent with the developmental-contextual framework and recognition of static, stable, and dynamic risk factors, the Biopsychosocial Model of Dodge and Pettit (2003) is a useful framework for understanding the development of chronic conduct problems, delinquency, and violence in adolescence. Dodge and Pettit (2003) identified the following social-information processing patterns that emerge across the development of violent youth as a function of biological predisposition (temperament, heart rate acceleration, etc.), a sociocultural context of poverty and racism, combined with harsh parenting and rejecting peer experiences. Characteristics they describe include:

1. Selective attention to hostile cues.
2. Hostile attributional biases when interpreting peer's intent that is ambiguous and interpretational errors when the intent is clear.
3. Ready access to aggressive responses and failure to access competent responses.

4. Valuing aggressive responses as morally acceptable and as relatively likely to lead to desired instrumental, interpersonal, and intrapersonal outcomes (or failure to foresee outcomes at all, with impulsive execution of the first behavioral response imagined).
5. Deficits in skills for enacting nonaggressive, assertive responses.

These characteristics are congruent with the hyper-vigilance and reactivity indicative of children who have lived in unsafe, coercive and nonempathic environments, and reflect extremes of ingrained defensive strategies. Adult criminality and domestic violence in their homes has often modeled antisocial attitudes and coercive styles of interpersonal interactions. For these youth physical safety, empathy, nurturance, and psychological safety may be so foreign that they cannot recognize or appreciate the need for a sense of safety. Betrayal of undefended trust has often provided evidence that supports dramatic hostility in their beliefs about human relationships.

For example, one youth who was adjudicated for rape and also had an extensive history of nonsexual conduct problems and delinquency, revealed the following core beliefs as he worked on treatment assignments:

- "I will get them before they get me."
- "Family don't care about me."
- "None of the family cares about my family."
- "Violence is my tipe (sic)."
- "I am made to do criminal stuff."
- "No one cares."
- "Is cool to be in gangs."
- "I get protection around homeboys."
- "My mom don't care about me because she is having relationships with other men."
- "F*** the world."
- "The world is full of gangs, drugs, sex, and violence."
- "Nobody would make it in this world with all this s***."
- "Gangs are cool because [they] are more than one person."
- "I will always have enemies any were (sic) I go."
- "All gangs are out to get me . . . I can't be safe at any place."
- "I need a gun to get them so they won't get me."
- "F*** every single person on this planet."

The higher risk and associated intensive treatment and supervision needs of these youth often require placement in secure residential facilities in the juvenile justice system. This is necessary to bring about the dramatic change from such beliefs to a worldview congruent with the goals and outcomes of treatment relevant to decreased risk of all types of aggression and abuse, as well as successful healthy prosocial functioning requiring significant intervention. The abuse-specific concepts are clearly relevant to the whole range of aggressive behaviors, and the goals of communication, empathy, and accountability remain imperatives.

Sex offense-specific treatment represents a discreet aspect in the context of evidence-based models that focus on the risk/need factors associated with general delinquency and youth violence. Chapter 17 identified these as: antisocial/procriminal attitudes, values, beliefs, and cognitive-emotional states; procriminal associates and isolation from anticriminal others; temperamental and personality factors conducive to criminal activity (i.e., psychopathy, weak socialization, impulsivity, restless aggressive energy, egocentrism, below average verbal intelligence, a taste for risk, weak problem-solving/self-regulation skills); familial factors; and low levels of personal educational, vocational, or financial achievement (Latessa, 2005). The cognitions associated with hostile masculinity need to be addressed as well as offering a Healthy Masculinity treatment component that may include mentoring by a strong male role model in the milieu (Hunter, 2006). Aggression Replacement Training (ART) (Glick, 2006; Goldstein, Glick, & Gibbs, 1998) has been identified as a preferred evidence-based institutional program model (Greenwood, 2008). Aggression Replacement Training is a multimodal intervention to train aggressive and violent prone youth:

- Social Skills Training (Structured Learning Training) → What to do in violence and aggressive-producing situations.
- Anger Control Training → What not to do.
- Moral Reasoning → View their world in a more fair and equitable manner, taking others' perspective in any given situation.

REFERENCES

Abel, G. G., Jones, C. D., Gabriel, W., & Harlow, N. (2009). A boy's experience of child sexual abuse: Factors that increase his risk of developing sexually abusive behavior. Submitted for publication.

Abrams, R., & Brecht, B. (1996). *Using the three R's in outpatient therapy with developmentally delayed adolescent sexual offenders.* Presentation at the 14th Annual ATSA Research & Treatment Conference—Marching Into the Future—Challenges, Directions, Solutions, New Orleans, LA.

Baker, S. (1996). *Integrating youth with special needs into outpatient adolescent sex offender group treatment.* Presentation at the 12th Annual Conference of the National Adolescent Perpetrator Network—Sexually Abusive Youth: Developmental Dilemmas and Opportunities, Minneapolis, MN.

Berliner, L., & Rawlings, L. (1991). *A treatment manual: Children with sexual behavior problems.* Seattle: Harborview Sexual Assault Center.

Blasingame, G. (2005). *Developmentally disabled persons with sexual behavior problems* (2nd ed.). Brandon, VT: Wood'N'Barnes Books/Safer Society Press.

Blasingame, G. (Ed.). (2006). *Practical treatment strategies for persons with intellectual disabilities: Working with forensic clients with severe and sexual behavior problems.* Brandon, VT: Wood'-N'Barnes Books/Safer Society Press.

Bonner, B., Walker, E., & Berliner, L. (1996). *Children with sexual behavior problems: Research based treatment.* Paper presented at the 11th International Congress on Child Abuse and Neglect, Dublin, Ireland.

Bumby, N. H., & Bumby, K. M. (2004). *Bridging the gender gap: Addressing juvenile females who commit sexual offenses.* In G. O'Reilly, W. L. Marshall, A. Carr, & R. C. Beckett (Eds.), *The handbook of clinical intervention with young people who sexually abuse* (pp. 369–381). New York: Brunner-Routledge.

Burton, D. L., & Meezan, W. (2004). Revisiting recent research on social learning theory as an etiological proposition for sexually abusive male adolescents. *Journal of Evidence Based Social Work, 1*, 41–80.

Camino, L. (2000). *Treating sexually abused boys.* San Francisco, CA: Jossey-Bass.

Chaffin, M., & Bonner, B. (1998). "Don't shoot, we're your children": Have we gone too far in our response to adolescent sexual abusers with sexual behavior problems. *Child Maltreatment: Journal of the American Professional Society on the Abuse of Children, 3*(4), 314–316.

Chesney-Lind, M., & Shelden, R. G. (2004). *Girls, delinquency, and juvenile justice* (3rd ed.). Belmont, CA: Wadsworth Publishing.

Colorado Sex Offender Management Board (CSOMB). (2009). *Notes from Developmental Disabilities subcommittee.* Unpublished manuscript.

Comte, M. (1988). *Treating the intellectually disabled sexual offender.* Paper presented at the First National Conference on the Assessment and Treatment of Intellectually Disabled Juvenile and Adult Sexual Offenders, Columbus, OH.

Cunningham, C., & MacFarlane, K. (1991). *When children molest children: Group treatment strategies for young sexual abusers.* Brandon, VT: Safer Society Press.

Cunningham, C., & MacFarlane, K. (1996). *When children abuse: Group treatment strategies for children with impulse control problems.* Brandon, VT: Safer Society Press.

Davies, D. (2004). *Child development: A practioner's guide* (2nd ed.). New York: The Guilford Press.

Denige, L. (1987). *Good touch, bad touch.* Norristown, PA: Rape Crisis Center of Montgomery County.

Dodge, K. A., & Pettit, G. S. (2003). A biopsychosocial model of the development of chronic conduct problems in adolescence. *Developmental Psychology, 39*(2), 349–371.

Finkelhor, D. (Ed.). (1986). *Sourcebook on child sexual abuse.* Thousand Oaks, CA: Sage.

Frey, L. L. (2006). Girls don't do that, do they? Adolescent females who sexually abuse. In R. E. Longo & D. S. Prescott (Eds.), *Current perspectives: Working with sexually aggressive youth and youth with sexual behavior problems* (pp. 255–272). Holyoke, MA: NEARI Press.

Friedrich, W., Beilke, R. L., & Urquiza, A. J. (1988). Behavior problems in young sexually abused boys. *Journal of Interpersonal Violence, 3,* 1–12.

Friedrich, W., Fisher, J., Broughton, D., Houston, M., & Shafran, C. R. (1991). Normative sexual behavior in children. *Pediatrics, 88*(3), 92–100.

Friedrich, W., Grambsch, P., Damon, L., Koverola, C., Wolfe, V., Hewitt, S., et al. (1992). The child sexual behavior inventory: Normative and clinical comparison. *Psychological Assessment, 4*(3), 303–311.

Friedrich, W. N., Davies, W. H., Feher, E., & Wright, J. (2003). Sexual behavior problems in preteen children: Developmental, ecological, and behavioral correlates. *Annuals of New York Academy of Science, 989,* 95–104.

Friedrich, W. N., Urquiza, A., & Bielke, R. (1986). Behavioral problems in sexually abused young children. *Journal of Pediatric Psychology, 11*(2), 47–57.

Garbarino, J. (2006). *See Jane hit: Why girls are growing more violent and what we can do about it.* New York: Penguin Press.

Giguere, R., & Bumby, K. (2007). *Female sex offenders.* Silver Spring, MD: Center for Sex Offender Management.

Gil, E. (1986). *A. guide for parents of young sex offenders.* Walnut Creek, CA: Launch Press.

Gil, E. (1993). Etiologic theories. In E. Gil and T. C. Johnson (Eds.), *Sexualized children* (pp. 53–64). Walnut Creek, CA: Launch Press.

Gilby, R., Wolf, L., & Goldberg, B. (1989). Mentally retarded adolescent sex offenders: A survey and pilot study. *Canadian Journal of Psychiatry 34*(6), 542–548.

Gilgun, C. (1982). *In a different voice: Psychological theory and women's development.* Cambridge, MA: Harvard University Press.

Glick, B. (2006). ART-A comprehensive intervention for aggressive youth. In B. Glick (Ed.), *Cognitive behavioral interventions for at-risk youth* (pp. 11-2-11-27). Kingston, NJ: Civic Research Institute.

Goldstein, A. P., Glick, B., & Gibbs, J. C. (1998). *Aggression replacement training: A comprehensive intervention for aggressive youth* (rev. ed.). Champaign, IL: Research Press.

Gray, A. S. (1991). *Setting a context: A balanced approach* [Audiotape]. Address given at the First National Conference on Sexually Aggressive and Sexually Reactive Children—Seeking a Balanced Approach, Burlington, VT.

Gray, A. S., Pithers, W., Busconi, A., & Houchens, P. (1997). Children with sexual behavior problems: An empirically derived taxonomy. *The Forum: Newsletter of the Association for the Treatment of Sexual Abusers (ATSA)*, 9(4), 10–11.

Grayston, A. D., & DeLuca, R. V. (1999). Female perpetrators of child sexual abuse: A review of the clinical and empirical literature. *Aggression and Violent Behavior, 4*, 93–106.

Greenwood, P. (2008). Prevention and intervention programs for juvenile offenders 18(2): Fall. From: http://www.futureofchildren.org

Herzog, D., & Money, J. (1993). Sexology and social work in the case of Klinefelters (47XXY) syndrome. *Mental Retardation, 3*(3), 161–162.

Hindman, J. (1983). *A. very touching book*. Durkee, OR: McClure-Hindman Associates.

Hunter, J. A. (2006). *Understanding sexually abusive youth: New research and clinical directions*. Broomfield, CO: Colorado Department of Human Services sponsored training.

Hunter, J. A. (2008). *Understanding sexually abusive youth: New research and clinical directions*. Ft. Collins, CO: Colorado Child and Adolescent Mental Health Conference.

Hunter, J. A. (2009). The sexual crimes of juveniles. In R. R. Hazelwood & A. W. Burgess (Eds.), *Practical aspects of rape investigation: A multidisciplinary approach*. CRC Press.

Hunter, J. A., Becker, J. V., & Lexier, L. J. (2006). *The female juvenile sex offender*. In H. E. Barbaree & W. L. Marshall (Eds.), *The juvenile sex offender* (2nd ed.) (pp. 148–165). New York: Guilford Press.

Hunter, J. A., Figueredo, A. J., Malamuth, N. M., & Becker, J. V. (2003). Juvenile sex offenders: Toward the development of a typology. *Sexual Abuse: A Journal of Research and Treatment, 15*(1), 27–48.

Isaac, C. (1986). *Identification and interruption of sexually offending behaviors in prepubescent children*. Paper presented at the 16th Annual Child Abuse and Neglect Symposium, Keystone, CO.

Johnson, T. C. (1988). Child perpetrators—Children who molest other children: Preliminary findings. *Child Abuse and Neglect, 12*, 219–229.

Johnson, T. C. (1991). *Understanding the sexual behaviors of young children*. SIECUS Report: August/September.

Johnson, T. C. (1992). *Child sexual behavior checklist—Revised*. Pasadena, CA: Author.

Johnson, T. C. (1993). Assessment of sexual behavior problems in preschool and latency-aged children. In A. Yates (Ed.), *Child and adolescent psychiatric clinics of North America* 2(3) (July), 431–449.

Johnson, T. C. (1995a). Children's natural and healthy sexual behaviors and characteristics of children's problematic sexual behaviors. *Believe the Children Newsletter, 12*(1) (Spring), 1–4.

Johnson, T. C. (1995b). *Treatment exercises for child abuse victims and children with sexual behavior problems*. Pasadena, CA: Author.

Johnson, T. C. (1998). *Helping children with sexual behavior problems—A guidebook for parents and substitute caregivers*. Self-published booklet.

Johnson, T. C., & Doonan, R. (2005). *Children, twelve and younger, with sexual behavior problems: What we know in 2005 that we didn't know in 1985*. In M. C. Calder (Ed.), *Children and young people who sexually abuse: New theory, research and practice developments* (pp. 32–58). Lyme Regis, Dorset: Russell House Publishing.

Kahn, T. J. (1990). *Pathways: A guided workbook for youth beginning treatment*. Orwell, VT: Safer Society Press.

Kahn, T. J. (1999). *Roadmaps to recovery* (2nd ed.). Orwell, VT: Safer Society Press.

Knopp, F. H., & Lackey, L. B. (1987). *Sexual offenders identified as intellectually disabled: A summary of data from forty treatment providers*. Brandon, VT: Safer Society Press.

Lane, S. (1991). *Special offender populations*. In G. Ryan & S. Lane (Eds.), *Juvenile sexual offending: Causes, consequences and correction* (pp. 299–332). Lexington, MA: Lexington Books.

Lane, S., & Lobanov-Rostovsky, C. (1997). Special populations: children, females, the developmentally disabled and violent youth. In G. Ryan & S. Lane (Eds.), *Juvenile sexual offending: Causes, consequences and correction* (2nd ed.) (pp. 322–359). San Francisco: Jossey-Bass.

Langstrom, N. (2002). Long-term followup of criminal recidivism in young sex offenders: Temporal patterns and risk factors. *Psychology, Crime and Law, 8,* 41–58.

Langstrom, N., & Grann, M. (2000). Risk for criminal recidivism among young sex offenders. *Journal of Interpersonal Violence, 15*(8), 855–871.

Latessa, E. J. (2005). *What works and what doesn't in reducing recidivism: The principles of effective intervention.* Vail, CO: Colorado Division of Youth Corrections Provider Council Conference.

Letendre, J. (2007). Sugar and spice but not always nice: Gender socialization and its impact on development and maintenance of aggression in adolescent girls. *Child and Adolescent Social Work Journal, 24*(4), 353–367.

Lindsay, W. R., Neilson, C. Q., Morrison, F., & Smith, A. H. (2001). A comparison of physical and sexual histories of sexual and non-sexual offenders with intellectual disability. *Child Abuse and Neglect, 25*(7), 989–995.

MacFarlane, K., & Cunningham, C. (1989). *Steps to healthy touching.* Mount Dora, FL: Kids Rights Publishers.

Marshall, W. L., Hudson, S. N., & Hodkinson, S. (1993). The importance of attachment bonds and the development of juvenile sex offending. In H. E. Barbaree, W. L. Marshall, & S. M. Hudson (Eds.), *The juvenile sex offender* (pp. 164–181). New York: Guilford.

Mathews, R., Hunter, J. A., & Vuz, J. (1997). Juvenile female sexual offenders: Clinical characteristics and treatment issues. *Sexual Abuse: A Journal of Research and Treatment, 9,* 187–199.

McGrath, R. J., Cummings, G., & Burchard, B. (2003). *Current practices and trends in sexual abuse management: The Safer Society 2002 national survey.* Brandon, VT: Safer Society Foundation.

Miccio-Fonseca, L. C., & Rasmussen, L. A. (2006). *Multiplex Empirically Guided Inventory of Ecological Aggregates for assessing sexually abusive adolescents and children—MEGA: Professional Manual.* San Diego, CA: Author.

Miner, M. (2008). *What attachment theory tells us about unique risks for adolescent boys to sexually offend.* Portland: National Adolescent Perpetration Network Conference.

Miner, M. H., Robinson, B. E., Knight, R. A., Berg, D., Swinburne-Romine, R., & Netland, J. (2010). Understanding sexual perpetration against children: Effects of attachment style, interpersonal involvement, and hypersexuality. *Sexual Abuse: A Journal of Research and Treatment, 22*(1) (March), 58–77.

Moffitt, T. (1993). Adolescence-limited and life-course persistent antisocial behavior: A developmental taxonomy. *Psychology Review, 100*(4), 674–701.

Murphy, W., Coleman, E., & Haynes, M. (1983). Treatment and evaluation of the mentally retarded sex offender. In J. G. Greer & I. R. Stuart (Eds.), *The sexual aggressor* (pp. 22–41). New York: Van Nostrand Reinhold.

Myers, B. A. (1991). Treatment of sexual offenses by persons with developmental disabilities. *American Journal on Mental Retardation, 95*(5), 563–569.

National Task Force on Juvenile Sexual Offending, National Adolescent Perpetration Network. (1993). The revised report. *Juvenile and Family Court Journal, 44*(4), 1–120.

O'Callaghan, D. (2006). Group treatment of young people with intellectual impairment who sexually harm. In R. E. Longo & D. S. Prescott (Eds.), *Current perspectives: Working with sexually aggressive youth and youth with sexual behavior problems* (pp. 273–324). Holyoke, MA: NEARI Press.

Patterson, S. (1986). *No, no seal.* New York: Random House.

Pithers, W. D., & Gray, A. (1998). The science of sex offenders: Risk assessment, treatment, and prevention: The other half of the story: Children with sexual behavior problems. *Psychology, Public Policy, and Law, 4,* 200.

Pithers, W. D., Gray, A. S., Cunningham, C., & Lane, S. (1993). *From trauma to understanding: A guide for parents of children with sexual behavior problems.* Brandon, VT: Safer Society Press.

Pond, A., & Brown, J. (1996). *Disclosure: Obtaining sexual histories from developmentally disabled youth.* Paper presented at the 12th Annual Conference of the National Adolescent Perpetrator Network, Minneapolis, MN.

Porter, E. (1986). *Treating the young male victim of sexual assault: Issues and intervention strategies.* Brandon, VT: Safer Society Press.

Rasmussen, L. (2000). *The trauma outcome process: An integrated model for guiding clinical practice with children with sexually abusive behavior problems.* (Submitted for publication.)

Rasmussen, L. A., Burton, J. E., & Christopherson, B. J. (1990). *Interrupting precursors to perpetration in males ages four to twelve.* Paper presented at the 5th Annual Training Conference—Confronting Sexual Offending, Albany, NY.

Rich, P. (2003). *Understanding, assessing, and rehabilitating juvenile sexual offenders.* Hoboken, NJ: John Wiley & Sons.

Robinson, S. (2002). *Growing beyond: A workbook for sexually abusive teenage girls (treatment manual).* Holyoke, MA: NEARI Press.

Robinson, S. (2006). Adolescent females with sexual behavior problems: What constitutes best practice? In R. E. Longo & D. S. Prescott (Eds.), *Current perspectives: Working with sexually aggressive youth and youth with sexual behavior problems* (pp. 273–324). Holyoke, MA: NEARI Press.

Rogers, N. (1992). *Results of a survey regarding the treatment of preadolescent sexually abusive behavior* (pp. 4–8). Interchange. (Newsletter of the National Adolescent Perpetrator Network). Denver: Kempe National Center.

Ryan, G. (1989). Victim to victimizer: Rethinking victim treatment. *Journal of Interpersonal Violence, 4*(3), 325–341.

Ryan, G. (1998). The relevance of early life experience to the behavior of sexually abusive youth. *The Irish Journal of Psychology, 19*(1), 32–48.

Ryan, G. (2000). Childhood sexuality: A decade of study. *Child Abuse and Neglect, 24*(1), 33–61.

Ryan, G. (2004a). Preventing violence and trauma in the next generation. *Journal of Interpersonal Violence, 20*(1), 132–141.

Ryan, G. (2004b). *Puberty and adolescence; addendum to primary, secondary, & tertiary perpetration prevention in childhood and adolescence.* Kempe Trainer Training Curriculum.

Ryan, G., and Associates (1998). *The web of meaning: A developmental-contextual approach in treatment of sexual abuse.* Brandon, VT: Safer Society Press.

Ryan, G., & Blum, J. (1994). *Childhood sexuality: A guide for parents.* Denver, CO Kempe Center.

Ryan, G., Blum, J., Sandau-Christopher, D., Law, S., Weber, F., Sundine, C., et al. (1988). *Understanding and responding to the sexual behavior of children: Trainer's manual.* Denver, CO: Kempe National Centre, University of Colorado Health Sciences Centre.

Ryan, G., & Lane, S. (Eds.). (1997). *Juvenile sexual offending: Causes, consequences and correction* (2nd ed.). San Francisco, CA: Jossey-Bass.

Ryan, G., Lindstrom, B., Knight, L., Arnold, L., Yager, J., Bilbrey, C., et al. (1989). *Sexual abuse in the context of whole life experience.* Paper presented at the 18th National Symposium on Child Abuse and Neglect, Keystone, CO.

Ryan, G., Yager, J., Sobicinski, J., & Metzner, J. (2002). *Informed supervision and therapeutic care for juveniles who commit sexual offenses.* Kempe Trainer Training Curriculum.

Schmidt, S., & Pierce, K. (2004). *NCSBY fact sheet: What research shows about female adolescent sex offenders.* National Center on Sexual Behavior of Youth. Center on Child Abuse and Neglect, University of Oklahoma Health Sciences Center.

Snyder, H. M., & Sickmund, M. (2006). *Juvenile offenders and victims: 2006 national report.* Washington, DC: U.S. Department of Justice, Office of Justice Programs, Office of Juvenile Justice and Delinquency Prevention.

Stermac, L., & Sheridan, P. (1993). *The developmentally disabled adolescent sex offender*. In J. E. Barbaree, W. L. Marshall, & S. M. Hudson (Eds.), *The juvenile sex offender* (pp. 235–242). New York: Guilford Press.

Stoops, A. L., & Baiser, M. L. (1996). *Bridging the gap in services for the adolescent sex offender with mental retardation*. Presentation at the 14th Annual ATSA Research and Treatment Conference—Marching Into the Future—Challenges, Directions, Solution, New Orleans, LA.

Straus, M. A., & Gelles, R. J. (1990). How violent are American families?: Estimates from the National Family Violence Resurvey and other studies. In M. A. Strays & R. J. Gelles (Eds.), *Physical violence in American families: Risk factors and adaptations to violence in 8,145 families* (pp. 95–112). New Brunswick, NJ: Transaction Books.

Terr, L. (1985). *Play therapy and psychic trauma: A preliminary report. Handbook of play therapy*. New York: John Wiley & Sons.

Terr, L. (1990). *Too scared to cry: Psychic trauma in childhood*. New York: Harper and Row.

Thompson, D., & Brown, H. (1998). *Response ability: Working with men with learning disabilities who have difficult or abusive sexual behaviors*. Brighton, England: Pavilion.

Ward, K., Trigler, J., & Pfeiffer, K. (2001). Community services, issues, and service gaps for individuals with developmental disabilities who exhibit inappropriate sexual behaviors. *Mental Retardation, 39*(1), 11–19.

Webster-Stratton, C. (2005). The incredibile years: A training series for the prevention and treatment of conduct problems in young children. In E. D. Hibbs & P. S. Jensen (Eds.), *Psychosocial treatments for child and adolescent disorders: Empirically based strategies for clinical practice* (2nd ed.). (pp. 507–555). Washington, DC: U. S. American Psychological Association.

Whitaker, M. (1986). *The low-functioning client*. Paper presented at the Second National Training Conference, Atlanta, GA.

Worling, J. R., & Curwen, T. (2000). Adolescent sexual offender recidivism: Success of specialized treatment and implications for risk prediction. *Child Abuse and Neglect, 24*(7), 965–982.

PART SIX

PERPETRATION PREVENTION

CHAPTER 22

The Public Health Approach

Primary, Secondary, and Tertiary Perpetration Prevention

GAIL RYAN

NUMEROUS ESTEEMED EXPERTS and national professional organizations have advocated that sexual abuse be viewed as a public health problem (see, for example, Freeman-Longo & Blanchard 1998; Kaufman, 2010; Krugman, Davidson, & U.S. Advisory Board on Child Abuse and Neglect, 1991). Public health approaches include: *primary prevention* aimed at the general population; *secondary prevention* to identify characteristics indicating greater risk for particular individual or categories of individuals and to provide some preventive intervention; and *tertiary prevention* to prevent identified problems from continuing (Ryan, 1998; Whitaker et al., 2008).

Abusive behavior is both predictable and preventable (Ryan, 2004). Empirical research has shown that how human beings grow and develop, how the brain functions, and how the individual interacts with others depends on and is influenced by all that surrounds them. There is also a growing body of evidence that illuminates factors associated with less than optimal outcomes for human beings (Gilgun, 1996; Strayhorn, 1988; Whitaker et al., 2008) and the static, stable, and dynamic risks associated with abusive behaviors (Ryan [2000b], see Chapter 7). Beginning in the genetics of conception, continuing through prenatal and postnatal processes, and extending into the domains of developmental, environmental, and experiential influences, both risks and protective factors are known. Primary prevention must assure that children acquire the skills and knowledge to support success and insist that they not be abusive (Ryan, 2002). Preventing, decreasing, and/or moderating risks and increasing health will prevent most children from becoming abusive.

SEXUAL ABUSE PERPETRATION

It is clear that sexually abusive behaviors do not suddenly appear in adolescence but rather have developed over time—often from early in childhood. Many teenagers in treatment for offending have been able to identify, in retrospect, abusive patterns of thinking and behavior that were present as early as age 5 (Law, 1987). Historically, the literature relevant to behavior problems in childhood has included references to sexual behavior problems, and the increased sexual acting out of children who have experienced physical or sexual abuse and neglect has been well documented (Conte, 1985; Friedrich, Urquiza, & Bielke, 1986; Ricci & Watson, 1989; Widom & Williams, 1996).

Although tremendous resources have been enlisted to respond to the incidence and impact of both child sexual abuse and adult sexual assaults, intervention strategies have failed to prevent the occurrence and prevention strategies have usually been aimed at potential victims. Certainly teaching self-protection and defense, identification and reporting of incidents, prosecution of offenders, and treatment programs are called for in response to this problem, but the ultimate solution is to prevent the development of offending so that future generations are no longer at risk. The only proactive approach to sexual abuse prevention is *perpetration prevention* rather than the reactive intervention responses that have been most common.

Reports of very young sexual perpetrators have supported greater awareness and identification of early perpetration behaviors (Cantwell, 1988; Cavanaugh-Johnson, 1988; Isaac, 1997), yet even the early identification of young children who are sexually abusing other children is a tertiary intervention, aimed at preventing the continuation of sexually abusive behavior that has already occurred.

Primary perpetration prevention requires social, cultural, and familial change in order to alter the earliest learning experiences of children in the family and in the community at large. Secondary perpetration prevention requires specialized intervention with children in groups known to be at greater risk than their age-mates to develop sexually aggressive or abusive behaviors.

Although research discussed in earlier chapters has illuminated a variety of factors that may increase the risk of abusive behaviors, every risk factor identified to date is also experienced by many who do not become abusive. The research supports the belief that risk factors are moderated by protective factors, that risks accumulate, and one's resilience in overcoming risks is unique to each individual, reflecting the relative balance of individual and environmental risks and assets. For every risk factor identified as overrepresented in those who sexually offend, there are corresponding protective factors that might moderate the power of those risks.

Prospective studies illustrate the risks and deficits that undermine optimal functioning and the protective factors that mediate risk and create resiliency, yet much of the knowledge that exists is not being put to use. For many of the most apparent risks, research already exists to prevent the risk itself. For example: prenatal care reduces risks that jeopardize health at birth; empathic parent-infant interaction and sensitive parenting reduce the risk of disordered attachment and negative internal working models of relationships; adequate stimulation develops skills for a wide range of pleasurable behaviors and combines with protection from unsafe environments and traumatic experiences to increase positive and decrease negative effects on the growth and development of the brain and the resultant neural pathways and sensitivities; and developmental skills support successful functioning for the child at each subsequent stage of life (Ainsworth, 1985; Bowlby, 1977; Brazelton & Cramer, 1990; Briggs, 1975; Chess & Thomas, 1984; Cicchetti, 1987; George & Solomon, 1989; Kotulak, 1997; Kurtz, 1994; Strayhorn, 1988).

There are many examples of preventive public health policies responding to recognized risks with effective preventive interventions. Physical risks to children's lives result in widespread preventive interventions such as vaccinations and seat belt laws, while developmental, emotional, and psychological risks often continue unaddressed. For example, seeing the risk of death or permanent physical disability (two outcomes that profoundly affect the adults who care about the child), led to significant public health efforts to prevent childhood brain injuries, including car restraints and recreational helmets.

The science exists to raise a much less abusive generation if preventive interventions and protective factors are introduced prior to the presence of risk. What seems lacking is a collective sense of adult responsibility to raise a generation of nonviolent children. Primary prevention must assure that babies are protected in utero, born healthy, well cared for by sensitive/empathic caregivers, protected from deviant exposure and trauma, exposed to nonabusive role modeling, acquire the skills and knowledge to support successful interactions and relationships, and be held accountable (personally responsible) for all types of abusive behavior (see Chapters 5, 7, and 15; Ryan, 2002, 2004).

Testing the validity of preventive interventions is a slow, expensive, and methodical science requiring large samples, random assignment to the preventive intervention or control groups, and long-term prospective follow-up. Resources tend to flow in the direction of identified problems much more than preventive interventions, perpetuating reactive rather than proactive strategies. Despite the impediments of scarce time and resources, a lot is known about preventing risks, including the risks associated with children becoming aggressive and abusive. The impediments to prevention are much more a matter of priorities and competing needs than a lack of knowledge.

PRIMARY PREVENTION FROM BIRTH

Engaging in abusive behavior requires the capacity to be abusive and the absence of effective inhibitions (Finkelhor, 1995). Primary perpetration prevention can specifically address two of the most common deficits apparent in all types of abuse: the lack of empathy and the misattribution of responsibility. These factors are not so much a product of deviant experience as they are deficits in human development; that is, the absence of something healthy (empathic deterrence and internal locus of control) more than the presence of something deviant. Primary prevention requires proactive rather than reactive care of children.

Empathy develops from birth in infants who are cared for by sensitive, consistent, empathic caregivers and should begin to be reflected in the infant's own interactions very early in life (Landry & Peters, 1992). Empathy is characterized by reading cues that indicate needs or emotions, interpreting the cue (attributing meaning), and validating responses that meet the need or express the emotion. Infants learn these three skills first in the experience of empathic care, then become able to read, interpret, and validate their own and others' cues.

Unfortunately, many times the advice given to parents and the subsequent actions are aimed at meeting the needs of babies according to adult agendas rather than in response to the infant's expression of emotion and need. Parents may be advised by pediatricians, parenting instructors, relatives, or other parents to disregard the infant's cues in order to prevent "spoiling" the child and in the interest of developing discipline and schedules. The most blatant examples are evident in proscribed feeding schedules (rather than feeding "on-demand"), in cynical interpretations of a baby's cries of distress, or disregard when the infant seeks intimacy, attention, or reassurance.

The notion that parents should control the infant's care rather than be responsive to the infant's expression of needs is a fundamental cultural mind-set. The parent who struggles to understand and respond to the baby's cues of distress may be chastened as "doting on" or "spoiling" the child and admonished regarding the need to avoid being "manipulated" by the child. Disregarding the infant's inherent need to manipulate the environment to meet one's needs, manipulation is then deemed negative rather than being viewed as evidence of effective communication. The community's empathy for the newborn's cry then gives way to judgment regarding the parent and the child. Such judgments distort attributions of responsibility and may encourage coercive styles of parenting.

Friends and family, pediatricians and health professionals, and even strangers in the community may offer advice in the form of rules for the parent that are designed to manipulate the child without regard for the child's legitimate need for empathic care. Of course the community is not unaware of the needs of children, and so it sanctions parents who "abuse" or "neglect" their child (although there is often intense controversy in defining those terms). Parents may be confused by mixed messages regarding their role in caring for the infant.

Those parents who bring to their relationship with the infant the developmental assets of empathy, secure attachment models, and a positive, assertive sense of self are usually able to provide a consistent empathic experience that is responsive to the infant's unique needs (even if they hear advice to the contrary). However, parents whose own internal representations of self and relationships are less secure, or who lack empathic skills and sensitivity, may rely on the "rules" of parenting and, although the child appears well-fed, clean, comfortable, and cared for, the child's expression of needs may diminish over time from lack of reinforcement. Thus, an appearance of health may exist despite the absence of empathic care. Such children may then be at risk to lack empathy in their own subsequent functioning and therefore may be less aware of their own needs and less sensitive to the needs of others (see Chapter 5).

The empathy deficit may not be manifest in any deviant functioning as long as the environment remains somewhat consistent and predictable and the individual's needs are not unusual. However, there is a risk that deviant exposure, stress, trauma, or unpredictable environmental factors may overwhelm the individual's internal resources. Failure to interpret their own needs accurately and attribute control and responsibility accurately puts them at risk of being similarly insensitive to the unique needs of others, including their own children as they become parents. Those who have not experienced validation and reinforcement of their own cues may be at risk for many harmful outcomes.

Consider for example, the infant who is taught through experience to disregard hunger as a cue for eating; this child might be at risk of developing eating disorders—either overeating or undereating—without regard for the body's cues regarding how much nutrition is needed. Such disorders might be subclinical (that is, not meet diagnostic criteria) throughout the life span or might become clinically apparent in the extremes, such as obesity or anorexia. Similarly, sexual functioning might not be affected as long as the environment and individual experience proceed along a normative, predictable course, but sexual functioning might become abusive when stress, trauma, or deviant exposure overwhelms the individual's internal resources and the individual fails to recognize, misinterprets, or does not feel responsible for cues of another's distress in sexual interactions.

Without empathic parenting, invalidation or disregard of the child's ability and responsibility to communicate his or her own needs may shift the locus of control early in life from the individual to the environment, creating a condition of risk for the external control seeking that is manifest in the abusive cycle and the misattributions of responsibility that are apparent in the thinking of abusive individuals. These risks may be exacerbated by changes in the culture and the community that expose more individuals to deviance or stress, as well as attitudes about violence, sexuality, and relationships. Certainly the infant who has not experienced or developed empathy and is then exposed to the risk factors already described in this book may be at greater risk to become abusive.

Although ideas about primary perpetration prevention are speculative and theoretical at this time, research does support the need for empathy in the care of infants and toddlers (sensitive parenting). When parent education, advice, and practice emphasize the value of respecting and responding to an infant's cues, perhaps more empathic interactions will result. Examples would be: when the advice says how much food one might expect the infant to need in a day and what cues might indicate when the baby is hungry, rather than advising "8 ounces every 4 hours" as a schedule; or when parents are encouraged to provide nourishing snacks between mealtimes when the child expresses hunger and to respect the child's lack of hunger as well, rather than avoiding snacks and then forcing the child to clean the plate at meals. This very basic respect for children's ability to express feelings and needs may provide the basis for children to recognize the needs of others.

Despite studies indicating that children should acquire and demonstrate empathic recognition and responses early in life, many early childhood educators do not expect children to be empathic because they believe that empathy requires abstract thinking (the role taking and perspective taking that creates a sympathetic response). If some educators and caregivers do not expect children to be empathic, they are not likely to model or promote empathic interaction as the optimal level of functioning. The concepts of modeling and the use of repetition and coaching empathic responses are embedded in Early Childhood Education (ECE) curriculum and within the national standards of the ECE profession. It is also included in many parenting curricula such as "Nurturing Parenting" and "Parents as Teachers" (Bavolek, 1985; Bavolek, Comstock, & McLaughlin, 2009; Bavolek, McLaughlin, & Comstock, 1983; Cowen, 2001; Devall, 2004).

Expressing concern for the lack of empathic recognition and responses, accurately attributing responsibility for abusive, insensitive, and aggressive behaviors when they are observed in play and in interactions with dolls and pets, and articulating the definition of abusive exposure in the community and media, are all responsible adult interventions that will not cause harm and may reduce the risk of children accepting, normalizing, and practicing abusive behaviors.

A parallel concern for parent educators should be any normalizing of aggression in sibling relationships. Parents may dismiss sibling violence, saying, "All kids fight." Distinctions must be made, however, between *sibling rivalry*, which is an assertion of uniqueness that facilitates personal identity and boundaries; *sibling conflicts*, which are the products of disagreements or conflicting needs and are resolved through mediation and compromise; and *sibling abuse*, which involve physical or verbal attacks that demonstrate a lack of empathic interaction. Sibling relationships may be an early indicator of internal working models for relationships and subsequent parenting, and the adults should correct coercive, intimidating, and abusive patterns.

PRIMARY PERPETRATION PREVENTION SPECIFICALLY RELEVANT TO CHILDHOOD SEXUALITY

Primary perpetration prevention can specifically address the risk of abusive sexuality by considering sexual development in the general population of all children. Recognizing that many sexually abused children are not identified, that all children are exposed to sexualized messages and information in the media and entertainment that seem to condone or even glorify sexual exploitation, and that models of sexualized compensation pervade many cultures, it is clear that children experience sexual learning throughout childhood. It is also clear that the development of sexuality begins in infancy and progresses throughout childhood (see Chapter 4). Yet many cultures traditionally have denied sexuality in childhood, redirecting and deterring children from open sexual exploration and discouraging acquisition of sexual information.

Sex education most often teaches the process or mechanics of reproduction with little or no mention of sexual behaviors or relationships. The interactions explicit in sexual relationships are often learned in secrecy and colored by guilt. Early childhood arousal has been defined as "genital discovery" and "genital exploration" and sexual feelings during childhood have been denied. It is not surprising that the majority of boys and girls who have been sexually exploited in childhood have preserved the secret of their abuse and that victims may internalize enormous burdens of guilt if they experience pleasure or arousal while being exploited.

Sexual learning prior to puberty has occurred within a social vacuum without the influence of societal norms, for better and for worse, so it is not surprising that children are often confused by sexual information, experiences, and feelings that occur without opportunity for validation, explanation, or correction. The secrecy surrounding sexuality during childhood not only protects the perpetrators of child sexual abuse but also prohibits both normative and corrective learning for children.

The traditional responses (or nonresponses) of ignoring, repressing, or punishing sexual behavior in childhood have failed to recognize the psychological and physiological motivations and reinforcements that are inherent in sexual interactions. Intimacy, arousal, and orgasm are powerful rewards in the process of sexual learning, so it is likely that sexual behaviors will persist and increase. Arousal patterns and sexual thoughts develop and progress over time. Knowledge and understanding of adolescent sexual offending has many implications in the consideration of prevention, and both primary and secondary models that specifically address the risk of deviant sexual development are possible.

Throughout the 1980s, adult awareness of the sexual behavior of children increased, as it was suggested that sexual behaviors might be diagnostic of a child victim's deviant experience. Unfortunately, when viewed as a symptom of child sexual abuse, all sexual behavior was seen as deviant and so management and modification were entirely reactive. However, childhood sexuality is not a pathological condition. The capacity for sexual arousal and function is inborn and the ways in which people behave sexually are learned: They are products of the environment and life experience. The motivation for sexual behaviors in early childhood is not always clear and may not be the same for every child. Early behaviors may be exploratory, imitative, or reactive but the question of origin or motivation in no way minimizes the need for understanding.

Having defined sexual abuse in terms of unlawfulness and harm; intimidation, coercion, and force; inequality; and lack of consent (National Task Force on Juvenile Sexual Offending, 1988), it becomes possible to differentiate problem behaviors from the normal range of sexual behavior in childhood (Ryan et al., 1988).

THE RANGE OF BEHAVIOR

Children exhibit a wide range of sexual behaviors, from the curious exploration of self and others in "playing doctor" to the aggressive 7-year-old who demanded sex at gunpoint in the school yard ("Boy, 7, Demands Sex at Gunpoint," *Rocky Mountain News*, 21 September, 1988; Denver, Colorado). Definition of this range of behaviors comes from the observations of caregivers and educators (Ryan et al., 1988), the self-reported memories of childhood sexual experiences by adults (Ryan et al., 1988), reports of childhood sexual behavior by sexually abusive children (Cantwell, 1988; Cavanaugh-Johnson, 1988; Law, 1987), and an extensive review of the literature on childhood sexuality (Ryan, 2000a). It is apparent that children do engage in sexual interactions with their peers as well as solitary sexualized behaviors. Additional studies of the range of sexual behavior in both clinical samples and general population controls have validated these earlier efforts (Friedrich, Fisher, Broughton, Houston, & Shafran, 1991; Friedrich 1992).

In studying the range of behavior observed in nonclinical samples, Cavanaugh-Johnson (1988) noted that these behaviors normally occur alone or between similar-aged peers, without coercion, and that the affect of the children is usually fun and teasing. Masturbation is common in toddlers and preschoolers, and attempts to touch or see the genitals of others commonly accompany the genital discovery and exploration of toddlers. The sexual behavior of young, sexually abused children may deviate from the norm in duration and frequency as some appear preoccupied with sexual themes for an extended period of time. These "sexually reactive" behaviors may include more explicit and precocious demonstrations and intensified masturbation, and may be accompanied by confused or anxious affect (Cavanaugh-Johnson, 1989).

The full range of sexual behaviors of children falls along a continuum including normal, problematic, and abusive behaviors (Ryan et al., 1988; Ryan, 2000). Within the normal range adult responses may be indicated to educate, redirect, or limit behavior, but the behavior itself is not deviant or problematic. As the behaviors move away from the norm, however, differential evaluation and corrective responses become desirable (see Table 22.1). It is important to note that many of the behaviors adults perceive to be problematic may be seen in many children occasionally as they experiment and imitate things they have seen or heard. Even so, these behaviors should be attracting attention and activating a response from adult educators and caregivers.

In considering the range of behavior in childhood, it becomes clear that most of these behaviors are not deviant in our culture in and of themselves. It is the relationship and interaction that define sexual abuse rather than an isolated behavior that occurs out of context. When the sexual abuse of children was first defined, age and behavior were the only factors considered. Even the sexual abuse of young children by adolescents has been defined on the basis of age and behavior (it is not difficult to know that a 17-year-old sodomizing a 4-year-old is abuse). However, with younger perpetrators and smaller age differences between two children,

Table 22.1

Range of Prepubescent Sexual Behavior

Normal	Genital or reproduction conversations with peers or similar-age siblings
	Show me yours/I'll show you mine with peers
	Playing "doctor"
	Occasional masturbation without penetration
	Imitating seduction (i.e., kissing, flirting)
	Dirty words or jokes within cultural or peer group norms
Yellow flags	Preoccupation with sexual themes (especially sexually aggressive)
	Attempting to expose others' genitals (i.e., pulling other's skirt up or pants down)
	Sexually explicit conversation with peers
	Sexual graffiti (especially chronic or impacting individuals)
	Precocious sexual knowledge
	Single occurrences of peeping, exposing, obscenities, pornographic interest, frottage
	Preoccupation with masturbation
	Mutual masturbation or group masturbation
	Simulating foreplay with dolls or peers with clothing on (for example, petting, french kissing)
Red flags	Sexually explicit conversations with significant age difference
	Touching genitals of others
	Degradation or humiliation of self or others with sexual themes
	Forced exposure of other's genitals[a]
	Inducing fear or threats of force
	Sexually explicit proposals or threats, including written notes
	Repeated or chronic peeping, exposing, obscenities, pornographic interests, frottage
	Compulsive masturbation, task interruption to masturbate
	Masturbation, including vaginal or anal penetration
	Simulating intercourse with dolls, peers, animals (i.e., humping)
No questions	Oral, vaginal, anal penetration of dolls, children, animals
	Forced touching of genitals
	Simulating intercourse with peers with clothing off
	Any genital injury or bleeding not explained by accidental cause

Source: Ryan et al. (1988).

[a]Although "force" is usually a factor in the "no question" range, restraining an individual in order to pull down pants or expose breasts does occur in the context of hazing among peers.

additional criteria are needed. The relationship of the involved children and the nature of the interaction must be evaluated. The same criteria apply in evaluating sexual interactions across the life span: consent, equality, and coercion. These factors have been defined in detail in Chapters 1 and 4.

Many parents fail to appreciate the seriousness of some behaviors that may have been more common in their own childhood but are now defined as "sexual offenses" or "sexual harassment." Educating both parents and children about the laws and defining abusive interactions is an important part of perpetration prevention. As in any other area of learning, the child's expectation is that adults will validate or correct behavior. An adult's failure to respond specifically to sexual behavior may confuse the child or be perceived as acceptance or approval.

RESPONDING TO SEXUAL BEHAVIORS

Most adults have considered the impact of the myths of their own upbringing and have moved toward less judgmental responses. Telling children they are "nasty" or bad because they touch their genitals or threatening to cut off the penis or the hand that masturbates are no longer thought to be reasonable in managing these behaviors.

As a result, adults' responses have become less specific and less punitive, but no less disapproving and no more enlightening. Children continue to be confused about an area of information that rightfully concerns them. While acknowledging the need for more informed responses, adults are often confused in the evaluation of sexual interactions involving same-aged children as well as the management of solitary sexualized behaviors.

The best way for adults to think through their responses to the sexual behaviors of children or adolescents is by asking: *"Is this behavior a problem? If so, what kind of problem is it?"* If a behavior cannot be defined as a problem then it probably isn't. However, there are many legitimate reasons why behavior might be a problem. Being abusive or illegal are two kinds of problems that are sometimes synonymous (abusive and illegal), and sometimes not (illegal but not abusive, or abusive but not illegal). Sexual behavior can also be a problem even if it is not abusive, if it poses a risk of harm to the person doing it. For example, behaviors that jeopardize health, risk unwanted pregnancy, stigmatize the person, or make them feel bad about themselves. Behavior can also be a problem for others if it makes others feel uncomfortable because it violates their beliefs or values or the norms of the family, peer group, or community.

WHEN IS SEXUAL BEHAVIOR A PROBLEM?

Behavior may be a problem for the child who is doing it if the behavior puts the child at risk, interferes with other developmental tasks, interferes in relationships, violates rules, is self-abusive, or lowers self-esteem.

Behavior may be a problem for others if the behavior causes others to feel uncomfortable, occurs in the wrong time or place, conflicts with family or community values or rules, or is abusive.

Behavior may be abusive if the behavior involves other children without consent, or if two children are not equal, or if one child is pressured or coerced by another child.

Behavior is always a problem when it violates the law, and children are often not taught the laws regarding juvenile sexual behavior until they have broken them.

By differentiating all the reasons sexual behaviors of children or adolescents could be a problem (i.e., *Problem for self; Problem for others; Problem because abusive and/or illegal*), adults can respond differently to different behaviors with reasonable, goal-oriented interventions. In every instance responses that foster communication, empathy, and accountability promote the development of healthy sexuality and the prevention of abuse.

It is also important for adults to think about the ways in which language may contribute to children's confusion. Distinctions must be made among privacy, secrecy, and surprise. The word *secret* is often misused to mean "a delay of awareness that enables a surprise" but may also be used to mean "exclusivity" or "never sharing." Most accurately, a secret is binding (never revealed), inhibiting/prohibiting external verification or feedback while protecting those involved from some consequence of disclosure. A *surprise*, on the other hand, is a temporary condition inherently dependent on disclosure (such as, what's for dessert, or what Santa will bring). *Privacy* most accurately reflects a "rightful lack of sharing" and "protection from intrusion," and implies self-ownership (personal boundaries/space).

While sexual abuse prevention programs for children have emphasized the "no more secrets" concept in an effort to encourage the child's disclosure of abusive experiences, adults have not been similarly educated to the "no secrets" rule. Secrecy can be a hard habit to break; for example, Christmas presents and other surprises have often been referred to as secrets. It is important for all adults to observe the "no secrets" rule with the understanding that adults cannot be sure children are safe if there are secrets. Secrecy allows sexual abuse to occur and to continue. Secrets protect perpetrators.

Having identified a sexual behavior of concern and having evaluated the interaction, adults can respond in ways designed to decrease the risk of abusive behavior and support healthy, prosocial development. It is important to realize that many sexual behaviors, even some that are very problematic, might be exhibited by many children once or occasionally, and even frequently among children who have been sexually abused.

It would not be helpful to overreact to a child who might be imitating language or behavior seen on television, talked about by others, or even experienced by the child. But it must be remembered that children look to the adults in their lives for verification, validation, and correction of what they are learning. They expect that adults will correct negative behavior. Failure to respond to sexually exploitive behavior may covertly support it; when no response occurs, the child's perception may be that the adult condones such behavior. When a nonspecific response occurs, the child may be confused. Suggested responses (Ryan et al., 1988) are specifically intended to be nonjudgmental, to label the behavior without labeling the child, and to foster universal goals that are not value-laden or based on personal opinions, but support the goals of healthy sexuality and perpetration prevention.

These universal goals are *communication* (articulating with words), *empathy* (recognition of affective cues), and *accountability* (accurate attributions of responsibility). Despite tremendous diversity and the controversies surrounding sex education for children, these approaches to evaluating and responding to the sexual behavior of children have been well-accepted as a model for consistent goal-oriented responses for more than two decades in the United States, United Kingdom, Canada, and Australia (Ryan, 2000a; Ryan & Blum, 1994; Ryan et al. 1988).

The first goal-oriented response is to label the behavior with words so the child has the language and permission to talk about it, and then to react at a personal level so the child hears that the behavior causes discomfort. The label is specific: what is seen (*"I see you touching Johnny's penis"*) or what is heard (*"I hear from Johnny that you touched his penis"*). This gives the child the language to discuss the behavior, avoids confusion concerning what behavior is problematic, and lets the child know that adults can discuss such matters. The reaction in the first response is nonjudgmental and not prohibiting. The reaction comes from a personal and empathic level: personal feelings (*"It makes me feel uncomfortable"*), and in some instances, pointing out signs that reflect others' feelings (*"Johnny was upset"*). The goal is primarily to foster empathic thought and consideration of others—to attach feelings to the behavior.

Fostering empathic recognition and responses requires that adults demonstrate and verbalize emotional expression in their own reactions. It is important that adults be honest and at the same time nonjudgmental in reacting to sexual behaviors— placing responsibility rather than blame and not making assumptions about what the child might be thinking or feeling. Too often adults tell the child what the adult thinks the child and others are feeling or thinking, but fail to express their own feelings. The child needs to be able to identify and communicate feelings for themselves. Adult instincts may minimize or deny the realities of negative feelings in children in order to preserve the myths of their carefree innocence and the adults' omniscient protection. In order to raise responsible people, adults must empower children with their own feelings and thoughts so they are allowed to express both anxiety and hurt and can be directed toward safe and empathic expression.

When problematic sexual behaviors reoccur after the adult has first responded, a second response would express the adult's concern that empathy has not been sufficient to control the behavior, and a rule might be made to prohibit the behavior. For example, *"I am very concerned because I see you touching Johnny's penis. I told you before that makes me uncomfortable and Johnny is upset. You need to stop doing that."*

The second response is still not judgmental but now adds a rule. By putting the emphasis of the first response on communication and empathy and reserving the prohibition for the second response, the child has the opportunity to think about, discuss, and internalize the adult's response. In the past, adult reactions to the sexual behavior of children have been prohibition without discussion (*"Don't let me catch you doing that again!"*), which may contribute to the risk of behaviors continuing in secret and certainly discourages opportunities for education, validation, or correction. Adults often feel compelled to make rules and use negative repressive messages. Holding off on prohibiting the behavior allows the adult to see whether their expression of discomfort is sufficient, which is a higher level of deterrence for behavior than simply following rules.

Finally, responses to children's sexual behaviors must include educating children about the laws that are relevant to sexual behaviors. As mentioned earlier, the legal consequences for children are often disproportionate to their culpability. Preventing children from engaging in illegal sexual behaviors is another aspect of perpetration prevention.

Although the first concern is always to prevent sexually exploitive behavior, a focus on the behavioral manifestation or symptoms of sexual abuse is a temporary intervention. Aggressive and nonempathic behaviors, as well as isolating and self-destructive behaviors, are manifestations of abuse issues, not definitive of the issue itself. The issues of sexual abuse lie deep in the experience of helplessness, betrayal, confusion, and fear (Ryan, 1989). Treatment of sexually abusive children is addressed in Chapter 20 (see also Cavanaugh-Johnson 1989; Gil & Johnson, 1993).

PRIMARY PERPETRATION PREVENTION IN ADOLESCENCE

Many differences exist in the range of behaviors (see Table 22.2) that are considered normal or problematic in adolescence. Some behaviors that are concerning in childhood become normal in adolescence, while others that were of less concern in childhood become problematic for the adolescent. The concept of a continuum of behaviors is again relevant.

Not surprisingly, many new areas of information and education become issues with adolescents. As the adolescent moves toward the establishment of adult relationships and sexual contact becomes more normative (Gadpaille, 1975), adolescents must become aware of moral, social, and familial values and rules regarding sexual behavior. Moral, social, or familial rules may discourage or restrict many behaviors that are not abnormal, developmentally harmful, or illegal when private, consensual, equal, and noncoercive. It is important that adults recognize the differences between behaviors that violate rules of the family from those that violate the law or are abusive.

Table 22.2
The Range of Post-Pubescent Sexual Behavior

Normal	Sexually explicit conversations with peers
	Obscenities and jokes within the cultural norm
	Sexual innuendo, flirting, and courtship
	Interest in erotica
	Solitary masturbation
	Hugging, kissing, holding hands
	Foreplay (petting, making out, fondling)[a]
	Mutual masturbation[a]
	Monogamist intercourse (stable or serial)[a,b]
Yellow flags	Sexual preoccupation, anxiety
	Pornographic interest
	Polygamist sexual intercourse (promiscuity)[c]
	Sexually aggressive themes, obscenities
	Sexual graffiti (especially chronic or impacting individuals)
	Embarrassment of others with sexual themes
	Violation of others' body space
	Pulling skirts up/pants down
	Single occurrences of peeping, exposing, frottage with known age-mates
	Mooning and obscene gestures[d]
Red flags	Compulsive masturbation (especially chronic or public)
	Degradation or humiliation of self or others with sexual themes
	Attempting to expose others' genitals
	Chronic preoccupation with sexually aggressive pornography
	Sexually explicit conversation with significantly younger children
	Touching genitals without permission (grabbing, goosing)
	Sexually explicit threats (verbal or written)
Illegal flags	(*illegal behaviors defined by law*)
	Obscene phone calls, voyeurism, exhibitionism, or frottage
	Sexual contact with significant age difference (child sexual abuse)
	Forced sexual contact (sexual assault)
	Forced penetration (rape)
	Sexual contact with animals (bestiality)
	Genital injury to others

[a]Moral, social, or familial rules may restrict, but these behaviors are not abnormal, developmentally harmful, or illegal when private, consensual, equal, and noncoercive.
[b]Stable monogamy is defined as a single sexual partner throughout adolescence. Serial monogamy indicates long-term (several months or years) involvement with a single sexual partner that may be preceded or followed by similar long-term monogamous relationships.
[c]Polygamist intercourse is defined as indiscriminate sexual contact with more than one partner during the same period of time.
[d]Mooning and obscene gestures have been called "Americana." Although many of the yellow flags are not necessarily outside the normal range of behavior exhibited in teenage peer groups, some evaluation and response is desirable in order to support healthy and responsible behavior.

The normality of human sexual interaction includes both risks and benefits that pose dilemmas for the adolescent. For adolescents who are sexually active, health and reproduction require specific cautions in order to prevent sexually transmitted diseases (including HIV) and unplanned pregnancy. It is important to note, however, that these issues are parallel to, but separate from, the consideration of sexually exploitive behavior. The identification of abusive interactions in adolescence continues to evaluate consent, equality, and coercion, and when youth reach the age of legal culpability, which is different in different states, the legality of behavior is an additional concern.

In responding to adolescent sexual behavior, it is even more important to differentiate the reasons why behavior is a problem. The same process is still helpful in evaluating adolescent behaviors by asking: *Is it a problem? If so, what kind of problem is it?* Identifying reasons why it might be a problem for self or others, as well as when it is abusive or illegal, continues to guide reasonable decisions about adolescent sexual behavior. Just as was true of children's behaviors, normal behaviors may occur in the wrong place or time and require limits, and behaviors of concern may be exhibited occasionally by many adolescents. The expectation that adults will validate and correct learning and behavior continues in adolescence.

Sexuality in adolescence is more apparent and in some ways the adult response may be more difficult. The goals of response to the adolescent's sexual behavior remain the same as the suggested response for children: to foster communication, empathy, and accountability in order to promote healthy and responsible sexuality and prevent exploitive behavior. This is dependent upon the adult's willingness to express feelings and encourage open communication. The adolescent may be cognitively more open to discussion, and intervention within the peer group is often desirable and possible. The peer culture's acceptance of sexually aggressive norms would be of major concern.

The conflicts characteristic of normal adolescent development sometimes make it even harder for adults to communicate their feelings and for adolescents to acknowledge theirs. Values influence the adult's beliefs, and the adolescent's expectation is often that an adult's response to sexual behavior will be judgmental rather than helpful or empathic. An adult response that encourages communication and focuses on feelings is often unexpected and may initially be unacknowledged or met with resistance or denial. By stressing one's feelings rather than rules or beliefs in the initial response, continued communication becomes more likely, and adults may have an opportunity to articulate their personal beliefs in a more didactic discussion at a later time.

Appreciation of the sexual dilemmas and confusion for youth in this culture is accelerated by awareness of the prevalence of sexual stimuli and sexually exploitive themes in the media, but the goals of accountability and empathy remain constant. In some communities, perpetration prevention curricula have been introduced into classrooms in order to educate middle school and high school students in avoidance of sexually exploitive attitudes (Kassees & Hall, 1987; Strong, Tate, Wehman, & Wyss, 1986), and numerous videotapes have been produced for adolescent audiences regarding responsible sexual behavior, identification of past victimization, and prevention of acquaintance rape. Despite these efforts, adolescents are often still unaware or misinformed regarding the laws and potential legal consequences of some behaviors; adults have a responsibility to make this information available.

SECONDARY PERPETRATION PREVENTION FOR AT-RISK GROUPS

When children do not experience consistent empathic care and do experience abuse, neglect, or trauma, they may be even more at risk than their peers. Identifying at-risk children creates the opportunity for secondary prevention interventions. Child protection should include perpetration prevention efforts with child victims of maltreatment or neglect as a priority, and mental health evaluators and therapists should be trained to recognize emerging sexual or abusive behavior problems in the referring and observed behavior problems of children they see.

Chapters 3, 4, 5, and 7 have described the body of research relevant to identification of factors that may increase the risk of sexually abusive behaviors. In summary, children who are known to have been exposed to or have experienced those risk factors (such as being sexually abused or otherwise maltreated; exposed to over-stimulating, nonnormative, or incomprehensible sexuality; exposed to sexualized models of compensation; been emotionally neglected, physically abused, abandoned, rejected, institutionalized, undersocialized; experienced parental loss or disruptions in early care and relationships), may constitute an at-risk group.

Such research offers some well-grounded hypotheses regarding the developmental and experiential factors that may, alone or in combination, increase the likelihood of abusive behaviors. Therefore, it is possible to infer that some individual children and some groups of children may be at greater risk to be abusive and some to perpetrate sexual abuse than the general population of children, even before any behavioral manifestation occurs.

Research also suggests that children who fail to develop positive attachment models and empathic relationship skills in the early years may be at greater risk than their peers for exploitive, abusive, and dysfunctional relationships. Current practices in treating youth who have already sexually offended operate in a "risk reduction-health promotion" paradigm, with the goal of helping kids be successful while insisting they not be abusive. Clearly, the same goal is desirable for all children, and is especially critical for those children known to be at-risk to perpetrate abusive and sexual offenses.

At-risk children are often overrepresented (and therefore accessible) in treatment programs for maltreated children, special education classrooms and emotionally/behaviorally disturbed (EBD) programs, foster care and adoptive homes, child protection caseloads, and residential child welfare facilities. When these individual children are referred for therapeutic services or specialized programs are developed for groups of these children, an opportunity exists for preventive intervention. Professionals and caregivers have numerous opportunities for secondary perpetration prevention strategies to be implemented in order to decrease the risk of these children developing abusive patterns of behavior and/or problematic sexual behaviors.

Having identified a cluster of issues that evoke similar defensive strategies and result in a variety of dysfunctional behaviors, it has been suggested that many of the same interventions that are used later in treating dysfunctional dynamics might be used preventively before behaviors occur (Ryan, 1989). Recent juvenile models such as described in Chapter 7 support a constellation of observable behaviors that are thought to represent "decreased risk" and "increased health." These are described as observable evidence of successful completion of treatment for juveniles who have sexually offended, yet could be demonstrated by anyone, even if they have never offended. It is now suggested (Ryan et al., 2002) that working with at-risk children to acquire the skills and knowledge to demonstrate those same outcomes might substantially reduce their risk of perpetration, without posing any risk of harm or unintended consequence.

The "outcomes relevant to decreased risk" that were described in Chapter 7 include: defining all that is abusive in terms of the risk of harm to self, others, or property; recognizing risks and using foresight and planning to moderate risks and manage stress; recognizing defensive reactions and dysfunctional coping patterns and interrupting them before engaging in potentially harmful behaviors; demonstrating functional coping skills when stressed; demonstrating empathic recognition and responses; making accurate attributions of responsibility; and rejecting abusive attitudes and behaviors.

These skills, knowledge, and actions are not only assets for someone who has been abusive but would support positive prosocial functioning for everyone, without any reference to personal abuse issues. Similarly, the "outcomes relevant to increased health" discussed in Chapter 7 simply represent the domains of human development that require skills for anyone to function as healthy, successful persons. Nothing in demonstrating these outcomes poses any risk of harm to self or others, or creates any stigma or prejudice. Therefore, making these the goals of secondary prevention for at-risk children and youth furthers the prevention of sexual abuse by implementing risk reduction/health promotion strategies before any victimization occurs.

Chapter 15 describes "Informed supervision and Therapeutic care" in concrete terms. The strategies described are useful in adult supervision and care of at-risk children and chronically acting out children with other types of abusive behaviors.

Although these are well grounded hypotheses about the causes and correction of abusive sexual behaviors, the proposed prevention strategies have not been subjected to randomized trials to prove a perpetration prevention effect. Nonetheless, when there is evidence of risk and a proposed intervention poses no risk but may reduce dysfunction and harm, it seems reasonable to implement the preventive intervention. Anecdotally, teaching caregivers of even very young children to define all abuse and to recognize and interrupt dysfunctional patterns with more functional skills has been included in training for alternative caregivers and special education professionals for many years, with positive feedback from those adults (Ryan & Blum, 1994; Ryan et al., 1988; Ryan, Yager, Sobicinski, & Metzner, 2002).

BASIC CONCEPTS FOR SECONDARY PERPETRATION PREVENTION

Perpetration prevention efforts in childhood are similar to those used to shape responsible behavior in other domains of human functioning, including adult modeling, teaching, and goal-oriented responses. Adults must resist the temptation to accept or excuse a child's abusive/exploitive behavior as symptomatic of the culture or the child's experience, and confront the beliefs that support abusive patterns of behavior. Dispelling the secrecy, communicating openly, expressing empathy, and holding children accountable for behavior are basic to the prevention of abusive behaviors and exploitive sexuality.

Helplessness, powerlessness, and a lack of control are issues that may trigger a defensive strategy. The concept of cyclical patterns that has been used to identify the dynamics surrounding sexual offenses can also be observed in other dysfunctional behaviors (Ryan, 1989). Adults caring for very young children are often able to recognize very simple, yet similar patterns of situations, emotions, thinking, and behavior surrounding problematic behaviors (see Figure 22.1).

Children who have experienced adversity are often trying to regain a sense of control and well-being, but harbor negative or unrealistic expectations in anticipation of interpersonal failures. These expectations may be fulfilled or avoided, either outcome resulting in the child's isolation or withdrawal. Attempts to regain control are often primitive and unsuccessful, increasing the child's frustration and anger

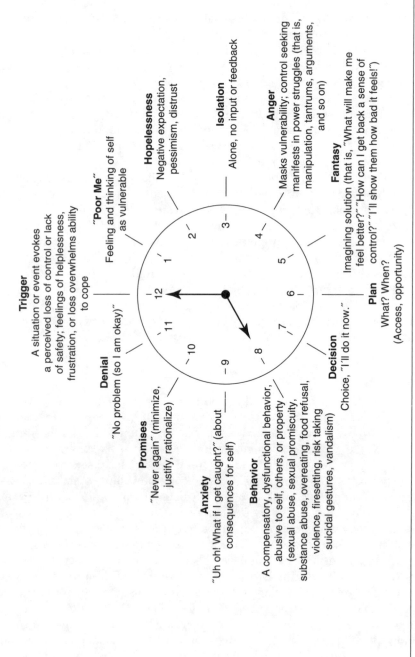

Trigger
A situation or event evokes
a perceived loss of control or lack
of safety; feelings of helplessness,
frustration, or loss overwhelms ability
to cope

"Poor Me"
Feeling and thinking of self
as vulnerable

Hopelessness
Negative expectation,
pessimism, distrust

Isolation
Alone, no input or feedback

Anger
Masks vulnerability; control seeking
manifests in power struggles (that is,
manipulation, tantrums, arguments,
and so on)

Fantasy
Imagining solution (that is, "What will make me
feel better?" "How can I get back a sense of
control?" "I'll show them how bad it feels!")

Plan
What? When?
(Access, opportunity)

Decision
Choice, "I'll do it now."

Behavior
A compensatory, dysfunctional behavior,
abusive to self, others, or property
(sexual abuse, sexual promiscuity,
substance abuse, overeating, food refusal,
violence, firesetting, risk taking
suicidal gestures, vandalism)

Anxiety
"Uh oh! What if I get caught?" (about
consequences for self)

Promises
"Never again" (minimize,
justify, rationalize)

Denial
"No problem (so I am okay)"

Figure 22.1   The High-Risk Cycle

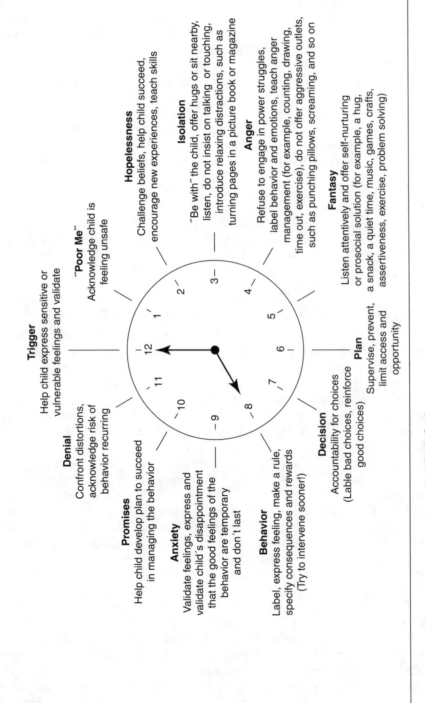

Figure 22.2 Adult Interventions in the High-Risk Cycle

Trigger
Help child express sensitive or
vulnerable feelings and validate

Denial
Confront distortions,
acknowledge risk of
behavior recurring

Promises
Help child develop plan to succeed
in managing the behavior

Anxiety
Validate feelings, express and
validate child's disappointment
that the good feelings of the
behavior are temporary
and don't last

Behavior
Label, express feeling, make a rule,
specify consequences and rewards
(Try to intervene sooner!)

Decision
Accountability for choices
(Lable bad choices, reinforce
good choices)

Plan
Supervise, prevent,
limit access and
opportunity

Fantasy
Listen attentively and offer self-nurturing
or prosocial solution (for example, a hug,
a snack, a quiet time, music, games, crafts,
assertiveness, exercise, problem solving)

Anger
Refuse to engage in power struggles,
label behavior and emotions, teach anger
management (for example, counting, drawing,
time out, exercise), do not offer aggressive outlets,
such as punching pillows, screaming, and so on

Isolation
"Be with" the child, offer hugs or sit nearby,
listen, do not insist on talking or touching,
introduce relaxing distractions, such as
turning pages in a picture book or magazine

Hopelessness
Challenge beliefs, help child succeed,
encourage new experiences, teach skills

"Poor Me"
Acknowledge child is
feeling unsafe

while reinforcing helplessness and poor self-image. As the child struggles to achieve control, the fantasy may be that some external source of gratification will compensate for negative experiences or that some behavior will "get back" what is missing. In this compensatory or retaliatory mode, the child imagines a solution, develops a plan, and decides to act. The behavior that follows may be self-abusive, re-abusive, or abusive of others. Simplistically, the victim who continues to operate within a victim identity maintains a victim stance that supports a worldview in which interactions will always or usually be abusive. The options are limited to revictimization, self-victimization, or victimization of others. For this child, the only adaptive response imaginable is to take control of the anticipated abuse rather than risk betrayal and helplessness.

Understanding the function of behavior and the progression of thinking that supports the choice of a compensatory or retaliatory behavior, adults can intervene in the pattern and disrupt the habituation of the avoidant pattern while working with the child to develop more functional coping skills (see Figure 22.2 on the previous page). Adults can be easily educated to use these "secondary prevention" strategies (Camino, 2000; Ryan, 2001; Ryan & Blum, 1994; Ryan et al., 2002), and many times report relief that they become proactive instead of simply reacting to bad behaviors after they occur.

Abuse is a multidimensional and dynamic phenomenon. No single intervention will assure prevention. However, both risks and protective factors are known that moderate or exacerbate the likelihood that a person will behave abusively. Putting that knowledge to work in the lives of children is the key.

TERTIARY PERPETRATION PREVENTION: JUVENILES AFTER TREATMENT

Primary and secondary prevention strategies address risk before the problem occurs. Tertiary prevention aims to prevent a problem from reoccurring. Everything that occurs in the system and in treatment after a juvenile commits a sexual offense is actually tertiary prevention. Prosecution, supervision, treatment, and care are all aimed at preventing further offending. Historically, the term "relapse prevention" was widely used in treatment and aftercare of sexual offending, modified from relapse prevention models in the addictions field (Pithers, 1990). Based in the assumption that anyone who had sexually offended would always be considered at risk to reoffend, the model supported a lifetime management approach.

For that minority of youth who continue to be high risk even after working hard in treatment, relapse prevention plans may still be useful in supporting lifetime vigilance (Leversee, 2003; Steen, 1993). However, since the research has shown that the majority of juveniles who have sexually offended do not "recidivate," the term is less useful in terms of aftercare planning for the majority of youth who successfully complete treatment. Nonetheless, many do continue to need some ongoing care or services beyond their completion of treatment.

Purposeful planning to support continued success beyond discharge should be a continuous part of treatment planning. Referring back to Chapter 7, static and stable risks will continue to be issues for the youth across the life span, along with the dynamic risks, which were referred to as more global than circumstantial. Losses such as employment, housing, relationships, and deaths are stressors for most people. Personal issues from the past also cause stress.

The ongoing assessment will be identifying risks that can be foreseen in the future for the youth. Just as the routine safety plans for daily activities have identified and moderated risks for the youth during treatment, aftercare plans can identify ongoing or foreseeable risks in order to maximize the youth's awareness and preparedness to meet new challenges successfully. Some will be sensitive issues or dynamics in the family that have not been adequately addressed to resolve them. Such issues must be acknowledged and defined as ongoing dilemmas for the youth.

It is useful for them to continue to recognize: (a) the risk of being abusive; (b) the risk of putting themselves in situations where someone might make an allegation that they have reoffended; and (c) the risk of being overwhelmed by stress or issues and responding with the old dysfunctional, defensive cycle. Essentially, aftercare plans address long-term risks, by looking forward across the life span. Just as foreseeing stress in daily activities desensitizes the stressors and allows thoughtful preparation to deal with stress from day to day, consciously acknowledging issues that are likely to continue or occur across the life span is the first step in preparing the youth to deal with those issues.

For older youth who have minimal risk factors and have done well in treatment, aftercare may be minimal. The younger the youth, the more likely it is that they will continue to need care and support from adult caregivers. Their caregivers may need to consult the therapist occasionally, but as youth return to the normalizing activities that they now have the skills to do successfully, most will do well. By foreseeing future stress points, the youth can be encouraged to remember and practice the preventive interventions they have learned in treatment and also encouraged to contact the therapist if they recognize risks that they did not foresee or if they have new issues arise.

Stress points for all people include major changes: moving, changing jobs, new relationships and relationships ending, marriage and divorce, birth of a child, loss of loved ones. For these youth, additional stressors can include the stigma of having sexually offended following them. This sometimes occurs through rumors or by persons bringing this up in times of conflict (especially in times of divorce when this issue may affect child custody and visitation), or when they are required to continue registering on registries that are readily accessible to the public, and some neighbor or co-worker becomes aware of the history.

Some youth will become eligible to petition the court to be relieved of registration at the end of probation and treatment, and for others the requirement may continue for many years before that is possible. The need to continue to re-register every few months or every year is a potential risk for youth in that it continues to trigger issues regarding the past, but there is also the risk that as life goes on they either forget or choose to miss those requirements. Failure to continue registration as required is a felony and there have been numerous cases of young adults in their mid- to late twenties being arrested and jailed for failure to re-register. The disruption this causes for those who have been working and living without problems can trigger a ripple effect in relationships, employment, and in the youth's mental health.

For some who continue to need treatment for co-occurring psychiatric disorders, the aftercare plan must include the referral and initiation of an ongoing relationship with a doctor who will continue the medical management of that disorder. For some who are not able to return home, the aftercare plan will include transition into emancipation programming designed to help them finish growing up and prepare to be independent. For some who are returning home, the aftercare plan may include some type of in-home family therapy such as MST, to support the parents resuming their parental role and maximize successful transition back to more normalizing activities.

By thinking of aftercare in terms of prevention, the needs of the youth that are foreseeable in the future can be addressed without assuming that all remain at risk to continue offending. It is important for the therapist to be very clear and direct in discussing the future with the youth prior to discharge. They need to be very aware that for the most part, they are at greatest risk to be rearrested for other types of delinquency and that as they become adults, avoiding all types of abusive behaviors becomes the evidence for them to demonstrate that they are no longer at risk.

Those youth who do continue to experience sexually abusive thoughts and arousal will need lifetime management strategies. For some, who continue to be easily triggered and become either angry or withdrawn, anger management strategies and conscious foresight and planning may continue to be necessary. For others, continually avoiding contact with young children will be necessary if they acknowledge the risk of being in situations that trigger pedophilic thoughts and arousal. Such youth would benefit from referral to an offense-specific therapist trained in treatment and management of adults for aftercare support.

Many youth benefit from involvement in community-based support groups or activities that are not limited to youth who have sexually offended but may be opportunities for more normalizing experiences. Ideally, it would be useful for providers to work together to create some type of ongoing support meeting that all youth who have successfully completed treatment for sexual offending could be invited to attend, either regularly for some or sporadically as needed. Such a support meeting could be facilitated by multiple therapists or programs and meet only once a week or once or twice a month, at some neutral designated location. This could be particularly beneficial for those who emancipate and, as young adults on their own, may not have anyone who can help them remember the lessons of treatment and provide informed responses when issues arise.

Youth need to hear that asking for help *before* they engage in any kind of problematic or abusive behavior is not a sign of failure, but a sign of strength. The ability to identify trustworthy sources of support and ask for help is a developmental asset. As the years go by, the longer they are successful as adults without significant behavioral dysfunction, it becomes possible to state: "Since the risk of sexual recidivism is low for juveniles who have sexually offended, and this individual has been functioning successfully as an adult, there is no evidence to suggest any particular risk of sexual offending." This should be the outcome for the majority of these youth.*

REFERENCES

Ainsworth, M. D. S. (1985). Attachments across the lifespan. *Bulletin of New York Academy of Medicine, 61*, 792–812.

Bavolek, S. J. (1985). Validation of the nurturing parenting program: Increasing the nurturing parenting skills of families in Head Start. *Research Report*.

Bavolek, S. J., Comstock, C. M., & McLaughlin, J. A. (2009). *The nurturing program*. Utah: Family Life Development.

Note: The author wishes to acknowledge the contributions of J. Blum, D. Sandau-Christopher, S. Law, F. Weber, C. Sundine, L. Astier, J. Teske, and J. Dale to the concepts of primary perpetration prevention in childhood, and to the members of the Kempe Study Group, authors of *The Web of Meaning*.

Bavolek, S. J., McLaughlin, J. A., & Comstock, C. M. (1983). *The nurturing parent program: A validated approach for reducing dysfunctional family interactions*. Final Report: NIMH.

Bowlby, J. (1977). The making and breaking of affectional bonds. *British Journal of Psychiatry, 130*, 201–210.

Brazelton, T. B., & Cramer, B. G. (1990). *The earliest relationship*. New York: Addison-Wesley.

Briggs, D. C. (1975). *Your child's self-esteem*. New York: Doubleday.

Camino, L. (2000). *Treating sexually abused boys*. San Francisco, CA: Jossey Bass.

Cantwell, H. (1988). Child sexual abuse: Very young perpetrators. *Child Abuse and Neglect: International Journal, 12*(4), 579–582.

Cavanaugh-Johnson, T. (1988). Child perpetrators: Children who molest children. *Child Abuse and Neglect: The International Journal, 12*(2), 219–229.

Cavanaugh-Johnson, T. (1989). *Human sexuality curriculum for parents and children*. Los Angeles: Children's Institute International.

Chess, S., & Thomas, A. (1984). *Origins and evolution of behavior disorders*. New York: Bruner/Mazel.

Cicchetti, D. (1987). Developmental psychopathology in infancy: Illustration from the study of maltreated youngsters. *Journal of Consulting and Clinical Psychology, 55*(6), 837–845.

Conte, J. (1985). The effects of sexual victimization on children: A critique and suggestions for future research. *Victimology: The International Journal, 10*(1), 10–30.

Cowen, P. S. (2001). Effectiveness of a parent education intervention for at-risk families. *Journal of the Society for Pediatric Nursing, 2*, 73–82.

Devall, E. (2004). Positive parenting for high-risk families. *Journal of Family and Consumer Sciences, 96*(4), 22–28.

Finkelhor, D. (1995). The victimization of children: A developmental perspective. *American Journal of Orthopsychiatry, 65*(2), 177–193.

Freeman-Longo, R. E., & Blanchard, G. T. (1998). *Sexual abuse in America: Epidemic of the 21st century*. Brandon, VT: Safer Society Press.

Friedrich, W. (1992). The child sexual behavior inventory: Normative and clinical comparison. *Psychological Assessment, 4*, 303–311.

Friedrich, W., Fisher, J., Broughton, D., Houston, M., & Shafran, C. R. (1991). Normative sexual behavior in children. *Pediatrics, 88*(3), 92–100.

Friedrich, W., Urquiza, A., & Bielke, R. (1986). Behavioral problems in sexually abused young children. *Journal of Pediatric Psychology, 11*(2), 47–57.

Gadpaille, W. J. (1975). Adolescent sexuality—A challenge to psychiatrists. *Journal of American Academy of Psychoanalysis, 3*(2), 163–177.

George, C., & Solomon, J. (1989). Internal working models of care-giving and security of attachment at age 6. *Infant Mental Health Journal, 10*, 222–227.

Gil, E., & Johnson, T. (1993). *Sexualized children*. Walnut Creek, CA: Launch Press.

Gilgun, J. (1996). Human development and adversity in ecological perspective. *Families in Society, 77*(8), 395–402, 459–476.

Isaac, C. (1987). *Identification and interruption of sexually offending behaviors in prepubescent children*. Paper presented at the 16th Annual Child Abuse and Neglect Symposium, Keystone, CO.

Kassees, J., & Hall, R. (1987). *Adolescent Sexual Abuse Prevention Project: Program curricula*. Wilmington, DE: Parents Anonymous of Delaware.

Kaufman, K. (Ed.) (In press, 2010). *The prevention of sexual abuse: A practitioner's sourcebook*. Holyoke, MA: NEARI Press.

Kotulak, R. (1997). *Inside the brain: Revolutionary discoveries of how the mind works*. Kansas City, MO: Andrews McMeel Publishing.

Krugman, R., Davidson, H., & U.S. Advisory Board on Child Abuse and Neglect. (1991). *Creating caring communities*. Washington, DC: USDHS.

Kurtz, H. (1984). The effects of victimization on acceptance of aggression and the expectations of assertive traits in children as measured by the general social survey. *Victimology, 9*(1), 166–173.

Landry, S., & Peters, R. D. (1992). Toward understanding of a developmental paradigm for aggressive conduct problems during the preschool years. In R. D. Peters, R. McMahon, & V. Quinsey (Eds.), *Aggression and violence throughout the lifespan* (pp. 1–30). Newbury Park, CA: Sage.

Law, S. (1987). *Clinical notes from client interviews.* Unpublished raw data.

Leversee, T. (2003). *Moving beyond sexually abusive behavior: A relapse prevention curriculum.* (Includes a therapist manual and a client workbook.) NEARI Press.

National Task Force on Juvenile Sexual Offending. (1988). Preliminary report. *Juvenile and Family Court Journal, 39*(2), 1–67.

Pithers, W. D. (1990). *Handbook of sexual assault.* New York: Plenum Press.

Ricci, L., & Watson, R. (1989). *Sexualized behavior seen by a child sex abuse diagnostic program in Maine.* Presentation of unpublished manuscript at trainers' workshop, Bar Harbor, ME.

Ryan, G. (1989). Victim to victimizer: Rethinking victim treatment. *Journal of Interpersonal Violence, 4*(3), 325–341.

Ryan, G. (1998). The relevance of early life experience to the behavior of sexually abusive youth. *The Irish Journal of Psychology, 19*(1), 32–48.

Ryan, G. (2000a). Childhood sexuality: A decade of study. *Child Abuse and Neglect, 24*(1), 33–61.

Ryan, G. (2000b). *Static, stable and dynamic risks and assets relevant to the prevention and treatment of abusive behavior.* Poster presentation at the First National Sexual Violence Prevention Conference, Dallas, TX.

Ryan, G. (2001). *Abuse: Stop the clock before it begins.* Cincinnati, OH: Creative Therapy Associates.

Ryan, G. (2002). Victims who go on to victimize others: No simple explanations. (Invited commentary.) *Child Abuse and Neglect: The International Journal, 26*(9), 893–907.

Ryan, G. (2004). Preventing violence and trauma in the next generation. *Journal of Interpersonal Violence, 20*(1), 132–141.

Ryan, G., & Blum, J. (1994). *Childhood sexuality: A guide for parents.* Denver, CO: Kempe Center, University of Colorado Health Sciences Center.

Ryan, G., Blum, J., Sandau-Christopher, D., Law, S., Weber, F., Sundine, C., et al. (1988). *Understanding and responding to the sexual behavior of children: Trainer's manual.* Denver, CO: Kempe Center, University of Colorado Health Sciences Center.

Ryan, G., Krugman, R., & Miyoshi, T. (1988). *Results of the early childhood experience survey.* Paper presented at the National Symposium on Child Abuse and Neglect, Keystone, CO.

Ryan, G., Yager, J., Sobicinski, M., & Metzner, J. (2002). *Informed supervision and therapeutic care for juveniles who commit sexual offenses.* Kempe Center Trainer Training Curriculum.

Steen, C. (1993). *The relapse prevention workbook for youth in treatment.* Brandon, VT: Safer Society Press.

Strayhorn, J. (1988). *The competent child.* New York: Guilford Press.

Strong, K., Tate, J., Wehman, B., & Wyss, A. (1986). *Sexual assault facts and effects.* Cumberland, WI: Human Growth and Development Program.

Whitaker, D., Le, B., Hanson, K. R., Baker, C. K., McMahon, P. M., Ryan, G., et al. (2008). Risk factors for the perpetration of child sexual abuse: A review and meta-analysis. *Child Abuse & Neglect: The International Journal, 32,* 529–548.

Widom, C. S., & Williams, L. (1996). *Cycle of sexual abuse. Research inconclusive about whether child victims become adult abusers.* Report to House of Representatives, Committee of Judiciary, Subcommittee on Crime. General Accounting Office, Washington, DC.

PART SEVEN

WORKING WITH SEXUAL ABUSE

CHAPTER 23

The Impact of Sexual Abuse
on the Interventionist

GAIL RYAN, SANDY LANE, and TOM LEVERSEE

PROFESSIONALS WHO INTERACT with dysfunctional populations are at risk personally, socially, and professionally. These risks stem from the realities, the beliefs, and the attributions of each individual and how each meets the challenges posed in the integration of this experience into his or her own worldview. Working in the area of sexual victimization raises issues on many different levels. These issues flow into each other, alternating from external to internal and personal to interpersonal. Each individual's experience of the impacts of this work proceeds along a different course in terms of the ordering and processing of the issues, but most workers face similar questions as their experience evolves.

In many ways the impact of this work parallels the impact of sexual abuse itself, and the effects have often been defended against in ways that parallel the dysfunctions of coping with sexual abuse. Denial and rationalization, secrecy and avoidance, disbelief, and victim blaming are all reactions that have supported the failure to define the risks of this work and prevented adequate protection and intervention on behalf of the professionals and paraprofessionals who work with sexual abuse cases. Burnout has been accepted as inevitable, and the involved systems have accepted staff turnover as if it were beyond their control. Workers have experienced dysfunctional impacts in their own lives without understanding the nature of their reactions. The acceptance of detrimental effects has been so pervasive that little has been done to confront the problem and protect workers from burnout or to identify healthy management strategies.

This chapter explores the worker's experience and anticipated impacts in hopes of promoting greater awareness in defining the mystery of burnout in order to promote healthier adaptation and coping. Burnout not only causes trained people to leave work, but also supports dysfunction in their work and personal lives. Just as intervention with every sexual abuse client must ultimately be based in accountability and empathy, systems and workers who intervene in sexual abuse must also apply accountability and empathy in their own functioning. Prevention can occur only through definition and understanding of the potential problems.

RELEVANT CONCEPTS

Burnout has been described in general terms by theorists and clinicians in many fields of work. In the areas of mental health, social services, and the helping professions, Maslach (1978), Maslach and Florian (1988), Spaniol (1986), and Warnath and Shelton (1976) are a few of the authors who have explored the symptomatology of burnout. Seligman's (1974, 1975) research on learned helplessness has been applied to understanding the depression that characterizes burnout. These theorists describe physical, psychological, and functional characteristics. Spaniol (1986) describes somatic aches and pains, reduced energy, and fatigue; Seligman (1974) notes the loss of appetites for food, sex, and social contact. Outwardly workers begin to slow down and retreat from their work: spending less time, initiating fewer voluntary responses, minimizing client contact, vacillating in decision making, avoiding confrontation of issues, and distancing themselves emotionally and intellectually. Internally, disillusionment, powerlessness, and apathy contribute to lower and lower expectations (Warnath & Shelton, 1976), and a negative cognitive set thwarts curiosity and decreases learning (Seligman, 1975).

Functioning and feelings are affected by one's perception of control. Helplessness is the psychological state that results when events seem uncontrollable (Seligman, 1974). When the outcome of one's work is controlled by others, the risks of detachment and depression increase. Irregardless of the skill or intensity of treatment and the progress made, the control continues to lie with the client, who may choose to use the help they receive or may disregard it and continue offending after treatment.

Whereas in many clinical, remedial, or rehabilitative settings results are reported in terms of measurable improvements or "cure," the treatment of those who sexually offend was historically based on a "no cure" model and "success" was difficult to measure. As Yochelson and Samenow (1976) stated in regard to the outcomes of treatment with criminal personalities, only time will tell. Therefore, therapists were left with little immediate gratification in treating those who sexually offend and long-term feedback was more likely related to failures than success.

As the recidivism data that has been discussed in earlier chapters began to accumulate, it has become apparent that rates of reoffending are actually much less than predicted and, especially with juveniles, the prognosis now appears much more optimistic. Of course, the client who is not known to have been rearrested cannot be assumed successful because such measures of recidivism are always questionable. However, as juvenile models have evolved into the current risk reduction/health promotion models, therapists now have observable measures to base decisions on. When youth actually demonstrate changes in their current functioning that provide evidence that they are now able to function differently, and foreseeable risks have been addressed in aftercare plans, the therapist now has a basis to feel they have met their responsibility and can experience some sense of closure as they discharge clients.

Nonetheless, the endless stream of new cases can still be discouraging. Warnath and Shelton (1976) describe the "Sisyphus syndrome" as a state of doom associated with the constant repetition of doing the same job again and again. The relentless procession of new sexual abuse cases may constitute the persistent assault on the clinician's assertiveness and adaptive coping that Richter's (1957) research parallels in terms of one's willingness to struggle to survive. The professional's willingness to leave the work may result from this inability to struggle against feelings of hopelessness and doom.

In the literature on burnout theorists have also suggested strategies of intervention and prevention. Seligman (1975) suggests that prevention is supported by teaching adaptive responses and escape mechanisms prior to exposure to uncontrollable situations. Spaniol (1986) concentrates more on primary prevention of risk rather than responses to the occurrence. Primary prevention of burnout includes awareness (correct information), adequate training and skills, adequate support from peers and colleagues, personal health and assertiveness, and shared responsibility and decision making. Others have suggested open communication, administrative empathy and support, and time away (vacations and sabbaticals) as other preventive measures. In many ways these preventive measures parallel the primary prevention of victimization by defining consensual involvement, balancing power and control, and eliminating coercion. For the professional, knowing what the work involves, evaluating the possible consequences, and making an informed choice to expose oneself to the risks counters the potential perception of a lack of control in the experience. Seligman's theory regarding teaching adaptive coping skills in advance might be viewed as a secondary level of burnout prevention that parallels secondary prevention concepts regarding sexual abuse (see Chapter 22).

Clinicians must recognize the defenses they use in their work. Many of the dysfunctional patterns of those who have sexually offended evolve from a maladaptive coping with their own victimization (Ryan, 1989). Just as it is recognized that many responses to sexual abuse were initially healthy, adaptive defenses for the victim, but become problematic when generalized over time (Conte, 1985), and clinicians are at risk to overgeneralize defenses in ways that become maladaptive. The details of sexual abuse are painful to hear and may be incomprehensible or overwhelming for the counselor. It is not only necessary but adaptive for therapists to defend themselves against this painful information. As these defense mechanisms are defined in Table 23.1, it is easy to conceptualize how each of the defenses may be used by therapists in order to remain objective and functional in the course of exposure to the details of sexual victimization or offending. It is initially adaptive and healthy to protect oneself from being overwhelmed by the experience. Nevertheless, coping does not equal resolution and overgeneralization of defense mechanisms becomes maladaptive over time. Clinicians must face and resolve the painful and confusing aspects of their work in order to prevent personal and professional dysfunction.

When the risks of the work are not managed and the worker becomes symptomatic, the effects become more difficult to counter and more resistant to intervention. The counselor who is experiencing burnout may become isolated from colleagues or seek out similarly affected peers in attempts to escape painful feelings. Denial and cynicism are frequent and escape mechanisms may parallel the dysfunction of clients. Drug and alcohol abuse, eating disorders, or promiscuity by workers may represent attempts to escape or avoid the issues and "feel better."

Maladaptive coping becomes self-perpetuating, and the counselor's own responses may be similar to the dysfunctional cycle of the client. Seligman (1974) suggests that interventions with burnout must be very directive to both teach and practice more functional coping patterns. Many professionals are lost to the field entirely when burnout occurs. However, even leaving the work does not

Table 23.1

Defense Mechanisms

Denial	Refusing to acknowledge consciously or perceive either internal or external realities that produce anxiety
Displacement	Redirection of distressing emotional energy toward less dangerous objects than the source of the distress
Dissociation	Separation of some mental or behavioral processes from one's perception in order to avoid overwhelming emotion
Identification with the aggressor	Assuming the patterns of thought or behavior of another person who represents an external source of frustration
Intellectualization	Using reasoning and logic to distance oneself from anxiety
Isolation	Separation of feeling from an idea or memory
Projection	Placing blame or responsibility on another in order to avoid internal or external sources of anxiety or conflict
Rationalization	Using logic to explain or justify irrational thoughts or behavior
Regression	Partial or total return to an earlier pattern of adaptation
Repression	An unconscious process that keeps unacceptable mental content out of consciousness
Sublimation	Channeling frustrated or intolerable energy into more gratifying activity
Suppression	Conscious repression
Withdrawal	Retreat or avoidance of sources of anxiety

Source: Adapted from Koplau and Sadock (1985, p. 498).

constitute a cure. The individual's mental health is jeopardized until the issues are resolved.

DEFINING THE ISSUES

Acquiring the knowledge necessary to anticipate and counter negative impacts requires careful exploration of the issues that sexual abuse work entails. In work with any criminal problem issues of community safety, victim protection, and personal safety are legitimate concerns that place tremendous responsibility on therapists and decision makers. These are the obvious worries of those who counsel those who have sexually offended, but there are also many covert issues attached to the work. Awareness of the risks these clients pose in the community, the vulnerability of potential victims, and the impact of abuse translates into a personal knowledge of one's own vulnerability and sensitivity to danger. Additionally, all sexual abuse work brings up issues from the past related to one's own sexual learning and experience, interpersonal relationships, and beliefs about humanity.

Many people who work in the field of child protection were themselves abused as children. In several surveys of participants at professional child abuse conferences, 45% of the multidisciplinary respondents reported histories of childhood sexual abuse (Ryan, Miyoshi, & Krugman, 1988). Others have chosen to work with dysfunctional problems because they have been touched by these problems in their relationships with others in their family or community. For some, working in the field of sexual abuse is motivated by the dissonance of abuse with their own view of the world. Many professionals enter social services, mental health, special education, or justice work and find that sexual abuse is a component in a majority of their cases.

One's own exposure to sexual abuse is the most recognized of covert issues and there are both advantages and disadvantages to having prior victims working in this field. Workers who are motivated to work with those who have offended by retaliatory or compensatory drives because of their own unresolved experiences with sexual abuse are ill advised to pursue this line of work. Survivors of sexual trauma may be particularly vulnerable due to post-traumatic stress reactions that may be triggered by this work. For those who choose or are chosen to become involved in the treatment of sexual abuse, a capacity for empathy and understanding and a desire to create a safer society support that choice.

Less obvious issues from the past involve memories of childhood sexual learning and the development of one's own sexuality. Ultimately, definition of deviancy in the sexual abuse client forces interventionists to question the normalcy of their own sexuality, sexual fantasies, and sexual experience. When forced to examine and question one's own experience, misinformation and lack of information regarding sexuality throughout life may raise many unanswerable questions. In the broadened definitions of Bolton, Morris, and MacEachron (1989), Finkelhor and Browne (1985), and Haynes-Seman and Krugman (1985), the abuse of sexuality, sexualized attention in family relationships, and traumatic or incomprehensible sexual experiences abound with such frequency in individual experience and the culture that few individuals are untouched by potentially abusive stimuli. Sexual abuse work confronts the defenses and assumptions that protect the average individual from being overwhelmed by the sexual fears and confusion of the times.

At every level of intervention—legal, medical, and psychological; education; investigation, prosecution, and correction; case manager and caregiver—all interventionists are exposed to a Pandora's Box of sexual abuse issues. For some the risks of this exposure are managed by the boundaries or the role of the profession and the definition of their own involvement with the problem. For others, distancing from the perceptual realities of sexual abuse serves to insulate them from the personal implications of the subject. However, in a survey of caseworkers, supervisors, and members of sexual abuse teams involved with incest cases at social service agencies, respondents reported many negative impacts that they attributed to the unpredictable and intrusive aspects of their work. Difficult aspects of the work included pain, sadness, nonsupportive systems, lack of recognition, inability to set boundaries, feelings of hopelessness, exhaustion, and distortion of power (Corman & Smith, 1986). Workers described changes in their sexuality and sexual fantasies, increased levels of anger, and a variety of sleep disturbances and psychosomatic complaints. These descriptions parallel those voiced by interventionists who work with both victims and perpetrators of sexual abuse.

Counselors of victims and perpetrators are exposed to the intimate perceptions and dysfunctions of their clients. When the dynamics of dysfunction become reflected in the professional's own perceptions and functioning due to existing personal issues or through transference and counter-transference in the therapeutic or correctional setting, the helping professional may become personally distressed or therapeutically ineffective. The risk of burnout in the helping professions (and especially in work with interpersonal violence and sexual abuse) has been acknowledged. It is interesting to note, however, that this risk is recognized much more than the pervasive and insidious effects of this work that change the individual's life in less obvious but more permanent ways.

EXTERNAL ISSUES

The external risks of working with those who have sexually offended are the worries that one loses sleep over: the incidence and prevalence of sexual abuse, the system's inability to protect potential victims, incidents of reoffending that may occur during treatment, and the system's failure to remove dangerous persons from the community. On a personal level these facts make therapists more aware of their own vulnerability, oversensitive to dangerous situations, and overprotective of children and other loved ones. Personal worries may be countered by locking doors, carrying disabling sprays, and educating children in self-protection, but the worry nevertheless persists. Contrary to popular belief, fear of the known may in this case be greater than fear of the unknown. Knowing the logic, rationale, and tactics of those who have sexually offended can only increase one's fear of their behavior. At the same time, confronting the distorted rationalizations of these clients strips away many of one's own cognitive defenses and may leave therapists feeling vulnerable.

At a more global level, the external worries of the sexual abuse worker are for the community based on an awareness of the risks these clients pose in the community, how sexual abuse occurs, the unpredictability of victimization, and the impact of abuse on the social structure. Therapists may become oversensitized to violence and explicit sexually exploitive influences in the culture and become more and more afraid for the community and themselves. They may experience television, movies, popular music, and advertising as aversive and consider the attitudes and humor of relatives and peers to be intolerable. Also at the external level, the therapist sees the developmental antecedents of sexually abusive behavior and must be afraid for all children who are experiencing similar developmental crises. Awareness of the vicious, unrelenting transmission of abusive behaviors from one generation to the next can be the most overwhelming of the external impacts.

Workers may experience a sense of alienation in the community or workplace as those who work with sexual assault victims often assume (inaccurately) that a therapist for those who have sexually offended is a protective advocate for sexually abusive behavior. Many who work with perpetrators confront hostility and emotional, volatile conflicts with those who are treating victims. Peers and co-workers may challenge or belittle the worker's belief in treatment by advocating severe punishment and alienation of those who have sexually offended. Those close to the interventionist may be unwilling or unable to be supportive because of their own personal issues. A sense of alienation gives rise to a defensiveness that isolates therapists even further.

Because many of these external issues are based in the culture, the community, and systems outside the therapeutic setting, the workers' frustrations and hopelessness are increased. The sociopolitical environment of fear, anger, and reactivity toward those who have sexually offended is evident in the evolution of increasingly punitive public policy responses (see Chapter 12). Working with this population, as well as advocating for public policy that is consistent with the empirical research, potentially exposes the professional to be a target of this reactivity.

Societal fear and anger may be internalized to some degree in the form of guilt and embarrassment, and professionals may experience a reluctance to speak openly about their work outside of professional circles. As with many other problems, the gap between knowledge and collective applications is a time of frustration for those who suggest solutions. This is not unique to sexual abuse work; consumer advocate Ralph Nader has stated that we have more problems than we deserve and more solutions than we apply. Much is known about the prevention and treatment of sexual abuse; much less is implemented and widely available to those who need it (Krugman, 1990). When the toll of this dilemma is measured in human suffering, the lack of access and resources supports helplessness and burnout.

INTERNAL ISSUES

Therapists must recognize that their own powerful emotions and beliefs may become issues in the therapeutic relationship. Every intervention takes place within the context of a relationship between the interventionist and the client. Whether distant, professional, or intimate every relationship adds to the worldview and perceptions of the parties involved. There are many internal issues that arise during work with sexual abuse clients.

AMBIVALENT EMOTIONS

As the therapist is exposed to the client's rage, fear, and disregard of others the professional's own affective memories are stirred and may become problematic. Reactions of rage, revulsion, fear, and disbelief arise from the therapist's own life experience and are processed through the fibers of the individual's own worldview. At the same time, the client's victim stance, poor self-image, and deprived life history trigger empathy, tolerance, and nurturance that may go beyond what is safe, rational, or therapeutic. The dichotomy between one's personal abhorrence of sexually abusive behavior and the desire to help an individual make positive changes can be stressful. The emotional tug-of-war that ensues can be frightening and exhausting for the therapist who loses perspective and is drawn into the negative or unrealistic expectations of the client. Denial of these emotions puts therapists at risk for covert expressions of victimization.

VICTIM OR AGGRESSOR IDENTIFICATION

Transference and counter-transference may occur in various phases of treatment. It is difficult to listen to the minute details of the process of victimization without reacting. Reactions may lead to identification with the victim and elicit feelings of fear, helplessness, or rage. At other times, identification with the aggressor may engender feelings of anger, confusion, dominance, or guilt. Some interventionists may identify with the client's power thrust and begin to believe that they are able to control the client. As the randomness of victim selection and the pervasiveness of exploitive dysfunction become apparent a therapist can easily feel overwhelmed. Identification with either the victim or the aggressor serves as a coping mechanism. This reaction is typically maladaptive and may be expressed in the worker's interpersonal inter-actions if the underlying issues are not resolved.

Power and Control

Exposure to power-based interactions and behaviors is unavoidable because that is the means that those who have sexually offended use to deal with their world (Lane, 1986). The client comes unwillingly into treatment due to the coercion or control of others and the treatment setting becomes a new setting in which manipulation and exploitation are tested. The client continues to engage in power and control inter-actions that boost his sense of adequacy and self-esteem. The therapist is often opposed, demeaned, or subtly victimized. There are times when it can become difficult to avoid engaging in the power game, and there are times when workers over-identify with power-based behaviors.

In some instances there is a qualitative difference in the reaction of the client to confrontation by males and by females, possibly based on the perceived ability to control females and subsequent need to discount that input in order to maintain their assumption (Lane, 1986). Inequality or conflict in the male-female co-therapy team may result from or be exacerbated by the power and control dynamics.

Power struggles and control battles with clients may also be replicated in interactions with the various intervening professionals and systems and may leave therapists feeling discounted, ineffectual, or helpless. The temptation for rules, control seeking, and structure is great, as is the risk of retaliatory or compensatory reactions.

Examination of Beliefs

As the therapist pursues the relentless scrutiny of the client's thoughts and beliefs, the examination of one's own worldview follows. It can be distressing to discover similarities in one's own patterns of coping, defenses, and beliefs; nevertheless, acknowledgment of one's own dysfunctional behaviors can enhance the therapist's patience and empathy with clients. The constant reexamination of one's beliefs and behavior often leads to changes in the therapist's own tolerance and accountability in personal relationships.

The worker's previous standards may become dissonant with new understand-ings acquired in the process of treating dysfunction. Disruptions in one's personal life lead the worker to question the assumptions that guide both work and personal decisions. As Maslach (1978) warns, sharp distinctions between personal and professional standards contribute to the risk of burnout.

Sexuality

Therapists cannot be repeatedly exposed to the ideation of sexual abuse without experiencing some effects on their own sexuality. The therapist who has been a victim of any part of a sexual act by a perpetrator may become distressed and need to work on that issue in his or her own therapy. The therapist who has unresolved adolescent sexuality issues may feel threatened or uneasy helping a youth with similar issues. Therapists with sexual dysfunctions of their own will become more aware of and more anxious about that area. Female workers who are covertly victimized during the process of treatment may transfer their fear or rage to all males they encounter or to the significant males in their lives. Male therapists who are covertly victimized may experience issues related to homosexuality, power, or even gender guilt (Lane, 1986).

Therapists may experience disinterest in sex at times, increased arousal at other times, or a complete shutdown of sexual desires. Deviant sexual images may intrude on fantasy or thought, and physiological arousal may occur in response to these images. When therapists experience arousal in response to a client's description of a sexually abusive behavior, it is likely associated with the therapist's own memory of a sexual behavior such as digital penetration, penile thrusting, vaginal secretions, erections, and the like. The therapist must be able to distinguish the normalcy of that association and response from the deviance of the behavior occurring in the context of an exploitive or violent interaction.

Therapists working with sexual abuse must anticipate that the sexual component of their work puts them at risk for sexual dysfunction, intrusive sexual images, deviant fantasies, and arousal. Both primary and secondary prevention concepts must be employed to support their own health and self-image and to counter the intrusion of work into their own sexual interactions. In almost every instance, the same techniques the therapist has used to help clients manage sexual thoughts and arousal or to restructure sexual fantasies can be used to manage the negative effects experienced by the interventionist. The danger is when the interventionist fails to use the interventions to stop the thoughts or suppress the arousal and instead ruminates on the problem, increasing its frequency and intensity and internalizing shame.

As therapists working with victims come to think of them as potential perpetrators, a proactive approach works toward prevention. Many issues relevant to offending must be explored with victims. Workers must be aware that they are simultaneously being oversensitized to sexual issues and exposed to vicarious sexual victimization.

Sexual arousal and intrusive sexual images are not the only issues to arise from the sexual nature of this work. Therapists may also struggle with feelings of intrusiveness and voyeurism when they inquire into the thoughts and feelings regarding sexual abuse. The therapist's discomfort and the subsequent self-examination are both useful in evaluating one's work, but should not automatically change the course of the treatment strategy. There is a very real need and a strong theoretical basis or rationale that supports the therapist's intrusive inquiry. Acknowledgment of one's own discomfort and empathy for the client's experience of the intrusive elements of the treatment process are appropriate and beneficial for the therapeutic relationship.

Much of the definition and restructuring of sexual thinking can be accomplished in anticipation of the client's needs in a more educational and informational format that minimizes the amount of intrusive investigation into the sexual thinking of the client. It is not possible, however, to treat sexual deviance without hearing from the individual the thoughts and fantasies that support and fuel the behavior. The intrusive and voyeuristic qualities associated with this aspect of the work are minimized in the context of an effective therapeutic group wherein alliances are less intimate, the client's self-disclosure is encouraged, and the defenses that allow self-observation are respected. While defining deviance and exploitation in his or her work, the therapist nevertheless recognizes that normal, healthy sexuality is a goal for the client. Workers must maintain some perspective of normality and celebrate healthy sexuality in their own lives (O'Brien, 1990).

ROLE TAKING

The intervening systems assign workers various roles that often include over-lapping or conflicting functions. The boundaries of one's role may at times be clear and at other times become enmeshed or rigid. There is a tendency for those in victim services to assume that their role is victim advocacy and that those working with those who have offended are in a corresponding role as advocates for the perpetrator (and his behavior). The betrayal of trust and intrusion inherent in sexual abuse may be expressed by workers becoming suspicious, rigid, intolerant, or oversensitive in these different roles. This conflict stems from the failure to think about all sexual abuse work in terms of prevention. The treatment of sexual abusers is typically motivated by the desire to reduce further victimization, and the common denominator in the roles of all who intervene is victim advocacy. There are times, however, when therapists must actively pursue resources and support in order to have the potential to succeed in the treatment of their clients. Treating those who have sexually offended is a preventive measure, not advocacy for sexually abusive behavior.

The unfortunate dilemma of inadequate resources for services for sexually abused children as well as remedial programs for the youth who has abused them is very real. Prioritizing time and dollars creates a debate regarding cause and effect similar to the proverbial dilemma of the chicken and the egg. If it is possible through treatment to stop those who have offended from victimizing others then there will be fewer victims and a corresponding reduction in the demand for those treatment services as well. On the other hand, if it is possible to intervene successfully with children who have been abused, their negative experience may be resolved without risk of long-term dysfunctions, including sexual perpetration against others. It is obvious why the allocation of limited resources fuels the role conflicts in this work.

Many workers are cast into multiple roles, working with victims and perpetrators, as well as with the systems and families involved. Work with each aspect may create an internal struggle that undermines the objectivity of the workers. The boundaries and conflicts become internalized within an individual and the subsequent dilemmas become very personal in the context of the therapeutic alliances that form. Co-therapy relationships may support or exacerbate these conflicts, or may be helpful in separating the issues.

At still another level, the therapist treating the one who has offended is often cast into rigid and conflicting roles by the client (Lane, 1986). At this level, role definition goes beyond the function and attacks the identity of the interventionist. The role assignment by the client is often extreme. The therapist may be seen as either all good or all bad: Madonna or whore, macho or effeminate, protector or abuser, advocate or foe. These role assignments are based in the client's world-views and beliefs, as are their definitions of their own roles in relationships. It is easy for the therapist to respond to the projection in dysfunctional ways. The challenge for the therapist in modeling more flexible roles is to maintain healthy boundaries and facilitate boundary respect among group members as well. Chal-lenging the stereotypes that facilitate objectification is an aspect of treatment with sexual abuse clients that must also be a part of supporting healthy interactions among the interventionists.

INTERPERSONAL ISSUES

The internal and external implications may be expressed in one's interpersonal relationships. Interpersonal impacts occur related to basic trust and empathy, responsibility, and accountability. Interactional difficulties are apparent in the multiplicity of roles that may lead to role confusion, blurring of personal and professional boundaries, and perceptual alienation among colleagues, family, and friends.

Being sensitized to exploitation and dysfunction opens one's eyes to the pervasiveness and risk of these negative qualities in all human relations. The dysfunctions that support or allow sexual offending are not black and white configurations, nor are they qualities that differ extensively from the personal characteristics of many who do not offend. The dynamics fall along a continuum from perfect to perverse. Cognitive manipulations of self and others are a constant part of our self-image and interactions. Emotional and physical gratifications are powerful reinforcers that motivate each of us in our relationships with others, as well as in our personal behavior. It is empathy that deters exploitation, and one's own capacity for empathy increases rather than diminishes sensitivity to the pervasiveness of dysfunction.

Dissonance in one's personal and professional standards can be problematic. Defining sexual abuse in terms of nonconsent, inequality, and coercion goes beyond sexual behavior into the realm of all interactions and relationships. In the therapeutic setting workers must be sensitive to coercion and manipulation in their own interactions and this sensitivity follows them back home. The style and tactics that have been the basis for giving and receiving nurturance in long-term relationships may be reevaluated in the light of the worker's increased understanding and fall short of his or her new standards regarding empathy, control, and trust. Faults and shortcomings in self and others may become dissonant in light of the worker's sensitivity and greater emphasis on accountability.

Challenging the defenses of the client increases the likelihood of similar challenges of one's personal defenses as well as those of friends, colleagues, and family members. As workers examine dysfunction in the life of clients, they are likely to reexamine their own life experiences as well. Sensitizing oneself to see the elements of the dysfunctional cycle in the daily lives of the client leads to the discovery of those same elements in one's own functioning. This discovery can shake the interventionists' view of their own competence and health, as well as their evaluation of others. Negative expectations, isolating behaviors, cognitive distortions, and control seeking may seem pervasive as the risk or presence of negative behavior is revealed in the daily functioning of self and others. Workers may begin to fear the presence of secret negative behavior in those close to them.

Being aware of the continuum of functionality, workers must accept that normal functioning is not perfect. For most, functioning falls along the middle of the continuum without clear delineation of the points that define optimal, acceptable, and unacceptable levels of responsibility. Similarly, most relationships are less than perfect as well. Differentiating between the dynamics of sexual abuse and the dynamics of one's own interactions and relationships is critical.

As the therapist becomes more and more sensitive to the issues, is propelled by curiosity and self-examination, or is excited by the positive implications and potential for change, his or her interpersonal relationships may be challenged, threatened, or jeopardized by the changes in his or her beliefs and expectations. One's spouse, partner, children, friends, and colleagues may be overwhelmed by what seem to them to be rapid changes and they may complain about the impact on their relationships. Workers must be cautious of overgeneralizing the techniques and expectations of their work into their personal relationships and at the same time be willing to accept the inevitable need for change in some aspects of their lives.

AGENCY ISSUES

Agencies that specialize in sexual abuse work, as well as interagency teams, are also at risk for dysfunction. Understanding that defense mechanisms are adaptive responses that protect individuals from being overwhelmed by adversity, stress, and painful experiences, it becomes clear that therapists must call on a variety of defenses to maintain their objectivity and function while dealing with the abhorrent details of sexual abuse. At the same time, knowing that the overgeneralization of defenses becomes problematic over time and supports dysfunctional outcomes, teams must be vigilant in order to avoid taking on the very characteristics present in the functioning of their clients. In their exposure to the details of sexual abuse, therapists experience sexual victimization and offending vicariously and are at risk to mirror the client's issues in their own interactions. Agencies specializing in the treatment of family dysfunction are at risk to function in similar roles within the agency. Incest programs have often reported discovery of victim, perpetrator, abuse-tolerant, and abuse-supportive dynamics occurring in staff relationships. Somatic complaints regarding the organization are evident and working conditions are maligned, with responsibility attributed to administrators, directors, and ancillary staff. O'Brien (1990) notes that even buildings become symptomatic in the perception of the workers, as if lack of space or old carpet were or could be responsible for one's stress. Those dynamics clearly contribute to the risk of burnout and high rates of staff turnover when workers' distortions of the impacts cause them to believe they are being victimized by the agency.

Professional staff are also at risk of overidentifying with their clientele to the extent that a process of normalization may occur. Staff may exhibit rescuing, increased minimization of behaviors or reactions, or acceptance of the client's victim stance. Normalizing may initially serve as an empathetic or coping response, but may result in blurred professional roles or changes in agency orientation. Agencies must work to keep perspective of safety and accountability issues, yet maintain a balance of intolerance of abusive sexual behaviors with supportive therapeutic interactions with the client.

PREVENTION AND INTERVENTION

Just as models have developed to support understanding, risk management, intervention, and prevention with those victimized or perpetrating sexual abuse, it is also possible to manage the risks associated with the work itself. To do so requires an understanding of the experience, recognition of symptoms, and purposeful planning for both prevention and intervention. Corman and Smith (1986), in processing the results of their survey on the effects of sexual abuse on staff, concluded that the manifestation of symptoms from the effects of sexual abuse work is not a measure of one's ability or inability to do the work, but rather that workers must monitor the impact on themselves and their co-workers and take responsibility for dealing with the stress.

In entering any challenging endeavor, the balance of risk and gain must be considered. One cannot accept a challenge without some anticipation of change. When accepting those who have sexually offended into treatment, the professional evaluates the needs and strengths of the individual and, on the basis of this assessment of amenability for treatment, the client is urged to accept the challenge to change. Workers and those who hire them must similarly evaluate the potential employee's own amenability to facilitate change and to accept the inevitable challenges, impacts, and personal change.

There is recognition in the field that this work can have negative effects and prospective workers need to be specifically cautioned that this is foreseeable. It is important to know the risk of negative impacts, although being changed by the work is not always a bad thing. Many practitioners acknowledge that they are better parents, partners, and children in their own familial relationships because of things they learn in working with dysfunctional families. The important thing is to be aware of the potential for changes and have the self-awareness and the collegial input to recognize dysfunctional reactions as they occur, without overgeneralizing defenses.

The potential worker's qualifications are an area of controversy in the field and many agencies and organizations are exploring the criteria of some minimal level of training, knowledge, and experience that would measure one's ability to work with juveniles who have sexually offended. It has been suggested that some combination of clinical and specialized training is required, but at a more personal level the individual's potential long-term success in this work is likely to be more related to personal characteristics than to the simple acquisition of skills and knowledge. Some of the qualifications that may be worth considering in pre-employment decisions include a genuine enjoyment of adolescents, comfort with one's own sexuality, an innate curiosity, a good sense of humor, and a patient, nurturing nature. Just as the client's functioning reflects the influences of his or her whole life experience, the worker's ability to succeed is influenced by his or her life experience as well. It is the stability and consistency of the individual's experience and self-image, along with positive sources of validation and correction that seem to mediate the risk of detrimental experiences having a negative outcome.

Just as prevention and intervention work with the client considers the situational, affective, cognitive, and behavioral aspects of their cycle and implements different strategies to counter each element of risk, burnout prevention must address each of these elements as well.

Situational variables present in the structure of the agency (as well as the specific therapeutic setting) can facilitate identification and management of many of the impacts. The atmosphere should support sharing of knowledge and responsibility and prohibit secrecy and scapegoating. Forums for learning, sharing, and conflict resolution (e.g., study groups, case processing, supervision, networking, and staff retreats) offer opportunities for open exploration of issues rather than denial. A clear statement of mission and goals that encompasses some vision of future directions counters the negative expectations and cynicism that support burnout. A peer culture based in accountability and empathy provides collegial support while allowing staff to both comfort and confront their peers. A consistent, shared awareness of the predictable issues facilitates recognition and intervention in symptoms as they arise.

Teamwork reduces isolation and allows for immediate validation or correction of erroneous perceptions and tough decisions. Co-therapy, outside consultation, and supervision reduce the worker's isolation. Networking with other programs and agencies reduces the secrecy and isolation that increases the risk of incestuous and exploitive dynamics among staff. Conferences and in-service training provide continuing education and support feelings of competence. The danger that similarly affected persons will reinforce maladaptive coping is countered by an open exchange of academic ideas in study groups, journal clubs, and book reviewing. Clinical dilemmas must be acknowledged at both the affective and cognitive levels, in a climate of curiosity that encourages exploration, resolution, and change.

Affectively, colleagues must facilitate sharing of emotional issues in a climate of empathy, openness, and permission. Minimization or denial of one's own feelings supports the denial of the feelings of one's colleagues, and pervasive minimizing of affect objectifies the interventionist. Lack of empathic peer support feeds the abuse-tolerant dynamic. Appropriate sharing encourages all staff to identify impacts and develop effective coping and resolution strategies. One of the strengths of those who work with children and adolescents is the good humor and enjoyment that supports both the clinician and the client in what might otherwise be intolerably painful circumstances. The collegial culture must monitor itself, however, for subtle shifts away from good humor into cynicism and sarcasm which, when pervasive, support objectification of clients and a lack of empathy for colleagues. Failure to interrupt this type of shift can develop into hurtful interchanges between staff members. The source of the hurt often parallels the affective triggers of the clients. Scapegoating, helplessness, and a lack of validation support hopelessness and feelings of doom. An ongoing process of feedback and insight provides validation and paves the way for intervention.

Cognitively, workers must constantly reconcile their own view of the world with the very different beliefs of the client. Colleagues must monitor professional interactions for subtle cognitive shifts away from accountability and empathy. While exposed to the sometimes overwhelming evidence of deceit and exploitation that pervade the life histories and the current functioning of the client, workers must remain grounded in their own experience of more rational and functional relationships.

Either consistently or intermittently, workers should seek out opportunities to work with or be exposed to nonclinical age-mates of their client population in order to maintain a sense of normality. The thoughts, feelings, and behaviors of the clients are often extremes or deviations and must not become one's measure of normalcy.

Although an emotional tug-of-war may result from the therapist's dual roles, purposefully planned involvement in victim services can be beneficial in maintaining one's perspective as well as countering the polarization of workers. The mutual exchange of workers from programs treating abused children and those who abused them promotes mutual goals and counters alienation, while providing external sources of validation and correction for both. The inclusion of victim therapist/ advocates on the multidisciplinary teams managing cases facilitates this process as well (Colorado Sex Offender Management Board, 2002).

Behaviorally, the symptoms of burnout often manifest in power and control behaviors and the abuse of self or others. Agencies can facilitate behavioral accountability by providing clear expectations and open communication. Workers can monitor themselves and each other for retaliatory or compensatory plans. Colleagues must be willing to confront their peers when client dysfunction is being reflected in current behavior. The culture within the agency should process problems as they arise and assist workers in recognizing the need for intervention and obtaining the help they need.

CONCLUSION

It may be that the risks of personal and professional impacts in the treatment of juveniles who have sexually offended are predictable and manageable. Pre-employment screening, ongoing training, peer consultation and supervision, and the open sharing of issues and responsibility minimize the negative risks of this work. It is equally important to acknowledge the unique individuality of each interventionist, appreciating the defenses that protect them in this work and supporting the strengths that keep them healthy. Each worker must find his or her own personal answers in order to survive in this work.

In explaining the challenge of staying sane while surrounded by misery, Hawkeye Pierce of the television series *M.A.S.H.* referred to the need for "mental anesthesia" with the following explanation: "If you get caught up in their misery too deeply, you can get into a hole you can't get out of." At the same time, anesthesia must be balanced with conscious, creative thinking. Always questioning what the current intervention can reveal about prevention is a good way to promote optimism and maintain health. Hopelessness and powerlessness must be countered by noticing and nurturing inner strengths and appreciating the importance of small changes in individual clients. Celebrating healthy relationships, positive sexuality, and peaceful pursuits are critical in the worker's ability to remain stable and grounded in a positive worldview.

Brandt Steele, in a personal communication with his staff (1990), suggests that one is never really an expert: "We are only curious people struggling to understand suffering and overcome it." Sexual abuse workers must give themselves permission to leave the work behind either temporarily or permanently. Sexual abuse has enough casualties. Colleagues must take care of themselves and of each other.

REFERENCES

Bolton, F., Morris, C., & MacEachron, A. (1989). *Males at risk.* Thousand Oaks, CA: Sage.

Colorado Sex Offender Management Board (CSOMB). (2002). *Standards and guidelines for the evaluation, assessment, treatment, and supervision of juveniles who have committed sexual offenses.* Colorado Department of Public Safety, Division of Criminal Justice.

Conte, J. (1985). The effects of sexual victimization on children: A critique and suggestions for future research. *Victimology: The International Journal, 10*(1), 10–30.

Corman, C., & Smith, H. (1986). Effects of sexual abuse on staff. *Colorado's Children, 5*(3), 1–3.

Finkelhor, D., & Browne, A. (1985). The traumatic impact of child sexual abuse: A conceptualization. *American Journal of Orthopsychiatry, 55*(4), 530–541.

Haynes-Seman, C., & Krugman, R. (1989). Sexualized attention: Normal interaction or precursor to sexual abuse? *American Journal of Orthopsychiatry, 59*(2), 238–245.

Koplau, H., Sadock, B. (Eds.) (1985). Comprehensive textbook of psychiatry. Baltimore: Williams & Wilkins.

Krugman, R. (1990). *Child sexual abuse.* Paper presented at the 22nd Ross Roundtable on Critical Approaches to Common Pediatric Problems, Washington, DC.

Lane, S. (1986). Potential emotional hazards of working with those who have sexually offended. *Interchange: Newsletter of the National Adolescent Perpetrator Network.* Denver, CO: Kempe National Center.

Maslach, C. (1978). Job burnout: How people cope. *Public Welfare, 36*(1), 56–58.

Maslach, C., & Florian, V. (1988). Burnout, job setting and self-evaluation among rehabilitation counselors. *Rehabilitation Psychology, 33*(2), 85–93.

O'Brien, M. (1990). *Child and adolescent perpetrators.* Paper presented at the Sexual Abuse Treatment Symposium, Breckenridge, CO.

Richter, C. (1957). On the phenomenon of unexplained sudden death in animals and man. *Psychosomatic Medicine, 19,* 191–198.

Ryan, G. (1989). Victim to victimizer: Rethinking victim treatment. *Journal of Interpersonal Violence, 4*(3), 325–341.

Ryan, G., Miyoshi, T., & Krugman, R. (1988). *Early childhood experience of professionals working in child abuse.* 17th Annual Symposium on Child Abuse and Neglect, Keystone, CO.

Seligman, M. (1974). Depression and learned helplessness. In R. J. Friedman & M. M. Katz (Eds.), *The psychology of depression.* Washington, DC: Winston and Sons.

Seligman, M. (1975). *Helplessness: On depression, development, and death.* New York: Freeman.

Spaniol, L. (1986). Program evaluation in psychosocial rehabilitation: A management perspective. *Psychosocial Rehabilitation Journal, 1*(1).

Warnath, C., & Shelton, J. (1976). The ultimate disappointment: The burned out counselor. *Personnel and Guidance Journal, 55*(4), 172–175.

Yochelson, S., & Samenow, S. (1976). *The criminal personality* (vol. 1). Northvale, NJ: Aronson.

Name Index

Subject Index